Schizophrenia

Schizophrenia

An International Follow-up Study

World Health Organization

Geneva

JOHN WILEY & SONS
Chichester · New York · Brisbane · Toronto

The designations employed and the presentation of the material in this publication do not imply the expression of any opinion whatsoever on the part of the Secretariat of the World Health Organization concerning the legal status of any country, territory, city or area or of its authorities, or concerning the delimitation of its frontiers.

The mention of specific companies or of certain manufacturers' products does not imply that they are endorsed or recommended by the World Health Organization in preference to others of a similar nature that are not mentioned. Errors and omissions excepted, the names of proprietary products are distinguished by initial capital letters.

Library of Congress Cataloging in Publication Data:

World Health Organization.
  Schizophrenia.

    1. Schizophrenia—Statistics.   2. Schizophrenia—
Prognosis.   3. Psychiatric research.   4. Psychiatry,
Transcultural.   I. Title.
RC514.W64 1979   616.8'982   78-17808

ISBN 0 471 99623 8

Typeset by Preface Ltd, Salisbury, Wilts
and printed by The Pitman Press,
Bath.

Contents

Preface ix

Historical perspective xi

Collaborating investigators xiii

Chapter 1   Aims and methods **1**

1.1   Aim 1
1.2   Design 2
1.3   Summary of results of initial examination of patients 6
1.4   Aims of the follow-up phase 8
1.5   Design of the follow-up phase 9

**Chapter 2   Selective review of results of previous follow-up studies of
schizophrenia and other psychoses** **11**

2.1   Introduction 11
2.2   Methodological problems in follow-up studies 11
2.3   Selective review of previous follow-up studies of schizophrenia . . 19
2.4   Conclusions 42

**Chapter 3   Feasibility of carrying out a multinational follow-up study of
patients with functional psychoses** **45**

3.1   Finding and reinterviewing patients and informants 45
3.2   Instruments 52
3.3   Co-ordination and organizational continuity 57
3.4   Summary and conclusions 58

Chapter 4   Reliability of methods and instruments **61**

4.1   Introduction 61
4.2   Concepts of reliability and validity 62
4.3   The intracentre reliability of the PSE 67
4.4   The intercentre reliability of the PSE 85
4.5   The reliability of the assessment of course and outcome
characteristics 91

Chapter 5 Characteristics of the study population and research settings during the follow-up period **95**

5.1 Characteristics of the study population at the time of second year follow-up 95

5.2 Characteristics of the field research centres during the follow-up period 102

Chapter 6 Course and outcome of patients with an initial evaluation diagnosis of schizophrenia **113**

6.1 Statistical approaches 115

6.2 Symptomatic picture at the time of second-year follow-up 117

6.3 Comparison of symptomatic picture at time of initial evaluation with the symptomatic picture at the time of second-year follow-up . 132

6.4 Course of illness in schizophrenic patients between initial evaluation and second-year follow-up 144

6.5 Outcome of schizophrenia in relation to age and sex 161

6.6 Summary of findings concerning the course and outcome of schizophrenic groups of patients during the follow-up period . . . 163

Chapter 7 Course and outcome of patients with an initial evaluation diagnosis other than schizophrenia **165**

7.1 Psychotic depression (ICD categories 296.0, 296.2, 298.0) 165

7.2 Mania (ICD category 296.1) 178

7.3 Other psychoses 191

Chapter 8 Comparison among diagnostic groups within and between centres . **193**

8.1 Comparison among psychotic diagnostic groups in terms of symptom picture at the time of second-year follow-up 193

8.2 Comparison among diagnostic groups in terms of clinical state at second-year follow-up 199

8.3 Comparison among diagnostic groups in terms of course during the interval between initial evaluation and second-year follow-up . . . 201

8.4 Course and outcome in terms of centres in developed and developing countries 221

8.5 Summary of comparisons of course and outcome among different diagnostic groups 221

Chapter 9 The concordant group and the subgroups of schizophrenia . . . **225**

9.1 The concordant and non-concordant groups 226

9.2 The subgroups of schizophrenia 239

9.3 Summary 251

Chapter 10 Predictors of course and outcome in schizophrenia and affective psychoses **253**

10.1 Introduction 253
10.2 Hypotheses about predictors of course and outcome 254
10.3 IPSS data and analyses used in the study of predictors 256
10.4 Predictors of two-year course and outcome of patients with clinical diagnosis of schizophrenia (ICD 295) 263
10.5 Prediction of course and outcome in affective psychoses 301
10.6 Discussion and conclusions 303

Chapter 11 Approaches toward assessment of the predictive validity of systems of classification of schizophrenia and other functional psychoses **313**

11.1 Introduction 313
11.2 Classification systems used in the study and criteria for the assessment of their validity 314
11.3 Clinical diagnosis at initial evaluation as a predictor of course and outcome 316
11.4 Discriminant function analysis of classification systems 322
11.5 Comparison of the predictive power of the four classifications . . . 354
11.6 Discussion and conclusions 362

Chapter 12 Discussion and conclusions . . . . , . **367**

12.1 The course and outcome of schizophrenia and other functional psychoses 367
12.2 Predictors of course and outcome . . . . , 375
12.3 Approaches toward the assessment of diagnostic validity 384
12.4 Feasibility of carrying out a large-scale transcultural follow-up study of patients with functional psychoses 388
12.5 Development of instruments and procedures for follow-up studies . . 390
12.6 Conclusions and hypotheses 391

Appendix 1 Summary of course and outcome of patients excluded from further analysis **397**

Appendix 2 Summary of data on patients who died during the follow-up period **403**

Appendix 3 Classification of patients on the basis of PSE ratings **409**

Appendix 4 Composition of CATEGO classes used in the analysis of the two-year follow-up data **413**

viii

Appendix 5   **Definition and measurement of reliability for dichotomous variables** 415

References 425

Author Index 430

Subject Index 432

Preface

Like the production of Volume 1 of the Report of the International Pilot Study of Schizophrenia (WHO, 1973), the planning and writing of this volume was a collaborative effort. Major aims and general approaches were identified and discussed at several meetings of all the collaborating investigators. Plans for the structure and content of the volume were developed by Dr R. Shapiro, Dr N. Sartorius, Dr A. Jablensky, Mr M. Kimura and Mr W. Gulbinat, who also carried out the main writing tasks. Drafts of the volume were discussed in detail by all the collaborating investigators during their meetings, and by an Advisory Group (Dr J. E. Cooper, Dr M. Katz, Dr M. Kramer, Dr C. A. Leon, Dr T.-Y. Lin, Dr R. A. Nadzharov, Dr R. Sadoun, Dr E. Strömgren, Dr L. A. Wienckowski, Dr J. Wing and Dr L. Wynne. In addition, an editorial working group consisting of Dr J. Bartko, Dr T.-Y. Lin, Dr R. Nadzharov, Dr N. Sartorius, Dr J. Strauss, Dr E. Strömgren and Dr J. Wing reviewed each draft in detail and provided comments which were incorporated into the final draft by Dr Shapiro and Dr Jablensky. The final draft was then circulated to all the collaborating investigators and additional suggestions were introduced prior to publication.

The handling and processing of the large amount of data presented in this volume was greatly facilitated by the work of Mrs G. Ernberg, research assistant. The report was retyped several times and we thank the many secretaries of the Office of Mental Health who helped with this task, particularly Mrs V. Cimato, Miss D. Codling, Mrs S. Fischer, Miss L. Lewis and Miss W. Knott.

The chapters and the people who wrote them are listed below:

Chapter 1: Aims and methods – Dr R. Shapiro, Dr N. Sartorius and Mr M. Kimura

Chapter 2: Selective review of results of previous follow-up studies of schizophrenia and other psychoses – Dr R. Shapiro and Dr R. Shader

Chapter 3: Feasibility of carrying out a multinational follow-up study of patients with functional psychoses – Dr R. Shapiro, Dr N. Sartorius, Dr A. Jablensky, Mr M. Kimura and Mrs G. Ernberg

Chapter 4: Reliability of methods and instruments – Mr W. Gulbinat

Chapter 5: Characteristics of the study population and research settings during the follow-up period – Dr R. Shapiro, Dr N. Sartorius, Dr A. Jablensky, Mr M. Kimura, Mrs G. Ernberg, and investigators from Field Research Centres.

Chapter 6: Course and outcome of patients with an initial evaluation diagnosis of schizophrenia – Dr R. Shapiro, Dr N. Sartorius, Dr A. Jablensky, Mr M. Kimura, Mr W. Gulbinat and Mrs G. Ernberg

Chapter 7: Course and outcome of patients with an initial evaluation diagnosis other than schizophrenia – Dr R. Shapiro, Dr N. Sartorius, Dr A. Jablensky, Mr M. Kimura, Mr W. Gulbinat and Mrs G. Ernberg

Chapter 8: Comparison among diagnostic groups within and between centres – Dr R. Shapiro, Dr N. Sartorius, Dr A. Jablensky, Mr M. Kimura, Mr W. Gulbinat and Mrs G. Ernburg

Chapter 9: The concordant group and the subgroups of schizophrenia – Dr R. Shapiro, Dr N. Sartorius, Dr A. Jablensky, Mr M. Kimura, Mr W. Gulbinat and Mrs G. Ernberg

Chapter 10: Predictors of course and outcome of schizophrenia and affective psychoses – Dr A. Jablensky, Mr W. Gulbinat, Dr N. Sartorius, Dr R. Shapiro, Mrs G. Ernberg and Mr J. Deppenthaler

Chapter 11: Approaches toward assessment of the predictive validity of systems of classification of schizophrenia and other functional psychoses – Dr A. Jablensky, Mr W. Gulbinat, Dr N. Sartorius, Dr R. Shapiro, Mrs G. Ernberg and Mr J. Deppenthaler

Chapter 12: Discussion and conclusions – Dr R. Shapiro, Dr A. Jablensky and Dr N. Sartorius

The volume is thus in a real sense the product of many hands, and the endeavour it records the work of many more.

Historical Perspective

In 1959 WHO convened an expert committee on the epidemiology of mental disorders (WHO, 1960). This committee reviewed the existing knowledge and stressed the need for reliable and valid data on the incidence and prevalence of mental disorders. The committee recommended that WHO should render assistance to activities concerned with psychiatric epidemiology in various countries of the world and coordinate and initiate research in this field. It felt that WHO should concentrate on problems which can be better solved through international coordination than by a single group and that it should explore the unique opportunities found in particular countries that require supplementation of the local effort. A series of studies were suggested which included studies aiming at a refinement of techniques of observation, classification, recording, and reporting of mental disorder and at the elucidation of problems of research design and studies of the influence of the sociocultural environment on the clinical condition and course of mental disorders. Other suggestions were made concerning studies on operational problems, such as the evaluation of psychiatric services and clinical research on problems of causation of psychiatric disorders.

The first steps to implement these recommendations were two important publications. One, by Dr D. D. Reid (1960) concentrated on epidemiological methods in the study of mental disorders. The second, by Dr T.-Y. Lin and C. C. Standley (1962) focused on the scope of epidemiology in psychiatry.

Almost at the same time an informal meeting took place in Dr M. Kramer's office in NIMH and Drs S. W. Greenhouse, M. Katz, T.-Y. Lin, B. Pasamanick and J. Zubin discussed the desirability and feasibility of studying the diagnostic process as a basis for developing effective methods for psychiatric epidemiology and crosscultural research.

A number of consultations and discussions followed that occasion until in 1964 WHO organized a scientific group meeting (WHO, 1964). This group, which was chaired by Dr R. Felix, recommended priorities for mental health research to WHO. The group put high priority on the development of methods necessary to carry out epidemiological research in a crosscultural setting. After the meeting of the scientific group in 1964, Dr Lin, in consultation with leading experts from several countries including Drs G. M. Carstairs, W. Caudill, E. Essen-Möller, R. Felix, M. Greenblatt, E. Gruenburg, M. Kramer. A. Lewis, E. Strömgren, J. K. Wing, L. Wynne and others, prepared the WHO meeting of investigators on comparative research on specific mental disorders in 1965. Discussion centred on WHO's research programmes in epidemiology of mental disorder and social psychiatry and an outline was produced for a long-term plan of studies in this area. Three basic papers were prepared for this meeting, one by Dr Lin, another by Dr Wing, and the third one by Dr Caudill. Consultations and work continued after this and several months later Drs Lin, Strömgren, Wing and Lin worked out an initial plan of the International Pilot Study of Schizophrenia (IPSS) which was presented to the meeting of investigators in the IPSS in 1966 (WHO, 1966). At the same time a grant was applied for and received from NIMH and thus the funds necessary for the project were made available using three sources: WHO, NIMH and the collaborating centres. Soon after that the IPSS started.

The spirit of collaboration which was so very important in producing the initial proposals continued to be an essential factor in the further development of this study. Each important decision was reached after many consultations and many people made contributions at various stages of the project.

Some of the collaborating investigators and consultants are no longer connected with this project, but their work and achievements were significant at the time they were made and remain so today.

Collaborating Investigators

Principal Investigators

Dr T.-Y. Lin (1965—70)
Dr N. Sartorius (1970—76))

Other Headquarters' Investigators

Miss E. M. Brooke (1967—70)
Dr F. Engelsmann (1967—68)
Dr G. Ginsburg   (1966—67)
Mr W. Gulbinat   (1974—76)
Dr A. Jablensky   (1974—76)
Mr M. Kimura   (1971—74)
Dr A. Richman   (1966—67)
Dr N. Sartorius   (1967—70)
Dr R. Shapiro   (1971—74)

Collaborating Investigators at the Field Research Centres

Aarhus   Dr E. Strömgren (Chief Collaborating Investigator) (1966—76)
            Dr A. Bertelsen (1970—76)
            Dr M. Fischer (1967—76)
            Dr C. Flach (1967—69)
            Dr N. Juel-Nielsen (1967)

Agra   Dr K. C. Dube (Chief Collaborating Investigator) (1966—76)
            Dr B. S. Yadav (1966—76)

Cali   Dr C. León (Chief Collaborating Investigator) (1966—76)
            Dr G. Calderon (1966—76)
            Dr E. Zambrano (1966—76)

Ibadan   Dr T. A. Lambo (Chief Collaborating Investigator) (1966—71)
            Dr T. Asuni (Chief Collaborating Investigator) (1971—76)
                (Collaborating Investigator) (1966—71)
            Dr M. O. Olatawura (1971—76)

London	Dr J. K. Wing (Chief Collaborating Investigator) (1965–76)
	Dr J. Birley (1966–68)
	Dr J. P. Leff (1968–76)
Moscow	Dr R. A. Nadzharov (Chief Collaborating Investigator) (1966–76)
	Dr N. M. Zharikov (1966–71)
Prague	Dr L. Hanzlicek (Chief Collaborating Investigator) (1967–76)
	Dr C.Škoda (1968–76)
Taipei	Dr C. C. Chen (Chief Collaborating Investigator) (1966–72)
	Dr M. T. Tsuang (1966–72)
Washington	Dr L. Wynne (Chief Collaborating Investigator) (1966–67)
	(Collaborating Investigator) (1968–76)
	Dr J. Strauss (Co-Chief Collaborating Investigator) (1975–76)
	(Chief Collaborating Investigator) (1968–75)
	(Collaborating Investigator) (1966–68)
	Dr W. Carpenter (Co-Chief Collaborating Investigator) (1975–76)
	(Collaborating Investigator) (1968–75)
	Dr J. Bartko (1971–76)

OTHER STAFF AND INDIVIDUALS WHO CONTRIBUTED
TO THE IPSS

Headquarters (WHO, Geneva)

Division of Mental Health

Various professional staff of the Division since 1965, and the following:

Research Assistants:	Mrs G. Ernberg (1973–76)
	Miss K. Barrett (1970–72)
	Miss A. Foster (1968–70)
Secretaries:	Mrs K. D. Ignoto (1969–76)
	Mrs S. Fischer (1972–76)
	Mrs V. M. Cimato (1972–76)
	Mrs J. Mamboury (1967–76)
	Miss S. Doyle (1972–76)
	Mrs M. Schwarz (1971–75)
	and many of the secretaries who previously worked in the Mental Health Unit

Division of Health Statistics:	Mr K. Uemura (1966–76)
	Mr W. Gulbinat (1968–74)
Data Processing Unit:	Mr J. P. Bansal (1968–76)

Other WHO Units: Staff of the Budget, Documents, Finance, Personnel, Travel, and other units were very helpful at various times throughout the project.

National Institute of Mental Health

Project Officers: Dr M. Kramer (1966–76)
   Dr H. Tuma (1967–69)

Members of Advisory Group: Dr M. Katz (1966–76)
   Dr L. Wienckowski (1968–76)

Aarhus

Psychiatrist: Dr N. Engkilde (1968–69)

Psychiatric Social Worker: Mrs L. Kann (1968–74)

Administrative, Secretarial and other Staff: Mrs J. Hildebrandt (1969–76); Mrs L. Aerø (1967–69); Mrs G. Spencer (1969–76)

Agra

Psychiatrists: Dr S. C. Jain (1973); Dr D. Parekh (1967–69, 1970–71)

Psychologists: Mr P. K. Chakraborty (1973); Mr A. Kumar (1967–76)

Psychiatric Social Worker: Mr S. P. Gupta (1967–76)

Statisticians: Mrs S. K. Handa (1967–70); Mr N. Kumar (1970–74, 1975–76)

Administrative, Secretarial and other Staff: Mr O. P. Chauhan (1967–74); Mrs L. N. Pillai (1975–76)

Cali

Psychiatrist: Dr C. Córdoba (1967–69)

Psychiatric Social Workers: Mrs L. de Gambetta (1967–69); Mrs R. de Guzman (1968–70)

Translator: Mrs D. de Zambrano (1967)

Administrative, Secretarial and other Staff: Mrs R. de Padilla (1968–70); Mr N. Ordoñez (1967–70); Miss Y. Otero (1967–69)

Ibadan

Psychiatrists: Dr M. O. Akindele (1969–71); Dr A. A. Marinho (1966–67); Dr C. O. Oshodi (1968–69); Dr T. Otolorin (1968–70)

Other Medical Officers: Dr X. Fernandez (1969–70); Dr V. O. Clairmonte (1969–70)

Psychologist: Mrs D. P. Dastoor (1966–72)

Psychiatric Social Workers: Mrs C. R. O. Barlow (1968–76); Mr J. Ojesina (1966–76)

Psychiatric Nursing Officers: Mr A. P. Coker (1966–76); Mr A. O. Oyeneye (1968–76)

Translators: Mr J. T. Erinle (1966–67); Mrs A. Johnson (1966–67); Mr J. Ojesina (1966–67); Miss E. O. Osanyin (1966–67); Mr A. O. Oyeneye (1966–67)

Administrative, Secretarial and other Staff: Mr J. Ogunniyi (1966–67)

London

Psychiatrist: Dr R. Hirschfeld (1970–71); Dr R. Prudo (1974–76)

Statisticians: Miss P. Dugard (1971–72); Miss J. Nixon (1972–76)

Programmers: Mrs C. Taylor (1966–70); Mrs J. Gourlay (1966–76)

Administrative, Secretarial and other Staff: Mrs L. Astell (1969–72); Miss E. Hicks (1972–75); Miss C. Durston (1975–76)

Moscow

Psychiatrists: Dr Khramelashvily (1973–76); Dr V. G. Levit (1966–72); Dr E. Lobova (1973–76); Dr E. S. Petrova (1966–72); Dr A. N. Popova (1968); Dr M. S. Popova (1966–68); Dr L. I. Teljuk (1969)

Psychiatric Social Workers: Ms M. V. Ivanova (1966–68); Ms G. S. Kozlova (1969); Ms S. P. Matjushina (1968–72)

Translators: Mrs L. G. Krasjuk (1966–72); Ms V. N. Shalirina (1968–72)

Prague

Psychiatrists: Dr T. Dostal (1968–76); Dr L. Kabešová-Gregová (1972–76); Dr E. Ledererová (1967–68); Dr St. Rúžička (1968); Dr M. Skodová-Formánková (1968–76); Dr O. Vinar (1967–69)

Psychiatric Social Workers: Ms B. Hlounová (1968–69); Ms M. Novotná (1969–76); Ms S. Pihrtová (1971); Ms H. Skátáková (1969–71)

Statisticians: Dr T. Husák (1971); Mr J. Janouch (1971–73)

Translators: Dr T. Dostal (1968–76); Dr E. Ledererová (1967–68); Mrs M. Semotánová (1969); Dr C. Škoda (1968–76)

Administrative, Secretarial and other Staff: Mrs H. Jiroutová (1968–76); Ms I. Kynclová (1969–71); Ms B. Prusiková (1968–69); Mrs D. Všetečková (1971–76)

Taipei

Psychiatrist: Dr W. S. Tseng (1968–72)

Psychologists: Miss M. Y. Wang (1968–72); Mr S. K. Yang (1967–72)

Psychiatric Social Workers: Miss F. M. Chen (1967–70); Miss H. C. Chang (1970–72); Miss M. L. Chiang (1966–72); Miss S. D. Yang (1969–72); Miss F. S. Yu (1967–69)

Statistician: Dr H. M. Chu (1967–72)

Washington

Psychiatrist: Dr A. Hawk (1973–76)

Psychologist: Dr J. Dent (1966–69)

Psychiatric Social Workers: Mr R. Blatchley (1968); Mrs D. Davenport (1968); Mr S. Hirsch (1968–69); Mr R. Savard (1968–69)

Statistician: Dr J. Bartko (1966–76)

Programmer: Mr K. Dorn (1969–70)

Administrative, Secretarial and other Staff: Miss R. Boesman (1969–76); Mrs E. Churgin (1970–76); Ms R. Silver (1967–69)

Consultants:
Dr G. M. Carstairs; Dr W. Caudill; Dr J. E. Cooper; Dr J. Dent: Dr E. Essen-Möller; Dr R. Felix; Dr J. Fleiss; Dr M. Greenblatt; Dr S. Greenhouse; Dr E. Gruenberg; Dr M. Hamilton; Dr M. Katz; Dr J. Klett; Dr M. Kramer; Dr A. Lewis; Dr T.-Y. Lin; Dr K. Rawnsley; Dr D. Robinson; Dr R. Sadoun; Dr A. V. Snezhnevskij; Dr J. Zubin

Participants at IPSS Meetings (unless mentioned above)
Dr J. McFie; Dr P. Schneider; Dr E. Slater; Dr J. Vana; Dr J. M. Velasco-Alzaga and WHO staff members. In addition, exchanges of visits of collaborating investigators were held during the course of the study, and other staff of the involved field research centres and various experts from other institutions attended these meetings.

CHAPTER 1

Aims and Methods

The International Pilot Study of Schizophrenia (IPSS) is a transcultural psychiatric investigation of 1202 patients in nine countries – Colombia, Czechoslovakia, Denmark, India, Nigeria, China, Union of Soviet Socialist Republics, United Kingdom and the United States of America. Volume 1 of the Report of the IPSS (WHO, 1973) presents a detailed account of the origins of the study as well as a description of the place of the IPSS in the World Health Organization's long-term programme in epidemiological and social psychiatry. To put the results of the two-year follow-up of the IPSS patients into perspective, a brief account of the aim, design and initial results of the study will be presented here.

1.1 AIM

Clinical, basic science and epidemiological studies of schizophrenia and other functional psychoses are being carried out throughout the world, but it is often difficult to compare the results of one study with those of another because of variability of diagnostic practice. Not only may investigators apply the diagnosis of schizophrenia to patients with very different clinical pictures, but the clinical state is often evaluated in a non-standardized and unspecified manner. Variability of diagnostic practice is a problem for research within one country. When transcultural investigations are undertaken, the problem is compounded by differences in the sociocultural backgrounds of patients and investigators, and by differences in training and theoretical orientation of investigators.

It was felt that the development of standardized method and procedures to overcome these difficulties, and the information that the use of such methods and procedures would produce, are crucial for obtaining knowledge on which to base the planning and evaluation of mental health services. Furthermore, it was felt that studies in genetics, aetiology, precipitation, treatment, prognosis, or course of schizophrenia would acquire meaning on a new level if they could, with confidence, be compared with one another.

The collaborating investigators were concerned with assessing the meaningfulness of the clinical distinction between schizophrenia and other psychiatric disorders within cultures; the effect of culture on the form and content of schizophrenia; the comparability of the clinical picture, course and outcome of schizophrenia and other functional psychoses across different cultures; and the development of methods of collecting data to make such assessments in a standardized, reliable and valid manner.

1

The aim of this study was thus to tackle certain basic methodological problems and to answer questions about the nature and distribution of schizophrenia. There were three major methodological questions:

1. Is it feasible to carry out a large-scale international psychiatric study requiring the coordination and collaboration of psychiatrists and mental health workers from different theoretical backgrounds and from widely separated countries with different cultures and socioeconomic conditions?

2. Is it possible to develop standardized research instruments and procedures for psychiatric assessment which can be reliably applied in a variety of cultural settings?

3. Can teams of research workers be trained to use such instruments and procedures so that comparable observations can be made both in developed and developing countries?

The major questions about the nature and distribution of schizophrenia that this study was intended to explore were:

1. In what sense can it be said that schizophrenic disorders exist in different parts of the world?

2. Are there groups of schizophrenic patients with similar characteristics present in every one of the countries studied?

3. Are there groups of schizophrenic patients whose symptoms differ in form or content from one country to another, and if so, are such differences the result of variations in diagnostic practice or are they true cultural differences in the manner of presentation of the various types of schizophrenia?

4. Does the clinical course and social outcome of schizophrenia in one country or group of countries differ from that in other countries?

5. How do the characteristics of schizophrenic patients compare with those of other psychoses in various countries?

6. Does the course of other psychoses differ from country to country?

The IPSS is a pilot study in the sense that it was intended, by providing answers to these questions, to lay scientific groundwork for future studies of schizophrenia and other psychiatric disorders.

1.2 DESIGN

In order to answer the questions outlined above, a comparative prospective study was designed. A series of psychotic patients was selected from among those contacting psychiatric services in nine countries. These patients were examined in a systematic and standardized fashion, and as many as possible have been followed up.

The IPSS has been carried out in three phases: the Preliminary Phase, the Initial Evaluation Phase and the Follow-up Phase. During the preliminary phase, administrative, operational and organizational procedures were established and tested. In the initial evaluation phase approximately 135 patients were selected and examined in each centre from among those patients contacting the centres during the one-year period from 1 April 1968 to 1 April 1969, according to procedures and methods developed during the preliminary phase. Two years following the initial evaluation of patients, they received a follow-up evaluation, which was repeated five years after their inclusion in the study.

1.2.1 Selection of field research centres and headquarters

Details of the criteria used for selecting field research centres are given in Volume 1 of the IPSS Report (WHO, 1973). Basically, the centres were chosen so that they would represent several of the major cultures of the world, and different levels of social and industrial development. Centres chosen had available at least one well-trained psychiatrist with knowledge and experience in epidemiological research, other trained psychiatrists and supporting staff, and a network of services, to detect a large enough number of likely and early cases of schizophrenia for implementing the study. The centres ultimately chosen were: University del Valle, Cali, *Colombia*; Psychiatric Research Institute, Prague, *Czechoslovakia*; Institute of Psychiatric Demography, Psychiatric Hospital, Aarhus, *Denmark*; Mental Hospital, Agra, *India*; Department of Psychiatry, University College Hospital, Ibadan, *Nigeria*; Department of Psychiatry, National Taiwan University Hospital, Taipei, *China*; Institute of Psychiatry, Academy of Medical Sciences of the USSR, Moscow, *USSR*; Institute of Psychiatry, London, *UK*; and National Institute of Mental Health, Bethesda, Maryland, *USA*.

The Mental Health Unit*, WHO, in Geneva was made the central organizing Headquarters for the study since it was well suited to handling the administrative problems of coordinating research activities and data analysis.

1.2.2 Selection of patients for the study

It was agreed that each series of patients should include an adequate number of young patients with functional psychoses of recent onset, covering the whole range of conditions including schizophrenia, mania, psychotic forms of depression, and borderline psychoses. To identify such patients, each field research centre assessed all patients contacting it with two screens, a demographic screen and a psychosis screen. These screens were designed to select patients with functional psychoses who would be likely to be available for long-term follow-up.

The Demographic Screen identified those patients who contacted each centre and (a) had resided or slept regularly in the catchment area for the last six months, and (b) were aged 15—44. It was decided to select only patients in this age group in order to avoid the inclusion of patients whose illness might be an early stage of presenile or senile psychosis at one end of the life-span, or childhood or juvenile schizophrenia at the other end. The residential requirement was designed to increase the likelihood of availability for follow-up.

*Now Division of Mental Health.

The Psychosis Screen identified all of those patients who passed the Demographic Screen who did not meet any one of a number of exclusion criteria and who met at least one of a number of inclusion categories.

Exclusion criteria were chosen to screen out (a) chronic patients, and (b) patients whose conditions may have been caused or significantly influenced by an organic condition. These categories were:

1. Severe psychotic symptoms in this episode probably continuously present for more than three years.

2. Total hospitalization of two years or more in the last five years, including readmissions.

3. Regular abuse of alcohol.

4. Abuse of drugs acting on the central nervous system.

5. Mental retardation with IQ estimated by a psychiatrist to be less than 70 before the onset of present illness.

6. Psychosis attributable to endocrine disorders (such as thyrotoxicosis, myxoedema, diabetes mellitus, of Cushing's disease).

7. Psychosis attributable to other metabolic or nutritional disorders, such as electrolyte disturbance, liver disease, vitamin deficiency.

8. Evidence of acute or chronic brain syndrome, effects of brain surgery and other organic psychoses, not already specified in 6 or 7 above.

9. Epilepsy.

10. Severe hearing difficulties or severe difficulties in speech production or language (bad stammer, foreign dialect, for example) which would impede the administration of the interview.

Since diagnostic practices vary, inclusion categories were symptoms rather than diagnostic labels. Inclusion categories were divided into (a) those whose presence automatically qualified the patient for inclusion, regardless of degree of symptomatology, and (b) those considered as a basis for inclusion only if present in severe degree. The first group consisted of delusions, hallucinations, gross psychomotor disorder and definitely inappropriate and unusual behaviour. The second group consisted of social withdrawal, disorders of form of thinking, overwhelming fear, disorders of affect, self-neglect, and depersonalization. Provisions were made to allow the local psychiatrist to include a patient that he felt was definitely psychotic, even if he did not demonstrate one of the inclusion symtoms. Later, in order to better demarcate psychotic depression, ten patients with neurotic depression were added to the series from each centre.

In all, the study population resulting from these screens consisted of 1202 patients, divided approximately equally over the nine centres. Of these patients 811 had a centre diagnosis of schizophrenia, 164 of affective psychosis, 29 of paranoid psychosis, 73 of other psychoses, 71 of neurotic depression and 54 had other diagnoses. Table 1.1 indicates the distribution of patients included at initial evaluation by diagnosis and centre.

The design of the IPSS did not include a specific attempt to select series of patients who were representative samples of all schizophrenic patients or of all

TABLE 1.1. PATIENTS INCLUDED IN THE STUDY, BY DIAGNOSTIC GROUP, BY CENTRE.

Diagnosis	ICD Code[1]	Field Research Centre									All Centres
		Aarhus	Agra	Cali	Ibadan	London	Moscow	Taipei	Washington	Prague	
Schizophrenia											
simple	295.0	6	4	2	7	2	–	–	1	5	31
hebephrenic	295.1	12	3	20	9	9	–	30	–	3	86
catatonic	295.2	2	27	3	10	3	4	3	1	1	54
paranoid	295.3	28	15	20	49	75	13	36	51	36	323
acute a)	295.4	–	10	29	5	1	11	4	15	4	79
latent b)	295.5	3	–	3	–	–	14	1	2	2	25
residual	295.6	–	1	–	–	1	–	–	1	–	3
schizo-affective	295.7	1	17	7	26	8	5	8	15	20	107
other specified c) d)	295.8	1	7	6	3	–	30	–	6	3	56
unspecified	295.9	–	17	11	11	1	–	3	3	1	47
Total		53	101	101	120	100	77	86	97	76	811
Affective Psychosis											
agitated depression	296.0	1	3	1	–	–	–	–	–	–	5
manic-depressive, depressed	296.2	19	5	1	8	4	10	3	4	19	73
manic-depressive, manic	296.1	20	20	3	4	6	1	2	2	8	66
others	296.3-6.9	4	–	–	1	4	2	5	2	2	20
Total		44	28	5	13	14	13	10	8	29	164
Paranoid States e)	297	10	–	–	1	–	–	9	–	9	29
Other Psychoses f)											
reactive depression	298.0	1	–	1	5	1	6	4	2	1	21
others	298.1-8.9, 299, 294	17	–	2	2	1	6	17	3	4	52
Total		18	–	3	7	2	12	21	5	5	73
All Psychosis		125	129	109	141	116	102	126	110	119	1077
Neurosis, Personality Disorders											
depressive neurosis	300.4	2	9	6	3	11	10	10	14	6	71
others	300.0-300.3, 300.5-301.9	2	2	12	1	–	28	1	8	–	54
Total		4	11	18	4	11	38	11	22	6	125
All Patients		129	140	127	145	127	140	137	132	125	1202

Note: Special diagnostic terms not found in the ICD, but used in some Centres, have been assigned as follows:
a) Periodic schizophrenia 295.4/5.5; b) Sluggish schizophrenia 295.5; c) Chronic undifferentiated schizophrenia 295.8;*
d) Shift-like schizophrenia 295.8/5.7; e) Acute paranoid psychosis 297.9/5.3; f) Psychogenic paranoid psychosis 298.9/7.9.
* In Volume I chronic undifferentiated schizophrenia was included under 295.6.
1. ICD categories correspond to categories of the 8th Revision of the International Classification of Diseases (WHO 1967).

patients with other functional psychoses seen at the centres. Nevertheless it is obviously of interest to have some idea of the degree to which the IPSS patients are typical of all patients seen at the centres. The collaborating investigators were asked therefore to give their impressions about the typicality of the series of patients from their centres. It was the general impression that, taking into consideration that very young, very old and chronic patients were excluded by design, the schizophrenic patients and the patients with affective psychoses included in the IPSS were for the most part typical, with regard to clinical characteristics, of all such relatively acute patients within the stated age-range admitted to the centres.

Each of the 1202 patients received an intensive initial evaluation by the research team at the field research centre. Each evaluation took a total of about five hours and resulted in the accumulation of some 1600 items of information. This information was elicited through the use of a series of standardized instruments developed or adapted for the study. Eight such instruments were used in the study, of which the three basic ones were the Present State Examination (PSE), the Psychiatric History Schedule (PH) and the Social Description Schedule (SD). A full description of the instruments and reliability data about their use is presented in Volume 1, of the IPSS Report, (WHO, 1973).

1.3 SUMMARY OF RESULTS OF INITIAL EXAMINATION OF PATIENTS

The results of the initial evaluation phase of the study provided answers to the methodological questions so far as the initial evaluation of patients in widely separated and socioculturally different settings. What was striking about the IPSS initial evaluation phase experience was that it demonstrated that it is possible to carry out effectively a large-scale transcultural investigation if careful attention is paid to developing central coordination and arranging frequent opportunities for face-to-face discussions of methodology and operational procedures.

Use of the Present State Examination during the initial evaluation of IPSS patients demonstrated that this instrument was acceptable to patients and clinicians in all of the cultures involved and, after translation and adaptations made on the basis of test use of the schedule in each centre, was applicable in all nine centres. The symptoms were readily comprehensible and rateable and the items translated fairly easily into languages of very different structure*. The reliability of the instrument was shown to be good, especially for items rated on the basis of patients' reports. Thus, the Present State Examination was subjected, during the initial evaluation phase of the study, to a fairly extensive test in nine different centres, and its acceptability, applicability and reliability were shown to be satisfactory. Other instruments were developed specially for this study. They are, therefore, less well standardized and the reliability is less rigorously determined than that of the PSE. The study demonstrated the difficulties of making comparable assessments of details of psychiatric history, social background and

*'ICD categories' correspond to categories of the Eighth Revision of the International Classification of Disease (WHO, 1967).

functional background, and made contributions to the development of techniques to overcome these difficulties.

The initial evaluation phase of the IPSS clearly demonstrated that teams of research workers can be trained to use standardized research instruments and procedures so that comparable observations can be made, both in developed and developing countries.

Questions about the nature and distribution of schizophrenia were approached by analysis of the psychopathology of patient groups, application of computer-simulated diagnosis, cluster analysis and the identification and description of a concordant group of schizophrenia on which three methods of classification agree.

Since all IPSS patients had been examined with the PSE, clinical profiles for the various diagnostic groups based on ratings on PSE items could then be compared between diagnostic groups and centres. Such comparisons indicated that the group of patients given a diagnosis of schizophrenia (ICD category 295)* in one centre, tended to have a symptom profile similar to that of patients given the same diagnosis in the other centres. This was also true of patients with psychotic depression (ICD categories 296.0, 296.2, and 298.0). The profiles of the schizophrenic patient groups and the psychotically depressed groups were markedly different from each other, both overall and within each centre in which numbers were large enough to make comparisons possible.

The symptom profiles of the schizophrenic groups of the different centres were characterized by high scores on lack of insight, predelusional signs (such as delusional mood, ideas of reference, perplexity), flatness of affect, auditory hallucinations, and experiences of control. Scores were also high on delusions, derealization, and disturbances of mood, although these were not uniformly as high as for the first-mentioned group of symptoms. Scores were relatively low across centres on qualitative psychomotor disorders (negativism, compliance, mannerisms, and similar abnormal behaviour), pseudohallucinations, and affective changes other than incongruous affect.

For the psychotically depressed patient groups, scores were high across all centres on affect-laden thoughts, neurasthenic complaints, lack of insight, depressed mood, and psychophysiological complaints. On the other hand, they were generally low on hallucinations, pseudohallucinations, and incongruity of affect.

An attempt was made to standardize the diagnostic principles that clinicians seem to use and to apply them, in the form of a computer program, to PSE data in order to obtain a completely standard reference classification (CATEGO). If the computer classification matched the diagnostic classification used by the participating psychiatrists, there could be little doubt (a) that the psychiatrists' diagnostic rules had been approximated in some precisely specifiable way in the computer's program of instructions, and (b) that certain common principles must apply throughout all the centres. In that case, either the computer classification or the psychiatrists' diagnoses could be used to answer the questions about the distribution of the major diagnostic groups in the nine series.

*A full discussion of the problems of translation that were encountered can be found in Chapter 6 of Volume 1 of the Report of the IPSS (WHO, 1973).

In fact, there was a very substantial measure of agreement between the CATEGO classification and clinical diagnosis (grouped into schizophrenia, mania, and psychotic depression) in seven of the centres, and a fair degree of agreement in the other two centres.

The results of analysis of the psychopathology of patient groups and the application of computer-simulated diagnosis thus indicate that the major functional psychoses are present in each of the centres studied and that the patients in any one of these groups are symptomatologically similar across centres and symptomatologically different from the patients in the other diagnostic groups.

Another approach to investigating the question of whether there are similar groups of schizophrenic patients in the different centres was to compare the results of clinical diagnosis, CATEGO classification and cluster analysis. It was felt that patients who receive both a clinical and CATEGO diagnosis of schizophrenia and who fall into clusters which select out schizophrenic patients, represent a group which would include few patients considered schizophrenic because of lack of standardization of the diagnostic process or because of culture-bound factors. This group of patients, on whom the three systems of classification agree, was referred to as the concordant group. It was demonstrated that there were concordant schizophrenics in every one of the nine series of patients, indicating that there is a very specific sense in which it can be said that there are similar groups of schizophrenic patients in every one of the nine centres in this study. Concordant schizophrenics showed a higher degree of similarity of symptom profiles across the different centres than all schizophrenic patients taken together.

Although most of the groups of schizophrenic patients were similar across centres, there were some groups of schizophrenic patients who had centre-specific characteristics. These patients were felt to be good subjects for further investigation to elucidate the possible role of culture on the form and content of schizophrenia.

IPSS data in this way provided fairly clear-cut answers, as far as the initial clinical picture is concerned, to the questions of the nature and comparability of schizophrenia and other functional psychoses in nine centres.

1.4 AIMS OF THE FOLLOW-UP PHASE

The purpose of the follow-up phase of the study was to provide additional data on which to base answers to the methodological questions, and questions about the nature and distribution of schizophrenia and other psychoses outlined above. The aims of this phase of the study can be stated as follows:

1. To determine the feasibility of carrying out a follow-up study of patients suffering from schizophrenia and other functional psychoses in the nine different centres.

2. To determine if it is possible to develop procedures for the standardized and reliable follow-up evaluation of patients with functional psychoses that will be applicable in different cultures.

3. To determine if the course and outcome of patients in the same diagnostic group are similar or different within and between cultures.

4. To determine if the course and outcome of patients in different diagnostic groups are similar or different within and between cultures.

5. To approach an assessment of the validity of classification of schizophrenia and other functional psychoses within and between cultures.

6. To determine whether it is possible to identify various symptomatic, past history and sociocultural characteristics of patients on initial evaluation which predict particular types of symptomatic, diagnostic, and social outcome.

7. To identify hypotheses about the nature of schizophrenia that can be tested in future studies.

In part the questions implicit in these aims can be answered on the basis of the two year follow-up evaluation of patients. Some of the questions will be more fully answered after the data of the five-year follow-up evaluation are analysed.

1.5 DESIGN OF THE FOLLOW-UP PHASE

In view of the long-term course often considered characteristic of schizophrenia, it was felt that in order to meet the aims of the study there should be an extended follow-up of as many patients originally included in the study as possible. The study design called for follow-ups at one year and two years, with longer-term follow-ups to be carried out if the two-year follow-up data indicated that they would be useful and feasible. The follow-up phase of the study was seen as an evolving process, in which data from evaluations at various points in time would make it possible to give progressively fuller answers to the questions posed at the beginning of the study. It was also envisaged that the follow-up instruments, methods, and procedures initially developed could be tested during the early parts of the follow-up phase, and that the experience thus gained would be used to improve and refine the instruments, methods and procedures to be used in later stages of the follow-up.

1.5.1 One-year trial follow-up

A trial follow-up was held after approximately one year. The purposes of this one-year follow-up were to form some estimate of how many patients it would be possible to follow-up after two years, to determine how the centres' procedures for follow-up of patients worked and how they might be altered for the second-year follow-up, and to assess how applicable the follow-up instruments were for work in the field.

Attempts were made to locate approximately half of the patients in each of the field research centres. It was determined that it was possible, using the resources available at the field research centres, to find more than 90 per cent of these patients approximately one year after their initial evaluation. This indicated that it was likely that at the second-year follow-up it would be possible to find a sizeable proportion of the initial population of patients included in the study.

This trial follow-up was very useful to the centres, as they were able to see what kinds of difficulties were involved in finding patients in each of their settings, and allowed them to make plans for efficient use of resources in the second-year follow-up.

Patients found were evaluated with the PSE, and the Follow-up Psychiatric History Schedule, Follow-up Social Description Schedule, and the Follow-up Diagnostic Assessment Schedule. The latter three schedules were developed during the course of the IPSS and were intended to provide data about the patients for the period between the initial evaluation and the time of follow-up. The PSE was used to gather symptomatic data about the patient during the 30-day period preceding the follow-up examination.

As a result of the experience in using the follow-up psychiatric history and social description schedules, a number of changes were introduced into these schedules to make them more applicable, and these altered schedules were used during the second-year follow-up phase of the study.

1.5.2 Second-year follow-up

The centres set out to evaluate every patient in their original series as close as possible to the second-year anniversary of their initial evaluation. Wherever possible, the patient was assessed with a PSE and follow-up PH, SD and DA schedules. Where this could not be attained, as much information as possible was obtained about the patient. If a patient could not be located or refused to be interviewed, attempts were made to interview relatives, or close friends. Any available case records of all patients were reviewed for information about the patient's condition during the interval since the time of the initial evaluation. The follow-up instruments will be described in detail in Chapter 3.

1.5.3 Fifth-year follow-up

As the experience gained from the second-year follow-up indicated that a five-year follow-up of IPSS patients would be both useful and feasible, such follow-up has been carried out and the findings are currently being analysed. It was felt that methodological difficulties encountered during the second-year follow-up, such as those related to the development of reliable instruments for assessing the psychiatric history of patients, could be further resolved during a five-year follow-up.

The current volume presents the results of the second-year follow-up phase of the IPSS. Before discussing the results, the available literature on follow-up studies of schizophrenia and other psychoses will be briefly reviewed.

CHAPTER 2

Selective Review of Results of Previous Follow-up Studies of Schizophrenia and Other Psychoses

2.1 INTRODUCTION

Early conceptualizations of schizophrenia emphasized both the symptoms considered to be characteristic of the disorder, and the nature of the course and outcome of the condition. One of Kraepelin's (1913) major accomplishments was to notice and call attention to the relationship between certain symptom patterns and prognosis. Eugen Bleuler's (1950) concept of schizophrenia also involved assumptions about both symptomatology and course. Thus, he defined schizophrenia in the following way:

> By the term 'dementia praecox' or 'schizophrenia', we designate a group of psychoses whose course is at times chronic, at times marked by intermittent attacks, and which can stop or retrograde at any stage, but does not permit a full *restitutio ad integrum*. The disease is characterized by a special type of alteration of thinking, feeling, and relation to the external world which appears nowhere else in this particular fashion.

M. Bleuler (1972) also noted that he had never discharged a schizophrenic patient from the hospital in whom he 'could not still see distinct signs of the disease; indeed, there are very few in whom one would have to search for such signs'.

Since the time of Kraepelin and E. Bleuler's (1950) study, there have been numerous follow-up studies of schizophrenia which have been designed to elucidate the nature of the course and outcome of schizophrenia. Before reviewing some of them, it may be useful to discuss the methodological problems that have made it difficult to come to clearer conclusions.

2.2 METHODOLOGICAL PROBLEMS IN FOLLOW-UP STUDIES

Bellak (1948), Langfeldt (1956) and Strömgren (1961), among others, have noted that it is difficult to compare follow-up studies of schizophrenia to one another because of the great differences in the methodologies of such studies. Methodological problems also make it difficult to assess what any particular study has contributed to the understanding of the course and outcome of schizophrenia.

11

These include problems of selection of schizophrenic patients, of definition of outcome criteria, variations in type and 'intensity' of follow up studies, choice of variables affecting outcome and the reliability of follow-up data.

2.2.1 Selection of schizophrenic patients

In many follow-up studies of schizophenia, patients are selected on the basis of having previously received a diagnosis of schizophrenia. Often, little is known or said about the criteria on which these previous diagnoses were based. In many studies, the diagnosis of patients has been made by many different psychiatrists over a long period of time. The differences in theoretical orientation or diagnostic practice between different psychiatrists, or within the same psychiatrist over the period of time involved, are usually not discussed in detail. Thus, little is actually known about what type of patient has been studied.

When diagnostic criteria are indicated, it is clear that the patients considered to be schizophrenic differ considerably from one study to another. Investigators differ with regard to what range of symptomatology they will include under the diagnosis of schizophrenia and the degree to which they take previous course and personality factors into consideration in making a diagnosis. When chronicity of previous course is an important factor in making the diagnosis of schizophrenia, it is difficult to tell whether subsequent chronicity is related to the nature of schizophrenia or to the previous chronicity itself.

Even when different investigators agree to use the same theoretical concepts of schizophrenia in diagnosing patients as schizophrenic, the assessment of the symptomatological and historical factors inherent in these concepts is largely unstandardized and of unknown reliability. Thus, patients that are described as similar may in fact not be similar.

Finally, different samples of schizophrenic patients may have difficult proportions of various subtypes of schizophrenia. Since it appears that the course and outcome of different subgroups may differ, the comparability of such samples is reduced if the distribution of the patients according to schizophrenic subtype is not included.

2.2.2 Types of outcome criteria

A second major methodological problem and source of difficulty in comparing results of different studies is the question of the types of criteria used to assess the outcome of schizophrenic patients. In some studies, a global assessment of outcome is used, without any specification of what has gone into the global assessment, and without any indication of the reliability of such assessments. Some studies have made extensive use of the concept of social outcome. Shepherd (1959) has called attention to the imprecision of this term and the need for more precise descriptions of factors which go into the assessment of social remission.

In some studies, outcome criteria are specified, but they may vary from one study to another. Thus, in one study, symptomatic improvement may be the criterion of improvement, in another, work adjustment may be the criterion, in a third, relationships with others may be used, while in a fourth, all three of these criteria may be studied. Brown (1959, 1966), among others has pointed out that improvement within one individual area does not necessarily correlate with improvement in other areas. Thus, for example, patients with rather severe symptoms may be able to work.

Even when studies use the same criteria of outcome, it may be difficult to compare their results because of differences in how these criteria are operationalized. In assessing work outcome, one investigator may consider the number of days worked, another the quality of the work performed, another movement up or down the hierarchy of occupational levels. Some authors separate the housewife role and student role from occupational categories, while other authors combine these categories and deal with them all as age-appropriate or situation-appropriate activities.

As difficult as social criteria may be within one culture, they are even more difficult to assess cross-culturally. The fact that someone is not employed indicates one thing about outcome in a highly industrialized setting where most people are employed, and another in a predominantly agricultural society where many individuals in the population are self-employed.

In many investigations, particularly those carried out a number of years ago, hospitalization was used as the only or the major criterion of outcome. However, length of hospital stay may indicate many things beside the condition of the patient: for example, the influence of nosocomial factors, hospital policy relating to discharge, attitudes of the responsible psychiatrists toward discharge, number of available hospital beds, presence of family support, availability of rehabilitation measures and disability pensions for psychiatric patients, etc.

Finally, a number of authors have underlined the complexity of the concept of the outcome of a psychiatric patient. Many variables are closely interrelated, and it is difficult to separate them from one another. Brown and collaborators (1966) have indicated that work success is dependent upon past employment record, attitudes toward discharge, and the personality of the patient. Harris and co-workers (1956) demonstrated a significant association between good clinical outcome and high employability rate. Kenniston, Boltax, and Almond (1971) have emphasized the fact that there are many dimensions involved in the assessment of outcome and that outcome results may vary according to which dimensions are focused on. They note that, in their own study, evaluation of a patient's condition appears to be strongly influenced by the nature of evaluation technique and the social structure of the setting in which it is carried out. They found high correlations among several follow-up measures, and concluded that these high correlations appeared to be a function of obtaining the informational basis for the scores at the same time and from the same person.

2.2.3 Type and intensity of follow-up

The vast majority of follow-up investigations are not purely prospective but are based on designs which are either retrospective or which contain both prospective and retrospective elements. Patients diagnosed as schizophrenic several years before are selected for follow-up evaluation, Their records are retrieved in order to re-examine the initial diagnosis and to extract information about presenting symptomatology, premorbid history, treatment and intervening course.

While efforts can be made to avoid bias, such designs allow the possibility of distortion, as the investigator often knows the outcome at the time that he is re-examining the diagnosis and historical material. Even when such evaluations are made without knowledge of the outcome assessment, the records usually contain considerable information about the course of the patient after the index episode, which may influence the investigator as he assesses the initial diagnosis, presenting symptomatology, and premorbid history. On the other hand, in a follow-up examination, the patient's mental state at the time of examination can colour his own memory for intervening events and influence the investigators' judgment.

A small number of prospective studies have been undertaken, but limitations in time and manpower or financial constraints, have generally resulted in compromises in information yield or design: the duration of follow-up may be short; assessment and criteria for diagnosis at admission may be lacking; the intensity of outcome assessments may vary across patients (some may be interviewed by the investigator, some by persons at the new location in which the subject now resides, some by telephone or letter, etc.); outcome criteria may be too abbreviated or pooled (despite low correlations among variables such as social relationships, heterosexual activity, work performance, manifest psychopathology, hospitalization status, etc.); and perhaps of most concern is the use of static assessments that do not reflect the subject's cumulative experiences since the diagnosis was made − the important issue of course as a dimension of outcome.

Another methodological difficulty of prospective studies is the fact that by their very nature they take a long time to carry out. Since they usually generate considerable data, conclusions may be further delayed by the time-consuming data analysis of large amounts of information. The long gap between initiation of the project and presentation of results may decrease the value of the study, since in the interim new treatment modalities may have been developed and changes in the psychosocial environment may have occurred that decrease the relevance of the results to the situation that obtains at the time of the completion of the study.

Jones (1974) has recently reviewed the methodological difficulties of prospective studies of individuals felt to be at a high risk of developing schizophrenia. He points out that one of the major difficulties with such studies is the development of useful criteria for indentifying a high-risk population. He notes that currently the most promising criterion is a genetic criterion, but cautions that such a criterion has the liability that sample collection on the basis of this criterion requires adequate psychiatric registers which are lacking in most parts of the world. Furthermore, Jones points out that even when such records are available, the cost of such sample collection is so high that such research is restricted to large, well-endowed projects.

It is perhaps an impossible task to carry out the ideal follow-up study which would involve:

1. a large heterogeneous sample containing well-defined, homogeneous sub-samples;

2. no attrition of the sample over time;

3. clear documentation of treatment, including assurance, for example, that the subject has taken the medication as prescribed;

4. consistent and reliable raters and consistent instrumentation so that assessments of change can be considered valid;

5. data collection points at regular intervals, spaced closely enough in time to permit a true prospectively generated picture of the subject's course;

6. some parallel population which would be studied less rigorously and less often to be sure that the intense investment of interest in, and contact with, these subjects had not distorted the nature of the course and outcome; and lastly,

7. availability of data about frequency and type of mental disorders in the general population in order to allow a judgement of representativeness of the follow-up samples.

Much can still be learned from less than ideal studies, but even here the logistics are extremely hard to manage. For example, May, Tuma, and Kraude (1965) undertook a two-year follow-up of 231 first admission schizophrenic patients with no significant history of prior treatment. They have pointed out that it took: (a) three years to plan the study, to develop instruments that could be used for baseline testing and subsequent evaluations over time, and to do pilot work with this design; (b) five years to obtain the sample from a single hospital; and (c) two additional years to conduct the follow-up on those subjects who entered in the last year of the collection of the sample. Thus, ten years went into data collection before any actual analyses of the data collected about follow up could be done. One can imagine the logistical difficulties of trying to carry out such a study for 20 years with an initial sample large enough to offset the inevitable attrition of the sample. Studies in some countries are facilitated by national registers which permit easier case finding, and in some countries and cultures there is less, or virtually no mobility for a sample. Investigations such as those conducted by Douglas (1960), which follow a representative sample of the general population, may also yield important results.

Finally, it should be noted that current follow-up studies of schizophrenia tell us little about the natural history of the disease, since they are almost all based on samples of patients admitted to the hospital, while there are very few based on outpatients at clinics or on schizophrenic patients diagnosed, treated, and followed up by general practitioners.

2.2.4 Variables affecting outcome

There is now considerable evidence to indicate that it is not sufficient to consider outcome only in terms of previous history and presenting clinical picture, but that environmental factors acting upon the patient after his identification as a patient are extremely important to examine.

2.2.4.1 Social and life history variables

In a series of studies, Brown and co-workers (Brown, 1959; Brown et al., 1962; Brown 1966; Brown, Birley, and Wing, 1972) have called attention to the important influence of social factors, such as the type of situation the patient returns to after hospitalization, on the subsequent course of schizophrenia. They have noted that not only is the type of environment the patient returns to an important factor, but that the quality of emotional interaction within that environment is also most important. These workers emphasize the need for careful and subtle assessments of the social environmental factors acting upon patients after discharge from the hospital if the course of schizophrenic patients is to be better understood. Brown (1966) has indicated his feeling that the ability to predict outcome will not be greatly improved until more attention is paid to the influence of environmental factors which the patient is likely to experience after discharge. In a follow-up study of 156 schizophrenic patients discharged after more than two years in a mental hospital, Brown (1959) noted that the percentage of patients able to remain out of the hospital for at least one year after discharge was higher for patients who left the hospital to live in lodgings or with siblings than in patients who went to live in hostels, with parents, or with their spouses.

Brown, Birley, and Wing (1972) found a high degree of emotional expression by relatives during the key admission to be strongly associated with symptomatic relapse nine months after discharge.

In assessing the outcome of schizophrenia attention should also be paid to the effect of important life events on the condition of patients, Brown and Birley (Brown and Birley, 1968; Birley and Brown, 1970) studied a series of schizophrenic patients who had experienced an acute onset or relapse within the three months preceding admission. The frequency of crises and life changes in these patients during the three months prior to admission was determined and compared to the frequency of such crises and changes in a general population group. It was found that in the patient group there was a much higher frequency of events that were independent of the patient's control in the three weeks prior to admission than in the general population group, but that the frequencies of such events during the three earlier three-week periods were similar for the two groups. The authors concluded that in the three weeks prior to the onset of the acute schizophrenic illnesses, there was a real increase in the rate of crises and life changes that could not have been brought about by abnormal behaviour on the patient's part and could not be considered to be an effect of biased reporting or a tendency to forget events which had occurred more than three weeks prior to interview.

These studies suggest that only limited conclusions can be drawn from outcome studies which do not take intervening environmental factors into consideration. They also indicate the difficulties of assessing outcome, since these intervening variables are subtle and complex ones to evaluate.

2.2.4.2 Treatment variables

In any study of outcome and course, a primary concern is the effect of any treatment intervention on the natural course of the illness. Hospitalization as a treatment has its effects, usually positive in the short run but often negative when it is extended too long. Goffman (1961) in the United States, Wing in Great Britain (1962) and Bhaskaran, Dhawan, and Mohan (1972) in India have all described the harmful effects of institutionalization. Rehabilitation and resocialization experiences and traditional interpersonal psychotherapies all make contributions and positively affect some patients.

Drug therapy has been an important factor in decreasing length of hospitalization, but its effects on long-term outcome are less clear. Ekblom and Lassenius (1964), among others, suggest that many chronic patients require at least two years of drug treatment before changes in their condition occur. Thus outcome assessed prior to two years after the onset of drug treatment would not reflect these changes. Controlled studies do rather consistently show the benefits of neuroleptic drugs for both chronic and acute schizophrenic patients during periods of hospitalization (Grinspoon, Ewalt and Shader, 1972).

Aftercare effects have also been studied, and the reports of Troshinsky and colleagues (1962), Gross (1961) and Hogarty and colleagues (1973) support the value of neuroleptics in the aftercare phase. These studies all employed random assignments and placebo controls, although they varied in their efforts to determine patients' drug-taking compliance.

Leff and Wing (1971) carried out a double-blind controlled trial of oral preventive medication in schizophrenia which showed that trifluoperazine or chlorpromazine taken orally was superior to placebo in preventing relapse. Hirsch and co-workers (1973) carried out a similar trial of an injectable form of fluphenazine with similar results.

In a double-blind placebo controlled trial of fluphenazine decanoate, Stevens (1973) set out to determine the effect of this treatment on the social burden of chronic schizophrenics on the community. She found that there was deterioration in family relationships in the placebo group manifested as an increase in the patients of agression, noisiness, talking about delusions, and socially embarrassing behaviour after withdrawal of active drug.

Feinsilver and Gunderson (1972) have reviewed five studies of the effectiveness of psychotherapy with schizophrenic patients. They limited their review to studies which they felt were potentially reproducible and which compared psychotherapeutically treated schizophrenic patients with appropriate control groups. They concluded that, taken together, the studies reviewed neither proved psychotherapy ineffective nor provided any strong evidence of its helpfulness.

A number of studies have emphasized the negative effect on severely mentally ill patients of impoverishing social environments both within and outside of hospitals and the beneficial effects of such social therapeutic measures as rehabilitation programmes, maintenance of contact with the community, the development of transitional facilities, and early discharge policies (Goffman, 1961; Barton, 1959; Bennett and Wing, 1963; Carse, Panton, and Watt, 1958; Wing and Brown, 1970, among others).

Since the comprehensiveness of social therapy programmes, the type and quality of psychotherapy and psychotherapists, and the adequacy of dosage of neuroleptics and the frequency with which patients take such medication, are all difficult things to assess in most studies, the treatment variable is a difficult one to control for in follow-up studies of schizophrenia which are not specifically designed to determine the effect of a particular therapeutic modality.

2.2.4.3 Cultural variables

When comparing the results of outcome studies carried out in different countries, in different parts of the same country, or even among different groups in the same geographical area, it is important to consider the possible effects of cultural or subcultural factors on outcome. For example, the attitudes towards mental illness among various cultural groups may have a marked effect on outcome, since they may affect the point in the course of schizophrenia at which a given patient will be brought to a medical facility for treatment. Furthermore, different cultures have different degrees of tolerance for certain types of symptoms. Thus, in some cultures patients with hallucinations and delusions are quite well tolerated within the community provided these symptoms are not accompanied by aggressive behaviour. In these cultures, it may be possible to return a patient with some residual thought disorder or disorder of perception to the community earlier than in other cultures. Different cultures have different types of family structure which may again influence the course and outcome of schizophrenia. In cultures with extended families, there may be more possibilities for the patient to return to the community than in cultures in which family ties are less extensive.

The stage of socioeconomic development of the society may also have an influence on outcome. Some schizophrenic patients may be more able to return to work in a rural society than in a highly industrialized society in which jobs involve complex and stressful situations.

In view of these and other effects on outcome, caution must be taken in comparing outcome across cultures. There is a great need for studies which will further elucidate the nature of the relationship between culture and the outcome of schizophrenia and other mental disorders.

2.2.5 Reliability of follow-up evaluations

Although considerable knowledge has been gained in recent years about the reliability of assessment of psychiatric symptoms, most of the studies of reliability of such assessment have been made on patients during a fairly acute phase of illness, while less is known about the reliability of symptom assessment during a follow-up phase, when symptoms are less dramatic and more subtle. When it comes to the question of the reliability of assessments of such factors as work, relationships with others, and adjustment to life in the community, the ground is even less firm. Reports of most follow-up studies of schizophrenia have included very little in the way of data indicating reliability of outcome assessments, and therefore often very little is known about the degree to which differences in outcome reflect true differences among patient groups and the degree to which these reflect differences among raters or within the same rater, in the assessment of the outcome criteria.

2.3 SELECTIVE REVIEW OF PREVIOUS FOLLOW-UP STUDIES
OF SCHIZOPHRENIA

With these points in mind, some of the previous studies of schizophrenia will now
be reviewed.

In view of the hundreds of follow-up studies of schizophrenia that have been
carried out, any current review of the field that wishes to do something more than
merely list previous studies must be a selective review. In the following sections,
studies have been selected for one or more of the following reasons: large numbers
of patients have been followed up; the follow-up period has been relatively long;
and criteria of diagnosis have been specified. They represent follow-up studies in a
variety of countries, and particular points not investigated in most other studies are
elucidated. The large field of follow-up studies has been subdivided into five
groups:

1. studies which present conclusions about the outcome of schizophrenia in
terms of the percentages of patients that are recovered, improved, unchanged, or
deteriorated after a follow-up period of a varying number of years. The definitions
of outcome groupings usually vary and the number of points on the continuum
between marked deterioration and complete recovery also varies;

2. studies which present data concerning the pattern of course of schizophrenia
over a number of years;

3. studies which consider the relationship between particular clinical, historical
and social factors and prognosis;

4. studies which compare the outcome of schizophrenia with the outcome of
other functional psychoses, particularly affective psychoses; and

5. crosscultural follow-up studies of schizophrenia.

Some of the studies selected belong to more than one of these groups and the
results of these studies will be discussed in several places.

2.3.1 Studies presenting conclusions about outcome

Langfeldt (1956) has pointed out that studies which reported the outcome of
dementia praecox (as the term was generally used before Bleuler broadened the
concept in 1911), consistently showed very low recovery rates, usually not more
than 2 to 5 per cent, while studies carried out later show much more variable
outcome results.

Thus, Kraepelin (1913) reported early recoveries in 12.6 per cent of patients
diagnosed by him as suffering from dementia praecox. Of these, most had
subsequent relapses, so that the percentage of lasting recoveries was 2.6 per cent,
while the percentage of patients either completely recovered or suffering only from
minor defects was 4.1 per cent; 17 per cent demonstrated social remission and the
others were considered to have deteriorated. Kraepelin quoted similar findings of
other psychiatrists indicating a low percentage of recovery: for example, Evensen's
finding that only 5 per cent of schizophrenics were subsequently fit for independent
living and work, Matuschek's data indicating a 2 to 3 per cent recovery among

TABLE 2.1.

Investigators	Country	Number of pts about whom FU inf.obtnd	Sample drawn from	Criteria for the diagnosis of schizophrenia	Length of follow-up
Malamud and Render (1939)	USA	309	all schizophrenics admitted to Iowa State Psychopathic Hospital, 1929-1936.	Essentially those of E. Bleuler.	2-9 years
Rennie (1939)	USA	456	all schizophrenic patients admitted to the Henry Phipps Psychiatric Clinic, 1913-1923.	Meyerian concept of parergasia.	1-26 years
Stalker (1939)	England	129	all first admiss. for schizophrenia, Royal Edinburgh Hospital, Mental & Nerv. Dis., 1932-1937.	specified as those described by Henderson and Gillespie (1936).	14 months- 6 years
Rupp and Fletcher (1939)	USA	608	all 1st admiss. for schizophrenia, Rhode Island St. Hospital, 1929-1934.	stated to be those outlined in the Statistical Manual of the National Committee for Mental Hygiene (6th ed., 1934).	5-10 years
Holmboe and Astrup (1957)	Norway	255	1st admiss. for acute schizo-phrenia or reac-tive psychosis with schizophrenic traits, Gaustad Hosp.,1938-1950.	presence of typical schizophrenic process symptoms, as des-cribed by Langfeldt.	6-18 years
Johnson (1958)	Sweden	82	1st admissions of all male patients 1938-1942.	pts. with symptoms which are essentially those considered typically schizo-phrenic by Langfeldt, and also patients felt to have "a schizo-phrenia simplex" deve-lopment. Not patients with confusional element in clinical picture.	11-18 years

Follow-up	Definition of outcome groups	Best 1	2	3	4	5	Worst 6	7	Dead
Personal re-examination by the authors or other staff psychiatrists.	Symptomatic and social adjustment criteria. Six groups: 1. complete recovery; 2. social recovery; 3. pronounced improvement with defect; 5. unimproved; 6. dead.	14%	8%	3%	7%	58%			10%
Inform.from pt., relatives,family physicians, & hospital records 51 pts. interviewed by a staff doctor; 118 rec. social serv. visit.	symptomatic and social adjustment criteria. 9 groups, which can be condensed to 4: 1. recovered; 2. partially productive; 3. non-productive; 4. hospitalized.	25%	12%	8%	56%				
Some personal interview psychiat. some interviews with relatives; some written report by pt.or relative.	symptomatic and social criteria. 5 groups: 1. complete remission; 2. social remission; 3. at home, improved. 4. remitted and relapsed; 5. unimproved.	12%	8%	9%	21%	50%			
394 personally re-examined; inform. about others from other sources.	symptomatic and social adjustment criteria. 4 groups: 1. much improved; 2. improved; 3. unimproved; 4. dead.	7%		15%		64%			15%
182 personally re-examined by authors, inform. about others from hospital records, letters, home visits to relatives & other sources.	symptomatic and social adjustment criteria. 6 groups: 1. recovered, with 1 psychotic episode; 2. recovered with 2 or more psychotic episodes; 3. improved; 4. deteriorated, not in need of public care; 5. slight deterioration, in public care; 6. severe deterioration, in public care.	29%	9%	20%	9%	11%	22%		
Personal re-examination.	Rated on a scale from 0-6, in which 0 indicates freedom from psychiatric symptoms, ability to enter into affectual contact, and complete social adjustment, and 6 indicates the most severe degree of psychic change. First three points considered to indicate good outcome and last 4 points considered to indicate bad outcome.	(1%	1%	9%)	(26%	26%	24%	13%)	

(1% 1% 9%) considered by author to be good outcome

(26% 26% 24% 13%) considered by author to be bad outcome

TABLE 2.1. continued.

Investigators	Country	Number of pts about whom FU inf. obtnd	Sample drawn from	Criteria for the diagnosis of schizophrenia	Length of follow-up
Astrup and Noreik (1966)	Norway	273	1st admiss. for functional psychosis, Gaustad Hosp., 1951-1957, with diagn. of schizophrenia at time of 1st discharge. Part of larger study of 706 pts. 1st admitted for functional psychosis.	Hospital diagnosis. Criteria not clearly stated. Said to represent a synthesis of the concepts of Kraepelin, Bleuler, and Meyer.	5-12 years
Henisz (1966)	Poland	178	1st admissions Pruszkow Mental Hosp. during the year 1956, given dx of schizophrenia on discharge.	Hospital diagnosis criteria unspecified.	7 years
Brown et al. (1966)	England	273	From screening of all pts. admitted to 3 mental hosp. in London in 1956, 1st admission & prev. admissions.	Stated to be basically those of Mayer-Gross, Slater & Roth (1954) - greatest weight given to characteristic delusions, hallucinations & speech disorders & catatonic disturbances.	5 years
Achte (1967)	Finland	96	1st admissions to Helsinki hosp. in 1950 & 1960. Part of larger study.	Essentially those of Langfeldt.	5 years
M. Bleuler (1972)	Switzerland	208	Representative sample of 653 schizophrenic pts. admitted to Burgholzli Hosp. during 1942 and 1943. Both 1st admiss. & pts. previously admitted.	Specified in detail - see text below.	20 years or more

Follow-up	Definition of outcome groups	Outcome Best 1 2 3 4 5 Worst 6 7	Dead

Follow-up	Definition of out-come groups	Best 1 2 3 4 5	Worst 6 7	Dead

66% re-examined personally; follow-up of others based on info. from relatives, hosp. records, public health officers and question-naires answered by patients.

Symptomatic and Social Adjustment criteria, together with sub-grouping according to Leonhard's subgroups of schizophrenia. 5 groups: 1 recovered; 2 improved; 3. schizophrenic per-sonality change; 4. slight schizophrenic deterioration; 5.severe schizophrenic deterior-ation.
1st 2 groups considered non-schizophrenic outcome groups, last 3 schizo-phrenic outcome groups.

(6% 10%)(17%44% 22%) consi-   considered dered by by authors authors to be to be   schizo- non-   phrenic schizo-   outcome. phrenic outcome.

Individual re-examination, hosp. inform. (102 pts.); questionnaires & letters of pts. & rela-tives (106 pts.)

Modification of the Hathaway scale. 5 groups: 1. no further trouble of original type; 2. good social adjust.; 3. inter-mit. good adjust.,relapses with hosp.; 4. readmitt. incapacitated at least once; 5. continuous trouble of original type.

17%   8% 16% 15% 44%

FU inform. from case records, OPD notes, records of MH departments, interviews with informants.

Symptomatic & social adjustment criteria. 3 groups: 1. functioning well; 2. still handicapped by symptoms; 3. still severely ill at follow up.

1st admissions
49%   23%   28%

admitted previously
30%   26%   44%

Most pts. re-interviewed. In larger series 144 person. by author, 36 inform. from other sources.

Symptomatic and social adjustment criteria. 5 groups: 1. complete recovery; 2. recovered from psychosis, possible mild defect state; 3. social recovery; 4. unable to work; 5. mental hosp. pt.

1950 series
(2%   5% 24%)(24% 38%)
1960 series
(8% 12% 31%)(20% 21%)
author consider: 1+2+3= social recovery;
4+5=no social recovery.

Personally followed by M. Bleuler throughout the follow-up period.

4 symptomatic outcome groups: 1. complete remission; 2. mild defect; 3. moderate defect; 4. severe defect.
Also 11 social outcome groups which can be condensed into good, moderate and poor.

1. symptomatic outcome
   all patients
20%   33%   24%   24%
   1st admissions only
23%   43%   19%   15%
2. social outcome
   all patients
31%   12%   55% (3% no stated
                        outcome)
   1st admissions only
40%   13%   41% (4% no stated
                        outcome)

hebephrenic cases and 5.5 per cent among catatonic cases, and Zablock's findings of no recovery among hebephrenic and catatonic patients.

Table 2.1 summarizes the results of a number of later follow-up studies of schizophrenia which present conclusions about outcome at a particular point in time. The studies cited were carried our in a number of different countries across the world, and involved relatively large numbers of patients who were followed up for relatively long periods of time.

Table 2.1 illustrates the difficulties of comparing the results of studies which utilize different definitions of schizophrenia, different outcome categories, and different methodologies and which were carried out at different points in time. There is a great variation among the findings of the different studies. One could make a case for schizophrenia having a good outcome or a bad outcome, depending on which study was selected. The percentage of first admission schizophrenic patients who were recovered or substantially improved at follow-up ranges between highs of 66 per cent in M. Bleuler's (1972) study (40 per cent if social functioning is considered rather than symptomatic outcome) and 49 per cent in the investigation of Brown and co-workers, (1966) and lows of 6.6 per cent in Rupp and Fletcher's (1939) study and 11 per cent in Johnson's (1958) follow-up of male schizophrenics.

This variation in percentage of patients with a relatively good outcome may not be due only to variations in the strictness of the definition of schizophrenia. Thus, although using somewhat different criteria, both Brown et al's., study and the Johnson study used a rather narrow definition of schizophrenia. However, the authors came to quite opposite conclusions. Brown and associates note that over one-half of all first admitted patients had an excellent five-year prognosis and required little aftercare and rehabilitation and constituted no major burden on families of community. Johnson, on the other hand, noting that only nine out of 82 male schizophrenic patients had a good outcome when followed up for 11–18 years after first admission, concluded that the prognosis for the patients studied was extremely unfavourable. The difference may be partly related to the fact that the patients in Johnson's study were first admitted in the period before neuroleptic drugs were available and before some of the recent advances in social therapies, while the patients in Brown et al's., study were first admitted in 1956, after neuroleptics were available and after the importance of social therapies was more generally recognized. In this context it should be pointed out that in comparing their results with those of previous workers over half a century, Brown and co-authors stressed that, considering the previous gloomy prediction of outcome of schizophrenia, the outcome was now more favourable than it ever had been for early cases.

The possibility that the time when the patients were first admitted may be more important than the narrowness of the diagnostic criteria with regard to outcome is also suggested by the fact that some of the earlier studies, such as those of Malamud and Render (1939), and Rennie (1939), in which a rather broad concept of schizophrenia was used, found some of the highest percentages of patients in the unimproved group (58 per cent for the Malamud and Render study, 63 per cent in Rennie's investigation).

Further evidence about the importance of the period in which the patients were first admitted is provided by Achté's (1967) study of two series of patients, one consisting of patients first admitted in 1950 and the other of patients first admitted in 1960. Comparing the five-year outcome of 45 patients in the 1950 series considered to have been schizophrenic according to rather strict criteria which were essentially those of Langfeldt (see below) with the five-year outcome of 51 patients in the 1960 series considered to be schizophrenic according to the same criteria, Achté concluded that the outcome of typical schizophrenia was definitely more favourable in 1960 than it had been ten years earlier. The percentage of cases with at least a social remission was 31 per cent in the 1950 series and 51 per cent in the 1960 series considered to be schizophrenic according to the same criteria Achté hand, Astrup and Norelk (1966) noted that both in their follow-up of patients admitted between 1951 and 1957 and their earlier follow-up of patients admitted between 1938 and 1950, 16 per cent of the schizophrenic patients had a 'non-schizophrenic' outcome. They concluded that it appeared that the prognostic significance of a diagnosis of schizophrenia had not changed despite the introduction of psychotropic drugs and considerably more social therapy and psychotherapy.

However, it is difficult to tell from the time patients were first admitted how much and what quality of care they had. Although, M. Bleuler's patients were first admitted before the current emphasis on the importance of social therapy of schizophrenia, it is clear from his work that his patients received care which had all the characteristics of good social therapy.

Thus, in considering what any individual study of group of studies contributes to knowledge about the outcome of schizophrenia, the characteristics of the study or studies must be carefully considered. In this respect, Bleuler's study warrants a more detailed consideration because of the great care with which it has been carried out, the fact that the author has personally followed the patients continuously over many years, and because of the careful consideration that he gives to diagnostic matters.

In 1972, Bleuler reported on the results of a 20-year or more follow-up of 100 male and 108 female schizophrenic patients admitted to Burgholzli Hospital in Zurich during the years 1942 and 1943. These patients are a representative sample of 267 male and 386 female schizophrenic patients admitted to the hospital during this period.

Patients with organic brain disorders were excluded. Patients were considered to be schizophrenic if they met certain criteria for psychosis and also demonstrated criteria felt to be specific for schizophrenia. In order to be considered psychotic, a patient had to exhibit at least three of the following:

1. confusion, so that a normal person would not be able to understand his way of thinking or would find it very hard to understand it — this symptom should be present not only in relation to strongly emotional matters;
2. completely incomprehensible emotional life;
3. severe excitation or stupor lasting more than a day and not explicable in formal psychological terms;

26

4. hallucinations over a long period of time;
5. delusions;
6. complete change in usual activities;
7. conviction on the part of healthy relatives and close associates that the ill person has become completely changed and that one cannot understand him any longer.

In determining which of the patients who met these criteria for psychosis should be diagnosed as schizophrenic, Bleuler considered the following characteristics to be of particular importance:

1. *Doppelte Buchführung* ('double bookkeeping') – it is possible to recognize normal intellectual capabilities in the patient even when he is suffering from severe psychotic symptoms;
2. schizophrenic thought disorder is present, which is clearly *not* any of the following: flight of ideas, disturbed chain of thought as a result of an acute exogenous psychosis, the result of labile attention, the result of lack of feeling for the situation, perseveration in organic disorders, confabulation, the result of dreamlike thinking during hysterical episodes, special religious thoughts in depressions;
3. loss of emotional contact as a result of a high degree of detachment of all affective expression;
4. severe depersonalization;
5. severe catatonia;
6. delusions which are frequent in schizophrenia and rare in other conditions, such as disorganized delusions and delusions not associated with depressed mood;
7. hallucinations which occur frequently in schizophrenia and rarely in other conditions, such as grotesque feelings of radiation, and hearing thoughts;
8. severe, secondary memory illusions and hallucinations in established primary memory.

In considering whether the patients would have been considered schizophrenic according to other schools of psychiatric thought, Bleuler notes that nine patients might have been considered schizo-affective, three might have been excluded because the illness started after the age of 60, three patients might have been excluded because the illness began with alcoholic hallucinosis, although the disorder continued and developed into a chronic psychotic disorder, while six patients had shortlasting psychotic episodes with schizophrenic symptoms related to a severe mental trauma and may have been called psychogenic psychoses or schizophrenic reactions by some psychiatrists. Two patients were borderline cases between schizophrenia and paranoia. Bleuler concluded that not more than 23 of the 208 patients would have been likely to have been diagnosed differently by other psychiatrists.

Of the 208 probands, 68 were first admissions. Bleuler personally followed up the patients, and personally examined their families, giving particular attention to 61 siblings of the probands having at least one hospitalization for a schizophrenic episode.

Bleuler divided patients into four outcome groups: complete remission, mild defect, moderate defect and severe defect. Of the 208 probands, 56 were considered to have demonstrated no stable type of outcome. Of the remainder, 20 per cent felt to be in complete remission, 33 per cent to demonstrate a mild defect, 24 per cent to demonstrate a moderate defect, and 24 per cent a severe defect. Thus, 53 per cent of patients, about whom a decision as to type of outcome could be made, were either judged to be in complete remission or to be suffering from a mild defect.

Of the 68 first admissions, 21 were considered to have demonstrated no stable type of outcome. Of the others, 23 per cent were judged as being in complete remission, 43 per cent had a mild defect, 19 per cent had a moderate defect, and 15 per cent had a severe defect. Thus, of the first admissions about whom a judgment as to type of outcome could be made, 66 per cent were felt to be in complete remission or to have a mild defect. There was thus a tendency for the first admissions to have a better outcome than the total cohort.

Bleuler also assessed patients in terms of social outcome, dividing them into groups which can be condensed as follows: (a) self-supporting, living outside an institution; (b) partly self-supporting, living outside an institution; (c) not self-supporting, or self-supporting only in periods; (d) constantly hospitalized or hospitalized for most of the time, moderately handicapped; (e) constantly hospitalized, severely disorganized; (f) no stable social condition reached.

Considering all of the probands, 31 per cent fell into group (a), 12 per cent into group (b), 8 per cent into group (c), 26 per cent into group (d), 21 per cent in group (e), and 3 per cent in group (f). Thus, combining groups (c), (d), and (e), 31 per cent of the patients had a good social outcome, 12 per cent a moderately good social outcome, and 55 per cent of the patients had a poor social outcome. For the group of first-admission patients, the percentages were 40 per cent in group (a), 13 per cent in group (b), 8 per cent in group (c), 20 per cent in group (d), 13 per cent in group (e), and 4 per cent in group (f).

Of the 208 probands, 10 per cent had one admission followed by discharge and no further admission, 73 per cent had more than one admission and more than one discharge, 10 per cent were discharged from the hospital after the first admission, and have been in the hospital constantly since the second admission, while 6 per cent have never been discharged and have been in the hospital constantly since the first admission. The corresponding figures for the first-admission probands only are 31 per cent, 47 per cent, 13 per cent, and 9 per cent.

2.3.2 Studies of the pattern of course of schizophrenia

The previously mentioned studies present results which for the most part indicate something about the outcome of schizophrenia after a certain number of years. However, a number of studies present data which are more related to the pattern of course of schizophrenia over a number of years and some of these will now be described. Some of the studies mentioned in the previous section also provide information about pattern of course, and such aspects of those studies will also be described here.

Müller (1951) carried out a 30-year follow-up study of a group of 100 schizophrenics first admitted to hospital in 1917—18, and a 15-year follow-up study of another group of 100 schizophrenic patients first admitted in 1933. Patients were selected on the basis of hospital diagnosis. Follow-up evaluations were made primarily on the basis of information obtained from letters and review of hospital charts. Patients were divided into seven groups, according to the type of course. The types of course and the percentages of patients that Müller felt exhibited each of them were as follows:

1. acute onset, recovered on discharge, remained in recovered state throughout follow-up period — 16 per cent;

2. acute onset, some subsequent attacks, but always discharged as recovered — 17 per cent;

3. acute onset progressing into chronic state — 12 per cent;

4. acute onset, subsequent attacks, initially recovery after attacks, but eventually progression into chronic state — 11 per cent;

5. insidious chronic course, with improvement to point where they can be discharged — 10.5 per cent;

6. insidious chronic course, continual need to be in an institution, or out of institution for only very brief periods — 30.5 per cent;

7. acute onset with death during the first attack or within first six months after the attack started — 3 per cent.

Arnold (1955) reported on a sample of 500 schizophrenic patients followed for three to 30 years. His results revealed:

1. a phasic course of illness leading to complete cure in 15.6 per cent;
2. a phasic course which then became shiftlike (new acute symptomatology followed by partial recovery) in 4 per cent;
3. a phasic course leading to deterioration on 0.4 per cent;
4. a phasic course which leads to deterioration punctuated by exacerbations of symptomatology in 3.4 per cent;
5. a shiftlike (some residual pathology) course in 9.6 per cent;
6. a shiftlike course leading to deterioration in 3.6 per cent;
7. a shiftlike course leading to deterioration punctuated by exacerbation in 14 per cent.
8. a gradual deterioration in 7.2 per cent;
9 a gradual deterioration punctuated by exacerbation in 38 per cent; and
10. mixed psychotic courses in 6.6 per cent.

In a follow-up of 344 patients observed personally over a period of 12 years and followed up for at least five years, Ey (1959) divided cases into five groups. The groups and the percentages of patients that Ey classified in each of them were:

1. severe forms (corresponding, according to Ey, to the Kraepelinian description of hebephrenia, catatonia and paranoid dementia, conditions which lead more or less rapidly to dementia) — 21.7 per cent;

2. intermediate forms (which Ey says correspond to Bleulerian schizophrenia, a large number of which, without ending in dementia, demonstrate autistic disintegration of the personality with typical defect) – 36.2 per cent;

Ey considers these first two groups to represent the central nucleus schizophrenia.

3. delusional marginal forms (systematized and fantastic delusions without marked disintegration) – 7 per cent;

4. marginal schizophrenic forms (cases which pose the problem of delimitation from neuroses) – 12.5 per cent;

5. acute or cyclical forms (cases which have shown one or several episodes, without chronic deterioration) – 22.6 per cent.

From among these patients, Ey studied 120 cases of acute delusional psychoses that were diagnosed as schizophrenia and were followed up for at least five years. He found that 44 per cent recovered without any after-effects for at least five years, 21 per cent had other acute episodes, without chronic organization of mental disturbance, while 35 per cent evolved as chronic schizophrenics with characteristic defect.

Ey indicates his feeling that the 65 per cent of acute delusional cases which had been diagnosed as schizophrenic but did not develop chronic deterioration were in fact misdiagnosed, and that they were not or did not become schizophrenic. He concludes that schizophrenia should be defined as a chronic delusional psychosis which progressively destroys the sense of reality and the relation of the person to his world, and that the acute delusional psychoses which do not go on to this type of chronic deterioration do not belong to the same genus. He feels that the subgroups of schizophrenia are nothing more than successive phases, stages, or different pathways of the regression into autism.

Another method of classification in which type of outcome is built into the classification system itself is that proposed by Snezhnevsky (1972). Snezhnevsky's system has two axes, a type of course axis and a syndrome axis. There are three major types of course of schizophrenia in this system: (a) continuous (sluggish, progredient, or malignant), (b) recurrent, and (c) shiftlike progressive. It is stressed that groups of syndromes are associated with particular types of course and that there is a 'stereotype' of each type of course, involving some regularities in the temporal sequence of the syndromes.

From 1965 to 1969, Liebermann (1974), using this classification system retrospectively assessed the course of 2021 schizophrenic patients from one catchment area in Moscow. The period assessed ranged from one to 50 years. He studied the relationship between type of course and age of onset of the disorder and noted that for a malignant course the peak age of onset was between 10 and 29 years, for shiftlike progressive schizophrenia the peak age of onset was from ages 20–28, and for periodic (recurrent) schizophrenia it was from ages 40–49. A malignant course was more frequent among males than among females while shiftlike and periodic courses were more frequent among females. Males tended to have an earlier age of onset than females for all types of course.

In the study of Brown et al. (1966) described in the previous section, the authors

TABLE 2.2. PATTERNS OF COURSE OF SCHIZOPHRENIC PATIENTS OBSERVED BY M. BLEULER.*

Pattern of course	Schizophrenic patients admitted until 1941	Schizophrenic patients admitted 1942-1943	Schizophrenic patients first admitted 1942-1943
I. Continuous patterns of evolution			
1. Acute onset leading to the most severe chronic end state (catastrophic schizophrenia)	5 - 18%	1% $\pm$ .69	0
2. Chronic onset leading to the most severe chronic end state	10 - 20%	12% $\pm$ 2.27	8% $\pm$ 3.34
3. Acute onset leading to chronic, moderate or mild end state	less than 5%	2% $\pm$ .97	6% $\pm$ 2.92
4. Chronic onset leading to moderate or mild end state (defect)	5 - 10%	23% $\pm$ 2.94	21% $\pm$ 5.01
II. Episodic course			
5. Episodic, leading to the most severe chronic end state (complete deterioration)	less than 5%	9% $\pm$ 1.99	5% $\pm$ 2.68
6. Episodic, leading to chronic moderate or mild end state (defect)	30 - 40%	27% $\pm$ 3.1	26% $\pm$ 5.4
7. Episodic, leading to recovery (benign form with only one single or several psychotic phases)	25 - 35%	22% $\pm$ 2.89	30% $\pm$ 5.64

* after Bleuler, M. (1972).

noted several aspects of the course of the first admission and previously admitted schizophrenics followed up for five years.

They found that 28 per cent of the first admitted and 48 per cent of the previously admitted patients showed a chronic course, with symptoms of at least moderate severity present nearly all the time; 27 per cent of first admissions and 29 per cent of patients previously admitted had an episodic course, with relatively symptom-free intervals, but recurrence throughout the five years. In 11 per cent of the first admissions and 14 per cent of those previously admitted, the disturbance occurred after the key discharge during the first year.

In his previously mentioned long-term follow-up of schizophrenic patients, M. Bleuler (1972) describes several main longitudinal patterns of the course of schizophrenia, and indicates the percentage of patients noted to demonstrate each pattern in his study of patients admitted between 1942 and 1943 and in an earlier study of patients followed until 1941. The patterns are divided into those demonstrating continuous evolution and those demonstrating episodic evolution. The patterns, and the percentage of patients demonstrating each of them in the two series are reported in Table 2.2.

Bleuler notes that there are also other, atypical courses, such as recovery after chronic evolution, or acute episodes after long-standing chronic evolution, but that these make up only about 5 per cent of the course in the 1941 or in the later material.

Bleuler points out that the evolution from acute episode to the most severe deterioration has decreased in frequency between the time of the earlier material and of the later material. He notes that the results indicate that there has been an increase in the percentage of patients with a chronic course that ends up in a moderate to mild defect, but that there has been no clear decrease in the percentage of patients with a chronic onset or episodic course that go on to the most severe chronic deterioration. Bleuler feels that his findings support the optimism of the view that treatment influences can decrease the percentage of patients with acute onset who go on to develop the course of catastrophic schizophrenia, but that they do not support the optimism of the view that such influences can decrease the percentage of patients with chronic onset or with episodic schizophrenia that progress to chronic deterioration.

2.3.3 Studies of prognostic factors

Since it was early noted by many investigators that the outcome of patients given the diagnosis of schizophrenia may vary greatly, even if a large percentage of patients have one particular type of outcome, many investigators have attempted to determine whether specific premorbid, past history, socio-demographic, course, or initial episode clinical factors are related to specific types of outcome. There have been large numbers of such studies.

This review will limit itself to a few of the major studies of some of the most frequently assessed possible predictors of outcome. A major part of the literature concerning prognostic factors has been concerned with making distinctions between two types of psychoses. These two types have variously been referred to as schizophrenia and schizophreniform psychoses, process and reactive schizophrenia and good outcome and bad outcome schizophrenia. The two groups have usually been claimed to differ on a variety of premorbid, acute symptomatological, and course factors. In view of the large number of studies revolving around such a dichotomy this area will be reviewed in some detail.

2.3.3.1 The schizophrenia complex versus the schizophreniform complex

Since so many subsequent studies of prognosis are based on Langfeldt's distinction between schizophrenia and schizophreniform psychoses, it is useful to review the development of Langfeldt's concepts. In *The Prognosis in Schizophrenia and the Factors Influencing the Course of the Disease*, published in 1937, Langfeldt reported the results of a catamnestic study of 100 patients. These patients were individuals admitted to the University Psychiatric Clinic at Vinderen during the years 1926–29, and whose diagnosis had been regarded at the clinic as 'unmistakably schizophrenia'. The patients were personally re-examined by Langfeldt in 1936 and divided by him into four outcome groups: *completely cured* (with regard to ability to receive impressions, apprehension, attention, and mental productiveness; no thought disorder or other psychotic symptoms); *partially cured* (mental condition stable for some years, slight anomalies in the form of mild disorders of thinking; or isolated symptoms to which the patient has adjusted – for example, a certain degree of autism; most of these patients were fully capable of working and were regular in their behaviour); *improved*: psychosis has shown a tendency to steady improvement or patient has been in a condition of more or less complete remission); *not cured* (the remainder – those continuing to have process symptoms and those that have passed into a final phase in which there has been no tendency toward improvement).

On follow-up, Langfeldt found that 17 patients were completely cured, four were cured, with defects, 13 were improved, and 66 were not cured. He then went back to the case histories, to investigate prognostic factors. He reviewed the symptomatology of the acute phase of the psychosis, and divided the patients into five main groups:

1. The purely paranoid conditions with primary delusions

    (a) 'dementia persecutiva' – cases with marked primary and clearly formed ideas of persecution;

    (b) 'physical influence delirium' – marked symptoms of influence and depersonalization without catatonic symptoms or formed ideas of persecution, but characterized by internal (physical) hallucinations;

    (c) pronounced projection syndromes – auditory hallucinations, visual hallucinations, thought projection, thought stealing, feelings of passivity and other symptoms of depersonalization;* feeling of loss of contact with reality, without formed delusions of persecution or prominent internal hallucinations.

---

*It should be noted that Langfeldt (1937; 1960) used the term 'depersonalization' to denote certain characteristic delusional experiences which should be distinguished from depersonalization as a symptom in some other disorders (neurosis, epilepsy, acute intoxications, or the so-called 'extreme states of consciousness').

2. Purely catatonic cases.
3. Catatonic—paranoid cases.
4. Hebephrenia-like.
5. Atypical (mainly characterized by pathoplastic features such as depression, hypochondriacal, hysterical, hypomanic symptoms, mild symptoms of depersonalization, vague projection symptoms, ideas of reference, occasionally with conspicious symptoms of other forms of psychosis.

Langfeldt's classification resulted in 20 cases of 'dementia persecutiva', eight with 'physical influence delirium', 20 with marked projection symptoms, 12 typical catatonic cases, 23 paranoid catatonic cases, four hebephrenia-like cases and 13 atypical cases.

Langfeldt then made the striking finding that of the 13 cases with atypical symptomatology. 11 were cured and two were cured with defect. He also noted that the typical catatonic cases seemed to have the worst prognosis, with none cured or cured with defect.

In view of his findings, Langfeldt concluded about the prognostic value of acute phase symptomatology that:

1. massive influence-depersonalization and derealization symptoms, schizophrenic conditions dominated by primary psychologically noncomprehensible delusions and other typical schizophrenic symptoms usually reflect a process which clearly leads towards severe mental deterioration;
2. typical catatonic cases usually have a poor prognosis;
3. atypical 'schizophreniform' symptomatology reveals manic-depressive, psychogenic, or pathoplastic trends, particularly when the psychogenic content reflects the precipitating situation. Clouding of consciousness and comprehensible self-reference tendencies and interpretations are usually prognostically favourable factors;
4. acute onset of a psychosis resembling schizophrenia usually has a good prognosis if it is not catatonic schizophrenia. These are usually schizophreniform, exogenously or psychogenically precipitated conditions.

Langfeldt thus felt that process symptoms included massive primary persecutory ideas, sensations of influence, depersonalization, derealization, and massive catatonic-stuporous symptoms, while atypical symptoms included manic-depressive, psychogenic and pathoplastic symptoms, clouding of consciousness and incoherence.

In *The Prognosis of Schizophrenia* (1956) Langfeldt summarized his views at that point about important prognostic factors in schizophrenia.

In considering the relationship between particular symptoms during the acute psychotic phase of schizophrenia and prognosis, Langfeldt concludes that the three principal types of 'genus schizophrenia' corresponding to Kraepelin's dementia praecox, are well circumscribed disorders with a typical symptomatology and a special type of course. He notes that he feels that special derealization and depersonalization symptoms in schizophrenia are so often associated with an unfavourable course that it must be assumed that they are in one way or another associated with the basic disorder. He concludes that the symptomatology associated with unfavourable prognosis is 'a symptomatology mainly characteristic of Kraepelin's dementia praecox types with the basic traits of autism and emotional blunting as stressed especially by E. Bleuler in his description of schizophrenia. Particularly unfavourable are those cases which are characterized by typical depersonalization and derealization symptoms in clear consciousness and absence of admixtures from other psychoses'. He also notes that in such cases the prognosis is poor, regardless of the type of onset. Other factors which Langfeldt feels are unfavourable for prognosis are (a) an emotionally and intellectually poorly developed personality; (b) no demonstrable precipitating factors; (c) insidious onset; (d) an unfavourable environment before and after the outbreak of the disease.

Factors he feels are associated with a favourable outcome are: (a) an emotionally and intellectually well-developed premorbid personality; (b) demonstrable precipitating factors; (c) acute onset; (d) a mental symptomatology characterized by a mixed picture, especially with admixture of manic-depressive traits, clouding of consciousness, or symptoms of organic (perhaps toxic) and psychogenic origin and without the 'typical' blunting of emotional life; (e) a favourable environment before and after the outbreak of the disorder, with a psychologically correct attitude on the part of those who surround the patient to his problems.

In a series of papers in the early 1940s Otto Kant made observations similar to those of Langfeldt. Reporting on the results of a study of 39 recovered schizophrenic patients, Kant (1940, 1941a) concluded that all of the recovered schizophrenic patients demonstrated some features that deviated from the classical picture of schizophrenia. Later Kant (1941b) compared this group of recovered patients with a group of 39 deteriorated patients that were inpatients at the time. He found that factors which he had noted to be prominent in the recovered group, such as acute onset, psychogenic precipitants, clouding of consciousness, extroversion, and pyknic physique were less frequently present in the deteriorated group, and he concluded that these factors deserved consideration as prognostic indicators.

A number of later studies were concerned with the distinction between schizophrenia and schizophreniform psychoses. Eitinger, Laane and Langfeldt (1958) followed up 154 patients admitted to the University Psychiatric Clinic, Vinderen, Oslo, from 1940 to 1949 who were discharged with a diagnosis of schizophrenia or schizophreniform psychosis. The series represented 19.8 per cent of all discharged patients. Eitinger and Laane personally examined and diagnosed all 154 patients on follow-up and divided them into four outcome groups (a) complete remission; (b) much improved; (c) improved; and (d) unchanged, perhaps even deteriorated. Langfeldt, meanwhile, independently and without knowledge of the follow-up results, reviewed the case histories and revised the discharge diagnosis on the basis of symptomatology present at the time of the initial admission, again classifying patients into two groups, schizophrenia and schizophreniform psychosis. Langfeldt also predicted the outcome of each patient in terms of the same four outcome groups used in the follow-up evaluation.

Langfeldt's reclassification resulted in 110 diagnoses of schizophrenia and 44 diagnoses of schizophreniform psychosis. At the follow-up evaluation 105 of Langfeldt's 110 schizophrenic cases were diagnosed by Eitinger and Laane as schizophrenia while five were diagnosed as schizophreniform cases. Of Langfeldt's 44 schizophreniform cases, 39 were given the diagnosis of schizophreniform psychosis at follow-up, and five were given the diagnosis of schizophrenia. There was also a striking agreement between Langfeldt's prognoses and the outcome noted at follow-up. Thus, on follow-up, 92 of Langfeldt's 110 schizophrenic patients were found to be unchanged or deteriorated, while only ten of his 44 schizophreniform psychoses had such a bad outcome.

The authors concluded that schizophrenia and schizophreniform psychoses probably represent two different groups of disorders, both from a symptomatological and prognostic point of view.

In a similar study, Stephens and Astrup (1963) attempted to predict outcome in a group of patients given the diagnosis at the time of discharge from the inpatient department of the Henry Phipps Psychiatric Clinic in Baltimore. The charts of 178 patients hospitalized between 1944 and 1954 were used. Diagnoses had been made by the psychiatrist in charge and the chief resident. Patients with diagnoses of paranoid state, schizoid personality and latent schizophrenia were excluded; 143 of the patients (80 per cent) were followed-up between five and 13 years after discharge by letter, telephone or personal contacts. Patients were graded into three categories on follow-up: *recovered* (either employed or doing housework without difficulty, no residual symptomatology of their psychoses); *improved* (no longer psychotic in any way, most of them employed or taking care of their homes, although they showed residual signs of the past illness and could not be considered entirely recovered); and *unimproved* (all of these were in psychiatric hospitals, except for four who were considered commitable although they were being taken care of at home by their relatives). At follow-up, 35 patients were rated as recovered, 72 as improved and 36 as unimproved.

Stephens and Astrup rediagnosed the patients retrospectively, on the basis of the case histories, before the follow-up results were known to them. They reclassified patients into four groups as follows: (a) a group made up of nine subgroups of Leonhard's 'systematic schizophrenia' and of the group 'early infantile autism'; (b) a group made of Leonhard's three forms of 'atypical schizophrenia'; (c) a group made up of Leonhard's three types of 'cycloid psychoses', as well as pseudoneurotic and pseudopsychopathic schizophrenia and depersonalization psychosis; (d) a group of reactive psychoses as described in the Scandinavian literature.

Patients in the first two groups were considered to be 'process' patients and those in the last two groups to be 'non-process' patients. At follow-up only two of the 97 non-process patients were rated unimproved, whereas about half of the 81 process patients were rated unimproved. The non-process groups had significantly more patients rated both improved and recovered on follow-up.

Welner and Strömgren (1958) carried out a genetic and clinical follow-up study of a group of schizophreniform psychoses considered to be benign and differentiated from the main group of more malignant schizophrenia by means of clinical criteria. A selection was made from 106 patients admitted to the Psychiatric

Clinic of the University of Copenhagen (during the years 1936–39) and the Department of Psychiatry of Aarhus (during the years 1945–50) were selected. The psychoses in these patients were characterized by several common schizophrenic symptoms, but at the same time also contained features suggesting a favourable prognosis. Absence of autism and the presence of catathymic features were the main clinical criteria for selecting patients. A follow-up carried out 1.5–20 years after admission (average 8.8 years) indicated that 72 probands were either cured or were suffering from non-schizophrenic abnormalities, while 30 patients went on to develop what appeared to be chronic schizophrenia. The expectancy of psychoses, particularly schizophrenia, among the siblings of the 72 patients that did not go on to a chronic schizophrenic course was significantly less than the corresponding expectancies for a group of 'true' schizophrenics, while the expectancy for neuroses and character disorders was significantly higher in the siblings of the schizophreniform patients. The authors concluded that the family picture indicated that the psychoses studied were not manifestations of a specific genetic factor. They also pointed out that it was not possible to differentiate with certainty between benign schizophreniform and more malignant schizophrenic psychoses during the acute phase since 30 of the original patients went on to suffer from what appeared to be chronic schizophrenia.

Vaillant (1962) reviewed a number of prognostic studies of schizophrenia which contrasted recovered schizophrenics with average or poor outcome schizophrenia, and on the basis of these studies selected six factors for further examination: (a) history of a blood relative with a psychotic depression; (b) acute onset; (c) confusion or disorientation during the acute episode; (d) absence of a schizoid adjustment; (e) a clear precipitating event and (f) presence of symptoms suggesting psychotic depression. He noted that all of these factors were correlated with recovery in schizophrenia in the studies of Kant and Langfeldt described above. Vaillant then selected 30 cases of recovered schizophrenics and a control group of 30 schizophrenics and compared the two groups with regard to the six prognostic factors. The patients were selected from among those admitted to the Massachussetts Mental Health Centre over a two-year period. Patients were followed in psychotherapy for a year or more, so that assessment of remission of schizophrenic symptoms was based on a longitudinal recording on the mental status. Recovered patients were those the resident psychiatrist following the patient considered: (a) were not now schizophrenic by any reasonable stretch of the imagination; (b) had resumed performance at the level of highest prior achievement; and (c) showed no flattening of affect, loose associations, or ideas of reference and had demonstrated the ability to achieve a gratifying relationship with at least one non-family member.

All six of the prognostic criteria proved to be significantly related to recovery. An attempt to separate the individual cases by the number of positive prognostic factors indicated that 97 per cent of the recovered group had three or more positive prognostic factors compared to 27 per cent of the unrecovered group with that many positive prognostic factors.

Vaillant (1964) investigated the predictive power of these same six factors and an additional factor, preoccupation with death, in two prospective studies, one a ten-year follow-up of 72 consecutive schizophrenic admissions to the Massachusetts Mental Health Center between 1947 and 1950, and the other a short-term follow-up study of 103 consecutive schizophrenic patients admitted during 1961 and 1962.

Case histories were rated for the presence of the seven prognostic factors and a prognostic score of 0–7 was given to each patient. Patients with scores of 4 or above were predicted to recover. Combining results for the two groups, it was found that subsequent clinical course was correctly predicted in 82 per cent of cases.

Stephens, Astrup and Mangrum (1966) in a similar study, followed up 350 patients diagnosed as schizophrenic and hospitalized at the Henry Phipps Psychiatric Clinic (Baltimore). Of those followed up for at least five years, 50 poor-outcome patients were identified and compared with a group of 50 recovered patients with at least a five-year follow-up. Case histories were rated for the presence or absence of 54 possible prognostic factors. Using the eight factors which showed a significant difference between the two groups at the $p < 0.01$ level (acute onset, precipitating factors, married, good premorbid history, depression, not schizoid, guilt, confusion or disorientation on admission), a scale was devised; 82 per cent of the recovered schizophrenics had scores of 4 or more on the scale, and 80 per cent of the deteriorated schizophrenics had scores of less than 4. The authors concluded that their work confirmed Vaillant's method of predicting schizophrenic remission and suggested that elaborate subclassifications of schizophrenia may be of less prognostic value than simpler methods which assign patients to a point on a prognostic continuum.

In the study by Achté described above (1967), the author classified patients into those suffering from typical schizophrenia (using criteria essentially the same as those of Langfeldt), those with a schizophreniform psychosis, and an intermediate group.

A five-year follow-up revealed that seven of 34 patients admitted for schizophreniform psychoses in 1950 developed typical schizophrenia later. Two additional such cases were noted at the time of the 1965 follow-up. A five-year follow-up of the 1960 series revealed that only one of the 25 schizophreniform patients had become typically schizophrenic.

Achté pointed out that the five-year outcome for patients with schizophreniform psychoses was highly significantly more favourable than for patients with typical schizophrenia. Of the 1950 patients with schizophreniform psychoses 62 per cent and 76 per cent of those in the 1960 series made a complete recovery within five years compared to 2 per cent and 8 per cent for typically schizophrenic patients; 83 per cent of the 1950 schizophreniform patients and 96 per cent of those in the 1960 series made a social recovery within five years compared to 31 per cent and 51 per cent for patients with typical schizophrenia.

2.3.3.2 Individual prognostic factors

In addition to those studies mentioned above, there have been many studies which have assessed the relationship between individual social, historical, course, and clinical factors and outcome. The results of two of the studies of large numbers of predictive factors will be briefly summarized. Further discussion of individual prognostic factors will be presented in Chapter 10.

Schofield *et al.* (1954) followed up 210 schizophrenic patients hospitalized in the psychiatric service of the University of Minnesota Hospital between 1938 and 1944, and indentified a good outcome group (28 per cent) and a poor outcome group (60 per cent). The good outcome group was made up of those patients who were found to have had no further difficulty or were making a good adjustment. The poor-outcome group was made up of those who were found to have spent over half of the follow-up period in a mental institution or had experienced difficulties which necessitated continuous care by their families. The two groups were rated and contrasted with respect to 200 personality, past history, and present illness factors. Of the 200 items, only 17 significant differences between the two groups were noted (ten would have been expected by chance if the 0.05 level of significance were used). The good-outcome group was differentiated from the poor-outcome group by shorter duration of illness prior to hospitalization, more rapid development of symptomatology; absence of previous episodes; poor school deportment; steady church attendance; good marital adjustment; affection towards mate; stereotypies; tensions; depression; tearfulness; disorientation for time; and absence of ideas of reference.

Simon and Wirt (1961) studied the relationship between prognostic factors and outcome in 80 first hospital admission patients diagnosed as schizophrenic. They investigated personality, historical, demographic and social history data, and 12 prognostic factors reported in the literature as having prognostic validity (affective expression, orientation, direction of aggression, type of onset, duration of illness, precipitating stress, marital status, school deportment, marital adjustment, presence of previous episodes, adjustment to the hospital, and presence of ideas of reference), in relationship to hospital course and outcome one year following hospitalization. They found three prognostic factors that discriminated between those who had improved at the time of discharge from the hospital and those who had not — exaggerated expression of affect, rapid onset of symptoms, and a brief rather than an extended period between the onset and hospitalization – all prognostically favourable at a statistically significant level. No reliable differences at discharge were found for such demographic data as age, ordinal position in family, number of siblings, educational level, religion, socioeconomic status, number of children or incidence of mental illness in the family.

Two social history factors predicted outcome of hospital treatment — 'absence of consistent parental figure', which predicted poor treatment response, and 'mother would do anything for the child', which predicted favourable outcome.

An analysis of detailed social histories indicated 13 behavioural variables which were found to differentiate good and poor outcome one year after hospitalization. These were: (a) poor outcome — no behaviour problem at school or home; lack of socialization during childhood; unwarranted threats by parents; poor heterosexual relationships; few adolescent and early adult interests; poor work history; inability to express aggression; possible organicity; inability to express feelings; and fears associated with school and peers: (b) good outcome — specific traumatic episodes which might have precipitated onset; good work history during childhood and adolescence; and marriage.

Further discussion of difficulties in the interpretation of results with respect to individual prognostic factors such as marital status, premorbid personality, social factors, duration of hospitalization at first admission, type on onset, and specific symptoms during acute psychotic phases will be presented in Chapter 10.

2.3.4. Studies which compare the outcome of schizophrenia with the outcome of other functional psychoses, particularly affective psychoses

There are few studies in which the same methodology is used to assess the course and outcome of a group of schizophrenic patients and the course and outcome of patients with other diagnoses. In the previously described study of Astrup and Noreik (1966), the authors reported on the outcome of patients with several different types of functional psychosis. They found that while 45 of 273 schizophrenic patients followed up were recovered or improved, all 38 of the manic-depressives followed up were recovered or improved. They also reported that 87 out of 107 patients given the diagnosis of depressive reactive psychoses, were recovered or improved at follow-up, while the figures for other reactive psychoses were: paranoid, 60 out of 113; hysterical 67 out of 82; and confusional, 3 out of 4. Of 89 schizophreniform patients, 52 were either recovered or improved at follow-up. It thus appears rather clear that in Astrup and Noreik's material the schizophrenic patients had a poorer outcome than patients with other functional psychoses.

Norris (1959) identified schizophrenic and manic-depressive groups of patients (among others) admitted to two observation units and three mental hospitals between 1947 and 1949, and followed them up through to the end of December 1951. Of the schizophrenic patients, 57 per cent were followed up for the entire follow-up period. From these results Norris concluded that the prognosis of schizophrenia is poor. She noted that two years after admission 60 per cent of the males and 65 per cent of the females were in mental hospitals, although not all of these had been hospitalized continuously throughout this period. Five years after admission, 51 per cent of the original males and 56 per cent of the original females were in mental hospitals. Schizophrenic males admitted in the first half of 1947 had spent an average of 136.5 weeks in mental hospitals by the end of 1951, while for women the figure was 130.9. Norris notes that on the average a schizophrenic patient admitted in any single year will be hospitalized 55 per cent of the time during the next five years.

In the same study, Norris found that at the end of the follow-up period 73 per cent of the manic-depressive patients were alive and out of the hospital. The average duration of hospitalization for men admitted in the first six months of 1947 was 70 weeks, while among women the figure was 75 weeks. Norris concludes that the findings indicate that manic-depressive states have, in the long run, a bad prognosis, but compared to schizophrenia the prognosis is good.

Norris compares the proportion of discharges to admissions by specified intervals for eight psychiatric disorders: schizophrenia, manic-depressive psychosis, psychoses of old age, epileptic psychoses, general paresis, other specified organic psychoses; psychoneuroses, and disorders of behaviour and character. She notes that of the six psychotic groups the manic-depressives had the best outcome. Two-thirds of the patients admitted with a manic-depressive diagnosis had been discharged by the end of six months. Over 80 per cent of the patients had been discharged at the end of two years. On the other hand, more than half of the schizophrenic patients were still in the hospital after six months, and more than a third after two years. However, she points out that even for the manic-depressive patients one-fifth had either died or were still in the hospital two years after admission.

The outcome for the psychoneurotic patients included in Norris's study was considerably better than for the psychoses, as four-fifths of the neurotic admissions had been discharged by the end of six months. However, between 5 and 8 per cent of neurotic patients had been in the hospital continuously for two years.

Shepherd (1957) has carried out a study which included a five-year follow-up of patients admitted to an English county mental hospital between 1945 and 1947. He found a considerable difference in outcome between those patients admitted with the diagnoses of schizophrenia and affective psychoses. The mean duration of hospitalization was nearly 40 months for the schizophrenics and 9.5 months for the affective patients. Of schizophrenics admitted for the first time between 1945 and 1947, 72 per cent were still in the hospital after six months, 48.2 per cent after two years, and 36.1 per cent after 54 months. Of the patients admitted for affective psychoses, 17 per cent were still in the hospital after six months, 6.6 per cent after two years and 2.8 per cent after 54 months. The 'unspecified' functional psychoses were found to be closer to the affective disorders in outcome than to the schizophrenic disorders.

2.3.5. Studies of course and outcome of schizophrenia in differing cultures

There is an insufficient body of knowledge about the course and outcome of schizophrenia in different cultures. No comparative studies have been published to date which have used standardized criteria for diagnosis and assessment of change and simultaneous selection of samples. A report by Murphy and Raman (1971) suggested that patients diagnosed as schizophrenic on the Island of Mauritius had more favourable outcomes than a British comparison group. The Mauritius cohort had a higher percentage of patients functioning 'normally and symptom-free' and the Mauritius patients had fewer relapses in the period between discharge and follow-up. The authors point out that no standardized criteria were used in making the diagnosis of schizophrenia. It should also be noted that the British comparison group is from a previous study and that the two studies are not directly comparable. An interesting finding in the presenting pictures of the Mauritius group suggests the possibility of cultural variation in symptomatology and its significance for outcome. Classification of outcome into healthy and disturbed was carried out, and presenting symptoms were then compared for these two outcome groups in the

Mauritius cohort. Further analysis of the data presented in this study indicates that two symptoms appear to have a different relationship to outcome in Mauritius than is suggested by the usual findings in Western culture studies. In most Western studies, excitement is usually associated with a relatively good outcome and social withdrawal is usually associated with a relatively poor outcome. In the Mauritius study, out of 61 patients with excitement on first admission, 31 were in the healthy-outcome group and 30 in the disturbed-outcome group. Of the 44 Mauritius patients with social withdrawal on first admission, 28 were in the healthy-outcome group and 16 in the disturbed-outcome group.

Rin and Lin (1962) noted that some patients from aboriginal tribes on Formosa recovered more easily than did those from the Chinese population. Katz, Sanborn, and Gudeman (1967) have observed differences among ethnic groups in Hawaii. Of particular interest was their finding that patients exhibited a pathology dependent upon the setting in which they were observed — hospital or community. Murphy (1969) has suggested that there may be cultural differences in responsiveness to psychotropic drugs. Thus, for example, Malaysian patients seem to respond to relatively low doses of phenothiazines.

Lambo (1968) has pointed out that prognostic criteria developed from Western studies are more applicable to Africans who have come into contact with Western culture than to those Africans who have not had such contact, particularly if they are illiterate.

In his paper on psychoses in Indonesia, Pfeiffer (1967) emphasized the similarities between schizophrenic pictures in Indonesia and Europe. He concluded that 'chronic defect states .. seem to be as frequent as in Europe and essentially conform to the usual forms'. He describes, on the other hand, 'acute confusional states' which occur in Indonesia and which can mimic acute schizophrenia but turn out to be of diverse aetiology (infections, hypovitaminosis, for example) and often tend to run a remitting course.

Cultural factors within the same country may change over time. Sakurai *et al.* (1964) in Japan have compared schizophrenic patients hospitalized at Kyushu University in 1939—41, 1947—49, 1952—54, and 1961—63. They noted that hebe-phrenics are admitted with the same frequency but that the frequency of catatonia has markedly decreased. Visual hallucinations and schizophrenic excitement have decreased in frequency and quiet and withdrawn behaviours have increased. The authors point out that as cultures change the clinical picture of schizophrenia can and does change. They cite changing value systems, changes in personality, diffusion of knowledge about mental health, expansion of social welfare systems, and advances in treatment as significant contributory factors.

Varga (1966) surveyed the case records of all psychotic patients treated in the psychiatric hospital of the University of Budapest in 1910 and 1960 (152 and 174 patients respectively) and came to the following conclusions:

1. the proportion of schizophrenic patients among those admitted to the Department was almost the same in 1910 and 1960;
2. there was a relative increase of paranoid symptomatology among the 1960 patients;

3. florid hallucinatory and delusional states were more frequent in 1910;

4. only a small part (16.7 per cent) of the schizophrenics in 1910 developed a dementia;

5. the readmission rate was higher in 1960.

Varga concluded that on the whole there were more similarities than differences between 1910 and 1960 schizophrenics.

There are many unanswered questions about the relation between culture and the clinical picture, pattern of course, and outcome of schizophrenia and other mental disorders. Crosscultural follow-up studies using standardized instruments and procedures are needed to further clarify the influence of culture on mental disorders.

2.4 CONCLUSIONS

Several points stand out from this selective review of the literature.

2.4.1 Methodological problems

Although hundreds of follow-up studies of schizophrenia have been carried out over the last three-quarters of a century, many of the methodological problems of carrying out such studies remain unresolved. In particular, a consideration of the literature suggests that the outcome of a psychiatric illness is an extremely complex thing to assess, and that a great many factors must be taken into consideration in arriving at conclusions about course and outcome. Not only are current methods of assessing the interaction of psychopathological, social, cultural, and treatment variables in relation to the outcome of schizophrenia not entirely satisfactory, but even in the assessment of the relationship between any one of these variables and the outcome of schizophrenia there remain considerable methodological problems. To take social factors as an example, the complexities of the type and quality of the interaction between schizophrenic patients and their families and the effects of such interactions on different phases of their illnesses are still only partially explored, and the methodologies for studying these factors are still undergoing development. The problem of how to assess the occupational adjustment of schizophrenic patients remains a difficult matter within one culture, let alone across cultures. The difficulties of assessing the reliability of informants in reporting intervening history remain largely unresolved. The problems of controlling for differences in intervening events in the lives of schizophrenic patients followed up over a period of years and of understanding the effects of such differences on course and outcome are only now being approached.

2.4.2 Comparability of different studies

As a result of the lack of standardization of diagnostic criteria, outcome criteria, and general methodological procedures, as well as of the fact that many other methodological problems remain unsolved, it is difficult to compare the results of one study with those of another. The increasing emphasis on standardization of methodology and particularly on standardization of diagnosis and classification will undoubtedly add to the comparability of the results of such studies. However, it should be recognized that since different researchers will attempt different ways of dealing with unresolved methodological problems, future studies of schizophrenia will most likely remain difficult to compare in at least certain areas for some years to come.

2.4.3 Results of previous studies

Although, for the reasons described below, it is difficult to compare the results of previous studies, some general conclusions can be made from the large body of data collected in such studies. In the first place, the studies cited in this review suggest that, despite improvements in social, psychopharmacological, and other treatments of schizophrenia, no matter how narrowly or broadly schizophrenia is defined, this disorder still has the potential to develop into a chronic disorder. Even in the studies of M. Bleuler and Brown *et al.,* those in which the highest percentages of patients had good outcomes, approximately one-half of the patients had a poor social outcome. Furthermore, the few studies that have used the same methodology to assess the outcome of schizophrenic patients and of patients with other functional psychoses suggest that the outcome of schizophrenic patients as a group appears to be worse than the outcome of groups of patients with other functional psychoses. Within the schizophrenic group itself, it seems clear that no matter how schizophrenia is defined, some patients go on to complete recovery and some go on to chronic, severe psychosis. A number of studies suggest that for groups of patients, certain particular, or clusters of, psychopathological, historical, socio-demographic, and cultural characteristics are associated with particular types of outcome. However, with regard to individual patients, it is still extremely difficult to predict type of course and outcome. This fact emphasizes the need to consider each schizophrenic patient, no matter what his history or presenting clinical picture, as a patient with a potentially good outcome, so that a self-fulfilling prophecy does not occur in which certain types of patients are assumed to have poor prognoses and the lack of enthusiasm about their ultimate outcome helps to fulfil the prediction.

2.4.4 Need for further work

Finally, it seems clear that further studies, designed to overcome some of the methodological difficulties of previous studies, are greatly needed. In particular, there is a great lack of prospective studies which utilize reliable and standardized methods for assessing patients and which include a follow-up of patients in several different cultures using such standardized methodology. It is therefore justified to hope that the results of the current study will help to clarify some of the unresolved questions about the nature of the course and outcome of schizophrenia.

CHAPTER 3

Feasibility of Carrying Out a Multinational Follow-up Study of Patients with Functional Psychoses

The first two aims of the second-year follow-up phase of the IPSS were concerned with determining the feasibility of carrying out a two-year follow-up study of patients suffering from schizophrenia and other functional psychoses in nine different countries and the feasibility of developing standardized, reliable and transculturally applicable instruments and procedures of assessing such patients.

Data available from the follow-up phase of the study will be used to examine this problem from the following aspects:

1. The feasibility of reinterviewing patients two years after initial evaluation and of gathering detailed information about their psychiatric and social history since the time of initial evaluation.

2. The feasibility of developing instruments and procedures for the standardized and reliable follow-up evaluation of patients with functional psychoses that will be applicable in different cultures.

3. The feasibility of maintaining coordination and organizational continuity within and among teams of researchers from widely separated countries over an extended period of time.

3.1 FINDING AND REINTERVIEWING PATIENTS AND INFORMANTS

3.1.1 Reinterviewing patients with the Present State Examination (PSE) Schedule

There are no previous studies which give an indication of how many psychotic patients in a variety of cultures can be found a considerable length of time after an initial evaluation. The results of the IPSS provide clear information about this point.

Table 3.1 indicates the percentage of patients at each field research centre (FRC) that it was possible to find and reinterview with a PSE at some point at least 21 months after the initial evaluation.

It can be seen from Table 3.1 that in every centre except London, it was possible to reinterview more than 70 per cent of the patients, that in five centres it was possible to reinterview more than 80 per cent of the patients, and that in two centres it was possible to reinterview more than 90 per cent of the patients. The

TABLE 3.1. PATIENTS REINTERVIEWED WITH PSE AT 2ND YEAR FOLLOW-UP

Centre	Aarhus	Agra	Cali	Ibadan	London	Moscow	Taipei	Washington	Prague	All Centres
Total patients at initial evaluation	130[1]	140	127	145	127	140	137	131[2]	125	1,202
Total patients reinterviewed with PSE	122	129	108	109	26	122	96	96	101	909
Percentage of patients reinterviewed with PSE	93.8	92.1	85.0	75.2	20.5[3]	87.1	70.1	73.3	80.8	75.6[4]

1) 129 patients in Volume I (WHO 1973). One patient (WHO No. 01-224, Diagnosis 295.3) was included in the analyses based on the PSE.

2) 132 patients in Volume I. One patient had two sets of schedules at IE (WHO No. 08-178, Diagnosis 295.7).

3) The low percentage of London patients re-interviewed with a PSE is the result of the limited numbers of staff available to carry out such interviews (see text).

4) Figure includes London FRC. 82.1% when excluding London FRC.

percentage of all patients reinterviewed for all centres combined was 75.6 per cent. The low number of reinterviewed patients in London was due to the limited staff resources. At the time of the follow-up, the London staff of the London FRC consisted of two psychiatrists, both of whom had full-time clinical and teaching responsibilities, and it was therefore not possible for them to make home visits. Most patients who were currently attending the outpatient clinic were reinterviewed with a PSE. Undoubtedly, with more staff, it would have been possible to reinterview a sizeable number of London patients. When the London figures are excluded, the percentage of patients reinterviewed for all centres combined was 82.1 per cent.

It can be noted from Table 3.1 that there was no clear difference between the centres in developed countries and in developing countries with regard to the number of patients that it was possible to reinterview. Of the two centres that were able to reinterview more than 50 per cent of the patients, one (Aarhus) is in a developed country and one (Agra) is in a developing country. Excluding London, where the special circumstances noted above played a part, the average percentage of patients reinterviewed in the four remaining centres in developed countries* was 83.75 (range 73.3−93.8), while in the three centres in developing countries* it was 84.1 (range 75.2−92.1).

Table 3.2 indicates, for those patients who did not have a follow-up PSE interview, the reason for which the PSE was not conducted.

It can be seen from Table 3.2 that only 2.9 per cent of the 1202 patients included in the study could not be traced. In four centres, Aarhus, London, Moscow and Taipei, every patient included in the study was traced. Of the patients who could not be traced, 23 were from the three centres in developing countries, and twelve were from centres in developed countries.

Of the patients who were traced, the largest group who did not have a PSE was the group of 98 in London. As noted above, this group was not reinterviewed because of lack of personnel to arrange for follow-up interviews. It is particularly noteworthy that in only 6.9 per cent of the 1202 patients did either the patient or his family refuse to allow a follow-up interview of the patient. This occurred most frequently in Taipei, Ibadan and Washington. Of the total patient series, 2.4 per cent died before a follow-up PSE could be carried out. There was no clear difference among centres as to the percentage of patients who died during the follow-up period. The causes of death of patients who died during the follow-up period are listed in Appendix 1. A great part of the 12.1 per cent not interviewed for other reasons could have been examined if more resources had been available.

Among the problems encountered by the field research centres in attempting to trace and reinterview patients were the lack of population registers in some centres,

*Throughout this volume, the Agra, Cali and Ibadan centres are referred to as centres in developing countries, because of the general socioeconomic conditions in India, Colombia and Nigeria. Taipei has not been included as a centre in a developing country because the characteristics of medical care facilities and the pattern of the leading cause of death in that centre resemble those of a centre in a developed country. Aarhus, London, Moscow, Washington and Prague are referred to as centres in developed countries.

TABLE 3.2. THE REASON WHY PSE INTERVIEW WAS NOT CONDUCTED

Centre	Aarhus	Agra	Cali	Ibadan	London	Moscow	Taipei	Washington	Prague	All Centres	%
Total patients at initial evaluation	130	140	127	145	127	140	137	131	125	1202	
Patient refused or family would not allow the interview	4	2	3	18	-	3	24	20	9	83	6.9
Patient traced — Patient died before PSE could be done	3	4	1	6	3	3	3	1	5	29	2.4
Interview not done for other reasons	1	1	5	3	98*	12	14	4	8	146	12.1
Patient not traced	-	4	10	9	-	-	-	10	2	35	2.9
Total	8	11	19	36	101	18	41	35	24	293	24.4
Percentage of patients at initial evaluation not interviewed at 2 year follow-up	6.2	7.9	15.0	24.8	79.5	12.9	29.9	26.7	19.2	24.4	

REASONS

* These patients were not interviewed because they were not regularly attending outpatient clinic, and there were not sufficient staff resources available to arrange for home visits (see text).

TABLE 3.3.   TIME INTERVAL BETWEEN INITIAL EVALUATION AND 2ND YEAR FOLLOW-UP PSE (COMPLETE MONTHS).

Months Centre	21	22	23	24	25	26	27	28	29	30	31	32	33	34	35	36	37	38	39	40	41	42	43	44	45	Total
Aarhus	1	10	31	22	26	13	5		1	2			1	1		3	1	2		1	1			1		122
Agra		3	56	29	19	11	5		1	3	1														1	129
Cali	2	13	45	37	4	4	1	1	1																	108
Ibadan		1	3	25	23	11	10	9	6	10	1		3	1			2		1				2		1	109
London			2	21	2		1																			26
Moscow		2	58	49	11	1																			1	122
Taipei	1		54	40					1																	95
Washington		3	41	37	6	4	1		1		1	1		1		1		1								95
Prague		5	22	30	17	12	8	2	2		1			1												101
Total	4	37	312	290	108	56	31	12	17	3	2	4	3	4	3	3	1	1	1	2	1		3		3	909

834 patients

the large size of the catchment area (in Agra, for example, the catchment area is 52 076 sq. km), lack of adequate transportion in rural areas, difficulties in finding specific houses because of changes in names of streets or lack of street names or numbers, seasonal variations in weather such as heavy rainstorm and suspicion of official-looking letters. The problems specific to each centre are described in further detail in Chapter 5.

It is thus striking that of the original 1202 patients, 97.1 per cent could be traced in a two-year follow-up study, and 75.5 per cent were reinterviewed. However, this information does not fully answer the question of how feasible it is to reinterview patients for a two-year follow-up, since the time when the follow-up interview was conducted plays an important role in the usefulness of the information gathered for a follow-up study. Thus, it was felt that the range of time within which a follow-up interview could be considered to be part of two-year follow-up analyses should be limited to three months on either side of the 24-month anniversary of the initial evaluation. For the purposes of the analyses presented later, only those patients who had a follow-up PSE between the 22nd and 27th months are included in analyses which involve follow-up PSE data.

Table 3.3 indicates, for the 909 patients who had a follow-up PSE interview, the time-interval between the initial evaluation and second year follow-up PSE.

It can be seen that 834 of the patients had a follow-up PSE between the 22nd and 27th month. Thus, setting out to reinterview as many patients as possible for a two year follow-up, the centres' staff were able to reinterview 69.4 per cent of the 1202 patients between the 22nd and 27th month.

The percentage of patients reinterviewed within the 22nd and 27th month by centre were: Aarhus, 82.3 per cent; Agra, 87.9 per cent; Cali, 81.9 per cent; Ibadan, 50.3 per cent; London, 20.5 per cent; Moscow, 86.4 per cent; Taipei, 68.6 per cent; Washinton, 70.0 per cent; and Prague, 75.2 per cent.

In the two centres, Aarhus and Ibadan, a relatively high number of patients were reinterviewed with a PSE after 27 months. The reason for this dispersion in Aarhus was shortage of psychiatrist-time. The patients interviewed later than scheduled did not answer letters of invitation to come to the hospital. Some of these were interviewed by a social worker with follow-up psychiatric history (PH) and social description (SD) schedules within the 22 to 27 months time-interval, and were later interviewed at home with a PSE when it was possible for a psychiatrist to make a home visit. In Ibadan, the dispersion was due to shortage of psychiatrist-time, and also to difficulties in locating patients becase of geographical mobility of patients, absence of adequate postal services to some areas, inadequate postal addresses, and illiteracy.

3.1.2. Patients with sufficient information to be included in analyses involving second-year follow-up data

All patients (834) who had a follow-up PSE done between the 22nd and 27th months also had at least some information available about past psychiatric and social history, and it was decided that all such patients had enough information available about the follow-up period to include them in follow-up analyses. In addition, there were 93 patients not reinterviewed with a PSE, but about whom there was detailed psychiatric and social history information available from other sources. It was felt that the information about these 93 was sufficiently detailed to warrant including them in analyses involving two-year follow-up data, making a total of 927 patients* about whom it was considered there was enough information to include them in such analyses.

Thus, of the 1202 patients given an initial evaluation, it was possible to obtain sufficient information about 77.1 per cent of them to include them in the basic follow-up patient material. The percentages by centre were Aarhus, 82.3 per cent; Agra, 90.7 per cent; Cali, 83.7 per cent; Ibadan, 50.3 per cent; London, 57.5 per cent, Moscow, 89.2 per cent; Taipei, 94.9 per cent; Washington, 70.2 per cent; and Prague, 76.8 per cent.

The data clearly indicate that in each of the nine centres of the study it was feasible to obtain detailed two year follow-up information about a high percentage of a series of mainly psychotic patients. In only two of the centres was the percentage less than 70 per cent. In London (57.5 per cent), the percentage seemed to be lower than in the other centres because of insufficient staff. In Ibadan (50.3 per cent) the main reason for the lower number was that for many patients complete information was obtained just outside the 22 to 27 months time-limit. Thus, nine Ibadan patients had detailed evaluations in the 28th month, six in the 29th month, and ten in the 30th month. Those 25 patients would have raised, to 68 per cent, the Ibadan percentage of patients about whom detailed information was collected.

3.1.3 Work required to find and interview patients and informants

Another aspect of the feasibility of carrying out a follow-up study is the amount of work required to carry it out. This section will describe the average amount of time per centre that it took to assess patients and will give some indication of the effort required to locate patients and informants to carry out such assessments.

The average time spent assessing a patient with all four of the major follow-up instruments was more than two hours; 1079 patients were assessed, and more than 2100 man hours were spent assessing IPSS patients with two-year follow-up schedules.

Although many of the patients and informants were interviewed at the field reasearch centre, a considerable amount of time was spent carrying out visits to patients' homes to interview either patients, informants, or both.

Almost 4000 manhours were spent carrying out home visits, and more than 1000 of those hours were spent by psychiatrists. The number of home visits required to gather follow-up information about patients differed markedly from centre to centre. For example, Aarhus and Cali were quite similar with regard to the

---

*Of the 927 patients, 24 were subsequently excluded from the basic follow-up group because of diagnostic considerations – see Chapter 5.

number of patients about whom sufficient information was gathered to include in the follow-up group. However, in Cali 81 home visits were required compared to 29 in Aarhus. Ibadan was the centre with the lowest percentage of patients included in the follow-up material (50.3 per cent), but which carried out the most home visits to gather information (104).

In addition to the time spent which can be documented with these figures, many more hours were spent at each centre telephoning and writing letters to make appointments, and carrying out the various administrative procedures necessary for coordinating the follow-up phase of the study. It can thus be seen that although the study has demonstrated the feasibility of carrying out a long-term follow-up of functional psychotic patients in nine countries, a great many manhours were necessary to make the study feasible.

3.2 INSTRUMENTS

One of the major aims of the IPSS was to determine if standardized instruments and procedures for assessing patients with functional psychosis could be developed that would be reliable and applicable in all of the nine centres. The report of the first part of this study (WHO, 1973) noted that initial evaluation data demonstrated that the PSE can be administered satisfactorily in various cultures and in widely different psychiatric centres, that intracentre reliability among interviewers using the PSE was high and intercentre reliability high enough to encourage crosscultural comparisons of the data, and that the more reliable items were those rated on the basis of patients' reports, while those with lower reliability consisted of items rated from observation of behaviour. The reliability of the PH and SD schedules was investigated less intensively because of the wide variety of conditions under which such schedules were filled out, and no definite conclusions were reached about the reliability of these schedules.

The follow-up phase aims included the determination of the applicability and reliability of follow-up instruments. The follow-up instruments will be described and their applicability discussed here. The question of reliability is discussed in detail in Chapter 4.

3.2.1 Description of follow-up instruments

Four main types of schedules were used during the follow-up phase of the IPSS: the Present State Examination (PSE), the Follow-up Psychiatric History schedule (FUPH), the Follow-up Social Description schedule (FUSD), and the Follow-up Diagnostic Assessment schedule (FUDA). The PSE has been described in detail in Volume 1 of the report of the IPSS (WHO, 1973). Table 3.4 presents a summary description of the other three instruments. In addition to these instruments, a number of administrative instruments and protocols were used, which for the most part remained the same as those used in the initial evaluation phase and were described in Volume 1 of the IPSS report (WHO, 1973).

3.2.1.1 Follow-up Psychiatric History schedule (FUPH)

Since there had been little previous work in the development of a standardized instrument for the transcultural collection of psychiatric history data, the preparation of the initial evaluation Psychiatric History schedule was considered by the investigators to be the first stage in the process of producing a useful instrument. The identification of items which would be applicable and useful in a variety of cultures was a particular problem with which the collaborating investigators attempted to deal. The experience of producing the initial evaluation instruments was of great help in preparing the follow-up instrument, but again there were many problems to be considered with regard to the applicability and usefulness of various types of follow-up data in different cultural settings.

The follow-up schedule was initially drafted by Headquarters, then discussed by all the collaborating investigators, and redrafted on the basis of these discussions. A draft schedule was then given a field trial in the field research centres, and on the basis of these experiences redrafted to produce the version used in the follow up phase. The main purpose of the follow-up psychiatric history schedule was to give a picture of the course of the patient's illness in the interval between the initial evaluation and the second-year follow-up evaluation.

The schedule includes a section which asks for a narrative account of the patient's course, including symptomatology and treatment, since the previous psychiatric history information was recorded. This is followed by a series of precoded questions intended to give a picture of the number of episodes and types of remissions that characterized the course of the patient's illness since the initial evaluation.

Another section of the schedule provides a symptom checklist to indicate symptomatology in the episode of inclusion noted after the previous psychiatric history schedule was filled in, symptomatology present in each of the subsequent episodes, and symptomatology present during the month prior to the filling in of the psychiatric history schedule.

The remainder of the schedule includes questions about contacts with psychiatrists and psychiatric services and other persons or organizations that the patient had contacted about his psychiatric problems since the previous evaluation, and about life events (divorce, birth of a child, for example) since the previous evaluation.

3.2.1.2 Follow-up Social Description schedule (FUSD)

Just as the development of the initial and follow-up psychiatric history schedules was viewed as beginning work in a relatively unexplored area, so the development of the initial and follow-up social depression schedules was viewed as the initial stage in the production of useful instruments for the transcultural description of social functioning. Again there were many problems relating to the identification of items which would be applicable and useful in different cultures, and the same process of drafting, discussions, redrafting, field testing, and redrafting was used.

TABLE 3.4. SCHEDULES USED IN THE FOLLOW-UP EXAMINATIONS.

Name and abbreviation for Schedule	Areas Assessed	Method for completing	Time covered	Source of Information	Time necessary for administering
Follow-up psychiatric history (FU-PH)	Type of remission; symptomatology between episodes; treatment; life history; history of use of alcohol and drugs; legal history.	Clinical interview; use of hospital records; interviews and correspondence with professionals; interviews and correspondence with informants.	Period since previous examination.	Patient; Informant; Professionals; Case records; others (e.g. coroner's inquest).	30-60 minutes
Follow-up Social Description (FU-SD)	Patient's residence; household; occupation; education; and social activities.	Clinical interview with patient; Use of hospital records; interviews and correspondence with professional and personal informants.	Period since last examination.	Patient; informant; professional sources.	30-60 minutes
Follow-up Diagnostic Assessment (FU-DA)	Diagnoses; Summary of findings; 2 diagnoses recorded, one using follow-up examination only, the other using all information available.	Analysis of material contained in other documents.	Second year follow-up and interval between initial evaluation and second year follow-up.	All documents; re-examination of patient if necessary.	10 minutes

TABLE 3.4. continued

Name and abbreviation for Schedule	Follow-up Documents done by	Layout	Type of Items	Available in	Data Processing	Type of Output
Follow-up psychiatric history (FU-PH)	Psychiatrist; psychologist or medical officer	Printed, 35 pages; information record on right-hand side only; left-hand side left completely blank throughout and can be used for interviewer's notes. Instructions given in text.	113 items; open-ended questions; Checklists; rating scales; dichotomous items.	Hindi; Danish; Spanish; Yoruba; Chinese; Russian; French and Czech.	Parts of schedule suitable for direct keypunching; transcription to coding sheets; content analysis of narrative accounts.	Ratings on items. Narrative accounts.
Follow-up Social Description (FU-SD)	Psychiatric social worker; psychologist; psychiatrist.	Printed, 29 pages; right-hand side of pages only used; left-hand side remained blank for interviewer's notes.	50 items; open-ended questions; check-lists; rating scales; dichotomous items.	as above	Parts of schedule suitable for direct keypunching. Transcription on coding sheets.	Ratings on items. Narrative accounts.
Follow-up Diagnostic Assessment (FU-DA)	Interviewing psychiatrist.	Printed, 4 pages, both sides used.	(i) 6 open-ended questions requiring summary of findings; (ii) Statement of diagnosis according to system used in centre; (iii) Checklist of ICD categories pertaining to functional psychiatric disorder; (iv) Rating scales for description of prognoses.	as above	Transcription to coding sheets.	Ratings on items. Diagnosis.

The main purpose of the follow-up social description schedule was to provide a picture of what had happened to the patient in the socioeconomic sphere since the previous evaluation. It includes questions which compare the patient's current situation to the average situation in his culture and questions which compare the patient's current situation with his situation at the time of the previous evaluation Areas covered include type of quality of residence; composition of household; length, quality and type of work; education; and social activities.

3.2.1.3 Follow-up Diagnostic Assessment schedule (FUDA)

The follow-up diagnostic assessment schedule requests the psychiatrist evaluating the patient at the time of second-year follow-up to state his diagnosis of the patient using follow-up information only, and to state his diagnosis of the patient using all information available. It also requests the psychiatrist to describe in narrative form the findings on which he bases his overall diagnosis of the patient, including symptomatology at initial and follow-up evaluations, physical and neurological findings and pertinent psychiatric and social history. It requests the psychiatrist to indicate his degree of uncertainty about the diagnosis, and to make predictions about the future course of the patient's illness.

3.2.2 Applicability of PSE during the follow-up period

During follow-up PSE interviews, the investigators made observations concerning the applicability of the PSE in their culture under field conditions at the time of the second-year follow-up. All the centres reported that there were no difficulties in administering the PSE under field conditions, and in general they found the PSE to be applicable at the time of follow-up. However, most investigators noted two difficulties with the PSE as a follow-up instrument: (a) that it was sometimes difficult to find a way to indicate on the PSE minor neurotic or psychosomatic symptoms and negative symptoms such as lack of ability to enjoy life, aimlessness, and difficulty relating to the interviewer, and (b) that in certain cases the interviewer felt that symptoms were present but that the patient had learned to deny them, and therefore answered all questions on the PSE in the negative, despite many probes from the interviewer.

3.2.3. Applicability and reliability of the follow-up psychiatric history and follow-up social description schedules

During this stage in the development of transcultural psychiatric history and social depression schedules the investigators have focused on questions of the applicability, usefulness, and adequacy of the items included. It was felt that until these basic issues were further resolved, it did not make sense to carry out detailed reliability tests of the items in the schedules. Reliability testing of psychiatric history and social description schedules was carried out in later stages of the IPSS when the investigators felt that they had arrived at schedules which were applicable, useful and adequate to cover the areas involved.

In general the centres found the follow-up PH and SD schedules applicable under field conditions. Some centres noted that the schedules were too long and that it was difficult to hold the attention and cooperation of the patient or relatives throughout. In some centres, certain of the items were found to be difficult to apply because they were not relevant to the culture. The investigators felt that progress had been made in developing transculturally applicable psychiatric history and social description schedules, but that considerable further work needed to be done to produce more satisfactory schedules, particularly on items relating to social functioning and work. It was also noted that it was quite difficult to use the precoded information to break the course of illness into episodes and intervals and that it was necessary to use the narrative account to do this. It was felt that in addition to items about specific behaviours of the patient, it would be useful to include global ratings of major course and outcome areas. It was also noted that often it was difficult to determine how reliable were the sources of information for filling in the schedules.

Follow-up instruments for the five-year follow-up phase were devised, taking these various difficulties into account, and it was hoped that these new instruments would represent a further step in the development of useful, applicable and reliable psychiatric history and social description instruments.

3.3 CO-ORDINATION AND ORGANIZATIONAL CONTINUITY

A striking finding of the follow-up phase of the IPSS is the demonstration that it is feasible to maintain co-ordination and organizational continuity within and among teams of researchers from widely separated countries over an extended period of time.

At no point in the study was there a break in the organizational functioning of the project. Although a high percentage of the original collaborating investigators at the field research centres (FRC) changed their position and duties within the centre, most were able to remain with the project from the planning stages, throughout the initial and two-year follow-up phases of the project, a period of more than four years. Of 20 collaborating investigators from the field research centres involved in the project in 1967, 17 were still with the project throughout 1971, to the end of the two-year follow-up phase data collection period, and 16 were still with the project throughout 1973, to the end of the period of second-year follow-up data analysis. This demonstrates one of the great advantages of involving local personnel in transcultural research, since such individuals are likely to remain in the centres involved throughout the length of the follow-up periods of such studies. Furthermore, when new investigators joined the IPSS, the local investigators could train them at the field research centres, making it easier to maintain continuity, since it was not necessary to send new investigators out of the country for training in the research procedures.

At Headquarters, the original principal investigator took up new duties after the completion of data collection of the initial evaluation phase, but continuity was maintained by his continuing to serve in an advisory capacity throughout the study, and by the fact that the new principal investigator had been working on the project at Headquarters for two years prior to becoming principal investigator.

Not only was the co-ordination of the study maintained over a long period of time, but investigators from different countries within the study began to co-ordinate work on substudies arising out of their IPSS work, leading to the beginnings of a network of centres interested and trained in transcultural psychiatric work, which had been one of the initial aims of the study

It is felt that three aspects of the organization of the IPSS contributed to the maintenance of co-ordination:

1. the existence of central co-ordination of the study from WHO Headquarters in Geneva;

2. the possibility of regular, frequent contact among the collaborating centres at meetings of all investigators, and small meetings during which investigators from one centre visited other centres to discuss and consider particular aspects of the study.

3. the development of special studies within the main study which stimulated collaborators to work closely together on particular areas of special mutual interest.

3.4 SUMMARY AND CONCLUSIONS

The second year follow-up phase of the IPSS has demonstrated that:

1. It is feasible to reinterview, assess the mental status of, and collect psychiatric and social history data about a high percentage of patients with functional psychoses two years after an initial evaluation in many different cultures. However, a great many manhours of work were required in all cultures to make such a follow-up feasible.

2. Within the framework of the IPSS there did not appear to be major differences between the feasibility of reassessing schizophrenic patients and the feasibility of reassessing patients in other diagnostic groups, psychotic and non-psychotic.

3. It is feasible to develop a standardized and applicable instrument for the follow-up evaluation of the mental status of patients given an initial evaluation diagnosis of a functional psychosis in different cultures. However, some difficulties were found in the application of the instrument in assessing very guarded patients or patients intent on denying the presence of their symptoms during the follow-up period and in assessing minor degrees of psychopathology present in patients who were no longer acutely ill. The reliability of this instrument during the follow-up phase will be discussed in detail in Chapter 4.

4. The development of transculturally applicable instruments for the follow-up of psychiatric and social history is a difficult task which requires a great deal of testing under field conditions, but it is feasible to develop such instruments.

5. Given central co-ordination, frequent opportunities for collaborating investigators to interact, and opportunities for continuing and expanding collaborative work, it is feasible to maintain organizational continuity and co-ordination within and among teams of psychiatric researchers from widely separated countries over an extended period of time.

CHAPTER 4

Reliability of Methods and Instruments

4.1 INTRODUCTION

Standardization of assessment is of particular importance in crosscultural psychiatric research and a prerequisite for its success is the availability of valid and reliable instruments. The three principal instruments used for data collection in the follow-up phase of the IPSS were the Present State Examination schedule (PSE), the Follow-up Psychiatric History Schedule (FUPH) and the Follow-up Social Description schedule (FUSD). In addition, the investigators provided narrative descriptions of the course and outcome of the patients which were coded and analysed at Headquarters.

The problems of reliability discussed in this chapter concern primarily the assessment of the patient's mental state at follow-up based on interviews in which the investigators used the PSE schedule. As regards the psychiatric history and social description schedules, at this stage of the project the investigators focused mainly on the applicability; usefulness and adequacy of the items included, and therefore no detailed reliability tests of these schedules were carried out.

However, information derived from these schedules was used in conjunction with the narrative descriptions of course and outcome, and data on the reliability of the coding procedure which was developed for the statistical analysis of course and outcome are reported.

As described in detail in Volume 1 of the IPSS report (WHO, 1973), the original items of the PSE were condensed into 129 units of analysis (UAs) corresponding to clinical symptoms and signs which formed the basis for further analysis. In addition, the 129 UAs were combined into 27 groups of units of analysis (GUAs) corresponding to broader areas of psychopathology. Therefore, the patient's symptomatic profile is defined by the 129 UAs and 27 GUAs respectively. The course and outcome profile is defined by six categories: length of episode of inclusion; proportion of time in the follow-up period during which the patient was in psychotic episodes; pattern of course; type of subsequent episodes; degree of social impairment; and overall outcome (see Chapter 6).

The scores used to record the patient's symptoms were the same for all 129 UAs: a symptom could be present, absent, indeterminate or questionable. In most of the statistical analyses no distinction was made between absent, indeterminate and questionable, and a symptom which was not rated as clearly present was considered as absent. Units related to the same major area of psychopathology (such as delusions, or auditory hallucinations, etc.) were grouped together, forming the 27 groups of units of analysis (GUAs) (see also Volume 1 on the IPSS report – WHO, 1973). The scores of the 27 groups of units of analysis (each including interrelated units or symptoms) represented the percentage of units rated as present, or positive, out of all units included in each particular group of units.

The categories used to rate the course and outcome of the disorder (defined in Chapter 6) were either nominal, like 'type of subsequent episodes' (including definitely schizophrenic, probably schizophrenic, affective, non-psychotic), or ordinal like 'degree of social impairment' (including none or mild, medium, severe). Thus, the variables used in the analyses were of three types: dichotomous (for example, units of analysis), continuous (for example, groups of units of analysis), and polychotomous (for example, some course and outcome-describing categories).

The problem of the reliability of the instruments designed to measure symptomatology can be approached from two points of view: reliability within and between the field research centres. In addition, a separate discussion is needed with regard to the categories describing course and outcome of the patients, which were defined and coded centrally at WHO Headquarters in Geneva on the basis of all information available, including the narrative descriptions of patient's progress. With the exception of one among them, the psychiatrists involved in this work did not come from field research centres, and should be considered an independent group of raters.

Before discussing in detail the reliability of assessments of symtomatology (sections 4.3 and 4.4) and course and outcome (section 4.5), the concepts of reliability and validity underlying the analyses reported in the present chapter will be summarized (section 4.2).

4.2 CONCEPTS OF RELIABILITY AND VALIDITY

4.2.1 The concept of validity of psychiatric rating scales

In psychometric theory the concept of validity is closely related to the purpose of the rating scale. Asking how valid a rating procedure is, Thorndike and Hagen (1969) stated, 'When we ask this question, we are inquiring whether the (procedure) measures what we want it to measure, all of what we want it to measure and nothing but what we want it to measure'. Several kinds of validity are usually distinguished, classified as content, construct, concurrent and predictive validity of which predictive and concurrent validity are often discussed under the heading criterion-oriented validity.

The PSE has been designed primarily as a guide to the structuring of the psychiatric interview in order to obtain a systematic coverage of all major areas of descriptive psychopathology. The question whether the items selected for this instrument are relevant and sufficient to serve its purpose, is a question of its content validity. In most instances the determination of content validity is based on expert judgments. With reference to psychological tests, Seibel (1968) wrote that 'in attempting to obtain content validity, test publishers usually rely on the judgments of recognized subject matter experts in the particular area covered by the test'. This approach is equally applicable to psychiatric rating scales and it underlies the development of the PSE. For a detailed description of the structure and content of the Present State Examination schedule the reader is referred to Volume 1 of the IPSS report (WHO, 1973).

Construct validity is another important aspect of rating scales development: 'If a score is intended to yield an index of some hypothetical characteristic which itself cannot be directly observed or measured, the attempt to verify, at least provisionally, that the test of scale yields results consistent with the investigator's hypothesis, involves the concept of construct validity' (Lyerly, 1973). The problem of construct validity has some special implications in crosscultural studies. The translation of an instrument into a different language may change the meaning of a construct; furthermore, a meaningful construct in one setting may be without an exact correspondent in another culture. In both instances the construct validity of the instrument will be affected. The PSE has been used extensively in a number of countries and it has been translated into several languages. However, as it was pointed out by Cronbach (1970),

> construct validation is difficult because so many diverse techniques are required to examine diverse hypotheses and counterhypotheses. Construct validation requires the integration of many studies. There is no such thing as a coefficient of construct validity. . . If the construct interpretation is taken seriously by the profession, its validity is challenged over and over again. The challenge consists of proposing a counterhypothesis; that is, an alternative construct to account for the test behaviour in whole or in part.

In view of such considerations, no special attempt was made in the follow-up phase of the IPSS to ascertain the construct validity of the PSE. For information related to the issues involved in the concept validity of the PSE, the reader is referred to Volume 1 of the IPSS report (WHO, 1973) and to Wing, Cooper and Sartorius (1973).

The main emphasis of the analysis reported in this chapter is, therefore, not on the validation of constructs underlying the PSE, although implicitly the findings presented probably do contribute to a better understanding of the meaning of the items used for describing symptomatology.

The situation is somewhat different as concerns the categories used to describe the course and outcome of the patients' conditions. Course and outcome were rated and coded 'centrally' at WHO Headquarters on the basis of all information available on each patient, including a narrative description provided by the field investigator (see section 4.5 for further details). Most of the categories utilized in the coding procedure – for example, length of the episode of inclusion, proportion of time during which the patient was in psychotic episodes, pattern of course, level of social impairment, etc. – have been used in previous studies to describe aspects of course and outcome in psychiatric patients. There is, however, less consensus on constructs such as 'course' and 'outcome' than there is on psychopathological categories and it can be assumed that the construct validity of categories designed to 'tap' course and outcome will only be ascertained as result of long-term cumulative research efforts.

In the present study, the emphasis of the analysis of course and outcome categories was on their capacity to discriminate between different diagnostic groups.

If there is a criterion to be predicted (relapses and remissions, future symptoms, social adjustment, for example), the concept of criterion-oriented, and more specifically, predictive validity is applicable. Does present symptomatology predict future symptom profiles? Do course and outcome categories discriminate between diagnostic groupings made on initial evaluation? Do symptoms predict course and outcome of the disorder? These and other related questions will be answered in subsequent chapters; the rest of the present chapter focuses on the reliability of the instruments and procedures, since the prerequisite for a scale or a measurement procedure to be valid is that it can be applied reliably. Previous work on the application of the PSE, in particular the findings presented in Volume 1 of the IPSS report (WHO, 1973), showed that symptom profiles derived from PSE ratings could measure symptomatology reliably, provided that the raters were sufficiently trained and experienced in the use of the schedule. The main emphasis of the reliability analysis reported here is firstly on quantifying the degree of reliability of PSE assessments during the follow-up phase and secondly on determining the reliability of the categories used to describe course and outcome, since the latter had not been explored during earlier stages of the IPSS.

4.2.2 The concept of reliability for psychiatric rating scales

A widely accepted definition of reliability is given by Guilford and Fruchter (1973): 'The reliability of any set of measurements is logically defined as the proportion of their variance that is true variance' and they continue to point out that 'one should speak of the reliability of a certain instrument applied to a certain population under certain conditions'. It is this conceptual framework which is adopted in the present chapter.

The underlying model for the above definition of reliability is that the measured score X_m is additively composed out of the true score X_r and an error increment X_e:

$$X_m = X_r + X_e$$

In the above terminology, the true score 'is assumed to be the genuine value of whatever is being measured, a value we should obtain if we had a perfect instrument applied under ideal conditions'. It is further assumed 'that the error components occur independently and at random . . . and that they are uncorrelated with the true values and with other measurements' (Guilford and Fruchter, 1973). Denoting by $\sigma_r{}^2$ and σ_m the variances of the true and measured scores respectively, the reliability coefficient r^2 then is, by definition

$$r^2 = \frac{\sigma_r^2}{\sigma_m^2} \ .$$

In practice, however, X_r and X_e are not directly measurable, hence σ_r^2 not known. Therefore, in order to assess the reliability of the rating procedures a group of

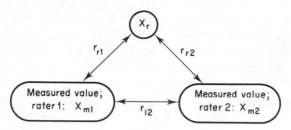

Figure 4.1 Model of rating correlation r_{r1} between real value X_r and measurement X_{m1} of rater 1; correlation r_{r2} between real value and measurement X_{m2} of rater 2, and correlation r_{12} between measurements of raters 1 and 2

patients may be assessed simultaneously and independently by two (or more) observers.

If two observers rate in this way a number of patients with regard to a specific characteristic, conceptually three correlations may be distinguished (see Figure 4.1) the correlation r_{r1} between the series of measurements of rater 1 and the true scores, the analogous correlation r_{r2} for the record rater and finally the correlation r_{12} between the measurement of raters 1 and 2. For characteristics of the continuous type, such as percentage of the follow-up period during which the patient was in psychotic episodes, r_{12} can be calculated as an ordinary (for example, Pearson) correlation coefficient or as an intraclass correlation coefficient. The square r_{r1}^2 of r_{r1}, as a coefficient of determination quantities the proportion of the total variance of the first rater's measurements that is true variance. Hence, by definition, r_{r1}^2 is the reliability of the instrument as used by rater 1 in the given situation. Similarly, r_{r2}^2 for the second rater. It can be shown that there is a functional relationship between the measurable correlation r_{12} between the observations of both raters and the indices of reliability* r_{r1} and r_{r2} of the rating instrument as used by the first and second rater respectively: $r_{12} = \sqrt{r_{r1}r_{r2}}$, i.e. the correlation between the measurements of the observers is the (geometric) mean of their indices of reliability and with the further assumption that the reliabilities of the raters are equal, i.e. $r_{r1}^2 = r_{r2}^2$, it follows that the index of reliability of the measurements equals the square root of the correlation between the measurements of both observers (Lord and Novick, 1968).

It is worth recalling the various assumptions underlying the above model of rating, which are important for understanding and interpreting measures of reliability. Firstly, they include the concept of a 'genuine' or true value of whatever is being measured and an error component induced by the rating procedure, Secondly, it is assumed that this error component occurs independently and at random which, for example, implies that a psychiatrist interviewing and rating ten patients will measure symptomatology with the same accuracy for the first as for the last one, in other words there is neither a learning nor a fatigue effect. Thirdly,

*The index of reliability is the square root of the reliability.

it is assumed that the error components do not correlate with the true values, which means ratings can be made with the same reliability for patients who really do have the symptom as for patients who, in fact, do not have it. Fourthly, it is assumed that different raters measure with similar reliability. This assumption, in many cases, is fulfilled approximately at most. However, it is evident from Figure 4.1 and from what has been said before, that (in the case of two-rater reliability exercises) the two different reliabilities r_{r1}^2 and r_{r2}^2 cannot be estimated on the basis of a single measurable correlation coefficient r_{12} between the ratings of both observers.

In principle, the definition of reliability of measurements given by Guilford and Fruchter, that is, the proportion of variance that is true variance, should refer equally to variables of the continuous type and to dichotomous or polychotomous characteristics. In the case of dichotomies, however (for example, for symptoms which may either be present or absent), the variance strongly depends upon the frequency of occurrence of the specific symptom. This is demonstrated by the following example: a psychiatrist may be able to ascertain correctly the presence or absence of a certain symptom in a clinical interview in, say, 90 per cent of the cases. The prevalence of the symptom in a series of patients may be 5 per cent; in other words in 95 per cent of the patients the symptom would be absent. It can be shown that the proportion of the variance that is true variance, i.e. the reliability of the measurements, in this instance, would be 0.24. On the other hand, still with the assumption that the psychiatrist measures correctly with a probability of 90 per cent, but rating a group of patients in which the proportion of subjects who do and do not have the symptom is equally distributed, i.e. 50 per cent, the reliability would be 0.64.

In many cases it is undesirable to work with a coefficient of reliability whose numerical value depends upon the distribution of the variable under consideration in the patient population. In the above sample, one would intuitively tend to describe the reliability of the rating procedure as 90 per cent or 0.9, i.e. as the probability that the psychiatrist rates correctly, regardless of whether the symptom is actually present in only 5 per cent or in 50 per cent of the patients. A modification of Guilford and Fruchter's definition of reliability which applies better to dichotomous, or more generally, polychotomous variables, would therefore be as follows: the reliability of any set of dichotomous (or polychotomous) measurements is defined as the proportion π of the measurements that are correct measurements, or, equivalently, as the probability π that the measurement is correct.

Like r^2, π is not directly measurable. However, if in a two-rater reliability exercise two participants rate independently and simultaneously a series of patients, their agreement can be calculated directly, similarly to the correlation r_{12} between the ratings made by two raters in the case of continuous variables. In Appendix 5 it is shown that a relation exists between the measurable agreement ratio between two raters and the reliabilities π_1 and π_2. If it can be assumed that the reliabilities of the two sets of ratings are equal (or at least similar) the π-values can be calculated directly from the agreement ratio in a way similar to the case of continuous variables where the reliability of the measurements equals the square

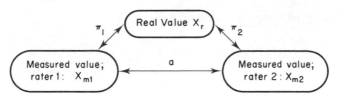

Figure 4.2   Model of rating for dichotomous variables. Probability π_1 that the first rater's measurement $X_{m\,1}$ is the true value X_r; probability π_2 that the second rater's measurement $X_{m\,2}$ is the true value; agreement ratio a of both raters' measurements

root of the correlation between the measurements made by the two observers. It is further shown that a π-value of 0.5 means that the rating procedure is not reliable so that $\pi = 0.5$ for dichotomous items should be interpreted in the same way as $r^2 = 0$ for continuous variables. Like r^2, the highest possible numerical value of π is 1.*

If it is considered unrealistic to assume that the two psychiatrists rate with equal reliability, the agreement ratio a can be used to estimate a sort of an average reliability for two raters involved in the rating process. For continuous variables this average reliability is the geometric mean of the individual reliabilities. For dichotomous items the average π-value is derived from the amount by which the individual π-values exceed the value of 'random' rating 0.5. This increment is the geometric mean of the increments of the individual π-values.†

Appendix 5 contains a more comprehensive discussion of the mathematical details.

4.3 THE INTRACENTRE RELIABILITY OF THE PSE

4.3.1 Methods

To assess the reliability with which the Present State Examination (PSE) schedule was used within the individual field research centres a series of rating exercises were carried out. During an exercise the same patient was rated independently by two psychiatrists of whom one conducted the interview (the second rater could ask clarifying questions if necessary). In another type of exercise, the patient was interviewed twice, each time by a different psychiatrist, on the same day. Since it was unlikely for major changes in the patient's mental state to occur within a day, it was felt that this type of rating exercise could be treated in the same way as the simultaneous rating exercises. A total of 53 rating exercises were performed,

---

*To compare the numerical values of reliability of the continuous type expressed as coefficients of determination (i.e. squares of correlation coefficients) with that of dichotomous variables expressed in terms of π the transformation $\pi^1 = 2\pi - 1$ is recommended.
†The average reliability π is related to the individual values π_1 and π_2 of raters 1 and 2 respectively by the formula:
$$\pi = 0.5 + \sqrt{(\pi'_1 - 0.5)(\pi_2 - 0.5)}.$$

distributed over field research centres as follows:

TABLE 4.1.   NUMBER OF SIMULTANEOUS RATING EXERCISES
(PAIRED INTERVIEWS BY FIELD RESEARCH
CENTRE) DURING THE 2ND YEAR FOLLOW-UP
PERIOD.

Aarhus	Agra	Ibadan	Moscow	Taipei	Washington	Total
5	12	21*	7	1	7	53

* One of the exercises was consecutive.

In Cali, London and Prague no rating exercises could be carried out. Since the number of simultaneous interviews per centre was small in Aarhus, Moscow, Taipei and Washington, no comparisons of the intracentre reliability of the PSE in the different centres would be meaningful. The purpose of the intracentre reliability exercises was to evaluate the overall performance of the instrument in different settings. Therefore, the data of all the 53 rating exercises were pooled.

As already described in detail in Volume 1 of the IPSS report (WHO, 1973), in each PSE interview, a total of 360 items were rated. This large body of information had to be condensed with a minimal loss of information.

Data can be condensed in several ways: items can be grouped or selected on the basis of clinical judgment; mathematical techniques such as factor analysis can be used; or both methods can be combined. The advantages and disadvantages of these different approaches have been discussed in detail in Volume 1 of the IPSS report. The method adopted to group PSE items relied upon a combination of clinical judgment and mathematical techniques. In this way the 360 items were collapsed into 129 units of analysis (UAs). The procedure was performed in several stages:

Stage 1: All collaborating investigators were requested to group the items in the PSE schedule into clinically meaningful groups corresponding to symptoms. A list of this kind was also produced at Headquarters. Three of the centres produced their own lists; others adopted the Headquarters' list with only slight modifications.

Stage 2: The four lists were studied in detail and a compound list was produced that took into account most of the suggestions received. It was encouraging that this could be done because it meant that the psychiatrists were in good agreement about which items compose symptoms, despite the fact that they had been trained in different schools and were working in different settings.

Stage 3: The compound list was assessed statistically, using the collected data, in two steps. In the first step the units of analysis were tested for statistical associations among the items using data on the first 700 patients; in the second step data on all the 1202 patients were used. Only one schedule per patient was utilized, excluding the second raters' schedules filled in during simultaneous interviews, as well as the second of the two schedules filled in during consecutive interviews.

TABLE 4.2.   COMPOSITION OF GROUPS OF UNITS OF ANALYSIS.*

Groups		Units of Analysis
1. Quantitative psychomotor disorder	1. 2. 3. 14.	Overactivity Retardation Stupor Repetitive movements
2. Qualitative psychomotor disorder	4. 5. 7. 9. 10. 11. 12. 13.	Negativism Compliance Stereotypies Grimacing Posturing Mannerisms Hallucinatory behaviour Waxy flexibility
3. Quantitative disorder of form of thinking (and speech)	15. 16. 18. 19. 124.	Flight of ideas Pressure of speech Mutism Restricted speech Distractibility
4. Qualitative disorder of form of thinking (and speech)	20. 21. 22. 23. 25. 26. 27.	Neologisms Klang association Speech dissociation Irrelevance Blocking Stereotypy of speech Echolalia
5. Affect-laden thoughts	28. 29. 30. 31.	Gloomy thoughts Elated thoughts Hopelessness Suicidal thoughts
6. Predelusional signs	33. 34. 35. 37.	Delusional mood Ideas of reference Questioning reasons for being Perplexity
7. Experiences of control	38. 39. 40.	Thought alienation Thoughts spoken aloud Delusions of control
8. Delusions	41. 42. 43. 44. 45. 46. 47. 48. 49. 50 51. 52. 53.	Persecution Guilt Self-depreciation Nihilistic Grandeur Reference Presence of delusional system Hypochondriacal Special mission Religious Fantastic Sexual Impending doom
9. Neurasthenic complaints	54. 55. 56. 57. 58. 59. 119.	Obsessive thoughts Worries Lack of concentration Memory difficulties Hypochondriacal Undecided Decreased interest
10. Lack of insight	60	Lack of insight
11. Distortion of self-perception	61. 63. 64.	Changed appearance Looking at self Break of self-identity
12. Derealization	62. 65.	Derealization Distortion of time perception

70

TABLE 4.2. Continued

Groups	Units of Analysis
13. Auditory hallucinations	66. Presence of verbal hallucinations 67. Voices speak to patient 69. Nonverbal auditory hallucinations 70. Presence of auditory hallucinations
14. "Characteristic" hallucinations	68. Voices speak full sentences 72. Voices discussing patient 73. Hallucinations from body 74. Voices comment on patient's thoughts 75. Voices speak thoughts
15. Other hallucinations	76. Visual 77. Tactile 78. Olfactory 79. Sexual 80. Somatic 81. Gustatory
16. Pseudo-hallucinations	82. Auditory 83. Visual
17. Depressed-elated	32. Special depression 84. Depressed mood 85. Observed elated mood
18. Anxiety, tension, irritability	86. Morose mood 88. Irritability 89. Tension 90. Situation anxiety 91. Anxiety
19. Flatness	92. Flatness 93. Apathy
20. Incongruity	95. Incongruity of affect
21. Other affective change	94. Ecstatic mood 97. Haughtiness 98. Ambivalence 101. Lability of affect 102. Ambitendence
22. Indication of personality change	8. Odd appearance and behaviour 103. Change of interest 104. Change of sex behaviour 105. Autism 106. Abnormal tidiness 110. Social withdrawal
23. Disregard of social norms	108. Disregard of norms 109. Self-neglect
24. Other behavioural change	6. Talking to self 17. Disorder of pitch 96. Giggling to self 100. Demonstrative
25. Psychophysical	111. Early waking 112. Worse in morning 113. Worse in evening 114. Diminished appetite 115. Sleep problems 116. Increased appetite 117. Increased libido 118. Decreased energy 120. Decreased libido 121. Constipation

TABLE 4.2. Continued.

Groups	Units of Analysis
26. Cooperation difficulties, circumstances related	125. Biological treatment 128. Environmental circumstances 129. Speech impediments
27. Cooperation difficulties, patient-related	36. Suspiciousness 122. Suggestibility 123. Poor rapport 126. Unwilling to cooperate 127. Inadequate description

* Five Units of Analysis (24 perseveration, 71 frequent auditory hallucinations, 87 groaning, 99 loss of emotion, and 107 increased interest) were excluded because they did not fit well into any of the groups and it was considered inappropriate to create 5 new groups to accommodate them.

Originally four ways of scoring individual units of analysis were envisaged. The simplest method was to use a dichotomy of the positive–negative (1–0) type. In this case a unit was considered positive, at least if one of the constituent items was rated as present, otherwise the unit was considered negative. In a second method of scoring the unit was considered: (a) positive if any one of the constituent items was positive; (b) negative if all items were rated either as absent or as not applicable, or (c) indeterminate in all other cases. In some special analyses a scaling system based on a clustering technique was adopted (see Volume 1 of IPSS report). In a fourth method provision was made for four values to be assigned to a unit: it was considered (a) positive if any one of the constituent items was rated positive; (b) negative if all items were rated as absent or as not applicable; (c) indeterminate if there were no positive ratings and at least one of the items was not rated; and (d) uncertain if all items were rated questionable. This last method was used in most of the analyses reported in Volume 1 of the IPSS report (WHO, 1973). In reliability assessments made at the time of the initial examination (Volume 1, Chapter 8 of the IPSS report) the score of a unit of analysis was the sum of the values of ratings made on all the constituent items of the unit divided by the maximum possible score for that unit.

Drawing upon the experience in analysing the initial evaluation data it was found possible to use the simplest scoring system in all the analyses reported in this volume. A unit of analysis is therefore either positive, i.e. the symptom present, if at least one of the items composing it was positive, or negative, i.e. the symptom is considered to be absent if none of the constituent items was rated as present. This system of scoring tends to increase the reliability of the units by an average of 5 per cent.

The reasons for condensing items into units of analysis apply, in certain analyses, to the units themselves, and therefore, further condensation was undertaken (Volume 1, Chapter 7.6 of the IPSS report). Psychopathology can be examined from the point of view of major areas of dysfunction, and the units describing such areas can be grouped together. For example, 'delusions of control' could be included under the general rubric of 'delusions' and 'auditory hallucinations in the third person' would be similarly included under 'hallucinations'. By applying this method of grouping 27 'groups of units of analysis' (GUAs) were obtained. A list of the GUAs with their constituent units and the PSE items contained in each, is shown in Table 4.2. The score of a group of units equals the proportion of its positive units.

4.3.2 The intracentre reliability of the 129 units of analysis (UAs)

The reliability of the 129 UAs is expressed in terms of the probability of making a 'correct' rating, π and of the two-rater agreement rate a. It turned out that on the whole, reliability was surprisingly high. On 59 out of the 129 units of analysis complete agreement was achieved in all of the 53 rating exercises, thus leading to an estimate of both reliability coefficients π and a of 1. For 34 UAs π was 0.99 ($a = 0.98$) and for 29 the reliability coefficient was between 0.97 and 0.98 (i.e. a between 0.94 and 0.96). Hence 122 out of the 129 UAs showed a reliability of 0.97 (i.e. a 0.94) or more. The three units 'suspiciousness', 'poor rapport' and 'inadequate description' all belonging to the group 'cooperation difficulties, patient-related' had π-values between 0.94 and 0.96 which correspond to agreement rates in the range of 0.89 and 0.92. Of similar reliability were the units 'early waking' and 'sleep problems' in the 'psychophysical' symptom group while both 'lack of insight' and 'flatness' had reliability estimates of $\pi = 0.96$ (i.e. $a = 0.92$).

The difference between the lowest and highest π values should, however, not be overestimated. Both values do not differ statistically significantly (at the 5 per cent level) and it cannot be excluded that they are due to random fluctuations only.

At first glance the reliability of the UAs seems to be extraordinarily high. The intraclass correlation coefficients which were calculated to estimate the UAs reliability at the time of the initial examination varied between 0.47 and 0.96 (see Volume 1 of the IPSS report, Table 8.3). But as already mentioned above, the

TABLE 4.3. INTRA-CENTRE RELIABILITY - NUMBER OF UNITS OF ANALYSIS BY MAGNITUDE OF π AND TWO-RATER AGREEMENT RATE.

π	Two-rater agreement rate a	No. of UAs
1.00	1.00	59
0.99	0.98	34
0.97 - 0.98	0.94 - 0.96	29
0.97 - 1.00	0.94 - 1.00	122

TABLE 4.4.   INTRA-CENTRE RELIABILITY - UNITS OF ANALYSIS
WITH LOWEST π AND CORRESPONDING a-VALUE.

Units of Analysis	π	a
Suspiciousness	0.95	0.91
Poor rapport	0.96	0.92
Inadequate description	0.94	0.89
Early waking	0.96	0.92
Sleep problems	0.95	0.91
Lack of insight	0.96	0.92
Flatness of affect	0.96	0.92

scores of the UAs were defined in a different way, namely as the proportion of positives of all the PSE items which define the corresponding unit of analysis, while in the present context the UAs are dichotomous. In addition, the intraclass correlation coefficient is not directly comparable to the probability π of correct rating, as discussed in section 4.2.2.

For the sake of comparability the probabilities π and the corresponding two-rater agreement rates were calculated for the reliability exercises carried out at the time of the initial examination. In general, figures obtained on initial evaluation were slightly lower; complete agreement was never reached while 118 of the units

TABLE 4.5.   UNITS OF ANALYSIS WITH LOWEST RELIABILITY
AT THE TIME OF THE INITIAL EXAMINATION.

Units of Analysis	π	a
Gloomy thoughts	0.92	0.85
Delusional mood	0.91	0.84
Perplexity	0.92	0.85
Anxiety	0.92	0.85
Flatness of affect	0.88	0.79
Apathy	0.93	0.87
Sleep problems	0.91	0.84
Suspiciousness	0.92	0.85
Poor rapport	0.92	0.85
Unwilling to cooperate	0.87	0.77
Inadequate description	0.88	0.79

of analysis had π-values between 0.93 and 0.99 (i.e. a-values between 0.87 and 0.98). The remaining 11 units and their respective reliability coefficients π and a are shown in Table 4.5 below.

Again the units in the groups 'patient related cooperation difficulties', 'psychophysical symptoms' and 'flatness' showed relatively low reliability coefficients. In addition, lower reliability was observed in the groups 'predelusional signs' and 'affect-laden thoughts'.

It is not easy to compare the reliability coefficients reported in the literature with the results of the IPSS data. Spitzer *et al.* (1970) describe the interjudge reliability of 22 symptoms based on their Psychiatric Status Schedule (PSS) and gave intraclass correlation coefficients with a medium 0.90. According to the remarks of section 4.2.2. this roughly corresponds to a π-value of 0.97. Wing *et al.* (1967) find correlation coefficients between 0.88 and 0.97 for six non-psychotic items and average values of 0.94 for items on delusions and hallucinations and of 0.91 for items on behavioural and speech abnormalities. The corresponding π-values would be 0.97, 0.99, 0.98 and 0.98 respectively. For eight dichotomized somatic symptoms the authors give an average agreement rate of 0.80 based upon a two-rater judgment. The corresponding π-value would be 0.89. Gurland *et al.* (1972) give the intraclass correlation coefficients of six factors derived from the Structured and Scaled Interview to Assess Maladjustment (SSIAM): social isolation 0.90 (0.97)*; work inadequacy 0.97 (0.99); friction with family 0.84 (0.96); dependence on family 0.88 (0.97); sexual dissatisfaction 0.78 (0.94); friction outside family 0.81 (0.95). This comparison shows that the reliability estimates based upon the IPSS data are very similar to those found by others.

As a conclusion of the intracentre reliability assessment of the 129 units of analysis, it can be stated that the PSE as used in the study is a very reliable tool to measure the patients' symptomatological profiles, if the original items are grouped into 129 UAs which are then dichotomized allowing for the ratings 'present' and 'not present' only. If rates of pairwise agreement are calculated as indicators of reliability it must be taken into account that a π-value of, say, 0.90 corresponds to an agreement rate of $\pi^2 + (1 - \pi)^2 = 0.82$. The agreement rate of 0.90 corresponds to a π-value of 0.95.

There is, however, another important aspect to be taken into account when interpreting the reliability of the measurements. Certain symptoms are extremely unlikely to occur frequently. For the 813 patients with PSE filled in at the time of the second year follow-up examination the proportions with positive UAs are shown below.

One of the assumptions for calculating π, i.e. the probability that a psychiatrist rates correctly, is that he is equally likely to make a correct rating both when the symptom is really present and when it is absent. This assumption may not always be realistic, especially for UAs which occur very rarely. In such cases it cannot be excluded that it is more difficult for a psychiatrist to recognize a symptom to be present than to judge correctly when it is absent. This implies that there exist, in

---

*The figures in brackets give the corresponding π-values.

TABLE 4.6.   FREQUENCY OF THE INDIVIDUAL UNITS OF
              ANALYSIS IN THE TOTAL SAMPLE AND IN THE
              INTRACENTRE RELIABILITY EXERCISES.

| | Units of Analysis | % Positive | |
No.	Description	In total sample	In reliability exercises
1	Overactivity	2.0	0.9
2	Retardation	3.7	9.4
3	Stupor	0.4	1.9
14	Repetitive movements	1.6	3.8
4	Negativism	1.0	1.9
5	Compliance	0.0	0.0
7	Stereotypies	1.0	1.9
9	Grimacing	2.2	0.9
10	Posturing	0.5	2.8
11	Mannerisms	4.9	2.8
12	Hallucinatory behaviour	2.1	1.9
13	Waxy flexibility	0.1	0.0
15	Flight of ideas	1.0	1.9
16	Pressure of speech	1.0	1.9
18	Mutism	1.6	1.9
19	Restricted speech	10.2	14.2
124	Distractibility	4.4	1.9
20	Neologisms	0.5	0.9
21	Klang association	0.7	0.0
22	Speech dissociation	6.0	5.7
23	Irrelevance	2.6	4.7
25	Blocking	2.6	0.0
26	Stereotypy of speech	0.2	1.9
27	Echolalia	0.1	0.0
28	Gloomy thoughts	11.9	11.3
29	Elated thoughts	7.0	7.5
30	Hopelessness	8.6	5.7
31	Suicidal thoughts	2.8	3.8
33	Delusional mood	9.0	6.6
34	Ideas of reference	15.4	4.7
35	Questions reason for being	0.7	0.0
37	Perplexity	4.3	7.5
38	Thought alienation	6.3	2.8
39	Thoughts spoken aloud	6.4	2.8
40	Delusions of control	4.3	1.9
41	Delusions of persecution	9.7	6.6
42	Delusions of guilt	3.1	4.7
43	Delusions of self-depreciation	7.9	8.5
44	Nihilistic delusions	1.1	1.9
45	Delusions of grandeur	3.8	3.8
46	Delusions of reference	11.6	4.3
47	Presence of delusional system	4.2	2.8
48	Hypochondriacal delusions	0.9	0.0
49	Special mission delusions	1.5	0.9
50	Religious delusions	3.2	2.8
51	Fantastic delusions	0.6	0.0
52	Sexual delusions	2.1	2.8
53	Delusions of impending doom	0.2	0.0
54	Obsessive thought	8.4	5.7
55	Worries	5.2	3.8
56	Lack of concentration	3.2	5.7
57	Memory difficulties	1.2	2.8
58	Hypochondriacal	14.2	14.2
59	Undecided	2.1	1.9
119	Decreased interest	3.6	3.8
60	Lack of insight	36.6	34.0

TABLE 4.6. continued.

| Units of Analysis | | % Positive | |
No. Description		In total sample	In reliable exercises
61	Changed appearance	2.8	3.8
63	Looking at self	0.6	0.0
64	Break of self-identity	1.4	0.0
62	Derealization	6.2	5.7
65	Distortion of time perception	1.4	0.9
66	Presence of verbal hallucinations	8.7	5.7
67	Voices speak to patient	7.6	5.7
69	Nonverbal auditory hallucinations	2.5	3.8
70	Presence of auditory hallucinations	9.4	5.7
68	Voices speak full sentences	5.2	4.7
72	Voices discussing patient	4.6	0.0
73	Hallucinations from body	0.9	0.0
74	Voices comment on patient's thoughts	3.7	4.7
75	Voices speak thoughts	3.0	1.9
76	Visual hallucinations	2.8	1.9
77	Tactile hallucinations	2.6	3.8
78	Olfactory hallucinations	2.1	1.9
79	Sexual hallucinations	1.2	1.9
80	Somatic hallucinations	1.5	1.9
81	Gustatory hallucinations	1.1	0.0
82	Auditory pseudo-hallucinations	2.1	2.8
83	Visual pseudo-hallucinations	0.9	0.0
32	Special depression	2.3	1.9
84	Depressed mood	6.5	11.3
85	Observed elated mood	3.0	0.9
86	Morose mood	0.6	1.9
88	Irritability	6.9	8.5
89	Tension	3.3	6.6
90	Situation anxiety	10.2	6.6
91	Anxiety	5.2	8.5
92	Flatness	20.6	11.3
93	Apathy	14.3	11.3
95	Incongruity of affect	7.1	4.7
94	Ecstatic mood	0.9	0.0
97	Haughtiness	1.8	0.9
98	Ambivalence	1.4	0.9
101	Lability of affect	7.0	5.7
102	Ambitendence	0.0	0.0
8	Odd appearance and behaviour	0.6	0.0
103	Change of interest	1.5	0.0
104	Change of sex behaviour	2.2	2.8
105	Autism	9.5	3.8
106	Abnormal tidiness	2.0	0.0
110	Social withdrawal	4.9	1.9
108	Disregard of norms	3.1	2.8
109	Self-neglect	6.7	1.9
6	Talking to self	2.7	1.9
17	Disorder of pitch	7.6	9.4
96	Giggling to self	3.6	3.8
100	Demonstrative	3.6	6.6
111	Early waking	8.7	18.9
112	Worse in morning	12.2	7.5
113	Worse in evening	5.2	6.6

TABLE 4.6. continued.

No.	Units of Analysis Description	% Positive In total sample	In reliable exercises
114	Diminished appetite	2.1	3.8
115	Sleep problems	6.9	16.0
116	Increased appetite	0.2	0.0
117	Increased libido	3.1	5.7
118	Decreased energy	1.5	4.7
120	Decreased libido	3.7	4.7
121	Constipation	1.0	0.0
125	Biological treatment	46.2	43.4
128	Environmental circumstance	6.5	6.5
129	Speech impediments	0.9	0.0
36	Suspiciousness	19.3	14.2
122	Suggestibility	1.6	0.9
123	Poor rapport	20.2	13.2
126	Unwilling to cooperate	20.1	14.2
127	Inadequate description	20.3	18.9
	Excluded UAs:		
24	Perseveration	0.6	0.0
71	Frequent auditory hallucinations	6.3	3.8
87	Groaning	0.7	4.7
99	Loss of emotions	2.7	3.8
107	Increased interest	3.1	8.5

fact, two probabilities for a correct rating: π_P and π_A, i.e. the probabilities to rate a present and an absent item correctly. If the true proportions of patients with the symptom present and absent are P and A respectively it can be shown that the two-rater agreement rate a estimates

$$P[\pi_P^2 + (1 - \pi_P)^2] + A[\pi_A^2 + (1 - \pi_A)^2].$$

Unfortunately, in most practical situations P and A, the true proportions of subjects with the symptom present and absent are not known. For example, unit of analysis 1, i.e. overactivity, is positive in 2 per cent of the total sample of 812 individuals. Therefore, if $P = 0.02$ and $A = 0.98$ are taken as estimates of P and A, with the two-rater agreement rate $a = 0.98$ the following relationship between k_P and π_A holds (Table 4.7).

The second part of Table 4.7 shows the relationship, if it is assumed that only 1 per cent of the patients examined really have a positive rating on unit of analysis 1 (i.e. $P = 0.01, A = 0.99$).

Since all the pairs of values for π_A and π_P are in agreement with the actual data, it cannot be excluded that the reliability for assessing correctly the symptom when it is really present is 0.5. In other words the data available allow the statement that only the absence of 'overactivity' can be determined with high reliability ($\pi^a = 0.99$) while nothing can be said about the reliability of measuring that symptom when it is really present.

It may be of interest to study the possible relationship between π_A and π_P for a symptom which is present more frequently, like unit of analysis 60, lack of insight.

TABLE 4.7.   UNIT OF ANALYSIS NO. 1 = OVERACTIVITY: RELATIONSHIP BETWEEN π_A AND π_P FOR DIFFERENT ASSUMPTIONS CONCERNING THE DISTRIBUTION OF THE SYMPTOM IN THE POPULATION.

a = 0.98		a = 0.98	
P = 0.02		P = 0.01	
A = 0.98		A = 0.99	

π_A	π_P	π_A	π_P
0.9903	1.0	0.9904	1.0
0.9920	0.9	0.9913	0.9
0.9936	0.8	0.9920	0.8
0.9946	0.7	0.9925	0.7
0.9953	0.6	0.9928	0.6
0.9955	0.5	0.9930	0.5

TABLE 4.8.   UNIT OF ANALYSIS NO. 60 = LACK OF INSIGHT: RELATIONSHIP BETWEEN π_A AND π_P FOR DIFFERENT ASSUMPTIONS CONCERNING THE DISTRIBUTION OF THE SYMPTOM IN THE POPULATION.

a = 0.93		a = 0.93	
P = 0.366		P = 0.20	
A = 0.634		A = 0.80	

π_A	π_P	π_A	π_P
0.87	1.00	0.95	1.00
0.90	0.99	0.96	0.96
0.92	0.98	0.97	0.92
0.94	0.97	0.98	0.88
0.96	0.96	0.99	0.84
0.98	0.95	0.99	0.80
1.00	0.94	1.00	0.75

In the total sample this symptom was present in 36.6 per cent of the cases. Again, taking 0.366 and 0.634 as estimates of P and A respectively, and based upon the two-rater agreement rate of $a = 0.96$, the relation between π_A and π_P is shown in Table 4.8.

In general, if the agreement ratio a is high but the reliability of rating not independent of the content of the item, and if the item is distributed evenly in the population, then the probabilities π_A and π_P for rating correctly an absent and a present symptom cannot be very different. In fact, if in one-half of the population the item is present and in the other half absent, and if the two-rater agreement ratio is, say, 0.90, π_P and π_A would range between 0.89 and 1.00. Table 4.6, however, shows that for most of the units of analysis the percentage of the patient population in which the particular symptom was absent was considerably higher than the percentage of patients in whom it was present. For most of those units of analysis it would be difficult to justify an *a priori* assumption that the reliabilities π_A and π_P for correct assessment are equal. Without such an assumption, however, the pooled reliability π would be strongly inflated by π_A, i.e. the probability of correctly assessing the unit of analysis if the symptom is absent, i.e. by the agreement on the absence of the symptom. In the same way it can be shown that in the case of symptoms with a prevalence of less than 4 per cent in the patient population and for which the agreement ratio is less than 0.98, it cannot be excluded that the reliability π_P for a correct assessment whether the symptom was really present would be 0.5. It must be emphasized here that this does not mean that the item cannot be assessed reliably. It simply means that on the basis of the data available a statement on the reliability of the measurements can only be made for patients who do not have the symptom, since information on patients who do have the symptom is lacking. Table 4.9 lists those UAs for which the data only allowed an estimation of the reliability π_A of measuring correctly the symptoms' absence. Sometimes the φ-coefficient ($\varphi = \sqrt{Z^2/N}$ where Z^2 is calculated on the basis of 2 x 2 contingency table and N is the total number of measurements in the table) is used to calculate the reliability in such situations. For unit of analysis 5 — compliance — there was complete agreement on the absence of this symptom among all the raters for all the patients. Evidently the φ-coefficient is zero. However, it would be counter-intuitive to state that the measurements are unreliable, since no better agreement could be achieved if the patients really did not have the symptom. Without making additional assumptions a single coefficient would be insufficient to describe adequately the reliability of the measurements.

4.3.3 The intracentre reliability of the 27 groups of units of analysis (GUAs)

The 27 groups of units of analysis (GUAs) are derived from the 129 UAs and the scores are the proportions of the positive units of analysis in the corresponding GUAs. One would therefore expect that a high reliability of the units implies a high reliability of the groups of units of analysis. The GUA 12 'derealization' is defined by the two units 'derealization' (UA 62) and 'distortion of time perception' (UA 65). If the reliability for those two units were independent, the probability π for

80

TABLE 4.9. UNITS OF ANALYSIS FOR WHICH SAMPLE INFORMATION IS INSUFFICIENT TO ESTIMATE THE RELIABILITY π_P FOR POSITIVE MEASUREMENTS, IF π_P IS DIFFERENT FROM THE RELIABILITY π_A FOR NEGATIVE MEASUREMENTS.

Units of Analysis	% positive in total sample
Overactivity	2.0
Grimacing	2.2
Posturing	0.5
Hallucinating behaviour	2.1
Mutism	1.6
Neologisms	0.5
Irrelevance	2.6
Delusions of guilt	3.1
Special mission delusions	1.5
Religious delusions	3.2
Sexual delusions	2.1
Memory difficulties	1.2
Distortion of time perception	1.4
Nonverbal auditory hallucinations	2.5
Voices comment on patient's thoughts	3.7
Tactile hallucinations	2.5
Auditory hallucinations	2.1
Observed elated mood	3.0
Groaning	0.7
Tension	3.3
Giggling to self	3.6
Haughtiness	1.8
Ambivalence	1.4
Change of sex behaviour	2.2
Increased interest	3.1
Disregard of norms	3.1
Decreased energy	1.5
Decreased interest	3.6
Decreased libido	3.7
Suggestibility	1.6

correctly rating GUA 12 would just be the product of the corresponding probabilities of UA 62 and UA 65, namely $\pi = 0.98 \times 0.99 = 0.97$. It is not certain that such an assumption would be realistic. It may well be that a high reliability in rating the unit 'derealization' would imply a high reliability in rating 'distortion of time perception'. Therefore, the π-values for the 27 GUAs were calculated directly (since in general the GUAs are no more dichotomous, the calculated π-values are conservative estimates in the sense described in Appendix 5). Those π-values and the agreement ratios upon which they are based, together with the lower and upper

TABLE 4.10.   GROUPS OF ANALYSIS WITH LOWEST INTRA-CENTRE RELIABILITY.

Groups of Units of Analysis	Reliability coefficient π	Agreement Ratio a
Predelusional signs	0.94	0.89
Delusions	0.94	0.89
Neurasthenic complaints	0.93	0.87
Anxiety	0.94	0.89
Psychophysical complaints	0.88	0.79
Cooperation difficulties patient-related	0.82	0.70

confidence limits (confidence coefficient 95 per cent) for the 27 GUAs are shown in Figure 4.3.

Twenty-one of the GUAs have a reliability coefficient of $\pi = 0.94$ or $a = 0.91$ or more. 'Predelusional signs' (GUA 6), 'delusions' (GUA 8), 'neurasthenic complaints (GUA 9), and 'anxiety' (GUA 18) show π-values between 0.90 and 0.94 (corresponding agreement ratios $a = 0.82$ and 0.89) while 'psychophysical complaints' (GUA 25) and 'co-operation difficulties, patient-related' (GUA 27) had π-values below 0.90 (i.e. $a = 0.82$).

However, as in the case of the UAs, not too much emphasis should be put on these differences of the estimates of π for GUAs since it cannot be excluded that they are due to random variations only.

In many publications on the reliability of psychiatric rating scales with continuous or polychotomous item scores the intraclass correlation coefficient is presented as an indicator of reliability. For reasons of comparability the intraclass correlation coefficients for the 27 GUAs were also calculated and are shown in Table 4.11.

Two observations can be made when comparing the intraclass correlation coefficients with the π-values: firstly, the correlation coefficients are numerically smaller than the probabilities π of correct rating and secondly, the range of their variation is considerably wider than that of the corresponding π-values. As already mentioned, the scale of the intraclass correlation coefficient ranges from -1 to $+1$ while π varies from 0.5 to 1.0, so the numerical values of both coefficients of reliability are not directly comparable. What is much more striking, however, is the difference in the variation. The intraclass correlation coefficients assume values between 0.37 and 1.00 while k varies between 0.85 and 0.99. The GUAs with the lowest intraclass correlation coefficients are GUA 12 'derealization' with $r = 0.41$, GUA 20 'incongruity' with $r = 0.37$, and GUA 23 'disregard of social norms' with $r = 0.37$. All these GUAs are composed of either one or two units of analysis which indicates that their scores are far from being continuous. The rates of complete

82

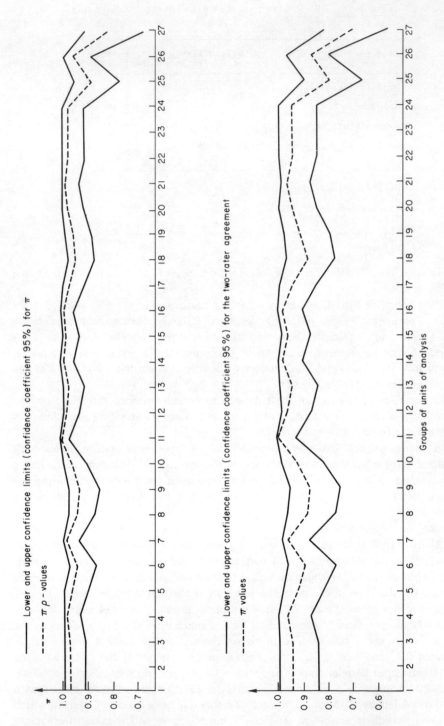

Figure 4.3   Intracentre reliability exercise

TABLE 4.11.   INTRA-CENTRE RELIABILITY - INTRACLASS CORRELATION
COEFFICIENTS FOR 27 GROUPS OF UNITS OF ANALYSIS.

Groups of Units of Analysis	Intra-class correlation coefficient
Quantitative psychomotor disorder	0.89
Qualitative psychomotor disorder	0.94
Quantitative disorder of form of thinking (and speech)	0.91
Qualitative disorder of form of thinking (and speech)	0.93
Affect-laden thoughts	0.93
Predelusional signs	0.58
Experiences of control	0.90
Delusions	0.93
Neurasthenic complaints	0.89
Lack of insight	0.83
Distortion of self-perception	1.00
Derealization	0.41
Auditory hallucinations	0.89
"Characteristic" hallucinations	0.86
Other hallucinations	0.89
Pseudo-hallucinations	0.66
Depressed-elated	0.84
Anxiety, tension, irritability	0.92
Flatness	0.77
Incongruity	0.37
Other affective change	0.79
Indication of personality change	0.64
Disregard for social norms	0.37
Other behavioural change	0.89
Psychophysical	0.91
Cooperation difficulties, circumstances-related	0.85
Cooperation difficulties, patient-related	0.77

pairwise agreement for these GUAs are 0.98, 0.97 and 0.97 respectively. Therefore, the intraclass correlation coefficient for ordinal scale categories with a small number of possible scores can be very misleading. In Section 4.4.3 on the intercentre reliability of the 27 GUAs this will be shown in more detail on the basis of examples.

One important characteristic of the patients at the time of the second-year follow-up examination is the sharply decreased level of their overall symptomatology in comparison with the initial assessment. At the time of the initial examination all the patients were in a psychotic episode while at the time of the two-year follow-up many of them were non-psychotic or even symptom-free. Therefore, only a relatively small percentage of the total sample population shows

84

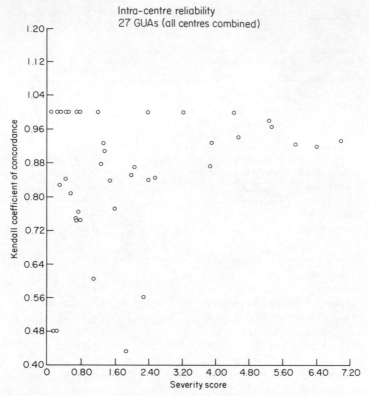

Figure 4.4   Relationship between severity score and reliability expressed as Kendall's coefficient of concordance. *Note*: Cases with severity score 0 are not included in this figure, since Kendall's coefficient of concordance is not defined, if there is no variation in the scores

positive symptoms (see Table 4.6). In such a situation the question emerges whether the reliability of rating correctly the presence of a symptom is as high as that of rating its absence. An attempt was made to test a related hypothesis on the basis of the actual data. For this purpose a severity score was calculated for each of the 53 patients in the rating exercises. This severity score was defined as the patient's average sum of all the 27 GUAs as rated by both psychiatrists. In addition, Kendall's coefficient of concordance was determined for each two-observer rating exercise. This coefficient measures the agreement of the overall profiles as judged by both observers. Its numerical value is 1, if both profiles are parallel, and 0 if both profiles are unrelated. The hypothesis was that with increasing severity the overall profile reliability in terms of Kendall's coefficient of concordance would decrease. The following graph (Figure 4.4) illustrates the actual relationship.

It is evident that the hypothesis cannot be supported by the data. No relationship between severity score and reliability can be demonstrated. There is no sample evidence that the reliability of rating symptoms as present differs from that of rating symptoms as absent.

4.3.4 Summary of the intracentre reliability assessment

The intracentre reliability of the Present State Examination schedule (PSE) was assessed on the basis of the data collected at the time of the two-year follow-up examinations of the patients. Fifty-three subjects were rated independently (but simultaneously) by two psychiatrists in six of the field research centres partici-pating in the study. The reliability of the 129 units of analysis and the corresponding 27 groups of units of analysis was expressed in terms of the probability π and the two-rater agreement ratio a upon which π is based. There was no sample evidence that this probability would depend on the real distribution of the symptom in the population. The overall level of the reliability was remarkably high: higher than $\pi = 0.93$ (i.e. $a = 0.87$) for all the UAs and less than π 0.94 only for the GUAs 25 and 27 ('psychophysical complaints' and 'co-operation diffi-culties, patient-related'). This is a slight improvement in comparison to the reliability achieved at the time of the initial examination where 10 of the 129 UAs had π-values smaller than 0.93 (based upon 190 rating exercises carried out in all the participating centres). These findings allow the conclusion that, within the field research centres, the PSE was a reliable instrument to assess the patients' symptomatological profiles.

4.4 THE INTERCENTRE RELIABILITY OF THE PSE

4.4.1 Methods

The fact that the PSE proved to be a reliable instrument within individual centres does not necessarily mean that the schedule was used in the same way in all the field research centres. For this reason a number of intercentre reliability exercises were performed.

Psychiatrists from the different field research centres participating in the IPSS met regularly and rated simultaneously and independently patients from videotape or film recordings of the interviews. Apart from the assessment of the crosscultural reliability of the rating instruments, a main purpose of these exercises was training. For the purpose of reliability analyses rating exercises were selected in which groups with a constant number of psychiatrists rated the patients. In total 26 rating exercises with nine psychiatrists each form the basis for the following intercentre reliability evaluation of the PSE.

4.4.2 The intercentre reliability of the 129 units of analysis

To quantify the reliability of the 129 UAs the probability π and the corresponding agreement ratio a were calculated in a similar way as described in the paragraph on intracentre reliability (section 4.3.2). However, in this context a rating exercise was considered 'successful' if all psychiatrists fully agreed on the rating of the unit of analysis. Since it is less likely that nine raters would agree completely on the presence or absence of a symptom than only two (as in the case of the intracentre exercises), it is not surprising that the proportion of successful rating exercises was considerably lower. However, the π-values do not depend upon the number of

86

TABLE 4.12.   INTER-CENTRE RELIABILITY.   NUMBER OF
UNITS OF ANALYSIS BY MAGNITUDES OF π
AND AGREEMENT RATES.

Probability π	Two-rater equivalent of nine-rater agreement rates	Number of UAs
0.97 - 1.00	0.94 - 1.00	71
0.95 - 0.96	0.91 - 0.92	31
0.92 - 0.94	0.85 - 0.89	21
0.92 - 1.00	0.85 - 1.00	123

raters in the exercise and to facilitate comparison between intracentre and intercentre reliability exercises in terms of agreement ratios the two-rater equivalents of the nine-rater agreement ratios are shown together with π. The overall level of π is still high, but about 5 per cent lower than for the intracentre exercises. Only two UAs reached a value $\pi = 1$ while 69 had a coefficient and reliability between 0.97 and 0.99 (agreement ratios 0.94 and 0.98 respectively) and 31 between 0.95 and 0.96 (agreement ratios between 0.91 and 0.96). The π-value ranged between 0.92 and 0.94 and the corresponding agreement rates between 0.85 and 0.89 for 21 UAs and the remaining six units had a reliability smaller than 0.92. Tables 4.12 and 4.13 summarize the findings.

It is interesting to note that the UAs in the groups 'co-operation difficulties, patient-related' and 'flatness' are again among the units with lowest reliability as in the intracentre results. On the other hand 'incongruity of affect' and 'biological treatment' could be rated very reliably within the centres (π-values and a-values 0.97 and 0.98, and 0.94 and 0.96 respectively). 'Lack of insight' and the units of

TABLE 4.13.   INTER-CENTRE RELIABILITY - UNITS OF
ANALYSIS WITH LOWEST RELIABILITY.

Units of Analysis	Probability π	Two-rater equivalents of nine-rater agreeement rates
Unwilling to cooperate	0.91	0.84
Inadequate description	0.91	0.84
Flatness of affect	0.83	0.72
Incongruity of affect	0.91	0.84
Biological treatment	0.90	0.82

the group 'psychophysical complaints' which were of relatively low reliability in the intracentre analyses (π of 0.95 and 0.96, and a of 0.91 and 0.92) were at the same level in the intercentre exercises, but with the general reliability decreased they were no longer at the lower end of the reliability scale.

4.4.3 The intercentre reliability of the 27 groups of units of analysis

The intercentre reliability of the 27 GUAs was determined in the same way as for the intracentre exercises. The lower and upper confidence limits (confidence coefficient 95 per cent) of the π-values and a-values for the corresponding GUAs are shown in the graph (Figure 4.5). The average π is 0.89 and the average a is 0.81, while it was $\pi = 0.96$ ($a = 0.92$) within the centres. The patterns of the reliability profiles for within and between-centre analyses are very similar. There are perhaps two more pronounced differences: GUA 22 ('indications of personality change'), with the lowest reliability coefficient of $\pi = 0.79$ ($a = 0.67$) in the intercentre exercises, was of average reliability within the centres. On the other hand, GUA 27 ('patient-related, co-operation difficulties'), with the lowest reliability in the intracentre exercises ($\pi = 0.82$, and $a = 0.70$), was rated in the intercentre exercises more reliably than 'predelusional signs', 'delusions', 'flatness' and 'indication of personality change'. The GUAs with lowest intercentre reliability are shown in the following table.

To facilitate the comparability of the results of the intercentre reliability assessment with similar exercises reported in the literature the intraclass correlation coefficients for the 27 GUAs together with the corresponding π-values are shown in Table 4.15.

As already mentioned, it is not surprising that the numerical values of the correlation coefficients are generally lower than the corresponding π-values, since the former are measured on a scale ranging from -1 to 1 while the scale of π ranges between 0 and 1. Therefore, the last column of Table 4.15 shows the numerical value r' derived from the intraclass correlation coefficients by adjusting for these scale differences: $r' = (r + 1)/2$. Like the probabilities π the transformed values vary between 0 and 1.

However, there remain striking differences for some of the GUAs particularly for quantitative psychomotor disorder (GUA 01), pseudohallucinations (GUA 16), incongruity (GUA 20), indication of personality change (GUA 22), disregard of social norms (GUA 23) and other behavioural characteristics (GUA 24). Pseudohallucinations (GUA 16) has the highest π-value and the lowest intraclass correlation coefficient. The high π-value is explained by the fact that in 19 out of the total of 26 reliability exercises all the nine participating raters agreed completely on the scores defining GUA 16. Therefore, $\pi^9 + (1 - \pi)^9 = 19/26$ and hence $\pi = 0.97$. However, most of the ratings made were of the absence of pseudohallucinations so that the π-value of 0.97 means a high probability of rating correctly the absence of this group of units. A statement on the reliability of assessing its presence cannot be made because of lack of relevant data unless it were known *a priori* that both probabilities were equal.

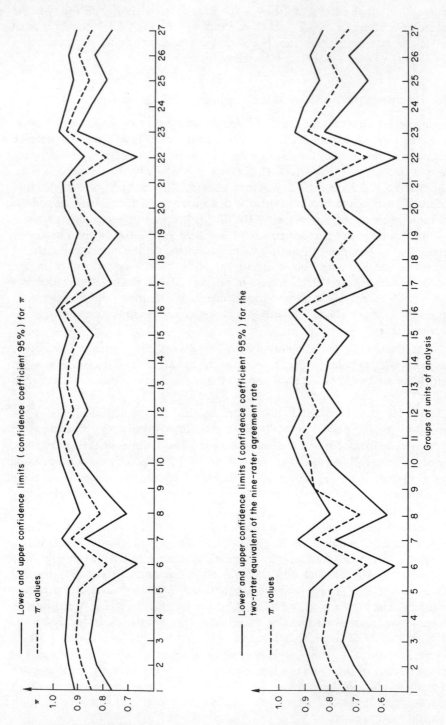

Figure 4.5　Intercentre reliability exercise

TABLE 4.14.   GROUPS OF UNITS OF ANALYSIS WITH THE
LOWEST INTER-CENTRE RELIABILITY.

Groups of Units of Analysis	Reliability coefficient	Two-rater equivalent of nine-rater agreement rates
Quantitative psychomotor disorder	0.85	0.75
Predelusional signs	0.79	0.67
Delusions	0.81	0.69
Depressed-elated	0.85	0.75
Flatness	0.83	0.72
Indication of personality change	0.79	0.67
Cooperation difficulties patient-related	0.85	0.75

The intraclass correlation coefficient r, on the other hand, estimates the proportion of variation of the measurements that is true variation. Since the raters agreed on the absence of this GUA in most of the patients assessed, there was little variation. A high proportion of this small variance was however due to disagreement between the observers, and for this reason r is very low. Taking r as an indicator of low reliability of the rating process would be misleading: if the patients do not have pseudohallucinations the raters can do no better than agree on the absence of this group of units of analysis. The particular group of 26 patients might not be suitable for a comprehensive evaluation of the reliability of assessing GUA 16, but it would be counter-intuitive to regard the measurements obtained as unreliable.

The discrepancies between the π and the r-values for GUA 01, 20, 22, 23 and 24 can be explained in the same way.

For the data of the intracentre reliability exercises the problem was discussed as to whether the level of the reliability depends on the severity of the patient's status overall symptomatology. The data did not support such a hypothesis. The same question was tested on the basis of the intercentre exercises and the results are shown in Figure 4.6.

In this analysis severity scores were defined in the same way as described before and the overall reliability of the symptomatological profile was quantified by Kendall's coefficient of concordance. It is easy to see that there is no sample evidence for any relationship between severity and reliability.

4.4.4 Summary of the intercentre reliability assessment

The intercentre reliability of the PSE was satisfactorily high. The π-coefficients for the symptoms in terms of the 129 UAs varied from 0.92 to 1.00 and for the 27

TABLE 4.15.   INTER-CENTRE RELIABILITY: COMPARISON
BETWEEN VALUES AND THE INTRACLASS
CORRELATION COEFFICIENT FOR 27 GROUPS
OF UNITS OF ANALYSIS.

Groups of Units of Analysis	Intraclass correlation coeff. r.	π-value	Adjusted intraclass corr.coeff. r.
Quantitative psychomotor disorder	(0.14)	0.85	0.57
Qualitative psychomotor disorder	0.56	0.89	0.78
Quantitative disorder of form of thinking (and speech)	0.56	0.90	0.78
Qualitative disorder of form of thinking (and speech)	0.52	0.90	0.76
Affect-laden thoughts	0.74	0.89	0.87
Predelusional signs	0.67	0.79	0.84
Experiences of control	0.83	0.93	0.92
Delusions	0.83	0.81	0.92
Neurasthenic complaints	0.45	0.88	0.73
Lack of insight	(0.65)	0.93	0.83
Distortion of self-perception	0.77	0.96	0.89
Derealization	(0.66)	0.91	0.83
Auditory hallucinations	0.90	0.95	0.95
"Characteristic" hallucinations	0.88	0.94	0.94
Other hallucinations	0.82	0.90	0.91
Pseudo-hallucinations	(0.10)	0.97	0.55
Depressed elated	0.41	0.85	0.71
Anxiety, tension, irritability	0.50	0.89	0.75
Flatness	(0.37)	0.83	0.69
Incongruity	(0.14)	0.91	0.57
Other affective change	(0.29)	0.93	0.65
Indication of personality change	0.36	0.79	0.68
Disregard of social norms	(0.29)	0.95	0.65
Other behaviour change	(0.30)	0.91	0.65
Psychophysical	0.69	0.86	0.85
Cooperation difficulties, circumstances-related	(0.52)	0.90	0.76
Cooperation difficulties, patient-related	0.59	0.85	0.80

GUAs they were in the range of 0.85—1.00. The corresponding agreement rates (two-rater equivalents) ranged between 0.85—1.00, and 0.75—0.94 respectively. However, the general level of reliability was about 5 per cent lower than in the intracentre exercises. 'Predelusional signs', 'delusions' and 'flatness' ranged at the lower end of the reliability scale within and between centres. On the other hand 'indication of personality change' which was of lowest reliability when rated in the between-centre exercises was of average reliability when rated within the centres, while 'co-operation difficulties, patient related' could be judged with the same reliability as most of the other items in the intercentre exercises, although it had lowest reliability when judged within the centres. It is important to note, however,

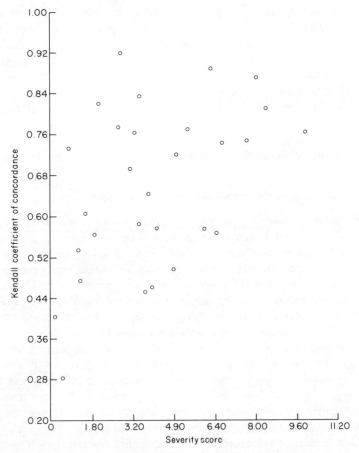

Figure 4.6   Intercentre reliability 1.27 GUAs (all centres combined)

that the numerical value of the reliability coefficient π of the latter item did not change so much (0.82 and 0.85 respectively). What really changed was the reliability of the other items of the rating scale. No relationship between severity of a patient's status and level of reliability could be demonstrated, an observation already made for the data of the intracentre exercises. The intraclass correlation coefficient turned out to be misleading when applied to items which can have three or fewer values only.

4.5 THE RELIABILITY OF THE ASSESSMENT OF COURSE AND OUTCOME CHARACTERISTICS

4.5.1 Method

Course and outcome of the patients' disorders were not measured directly by structured rating scales as was the case with symptom profiles. The ratings were made at WHO Headquarters by a group of psychiatrists using information contained in the Psychiatric History (PH) and Social Description (SD) schedules and the narrative history. To evaluate the reliability of the assessment and coding of the main categories describing course and outcome (that is, social functioning, length of episode of inclusion, proportion of time in psychotic episodes, pattern of course and overall outcome), two series of rating exercises were carried out at WHO Headquarters. In the first series, the PH and SD information and the narrative assessments of 26 patients were rated independently by four psychiatrists and in the second the data on 22 patients were rated independently by a pair of psychiatrists, one of whom also participated in the four-rater exercises.

4.5.2 The reliability of the course and outcome categories

None of the five course and outcome categories were defined as dichotomies. As already outlined in the introduction, pattern of course represents a nominal scale variable with eight possible scores while the remaining four categories are ordinal scale items. An exact estimate of the probability of correct rating can be given for dichotomous variables and for polychotomous categories only under the assumption that the likelihood for wrong judgment does not depend upon the real content of the variable under consideration. However, the π-value calculated by applying the formula for dichotomous items provides a lower limit of the real π. Both this conservative estimate of π and the π derived under the assumption of equal probabilities for 'wrong' rating were calculated for each of the five course and outcome categories in both series of rating exercises. In addition, the two-rater agreement rates for the two-rater exercises and the two-rater equivalents of the four-rater agreement rates were computed. The results are summarized in Table 4.16. Three main conclusions can be derived from this table.

Firstly, the level of reliability of course and outcome ratings is lower than the level of reliability of symptomatological characteristics obtained from the PSE. The order of magnitude of the reliability coefficients π for the course and outcome is comparable with the lower end of the reliability scale for the groups of units of analysis in the intercentre exercises. The only exception is 'social functioning' with the levels of 'no or mild', 'moderate', 'severe' and 'unknown' impairment. This item turned out to be unreliable in the sense that the actual π-value obtained was 0.50. Therefore, it was decided to collapse the levels of 'social functioning' and to distinguish only between 'no, mild or moderate', 'severe', and 'unknown' degree of social impairment. The π-values thus obtained were as follows.

Course and outcome category	Four-rater exercise		Two-rater exercise	
	conservative	equal prob.	conservative	equal prob.
Social functioning (three levels only)	0.86	0.86	0.85	0.86

In all analyses reported in further chapters 'social functioning' is used as a three-level variable. With this proviso the reliability of the course and outcome categories could be considered satisfactory.

TABLE 4.16. RELIABILITY OF COURSE AND OUTCOME CATEGORIES IN TWO SERIES OF RATING EXERCISES.

Course and Outcome Category	Rating Exercises with						
	4 Psychiatrists Involved			2 Psychiatrists Involved			Test: $\pi=\frac{1}{2}$
	2-rater equivalent of 4-rater agreement rate	Conservative π	Equal probability π	Agreement rate	Conservative π	Equal probability π	Level of Significance
Social functioning	0.50	0.50	0.52	0.50	0.50	0.56	0.200 not rejected
Length of episode of inclusion	0.76	0.86	0.86	0.58	0.70	0.76	0.001 rejected
Time psychotic	0.62	0.74	0.75	0.63	0.75	0.79	0.001 rejected
Pattern of course	0.73	0.84	0.84	0.67	0.79	0.81	0.001 rejected
Overall Outcome	0.64	0.77	0.77	0.63	0.75	0.79	0.001 rejected

The second conclusion is that the conservative estimate of π and the value calculated under the assumption of equal probabilities of misjudging are practically identical, in particular when based upon the data from the four-rater exercises.

The third conclusion is that there is a remarkable consistency in the reliability of different groups of psychiatrists. The reliability coefficients for the course and outcome categories were very similar in the two series of rating exercises. Only 'length of episode of inclusion' was rated less reliably in the group of rating exercises carried out by a pair of psychiatrists. The difference, however, is not statistically significant at the 5 per cent level.

4.5.3 Summary of the reliability assessment of course and outcome

The reliability of the categories describing course and outcome of the patients' disorders, i.e. social functioning, length of episode of inclusion; proportion of time in psychotic episodes, pattern of course, and overall outcome was lower than the reliability of the groups of units of analysis in the intercentre exercises: π ranged between 0.70 and 0.85, and the corresponding agreement rates (two-rater equivalents) between 0.58 and 0.75. It was not possible to distinguish reliably between mild and moderate social impairment. Therefore 'social functioning' had to be described by three scores only: severe, not severe, or unknown degree of social impairment. The reliability coefficient π for this grouping was 0.85 (agreement rate $a = 0.75$). The reliability of rating the categories describing the patients' course and outcome was similar for all psychiatrists taking part in the rating exercises and sufficiently high to allow the various analyses reported in the following chapters.

CHAPTER 5

Characteristics of the Study Population and Research Settings during the Follow-up Period

5.1 CHARACTERISTICS OF THE STUDY POPULATION AT THE TIME OF SECOND-YEAR FOLLOW-UP

As indicated in Chapter 3, it was possible to obtain sufficient information about 927 of the 1202 patients initially included in the study to include them in the basic follow-up patient material. Of these 927, 24 were subsequently excluded because of diagnostic considerations (see Appendix 1). These excluded cases fall into two groups. The first group consists of 21 patients, about whom data collected early in the episode of inclusion indicated that they should have been excluded because of one of the exclusion criteria. For example, a patient included because he had hallucinations, (an inclusion symptom), who was noted three weeks after inclusion in the study to have an abnormal EEG suggestive of temporal lobe epilepsy, would fall into this group. The second group consisted of three patients who, during the course of the follow-up period, developed a condition which would make it difficult to compare them meaningfully with other follow-up patients. For example, a patient within an initial evaluation diagnosis of schizophrenia, who subsequently developed a severe neurological condition with organic brain symptoms, would fall into this group. Patients in both groups were excluded from the main follow-up analyses, but have been followed up, and their course during the follow-up period is described separately in Appendix 1. The final follow-up study population thus consists of 906 patients. Table 5.1 indicates the distribution of patients excluded by centre.

5.1.1 Diagnostic distribution of follow-up study population by centre

Table 5.2 indicates the diagnostic distribution by centre of the 906 patients about whom detailed past history (PH) and social description (SD) information concerning the follow-up period is available. This distribution of patients is thus relevant to all analyses which involve second-year follow-up PH and SD data.

Not all of these patients had a PSE between the 22nd and 27th month of this study. Table 5.3 indicates the diagnostic distribution by centre of the 813 patients who were assessed with a PSE between the 22nd and 27th month of the study. This

TABLE 5.1. DISTRIBUTION OF PATIENTS EXCLUDED FOR DIAGNOSTIC REASONS, BY CENTRE.

	Aarhus	Agra	Cali	Ibadan	London	Moscow	Taipei	Washington	Prague	All Centres
Number of patients with PSE 22-27 months after initial examination or with detailed follow-up PH and follow-up SD information	107	127	105	73	73	124	130	92	96	927
Number of patients excluded for diagnostic reasons	5	1	4	1	–	4	1	5	–	21
Number of patients for whom sufficient 2nd year follow-up information available	102	126	101	72	73	120	129	87	96	906
Number of patients with PSE done 22-27 months after initial examination	107	123	104	73	26	121	94	92	94	834
Number of patients excluded for diagnostic reasons	5	1	4	1	–	4	1	5	–	21
Number of patients with PSE done 22-27 months without those excluded for diagnostic reasons	102	122	100	72	26	117	93	87	94	813

TABLE 5.2. DISTRIBUTION OF BASIC FOLLOW-UP STUDY POPULATION BY INITIAL EVALUATION DIAGNOSIS AND CENTRE

Diagnosis	ICD Code	Aarhus	Agra	Cali	Ibadan	London	Moscow	Taipei	Washington	Prague	All Centres
Schizophrenia											
simple	295.0	5	4	2	2	2	-	1	3	4	23
hebephrenic	295.1	12	3	16	5	7	-	29	1	2	74
catatonic	295.2	2	20	9	6	2	-	3	1	-	43
paranoid	295.3	25	12	15	23	40	11	33	32	28	219
acute	295.4	-	9	22	3	-	12	2	10	3	61
latent	295.5	3	-	2	-	1	12	1	2	-	20
residual	295.6	-	-	-	-	1	-	-	-	1	2
schizo-affective	295.7	1	16	6	17	6	4	8	10	15	83
other specified	295.8	1	3	6	2	-	30	-	5	-	49
unspecified	295.9	-	25	-	5	-	3	3	2	-	35
Total		49	92	78	63	58	69	80	65	55	609
Affective Psychosis											
agitated depression	296.0	1	3	1	-	-	-	-	-	-	5
manic-depressive, depressed	296.2	12	4	1	3	2	10	3	3	18	56
manic-depressive, manic	296.1	17	18	2	2	3	1	2	1	7	53
others	296.3-6.9	3	-	1	3	3	1	3	1	1	12
Total		33	25	4	5	8	12	8	5	26	126
Paranoid States	297	9	-	-	-	-	-	9	-	5	23
Other Psychoses											
reactive depression	298.0	-	-	1	1	1	5	4	-	1	13
others	298.1-8.9 299	9	-	2	1	-	5	17	2	3	39
Total		9	-	3	2	1	10	21	2	4	52
All Psychoses		100	117	85	70	67	91	118	72	90	810
Neurosis - Personality disorders											
depressive neurosis	300.4	-	7	5	2	6	9	10	10	6	55
others	300.0-0.3 300.5-301.9	2	2	11	-	-	20	1	5	-	41
Total		2	9	16	2	6	29	11	15	6	96
All Patients		102	126	101	72	73	120	129	87	96	906

98

TABLE 5.3. DISTRIBUTION OF PATIENTS ASSESSED WITH 2ND YEAR FOLLOW-UP PSE 22-27 MONTHS AFTER INITIAL EVALUATION BY INITIAL EVALUATION DIAGNOSIS AND CENTRE.

Diagnosis	ICD Code	Aarhus	Agra	Cali	Ibadan	London	Moscow	Taipei	Washington	Prague	All Centres
Schizophrenia											
simple	295.0	5	4	2	2	-	-	1	3	3	20
hebephrenic	295.1	12	2	16	5	3	-	21	-	2	61
catatonic	295.2	2	19	9	6	1	-	1	1	-	39
paranoid	295.3	25	11	15	23	16	11	28	32	27	188
acute	295.4	-	8	22	3	-	12	2	10	3	60
latent	295.5	3	-	2	-	-	12	-	2	-	19
residual	295.6	-	1	-	1	-	-	-	-	-	1
schizo-affective	295.7	1	16	6	17	1	4	-	10	15	77
other specified	295.8	1	3	5	2	-	27	7	5	2	45
unspecified	295.9	-	25	-	5	-	-	1	2	-	33
Total		49	88	77	63	21	66	61	65	53	543
Affective Psychosis											
agitated depression	296.0	1	3	1	-	-	-	-	-	-	5
manic-depressive, depressed	296.2	12	4	1	3	2	10	3	3	18	56
manic-depressive, manic	296.1	17	18	2	-	2	1	1	1	7	51
others	296.3-6.9	3	-	-	1	1	1	3	1	1	10
Total		33	25	4	5	5	12	7	5	26	122
Paranoid States	297	9	-	-	-	-	-	5	-	5	19
Other Psychoses											
reactive depression	298.0	-	-	1	1	-	5	3	-	1	11
others	298.1-8.9	9	-	2	1	-	5	12	2	3	34
	299										
Total		9	-	3	2	-	10	15	2	4	45
All Psychosis		100	113	84	70	26	88	88	72	88	729
Neurosis, Personality Disorders											
depressive neurosis	300.4	-	7	5	2	-	9	4	10	6	43
others	300.0-0.3 300.5-1.9	2	2	11	-	-	20	1	5	-	41
Total		2	9	16	2	-	29	5	15	6	84
All Patients		102	122	100	72	26	117	93	87	94	813

distribution of patients is thus relevant to all analyses which involve second-year follow-up PSE data.

5.1.2 Distribution of follow-up study population by age, sex and marital status

The percentage of patients in each age (15—24, 25—34, 35—44) and sex group on initial evaluation, about whom detailed past history and social description information concerning the follow-up period is available, was calculated.

For all centres combined there were no age or sex groups from which patients were lost to follow-up more frequently than from other groups. The same was true for most individual centres except that in London relatively few of the males initially in the 25—34 age group are in the follow-up material, and in Aarhus relatively few of the females initially in the 15—24 age group are in the follow-up material, but neither of these differences is statistically significant.

The percentage of patients in each age and sex group on initial evaluation that was reassessed with a PSE 22 to 27 months after the initial evaluation was also calculated. Again, for all centres combined and for individual centres, there was no age and sex group in which a significantly higher percentage of patients was lost to follow-up than in the other groups. The same analysis was done for marital status on initial evaluation and again there were no significant differences between the initial evaluation and follow-up evaluation distributions.

Thus, the IPSS experience suggests that in carrying out long-term follow-up studies of patients with functional psychoses in different cultures, it is no easier to follow-up males than females, patients in one age group than in another (within the 15—44 age span) or patients in one diagnostic group than in another diagnostic group.

Although there were no differences in the percentages of patients in the various age, sex and marital status groups that were followed up, since there were some differences on these variables in some centres on initial evaluation, there are also some differences on follow-up.

Tables 5.4 and 5.5 present, for each centre and for all centres combined, the distribution of the basic follow-up material at initial evaluation by age, sex, marital status and socioeconomic status for schizophrenic patients and for all patients. It can be seen than in Aarhus and Agra there were considerably more males than females in the followed-up schizophrenic group, while in Moscow and Washington there were considerably more females than males. There was a high proportion of single schizophrenics included in the follow-up material in Aarhus, Cali, London and Taipei, and a high proportion of married schizophrenics included in Agra. Taipei, Agra and Cali had a relatively large number of schizophrenic patients under the age of 30 at initial evaluation in the basic follow-up material, while Aarhus and Washington had a relatively small number of such patients in this material. In Ibadan a high percentage of the basic follow-up material was in the lowest socioeconomic status group (as rated by social workers) at initial evaluation.

TABLE 5.4. DISTRIBUTION OF BASIC FOLLOW-UP STUDY POPULATION BY SOCIODEMOGRAPHIC CHARACTERISTICS OF INITIAL EVALUATION. SCHIZOPHRENIC PATIENTS.

		Aarhus	Agra	Cali	Ibadan	London	Moscow	Taipei	Washington	Prague	All Centres
Sex	Male	32	58	42	31	34	27	38	18	23	303
	Female	17	34	36	32	24	42	42	47	32	306
Age	15-19	5	18	16	7	10	7	28	6	6	103
	20-24	11	19	27	12	15	13	24	13	11	145
	25-29	9	22	16	24	11	13	12	14	13	134
	30-34	11	12	10	11	4	13	11	9	7	88
	35-39	6	15	8	8	8	15	3	8	7	78
	40-44	7	6	1	1	10	7	2	15	11	60
	45-49	-	-	-	-	-	1	-	-	-	1
Marital Status	Single	37	16	53	28	45	33	58	25	32	327
	Married	7	73	21	33	10	31	22	31	16	244
	Cohabiting	-	-	3	-	1	-	-	2	-	4
	Widowed	-	1	-	-	-	-	-	-	-	3
	Divorced	5	-	-	2	-	4	-	4	6	21
	Separated	-	2	1	-	2	1	-	3	1	10
Socio-economic status	1 (Highest)	-	2	1	-	1	-	2	-	2	8
	2	3	13	11	6	8	11	2	4	6	64
	3	19	29	25	12	14	37	28	37	33	234
	4	27	34	29	16	29	11	19	14	14	193
	5 (Lowest)	-	12	11	26	5	-	3	3	-	60
	Not Known	-	2	1	3	1	10	26	7	-	50

TABLE 5.5. DISTRIBUTION OF BASIC FOLLOW-UP STUDY POPULATION BY SOCIODEMOGRAPHIC CHARACTERISTICS OF INITIAL EVALUATION. ALL PATIENTS.

		Aarhus	Agra	Cali	Ibadan	London	Moscow	Taipei	Washington	Prague	All centres
Sex	Male	57	80	45	33	41	39	63	24	34	416
	Female	45	46	56	39	32	81	66	63	62	490
Age	15-19	9	23	18	8	14	7	38	7	7	131
	20-24	17	20	31	14	19	21	34	17	19	192
	25-29	17	27	20	26	13	19	21	16	22	181
	30-34	18	24	17	15	6	30	17	17	11	155
	35-39	20	22	11	8	9	19	10	12	16	127
	40-44	21	10	4	1	12	23	9	18	21	119
	45-49	-	-	-	-	-	-	-	-	-	1
Marital Status	Single	55	20	63	31	51	40	81	26	40	407
	Married	36	102	32	39	18	63	48	47	46	431
	Cohabiting	-	-	5	-	1	-	-	-	-	6
	Widowed	-	2	-	-	-	3	-	3	-	8
	Divorced	7	-	-	2	-	13	-	5	9	36
	Separated	4	2	1	-	3	1	-	6	1	18
Socio-economic status	1 (Highest)	-	2	1	1	2	-	2	-	3	11
	2	15	15	12	6	11	24	8	5	16	112
	3	35	49	36	16	19	66	50	47	60	378
	4	49	45	39	17	35	16	33	18	17	269
	5 (Lowest)	1	13	11	27	5	-	4	3	-	64
	Not known	2	2	2	5	1	14	32	14	-	72

5.2 CHARACTERISTICS OF THE FIELD RESEARCH CENTRES DURING THE FOLLOW-UP PERIOD

This section contains a description of those characteristics of the field research centres and the catchment areas they serve that are relevant to an understanding of the ability of the centre to locate patients (for example, presence or absence of patient registers and residence registers of the population, mobility of the population) and those factors that may have influenced the outcome of the patient (for example, local employment conditions, availability of hospital beds, availability of different kinds of treatment).

5.2.1 Aarhus

There were no difficulties in locating a person in the Aarhus catchment area. There is a National Register to which everybody reports a change of address. The National Register is administered in cooperation with other instititutions such as health insurance, social welfare institutions, etc. and is extremely efficient, probably because it is accepted by the population and has been in use since 1924.

For the follow-up study it was also possible to obtain information from the Central Psychiatric Register (which covers all psychiatric hospitals and departments in Denmark) about contacts with psychiatric services.

Most of the patients stayed within the catchment area, but even though some moved to other areas of Denmark, the distances were not as great as to make an interview inpossible.

The majority of the patients came to the hospital after receiving letter(s) of invitation, but about one-third did not answer and were visited in their homes. Only a very few refused interviews.

In Denmark health insurance is obligatory and hospital treatment — inpatient as well as outpatient — is free. Psychotropic drugs are rather inexpensive for patients as the health insurance pays about three-quarters of the actual price.

A large proportion of the patients who have been admitted are followed as outpatients after discharge. For patients who for some reason do not go back to their previous home after discharge, halfway hostels are available. If such an arrangement is not suitable a psychiatric social worker helps the patient to find accommodation if such help is required.

During inpatient stay many of the patients attend the hospital's sheltered workshops and some continue to work there after discharge. For patients who are not able to support themselves to the degree they did before admission a monthly allowance is paid either for a period during which the patient is trained for another job or as a permanent disability pension. The unemployment rate was low during the follow-up period.

5.2.2 Agra

Resident registers of the population are not maintained in Agra. Although it is possible to get information from other records such as municipal registers, voters' lists, or tax records, these do not cover all persons and it is often difficult to get these records or to go through them. Therefore it may be difficult to locate the patient, unless he happens to come to the hospital for treatment, or a follow-up contact is established. Information about a patient's psychiatric status can only be obtained by personal contact.

When a patient moves away from his given address, he can be traced from information obtained from other family members or neighbours. Whereabouts and addresses could be checked through the police, the local postmaster or the village headman.

Out of 140 patients in the study, 22 shifted their residence — five moved from rural to rural areas (three within the same town and one from one town to another); three moved from rural to urban areas and three cases were untraceable. Seven patients migrated to distant places outside of the catchment area. There was no movement from urban to rural area.

The majority of the patients lived in rural areas with inadequate roads and means of transport. Travel to these areas had to be done by bicycle, bullock cart, mule or on foot. Sometimes, it took as much as three days to reach the patient and complete the schedules. The catchment area of the field research centre covers 52 076 sq. km. Houses in many localities are not numbered; locating them is difficult.

Cooperative and hospitable attitudes of the patients and their family members — common features of Indian society — facilitated good contact. Initial difficulties in follow-up contact were easily overcome and once contact was made, there was usually no occasion to expect refusal unless the patient was very disturbed. In the second-year follow-up there was only a single instance of refusal due to the patient's excited state.

A registered letter is often refused or the addressee may hide himself, fearing that it might be a court notice. Such a letter may be refused for other reasons, such as because of the stigma of a mental hospital contact, the wish to avoid identification as a mental patient, disinclination to divulge information to a marital partner or his/her relations, and hiding mental illness from employers. Time and money necessary for a visit to the hospital are also frequently lacking, even if the letter is received.

The communities, particularly in villages, are closely knit and it is relatively easy to locate patients since nearly all the members of the locality have knowledge about who is the one who had mental illness and was treated at the Mental Hospital, Agra.

Extremes of temperature in summer and flooding of the countryside during the monsoons made visits difficult in these seasons. Other impediments are festive and marriage seasons and harvesting time when the patient or his relatives are too busy to be contacted.

The Chief Collaborating Investigator was also the Medical Superintendent of the Hospital and could adjust the organizational procedures of the Hospital so as to facilitate IPSS activities.

All the admissions to the hospital were made by the Superintendent of the Hospital who could thus identify patients who happen to be in the IPSS and whose follow-up is due. Other staff members of the Agra Field Research Centre were also involved in the activities of the Out-Patient Department. Psychiatric and social histories, for example, of all the new cases were written up by them. All patients included in the study were thus seen by IPSS staff whenever they come to hospital for inpatient or outpatient treatment. The hospital medical staff, particularly those involved in postgraduate training, had spent their afternoons in the research wing of the hospital where the field research centre is located and cooperated in IPSS activities.

There are no psychiatric facilities available to the patients in the catchment area other than the Agra Mental Hospital (718 beds), and the departments of neuropsychiatry at the S.N. Medical College, Agra and Lala Lajpat Rai Hospital, Manpur. The last two had few practising neuropsychiatrists during the years of this study. The Mental Hospital, Agra, on the other hand, is a well-known treatment centre in the area and most patients seeking psychiatric treatment generally make use of this facility. The popularity of the Hospital coupled with non-availability of other psychiatric facilities in the area have been a considerable help in carrying out the follow-up study.

The belief that the patient is possessed by some 'evil' or 'good' spirit is a widespread one. The acceptance of the faith-healers, wisemen of the village and practitioners of magic and religious cures, is found in almost every locality, which was often the reason for which patients did not come to the hospital for follow-up or for treatment.

Nearly all patients were found to be engaged in some form of work. Only a few, particularly chronic schizophrenics and neurotic depressives, having settled at a lower level of effeciency, were doing nothing or very little. Family acceptance of the sick person was a notable feature but the community at times had ambivalent attitudes towards the mentally ill. Misconceptions and superstitious beliefs about mental illnesses may partly be responsible for this phenomenon.

Work in the rural setting is mostly collective, agricultural, and often does not require particular skills. Many occupations are passed from father to son. Thus, competitive situations seldom exist. The occupational pursuits do not usually require fine skill and adaptability and often do not demand much effort or strain. The level of efficiency therefore is not a major consideration. Employment conditions in the country usually do not have any untoward effects on most patients. Many females do not go out to work.

Generally, patients remain busy in working seasons and cannot attend the field research centre during such months. Females have domestic responsibilities like cooking, cleaning, caring for children, etc. which make heavy demands on their time.

Although the joint family system is weakening, the background structure still persists providing shelter, supervision and help to the sick person. This plays an important role in the course and outcome of illness.

Ignorance within a large part of the population about the nature of mental illnesses also plays a significant role in course and outcome. Misconceptions about mental illness may at times deprive the mentally ill from receiving treatment, cause late referral to a psychiatric facility and premature discontinuation of treatment. Poverty is also sometimes responsible for lack of proper treatment. Prescriptions for maintenance treatment, check-ups are usually not followed.

5.2.3 Cali

In Cali there are no case registers or other types of retrieval systems for information about mental patients. Most of the patients are tenants rather than house-owners and the addresses supplied at initial examination changed in many cases. Forwarding addresses are usually not provided. Although in each case, after discharge from the episode of inclusion, appointments were given for the outpatient clinics, only a small proportion of patients kept these appointments. Many patients were either too poor to pay transportation fares to come to the hospital or unable to leave their homes (especially housewives). Home visits had to be arranged, or special transportation provided.

The nomenclature of the streets of Cali was changed in the intervening period and in some cases it was not possible to locate the dwellings. No central registration system for addresses exists in the Colombian cities. Very few patients could be located by telephone either at work or at home, and they very seldom responded to letters, did not keep appointments or changed them; the great majority of contacts, therefore, had to be made through home visits. Quite often, the patients had to be traced through neighbours, relatives or employers.

Case-histories of all patients included in the IPSS had a notice alerting hospital personnel about the fact that these patients were needed for a special study and requesting that a member of the research team be contacted immediately, should the patients in question attend the hospital. Other methods for case finding included systematic scanning of hospitals, clinics, health centres, community centres, jails and neighbourhood stores, as well as radio messages sent through local stations.

The average stay of patients in the hospital is about 28 days. During this period, all medications are provided by the hospital. On discharge, in most cases, patients are requested to continue on the prescribed medication but quite often they are not able to afford to buy these medicines.

In general, the family reinforces the fear patients have about psychiatric drugs. Somnolence and akinetic symptoms are almost seen as toxic or stultifying effects of the treatment. As a result, in many cases, medication is discontinued by the patient. Appointments to the outpatient department are not kept in the majority of cases and those who come only do so for two or three times. The widespread use of cannabis, especially in young male patients, could be regarded as a possible complicating factor, in need of further evaluation.

With regard to readjustment to family life and work after discharge, an important factor may be the apparently high level of tolerance of relatives and friends for symptoms of mental disorder. This seems to apply especially to disorders of thought rather than to behavioural disorders (particularly agitation). Degree of family cohesion, in terms of persistence or disintegration of the family unit, may also be a significant factor for influencing outcome.

Changes in demographic conditions such as marital status, and changes in the socioeconomic situation may also play an important role. The proportion of unemployment in Cali (about 17 per cent) possibly places an extra amount of stress on expatients who have to compete for jobs with people who are and have been healthy.

5.2.4 Ibadan

There is no resident register for the population of the catchment area around Ibadan. The population is highly mobile. The most important reason for this mobility are the strong family ties between component family units. If a young man seeks employment outside his usual place of domicile, he goes to a place where a relative is already established; there he is guaranteed food and shelter until he finds employment. If he wishes, as is often the case, to attend one of the many yearly festivals away from home, he travels out to a relative. It is not uncommon for a visit planned to be short to become protracted; members of the family may overstay their welcome in such circumstances. This has resulted in patients being as far as 250 miles from the field research centre by the time of the follow-up which created problems of distance and of tracing the patient. In the catchment area, the houses are either not numbered or the system of numbering makes the tracing a very irksome duty. Finally, patients spend long periods of the year in small hamlets which are essentially farming communities, coming to the towns and cities at festival periods. Most of these farming communities are only accessible by bush paths.

There is no psychiatric case register in Ibadan and hospital treatment can be very expensive. This is one of the reasons why patients often end up in a residential facility of a traditional healer. A number of follow-up interviews were in fact done by the centre staff with patients who had been found in such facilities.

The symptomatic picture between the initial evaluation and the second-year follow-up could also be affected by factors related to general underdevelopment. Poor level of public hygiene, illiteracy, ignorance, malnutrition, etc., all produce not only obvious physical ill-health but may also reinforce psychological symptoms.

Another important factor that could affect outcome is distance of patients from the treatment centres. The long distances patients have to travel for follow-up often prevent them from attending. Failure to come for follow-up may have contributed to the relapses, and may also have been the result of the belief that cures are permanent, once they have occurred. On the other hand, the involvement of relatives in the treatment programme of patients may contribute to better outcome, and it makes possible the identification of relationship problems which can be solved.

The Ibadan FRC included several facilities – the Aro Neuropsychiatric Hospital, Abeokuta, where the majority of the patients were treated; the Department of Psychiatry of the University College Hospital, Ibadan; and the Aro Psychiatric Village. Owing to considerable pressure on psychiatric beds, patients are sometimes discharged sooner than is ideal, particularly from the University Department.

Readmission of relapsed cases cannot always be guaranteed and relatives have to take their sick members back over long distances sometimes with no money to buy expensive psychiatric drugs. That relapse comes so soon after leaving hospital often confirms the general belief in many sections of the population that mental illness is incurable or is better taken care of by traditional healers. There are also differences in outcome and relapse rates of patients treated in the University Department hospitals and those treated under the village system; the latter have fewer relapses and better outcome.

In the area of relationship with others, the situation in which all members of the family or many members of the village contribute towards the heavy expenses of treatment (transport, drug, fees, etc.) can be disturbing to the patient. Many rightly feel that they are a burden to their family or their community. A relapse is not always taken kindly by the relatives.

Patients who come from the rural areas find it relatively easy to get back to their farming or petty trading. Those in the cities are worse off, since the rate of unemployment is so high that few patients can find jobs, gain subsistence or meet their family obligations.

5.2.5 London

The psychiatric facilities in the London centre provide a comprehensive service for the local population of Camberwell in the South-East of London, and also accept patients from other parts of London and from the rest of the United Kingdom. The reputation of the Maudsley Hospital also attracts patients from other countries.

Of the London IPSS sample 31.5 per cent were local patients from Camberwell. This is a completely urban area, mostly inhabited by working-class people, but with a middle-class area in the south. People born outside the United Kingdom constitute about 10 per cent of the population. A psychiatric register was established in 1965 to cover the Camberwell population. This provided help in tracing the 31.5 per cent of the IPSS sample who came from Camberwell. The remainder of the sample are considerably more difficult to trace, particularly those who came from outside London and from abroad.

At the time of the second-year follow-up there were only two members of staff of the field research centre. Both were psychiatrists committed to full-time clinical and teaching duties in addition to research. This made it impossible to undertake a comprehensive follow-up and certain limits were imposed. The PSE was administered only to those patients who were readily available by reason either of current inpatient status or of regular attendance at the outpatient department. In addition a few patients were seen in their homes because they happened to be included in another ongoing follow-up study. Detailed information was available in the case-notes of patients who continued to attend the outpatient department after their episode of inclusion or who were readmitted to the Maudsley Hospital during the second-year follow-up period. These case-notes are usually well kept and detailed, as the doctors responsible for them are undergoing intensive postgraduate training. Patients who lost contact with the hospital soon after their episode of inclusion had no further information recorded in their case-notes and consequently were lost to the second-year follow-up.

A sufficient number of hospital beds is reserved for Camberwell patients, and there is never any difficulty in arranging such admission at short notice. Patients from other areas may not be admitted to the Maudsley Hospital if there is a shortage of beds but could be referred to their catchment area hospital. Length of stay in hospital is not entirely determined by the patient's clinical state. A study of patients remaining in hospital more than six months showed that in many cases patients were free of symptoms but could not be discharged because of lack of suitable accommodation. There is a national shortage of housing which is particularly bad in London. Furthermore, very little hostel accommodation for psychiatric patients is provided in Camberwell. Throughout the second year of follow-up the national level of unemployment remained at its highest for many years.

5.2.6 Moscow

The close links of the Institute of Psychiatry of the Academy of Medical Sciences of the USSR (in which the field research centre is located), with a number of medical institutions in Moscow, the well-functioning dispensary services, the easily accessible and well-organized case registers of hospitals and dispensaries, and the city information services all facilitated the work of the centre in carrying out the follow-up.

During the follow-up period there was an increased migration of patients into the catchment area. This was the result of the building of new housing units in Moscow and of administration changes in the delineation of city wards. However, this migration was a intracity migration and it did not seriously affect the centre's ability to locate patients for follow-up, since it was possible to keep track of the migration of patients through the network of psychiatric dispensaries and the information services of the city population register.

Many patients were reluctant to come for the follow-up re-examination. It was often necessary to make repeated telephone calls, send letters and to have a special research assistant make contact with the patients before they would come for follow-up. Some of the patients had to be seen in their homes. At times this made it necessary for a psychiatrist to make two or three trips over a considerable distance.

A factor which would be expected to influence favourably the course and outcome of IPSS patients in Moscow is the availability and accessibility of follow-up post-hospital care and of facilities for occupational retraining and placement. Such work is coordinated by the psychiatric dispensaries which operate on a catchment area basis and have the capacity to provide comprehensive outpatient services immediately after discharge of patients from hospitals. In addition, a proportion of patients with functional psychoses can be managed almost entirely on an outpatient basis even in periods of exacerbation of symptoms, due to the well-organized system of domiciliary visits by psychiatrists, psychiatric nurses and social workers.

5.2.7 Taipei

It was possible to locate all IPSS cases in Taipei at the time of second-year follow-up, and to obtain sufficient data for inclusion in the second-year follow-up material for over 90 per cent of those patients. This was made possible through the assistance of the excellent postal service, the cooperation of the patients' relatives, friends, and neighbours, the well-established census registration system, and very convenient transportation in the area served by the centre. The mobility of IPSS cases was higher than expected; 28 (20.4 per cent) of the 137 patients initially evaluated had moved with their families away from their registered address before the time of the second-year follow-up, and 33 more cases (24.1 per cent) had left their original family to live in another place because of marriage, work, study, military service, visits to relatives abroad, or for reasons of health since the initial examination. About two-fifths of the cases responded to the first letter sent by the field research centre and came to it to give PH and SD data whether they had changed their address or not. Eventually the PH and SD data for 74 cases was obtained at our field research centre office, and for 63 cases at their home or other hospitals.

As a central psychiatric case register has not been set up, it was necessary to contact psychiatric facilities to obtain information on the treatment course of some patients during the follow-up period. However, it was not possible to obtain as complete information from other psychiatric facilities as from the four psychiatric facilities involved in the IPSS.

A factor with likely influence on outcome of mental illness was the degree of the patients' participation in drug treatment, since only a limited number of patients were treated with a psychotherapeutic approach in the psychiatric facilities. Medical insurance for government employees covers psychiatric illness but labourers' insurance does not. Although some social welfare services helped poor patients receive psychiatric treatment free of charge most of the mentally ill have to pay treatment fees by themselves. The short duration of hospitalization and the irregularity of outpatient visits, which were partly the result of the difficulty of the patients' families in paying expensive treatment fees, may have contributed to lack of improvement at the time of the second-year follow-up.

As no prescription is needed to obtain drugs other than narcotics in Taipei some patients went to local drug stores to get drugs for self-medication when their mental illness took a chronic course. A few patients went to see herbalists or religious healers but this seemed to prolong their course of treatment.

The unemployment problem, serious enough even for healthy people, and the stigma attached to mental illness in the society, seemed to affect the outcome of psychiatric disorders to some extent.

5.2.8 Washington

Prince Georges County, the catchment area of the Washington field research centre, is a heterogeneous population area including urban, suburban and rural sections. The population in the urban and suburban sections tends to be one of the geographically most mobile in the United States. Several patients from the cohort had moved, over distances of up to 4800 km by the time the two-year follow-up interviews were carried out. This disadvantage was counteracted by the surprising ease with which intensive and extensive telephone interviews were possible. Interviews were held with patients who had moved to Florida, Louisiana and California. In none of these did the investigators have any difficulty asking even very personal questions. In fact, the subjects were interested to hear how things had gone with the study and were most helpful and frank in participating.

A somewhat more difficult problem related to the nature of the catchment area arose from the small matrix of social relationships that many people had. Once such patients moved from their original neighbourhood, there was sometimes no way to trace them. If they moved from one small town to another, frequently none of the friends or neighbours in the old town knew enough about the new area to suggest where such patients had moved. Thus, although the names of relatives and informants were noted at the initial evaluation, if these people could not be located, then it was almost impossible to trace the patients who had also moved.

Throughout the IPSS, the Washington collaborating investigators were constantly impressed by the fact that health care provision in the Washington area is less regionalized than in the other centres of the IPSS. Patients from the Washington area might be treated anywhere within a 72 km radius or more. This radius included the large cities of Baltimore and Washington and different hospital systems including federal mental health hospitals, state hospitals, private hospitals, and other facilities, all totally independent of one another. Besides this, a patient could move 24 km or so from Maryland to Virginia and then have access to an entirely new set of psychiatric treatment facilities. This meant that contact with many hospitals had to be maintained, and sometimes it was particularly difficult to trace patients who had slipped into another hospital system. Follow-up outpatient treatment facilities, when available, were even more decentralized than inpatient facilities. On the other hand, the existence of the Maryland Register had made it possible for the investigators to analyse in advance the percentage of patients from Prince Georges County hospitalized and otherwise treated at each facility. This helped them to determine the facilities to which they needed to remain particularly closely linked.

Unemployment during the follow-up period was at a moderate level (about 5 per cent), especially in semiskilled and unskilled positions. There was, however, a special problem for professional workers, such as teachers and engineers, for whom jobs had become increasingly difficult to find. For these reasons, patients who usually held or were content to have jobs in non-professional categories had considerably greater opportunity for re-employment following hospitalization than those few subjects in more professionally oriented positions.

Opportunities for social relationships following discharge varied greatly. Those patients who returned to family settings or who had had close friends prior to admission and returned to their previous living situation had considerable opportunity to renew these relationships. Generally speaking, not much prejudice against discharged mental patients was reported in terms of social relations, and friends were most frequently described as understanding and sympathetic. On the other hand, those patients who had lived alone or became estranged from their families prior to or during hospitalization found themselves returning to living conditions in this area of high geographical mobility in which social isolation had to be actively avoided. Because of the large geographical area involved and the loosely organized regional responsibility of social agencies, social rehabilitation programmes, although available, had great difficulty following patients who did not spontaneously continue in programmes offered.

Similar conditions influenced follow-up treatment. In this area where a large population mass and geographical mobility were combined with heterogeneous independent facilities for providing care, patients were easily lost to further care unless they followed up with programmes on their own. Nevertheless, outpatient treatment facilities were available for those desiring to use them.

Taken together, these conditions favoured those patients who already had personal and social resources to resume their active social life and continue treatment and made it somewhat more difficult for those patients who tended to be withdrawn, or not to seek or follow-up on care offered, or who had minimal social resources either from families or friends. In this sense, then, the conditions in the area favoured those patients who already had better prognostic characteristics.

5.2.9 Prague

Information from the resident register is available at official request, but it was used to trace the IPSS patients in only very few cases. The mobility of the population is not very high because of the administrative limitations of immigration to Prague, the shortage of flats and the availability of many working opportunities in Prague. The catchment area of IPSS sample was identical with the administrative boundaries of the city of Prague. There were, therefore, no serious difficulties in locating patients.

The unified state-organized structure of the health outpatient and inpatient services greatly facilitated the carrying out of the follow-up phase of the study, as did also the status of the Research Institute as a Ministry of Health institution.

The relatively high proportion of patients still in treatment or in contact with the services at second-year follow-up was probably due to the availability of psychiatric care which is free, to the relative anonymity of living in a large city and to the special interest shown by the IPSS staff in the aftercare of patients included in the study.

Long-term lithium prophylactic treatment was given to some of the IPSS patients for research and treatment purposes. This might have contributed to the prolongation of their outpatient treatment status as well as to a longer personal contact of the patient and his relatives with the research psychiatrists in some cases. The number of inpatient treatment episodes may have been influenced by (a) ready availability of the beds of the Psychiatric Research Institute for the hospitalization of IPSS patients, and (b) a higher status of hospitalization in the Institute in comparison with hospitalization in a mental hospital, lowering the resistance of patients and relatives to early hospitalization at the very beginning of a new attack of illness.

A long duration of inpatient treatment of some patients in the IPSS series might have been due to the lack of opportunity for partial hospitalization (day and night treatment) in Prague. At the same time, during the two-year follow-up many IPSS patients were treated in the Institute's wards as day patients though they were formally assigned to inpatient status for administrative reasons.

CHAPTER 6

Course and Outcome of Patients with an Initial Evaluation Diagnosis of Schizophrenia

Volume 1 of the IPSS report (WHO, 1973) presents data indicating that groups of schizophrenic patients with similar psychopathological characteristics could be identified in each of the nine centres of the study, and that the characteristics of these groups of patients were significantly different from those of groups of patients with other major functional psychoses. These findings gave important support for the supposition that schizophrenia can be reliably identified on the basis of a characteristic clinical picture at the time of an individual episode, and that patients with this clinical picture can be found in all of the cultures involved in this study. If it can be shown that the patients identified as schizophrenic in the nine centres on the basis of the clinical picture on initial evaluation are similar to one another with regard to course and outcome, and are different in this respect from patients with other functional psychoses, further evidence will have been provided that the diagnosis of schizophrenia is useful and meaningful.

There are a number of hypotheses about the course of schizophrenia which are inherent in many past and current concepts of the nature of schizophrenia and which can be considered in the light of findings of follow-up studies. These hypotheses include the following:

1. That a high percentage of patients diagnosed as schizophrenic will be severely socially disabled in their subsequent lives, and that the percentage of schizophrenic patients with such disability will be higher than in patients with other functional psychoses.

2. A high percentage of patients diagnosed as schizophrenic will have psychotic symptoms* for a considerable part of their subsequent lives and schizophrenic patients will usually be psychotic for a larger percentage of their lives than patients with other functional psychoses.

3. The majority of schizophrenic patients will not have full remissions after acute psychotic episodes, and a smaller percentage of schizophrenic patients. will have such remissions than patients with other functional psychoses.

---

*Throughout this volume the term psychotic symptoms refers to those symptoms indicated in Appendix 3, and patients are considered to be psychotic if they meet the criteria outlined in that Appendix and in section 6.2.3 of this chapter.

4. The percentage of schizophrenic patients who show symptomatic improvement over time will be lower than the percentage of patients with other functional psychoses showing such improvement.

5. When patients initially diagnosed as schizophrenic have episodes of illness subsequently during their lives these will be similar to one another in the type of symptoms that they demonstrate and these symptoms will be different from the symptoms that patients initially given a diagnosis of one of the other functional psychoses will have later in their lives.

6. There are a variety of courses and outcomes of schizophrenia. These tend to be associated with particular symptomatic, past history and sociodemographic characteristics of patients, and may also vary according to the subtypes of schizophrenia.

7. The course of schizophrenia may vary from one sociocultural setting to another.

Some of these hypotheses have recently been questioned both from within and outside of the psychiatric field. The statement of these hypotheses does not indicate that the investigators necessarily ascribe to them, but rather that they represent important areas for empirical investigation.

The review of previous follow-up studies presented in Chapter 2 indicates that such studies shed a limited amount of light on these hypotheses. In the first place, there are no previous large-scale crosscultural follow-up studies of schizophrenia and other functional psychoses. Secondly, those intracultural follow-up studies which have been done have been carried out primarily in Western cultures. Thirdly, those intracultural follow-up studies which have been done in Western cultures for the most part have not been entirely prospective or have not utilized standardized assessments and offer little information about the reliability of the original diagnosis. Therefore, conclusions that can be drawn from previous follow-up studies are limited, and those results which do exist must be interpreted with caution.

A two-year follow-up period is not long enough to fully examine many of these hypotheses. Therefore longer-term follow-up of IPSS patients has been carried out, and analysis of five-year follow-up data is now under way. However, an initial examination of these hypthoses can be made on the basis of the second-year follow-up data.

Although the term 'outcome' is usually used to indicate the situation existing at the end of an illness and the term 'course' to indicate what has happened between two points in time, it is difficult to make a useful distinction between these two terms in a follow-up study of schizophrenia when the period of the follow-up has been only two years. Therefore, in this volume the terms course and outcome are used together to refer to all parameters giving an idea of what has happened to the patients during the two-year period after their initial evaluations.

In order to consider the hypotheses listed above, IPSS data was used to carry out the following analyses:

1. A comparison of the symptomatic picture of patients at the time of second-year follow-up within and between diagnostic groups (defined by initial evaluation diagnosis) and within and between centres.

2. A comparison of the symptomatic picture of patients at the time of initial evaluation with the symptomatic picture of the same patients at the time of the second-year follow-up.

3. An assessment of the type of course of patients during the interval between the time of initial evaluation and the second-year follow-up. This assessment includes an estimate of the length of the episode of inclusion, the proportion of the follow-up period spent in a psychotic episode, the number and type of subsequent psychotic episodes, the pattern of episodes and the level of social functioning during the follow-up period.

4. The identification of various symptomatic, sociodemographic and past history characteristics of patients at the time of initial evaluation which seem to predict the type of outcome.

In this chapter and the next the course and outcome of patients in the same diagnostic group will be discussed. This chapter will be concerned with the course and outcome of patients with an initial evaluation diagnosis of schizophrenia. Chapter 7 will discuss the course and outcome of patients in the following diagnostic groups on initial evaluation: psychotic depression (ICD categories 296.0, 296.2, 298.0); mania (296.1) and other psychoses. Chapter 8 will deal with comparisons of course and outcome of patients in different diagnostic groups. Chapter 9 will consider findings in terms of the concordant group and the subgroups of schizophrenia. The relationship between symptomatic, sociodemographic, and past history characteristics of patients on initial evaluation and course and outcome will be explored in Chapter 10, while Chapter 11 will, among other things, discuss the results of the analyses presented in Chapters 6 to 10 in light of the hypotheses listed above.

6.1 STATISTICAL APPROACHES

Before considering the two-year course and outcome of the initial evaluation schizophrenic patients, the statistical approaches used in this chapter and the following three chapters will be described.

In these chapters, as in Volume 1 of the report of the IPSS (WHO, 1973), the symptom profiles of groups of patients are compared by assessing the distances between profiles and by comparing the shapes of profiles. Differences between two profiles in terms of distance indicate that the patient groups differ with regard to degree of symptomatology, while differences in the shapes of two profiles indicate that the patient groups differ with regard to type of symptoms.

The statistical techniques used in this context are classical models of the analysis of variance modified by Greenhouse and Geisser (1959). An analysis of variance (ANOVA) is a parametric method which, as used here, compares every patient to every other patient, uses absolute scores to determine parallelism of symptom profiles, and takes into consideration interaction among different symptoms. Since for most of the analyses in the following chapters the groups to be compared are composed of a large number of patients, and as by nature data do not meet all of the requirements for parametric analyses, a high level of significance, $p = 0.001$, has been chosen. Throughout these chapters, whenever the differences between profiles are said to be statistically significant, p is equal to or less than 0.001.

The ANOVA analysis gives an indication of whether two symptom profiles are significantly different from one another. To give an indication of the degree of similarity between the shapes of profiles, a rank order correlation coefficient was calculated, as described by Kendall, for each pair of symptom profiles as a measure of the concordance of rank order of average scores.

The course and outcome variables relating to what happened during the interval between initial evaluation and second-year follow-up (length of episode of inclusion, percentage of time psychotic, pattern of course, type of subsequent episode, degree of social impairment, and overall outcome) were categorized even when they could have been measured on a continuous scale. Comparison of two or several groups of patients on these variables thus means comparison of the frequency distributions of the groups with respect to the variable under consideration. For some of the course and outcome variables the distributions cannot be expected to be symmetrical, because of the nature of the variables. Therefore comparisons are carried out in terms of distributions rather than only in terms of central tendencies or other single parameters.

The large number of possible comparisons that can be made with the data for any one of these course and outcome variables creates some difficulties for statistical analyses. For each variable, patients are placed into five or more outcome groups. Since there are nine centres, and since for some comparisons the outcome groups are considered not only separately but also in combination, there is a very large number of possible comparisons. It did not seem reasonable to do statistical analyses for all possible comparisons within any individual variable, since this would have involved more than 250 analyses for some variables. With such a large number of comparisons many results would have been expected to reach the usual levels of significance just by chance. Therefore, for most of the analyses considering these course and outcome variables, two major questions were assessed:

1. Do the distributions of the patient groups in the different centres (or different diagnostic groups) differ significantly from one another? If the overall differences are statistically significant, then those differences within particular parts of the distributions which seem most striking are described.

2. Are the distributions for the group of centres in developing countries and the group of centres in developed countries alike within each group and different between the two groups?

On the basis of this stategy for the analyses, the chi-square technique was selected as an appropriate statistical method of examining the questions defined. However, the questions described above relate to exactly the same data. Thus the chi-square test statistics are correlated and the usual p-values are biased. For this reason, Bonferroni's chi-square technique has been applied so that the number of tests based on the same data is taken into account. Throughout this chapter and the three following chapters, when differences on course and outcome comparisons are said to be significant, p is equal to or less than 0.01.

It is evident that not all of the interesting patterns of data under study can be foreseen, so that it was not possible to define all possible interesting hypotheses in advance, before the data were seen. It is well known that questions posed on the basis of a certain set of data should not be answered by means of statistical significance tests carried out for the same data. However, interesting findings which can be seen when the data are examined should be described so that pertinent hypotheses can be tested in future studies and surveys.

6.2 SYMPTOMATIC PICTURE AT THE TIME OF SECOND-YEAR FOLLOW UP

One aspect of the course and outcome of patients given a particular psychiatric diagnosis is the nature of the symptoms which characterize these same patients at some specified point after they have been given the diagnosis. In the case of the IPSS it was possible to determine for patients given a particular diagnosis the nature of the symptoms which characterized them two years later. This section will consider this topic for schizophrenic patients, both within and across centres. It focuses particularly on the question of whether patients given the diagnosis of schizophrenia on initial evaluation have symptomatic clinical pictures at the time of the second-year follow-up, which are similar to one another.

The symptomatology of patient groups has been considered primarily in terms of the frequency of units of analysis (UAs) and average percentage scores on groups of units of analysis (GUAs). A full description of these terms is given in Volume 1 of the report of the IPSS, and a summary in Chapter 4 of this volume.

A full list of the GUAs and the UAs included within them is presented in Appendix 3.

6.2.1 Symptom profiles

6.2.1.1 Groups of units of analysis (GUAs)

Table 6.1 presents, for groups of patients diagnosed as schizophrenic on initial evaluation, the average percentage scores on groups of units of analysis at the time of second-year follow-up by centre and for all centres combined.

The most striking feature of Table 6.1 is that in general the scores on the GUAs across the centres were quite low. The only GUAs on which scores were relatively high across most centres were lack of insight, flatness of affect, cooperation difficulties, circumstances related, and co-operation difficulties, patient related. Scores were relatively high on predelusional signs in four centres (London, Moscow, Taipei and Washington), on affect-laden thoughts in three centres (London, Moscow and Washington), on incongruity of affect in three centres (Aarhus, Moscow and Taipei), on auditory hallucinations in three centres (Aarhus, London and Taipei), and on derealization in two centres (Aarhus and London). Several symptoms had relatively high scores in only one centre: quantitative disorder of form of thinking and speech (Aarhus), neurasthenic complaints (Moscow),

TABLE 6.1.   AVERAGE PERCENTAGE SCORES ON 27 GROUPS OF UNITS OF ANALYSIS AT 2ND YEAR FOLLOW-UP. ALL SCHIZOPHRENIC PATIENTS.

Groups of Units of Analysis	Aarhus N=49	Agra N=88	Cali N=77	Ibadan N=68	London N=21	Moscow N=66	Taipei N=61	Washington N=65	Prague N=53	All centres N=543
Quantitative psychomotor disorder	6	2	-	1	3	1	3	1	-	2
Qualitative psychomotor disorder	3	1	1	-	2	5	-	-	2	1
Qualitative disorder of form of thinking	11	3	1	1	1	6	7	3	1	4
Quantitative disorder of form of thinking	5	3	1	1	2	3	3	1	3	2
Affect-laden thoughts	4	3	6	3	10	11	4	13	3	6
Predelusional signs	8	4	9	5	13	11	13	10	6	8
Experiences of control	17	3	7	4	4	5	11	8	5	7
Delusions	6	3	4	2	2	5	6	6	3	4
Neurasthenic complaints	4	4	4	2	4	10	5	4	6	5
Lack of insight	59	29	38	17	28	65	59	35	50	42
Distortion of self-perception	2	1	1	2	6	1	2	2	-	1
Derealization	12	1	2	2	11	1	4	8	1	4
Auditory hallucinations	12	6	9	9	16	4	13	5	6	8
"Characteristic" hallucinations	8	3	5	6	6	3	3	-	3	4
Other hallucinations	4	1	2	1	1	2	1	4	1	2
Pseudohallucinations	-	5	5	5	2	3	2	3	-	1
Depressed-elated	4	2	2	2	6	6	1	2	2	2
Anxiety, tension, irritability	2	1	2	2	6	6	4	7	-	4
Flatness	32	25	8	8	9	50	27	11	24	22
Incongruity	18	6	10	5	4	30	11	4	-	9
Other affective change	1	1	5	1	1	3	1	2	-	1
Indication of personality change	7	3	3	1	3	7	4	3	1	4
Disregard of social norms	8	7	5	3	2	16	4	6	4	6
Other behavioural change	8	4	3	3	1	4	4	3	2	4
Psychophysical disorders	2	3	1	3	7	5	3	1	3	3
Cooperation difficulties, circumstances-related	29	2	13	17	28	19	18	21	30	18
Cooperation difficulties, patient-related	37	12	16	8	15	34	30	15	16	20

experiences of control (Taipei), and disregard for social norms (Moscow). For all other GUAs the scores were low across all centres. In three centres, Agra, Cali and Ibadan, the scores were generally lower than in the other centres.

Thus, it can be seen from examining this table that at the time of the second-year follow-up there was not a high degree of psychopathology present among patients who were considered schizophrenic at the time of initial evaluation. The schizophrenic groups scored low on such positive* psychotic symptoms as delusions, characteristic auditory hallucinations, other hallucinations, and distortions of self-perception, although in three centres the scores were relatively high on auditory hallucinations (other than characteristic auditory hallucinations). The symptoms which were present tended to be negative† and non-specific † symptoms, such as flatness of affect, lack of insight, and difficulties in co-operating.

ANOVA analysis was carried out for centre-by-centre comparisons to determine if the shapes of the symptom profiles were significantly different from one another. The only centre in which the profiles showed significant differences from the profiles of other centres was Moscow. The second-year follow-up profile of the Moscow schizophrenic patients was significantly different from the profiles of the schizophrenics followed up in Agra, Cali, Ibadan and Washington. As noted in Volume 1 of the IPSS report the diagnosis of schizophrenia in Moscow appears to be made on the basis of criteria which lay greater emphasis on the course of illness. The differences of the follow-up profiles of the Moscow schizophrenic patients may also reflect the fact that in the Moscow patients neurotic and affective symptoms were more frequently rated as present during remissions from psychotic episodes than in other centres.

To assess the degree of similarity in the shapes of the profiles in the different centres, Kendall's τ-values were calculated for comparisons between all possible pairs of centres. The results were consistent with the findings of the ANOVA analyses, and as for most of the comparisons, there was a high degree of similarity. Three centres were each involved in three comparisons which showed a low degree of similarity: Agra, London and Moscow. The reason that for a few of the comparisons the results of the ANOVA and τ analyses were not completely consistent is probably the fact that when profile scores are low, as they are at the second-year follow-up, small differences in score may make considerable differences in rank order, while comparisons of profiles carried out with ANOVA are based on absolute scores rather than rank orders.

---

*Throughout this chapter and the rest of the volume, the terms positive psychotic symptoms, negative psychotic symptoms, and non-specific symptoms are used. The term 'positive psychotic symptoms' is used to refer to those symptoms which suggest a psychosis and which consist of the presence of a characteristic not usually present. Delusions and hallucinations are examples of such positive psychotic symptoms. The term 'negative psychotic symptoms' is used to refer to those symptoms which suggest a psychosis, but which consist of the absence of a characteristic which is usually present — flatness of affect is an example of such a negative symptom. A full list of those symptoms considered in the study to be either definitely or possibly psychotic is presented in Appendix 3. The term 'non-specific symptoms' is used to refer to symptoms which are not very discriminating between diagnostic categories, tension, anxiety and difficulties in cooperation are examples of such symptoms.
†See Appendix 3 for operational definitions.

One difficulty in interpreting these results is the fact that at the time of the second year follow-up the patients were in various phases of illness. Thus, some may have been still psychotic, some in partial remission, and others in full remission. The lumping of these patients together may obscure the degree of similarity in the psychopathology of patients at follow-up. Therefore, the above analyses were repeated, including only those patients who on follow-up were psychotic*.

There were 202 patients with an initial evaluation diagnosis of schizophrenia who were psychotic at the time of the second-year follow-up. Of the remaining 341 followed-up schizophrenics, 169 were symptomatic but not psychotic and 172 were asymptomatic at the time of the second-year follow-up.

Table 6.2 presents scores on 27 GUAs for followed-up schizophrenics who were psychotic at the time of second-year evaluation. It can be seen from this table that scores were relatively high across most centres on affect-laden thoughts, predelusional signs, experiences of control, lack of insight, auditory hallucinations, 'characteristic' auditory hallucinations, flatness of affect, incongruity of affect, and co-operation difficulties, patient- and circumstance-related. Scores were relatively high in four centres on delusions, anxiety and other behavioural changes (for example, talking or giggling to self or disorders of pitch of voice).

ANOVA analysis for centre-by-centre comparisons of these second-year follow-up symptom profiles indicates that there are no significant differences between centres with regard to these profiles. τ-Values for comparisons between all possible pairs of centres indicates that the only centre in which the profile does not show a high degree of similarity with the profiles of all other centres is Washington. There was a relatively low degree of similarity between the Washington profile and the profiles in Aarhus, Agra, Ibadan, Moscow and Prague.

Thus, a consideration of only those schizophrenic patients who were psychotic at the time of second-year follow-up indicates that these patients have similar profiles across centres.

Figure 6.1 compares the second-year follow-up profiles of initial evaluation schizophrenic patients who were psychotic at follow-up and the profiles of initial evaluation schizophrenic patients who were symptomatic but not psychotic at the time of second-year follow-up. It can be seen from this figure that the profile for the symptomatic but non-psychotic patients is flat. The groups of units of analysis on which there were more than minimal scores were lack of insight, flatness of affect, and co-operation difficulties. ANOVA and τ interaction level analyses for those intercentre comparisons possible indicate that the second-year follow-up profiles of the symptomatic but non-psychotic patients are similar across centres.

It thus appears from these analyses that of the 543 followed-up schizophrenics, 202 were psychotic at the time of second-year follow-up, and the symptomatic profiles of these patients were similar to one another from centre to centre. Most of the pathology in the profile of the entire followed-up group was accounted for by these 202 patients, 172 patients were asymptomatic at the time of second-year

*See Appendix 3 for operational definitions.

TABLE 6.2. AVERAGE PERCENTAGE SCORES ON 27 GROUPS OF UNITS OF ANALYSIS AT 2ND YEAR FOLLOW-UP. INITIAL EXAMINATION SCHIZOPHRENICS CONSIDERED PSYCHOTIC AT FOLLOW-UP.

Groups of Units of Analysis	Aarhus N=30	Agra N=28	Cali N=26	Ibadan N=16	London N=9	Moscow N=25	Taipei N=25	Washington N=25	Prague N=18	All centres N=202
Quantitative psychomotor disorder	7	7	1	6	8	5	8	5	3	5
Qualitative psychomotor disorder	4	6	2	4	6	8	2	2	6	4
Qualitative disorder of form of thinking	13	9	1	4	4	12	12	3	4	8
Qualitative disorder of form of thinking	11	11	7	6	5	2	8	3	7	6
Affect-laden thoughts	5	11	16	14	17	19	11	26	6	14
Predelusional signs	12	13	28	20	31	26	26	25	17	21
Experiences of control	28	12	22	17	18	4	27	23	17	19
Delusions	10	9	13	9	9	14	12	17	10	12
Neurasthenic complaints	5	10	7	8	9	19	10	9	9	10
Lack of insight	70	71	81	56	44	92	84	60	72	73
Distortion of self-perception	4	-	5	2	15	3	7	7	-	4
Derealization	18	4	6	9	17	4	8	22	-	10
Auditory hallucinations	20	21	28	36	39	13	34	14	19	23
"Characteristic" hallucinations	14	11	17	20	15	8	11	2	11	12
Other hallucinations	7	4	7	4	4	6	9	11	6	7
Pseudohallucinations	-	-	8	10	6	2	4	8	2	5
Depressed-elated	8	1	6	7	11	12	5	3	-	6
Anxiety, tension, irritability	4	3	12	34	13	11	8	12	-	8
Flatness	40	75	21	19	17	60	52	16	39	42
Incongruity	23	18	15	2	-	52	24	12	-	20
Other affective change	3	4	3	3	-	2	4	6	3	3
Indication of personality change	11	11	7	7	7	11	10	8	8	8
Disregard of social norms	10	23	8	3	6	32	6	16	6	14
Other behavioural change	11	13	8	14	3	15	9	7	6	10
Psychophysical disorders	3	7	3	8	12	7	4	4	3	5
Cooperation difficulties, circumstances-related	29	6	15	19	29	21	18	29	33	21
Cooperation difficulties, patient-related	41	36	25	31	22	64	50	27	31	38

122

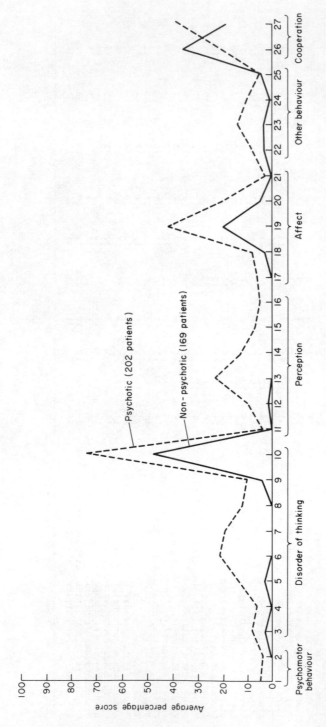

Figure 6.1   Comparison of second-year follow-up symptom profiles of initial evaluation schizophrenics considered psychotic at follow-up, and schizophrenics considered symptomatic but not psychotic at follow-up. Groups of units of analysis: 1 Quantitative psychomotor disorder. 2 Qualitative psychomotor disorder. 3 Quantitative disorder of thinking. 4 Qualitative disorder of form of thinking. 5 Affect-laden thoughts. 6 Predelusional signs. 7 Experiences of control. 8 Delusions. 9 Neurasthenic complaints. 10 Lack of insight. 11 Distortion of self-perception. 12 Derealization. 13 Auditory hallucinations. 14 'Characteristic' hallucinations. 15 Other hallucinations. 16 Pseudohallucinations. 17 Depressed—elated. 18 Anxiety, tension, irritability. 19 Flatness. 20 Incongruity. 21 Other affective change. 22 Indication of personality change. 23 Disregard for social norms. 24 Other behavioural change. 25 Psychophysical disorders. 26 Co-operation difficulties, circumstances-related. 27 Co-operation difficulties, patient-related

follow-up and the remaining 169 patients were characterized almost exclusively by lack of insight, flatness of affect, and co-operation difficulties.

6.2.1.2 The 15 most frequent units of analysis (UAs)

Symptom profiles based on groups of units of analysis give a picture of the nature of the psychopathology of patient groups in terms of broad areas of psychopathology. However, it is useful to consider how the patient groups compare on specific symptoms. For example, as the group of units 'delusions' is composed of 13 separate types of delusions, a group of patients, all of whom had delusions of persecution and none of whom had any other delusions, would receive a low score on the group of units, 'delusions', although delusions of persecution would be among the most frequent symptoms for the patient group. Units of analysis represent more specific areas of psychopathology. Therefore, the schizophrenic patient groups will be compared in terms of the 15 most frequent units of analysis on second-year follow-up.

Table 6.3 shows, for patients diagnosed schizophrenic on initial evaluation, the 15 most frequently positive units of analysis for all centres combined and for each centre. It can be seen from this table that the most frequently present symptoms on the unit of analysis level are such negative symptoms and non-specific symptoms as lack of insight, flatness of affect, poor rapport, inadequate description of problems, suspiciousness, unwillingness to co-operate and apthy. This finding is similar to the conclusion that can be drawn from the scores on the groups of units of analysis. Although they were not present as frequently as the above symptoms, some positive psychotic symptoms, such as delusions of reference and persecution and auditory hallucinations, are relatively frequently present in some centres. Thus, for example, delusions of reference were present in 18.9 per cent of patients in Prague, 18 per cent in Taipei, 16.9 per cent in Cali and 16.7 per cent in Moscow, although they were present in only 7.9 per cent of patients in Ibadan and 4.5 per cent in Agra. These findings are also consistent with the findings from analyses of the scores on groups of units of analysis.

Table 6.4 presents the number of UAs that were among the 15 most frequent in centre-by-centre comparisons for all possible pairs of centres. This table again suggests a considerable degree of similarity among the psychopathology of schizophrenic patient groups at the time of second-year follow-up.

Although there is considerable similarity among the centres with regard to the symptoms which characterize the schizophrenic patient groups at the time of second-year follow-up, there are considerable differences in the percentages of patients who have such symptoms. In Aarhus, Moscow, Taipei, and Prague the percentage of patients with symptoms was higher than in the other centres. In Ibadan, the percentage of patients with symptoms was particularly low. For example, considering the most frequent symptom in each centre, the percentage of patients with that symptom in Aarhus was 69.4, in Moscow 65.2, in Taipei 59.0, and Prague 50.9, while in Ibadan it was only 17.5. This suggests that when patients had symptoms on second-year follow-up, they tended to be of the same pattern

TABLE 6.3. 15 MOST FREQUENT UAS AT THE TIME OF 2ND YEAR FOLLOW-UP, ALL SCHIZOPHRENIC PATIENTS.

Rank (R)	All centres combined N = 543	Score (S)	Aarhus N=49		Agra N=88		Cali N=77		Ibadan N=63		London N=21		Moscow N=66		Taipei N=61		Washington N=65		Prague N=53	
			R	S	R	S	R	S	R	S	R	S	R	S	R	S	R	S	R	S
1	Lack of insight	42.5	2	59.2	1	29.5	1	39.0	1	17.5	1	28.6	1	65.2	1	59.0	1	35.4	1	50.9
2	Flatness	27.1	3=	44.9	4	25.0	12=	11.7	7=	9.5		9.5	2	57.6	6	29.5	3=	21.5	3	30.2
3	Poor rapport	26.3	1	69.4	5	14.8	2	26.0	14=	7.9	5=	19.0	3	48.5	4=	32.8	14=	12.3	11=	13.2
4=	Inadequate description	25.2	5	38.8	2=	26.1	6=	19.5	7=	9.5	5=	19.0	5	42.4	4=	32.8	5	20.0	8	17.0
4=	Suspiciousness	25.2	3=	44.9	13	11.4	6=	19.5	7=	9.5	5=	19.0	6	40.9	2	44.3	3=	21.5	4=	22.6
6	Unwilling to cooperate	24.5	7	32.7	7=	12.5	10	15.6	2	12.7	5=	19.0	7	37.9	3	39.3	2	24.6	2	32.1
7	Apathy	18.8	11	20.4	2=	26.1	14=	9.1	14=	7.9		9.5	4	43.9	8	24.6	9	1.5	6=	18.9
8	Ideas of reference	18.0	7=	16.3	7=	12.5	4	23.4	14=	4.8	2=	23.8	8	21.2	7	27.9	9	15.4	4=	22.6
9	Delusions of reference	14.2		12.2		4.5	9	16.9	14=	7.9	12	14.3		16.7	11=	18.0	8	16.9	6=	18.9
10	Restricted speech	12.9	6	36.7	6	13.0		2.6		4.8		4.8	10	28.8	15	16.4		4.6		3.8
11=	Delusions of persecution	12.7		12.2	7=	12.5		7.8	3=	11.1		0		13.6	9	23.0	11	13.8	11=	13.2
11=	Hypochondriacal (neurasthenic complaints)	12.7		2.0	7=	12.5	3	24.7	14=	7.9		4.8	14	22.7	11=	18.0		6.2		3.8
11=	Autism	12.7	8	28.6	7=	12.5	6=	19.5		3.2		9.5		4.5	10	19.7	14=	12.3		3.8
14	Presence of auditory hallucinations	11.6		14.3		1.1	12=	11.7	3=	11.1	2=	23.8		6.1	11=	18.0		10.8		9.4
15	Presence of verbal hallucinations	10.7		14.3		0	12=	11.7	7=	9.5	2=	23.8		7.6	11=	18.0		3.1		9.4

TABLE 6.4. NUMBER OF UNITS OF ANALYSIS AMONG THE 15 MOST FREQUENT FOR BOTH MEMBERS OF EACH PAIR OF CENTRES AT TIME OF 2ND YEAR FOLLOW-UP. ALL SCHIZOPHRENIC PATIENTS.

	Aarhus	Agra	Cali	Ibadan	London	Moscow	Taipei	Washington	Prague
Aarhus	-								
Agra	9	-							
Cali	7	9	-						
Ibadan	7	9	11	-					
London	6	8	11	13	-				
Moscow	8	10	7	8	7	-			
Taipei	9	12	13	12	12	9	-		
Washington	10	9	11	9	10	6	10	-	
Prague	7	9	8	10	11	8	10	9	-

from centre to centre, but that patients in some centres had symptoms less frequently than patients in other centres.

In the discussion of the groups of units of analysis symptom profiles, it was mentioned that there may be a problem in interpreting the data, since patients in different stages of illness are lumped together. The same problem exists when considering the 15 most frequently positive units of analysis. Therefore, these were recalculated in terms of patients who were psychotic at the time of follow-up.

Table 6.5 shows, for initial evaluation schizophrenic patients who were psychotic at the time of second-year follow-up, the 15 most frequently positive units of anlysis for all centres combined and for each centre. It can be seen by comparing this table with Table 6.3 that there is a very great similarity between the 15 most frequent UAs for the group of all schizophrenics and the 15 most frequent UAs for the psychotic schizophrenics. The only differences are that restricted speech and neurotic hypochondriasis drop out of the 15 most frequent for those initial evaluation schizophrenics who are still psychotic at the time of the second-year follow-up, and are replaced by delusional mood and voices speaking to the patient. The percentages of patients with a positive score on individual units of analysis are much higher for the psychotic group.

Furthermore, it can be seen by comparing the two tables that most of the second-year follow-up psychopathology of the group of all schizophrenics followed up is accounted for by the psychotic group. Thus, for example, of the 147 patients with flatness of affect (27.1 per cent of the 543 schizophrenics followed up), 105 (52 per cent of 202 that were psychotic at follow-up), are among the psychotic group. Of course, by definition, the scores on UAs representing psychotic symptoms, such as hallucinations and delusions, are accounted for only by the psychotic patients.

Table 6.6 presents, for initial evaluation schizophrenics that were psychotic on second-year follow-up, the number of UAs that were among the 15 most frequent for both members of each pair of centres. It can be seen from this table that there is a high degree of similarity between the centres with regard to the psychopathology of their psychotic patient groups. The similarity between Washington and Moscow and the other centres is less than it is among the other seven centres.

Thus, a consideration of symptom profiles suggests that at the time of second-year follow-up groups of patients diagnosed as schizophrenic are for the most part similar from centre to centre. When those patients initially diagnosed as schizophrenic who were psychotic at the time of second-year follow-up are considered separately, it is seen that the groups of these patients in the various centres are similar to one another. Furthermore, the initial evaluation schizophrenic patients who were symptomatic but not psychotic at the time of second-year follow-up demonstrated very little psychopathology, with more than minimal scores only on flatness of affect, lack of insight, and co-operation difficulties; 172 of the 543 initial evaluation schizophrenic patients followed up were totally asymptomatic at the time of second-year follow-up. Although centres were quite similar with regard to the pattern of symptoms characterizing the schizophrenic group of patients at second-year follow-up, there were considerable differences

TABLE 6.5. 15 MOST FREQUENT UNITS OF ANALYSIS AT THE TIME OF 2ND YEAR FOLLOW-UP, SCHIZOPHRENIC PATIENTS CONSIDERED PSYCHOTIC AT THE TIME OF 2ND YEAR FOLLOW-UP.

Rank (R)	All centres combined (N = 202)	Score (S)	Aarhus N=30		Agra N=28		Cali N=26		Ibadan N=16		London N=9		Moscow N=25		Taipei N=25		Washington N=25		Prague N=18	
			R	S	R	S	R	S	R	S	R	S	R	S	R	S	R	S	R	S
1	Lack of insight	74.3	2	70.0	3=	75.0	1	80.8	1	56.3	4=	44.4	1	96.0	1	88.0	1	60.0	1	72.2
2=	Suspiciousness	52.0	4=	50.0	12	35.7	6=	38.5	5=	37.5	7=	33.3	2	84.0	2	72.0	2	52.0	5	50.0
2=	Flatness	52.0	3	63.3	1=	78.6	14=	26.9	5=	37.5		22.2	5=	72.0	3=	60.0	12=	32.0	6	44.4
4	Inadequate description	49.5	4=	50.0	3=	75.0	14=	26.9	5=	37.5	7=	33.3	3	80.0	3=	60.0	6=	36.0	14=	22.2
5	Poor rapport	48.0	1	76.7	5	46.4	4=	42.3	12=	31.3	7=	33.3	3	80.0	3=	60.0		12.0	14=	22.2
6	Ideas of reference	45.1	13=	23.3	7=	39.3	2	69.2		18.8	1=	55.6	7=	52.0	6=	56.0	6=	36.0	3	61.1
7	Unwilling to cooperate	44.1	10	33.3	7=	39.3		23.1	2=	43.8		11.1	5=	72.0	6=	56.0	5	40.0	2	66.7
8	Delusions of reference	38.1		20.0		25.0	3	50.0	12=	31.3	7=	33.3	13	44.0	10=	44.0	3=	44.0	4	55.6
9	Delusions of persecution	34.2		20.0	7=	39.3		23.1	2=	43.8		0		36.0	6=	56.0	6=	36.0	7	38.9
10	Apathy	33.2		16.7	1=	78.6		15.4	12=	31.3		11.1	12	48.0	9	48.0		0	8=	33.3
11	Presence of auditory hallucinations	31.2	13=	23.3	15=	28.6	8=	34.6	2=	43.8	1=	55.6	15	44.0	10=	44.0		28.0	10=	27.8
12	Autism	29.7	6	43.3	7=	39.3	6=	38.5		12.5		22.2	12	40.0	13=	40.0	12=	32.0		5.6
13	Presence of verbal hallucinations	28.7	13=	23.3	15=	28.6	8=	34.6	5=	37.5	1=	55.6	20	44.0	10=	44.0		8.0	10=	27.8
14	Delusional mood	26.2		16.7		7.1	4=	42.3	12=	31.3	4=	44.4	36	36.0	15=	36.0		28.0		5.6
15	Voices speak to patient	25.3	13=	23.3		25.0	8=	34.6	5=	37.5	7=	33.3	12	40.0	13=	40.0		8.0	14=	22.2

TABLE 6.6. NUMBER OF UNITS OF ANALYSIS AMONG THE 15 MOST FREQUENT FOR BOTH MEMBERS OF EACH PAIR OF CENTRES AT TIME OF 2ND YEAR FOLLOW-UP. SCHIZOPHRENIC PATIENTS CONSIDERED PSYCHOTIC AT FOLLOW-UP.

	Aarhus	Agra	Cali	Ibadan	London	Moscow	Taipei	Washington	Prague
Aarhus	-	11	12	10	8	10	11	8	11
Agra		-	9	10	7	8	12	8	12
Cali			-	13	13	8	13	6	10
Ibadan				-	11	7	13	7	12
London					-	6	11	5	9
Moscow						-	9	6	9
Taipei							-	8	13
Washington								-	8
Prague									-

among centres with regard to the actual percentages of patients with individual symptoms.

However, it must be kept in mind that these conclusions about similarity are based on the comparison of groups of patients in terms of scores on all symptoms, without giving weight to particular symptoms. Therefore these analyses should be complemented by a more clinical approach in which symptoms are clinically weighted and patients considered individually. The IPSS patients have thus been compared on the basis of CATEGO classification at the time of second-year follow-up.

6.2.2 CATEGO

CATEGO is a computer program for classifying psychiatric patients on the basis of PSE input. The rules of classification are similar to those used by clinicians in many parts of the world but particularly in Europe. It was shown in Volume 1 of the IPSS report (WHO, 1973) that, with the exception of certain cases in Moscow and Washington, there was a fairly close correspondence between broad CATEGO classes and the clinical diagnoses given in the centres. When based solely on PSE data, the CATEGO classes constitute a descriptive summary of the predominant symptoms present at the time of examination and can therefore be used to compare different groups. Definitions of the CATEGO classes are presented in Appendix 4.

Table 6.7 presents, for each centre, the proportion of patients with an initial clinical diagnosis of schizophrenia assigned to each of the main CATEGO classes at the time of second-year follow-up.

TABLE 6.7. PERCENTAGE DISTRIBUTION OF PATIENTS WITH INITIAL EVALUATION CLINICAL DIAGNOSIS OF SCHIZOPHRENIA BY CATEGO CLASS ASSIGNED ON THE BASIS OF PSE DATA AT THE TIME OF 2ND YEAR FOLLOW-UP.

Centre	No. of patients	CATEGO classes							Total
		S	P	O	M	D	R+N+	Other	
Aarhus	48	31	6	21	10	3	6	23	100
Agra	88	13	3	7	-	1	6	70	100
Cali	77	22	5	3	3	-	5	62	100
Ibadan	63	11	5	-	-	-	8	76	100
London	21	33	-	5	-	5	9	48	100
Moscow	66	12	14	18	14	3	9	30	100
Taipei	61	25	11	8	3	-	7	46	100
Washington	65	20	11	5	6	-	9	49	100
Prague	53	11	11	11	6	-	4	57	100
All centres	542	18	8	8	5	1	7	53	100

130

TABLE 6.8.   PERCENTAGE DISTRIBUTION OF PATIENTS WITH
INITIAL EVALUATION CLINICAL DIAGNOSIS OF
SCHIZOPHRENIA CONSIDERED PSYCHOTIC AT
FOLLOW-UP BY CATEGO CLASS ASSIGNED ON THE
BASIS OF PSE DATA AT THE TIME OF 2ND YEAR
FOLLOW-UP.

Centre	No. of patients	CATEGO classes							
		S	P	O	M	D	R+N+	Other	Total
Aarhus	30	47	10	13	10	3	10	7	100
Agra	28	39	11	18	-	4	14	14	100
Cali	26	57	12	-	4	-	12	15	100
Ibadan	16	44	19	-	-	-	25	12	100
London	9	78	-	11	-	11	-	-	100
Moscow	25	32	24	12	8	8	12	4	100
Taipei	25	60	16	-	4	-	12	8	100
Washington	25	52	28	4	4	-	8	4	100
Prague	18	34	22	11	11	-	-	22	100
All centres	202	48	16	8	5	2	11	10	100

Chi-square analysis indicates that there are no significant differences among centres $(p < 0.1)$ with regard to the percentage of patients in CATEGO class S (representing a central schizophrenic group). Within any individual centre, the patients who had an initial evaluation diagnosis of schizophrenia fell into a variety of CATEGO class representing a definite psychosis (S, P, O, M or D). Table 6.8 presents the results of a similar analysis including only those initial evaluation schizophrenic patients who were considered psychotic at the time of second-year follow-up according to the criteria described in Appendix 3. Chi-square analysis indicates that there are no significant differences among centres with regard to the percentage of patients in CATEGO class S. It can also be seen that more patients fall into CATEGO class S than into any other class, and that when CATEGO class S and CATEGO class P (representing paranoid psychoses) are taken together, 50 per cent or more of patients in each centre fell into one of these classes. However, a percentage of patients in every centre fell into other CATEGO classes. In Ibadan, 25 per cent of patients fell into the CATEGO classes representing retarded and neurotic depression, while in London and Prague none of the patients fell into these classes.

Thus, it appears that although symptom profiles indicate that initial evaluation schizophrenic patients are symptomatologically similar from centre to centre at second-year follow-up, the CATEGO classifications of these patients at second-year follow-up suggest a certain variation of clinical syndromes at that time.

6.2.3 Presence or absence of psychotic and other symptoms at second-year follow-up

It is possible to consider the clinical conditions of patients at second-year follow-up in terms of the presence or absence of psychotic symptoms and the presence or absence of any symptoms.

Patients were divided into those who at second-year follow-up had at least one clearly psychotic* or three possibly psychotic symptoms*; those who were symptomatic, but did not have at least one clearly psychotic or at least three possibly psychotic symptoms; and those characterized by no symptoms at all†.

It has been noted above that at the time of second-year follow-up for all centres combined 202 initial evaluation schizophrenic patients were psychotic, 169 were symptomatic but not psychotic, and 172 were asymptomatic.

Figure 6.2 indicates the percentage of followed-up schizophrenic patients that fell into each one of these groups at the time of second-year follow-up, by centre. Chi-square analysis indicates that the differences among the centres are statistically significant ($p < 0.01$). It can be seen from Figure 6.2 that the Ibadan schizophrenic group was characterized by the highest percentage of asymptomatic (57 per cent)

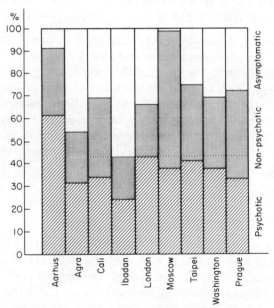

Figure 6.2   Percentage of followed-up initial evaluation schizophrenic patients, psychotic, non-psychotic and asymptomatic at second-year follow-up

*See Appendix 3 for list of symptoms that were considered definitely and possibly psychotic symptoms.
†These symptom-free patients were symptom-free in the sense that evaluation with the PSE did not reveal them to have any symptoms. It is possible that mild neurotic or psychosomatic symptoms not covered by the PSE may have been present.

and the lowest percentage of psychotic (25 per cent) patients at the time of the second-year follow-up. Aarhus was the centre with the highest percentage of patients psychotic at second-year follow-up (61 per cent), and next to the lowest number of patients asymptomatic (8 per cent). Moscow had the lowest percentage of asymptomatic patients (2 per cent).

For all centres combined 63 per cent of patients were not psychotic at the time of second-year follow-up, and this percentage varied between 75 per cent in Ibadan and 39 per cent in Aarhus.

Since it is possible that the relatively high percentage of non-psychotic patients at the time of second-year follow-up might have been due to a selection process in which those patients whom it was possible to follow-up were the most likely to be non-psychotic, the initial evaluation profile of the second-year follow-up psychotic and non-psychotic patients were compared. There were no significant differences between the initial evaluation profiles of these two groups in any centre, indicating that the findings cannot be explained by the existence of such a bias.

6.3 COMPARISON OF SYMPTOMATIC PICTURE AT TIME OF INITIAL EVALUATION WITH THE SYMPTOMATIC PICTURE AT THE TIME OF SECOND-YEAR FOLLOW-UP

Another way to consider the nature of the course and outcome of the patient group originally diagnosed as schizophrenic is to compare the profile of the group at the time of initial evaluation with the group profile of the same patients at the time of second-year follow-up. Such a comparison gives an indication of how consistent the symptom picture of these patients is over time, and allows a qualitative assessment of the two-year outcome of schizophrenia in these patients, which can be used for comparing the outcome of the schizophrenic groups in different centres, and which can later also be used for comparing outcome across diagnostic groups.

6.3.1 Symptom profiles

6.3.1.1 Groups of units of analysis (GUAs)

ANOVA analyses were carried out to determine how different the initial evaluation and second-year follow-up profiles in each centre are with regard to the distances between the symptom profiles and the shapes of the symptom profiles.

These analyses indicate that the difference between the initial evaluation and second-year follow-up profiles in terms of distance is significant in every centre. This supports the finding from analysis of the second-year follow-up profiles that there is a very low level of psychopathology among the patient groups at the time of second-year follow-up.

When ANOVA was used to compare the shapes of the initial evaluation and second-year follow-up profiles in each centre, it was found that there were significant differences in four centres, Moscow, Agra, Cali and Ibadan. As noted previously, the Moscow schizophrenic patients may have been rated higher on presence of neurotic and affective symptoms during remissions than those in other centres. In Agra, Cali and Ibadan there were many initial evaluation schizophrenic patients with little or no psychopathology at the time of second-year follow-up. To determine if the initial evaluation and second-year follow-up profiles of patients who demonstrated considerable psychopathology at the time of second-year follow-up are similar, ANOVA analyses were repeated for those patients who were psychotic at the time of second-year follow-up. It was found that there were no significant differences between the profiles in any of the centres.

τ-Values were calculated to determine the degree of similarity between initial evaluation and second-year follow-up profiles in each centre, and the results indicated a high degree of similarity in all centres except Moscow*.

Thus, it appears that the schizophrenic groups of patients showed much less symptomatology at the time of second-year follow-up than they did at the time of the initial evaluation, but when they did demonstrate symptomatology, it was similar to the symptomatology that was present at the time of initial evaluation.

To consider what symptoms account for this similarity, it is necessary to consider the symptom profiles further.

Figure 6.3 presents the symptom profile of scores on 27 GUAs for all schizophrenics reassessed with a PSE at the time of the second-year follow-up and the symptom profile of the same patients at the time of initial evaluation. It can be seen again from this figure that the level of symptomatology has markedly decreased at the time of second-year follow-up. On initial evaluation the profile is characterized by high scores on positive psychotic symptoms such as delusions, hallucinations, and experiences of control and on negative and non-specific symptoms such as flatness of affect, lack of insight, and co-operation difficulties. Scores on both types of symptoms decreased at the time of second-year follow-up, but the decrease was most striking in the positive psychotic symptoms. Thus, it can be seen that the scores on predelusional signs, experiences of control, delusions, distortion of self-perception, derealization, auditory hallucinations, and characteristic auditory hallucinations are strikingly decreased on second-year follow-up, while the scores on items such as flatness of affect, incongruity of affect, indication of personality change and co-operation difficulties, though decreased, are less markedly decreased than for the more acute, positive symptoms. This suggests that what accounts for the similarity of profiles between the initial and second-year follow-up evaluations are primarily similarities in negative and non-specific symptoms.

Figure 6.4 presents the analogous profiles for those initial evaluation schizophrenics who were psychotic at the time of second-year follow-up. Again, it can be

---

*It should be kept in mind that using rank order of symptoms to consider similarity of the same group on two occasions does not take into account how many patients are symptomatic. Thus, if on the second occasion 90 per cent of patients are completely asymptomatic, and in the 10 per cent of patients who are symptomatic, the symptoms are present in the same rank order of frequency as the initial evaluation rank order for all patients, then τ will be high, although most of the patients are symptom free and quite different from their initial symptomatic status. ANOVA analyses do not cause the same problem, since comparisons are based on absolute scores rather than ranks.

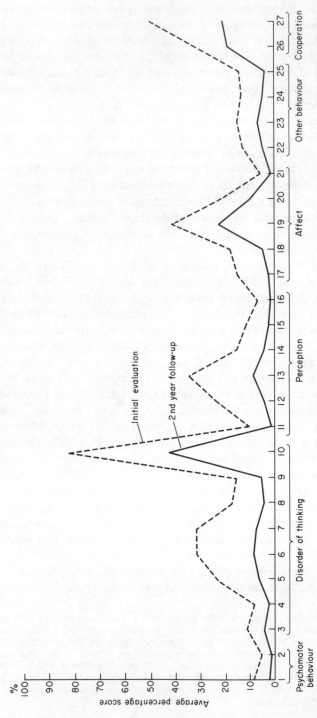

Figure 6.3   Comparison of scores of 27 GUAs at initial evaluation and second-year follow-up. All schizophrenia (543 patients). Groups of units of analysis: 1 Quantitative psychomotor disorder. 2 Qualitative psychomotor disorder. 3 Quantitative disorder of form of thinking. 4 Qualitative disorder of form of thinking. 5 Affect-laden thoughts. 6 Predelusional signs. 7 Experiences of control. 8 Delusions. 9 Neurasthenic complaints. 10 Lack of insight. 11 Distortion of self-perception. 12 Derealization. 13 Auditory hallucinations. 14 'Characteristic' hallucinations. 15 Other hallucinations. 16 Pseudohallucinations. 17 Depressed—elated. 18 Anxiety, tension, irritability. 19 Flatness. 20 Incongruity. 21 Other affective change. 22 Indication of personality change. 23 Disregard for social norms. 24 Other behavioural change. 25 Psychophysical disorders. 26 Co-operation difficulties, circumstances-related. 27 Co-operation difficulties, patient-related

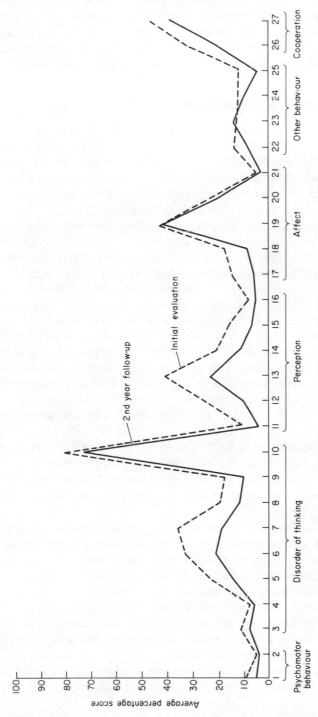

Figure 6.4 Comparison or 27 GUAs at initial evaluation and second-year follow-up. Initial evaluation schizophrenics considered psychotic at follow-up (202 patients). Groups of units of analysis: 1 Quantitative psychomotor disorder. 2 Qualitative psychomotor disorder. 3 Quantitative disorder of form of thinking. 4 Qualitative disorder of form of thinking. 5 Affect-laden thoughts. 6 Predelusional signs. 7 Experiences of control. 8 Delusions. 9 Neurasthenic complaints. 10 Lack of insight. 11 Distortion of self-perception. 12 Derealization. 13 Auditory hallucinations. 14 'Characteristic' hallucinations. 15 Other hallucinations. 16 Pseudohallucinations. 17 Depressed—elated. 18 Anxiety, tension, irritability. 19 Flatness. 20 Incongruity. 21 Other affective change. 22 Indication of personality change. 23 Disregard for social norms. 24 Other behavioural change. 25 Psychophysical disorders. 26 Co-operation difficulties, circumstances-related. 27 Co-operation difficulties, patient-related

seen that scores on positive psychotic symptoms showed a greater decrease than scores on negative and non-specific symptoms, but the differences in the decrease on the different types of symptoms are much less marked than in the case of the profiles of all schizophrenics. Thus, the similarity in profiles for these patients appears to be due to similarities in positive, negative, and non-specific symptoms.

6.3.1.2 15 most frequent units of analysis (UAs)

Another way to compare the symptom profiles on initial evaluation and second-year follow-up is to compare symptoms which occur most frequently in the patient group on each of the two occasions. Table 6.9 presents the 15 most frequent units of analysis on initial evaluation and second-year follow-up for all centres combined. Table 6.10 indicates by centre those units of analysis which were among the 15 most frequent units of analysis on both occasions.

It can be seen from Table 6.9 that for all centres combined there was considerable similarity between the symptoms which characterized the schizophrenic patients on the two occasions, as 11 of the symptoms which were among the 15 most frequent on initial evaluation were also among the 15 most frequent at the time of the second-year follow-up. The symptoms which characterized the schizophrenic patients on initial evaluation were both positive and negative symptoms. Although the percentages of patients with symptoms decreased for both of these types of symptoms, there was a more striking decrease for the positive psychotic symptoms. Thus, the percentage of patients with delusions of reference decreased from 50.3 per cent on initial evaluation to 14.2 per cent on second-year follow-up, for delusions of persecution from 48.1 to 12.7 per cent, delusional mood from 47.5 to 10.5 per cent, presence of auditory hallucinations 43.8 to 11.6 per cent, voices speaking to patient from 36.3 to 9.4 per cent and thought alienation from 33.5 to 7.4 per cent.

The four symptoms which dropped out of the 15 most frequent list at the time of second-year follow-up were delusional mood, voices speaking to patient, gloomy thoughts, and thought alienation, while those which replaced them were more negative symptoms: apathy, restricted speech, non-delusional hypochondriacal complaints and autism.

Thus, the results of comparison of the 15 most frequent units of analysis confirms the findings of analysis at the GUA level that the patient groups on the two occasions are quite similar, and that the similarity is mainly due to the continued presence on follow-up of negative and non-specific symptoms, while the positive psychotic symptoms tend to disappear.

Table 6.10 demonstrates that within individual centres there was also a considerable degree of similarity between the symptoms that characterized the patient groups on the two occasions. The number of symptoms among the 15 most frequent on both occasions varied between 6 and 14.

Tables 6.11 and 6.12 present the analogous figures for those initial evaluation schizophrenics who were psychotic at the time of second year follow-up. These

TABLE 6.9.   COMPARISON OF THE 15 MOST FREQUENT UNITS
             OF ANALYSIS AT INITIAL EVALUATION AND 2ND
             YEAR FOLLOW-UP.   ALL SCHIZOPHRENIC PATIENTS,
             ALL CENTRES COMBINED.

Units of Analysis	Rank order at IE	Score at IE	Rank Order at 2FU	Score at 2FU
Lack of insight	1	82.7	1	42.5
Inadequate description	2	67.2	4 =	25.2
Suspiciousness	3	60.0	4 =	25.2
Unwilling to cooperate	4	57.3	6	24.5
Ideas of reference	5	55.1	8	18.0
Flatness	6	51.0	2	27.1
Delusions of reference	7	50.3	9	14.2
Poor rapport	8	49.5	3	26.3
Delusions of persecution	9	48.1	11 =	12.7
Delusional mood	10	47.5	16	10.5
Presence of auditory hallucinations	11	43.8	14	11.6
Presence of verbal hallucinations	12	37.9	15	10.7
Voices speak to patient	13	36.3	18	9.4
Gloomy thoughts	14	35.7	19	9.2
Thought alienation	15	33.5	27	7.4
Apathy	19	30.4	7	18.8
Restricted speech	52	17.5	10	12.9
Hypochondriacal (neurasthenic complaints)	32	21.7	11 =	12.7
Autism	18	30.7	11 =	12.7

tables demonstrate that there was a striking similarity between the initial evaluation and second-year follow-up symptomatology for these two groups of patients. Of the 16 most frequent units (two units tied for fifteenth) for this group on initial evaluation, 14 units were among the 15 most frequent at the time of second-year follow-up, for all centres combined. In individual centres, Moscow was the only centre in which there were less than 11 UAs which were among the 15 most frequent on both occasions. Again, the biggest decreases in scores occurred for positive psychotic symptoms, but the magnitude of this decrease was of course much less than for the group of all schizophrenics.

138

TABLE 6.10.   NUMBER OF UNITS OF ANALYSIS AMONG THE 15
MOST FREQUENT ON BOTH INITIAL EVALUATION
AND 2ND YEAR FOLLOW-UP.   ALL SCHIZOPHRENIC
PATIENTS.

Aarhus	Agra	Cali	Ibadan	London	Moscow	Taipei	Washington	Prague	All centres
8	10	12	11	12	6	12	14	12	11

The units of analysis that are among the 15 most frequent on
both evaluations are listed below in the order of rank at Initial
Evaluation.   The names of the units of analysis are listed on the
following page.

Aarhus	Agra	Cali	Ibadan	London	Moscow	Taipei	Washington	Prague	All centres
60	60	60	60	60	60	60	127	60	60
127	127	34	126	33	127	36	126	126	127
126	36	33	36	34	123	34	36	127	36
92	92	127	70	46	36	41	62	34	126
123	93	46	127	62	126	123	46	46	34
36	41	123	41	39	29	46	92	92	92
105	34	66	66	66		126	60	36	46
38	123	70	92	67		127	123	56	123
	109	36	67	36		66	33	93	41
	126	67	46	71		70	28	123	70
		92	71	2		92	41	22	66
		126		111		58	105	41	
							34		
							37		

UNITS OF ANALYSIS LISTED IN TABLE 6.10.

	Units of Analysis	Number of centres in which unit of analysis among 15 most frequent
2	Retardation	1
22	Speech dissociation	1
28	Gloomy thoughts	1
29	Elated thoughts	1
33	Delusional mood	3
34	Ideas of reference	6
36	Suspiciousness	9
37	Perplexity	1
38	Thought alienation	1
39	Thoughts spoken aloud	1
41	Delusions of persecution	5
46	Delusions of reference	6
56	Lack of concentration	1
58	Hypochondriacal	1
60	Lack of insight	9
62	Derealization	2
66	Presence of verbal hallucinations	4
67	Voices speak to patient	3
70	Presence of auditory hallucinations	3
71	Presence of frequent auditory hallucinations	2
92	Flatness	7
93	Apathy	2
105	Autism	2
109	Self-neglect	1
111	Early waking	1
123	Poor rapport	7
126	Unwilling to cooperate	8
127	Inadequate description	8

TABLE 6.11.   COMPARISON OF THE 15 MOST FREQUENT UNITS
OF ANALYSIS AT INITIAL EVALUATION AND
2ND YEAR FOLLOW-UP.   SCHIZOPHRENICS, ALL
CENTRES COMBINED.   ONLY PATIENTS CONSIDERED
PSYCHOTIC AT THE TIME OF 2ND YEAR FOLLOW-UP.

Units of Analysis	Rank order at IE	Score at IE	Rank order at 2FU	Score at 2FU
Lack of insight	1	82.7	1	74.3
Inadequate description	2	69.8	4	49.5
Suspiciousness	3	66.3	2=	52.0
Ideas of reference	4	60.9	6	45.1
Delusions of reference	5	58.4	8	38.1
Unwilling to cooperate	6	57.4	7	44.1
Flatness	7	55.9	2=	52.0
Delusional mood	8=	54.5	14	26.2
Delusions of persecution	8=	54.5	9	34.2
Poor rapport	10	53.0	5	48.0
Presence of auditory hallucinations	11	50.0	11	31.2
Presence of verbal hallucinations	12	43.6	13	28.7
Voices speak to patient	13	41.1	15	25.3
Gloomy thoughts	14	37.1	21=	10.4
Thought alienation	15=	36.6	21=	10.4
Autism	15=	36.6	12	29.7
Apathy	19	32.2	10	33.2

6.3.2 CATEGO

Since the above profile comparisons of patients on initial evaluation and second-year follow-up do not give weights to different symptoms and are done in terms of groups it is useful also to carry out comparisons with a method that gives clinical weights to symptoms and considers individual patients. Thus it is possible to consider how consistent the clinical picture of schizophrenia is between initial evaluation and second-year follow-up by determining how many patients given an initial evaluation diagnosis of schizophrenia were in the same CATEGO class on both initial evaluation and second-year follow-up.

Table 6.13 presents, for initial evaluation schizophrenic patients who were considered to be psychotic on follow-up, the percentage that fell into the same CATEGO class on initial evaluation and second-year follow-up. It can be seen from Table 6.13 that the percentage was quite high across all centres. These results suggest that when patients were psychotic on both occasions, the clinical type of psychosis they presented tended to be the same on both occasions.

The above analyses were carried out on data available from a standardized assessment of the patients' mental status at the initial evaluation and at the time of second-year follow-up. These analyses indicate that:

1. Groups of patients initially diagnosed as schizophrenic in nine different centres and shown to be symptomatologically similar to one another at the time of initial evaluation remained similar to one another at the time of second-year follow-up. At second-year follow-up the level of psychopathology of these patient groups was generally low, and consisted mainly of negative and non-specific symptoms such as flatness of affect, poor rapport, apathy, lack of insight and cooperation difficulties.

2. Of the 543 initial evaluation schizophrenics followed up, at the time of the second-year follow-up 202 were psychotic, 169 were symptomatic but not psychotic, and 172 were asymptomatic. The percentage of followed-up schizophrenics that were psychotic at second-year follow-up ranged between 61 per cent in Aarhus and 25 per cent in Ibadan. The percentage of followed-up schizophrenics that were asymptomatic at second-year follow-up ranged between 58 per cent in Ibadan and 2 per cent in Moscow. The level of psychopathology was particularly low in the schizophrenic groups in Agra, Cali and Ibadan. When patients who were psychotic at the time of second-year follow-up were considered separately, it was found that the groups of such patients in the different centres were symptomatologically similar to one another. These patients demonstrated positive, negative, and non-specific symptoms, while the symptomatic but not psychotic patients were characterized almost exclusively by flatness of affect, lack of insight, and cooperation difficulties.

3. Since the methods of profile comparison used do not give different weights to different symptoms and consider groups of patients, the patients were also compared at the time of second-year evaluation in terms of CATEGO classification, a method which gives clinical weights to symptoms and which considers individual patients. When the second-year follow-up CATEGO classifications of patients initially diagnosed as schizophrenic were compared, it was noted that there was a variety of clinical syndromes at that time, and that in most centres less than half of the patients were placed in a CATEGO class that represented a definitive psychosis. Of those patients that were psychotic at follow-up, more patients fell into CATEGO class S (representing schizophrenia) than into any other class, and 50 per cent or more of patients in every centre fell into either CATEGO class S or P (representing paranoid psychosis).

4. When initial evaluation profiles of schizophrenic patients were compared to the profiles of the same patients at the time of second-year follow-up, it was noted that there was considerable similarity between the symptomatological pictures of the groups of schizophrenic patients on both occasions. At initial evaluation the schizophrenic group of patients had positive psychotic symptoms – such as hallucinations and delusions, negative symptoms – such as flatness of affect, and non-specific symptoms – such as anxiety, tension and irritability, lack of insight

TABLE 6.12.   NUMBER OF UNITS OF ANALYSIS AMONG THE 15
               MOST FREQUENT ON BOTH INITIAL EVALUATION
               AND 2ND YEAR FOLLOW-UP SCHIZOPHRENIC
               PATIENTS CONSIDERED PSYCHOTIC AT TIME OF
               2ND YEAR FOLLOW-UP.

Aarhus	Agra	Cali	Ibadan	London	Moscow	Taipei	Washington	Prague	All centres
12	12	11	13	-	7	13	12	14	14

The units of analysis that are among the 15 most frequent on
both evaluations are listed below in the order of rank at Initial
Evaluation.   The names of the units of analysis are listed on the
following page.

Aarhus	Agra	Cali	Ibadan	London	Moscow	Taipei	Washington	Prague	All centres
60	60	60	36		60	60	127	60	60
126	127	33	70		127	36	92	34	127
127	93	34	71		36	41	36	127	36
36	92	127	41		123	46	126	126	34
123	36	46	67		34	123	62	46	46
92	34	66	126		46	34	41	36	126
105	123	67	46		126	33	46	55	92
34	41	70	60			127	105	41	33
70	19	123	66			70	36	56	41
66	70	36	33			66	34	92	123
67	126	92	28			67	43	66	70
38	66		92			126	60	70	66
			127			92		93	67
								123	105

UNITS OF ANALYSIS LISTED IN TABLE 6.12.

Units of Analysis	Number of centres in which unit of analysis among 15 most frequent
19 Restricted speech	1
28 Gloomy thoughts	1
30 Hopelessness	-
33 Delusional mood	3
34 Ideas of reference	7
36 Suspiciousness	8
38 Thought alienation	1
41 Delusions of persecution	5
43 Self-depreciation	1
46 Delusions of reference	6
55 Worries	1
56 Lack of concentration	1
60 Lack of insight	8
62 Derealization	1
66 Presence of verbal hallucinations	6
67 Voices speak to patient	4
70 Presence of auditory hallucinations	6
71 Presence of frequent auditory hallucinations	1
92 Flatness	7
93 Apathy	2
105 Autism	2
123 Poor rapport	6
126 Unwilling to cooperate	7
127 Inadequate description	8

TABLE 6.13.   PERCENTAGE OF PATIENTS WITH INITIAL EVALUATION CLINICAL
DIAGNOSIS OF SCHIZOPHRENIA, WHO HAD THE SAME CATEGO
CLASSIFICATION AT 2ND YEAR FOLLOW-UP AS AT INITIAL
EVALUATION.   ONLY PATIENTS CONSIDERED PSYCHOTIC AT 2ND
YEAR FOLLOW-UP.

Aarhus N=30	Agra N=28	Cali N=26	Ibadan N=16	London N=9	Moscow N=25	Taipei N=25	Washington N=25	Prague N=18	All Centres N=202
80	79	73	88	100	88	88	78	94	83

and co-operation difficulties. At the time of second-year follow-up the patients demonstrated much less pathology in all three types of symptoms than on initial evaluation, but the decrease was most marked in the positive, psychotic symptoms. Thus, the similarity of the symptom profiles on the two occasions was primarily due to similarities in negative and non-specific symptoms. When the comparisons were carried out for patients who were psychotic at the time of second-year follow-up, it was found that the symptomatology on the two occasions was significantly similar in all centres. This similarity was due to similarity in positive psychotic, negative and non-specific symptoms.

5. When the similarity of clinical picture between initial evaluation and second-year follow-up was considered in terms of the percentage of patients with an initial evaluation diagnosis of schizophrenia who had the same CATEGO classification on both occasions, it was noted that those patients that were psychotic on both initial evaluation and second-year follow-up tended to present the same clinical type of psychosis on the two occasions. The percentage of such patients who were placed into the same CATEGO class on both occasions ranged between 72 per cent in Washington and 100 per cent in London.

In order to further consider the nature of the course and outcome of schizophrenia within and among centres, additional analyses were carried out on data concerning the interval between the initial evaluation and second-year follow-up.

6.4 COURSE OF ILLNESS IN SCHIZOPHRENIC PATIENTS BETWEEN INITIAL EVALUATION AND SECOND-YEAR FOLLOW-UP

The course of illness in schizophrenic patients during the interval between initial evaluation and second-year follow-up was compared in terms of the length of the episode of inclusion*, the percentage of the follow-up period spent in psychotic episodes, pattern of course, type of subsequent episodes, degree of social impairment during the follow-up period, the percentage of the follow-up period spent out of the hospital, and overall outcome. Assessments of each of these factors in the form of ratings were made by five psychiatrists who reviewed the narrative and precoded portions of the follow-up psychiatric history and social description schedules and the follow-up diagnostic assessment schedules. The reliability of their

*The episode in which the patient was at the time of inclusion in the study.

assessments has been discussed in Chapter 4. It should be kept in mind, in considering the analyses involving psychiatric history information that such analyses are not based on data known to be as reliable as the data on which the symptom profile analyses have been based (see also Chapter 3, where this issue is discussed).

In the tables throughout this section, the figures refer to those patients given an initial evaluation diagnosis of schizophrenia who were followed up and about whom there was sufficient information available to form an estimate concerning the factor being assessed.

As noted in section 6.1 chi-square tests have been used to assess the statistical significance of differences between centres and groups of centres. When a number of different tests are carried out on the same data, Bonferroni's chi-square technique has been applied. Whenever differences are stated to be statistically significant, p is equal to or less than 0.01.

6.4.1 Length of episode of inclusion for patients with an initial evaluation diagnosis of schizophrenia

Table 6.14 presents the percentage distribution of schizophrenic patients by length of the episode of inclusion. Patients in group 1 remained in the episode of inclusion up to one month, those in group 2 one month up to three months, in group 3 three months up to nine months, in group 4 nine months up to 18 months and in group 5 18 months or more. The length of episode of inclusion does not refer to length of time hospitalized, since it was felt that this factor is likely to be influenced by local sociocultural factors and availability of services. Rather, an estimate was made from the follow-up psychiatric history of when the episode of inclusion was over. The length of hospitalization was assessed separately (see section 6.4.6. below). The end of the episode was considered to be the time of the disappearance of the main symptoms of the illness which had been prominent during the episode. If the episode was a psychotic one, the time of recovery from such positive psychotic symptoms as delusions, other thought disorder, and hallucinations was rated as the end of the episode, although some secondary or minor symptoms might persist.

It can be seen from the table that for all centres combined, 27 per cent of patients were in the episode of inclusion for 18 months or longer while the length of the episode of inclusion had been less than one month for 28 per cent of patients. Combining groups 1 and 2 and 4 and 5 indicates that for 56 per cent of patients the episode of inclusion lasted less than three months, while for 30 per cent of patients it lasted for nine months or longer.

The centres differ significantly with regard to the distribution of patients into the six groups. A high percentage of patients were in the episode of inclusion for 18 months or longer in Aarhus (50 per cent) and Washington (47 per cent) while in Ibadan only 6 per cent of patients were in the episode of inclusion for that long. Five centres had a high percentage of patients in whom the episode of inclusion lasted less than one month: Cali (36 per cent), Ibadan (36 per cent), Moscow (35 per cent), Agra (34 per cent), and Washington (32 per cent). In Prague, only 10 per

TABLE 6.14. PERCENTAGE DISTRIBUTION OF SCHIZOPHRENIC PATIENTS BY LENGTH OF EPISODE OF INCLUSION AND BY CENTRE.

Centre	No. of patients	1 <1 month	2 1-3 months	3 3-9 months	4 9-18 months	5 >18 months	Total	Mean
Aarhus	48	19	23	4	4	50	100	13.9
Agra	92	34	31	13	2	20	100	7.1
Cali	75	36	25	8	3	28	100	8.1
Ibadan	61	36	36	20	2	6	100	3.8
London	58	24	22	16	7	31	100	9.8
Moscow	68	35	31	13	3	18	100	6.4
Taipei	79	16	34	18	4	28	100	9.3
Washington	38	32	13	5	3	47	100	12.6
Prague	49	10	29	24	4	33	100	11.0
All centres	568	28	28	14	3	27	100	8.6

cent of patients fell into the less than one month group, in Taipei 16 per cent fell into this group, and in Aarhus 19 per cent of patients had an episode of inclusion lasting less than one month.

Combining Groups 1 and 2 and Groups 4 and 5, it can be seen that the episode of inclusion lasted less than three months for a very high percentage of patients in Ibadan (72 per cent), Moscow (66 per cent), Agra (65 per cent) and Cali (61 per cent). In two centres the percentage of patients in whom the episode of inclusion lasted nine months or longer was very high: Aarhus (54 per cent), and Washington (50 per cent). Ibadan had only 8 per cent of patients in whom the episode of inclusion lasted longer than nine months.

The percentage of such patients was also low in Moscow (21 per cent) and Agra (22 per cent).

The figures also show that in all centres patients who were still in the episode of inclusion after nine months were likely to remain in the episode of inclusion for at least 18 months.

The last column of Table 6.14 indicates the mean length of the episode of inclusion in months for all centres combined and by centre. The mean length of the episode of inclusion was 8.6 months for all schizophrenics. Among the centres, the means ranged from 3.8 months in Ibadan to 13.9 months in Aarhus.

It can be seen from Table 6.14 that schizophrenic patients in the centres in the developing countries had a better two-year course and outcome on this variable than those in the centres in developed countries. Chi-square analysis was carried out to assess the homogeneity of results on this variable among the centres in the developed countries and among the centres in developing countries*. The analyses indicated that the centres in developing countries were homogeneous, but the centres in developed countries were not. When Moscow was removed the group of centres in developed countries became homogeneous and the differences between the two groups were significant.

6.4.1.1 Summary

It appears that for all centres combined the episode of inclusion lasted less than three months for the majority of schizophrenic patients, and less than one month for approximately one-quarter of schizophrenic patients. Approximately one-quarter were in the episode of inclusion for 18 months or longer. However, when the figures are considered by individual centres, it appears that in four centres – Ibadan, Moscow, Agra and Cali – a high percentage of patients had an episode of inclusion which lasted less than three months; in three centres – Ibadan, Moscow and Agra – a relatively low percentage of patients had an episode of inclusion which lasted more than nine months; in one centre, Aarhus, a relatively low percentage of patients had an episode of inclusion which lasted less than three months and a high percentage of patients had an episode of inclusion which lasted

---

*As noted in Chapter 3, Taipei was not grouped with the centres in developing countries because of the high ratio of physicians to general population, availability of medical facilities, and pattern of leading causes of death.

more than nine months; and in three centres (London, Washington and Prague) the percentages of patients who had an episode which lasted less than three months and more than nine months were approximately the same. The two extreme centres were Aarhus and Ibadan, with Aarhus patients tending to have long episodes of inclusion and Ibadan patients tending to have short episodes of inclusion. The mean length of the episode of inclusion for all schizophrenics was 8.6 months ranging from 3.8 months in Ibadan to 13.9 months in Aarhus. For schizophrenics from the three centres in developing countries (Agra, Cali and Ibadan) the mean length of the episode of inclusion was 6.3 months, while for those from the five centres* in developed countries it was 10.7 months.

When the distribution for patients in the group of centres in developed countries and in the group of centres in developing countries were compared within and between the groups, it was found that the two-year course and outcome on this variable was significantly different between the two groups, with schizophrenic patients in the developing countries group having a better course and outcome than those in the developed countries.

6.4.2 Percentage of follow-up period spent in a psychotic episode by patients with an initial evaluation diagnosis of schizophrenia

The follow-up psychiatric histories were reviewed to estimate the percentage of the follow-up period that each followed-up patient had spent in a psychotic episode. A psychotic episode was an episode which the psychiatrists rating the follow-up schedules considered to be definitely schizophrenic, probably schizophrenic, an affective psychosis, or 'another psychosis'. Usually these episodes were characterized by clearly psychotic symptoms, such as hallucinations, delusions, or experiences of control.

The results are presented in Table 6.15 which shows that when all centres are considered together, 17 per cent of the patients were in a psychotic episode for 5 per cent or less of the follow-up period, while 28 per cent were in a psychotic episode for more than 75 per cent of the follow-up period.

Chi-square analysis indicates that the centres differ significantly with regard to the distribution of patients into the five groups. A relatively high percentage of the schizophrenics were in a psychotic episode for 5 per cent or less of the follow-up period in Ibadan (29 per cent) and Agra (27 per cent), while a relatively low percentage of schizophrenic patients were in a psychotic episode for 5 per cent or less of the follow-up period in Taipei (7 per cent), Prague (7 per cent) and London (9 per cent).

In Aarhus 48 per cent of the patients were in a psychotic episode for more than 75 per cent of the follow-up period: On the other hand only 7 per cent of the Ibadan patients were in a psychotic episode for more than 75 per cent of the time.

Of all schizophrenic patients followed up, 39 per cent were in a psychotic

*As noted in Chapter 3, Taipei was not grouped with the centres in developing countries because of the high ratio of physicians to general population, availability of medical facilities, and pattern of leading causes of death.

TABLE 6.15. PERCENTAGE DISTRIBUTION OF SCHIZOPHRENIC PATIENTS BY PERCENTAGE OF FOLLOW-UP PERIOD SPENT IN PSYCHOTIC EPISODES AND BY CENTRE.

Centre	No. of patients	1 1-5%	2 6-15%	3 16-45%	4 46-75%	5 76-100%	Total	Mean
Aarhus	46	13	22	13	4	48	100	53.2
Agra	92	27	24	22	8	19	100	28.7
Cali	68	21	19	26	6	28	100	34.5
Ibadan	61	29	36	25	3	7	100	16.3
London	58	9	17	28	10	36	100	46.8
Moscow	63	14	26	35	6	19	100	29.6
Taipei	77	7	19	30	13	31	100	43.3
Washington	34	20	12	15	6	47	100	46.4
Prague	44	7	20	30	7	36	100	49.4
All centres	543	17	22	26	7	28	100	37.1

episode for 15 per cent or less of the follow-up period. In two centres the percentage of such patients was quite high — Ibadan (65 per cent) and Agra (51 per cent).

Of all schizophrenics followed up 35 per cent were in a psychotic episode for more than 45 per cent of the time. High percentages of such patients were found in Washington (53 per cent), Aarhus (52 per cent), London (46 per cent), Taipei (44 per cent) and Prague (43 per cent). In Ibadan, only 10 per cent of patients were psychotic for 45 per cent or more of the follow-up period.

The last column in Table 6.15 indicates the mean percentage of the follow-up period spent in a psychotic episode for all centres combined and by centre. It can be seen that the mean time spent in a psychotic episode by schizophrenic patients was 37.1 per cent of the follow-up period. Centres in which the mean was high were Aarhus (53.2 per cent), Prague (49.4 per cent), London (46.8 per cent), Washington (46.4 per cent) and Taipei (43.3 per cent). The percentage of the follow-up period spent in a psychotic episode was particularly low in Ibadan (16.3 per cent).

Comparisons within and between the developing and developed groups of centres indicated that these are homogeneous groups which differ significantly from one another. More patients in developing than in developed centres spent less than 15 per cent of the follow-up in a psychotic episode, and fewer patients in the developing centres spent more than 45 per cent of this period in such an episode.

The percentage of the follow-up period that schizophrenic patients spent in any episode, psychotic or non-psychotic, was also calculated, and the figures were very little changed from the figures for psychotic only episodes. This indicates either that when the schizophrenic patients had subsequent episodes, those episodes were usually psychotic, or that the narrative histories were more likely to record psychotic than non-psychotic episodes.

6.4.2.1 Summary

About one-third of all the schizophrenics followed up were in a psychotic episode for more than 145 per cent of the follow-up period, a quarter were psychotic between 16 per cent and 45 per cent of the time, and almost 40 per cent for 15 per cent or less of the time. The mean percentage of the follow-up period that schizophrenic patients spent in a psychotic episode was 37.1 per cent. In Ibadan and Agra a relatively high proportion of schizophrenics spent only a small part of the follow-up period in a psychotic episode, and the mean percentage of the follow-up period spent in such an episode was below the mean for all schizophrenics. In Washington, Aarhus, London, Taipei and Prague, a relatively high proportion of patients spent a large part of the follow-up period in a psychotic episode and the mean percentage time spent in such an episode was higher than for all schizophrenics. Cali and Moscow patients were intermediate, and the mean percentage of time spent in episodes of illness was somewhat lower than the mean for all schizophrenics.

In the centres in developing countries there were more patients who spent less than 15 per cent of the follow-up period in a psychotic episode and fewer patients that spent more than 45 per cent of this period in such an episode than in the centres in the developed countries.

6.4.3 Pattern of course of schizophrenic patients in the interval between initial evaluation and second-year follow-up

On the basis of assessment of interval histories, followed-up schizophrenic patients were assigned to one of seven groups, depending on the pattern of course they demonstrated during the interval between the initial evaluation and the second-year follow-up. Patients in group 1 are those who had a full remission after the episode of inclusion and no further episodes; in group 2 those who had a partial remission after the episode of inclusion and no subsequent episodes; in group 3 those who had at least one non-psychotic episode after the episode of inclusion and full remissions between all episodes; in group 4 those who had at least one non-psychotic episode after the episode of inclusion and did not have full remissions between all episodes; group 5, those who had at least one subsequent psychotic episode and full remission between all episodes; group 6 those who had at least one subsequent psychotic episode and who did not have full remissions between all episodes; and group 7, those who were still in the episode of inclusion at the time of the second-year follow-up. The results are presented in Table 6.16.

There are several striking results presented in this table. Considering the figures for all centres combined, it can be seen that 27 per cent of the schizophrenic patients followed up had a full remission after the episode of inclusion and no subsequent episodes while a further 17 per cent had no subsequent episodes, but had only a partial remission. This means that 44 per cent of the schizophrenic patients had no episodes after the episode of inclusion.

The centres differ significantly with regard to the distribution of patients into the pattern of course groups. It is particularly noteworthy that in two centres more than 50 per cent of the schizophrenics had a full remission after the episode of inclusion, with no further episodes during the two-year follow-up period — Ibadan (58 per cent) and Agra (51 per cent).

Combining groups 5, 6 and 7 gives an indication of the percentage of schizophrenic patients who were either still in the episode of inclusion at the time of second-year follow-up or who had had at least one subsequent psychotic episode. For all centres combined, 55 per cent of patients fell into these categories. Only in Agra and Ibadan was the percentage of such patients less than 50. The centres with the highest percentages of patients in groups 5, 6 and 7 were Aarhus (71 per cent), London (67 per cent), Cali (65 per cent) and Washington (63 per cent).

In Ibadan and Agra, a high percentage of patients had full remissions either after the initial episode or after subsequent psychotic episodes. Combining groups 1 and 5, it can be seen that the percentage of such patients was 80 per cent in Ibadan and 66 per cent in Agra.

The centres in developed countries are homogeneous with regard to the distribution of patients into pattern of course groups. The developing centres are not homogeneous, but when Cali is dropped they become homogeneous, and the

TABLE 6.16. PERCENTAGE DISTRIBUTION OF SCHIZOPHRENIC PATIENTS BY PATTERN OF COURSE GROUP AND BY CENTRE.

Centre	No. of patients	Pattern of course groups							
		1 Only episode of inclusion, full remission	2 Only episode of inclusion, incomplete remission	3 Subsequent non-psychotic episodes, full remission	4 Subsequent non-psychotic episodes, incomplete remission	5 Subsequent psychotic episodes, full remission	6 Subsequent psychotic episodes, incomplete remission	7 Still in episode of inclusion	Total
Aarhus	48	6	23	-	-	4	17	50	100
Agra	90	51	7	-	-	15	7	20	100
Cali	77	19	16	-	-	13	26	26	100
Ibadan	59	58	8	-	2	22	3	7	100
London	57	23	7	-	3	12	25	30	100
Moscow	69	7	30	-	3	10	32	18	100
Taipei	79	27	20	-	-	6	20	27	100
Washington	38	21	16	-	-	-	16	47	100
Prague	53	17	25	-	-	9	19	30	100
All centres	570	27	17	-	1	11	18	26	100

differences between the developed and developing centres are significant.

Groups 1 and 2 which represent those patients who had no subsequent episodes after the episode of inclusion, were further analysed in terms of the length of the episode of inclusion. It was found that 12 per cent of followed-up schizophrenic patients had an episode of inclusion that lasted less than one month, followed by a full remission and no subsequent episodes, and 20 per cent had an episode of inclusion that lasted less than three months, followed by a full remission and no subsequent episodes. The differences among the centres are statistically significant. What is particularly interesting is that in Ibadan, 36 per cent of followed-up schizophrenics had an episode of inclusion which lasted less than one month, followed by full remission throughout the follow-up period, and 46 per cent had an episode of inclusion that lasted less than three months and was followed by full remission lasting throughout the follow-up period. The corresponding percentages for Agra are 27 and 40 per cent, while at the other extreme, the corresponding figures for Aarhus were 2 per cent, and 6 per cent, and for Moscow 1 per cent, and 4 per cent. The differences between Agra and Ibadan, on the one hand, and the developed countries on the other, are statistically significant.

6.4.3.1 Summary

More than half of all schizophrenics either remained in the episode of inclusion throughout the follow-up or had at least one subsequent psychotic episode during the follow-up, and more than one-quarter of schizophrenic patients had a full remission after the episode of inclusion and no subsequent episodes. Of all schizophrenic patients followed up 20 per cent had an episode of inclusion that lasted less than three months, with full remission and no subsequent episodes. A high percentage of patients in Ibadan and Agra demonstrated a pattern of course characterized by a short episode of inclusion and subsequent full remission lasting throughout the follow-up period. Aarhus, London, Cali and Washington had a high percentage of schizophrenic patients who remained in the episode of inclusion throughout the follow-up period, or who had subsequent psychotic episodes. The differences between Ibadan and Agra, on the one hand, and the developed centres, on the other, with regard to the distributions into pattern of course groups, are statistically significant.

6.4.4 Types of subsequent episodes

Another aspect of the course of patients who have subsequent episodes is the type of subsequent episodes. 174 of the 609 schizophrenics* followed up had episodes of illness after the episode of inclusion which could be characterized as to type.

On the basis of the follow-up history data, episodes during the follow-up period were classified as definitely schizophrenic; probably schizophrenic; affective

*Figure refers to all patients for whom sufficient information was available to make these ratings regardless of whether they were examined with a PSE.

TABLE 6.17.   PERCENTAGE OF DISTRIBUTION OF FOLLOWED UP SCHIZOPHRENIC PATIENTS WITH SUBSEQUENT EPISODES, BY TYPE OF EPISODE.

Centre	No. of patients	Type of subsequent episode									Total
		1	2	3	4	5	Both 1+2	1 or 2 +3	Both 1+4	Both 3+4	
Aarhus	9	44	44	-	-	-	-	-	12	-	100
Agra	21	29	38	19	-	9	5	-	-	-	100
Cali	29	24	48	24	-	4	-	-	-	-	100
Ibadan	17	35	35	18	12	-	-	-	-	-	100
London	24	46	34	4	8	-	-	-	4	4	100
Moscow	31	32	26	32	7	-	-	3	-	-	100
Taipei	21	57	33	5	-	-	5	-	-	-	100
Washington	10	20	60	10	-	10	-	-	-	-	100
Prague	15	40	46	7	-	-	-	7	-	-	100
All centres	177	36	39	16	3	2	1	1	1	1	100

Types of episodes: 1 = only definitely schizophrenic episodes.
                     2 = only probably schizophrenic episodes.
                     3 = only affective psychotic episodes.
                     4 = only non-psychotic episodes.
                     5 = only other psychotic episodes.

psychosis; other psychoses; and non-psychotic. Episodes which were felt to meet the WHO/ICD glossary criteria for schizophrenia were rated as schizophrenic. Episodes which were felt to meet the WHO/ICD glossary criteria of involutional melancholia, manic-depressive psychosis, other or unspecified affective psychoses, or reactive depressive psychosis were rated as affective episodes. The 'probably schizophrenic' category was used for those episodes which met the glossary criteria for paranoid states and those which were not clearly schizophrenic according to the ICD glossary but were closer to the criteria for schizophrenia than for any other diagnostic category. Episodes meeting the glossary criteria of other and unspecified psychoses were rated as 'other psychosis' and any episode which did not meet the glossary criteria for any of the psychotic categories was classified as non-psychotic.

Table 6.17 indicates the percentage distribution of these patients by type of subsequent episodes, by centre and for all centres combined.

From this table it can be seen that 76 per cent of those schizophrenic patients with subsequent episodes had only definitely schizophrenic episodes (category 1), only probably schizophrenic episodes (category 2), or a combination of these two types of episodes. Of schizophrenic patients with subsequent episodes 16 per cent had only affective psychotic episodes. Only 5 per cent had subsequent non-psychotic episodes (category 4, category 1 + 4, and category 3 + 4), 2 per cent had only other psychotic episodes and 1 per cent had both probably schizophrenic and affective psychotic episodes.

Thus, of those schizophrenic patients who did have subsequent psychotic episodes, the vast majority had definitely or probably schizophrenic episodes, but 16 per cent did have subsequent affective psychotic episodes.

It is difficult to make comparisons in terms of individual centres because the numbers of patients involved are rather small, but in all centres the majority of schizophrenic patients with subsequent episodes had schizophrenic or probably schizophrenic episodes. In Moscow 33 per cent of patients had subsequent affective psychotic episodes, while in London only 4 per cent of patients had such subsequent episodes.

6.4.5 Degree of social impairment during the two-year follow-up period

The follow-up schedules were reviewed in order to make a global assessment of the degree of social impairment suffered by each patient during the follow-up period. This assessment took into account the patient's occupational adjustment, relationship with friends, and degree of social interaction. Initially, the patients were divided into three groups: those with no impairment, those with mild or moderate impairment, and those with severe impairment. However, when the division of patients was done in this way the inter-rater reliability was not sufficiently high to warrant carrying out further analyses. Then the patients were divided into two groups, those with severe impairment and those without severe impairment. When the patients were divided in this way, the inter-rater reliability was high. For this reason the analyses were done using the severe impairment/no severe impairment dichotomy.

TABLE 6.18.   PRESENCE OR ABSENCE OF SEVERE SOCIAL
               IMPAIRMENT DURING FOLLOW-UP PERIOD BY
               CENTRE.

All schizophrenic patients

Centre	No. of patients	No severe impairment (%)	Severe impairment (%)	Total
Aarhus	48	67	33	100
Agra	89	82	18	100
Cali	78	78	22	100
Ibadan	63	95	5	100
London	58	62	38	100
Moscow	68	79	21	100
Taipei	80	80	20	100
Washington	47	68	32	100
Prague	54	67	33	100
All centres	585	77	23	100

Table 6.18 presents the percentage of patients with severe social impairment during the follow-up period by centre and for all centres combined. It can be seen from the table that 23 per cent of follow-up schizophrenics were considered to have had severe social impairment during the follow-up period. The differences among the centres are statistically significant. Only 5 per cent of patients in Ibadan were considered to have severe social impairment, while 38 per cent of London patients, 33 per cent of Aarhus and Prague patients, and 32 per cent of Washington patients had such impairment. In addition to Ibadan, four centres had a smaller percentage of severely impaired patients than the percentage for all centres combined — Agra (18 per cent), Taipei (20 per cent), Moscow (21 per cent), and Cali (22 per cent). The average percentage of patients with severe impairment from the three centres in developing countries was 15 per cent, while for the patients in the five centres in developed countries it was 32.4 per cent. The developing centres and the developed centres differ significantly from one another with regard to this variable.

6.4.6 Percentage of follow-up period in which schizophrenic patients were out of the hospital

One aspect of the type of social outcome patients have is the percentage of time in their lives that they can stay out of a hospital. The percentage of time during the follow-up period that schizophrenic patients stayed out of the hospital was

TABLE 6.19. PERCENTAGE DISTRIBUTION OF SCHIZOPHRENIC PATIENTS BY PERCENTAGE OF FOLLOW-UP PERIOD SPENT OUT OF HOSPITAL AND BY CENTRES.

Centre	No. of patients	Percentage of follow-up period during which patient was out of hospital					Total	Mean (days)
		1 >90%	2 75-90%	3 50-75%	4 25-50%	5 <25%		
Aarhus	47	36	31	11	11	11	100	538
Agra	92	63	32	3	2	-	100	668
Cali	78	78	19	3	-	-	100	689
Ibadan	58	85	12	3	-	-	100	711
London	58	33	22	24	9	12	100	516
Moscow	66	44	39	12	2	3	100	616
Taipei	79	58	28	10	4	-	100	639
Washington	29	38	35	17	-	10	100	556
Prague	38	26	34	21	16	3	100	546

calculated by centre for followed-up schizophrenics and the results are presented in Table 6.19.

The results of this analysis must be interpreted with caution, because the differences may reflect differences in the tolerance of the various cultures for psychotic patients within the community or differences in the availability of hospital beds. There is no figure for all field research centres combined because the possible effect of these variables on the figures makes is misleading to combine figures from different centres. The centres differ significantly with regard to the distribution of patients into the groups presented in the table.

It can be seen from the table that a high percentage of patients were out of the hospital for more than 90 per cent of the follow-up period (> 657 days) in Ibadan (85 per cent), Cali (78 per cent), Agra (63 per cent) and Taipei (58 per cent). It is quite striking that 97 per cent of the Ibadan and Cali patients and 95 per cent of the Agra patients remained out of the hospital for more than three-quarters of the follow-up period (> 548 days).

On the other extreme, in three centres a relatively high percentage of patients remained out of the hospital for only one-quarter of the follow-up period (182 days) or less — London with 12 per cent, Aarhus with 11 per cent and Washington with 1 per cent. In Aarhus, 22 per cent of the patients remained out of the hospital for 50 per cent (365 days) or less of the follow-up period, while the figure in London was 21 per cent and in Prague 19 per cent.

Chi-square analysis indicates that the patients in the centres in the three-developing countries spent a significantly greater percentage of the follow-up period out of the hospital than patients in centres in other countries ($P < 0.01$), but again this may have been the result of differences in socioeconomic conditions and differences in the availability of hospital beds, rather than of differences in the patients.

6.4.7 Overall outcome

Each of the factors described above — symptomatic outcome, length of episode of inclusion, percentage time spent in a psychotic episode, pattern of course, type of subsequent episodes, degree of social impairment, and length of time out of the hospital — is one aspect of the course and outcome of a disorder. It is useful to examine each of these factors separately, in order to separate out the differences among the various centres according to each factor. However, it is also useful to have some sort of overall outcome grouping, both for use as a summary statement about outcome and for use in evaluating possible predictors of outcome. Therefore, three variables concerning the course and outcome of the IPSS patients were combined to form five overall outcome groups. The three variables are percentage of follow-up period spent in a psychotic episode, presence or absence of severe social impairment, and type of remission after episodes (full remission or no full remission). The composition of the five groups is shown in Table 6.20. Thus, the 'best' is group 1 (less than 15 per cent of follow-up period in psychotic episodes, no severe social impairment and full remission) and the 'worst' outcome group is

TABLE 6.20. COMPOSITION OF OVERALL OUTCOME GROUPS.

	0 - 15				16 - 45				46 - 75				76 - 100			
% of follow-up period in psychotic episodes																
Severe social impairment (SI) or no severe social impairment (NSI)	NSI		SI		NSI		SI		NSI		SI		NSI		SI	
Full remission (FR) or no full remission (NFR)	FR	NFR	FR	NFR	FR	NFR	FR	NFR	FR	NFR	FR	NFR	FR	NFR	FR	NFR
Overall outcome group	1	2	3	3	3	3	3	3	3	3	4	5	4	4	5	5

160

TABLE 6.21.   PERCENTAGE DISTRIBUTION OF SCHIZOPHRENIC
               PATIENTS BY OVERALL OUTCOME GROUP AND BY
               CENTRE.

Centre	No. of patients	overall outcome groups					Total
		1	2	3	4	5	
Aarhus	48	6	29	17	17	31	100
Agra	88	48	18	13	6	15	100
Cali	72	21	32	19	13	15	100
Ibadan	58	57	29	7	2	5	100
London	58	24	12	23	10	31	100
Moscow	66	9	39	32	9	11	100
Taipei	78	15	23	27	20	15	100
Washington	31	23	16	16	26	19	100
Prague	44	14	20	27	9	30	100
All centres	543	26	25	20	11	18	100

group 5 (more than 75 per cent of follow-up period in psychotic episodes, severe social impairment and without any full remissions between episodes).

The percentage distribution of followed-up schizophrenic patients by overall outcome group is presented in Table 6.21.

The table indicates that 26 per cent of all followed-up schizophrenics fell into the best-outcome group, while 18 per cent fell into the worst group; 51 per cent were in one of the two best groups while 29 per cent were in one of the two worst groups.

The differences among the centres with regard to the distribution of patients into the five overall outcome groups are statistically significant. In Ibadan and Agra, a high percentage of patients fell into the best-outcome group, 57 per cent for Ibadan and 48 per cent for Agra. Only 6 per cent of Aarhus patients and 9 per cent of Moscow patients were in the best-outcome group. In three centres a high percentage of patients fell into the worst-outcome group: Aarhus (31 per cent), London (31 per cent) and Prague (30 per cent). Only five per cent of the Ibadan patients fell into this group.

Combining the figures for groups 1 and 2 and for groups 4 and 5, it is noted that the percentage of patients in the two best groups was very high in Ibadan (86 per cent) and Agra (66 per cent). In contrast, in three centres the percentage of patients falling into the two worst groups was high — Aarhus (48 per cent), Washington (45 per cent) and London (41 per cent). Only 7 per cent of Ibadan patients fell into the two worst groups. The differences between the Ibadan and Agra patients, on the one hand, and the centres in developed countries on the other hand, with regard to the distribution of patients into the five outcome groups, are statistically significant.

6.4.7.1 Summary

Using this overall outcome grouping as a criterion, patients in Ibadan had the best outcome, with the highest percentage of patients in the best-outcome group and the lowest percentage of patients in the worst-outcome group. Agra patients had the next best outcome, with the second highest percentage in the best group and a low percentage in the worst group. Aarhus patients seemed to have the worst outcome, with the lowest percentage of patients in the best group and the highest percentage (with London) of patients in the worst group. London and Prague had relatively high percentages of patients in the worst group and a relatively low percentage of patients in the two best groups. Cali had a low percentage of patients in the worst group and a relatively high percentage of patients in the two best groups. In Moscow and Taipei, a high percentage of patients fell into the middle group. Washington had a relatively high percentage of patients in the two worst groups. Considering the findings for all centres combined, 51 per cent of patients fell into the two best groups, 29 per cent into the two worst groups and 20 per cent into the middle group.

6.5 OUTCOME OF SCHIZOPHRENIA IN RELATION TO AGE AND SEX

Table 6.22 presents the distribution of schizophrenic patients among overall outcome groups by age and sex. It can be seen that there appears to be a differential between the proportion of males and females that fall into the worst overall outcome group. Thus, 61 out of 303 males (20 per cent) and 37 out of 305 females (12 per cent) fall into this group.

Intracentre comparisons of outcome by sex indicate that the differences between the sexes occurred mainly in four centres — Agra, London, Taipei and Prague. In each of these centres there was a higher percentage of females in the best-outcome group (in the second best-outcome group in the case of Taipei) and a higher percentage of males in the worst-outcome group. There do not appear to be any differences between patients in centres in developing and developed centres with regard to the relationship between sex and outcome.

The result lend some support to the hypothesis that younger males have a poorer outcome than older females. The age-range was restricted by the inclusion criteria, but nevertheless it is noteworthy that there was a lower percentage of males under 20 in the best overall outcome group (17 per cent) than of females 35 or over in this group (24 per cent), while there was a higher percentage of males under 20 in the worst overall outcome group (25 per cent) than of females 35 or over (14 per cent).

Chi-square analysis of Table 6.22 indicates that the differences among age and sex groups with regard to overall outcome described above do not reach the level

TABLE 6.22. PERCENTAGE DISTRIBUTION OF SCHIZOPHRENIC PATIENTS BY OVERALL OUTCOME, AGE AND SEX.

Age-groups	No. of patients		Outcome groups										Not known		Total	
Sex	M	F	1 M	1 F	2 M	2 F	3 M	3 F	4 M	4 F	5 M	5 F	M	F	M	F
15-19	64	39	17	31	23	28	14	18	13	5	25	10	8	8	100	100
20-24	76	69	24	23	26	22	16	17	11	16	14	13	9	9	100	100
25-29	68	66	21	27	21	20	25	18	7	11	19	11	7	13	100	100
30-34	49	39	26	18	25	28	12	15	8	8	23	13	6	18	100	100
35-39	28	50	14	30	29	14	14	16	14	12	22	14	7	14	100	100
40-44	18	41	17	17	16	15	33	25	6	7	22	12	6	24	100	100
45-49	-	1	-	-	-	-	-	(100)	-	-	-	-	-	-	-	(100)
Total	303	305	21	24	24	21	18	18	10	11	20	12	7	14	100	100

of statistical significance. Therefore, at this stage it is not possible to determine if these differences reflect chance variations or true differences in outcome.

More detailed analyses of outcome by age and sex, for each outcome measure and by centre will be published separately.

6.6 SUMMARY OF FINDINGS CONCERNING THE COURSE AND OUTCOME OF SCHIZOPHRENIC GROUPS OF PATIENTS DURING THE FOLLOW-UP PERIOD

The previous sections have reviewed various aspects of the course and outcome of IPSS schizophrenic patients during a two-year follow-up period. The following major points stand out from this review:

1. Some of the schizophrenic patients had an extremely good two-year course and outcome. Of all schizophrenics followed up 12 per cent had an episode of inclusion which lasted less than one month, followed by a full remission which lasted through the follow-up period. 26 per cent of all schizophrenics followed up spent less than 15 per cent of the follow-up period in a psychotic episode, did not suffer severe social impairment, and had full remissions after episodes.

2. At the other extreme, some of the schizophrenic patients had a very bad outcome: 18 per cent were either in a psychotic episode for more than three-quarters of the follow-up period and suffered severe social impairment or were psychotic for 46 to 75 per cent of the follow-up period, without full remission and suffered severe social impairment; 26 per cent were still in the episode of inclusion at the time of follow-up.

3. Fifty-one per cent of all schizophrenics fell into the two best overall outcome groups, 29 per cent fell into the two worst groups and 20 per cent fell into the middle group.

4. At the time of second-year follow-up, 37 per cent (202 out of 543) of schizophrenic patients followed up were psychotic, 31 per cent (169 out of 543) were symptomatic but not psychotic, and 32 per cent (172 out of 543) were asymptomatic.

5. The nature of the course and outcome of schizophrenia varied considerably among centres. Ibadan patients clearly had the best course and outcome: 72 per cent had an episode of inclusion that lasted less than three months; 46 per cent had an episode of inclusion that lasted less than three months followed by a full remission and no further episodes; 65 per cent were in psychotic episode for 15 per cent or less of the follow-up period; 97 per cent remained out of the hospital for more than three-quarters of the follow-up period; and 57 per cent fell into the best overall outcome group, while only 5 per cent fell into the worst overall outcome group. Agra patients had the next best course and outcome for most of the factors considered, including overall outcome.

Aarhus patients had the worst course and outcome: 50 per cent were still in the episode of inclusion at the time of second-year follow-up; 31 per cent fell into the worst overall outcome group and only 6 per cent into the best group. The other centres varied according to the factor being assessed. In general Cali and Moscow patients had an intermediate outcome, and Washington, Taipei and Prague patients a relatively poor outcome.

For all variables considered, the schizophrenic patients in Ibadan, Agra, and Cali (all centres in developing countries) tended to have a better outcome on average than the schizophrenic patients in the other six centres (except for Cali on pattern of course). Chi-square analysis indicates that the results are statistically significantly similar within the three centres in developing countries and within the centres in developed countries, and that the differences between these two groups are statistically significant for percentage of time psychotic and presence of severe social impairment. The schizophrenic patients in Agra and Ibadan had a better outcome on every variable than those in Aarhus, London, Washington, and Prague, with Cali and Moscow being intermediate on some variables. (Taipei was not included in these analyses for the reasons indicated earlier.)

6. Of schizophrenic patients who had subsequent episodes, the vast majority had episodes that were schizophrenic or probably schizophrenic. However, 16 per cent of schizophrenics who had subsequent episodes had only subsequent affective psychotic episodes.

7. The symptom profiles of the groups of patients given an initial evaluation diagnosis of schizophrenia were for the most part similar to one another at the time of the second-year follow-up. The groups at follow-up were characterized mainly by negative and non-specific symptoms rather than by positive psychotic symptoms. The level of psychopathology in the schizophrenic patient groups was in general low at the time of second-year follow-up, and was particularly low in the three centres in developing countries, Agra, Cali and Ibadan.

8. Comparison of the initial evaluation and second-year follow-up profiles of groups of patients diagnosed as schizophrenic at initial evaluation indicate that the group profiles on the two occasions are significantly similar to one another. This similarity appears to be accounted for mainly by similarity in negative and non-specific symptoms.

9. Analyses based on CATEGO classification, a method which gives clinical weights to symptoms and which considers individual patients, indicated that in most centres less than half of patients were placed in a CATEGO class that represented a definite psychosis at the time of follow-up in all centres. A high percentage of patients that had an initial evaluation diagnosis of schizophrenia and that were psychotic at second-year follow-up fell into the same CATEGO class on both occasions. This indicates that those schizophrenic patients that were psychotic at follow-up tended to have the same type of psychosis they presented at initial evaluation.

These findings will be compared with those for other diagnostic groups in Chapter 8. The course and outcome of the subgroups of schizophrenia will be described in Chapter 9. The implication of all of these findings for the hypotheses concerning the nature of schizophrenia stated at the beginning of this chapter will be discussed in Chapter 11.

CHAPTER 7

Course and Outcome of Patients with an Initial Evaluation Diagnosis other than Schizophrenia

This chapter will review the data concerning the two-year course and outcome of patients with initial evaluation diagnosis of psychotic depression, mania and other psychoses.*

7.1 PSYCHOTIC DEPRESSION (ICD CATEGORIES 296.0, 296.2, 298.0)

7.1.1 Symptomatic picture at the time of follow-up

7.1.1.1 Symptom profiles – Groups of Units of Analysis (GUAs)

Table 7.1 presents, for the groups of patients diagnosed as having a psychotic depression on initial evaluation, the average percentage scores on groups of units of analysis at the time of second-year follow-up. Psychotic depression refers to the ICD diagnoses of involutional melancholia, manic-depressive psychosis, depressed and reactive depressive psychosis. The figures are given for all centres combined, and for Aarhus, Moscow and Prague. †

It can be seen from this table that the level of psychopathology for these groups of patients at the time of the second-year follow-up was extremely low. There are only seven GUAs in which at least one centre had more than a minimal score (10 per cent) — affect-laden thoughts; lack of insight; depressed-elated: flatness of affect; other affective changes; psychophysical symptoms and cooperation difficulties, circumstances-related. It is striking that scores on GUAs representing positive psychotic symptoms such as delusions, experiences of control, auditory hallucinations, other hallucinations and derealization were never higher than 2. Thus, it can be said that these patient groups had very little in the way of

---

*As the groups of patients given non-psychotic diagnoses at initial evaluation were extremely heterogeneous and differed greatly from centre to centre, and as the numbers of patients with the same specific diagnosis in different centres were quite small, analyses were not carried out for this group of patients.

†Throughout this volume, statistical analyses in general were done for patient groups with 15 or more patients. Moscow and Prague have 15 or more patients. Aarhus, with 13 patients, is included for descriptive purposes. The profile of the ten patients who were psychotic at the second-year follow-up is also presented for descriptive purposes.

TABLE 7.1. AVERAGE PERCENTAGE SCORES ON 27 GROUPS OF UNITS
OF ANALYSIS AT 2ND YEAR FOLLOW-UP. PSYCHOTIC
DEPRESSION.

Groups of Units of Analysis	Aarhus N=13	Moscow N=15	Prague N=19	All Centres N=72
Quantitative psychomotor disorder	1	3	-	1
Qualitative psychomotor disorder	-	-	-	-
Quantitative disorder of form of thinking	6	1	1	2
Qualitative disorder of form of thinking	-	-	-	-
Affect-laden thoughts	13	9	2	7
Predelusional signs	7	1	2	4
Experiences of control	2	-	-	1
Delusions	1	2	-	1
Neurasthenic complaints	4	9	5	6
Lack of insight	38	26	10	19
Distortion of self-perception	-	2	-	1
Derealization	-	-	-	2
Auditory hallucinations	-	-	-	2
"Characteristic" hallucinations	-	-	-	-
Other hallucinations	-	-	-	-
Pseudohallucinations	-	-	-	-
Depressed-elated	2	13	1	4
Anxiety, tension, irritability	4	5	3	5
Flatness	3	19	5	7
Incongruity	-	-	-	-
Other affective change	1	11	1	3
Indication of personality change	1	4	1	2
Disregard of social norms	-	-	-	-
Other behavioural change	5	3	-	2
Psychophysical disorders	3	14	7	7
Cooperation difficulties, circumstances-related	28	13	24	17
Cooperation difficulties, patient-related	4	7	4	5

symptomatology at the time of second-year follow-up, and what symptoms they did demonstrate were primarily affective and non-specific symptoms, with a striking lack of positive psychotic symptoms.

The shapes of symptom profiles of Moscow and Prague, the only two centres with 15 or more patients, were statistically compared using ANOVA analysis, and the profiles did not show significant difference. The τ-value for the comparison of the profile in these two centres was calculated, and the τ-value was 0.71 which indicates a high degree of similarity. Thus, it can be said that the symptom profiles of the psychotic depressive patients in these two centres were significantly similar to one another at the time of the second-year follow-up.

There were ten follow-up patients with an initial evaluation diagnosis of psychotic depression who were psychotic at the time of second-year follow-up according to the criteria described in section 6.2.3. These patients were characterized mainly by affect-laden thoughts, predelusional signs, derealization, auditory hallucinations, depressed-elated symptoms, anxiety, flatness of affect, psychophysical signs and co-operation difficulties.

7.1.1.2 Symptom profiles – 15 most frequent Units of Analysis (UAs)

The 15 most frequently positive units of analysis for the psychotic depressive groups are presented in Table 7.2. It can be seen from this table that on the unit of analysis level those symptoms which were present among these groups of patients at the time of second-year follow-up were primarily depressive symptoms, and that the centres are rather similar to one another with regard to symptoms which were among the 15 most frequent in their psychotically depressed groups of patients.

The symptom of feeling worse in the morning was present in 30.6 per cent of all

TABLE 7.2. 15 MOST FREQUENT UNITS OF ANALYSIS AT THE TIME OF 2ND YEAR FOLLOW-UP. PSYCHOTIC DEPRESSION.

R	All centres combined N = 72	S	Aarhus N=13 R	S	Moscow N=15 R	S	Prague N=19 R	s
1	Worse in morning	30.6	2=	23.1	2	58.3	1	36.8
2	Lack of insight	19.4	1	38.5	4=	26.7	4=	10.5
3	Early waking	16.7			4=	26.7	2	26.3
4=	Gloomy thoughts	15.3	2=	23.1	3	33.3		
4=	Hypochondriacal (neurasthenic complaints)	5.3			4=	26.7	4=	10.5
6=	Hopelessness	13.9	6=	15.4				
6=	Situation anxiety	13.9	2=	23.1	1	60.0	4=	10.5
6=	Lability of affect	13.9						
9	Obsessive thoughts	9.2					3	21.1
10=	Delusional mood	8.3	6=	15.4			8=	5.3
10=	Anxiety	8.3					8=	5.3
10=	Sleep problems	8.3	6=	15.4			8=	5.3
10=	Inadequate description	8.3			8=	20.0	8=	5.3
10=	Flatness	8.3			8=	20.0	8=	5.3
10=	Social withdrawal	8.3					8=	5.3
10=	Unwilling to cooperate	8.3					4=	10.5

168

psychotic depressive patients followed up. Other depressive symptoms among the highest for all centres combined were early waking, gloomy thoughts, and hopelessness.

7.1.1.3 CATEGO

The similarity of psychotically depressed patients at the time of second-year follow-up was also assessed by comparing their CATEGO classifications at the time of second-year follow-up. These are presented in Table 7.3. It can be seen that the vast majority of patients fell into CATEGO classes which do not represent definite psychosis. This finding is consistent with the profile analyses which indicated that at second-year follow-up the level of symptomatology of these patients was low and that there was a striking lack of positive psychotic symptoms. Out of patients with an initial evaluation diagnosis of psychotic depression 22 per cent fell into CATEGO class representing retarded or neurotic depression at second-year follow-up, while 3 per cent fell into the CATEGO class representing psychotic depression.

TABLE 7.3.   PERCENTAGE DISTRIBUTION OF PATIENTS WITH INITIAL EVALUATION DIAGNOSIS OF PSYCHOTIC DEPRESSION BY CATEGO CLASS ASSIGNED ON THE BASIS OF PSE DATA AT THE TIME OF 2ND YEAR FOLLOW-UP.

Centre	No. of patients	S	P	O	M	D	R+N+	Other	Total
Moscow	15	-	7	-	-	7	33	53	100
Prague	19	-	5	-	-	-	21	74	100
All centres	72	3	3	1	-	3	22	68	100

7.1.1.4 Presence or absence of psychotic and other symptoms at second-year follow-up

The followed-up psychotic depressive patients were categorized into three groups according to their second-year follow-up symptomatological picture – psychotic; symptomatic but not psychotic; and asymptomatic* – using the same criteria as described in section 6.2.3. It was found that 14 per cent (10 out of 72) of the patients were psychotic, 47 per cent (34 out of 72) were symptomatic but not psychotic, and 38 per cent (28 out of 72) were asymptomatic* at the time of second-year follow-up.

7.1.2 Comparison of symptomatic picture at the time of initial evaluation with the symptomatic picture at the time of second-year follow-up

7.1.2.1 Symptom profiles – Groups of Units of Analysis (GUAs)

Figure 7.1 shows the symptom profiles on the GUA level for all psychotic depressive patients at the time of initial evaluation and at the time of second-year

*As indicated in Chapter 6, these asymptomatic patients were symptom-free in the sense that evaluation with the PSE did not reveal them to have any symptoms. It is possible that mild neurotic or psychosomatic symptoms not covered by the PSE may have been present.

169

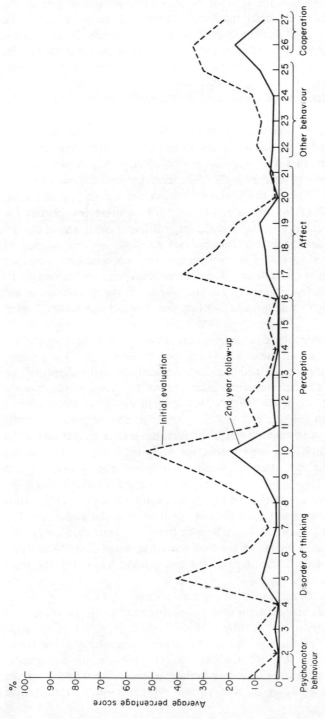

Figure 7.1 Comparison of scores of 27 GUAs at initial evaluation and second-year follow-up. Psychotic depression (72 patients). Groups of units of analysis: 1 Quantitative psychomotor disorder. 2 Qualitative psychomotor disorder. 3 Quantitative disorder of form of thinking. 4 Qualitative disorder of form of thinking. 5 Affect-laden thoughts. 6 Predelusional signs. 7 Experiences of control. 8 Delusions. 9 Neurasthenic complaints. 10 Lack of insight. 11 Distortion of self-perception. 12 Derealization. 13 Auditory hallucinations. 14 'Characteristic' hallucinations. 15 Other hallucinations. 16 Pseudohallucinations. 17 Depressed—elated. 18 Anxiety, tension, irritability. 19 Flatness. 20 Incongruity. 21 Other affective change. 22 Indication of personality change. 23 Disregard for social norms. 24 Other behavioural change. 25 Psychophysical disorders. 26 Co-operation difficulties, circumstances-related. 27 Co-operation difficulties, patient-related

follow-up. It can be seen that the level of psychopathology at the time of the second-year follow-up is much lower than at the time of initial evaluation. The most striking changes are those relating to the depressive symptoms. Thus, the score on affect-laden thoughts fell from 38 to 7, and on depressed-elated symptoms from 36 to 4. The score on quantitative psychomotor disorder, which includes retardation and stupor, fell from 12 to 1. Also there is an almost complete absence of any positive psychotic symptoms, such as delusions, at the time of the second-year follow-up.

ANOVA analyses of the distances between the initial evaluation and second-year follow-up profiles and of comparisons of the shapes of the initial evaluation and second-year follow-up profiles were carried out for all centres combined and for Moscow and Prague, the two centres with 15 or more patients followed up. The analysis of the distance between the initial evaluation and second-year follow-up profiles in Moscow and Prague indicates that in each of these two centres the profiles on the two occasions were significantly different with regard to the amount of psychopathology present. The analyses also indicate that in each of these two centres the *shapes* of the profiles on the two occasions were not significantly different from one another. Kendall's τ-values were also calculated to assess the degree of similarity of the shapes of the profiles on the two occasions and these indicated a very high level of similarity of pattern of psychopathology in each of the two centres.

For all centres combined, the same findings are noted, except that the ANOVA analyses indicate significant differences in the shapes of the profiles. The seeming contradiction between the τ-value and the ANOVA analysis of the shapes of the profiles is explained by the fact that τ considers the average group profile in terms of rank order of symptoms, while the ANOVA analysis compares the profile of each individual patient on one occasion with the profiles of all other patients on the other occasion in terms of absolute scores. Therefore, the results suggest that at the time of second-year follow-up a large percentage of patients improved, while for those who had symptoms the pattern of symptomatology remained similar to that on initial evaluation. This suggestion is supported by a comparison of the second-year follow-up profiles of the ten patients who were psychotic at that time with the profiles of those same ten patients at the time of initial evaluation. The profiles are presented in Figure 7.2. It can be seen from this figure that the profiles of these patients were fairly similar on the two occasions; τ and ANOVA analyses were not carried out for the comparison of the two profiles because of the small number of patients involved.

From these analyses and the previous consideration of Figure 7.1, which indicated the marked decrease in depressive symptoms and the virtual absence of positive psychotic symptoms on second-year follow-up, it appears that for most patients with psychotic depression on initial evaluation the similarity in pattern of symptomatology primarily reflects similarity in the pattern of non-specific symptoms. For the few patients who were psychotic at second-year follow-up, the similarity also reflects similarity in the pattern of psychotic and depressive symptoms.

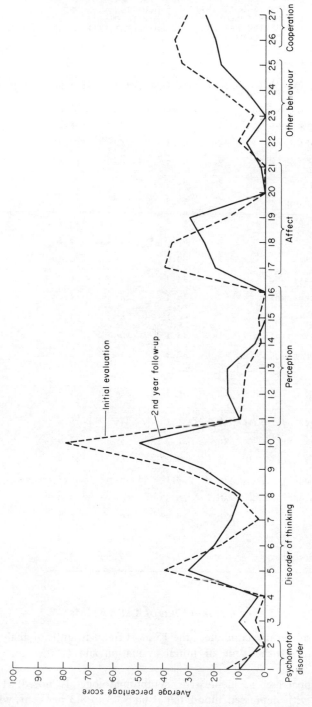

Figure 7.2 Comparison of scores of 27 GUAs at initial evaluation and second-year follow-up. Initial evaluation psychotic depressive patients considered psychotic at follow-up (10 patients). Groups of units of analysis: 1 Quantitative psychomotor disorder. 2 Qualitative psychomotor disorder. 3 Quantitative disorder of form of thinking. 4 Qualitiative disorder of form of thinking. 5 Affect-laden thoughts. 6 Predelusional signs. 7 Experiences of control. 8 Delusions. 9 Neurasthenic complaints. 10 Lack of insight. 11 Distortion of self-perception. 12 Derealization. 13 Auditory hallucinations. 14 'Characteristic' hallucinations. 15 Other hallucinations. 16 Pseudohallucinations. 17 Depressed—elated. 18 Anxiety, tension, irritability. 19 Flatness. 20 Incongruity. 21 Other affective change. 22 Indication of personality change. 23 Disregard for social norms. 24 Other behavioural change. 25 Psychophysical disorders. 26 Co-operation difficulties, circumstances-related. 27 Co-operation difficulties, patient-related

172

TABLE 7.4. COMPARISON OF THE 15 MOST FREQUENT UNITS
OF ANALYSIS AT INITIAL EVALUATION (IE) AND
2ND YEAR FOLLOW-UP (2FU). PSYCHOTIC
DEPRESSIVE PATIENTS (72 PATIENTS), ALL
CENTRES COMBINED.

Units of Analysis	Rank order at IE	Score at IE	Rank order at 2FU	Score at 2 FU
Depressed mood	1	83.3	10=	8.3
Gloomy thoughts	2=	65.3	4=	15.3
Hopelessness	2=	65.3	6=	13.9
Early waking	4	64.5	3	16.7
Worse in morning	5	55.6	1	30.6
Lack of insight	6	52.8	2	19.4
Anxiety	7=	50.0	10=	8.3
Sleep problems	7=	50.0	10=	8.3
Self-depreciation	9=	44.4	18	6.9
Lack of concentration	9=	44.4	28=	4.2
Retardation	11=	43.1	28=	4.2
Inadequate description	11=	43.1	10=	8.3
Decreased energy	13	40.3	34	2.8
Undecided	14	37.5	28=	4.2
Tension	15	36.1	28=	4.2
Hypochondriacal delusions	17=	31.9	4=	15.3
Situation anxiety	26=	22.2	6=	13.9
Lability of affect	46	9.7	6=	13.9
Obsessive thoughts	36	18.1	9	9.2
Delusional mood	30=	20.8	10=	8.3
Flatness	30=	20.8	10=	8.3
Social withdrawal	17=	31.9	10=	8.3
Unwilling to cooperate	26=	22.2	10=	8.3

7.1.2.2 Symptom profiles – 15 most frequent Units of Analysis (UAs)

Table 7.4 presents, for all centres combined, the 15 most frequent units of analysis for followed-up patients at the time of initial evaluation and at the time of second-year follow-up.

Again, a striking decrease in depressive symptomatology is noted. The percentage of patients with depressed mood fell from 83.3 to 8.3 per cent, with gloomy thoughts from 65.3 to 15.3 per cent, with hopelessness from 65.3 to 13.9

per cent, early waking from 64.5 to 16.7 per cent, and sleep problems from 50.0 to 8.3 per cent. The one clearly psychotic symptom among the 15 most frequent UAs at the time of initial evaluation, delusions of self-depreciation, fell from 44.4 to 6.9 per cent. Retardation fell from 43.1 to 4.2 per cent. On the other hand, non-specific symptoms, while decreasing in frequency, did not decrease as strikingly as the depressive and psychotic symptoms.

7.1.2.3 CATEGO

The similarity of the initial evaluation and second-year follow-up clinical pictures of psychotically depressed patients was further compared by determining how many patients had the same CATEGO classification on both occasions.

Out of the 72 patients with an initial evaluation diagnosis of psychotic depression 33 were in the same CATEGO class on both initial evaluation and second-year follow-up.

7.1.3 Course of psychotic depressive patients between initial evaluation and second-year follow-up

The course of illness of psychotically depressed patients during the interval between initial evaluation and second-year follow-up was considered in terms of length of episode of inclusion, percentage of follow-up period spent in a psychotic episode, pattern of course, type of subsequent episodes, degree of social impairment during the follow-up period, percentage of follow-up period spent out of hospital and overall outcome grouping. The findings for all of these factors except type of subsequent episode, which will be described separately, are presented in Table 7.5. Figures are presented for all centres combined and for the two centres with 15 or more patients.

7.1.3.1 Length of episode of inclusion

It can be seen from this table that 39 per cent of all followed-up psychotically depressed patients had an episode of inclusion which lasted less than one month, and 60 per cent had an episode of inclusion which lasted less than three months. Only 9 per cent had an episode of inclusion which lasted 18 months or longer and only 12 per cent had an episode of inclusion which lasted nine months or longer. The mean length of the episode of inclusion was 4.5 months. There were no significant differences between the distribution of patients among the five groups in Moscow and the distribution in Prague. The mean length of the episode of inclusion was five months in Moscow and 4.9 months in Prague.

7.1.3.2 Percentage of time spent in a psychotic episode

Out of all psychotically depressed patients followed up 26 per cent spent 5 per cent or less of the follow-up period in a psychotic episode, and 54 per cent spent 15 per cent or less of the follow-up period in such an episode. On the other extreme, only

TABLE 7.5. COURSE AND OUTCOME OF PATIENTS WITH A
DIAGNOSIS OF PSYCHOTIC DEPRESSION AT INITIAL
EVALUATION.   PERCENTAGE DISTRIBUTION BY 2
YEAR COURSE AND OUTCOME GROUPS.

Length of episode of inclusion

Centre	No. of patients	1 <1 month	2 1-3 months	3 3-9 months	4 9-18 months	5 >18 months	Total	Mean
All centres	71	39	21	28	3	9	100	4.5
Moscow	15	40	20	27	-	13	100	5.0
Prague	18	22	22	44	6	6	100	4.9

Percentage of follow-up time spent in psychotic episodes

Centre	No. of patients	1 1-5%	2 6-15%	3 16-45%	4 46-75%	5 76-100%	Total	Mean
All centres	68	26	28	25	12	9	100	21.3
Moscow	15	27	33	27	-	13	100	22.9
Prague	17	12	23	41	12	12	100	24.9

Pattern of course

Centre	No. of patients	1	2	3	4	5	6	7	Total
All centres	73	35	21	3	-	11	23	7	100
Moscow	15	20	27	-	-	13	33	7	100
Prague	19	26	26	-	-	16	26	6	100

Pattern of course groups:

1 = full remission after episode of inclusion, no further episodes.
2 = incomplete remission after episode of inclusion, no further episodes.
3 = one or more non-psychotic episodes after episode of inclusion, full remission between all episodes.
4 = one or more non-psychotic episodes after episode of inclusion, at least one incomplete remission.
5 = one or more psychotic episodes after episode of inclusion, full remission between all episodes.
6 = one or more psychotic episodes after episode of inclusion, at least one incomplete remission.
7 = still in episode of inclusion.

TABLE 7.5. continued

Level of social functioning

Centre	No. of patients	No severe impairment	Severe impairment	Total
All centres	73	90	10	100
Moscow	15	87	13	100
Prague	19	89	11	100

Percentage of follow-up period spent out of hospital

Centre	No. of patients	1 >90%	2 75-90%	3 50-75%	4 25-50%	5 <25%	Total	Mean (days)
Moscow	13	62	8	15	-	15	100	568
Prague	17	47	35	18	-	-	100	646

* There is no figure for all centres combined because the
possible effects of sociocultural and hospital procedure
variables on the figures make it undesirable to combine
figures from different centres.

Overall outcome

Centre	No. of patients	1 Very favourable	2 Favourable	3 Inter-mediate	4 Unfav-ourable	5 Very unfav-ourable	Total
All centres	70	39	31	19	4	7	100
Moscow	15	40	26	20	7	7	100
Prague	18	17	44	28	-	11	100

9 per cent of psychotic depressives spent more than 75 per cent of the follow-up period in a psychotic episode, while 21 per cent spent more than 45 per cent of the follow-up period in such an episode. The mean percentage of the follow-up period spent in a psychotic episode was 21.3 per cent. There were no significant differences between Moscow and Prague with regard to percentage of time spent in a psychotic episode.

7.1.3.3 Pattern of course

In 34 per cent of psychotic depressives the episode of inclusion was followed by a full remission and no subsequent episodes, while in an additional 21 per cent it was followed by a partial remission with no subsequent episodes. Thus, 56 per cent of psychotic depressives had a full or partial remission after the episode of inclusion and no subsequent episodes.

Seven per cent of psychotic depressive patients followed up were still in the episode of inclusion at the time of second-year follow-up, while 34 per cent had had psychotic episodes after the episode of inclusion. Prague and Moscow were similar with regard to the pattern of course of psychotically depressed patients.

Considering in more detail the psychotic depressives who had a full remission after the episode of inclusion, and no subsequent episodes, it was found that 16 per cent of all psychotically depressed patients followed up had an episode of inclusion which lasted less than one month, followed by full remission and no further episodes, while 26 per cent had an episode of inclusion which lasted less than three months, followed by a full remission throughout the follow-up period.

7.1.3.4 Type of subsequent episodes

Twenty-seven psychotically depressed patients had subsequent episodes. Of these none had a definitely schizophrenic episode, two had a probably schizophrenic episode, 23 had effective psychotic episodes, and two had neurotic episodes. Thus, it can be seen that the vast majority of psychotic depressives having subsequent episodes had affective psychotic episodes, and only two had a probably schizophrenic subsequent episode.

7.1.3.5 Degree of social impairment during the follow-up period

Using the criteria described under section 6.4.5 psychotic depressive patients were categorized into two groups — those suffering from severe social impairment during the follow-up period and those not suffering from severe social impairment during this period. It can be seen from Table 7.5 that 10 per cent of psychotic depressives suffered from severe social impairment, while 90 per cent did not. Moscow and Prague were quite similar with regard to the percentage with severe social impairment, 13 per cent and 11 per cent respectively.

7.1.3.6 Percentage of follow-up period spent out of the hospital

There were no significant differences between Moscow and Prague with regard to the percentage of follow-up period spent out of the hospital. Since these two centres are similar with regard to sociocultural conditions and availability of services, it is reasonable to make a direct comparison of the figures.

7.1.3.7 Overall outcome

Psychotic depressive patients were classified into one of five overall outcome groups, using the same criteria as described in section 6.4.7; here 34 per cent fell into the best overall outcome group (less than 15 per cent of the follow-up period spent in a psychotic episode, no severe social impairment, and full remission), while only 7 per cent fell into the worst overall outcome group (more than 75 per cent of the follow-up period spent in a psychotic episode, or 46 to 75 per cent of the follow-up period spent in a psychotic episode and severe social impairment), 70 per cent fell into the two best groups, while only 11 per cent fell into the two worst groups. There were no significant differences between Moscow and Prague with regard to overall outcome.

7.1.4. Summary of findings concerning the course and outcome of psychotically depressed patients during the follow-up period

The previous three sections have reviewed various aspects of the course and outcome during a two-year follow-up period of IPSS patients given an initial evaluation diagnosis of psychotic depression. The following main points stand out from this review.

1. A fairly high percentage of patients given an initial evaluation diagnosis of psychotic depression had a very good two-year course and outcome: 39 per cent (27 out of 70) of all psychotic depressive patients spent less than 15 per cent of the follow-up period in a psychotic episode, did not suffer from any severe social impairment, and had full remissions; 16 per cent (12 out of 73) had an episode of inclusion which lasted less than one month, followed by a full remission and no subsequent episodes.

2. A very small percentage of patients given an initial evaluation diagnosis of psychotic depression had a very poor course and outcome: only 12 per cent (8 out of 71) had an episode of inclusion which lasted nine months or longer; only 9 per cent (6 out of 68) spent more than 75 per cent of the follow-up period in a psychotic episode; only 7 per cent (5 out of 73) were still in the episode of inclusion at the time of second-year follow-up; only 10 per cent (7 out of 73) suffered severe social impairment during the follow-up period; and only 7 per cent (5 out of 70) fell into the worst overall outcome group.

3. Seventy per cent (49 out of 70) of all psychotic depressives followed up fell into the best overall outcome groups; 11 per cent (8 out of 70) fell into the two

178

worst overall outcome groups; and 19 per cent (13 out of 70) fell into the middle group.

4. At the time of second-year follow-up 14 per cent (10 out of 72) of followed-up patients with an initial evaluation diagnosis of psychotic depression were psychotic; 47 per cent (34 out of 72) were symptomatic but not psychotic at this time; and 39 per cent (28 out of 72) were asymptomatic.

5. Since the numbers of psychotic depressive patients followed up in the individual centres were small, it is difficult to make comparisons between centres. For the two centres which had 15 or more followed-up patients, Moscow and Prague, there were no significant differences in the two-year course and outcome.

6. Of the psychotically depressed patients who had subsequent episodes, the vast majority had only affective psychotic episodes, and none had a definitely schizophrenic and only two had a probably schizophrenic subsequent episode.

7. The patient group initially diagnosed as psychotically depressed was characterized at follow-up mainly by depressive and non-specific symptoms. Positive psychotic symptoms were rare. The level of psychopathology of this patient group at the time of second-year follow-up was very low.

The symptom profiles of the groups of patients given an initial evaluation diagnosis of psychotic depression were significantly similar to one another at the time of second-year follow-up, for the two centres with a large enough number of followed-up patients to make comparisons.

8. Comparison of the initial evaluation and second-year follow-up profiles of psychotically depressed patients indicates that the group profiles are similar to one another. The similarity appears to be accounted for mainly by similarity in non-specific symptoms. The profile of the ten patients who were psychotic at the time of second-year follow-up was similar to the initial evaluation profile of the same ten patients.

9. Analyses based on CATEGO classification indicated that at second-year follow-up the vast majority of patients fell into CATEGO classes which do not represent definite psychoses – 22 per cent of patients with an initial evaluation diagnosis of psychotic depression fell into a CATEGO class representing retarded or neurotic depression, while 3 per cent fell into the CATEGO class representing psychotic depression; 33 of the 72 patients followed up fell into the same CATEGO class on both initial evaluation and second-year follow-up.

These findings will be compared with those for other diagnostic groups in Chapter 8.

7.2 MANIA (ICD CATEGORY 296.1)

7.2.1 Symptomatic picture at the time of second-year follow-up

7.2.1.1 Symptom profiles – Groups of Units of Analysis (GUAs)

Table 7.6 presents, for the group of patients given the diagnosis of manic-depressive psychosis, manic type, on initial evaluation, the average percentage scores on groups

TABLE 7.6.   AVERAGE PERCENTAGE SCORES ON 27 GROUPS OF UNITS
OF ANALYSIS AT 2ND YEAR FOLLOW-UP.   MANIA.

Groups of Units of Analysis	Aarhus N=17	Agra N=18	All Centres N=51
Quantitative psychomotor disorder	1	1	2
Qualitative psychomotor disorder	-	-	-
Quantitative disorder of form of thinking	9	3	7
Qualitative disorder of form of thinking	2	-	1
Affect-laden thoughts	13	4	8
Predelusional signs	7	2	4
Experiences of control	9	-	4
Delusions	6	2	5
Neurasthenic complaints	4	2	2
Lack of insight	29	27	27
Distortion of self-perception	3	-	1
Derealization	2	-	1
Auditory hallucinations	14	4	9
"Characteristic" hallucinations	5	2	3
Other hallucinations	-	-	1
Pseudohallucinations	8	-	2
Depressed-elated	11	3	10
Anxiety, tension, irritability	5	1	3
Flatness	5	2	3
Incongruity	-	-	-
Other affective change	4	2	3
Indication of personality change	5	-	2
Disregard of social norms	2	2	3
Other behavioural change	5	1	3
Psychophysical disorders	7	4	6
Cooperation difficulties, circumstances-related	23	-	18
Cooperation difficulties, patient-related	11	6	9

TABLE 7.7.   15 MOST FREQUENT UNITS OF ANALYSIS AT THE
              TIME OF 2ND YEAR FOLLOW-UP, ALL CENTRES
              COMBINED.   MANIA (51 PATIENTS).

Rank	Units of Analysis	Score
1	Lack of insight	27.4
2=	Elated thoughts	19.6
2=	Early waking	19.6
4	Observed elated mood	15.7
5	Worse in morning	13.7
6=	Ideas of reference	11.8
6=	Self-depreciation	11.8
6=	Presence of verbal hallucinations	11.8
6=	Voices speak to patient	11.8
6=	Presence of auditory hallucinations	11.8
6=	Depressed mood	11.8
6=	Sleep problems	11.8
6=	Unwilling to cooperate	11.8
14=	Flight of ideas	9.8
14=	Pressure of speech	9.8
14=	Hopelessness	9.8
14=	Delusion of grandeur	9.8
14=	Delusion of reference	9.8
14=	Religious delusions	9.8
14=	Increased libido	9.8
14=	Poor rapport	9.8
14=	Distractibility	9.8
14=	Inadequate description	9.8

of units of analysis at the time of second-year follow-up. Only two centres, Aarhus
and Agra had 15 or more such patients followed up.

It can be seen from this table that the level of psychopathology for the manic
patients was very low at the time of second-year follow-up. There were only six
GUAs on which there was more than a minimal score (10 per cent) in at least one
centre: affect-laden thoughts; lack of insight; auditory hallucinations; depressed-
elated symptoms; co-operation difficulties, circumstances-related; and co-operation
difficulties, patient-related. Scores were low on GUAs which represent positive
psychotic symptoms, except on auditory hallucinations in Aarhus. The Aarhus

patients tended to have somewhat higher scores than the Agra patients. Agra patients had no score over six except on lack of insight. For all centres combined, only lack of insight, depressed-elated symptoms, and co-operation difficulties related to circumstances had scores of 10 or more. Thus, it can be seen that the manic patients showed very little psychopathology at the time of second-year follow-up, and what symptoms they did show were primarily non-specific and affective symptoms. The shapes of the symptom profiles of manic patients in Aarhus and Agra were statistically compared by ANOVA analysis, which indicated that the profiles are not significantly different. The τ value for comparison of the two profiles indicated that the profiles have a high degree of similarity.

The 15 most frequently positive units of analysis for the manic group of patients, all centres combined, are presented in Table 7.7.

It can be seen that at the UA level the symptoms which characterized the manic patients at the time of second-year follow-up were mainly affective symptoms: elated thoughts (19.6 per cent) of patients; early waking (19.6 per cent); observed elated mood (15.7 per cent); worse in morning (13.7 per cent); sleep problems, delusions of self-depreciation, and depressed mood (all 11.8 per cent). A relatively high percentage of patients had positive psychotic symptoms at the time of second-year follow-up: 11.8 per cent delusions of self-depreciation; 11.8 per cent auditory hallucinations; 9.8 per cent delusions of reference and 9.8 per cent delusions of grandeur.

7.2.1.2 CATEGO

The similarity of manic patients at the time of second-year follow-up was also assessed by comparing their CATEGO classifications at the time of second-year follow-up. These are presented in Table 7.8. It can be seen that 70 per cent of the manic patients followed up fell into CATEGO classes which do not represent definite psychoses; 10 per cent fell into CATEGO class M (representing mania) and 14 per cent into either CATEGO class S (representing schizophrenia) or P (representing paranoid psychosis). These results are consistent with the profile analyses presented above, which indicated that the manic patients had a low level of psychopathology at second-year follow-up; 10 per cent of the manic patients fell into CATEGO class R or N at follow-up (representing retarded and neurotic depression). Only 18 per cent of Agra manics followed up fell into a CATEGO class representing a definite psychosis, compared to 41 per cent of followed-up manics in Aarhus; 12 per cent of Aarhus manic patients fell into a CATEGO class representing retarded or neurotic depression at follow-up, while none of the Agra manic patients fell into such a CATEGO class at follow-up.

7.2.1.3 Presence or absence of psychotic and other symptoms at second-year follow-up

The manic patients were characterized into three groups according to their clinical condition at second-year follow-up — psychotic, symptomatic but not psychotic,

TABLE 7.8.   PERCENTAGE DISTRIBUTION OF PATIENTS WITH
INITIAL EVALUATION CLINICAL DIAGNOSIS OF
MANIA BY CATEGO CLASS ASSIGNED ON THE BASIS
OF PSE DATA AT THE TIME OF 2ND YEAR
FOLLOW-UP.

Centre	No. of patients	CATEGO classes							
		S	P	O	M	D	R+N+	Other	Total
Aarhus	17	17	-	12	12	-	12	47	100
Agra	18	6	6	-	6	-	-	82	100
All centres	51	12	2	6	10	-	10	60	100

and asymptomatic – using the criteria described in section 6.2.3. It was found that 25% of manic patients were psychotic at the time of second year follow up, 37% were symptomatic but not psychotic, and 37% were asymptomatic.

7.2.2 Comparison of symptomatic picture at the time of initial evaluation with the symptomatic picture at the time of second-year follow-up

7.2.2.1 Symptom profiles – Groups of Units of Analysis (GUAs)

Figure 7.3 shows the symptom profiles on the GUA level for all manic patients at the time of initial evaluation and at the time of second-year follow-up. It can be seen that the level of psychopathology was considerably lower at the time of second-year follow-up. The GUAs on which scores decreased most dramatically were derealization (14 to 1), incongruity of affect (9 to 0), disregard for social norms (23 to 3), other behavioural changes, which includes demonstrative behaviour (20 to 3), and co-operation difficulties, patient-related (36 to 9). Scores on the affective GUAs such as affect-laden thoughts, and depressed-elated symptoms, did decrease, but not any more than for most other GUAs. Thus, it appears that the manic patients lost most of their grossly inappropriate behaviour, but retained a fair amount of their affective symptoms.

ANOVA analyses of the distance between the initial evaluation and second-year follow-up profiles and of comparisons of the shapes of the initial evaluation and second-year follow-up profiles were carried out for all centres combined and for Aarhus and Agra. The analysis of the distance between the initial evaluation and second-year follow-up profiles indicates that in Agra the profiles on the two occasions were significantly different, while in Aarhus the differences did not quite reach the 0.001 level of significance ($p = 0.003$) with regard to the amount of psychopathology present. The analyses indicate that in both centres the shapes of the profiles were not significantly different on the two occasions; τ values were calculated to assess the degree of similarity of the shapes of the profiles on the two occasions, and these indicated a high level of similarity of pattern of symptomatology in each of the two centres.

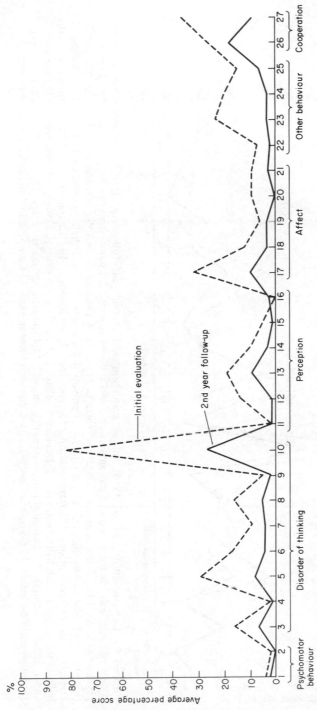

Figure 7.3 Comparison of scores of 27 GUAs at initial evaluation and second-year follow-up. Mania (51 patients). Groups of units of analysis: 1 Quantitative psychomotor disorder. 2 Qualitative psychomotor disorder. 3 Quantitative disorder of form of thinking. 4 Qualitative disorder of form of thinking. 5 Affect-laden thoughts. 6 Predelusional signs. 7 Experiences of control. 8 Delusions. 9 Neurasthenic complaints. 10 Lack of insight. 11 Distortion of self-perception. 12 Derealization. 13 Auditory hallucinations. 14 'Characteristic' hallucinations. 15 Other hallucinations. 16 Pseudohallucinations. 17 Depressed—elated. 18 Anxiety, tension, irritability. 19 Flatness. 20 Incongruity. 21 Other affective change. 22 Indication of personality change. 23 Disregard for social norms. 24 Other behavioural change. 25 Psychophysical disorders. 26 Co-operation difficulties, circumstances-related. 27 Co-operation difficulties, patient-related

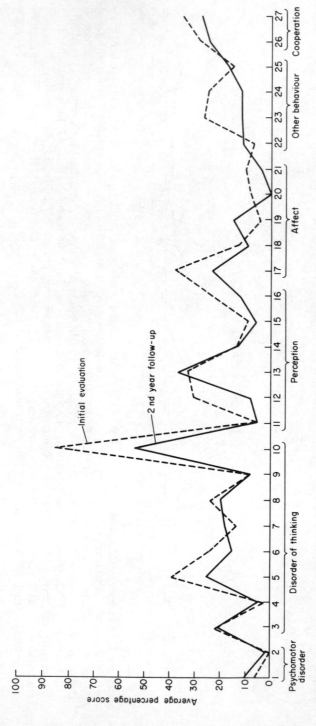

Figure 7.4 Comparison of 27 GUAs at initial evaluation and second-year follow-up. Initial evaluation manic patients considered psychotic at follow-up (13 patients). Groups of units of analysis: 1 Quantitative psychomotor disorder. 2 Qualitative psychomotor disorder. 3 Quantitative disorder of form of thinking. 4 Qualitative disorder of form of thinking. 5 Affect-laden thoughts. 6 Predelusional signs. 7 Experiences of control. 8 Delusions. 9 Neurasthenic complaints. 10 Lack of insight. 11 Distortion of self-perception. 12 Derealization. 13 Auditory hallucinations. 14 'Characteristic' hallucinations. 15 Other hallucinations. 16 Pseudohallucinations. 17 Depressed—elated. 18 Anxiety, tension, irritability. 19 Flatness. 20 Incongruity. 21 Other affective change. 22 Indication of personality change. 23 Disregard for social norms. 24 Other behavioural change. 25 Psychophysical disorders. 26 Co-operation difficulties, circumstances-related. 27 Co-operation difficulties, patient-related

When the profiles of all centres combined were considered, ANOVA analyses indicated that the initial evaluation and second-year follow-up profiles are significantly different from one another in terms of both the distance between the profiles and in terms of the shapes of the profiles. On the other hand, τ analysis indicated a high degree of similarity in the shape of the profiles. These results probably reflect the fact that the shapes of the profiles on the two occasions in at least some of the centres other than Aarhus and Agra, are not similar. The reason that, for the profiles of all centres combined, τ indicates significant similarity between profiles on the two occasions, while ANOVA indicates significant difference, is that τ considers the average profiles on the two occasions in terms of rank order of symptoms, while ANOVA compares each individual patient's profile on one occasion, with all other patient's profiles on another occasion in terms of absolute scores. These findings suggest that a high percentage of the manic patients improved, and that for those who had symptoms at second-year follow-up, the pattern of symptomatology remained similar to that on initial evaluation.

Figure 7.4 compares the initial evaluation and the second-year follow-up profiles of the 13 initial evaluation manic patients who were psychotic (according to the criteria outlined in section 6.2.3.) at the time of second-year follow-up. It can be seen from this figure that the profiles are fairly similar. Statistical profile analyses were not carried out because of the small number of patients.

7.2.2.2 15 most frequent Units of Analysis (UAs)

Table 7.9 presents, for followed-up manics, all centres combined, the 15 most frequently positive units of analysis at the time of initial evaluation and at the time of second-year follow-up. It can be seen that there is considerable similarity among the symptoms which characterize the patients on the two occasions, as 12 of the symptoms which were among the 15 most frequent at the time of initial evaluation were also among the 15 most frequent at second-year follow-up. The most striking changes were on delusions of persecution where the percentage of patients with the symptom fell from 49 to 7.8 and suspiciousness where the percentage fell from 47 to 7.8.

7.2.2.3 CATEGO

The similarity of the initial evaluation and second-year follow-up clinical pictures of manic patients was further compared by determining how many patients had the same CATEGO classification on both occasions. Only ten of the 51 followed-up manic patients had the same CATEGO classification on both occasions.

7.2.3 Course of manic patients in the interval between initial evaluation and second-year follow-up

The course of illness in manic patients was considered in terms of the same factors as for schizophrenia and psychotic depression and the results are presented in Table

TABLE 7.9.   COMPARISON OF THE 15 MOST FREQUENT UNITS OF
             ANALYSIS AT INITIAL EVALUATION AND AT 2ND
             YEAR FOLLOW-UP, MANIA, ALL CENTRES COMBINED.

Units of Analysis	Rank order at IE	Score at IE	Rank order at 2 FU	Score at 2 FU
Elated thoughts	1	88.2	2=	19.6
Lack of insight	2=	82.3	1	27.4
Observed elated mood	2=	82.3	4	15.7
Delusions of grandeur	4=	54.9	14=	9.8
Unwilling to cooperate	4=	54.9	6=	11.8
Delusions of persecution	6=	49.0	25=	7.8
Early waking	6=	49.0	2=	19.6
Inadequate description	6=	49.0	14=	9.8
Suspiciousness	9	47.0	25=	7.8
Increased interest	10=	41.2	14=	9.8
Sleep problems	10=	41.2	6=	11.8
Ideas of reference	12	39.2	6=	11.8
Flight of ideas	13=	33.3	14=	9.8
Disorder of pitch	13=	33.3	25=	7.8
Demonstrative	13=	33.3	64	2.0
Worse in morning	43	11.8	5	13.7
Self-depreciation	51=	7.8	6=	11.8
Presence of verbal hallucinations	23=	23.5	6=	11.8
Voices speak to patient	23=	23.5	6=	11.8
Presence of auditory hallucinations	23=	23.5	6=	11.8
Depressed mood	51=	7.8	6=	11.8
Pressure of speech	39	13.7	14=	9.8
Hopelessness	51=	7.8	14=	9.8
Delusions of reference	19	27.4	14=	9.8
Religious delusions	28	19.6	14=	9.8
Increased libido	17=	29.4	14=	9.8
Poor rapport	26	21.6	14=	9.8
Distractibility	17=	29.4	14=	9.8

7.10 except for type of subsequent episodes, which will only be described in the
text. Figures are presented for all centres combined and for the two centres with 15
or more patients. In considering the comments about statistical significance for the
comparisons between Aarhus and Agra, it should be kept in mind that the numbers
of patients involved are small.

7.2.3.1 Length of episode of inclusion

It can be seen from this table that in 45 per cent (24 out of 53) of manic patients,
the episode of inclusion lasted less than one month and in 79 per cent (42 out of

53) it lasted less than three months. Only 2 per cent (1 out of 53) of manic patients had an episode of inclusion which lasted nine months or longer. The mean length of the episode of inclusion for manic patients was 2.5 months. There was no significant difference between the distribution of patients among the five groups in Aarhus and Agra.

7.2.3.2 Percentage of time spent in a psychotic episode

Out of the manic patients followed up 17 per cent (9 out of 52) spent 5 per cent or less of the follow-up period in a psychotic episode, and 54 per cent (28 out of 52) spent 15 per cent or less of the follow-up period in such an episode. At the other extreme only 4 per cent (2 out of 52) of manic patients were in a psychotic episode for more than 75 per cent of the follow-up period, and only 9 per cent (5 out of 52) were in a psychotic episode for more than 45 per cent of the time. The mean percentage of the follow-up period spent in a psychotic episode by manic patients was 16.8 per cent. There were no significant differences between Agra and Aarhus with regard to percentage of the follow-up period patients spent in a psychotic episode.

7.2.3.3 Pattern of course

In 29 per cent (15 out of 51) of manic patients, the episode of inclusion was followed by a full remission and no further episodes, while in an additional 10 per cent (5 out of 51) it was followed by a partial remission and no subsequent episodes.

Two per cent of the manic patients (1 out of 51) were still in the episode of inclusion at the time of the second-year follow-up and 59 per cent (30 out of 51) had subsequent psychotic episodes after the episode of inclusion. There were no statistically significant differences in the distributions by patterns of course between Aarhus and Agra.

Considering in more detail the manics who had a full remission after the episode of inclusion, and no subsequent episodes, it was found that 14 per cent of all manics followed up had an episode of inclusion which lasted less than one month, followed by full remission and no further episodes, and 27 per cent had an episode of inclusion which lasted less than three months followed by full remission and no further episodes.

7.2.3.4 Type of subsequent episodes

Thirty-two manic patients had subsequent episodes. Of these, one had subsequent episodes considered to be definitely schizophrenic, four had subsequent episodes considered to be probably schizophrenic, 26 had subsequent episodes considered to be affective psychotic episodes, and one had an episode classified as 'other psychosis'.

TABLE 7.10.   COURSE AND OUTCOME OF PATIENTS WITH A DIAGNOSIS
OF MANIA AT INITIAL EVALUATION.   PERCENTAGE
DISTRIBUTION BY COURSE AND OUTCOME.

Length of episode of inclusion

Centre	No. of patients	1 <1 month	2 1-3 months	3 3-9 months	4 9-18 months	5 >18 months	Total	Mean
All centres	53	45	34	19	-	2	100	2.5
Aarhus	17	65	12	23	-	-	100	2.0
Agra	18	39	44	17	-	-	100	2.2

Percentage of follow-up period spent in psychotic episodes

Centre	No. of patients	1 1-5%	2 6-15%	3 16-45%	4 46-75%	5 76-100%	Total	Mean
All centres	52	17	37	37	5	4	100	16.8
Aarhus	17	18	29	47	-	6	100	17.2
Agra	18	22	33	39	6	-	100	13.3

Pattern of course

Centre	No. of patients	1	2	3	4	5	6	7	Total
All centres	51	29	10	-	-	51	8	2	100
Aarhus	16	13	13	-	-	56	18	-	100
Agra	18	50	6	-	-	44	-	-	100

Pattern of course groups:

1 = full remission after episode of inclusion, no further episodes.
2 = incomplete remission after episode of inclusion, no further
    episodes.
3 = one or more non-psychotic episodes after episode of inclusion,
    full remission between all episodes.
4 = one or more non-psychotic episodes after episode of inclusion,
    at least one incomplete remission.
5 = one or more psychotic episodes after episode of inclusion,
    full remission between all episodes.
6 = one or more psychotic episodes after episode of inclusion,
    at least one incomplete remission.
7 = still in episode of inclusion.

TABLE 7.10. continued

Level of social functioning

Centre	No. of patients	No severe impairment	Severe impairment	Total
All centres	53	91	9	100
Aarhus	17	82	18	100
Agra	18	94	6	100

Percentage of follow-up period spent out of hospital

Centre *	No. of patients	>90%	75-90%	50-75%	25-50%	<25%	Total	Mean (days)
Aarhus	17	47	35	12	6	-	100	650
Agra	18	67	28	5	-	-	100	667

* There is no figure for all centres combined because the possible effects of sociocultural and hospital procedure variables on the figures make it undesirable to combine figures from different centres.

Overall outcome

Centre	No. of patients	1 Very favourable	2 Favourable	3 Inter-mediate	4 Unfav-ourable	5 Very unfav-ourable	Total
All centres	51	49	31	12	6	2	100
Aarhus	17	41	29	24	-	6	100
Agra	18	55	33	6	6	-	100

7.2.3.5 Degree of social impairment during the follow-up period

Using the criteria described under 6.4.5. manic patients were categorized into those suffering from severe social impairment and those not suffering from such impairment during the follow-up period. It can be seen from Table 7.10 that, overall, 9 per cent (5 out of 53) were considered to have severe social impairment; and 91 per cent (48 out of 53) were not considered to have such impairment. There was no significant difference between Aarhus and Agra with regard to the number of manic patients with severe social impairment.

7.2.3.6 Percentage of follow-up period spent out of hospital

Sixty-seven per cent (12 out of 18) of Agra manics and 47 per cent (8 out of 17) of Aarhus manics spent more than 90 per cent of the follow-up period out of the hospital; 95 per cent (17 out of 18) of Agra manics and 82 per cent (14 out of 17) of Aarhus manics spent more than 75 per cent of the follow-up period out of the hospital. The differences are not significant.

7.2.3.7 Overall outcome

Manic patients were classified into one of five overall outcome groups, according to the same criteria described in Chapter 6, section 6.4.7. Forty-nine per cent (25 out of 51) fell into the best outcome group (less than 15 per cent of the follow-up period in a psychotic episode, no severe social impairment, and full remissions), while only 2 per cent (1 out of 51) fell into the worst overall outcome group (more than 75 per cent of the follow-up period in a psychotic episode or 46 to 75 per cent of the follow-up period in a psychotic episode and severe social impairment); 80 per cent fell into the two best groups, 8 per cent fell into the two worst groups, with 12 per cent in the middle group. Aarhus and Agra manics were quite similar with regard to overall outcome grouping.

7.2.4 Summary of findings concerning the course and outcome of manic patients during the follow-up period

1. A fairly high percentage of patients given an initial evaluation diagnosis of manic-depressive psychotic, manic type had a very good two-year course and outcome: 49 per cent spent less than 15 per cent of the follow-up period in a psychotic episode, did not suffer severe social impairment, and had full remissions; 27 per cent had an episode of inclusion which lasted less than three months and which was followed by a full remission and no subsequent episodes.

2. A very small percentage of patients given an initial evaluation diagnosis of manic depressive psychosis, manic type, had a very severe course and outcome: only 2 per cent had an episode of inclusion which lasted nine months or longer; only 4 per cent spent 75 per cent or more of the follow-up period in a psychotic episode; only 2 per cent were still in the episode of inclusion at the time of the second-year follow-up; only 9 per cent were considered to suffer from severe social impairment; and only 2 per cent fell into the worst overall outcome group.

3. Eighty per cent of all manics fell into the two best overall outcome groups; 8 per cent fell into the two worst overall outcome groups; and 12 per cent fell into the middle group.

4. At the time of the second-year follow-up, 25 per cent of the manic patients were psychotic, 37 per cent were symptomatic but not psychotic, and 37 per cent were asymptomatic.

5. Since the numbers of manic patients followed up in individual centres was small, it is difficult to make comparisons between centres. Comparing the two centres with more than 15 manics followed up, Aarhus and Agra, it is noted that for all criteria there are no statistically significant differences between the two centres.

6. Of the 32 manic patients who had subsequent episodes, the vast majority (26) had affective psychotic episodes, although a few (five) had schizophrenic or probably schizophrenic episodes.

7. The symptom profile of the manic group of patients at the time of second-year follow-up was characterized mainly by affective and non-specific symptoms, although some patients had positive psychotic symptoms. The level of psychopathology at the time of second-year follow-up was, in general, low.

8. Comparison of the initial evaluation and second-year follow-up profiles of manic patients indicates that the group profiles on the two occasions are similar to one another.

9. At second-year follow-up, 70 per cent of patients with an initial evaluation diagnosis of mania were classified in CATEGO classes that do not represent definite psychoses. Only 10 per cent classified in CATEGO class M (representing mania); 10 per cent were classified in CATEGO class R or N (representing retarded and neurotic depression.)

These findings will be compared with those for other diagnostic groups in Chapter 8.

7.3 OTHER PSYCHOSES

Analyses of course and outcome similar to those described in the previous three sections were carried out for the group of other psychoses. This group is composed of 62 patients with the following initial evaluation diagnoses: paranoia, involutional paraphrenia, other paranoid states, reactive excitation, reactive confusion, acute paranoid reaction, unspecified reactive psychosis, and unspecified psychosis. The main findings were:

1. A high percentage of patients in this group had a very good two-year course and outcome: 39 per cent spent less than 15 per cent of the follow-up period in a psychotic episode, did not suffer severe social impairment during the follow-up period, and had full remissions; 28 per cent had an episode of inclusion which lasted less than three months, followed by a full remission which lasted throughout the follow-up period.

2. Some of the patients in this group had a very bad two-year course and outcome: 20 per cent had an episode of inclusion which lasted nine months or

longer and 15 per cent were still in the episode of inclusion at the time of the second-year follow-up. However, only 8 per cent were considered to have suffered from severe social impairment during the follow-up period, and only 3 per cent fell into the worst overall outcome group.

3. Out of all patients in this group 67 per cent fell into the two best overall outcome groups, 14 per cent fell into the two worst overall outcome groups, and 19 per cent fell into the middle group.

4. The mean length of the episode of inclusion was 5.7 months. The mean percentage of the follow-up period spent in a psychotic episode was 24.1 per cent.

5. At the time of the second-year follow-up, 28 per cent (15 out of 53) of the patients in this group were psychotic, 43 per cent (23 out of 57) were symptomatic but not psychotic, and 28 per cent (15 out of 53) were asymptomatic.

6. Sixteen patients in this group had subsequent episodes. Of these, two had an episode considered to be definitely schizophrenic, six had episodes considered to be probably schizophrenic, one had an affective psychotic episode, four had non-psychotic episodes, one had an episode characterized as 'other psychosis' one had a mixture of an affective psychosis episode with a probably schizophrenic episode, and in one patient the subsequent episode could not be classified.

7. The level of psychopathology of this patient group on second-year follow-up was very low, and symptoms which characterized the group were mainly non-specific symptoms.

8. Comparisons of the initial evaluation and second-year follow-up profiles indicates that the group profiles on the two occasions were significantly similar in pattern, although the levels of psychopathology were significantly different.

9. Of the patients in this group 64 per cent fell into a CATEGO class which does not represent a definite psychosis at the time of second-year follow-up; 21 per cent of patients fell into the same CATEGO class on both initial evaluation and second-year follow-up, and 80 per cent of those patients who were psychotic on second-year follow-up fell into the same CATEGO classification on both occasions.

Since the category 'other psychoses' is a heterogeneous category, the composition of which may vary from centre to centre, intercentre comparisons were not made.

These findings will be compared with those for other diagnostic groups in Chapter 8.

CHAPTER 8

Comparison among Diagnostic Groups Within and Between Centres

In the previous two chapters, the results of analyses were used to provide a picture of the course and outcome of patients in the same diagnostic group, within and between centres. As a consideration of many of the hypotheses listed at the beginning of Chapter 6 involves comparisons between diagnostic groups, this chapter will utilize the results of the same analyses to make comparisons among different diagnostic groups, within and between centres. For most of the comparisons, the following groups will be considered: schizophrenia, psychotic depression, mania, and other psychoses. Comparisons will be made within and between centres for patient groups in which there were at least 15 patients followed up. As in Chapters 6 and 7, the groups are defined in terms of the diagnosis of patients at the time of initial evaluation.

8.1 COMPARISON AMONG PSYCHOTIC DIAGNOSTIC GROUPS IN TERMS OF SYMPTOM PICTURE AT THE TIME OF SECOND-YEAR FOLLOW-UP

8.1.1 Groups of Units of Analysis (GUAs)

Volume 1 of the report of the IPSS (WHO, 1973) indicated that the symptom pictures of the major functional psychoses were distinguishable from one another at the time of initial evaluation. To determine if this was still true at the time of follow-up evaluation, the second-year follow-up profiles of the following pairs of diagnostic groups were compared: schizophrenia-psychotic depression; schizophrenia-mania, and schizophrenia-other psychosis. Figure 8.1 presents these comparisons graphically. It can be seen that the second-year follow-up profiles of all of the psychoses are quite similar to one another. The only GUAs on which there was higher than a minimum score of 10 per cent for any diagnostic group were lack of insight, flatness of affect, co-operation difficulties (circumstances-related) and co-operation difficulties (patient-related). The schizophrenic group was the only group with a relatively high score of flatness of affect, and scored highest on lack of insight and co-operation difficulties. None of the diagnostic groups had high scores on any of the GUAs representing positive psychotic symptoms such as hallucinations or delusions. The manic patients had the highest score on depressed-elated symptoms (10 per cent). The schizophrenic patients had the highest score on disregard for social norms (6 per cent).

194

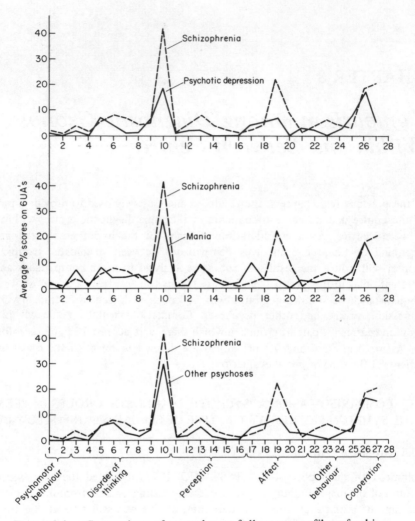

Figure 8.1   Comparison of second-year follow-up profiles of schizophrenia with profiles of psychotic depression, mania and other psychoses. Groups of units of analysis: 1 Quantitative psychomotor disorder. 2 Qualitative psychomotor disorder. 3 Quantitative disorder of
form of thinking. 4 Qualitative disorder of form of thinking. 5
Affect-laden thoughts. 6 Predelusional signs. 7 Experiences of control.
8 Delusions. 9 Neurasthenic complaints. 10 Lack of insight. 11 Distortion of self-perception. 12 Derealization. 13 Auditory hallucinations. 14 'Characteristic' hallucinations. 15 Other hallucinations.
16 Pseudohallucinations. 17 Depressed–elated. 18 Anxiety, tension,
irritability. 19 Flatness. 20 Incongruity. 21 Other affective change. 22
Indication of personality change. 23 Disregard for social norms. 24
Other behavioural change. 25 Psychophysical disorders. 26 Co-operation difficulties, circumstances-related. 27 Co-operation difficulties,
patient-related

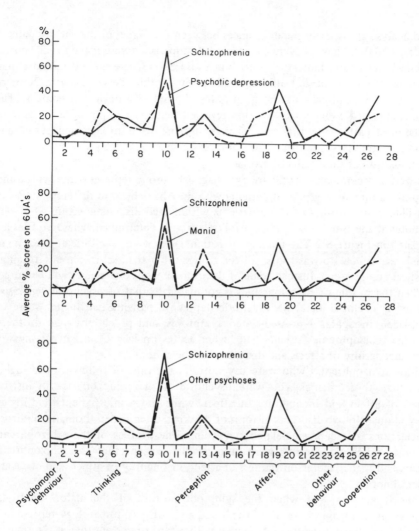

Figure 8.2 Comparison of second-year follow-up profiles of schizophrenia with profiles of psychotic depression, mania and other psychoses. Patients considered psychotic at follow-up. Groups of units of
analysis: 1 Quantitative psychomotor disorder. 2 Qualitative psychomotor disorder. 3 Quantitative disorder of form of thinking. 4 Qualitative disorder of form of thinking. 5 Affect-laden thoughts. 6 Predelusional signs. 7 Experiences of control. 8 Delusions. 9 Neurasthenic
complaints. 10 Lack of insight. 11 Distortion of self-perception. 12
Derealization. 13 Auditory hallucinations. 14 'Characteristic' hallucinations. 15 Other hallucinations. 16 Pseudohallucinations. 17 Depressed—elated. 18 Anxiety, tension, irritability. 19 Flatness. 20 Incongruity. 21 Other affective change. 22 Indication of personality
change. 23 Disregard for social norms. 24 Other behavioural change.
25 Psychophysical disorders. 26 Co-operation difficulties, circumstances-related. 27 Co-operation difficulties, patient-related

To analyse statistically the differences between the shapes of the various pairs of profiles, ANOVA analyses were carried out. Comparisons were made for all centres combined and within individual centres in those cases where there were more than 15 patients followed up in both diagnostic groups within the same centre. None of the pairs of second-year follow-up profiles showed significant differences. The initial results of Kendall's τ calculation revealed that the group profile scores were for the most part so low that small changes in score made for large changes in rank order. Therefore it was felt that it was not reasonable to proceed with such-analyses for comparison of these pairs of profiles.

Since the second-year profile for any diagnostic group represents the symptomatological picture of a group of patients who may have been in different stages of their illness, the profiles of those patients within each diagnostic group who were psychotic at the time of second-year follow-up were determined. These profiles are compared in Figure 8.2 The number of patients who were psychotic at the time of second-year follow-up was too small for groups other than schizophrenia to allow statistical comparisons. Instead some of the more obvious differences will be noted.

When the profile of schizophrenics is compared to that of psychotic depressive patients, it is noted that the psychotic depressive patients had higher score on affect-laden thoughts, depressed-elated symptoms, and psychophysical disorders, while the schizophrenic patients had higher scores on lack of insight, flatness of affect, incongruity of affect, and disregard for social norms.

Those schizophrenics who were psychotic at the time of follow-up had higher scores than those manics who were psychotic at that time on lack of insight, flatness of affect and incongruity of affect, while the manic patients had higher scores on quantitative disorders of form of thinking, affect-laden thoughts, auditory hallucinations and depressed-elated symptoms. The profiles of the schizophrenic and other psychotic patients were quite similar, except that the schizophrenic patients had higher scores on flatness of affect, incongruity of affect, and disregard for social norms.

Thus it appears that when the symptom profiles of the major functional psychoses are compared in terms of the broad areas of symptomatology represented by the GUAs, the groups are quite similar with regard to one another at the time of second-year follow-up. When only patients in a psychotic episode at the time of second-year follow--up are considered, the patients with affective psychoses appear to demonstrate more affective and fewer negative symptoms than the schizophrenic patients. Numbers are not large enough to make a statement about statistical significance of these differences.

8.1.2 Units of Analysis (UAs)

To get a clearer picture of what symptoms were most prominent in different diagnostic groups among those patients who were symptomatic at the time of second-year follow-up, it is useful to consider the units of analysis which were most frequently positive for each of the diagnostic groups. Table 8.1 compares among

TABLE 8.1. COMPARISON AMONG DIAGNOSTIC GROUPS OF 15 MOST FREQUENTLY POSITIVE UNITS OF ANALYSIS AT TIME OF 2ND YEAR FOLLOW-UP. FIGURES IN BRACKETS SHOW THE PERCENTAGE POSITIVE RATINGS OF THE UNITS OF ANALYSIS WITHIN THE RESPECTIVE GROUP OF PATIENTS.

Rank Order	Schizophrenia	Psychotic depression	Mania	Other psychoses
1	Lack of insight (42.5)	Worse in morning (30.6)	Lack of insight (27.4)	Lack of insight (30.2)
2	Flatness (27.1)	Lack of insight (19.4)	Elated thoughts (19.6)	Unwilling to cooperate (22.6)
3	Poor rapport (26.3)	Early waking (15.3)	Early waking (19.6)	Inadequate description (20.8)
4	Suspiciousness (25.2)	Gloomy thoughts (15.3)	Elated mood (15.7)	Suspiciousness (18.9)
5	Inadequate description (25.2)	Hypochondriacal (15.3)	Worse in morning (13.7)	Ideas of reference (17.0)
6	Unwilling to cooperate (24.5)	Hopelessness (13.9)	Ideas of reference (11.8)	Gloomy thoughts (15.1)
7	Apathy (18.8)	Situation anxiety (13.9)	Self-depreciation (11.8)	Poor rapport (15.1)
8	Ideas of reference (18.0)	Lability of affect (13.9)	Verbal hallucinations (11.8)	Worse in morning (11.3)
9	Reference (14.2)	Obsessive thoughts (9.2)	Voices speak to patient (11.8)	Delusions of reference (9.4)
10	Restricted speech (12.9)	Delusional mood (8.3)	Auditory hallucinations (11.8)	Delusional mood (9.4)
11	Persecution (12.7)	Anxiety (8.3)	Depressed mood (11.8)	Tension (9.4)
12	Hypochondriacal (12.7)	Sleep problems (8.3)	Sleep problems (11.8)	Obsessive thoughts (9.4)
13	Autism (12.7)	Inadequate description (8.3)	Unwilling to cooperate (11.8)	Observed elated mood (9.4)
14	Auditory hallucinations (11.6)	Flatness (8.3)	Flight of ideas (9.8)	Situation anxiety (9.4)
15	Verbal hallucinations (10.7)	Social withdrawal (8.3)	Pressure of speech (9.8)	Flatness (9.4)
		Unwilling to cooperate (8.3)	Hopelessness (9.8)	Worse in morning (9.4)
			Delusions of grandeur (9.8)	
			Delusions of reference (9.8)	
			Religious delusions (9.8)	
			Increased interest (9.8)	

diagnostic groups the 15 most frequently positive units of analysis at the time of second-year follow-up.

It can be seen that the most frequently positive units of analysis for the schizophrenic patient group are mainly negative and non-specific symptoms such as flatness of affect, lack of insight, poor rapport, co-operation difficulties, suspiciousness, and apathy. On the other hand, for the psychotic depressive group and the manic group, the most frequently positive units of analysis are mainly affective symptoms. There are no positive psychotic symptoms among the 15 most frequently positive UAs for the psychotic depressive group, while delusions of self-depreciation and auditory hallucinations were present among 11.8 per cent of the manic patients; 14.2 per cent of the schizophrenic patients had delusions of reference at the time of follow-up, 12.7 per cent had delusions of persecution, and 11.6 per cent had auditory hallucinations. In the 'other psychosis' group, both affective symptoms (such as gloomy thoughts) and non-specific symptoms (such as lack of insight, poor rapport, and co-operation difficulties) were among the most frequently positive UAs; 9.4 per cent had delusions of reference at the time of the second-year follow-up.

When only patients in a psychotic episode at the time of second-year follow-up are considered, the patients with an initial evaluation diagnosis of an affective psychosis appeared to demonstrate more affective and fewer negative symptoms than the schizophrenic patients.

8.1.3 CATEGO

Another way of comparing second-year follow-up symptom profiles of patients given different initial evaluation diagnoses is to compare their CATEGO classifications at the time of second-year follow-up. Table 8.2 indicates for groups given an initial evaluation diagnosis of schizophrenia, psychotic depression, mania, or other psychosis, the percentage of patients who fell into each CATEGO classification.

It can be seen from this table that only 10 per cent of the psychotic depressive patients followed up fell into a CATEGO class representing definite psychosis, while 40 per cent of the initial evaluation schizophrenics followed up fell into such a class at the time of second-year follow-up. The manic and other psychosis groups were in between, with 30 per cent and 37 per cent respectively falling into a CATEGO class representing definite psychosis. Out of initial evaluation schizophrenic patients 18 per cent fell into CATEGO class S at second-year follow-up compared to only 3 per cent of psychotic depressive patients followed-up, while 12 per cent of initial evaluation manic patients and 9 per cent of patients in the other psychosis group fell into this class on follow-up; 22 per cent of psychotic depressive patients, 10 per cent of manic patients, 9 per cent of other psychosis patients, and 7 per cent of schizophrenic patients fell into CATEGO classes R or N representing retarded and neurotic depression.

Thus, in terms of CATEGO results the clearest differences were between schizophrenia and psychotic depression, with more schizophrenics than psychotic depressive patients falling into a psychotic and schizophrenic category at the time

TABLE 8.2. COMPARISON AMONG DIAGNOSTIC GROUPS OF 2ND YEAR
FOLLOW-UP CATEGO CLASSIFICATION.

2nd year follow-up CATEGO classification	Initial Evaluation Clinical Diagnosis			
	Schizophrenia N=542	Psychotic Depression N=72	Mania N=51	Other Psychoses N=53
S	18	3	12	9
P	8	3	2	8
O	8	1	6	8
M	5	-	10	8
D	1	3	-	-
R+N+	7	22	10	9
Other	53	68	60	58
Total	100	100	100	100

of second-year follow-up, and more psychotic depressive than schizophrenic patients falling in a category denoting a retarded or neurotic depression at second-year follow-up.

8.2 COMPARISON AMONG DIAGNOSTIC GROUPS IN TERMS OF CLINICAL STATE AT SECOND-YEAR FOLLOW-UP

As described in Chapter 6, patients were categorized according to their clinical state at the time of second-year follow-up as psychotic, symptomatic but not psychotic, and asymptomatic. Table 8.3 compares the results among the diagnostic groups of schizophrenia, psychotic depression, mania and other psychosis for all centres combined.

It can be seen that the schizophrenic group had the highest percentage of patients who were psychotic at the time of second-year follow-up. The difference between the distributions into the three categories is statistically significant for the

TABLE 8.3. PERCENTAGE OF PATIENTS PSYCHOTIC, SYMPTOMATIC BUT
NOT PSYCHOTIC AND ASYMPTOMATIC AT 2ND YEAR FOLLOW-
UP BY INITIAL EVALUATION DIAGNOSTIC GROUPS.

Diagnostic group	No. of Patients	Psychotic	Symptomatic but not psychotic	Asymptomatic	Total
Schizophrenia	543	37	31	32	100
Psychotic depression	72	14	47	39	100
Mania	51	26	37	37	100
Other psychoses	53	28	44	28	100

TABLE 8.4. INTRA-CENTRE COMPARISONS OF PERCENTAGES OF PATIENTS PSYCHOTIC, SYMPTOMATIC BUT NOT PSYCHOTIC AND ASYMPTOMATIC AT 2ND YEAR FOLLOW-UP, BY INITIAL EVALUATION DIAGNOSTIC GROUP.

Centre	Diagnostic group	No. of patients	Psychotic	Symptomatic but not psychotic	Asymptomatic	Total
Aarhus	Schizophrenia	49	61	31	8	100
	Mania	17	35	59	6	100
	Other Psychoses	18	44	39	17	100
Agra	Schizophrenia	88	32	12	56	100
	Mania	18	11	22	67	100
Moscow	Schizophrenia	66	38	61	1	100
	Psychotic Depression	15	20	80	-	100
Taipei	Schizophrenia	61	41	33	26	100
	Other Psychoses	17	18	41	41	100
Prague	Schizophrenia	53	34	38	28	100
	Psychotic Depression	19	5	58	37	100

comparison of schizophrenia with psychotic depression. A high percentage of patients in all groups were asymptomatic at second-year follow-up, ranging from 28 per cent for the other psychotic group to 39 per cent for the psychotic depression group.

Table 8.4 presents the results of the same analyses within individual centres for those diagnostic groups with more than 15 patients followed up.

In all centres the percentage of schizophrenics who were psychotic at second-year follow-up, was higher than the percentage of patients in the other diagnostic groups who were psychotic at that time, but the differences were significant only in Prague, between schizophrenia and psychotic depression. However, this trend supports the finding from all centres combined that more schizophrenic patients than other patients were psychotic at the time of second-year follow-up.

8.3 COMPARISON AMONG DIAGNOSTIC GROUPS IN TERMS OF COURSE DURING THE INTERVAL BETWEEN INITIAL EVALUATION AND SECOND-YEAR FOLLOW-UP

In Chapters 6 and 7, for each diagnostic group, the course of illness was considered during the interval between initial evaluation and second-year follow-up in terms of length of episode of inclusion, percentage of follow-up period spent in a psychotic episode, pattern of course, type of subsequent episode, degree of social impairment during the follow-up period, percentage of follow-up period spent out of hospital, and overall outcome. This section will reconsider those findings, making comparisons among diagnostic groups for all centres combined and within individual centres. In this section, whenever differences are stated to be significantly different, p is equal to or less than 0.01.

8.3.1. Length of the episode of inclusion

8.3.1.1 All centres combined

Table 8.5 presents the percentage distribution of patients in each diagnostic group by length of episode of inclusion and the mean length of the episode of inclusion for each diagnostic group. Chi-square analysis indicates that the diagnostic groups differ significantly ($p < 0.01$) with regard to the distribution of patients into the five lengths of episode of inclusion of groups. When the distributions for the three non-schizophrenic groups were compared, the differences were also statistically significant. It can be seen that the manic patients tended to have the shortest episodes of inclusion, with 45 per cent of manic patients having an episode of inclusion which lasted less than one month, 79 per cent having an episode of inclusion which lasted less than three months, and only 2 per cent having an episode of inclusion which lasted nine months or longer. The mean length of the episode of inclusion among manic patients was 2.5 months. The schizophrenic patients tended to have the longest episodes of inclusion. In 28 per cent of them

TABLE 8.5. PERCENTAGE DISTRIBUTION OF PATIENTS IN EACH PSYCHOTIC DIAGNOSTIC GROUP BY LENGTH OF EPISODE OF INCLUSION.

All centres combined

Diagnostic group	No. of patients	<1 month	1-3 months	2 months	3 months	3-9 months	4 9-18 months	5 >18 months	Total	Mean (months)
Schizophrenia	568	28	28		14		3	27	100	8.6
Psychotic depression	71	39	21		28		3	9	100	4.5
Mania	53	45	34		19		-	2	100	2.5
Other psychoses	61	31	36		13		5	15	100	5.7

the episode of inclusion lasted less than one month, in 56 per cent less than three months, in 27 per cent 18 months or longer and in 30 per cent nine months or longer. The mean length of the episode of inclusion for schizophrenic patients was 8.6 months. The psychotic depressive patients were rather close to the manic patients, tending to have only slightly longer episodes of inclusion: in 39 per cent, the episode of inclusion lasted less than one month, in 60 per cent, it lasted less than three months, in 12 per cent nine months or more, and in 9 per cent eighteen months or more. The mean length of the episode of inclusion was 4.5 months. The results for the 'other psychosis' group were closer to those for the schizophrenic group than to those for the affective psychosis groups.

Using the length of the episode of inclusion as the criterion, it can thus be seen that manic patients had the best outcome, followed closely by patients with psychotic depression, while schizophrenic patients had the worst outcome.

8.3.1.2 Intra-centre comparisons

Table 8.6 presents the same analyses for those within centre comparisons that were possible.

Schizophrenia — mania. In Aarhus and Agra it was possible to compare the length of the episode of inclusion of manic patients with that of schizophrenic patients. It can be seen that in Aarhus there was a striking difference between the two groups: the mean length of the episode of inclusion was 13.9 months among the schizophrenic patients, and two months among the manic patients. In schizophrenic patients the episode of inclusion lasted 18 months or longer in 50 per cent and nine months or longer in 54 per cent, less than one month in only 19 per cent and less than three months in 42 per cent. No Aarhus manics had an episode of inclusion which lasted nine months or longer, while in 65 per cent, it lasted less than one month and in 77 per cent less than three months. These differences are statistically significant. In Agra, 22 per cent of the schizophrenics and none of the manics had an episode of inclusion which lasted nine months or longer. The differences in distributions did not reach the level of statistical significance.

Schizophrenia — psychotic depression. It was possible to compare schizophrenia and psychotic depression in terms of the length of the episode of inclusion in Moscow and Prague. It can be seen that in Moscow the psychotic depressive patients did somewhat better than the schizophrenic patients, with a smaller percentage of patients falling into groups four and five but the differences are not statistically significant. In Prague, a higher percentage of schizophrenic than psychotically depressed patients were in the episode of inclusion for 18 months or more (33 per cent compared to 6 per cent) and the mean length of the episode of inclusion for the schizophrenic patients was 11.0 months compared to 4.9 months for the psychotically depressed group, but there were no statistically significant differences between the two groups with regard to the distribution of patients by the length of episode of inclusion.

TABLE 8.6. PERCENTAGE DISTRIBUTION OF PATIENTS IN EACH PSYCHOTIC DIAGNOSTIC GROUP BY LENGTH OF EPISODE OF INCLUSION.

Centre	Diagnostic group	No. of patients	1 <1 month	2 1-3 months	3 3-9 months	4 9-18 months	5 >18 months	Total	Mean (months)
Aarhus	Schizophrenia	48	19	23	4	4	50	100	13.9
	Mania	17	65	12	23	-	-	100	2.0
	Other psychoses	18	28	33	11	6	22	100	8.1
Agra	Schizophrenia	92	34	31	13	2	20	100	7.1
	Mania	18	39	44	17	-	-	100	2.2
Moscow	Schizophrenia	68	35	31	13	3	18	100	6.4
	Psychotic depression	15	40	20	27	-	13	100	5.0
Taipei	Schizophrenia	79	16	34	18	4	28	100	9.3
	Other psychoses	26	35	31	15	4	15	100	5.5
Prague	Schizophrenia	49	10	29	24	4	33	100	11.0
	Psychotic depression	18	22	22	44	6	6	100	4.9

Schizophrenia – other psychoses. When schizophrenia is compared to other psychoses in Aarhus, it is found that schizophrenic patients tend to have a lower percentage of patients with short episodes of inclusion and a higher percentage of patients with long episodes of inclusion, but the differences in the distribution are not statistically significant. The mean length of the episode of inclusion was shorter in the 'other psychosis' group (8.1 months compared to 13.9 months). In Taipei, a lower percentage of schizophrenics than of patients in the 'other psychosis' group were in the episode of inclusion for less than one month, but the differences in the distributions among the outcome groups were not significant. The mean for the other psychosis group was shorter than for the schizophrenic group.

Thus, although the intracentre differences for the most part did not reach the level of statistical significance, the trends in the individual centres support the finding for all centres combined that schizophrenic patients had longer episodes of inclusion than patients in the other psychotic diagnostic groups.

8.3.2 Percentage of follow-up period spent in psychotic episodes

8.3.2.1 All centres combined

The percentage distribution of patients in each diagnostic group by percentage of time spent in psychotic episodes is presented in Table 8.7.

It can be seen that the schizophrenic patients tended to spend a greater percentage of the follow-up period in psychotic episodes than patients in the other psychotic diagnostic groups. The differences among the four diagnostic groups with regard to the distribution of patients into the five outcome groups are statistically significant. The mean percentage of the follow-up period spent in psychotic episodes by schizophrenic patients was 37.1 per cent, which was higher than the means for the other diagnostic groups.

Patients in the three non-schizophrenic groups were rather similar with regard to the percentage of the follow-up period spent in psychotic episodes although fewer manic patients than patients in the other two groups were in psychotic episodes for more than 75 per cent of the follow-up period or more than 45 per cent of the follow-up period. The distributions for the three non-schizophrenic groups are not significantly different.

8.3.2.2 Intra-centre comparisons

Table 8.8 presents the same analysis for those within-centre comparisons that are possible.

Schizophrenia – mania. Schizophrenia and mania were compared in Aarhus and Agra. In Aarhus, the differences between the two diagnostic groups almost reached the 0.01 level of statistical significance ($p < 0.025$). More Aarhus schizophrenics than Aarhus manics were in psychotic episodes for more than 75 per cent of the follow-up period and for more than 45 per cent of the follow-up period.

TABLE 8.7. PERCENTAGE DISTRIBUTION OF PATIENTS IN EACH PSYCHOTIC DIAGNOSTIC GROUP BY PERCENTAGE OF FOLLOW-UP PERIOD SPENT IN A PSYCHOTIC EPISODE.

All centres combined

Diagnostic group	No. of patients	1 -5%	2 6-15%	3 16-45%	4 46-75%	5 76-100%	Total	Mean
Schizophrenia	543	17	22	26	7	28	100	37.1
Psychotic depression	68	26	28	25	12	9	100	21.3
Mania	52	17	37	37	5	4	100	16.8
Other psychoses	55	20	34	27	4	15	100	24.1

207

TABLE 8.8. PERCENTAGE DISTRIBUTION OF PATIENTS IN EACH PSYCHOTIC DIAGNOSTIC GROUP BY PERCENTAGE OF FOLLOW-UP PERIOD SPENT IN A PSYCHOTIC EPISODE.

Centre	Diagnostic group	No. of patients	1 -5%	2 6-15%	3 16-45%	4 46-75%	5 76-100%	Total	Mean
Aarhus	Schizophrenia	46	13	22	13	4	48	100	53.2
	Mania	17	18	29	47	-	6	100	17.2
	Other psychoses	18	28	33	11	6	22	100	32.5
Agra	Schizophrenia	92	27	24	22	8	19	100	28.7
	Mania	18	22	33	39	6	-	100	13.3
Moscow	Schizophrenia	63	14	26	35	6	19	100	29.6
	Psychotic depression	15	27	33	27	-	13	100	22.9
Taipei	Schizophrenia	77	7	19	30	13	31	100	43.3
	Other psychoses	23	17	35	31	4	13	100-	21.9
Prague	Schizophrenia	44	7	20	30	7	36	100	49.4
	Psychotic depression	17	12	23	41	12	12	100	24.8

Differences between schizophrenic patients and manic patients in Agra did not reach the level of statistical significance, although more schizophrenics than manics spent more than 45 per cent of the follow-up period in psychotic episodes. The mean percentage of time spent in psychotic episodes by schizophrenics in Aarhus was 53.2 per cent while for manics it was 17.2 per cent. In Agra, schizophrenic patients spent an average of 28.7 per cent of the follow-up period in psychotic episodes compared to 13.3 per cent of manic patients.

Schizophrenia – psychotic depression. There were no significant differences between the distribution of schizophrenic patients among the five groups and the distribution of depressive patients among these groups in either Moscow or Prague. The mean percentage of the follow-up period spent in psychotic episodes was 29.6 per cent for schizophrenic patients in Moscow and 22.9 per cent for Moscow psychotic depressives. In Prague, the mean was 49.4 per cent for schizophrenic patients and 24.8 per cent for psychotic depressive patients.

Schizophrenia – other psychoses. In both Aarhus and Taipei, the schizophrenic patients tended to spend a greater percentage of the follow-up period in psychotic episodes than the patients in the other psychoses group, but the differences are not statistically significant. The mean percentage of the follow-up period spent in psychotic episodes was higher for the schizophrenia group than for the other psychoses group in both centres.

Thus, the trends noted in the intracentre comparisons tend to confirm the findings from the comparisons for all centres combined that schizophrenic patients spent a higher percentage of the follow-up in psychotic episodes than did patients in other psychotic diagnostic groups.

8.3.3 Pattern of course

8.3.3.1 All centres combined

Table 8.9 presents the percentage distribution of patients in each diagnostic group by pattern of course group.

The differences among the four diagnostic groups with regard to the distribution of patients among the pattern of course groups are statistically significant. It can be seen that the pattern of course was more severe in the schizophrenic group than in the other groups. The schizophrenic group had the highest percentage of patients still in the episode of inclusion at the time of second-year follow-up (group 7), the highest percentage of patients either still in the episode of inclusion at second-year follow-up or with subsequent psychotic episodes without full remissions (group 6 and group 7), and the lowest percentage of patients in whom the episode of inclusion or a subsequent episode was followed by a full remission (groups 1 and 5).

Among the diagnostic groups, the psychotic depressive group had a relatively high percentage of patients in whom the episode of inclusion was followed by a full remission lasting throughout the follow-up period, and a relatively low percentage

TABLE 8.9. PERCENTAGE DISTRIBUTION OF PATIENTS IN EACH PSYCHOTIC DIAGNOSTIC GROUP BY PATTERN OF COURSE.

All centres combined

Diagnostic group	No. of patients	1 Only episode of inclusion full remission	2 Only episode of inclusion incomplete remission	3 Subsequent non-psychotic episodes full remission	4 Subsequent non-psychotic episodes incomplete remission	5 Subsequent psychotic episodes full remission	6 Subsequent psychotic episodes incomplete remission	7 Still in episode of inclusion	Total
Schizophrenia	570	27	17	-	1	11	18	26	100
Psychotic depression	73	35	21	3	-	11	23	7	100
Mania	51	29	10	-	-	51	8	2	100
Other psychoses	60	35	23	5	2	10	10	15	100

of patients still in the episode of inclusion at the time of the second-year follow-up. A high percentage of manic patients had subsequently psychotic episodes with full remissions between episodes while a low percentage of manic patients were either still in the episode of inclusion or had subsequent psychotic episodes without full remissions between episodes. A relatively high percentage of patients in the other psychosis group were in the worst (group 7) pattern of course group.

Thus, considering all centres combined, it appears that schizophrenics had the most severe pattern of course. The manic and psychotic depressive groups had a relatively high percentage of patients with subsequent psychotic episodes followed by full or partial remission, while the 'other psychoses' group had a relatively high percentage of patients still in the episode of inclusion. The distribution for the three non-schizophrenia groups are significantly different.

A fairly high percentage of patients in all four psychotic diagnostic groups had an episode of inclusion which lasted less than three months and which was followed by a full remission and no further episodes: 28 per cent for other psychoses, 27 per cent for mania, 26 per cent for psychotic depression and 20 per cent for schizophrenia. The differences are not statistically significant.

8.3.3.2 Intracentre comparisons

Table 8.10 presents the results of the pattern of course analysis for those intracentre comparisons that were possible.

Schizophrenia – mania. In Aarhus the distribution of the schizophrenic and manic patients into the pattern of course groups was significantly different. A higher percentage of schizophrenic patients than of manic patients were still in the episode of inclusion at the time of the second-year follow-up or had had subsequent psychotic episodes without full remissions between episodes; 50 per cent of the schizophrenic patients and none of the manic patients were still in the episode of inclusion at follow-up. A higher percentage of the manic patients than of the schizophrenic patients had had subsequent psychotic episodes with full remissions between episodes. The same trends were noted in Agra, although probably because of the small number of patients, the differences in distribution among the outcome groups did not reach the level of statistical significance.

Schizophrenia–psychotic depression. In both Moscow and Prague a higher percentage of schizophrenic patients than of psychotic depressive patients were still in the episode of inclusion at the time of second-year follow-up, while a higher percentage of psychotic depressive patients than of schizophrenic patients had an episode of inclusion which was followed by a full remission and no subsequent episodes. However, the differences in distribution among the outcome groups are not statistically significant.

Schizophrenia – other psychoses. Table 8.10 indicates that in both Aarhus and Taipei, a higher percentage of schizophrenic patients than of patients in the other

211

TABLE 8.10. PERCENTAGE DISTRIBUTION OF PATIENTS IN EACH PSYCHOTIC DIAGNOSTIC GROUP BY PATTERN OF COURSE.

Centre	Diagnostic group	No. of patients	1 only episode of inclusion, full remission	2 only episode of inclusion, incomplete remission	3 subsequent non-psychotic episodes, full remission	4 subsequent non-psychotic episodes, incomplete remission	5 subsequent psychotic episodes, full remission	6 subsequent psychotic episodes, incomplete remission	7 subsequent still in episode of inclusion	Total
Aarhus	Schizophrenia	48	6	23	-	-	4	17	50	100
	Mania	16	13	13	-	-	56	18	-	100
	Other psychoses	18	33	45	-	-	-	-	22	100
Agra	Schizophrenia	90	51	7	-	-	15	7	20	100
	Mania	18	50	6	-	-	44	-	-	100
Moscow	Schizophrenia	69	7	30	-	3	10	32	18	100
	Psychotic depression	15	20	27	-	-	13	33	7	100
Taipei	Schizophrenia	79	27	20	-	-	6	20	27	100
	Other psychoses	25	40	12	-	-	12	20	16	100
Prague	Schizophrenia	53	17	25	-	-	9	19	30	100
	Psychotic depression	19	26	26	-	-	16	26	6	100

psychoses group were still in the episode of inclusion at the time of second-year follow-up, or had had subsequent psychotic episodes without full remissions, while a higher percentage of patients in the other psychoses group than in the schizophrenic group had an episode of inclusion which was followed by a full remission and no subsequent episodes. The differences in distribution among the outcome groups were statistically significant in Aarhus, but not in Taipei.

Thus, the results of intracentre comparisons support the finding of the analyses for all centres combined that schizophrenic patients had a pattern of course which was different from, and more severe than the patterns of course of the patients in the other psychotic diagnostic groups.

8.3.4. Type of subsequent episodes

During the follow-up period, 251 of the patients who had an initial evaluation diagnosis of schizophrenia, psychotic depression, mania, or other psychoses had episodes after the episode of inclusion about which enough information was available to characterize the episodes. On the basis of the follow-up history data, episodes during the follow-up period were classified as definitely schizophrenic, probably schizophrenic (including paranoid and schizo-affective episodes), affective illnesses, other psychotic episodes and non-psychotic episodes. The criteria used are described in section 6.4.4. Table 8.11 indicates the percentage distribution of followed-up patients in each psychotic diagnostic group with subsequent episodes, by type of episode.

It can be seen from this table that the vast majority of schizophrenic patients with subsequent episodes had either definitely schizophrenic or probably schizophrenic episodes, although 16 per cent of them had only subsequent affective psychotic episodes. Of the 27 psychotic depressive patients with subsequent episodes, the vast majority had affective psychotic episodes, none had a definitely schizophrenic episode, and two (7 per cent) had probably schizophrenic episodes.

Thirty-two manic patients had subsequent episodes. The vast majority of these had affective psychotic episodes, one had a definitely schizophrenic episode, and four had probably schizophrenic episodes. Of the fifteen patients in the other psychoses group who had subsequent episodes, two had episodes considered to be definitely schizophrenic, six had episodes considered to be probably schizophrenic, one had an episode of affective psychosis, one had an episode classified as other psychotic episode, four had non-psychotic episodes, and one had a combination of affective psychotic and probably schizophrenic episodes.

When the schizophrenic, affective psychosis, and other psychoses groups are compared with regard to the percentages of patients with definitely or probably schizophrenic subsequent episodes on the one hand, and affective psychotic subsequent episodes on the other hand, the differences are statistically significant. The differences between the affective psychosis group and the other psychoses group are also statistically significant.

Thus, it appears that when the schizophrenic patients had subsequent episodes, they tended to have schizophrenic episodes, when psychotic depressive patients

TABLE 8.11.   PERCENTAGE DISTRIBUTION OF PATIENTS IN EACH PSYCHOTIC DIAGNOSTIC GROUP WITH SUBSEQUENT EPISODES, BY TYPE OF EPISODE.

Type of subsequent episode

Diagnostic group	No. of patients	1	2	3	4	5	Both 1+2	1 or 2 +3	Both 1+4	Both 3+4	Total
Schizophrenia	177	36	39	16	3	2	1	1	1	1	100
Psychotic depression	27	-	7	86	7	-	-	-	-	-	100
Mania	32	3	13	81	-	3	-	-	-	-	100
Other psychoses	15	13	40	7	26	7	-	7	-	-	100

Types of episodes: 1 = only definitely schizophrenic episodes.

2 = only probably schizophrenic episodes.

3 = only affective psychotic episodes.

4 = only non-psychotic episodes.

5 = only other psychotic episodes.

214

TABLE 8.12.   TYPE OF SUBSEQUENT EPISODE AND INITIAL DIAGNOSIS.

Type of subsequent episode	Probability that the initial diagnosis was					
	Schizophrenia	Affective psychosis			Other psychoses	Other diagnoses
		Mania	Depression	Total		
Definitely schizophrenic	95.5	1.5	-	1.5	3.0	-
Affective psychosis	30.4	28.3	25.0	53.3	1.0	15.3
Probably schizophrenic	85.0	5.0	2.5	7.5	7.5	-
Other psychosis	57.1	14.3	-	14.3	14.3	14.3

and manic patients had subsequent episodes they tended to have affective psychotic episodes, and when patients in the other psychoses group had subsequent episodes, they had various types of episodes, but mainly schizophrenic episodes.

However, it should be noted that a fairly high percentage (16 per cent) of the schizophrenic patients who had subsequent psychotic episodes had only affective psychotic episodes, while five of the 32 manic patients with subsequent episodes had definitely or probably schizophrenic episodes.

The numbers of patients who had subsequent episodes were too small to allow intracentre comparisons.

The data about the type of subsequent episode can also be used to assess what was the probability that someone with a specific psychotic type of subsequent episode had been given the initial diagnosis of schizophrenia, mania, depression, other psychosis or a non-psychotic diagnosis. It can be seen from Table 8.12 that patients who had a subsequent psychotic episode of schizophrenic type had a very high probability of having been given an initial evaluation of schizophrenia (95.5 per cent), while those with a subsequent psychotic episode of affective type had a high probability of having been given an initial evaluation diagnosis of affective psychosis (53.3 per cent). For patients with a subsequent episode of a probably schizophrenic type the probability of having been given the diagnosis of schizophrenia was 85 per cent, of affective psychosis 7.5 per cent, and of other psychoses 7.5 per cent. The patients who had a subsequent episode of the other psychoses type were most likely diagnosed as schizophrenic on initial examination.

8.3.5 Degree of social impairment during the follow-up period

8.3.5.1 All centres combined

Table 8.13 indicates, for each psychotic diagnostic group, the percentage of patients considered to have suffered from severe social impairment during the

TABLE 8.13. PRESENCE OR ABSENCE OF SEVERE SOCIAL IMPAIRMENT DURING FOLLOW-UP PERIOD BY PSYCHOTIC DIAGNOSTIC GROUP.

All centres combined

Diagnostic group	No. of patients	No severe impairment (%)	Severe impairment (%)	Total
Schizophrenia	585	77	23	100
Psychotic depression	73	90	10	100
Mania	53	91	9	100
Other psychoses	61	92	8	100

follow-up period. It can be seen that more than twice as high a percentage of schizophrenic patients than of patients in each of the other psychotic diagnostic groups were considered to have had severe impairment during the follow-up period. The differences among the four diagnostic groups with regard to the number of patients with severe social impairment are statistically significant. The differences among the three non-schizophrenic groups are not statistically significant.

8.3.5.2 Intracentre comparisons

The results of the same analysis for those intracentre comparisons that were possible are presented in Table 8.14. A higher percentage of schizophrenics than of patients in the other diagnostic categories were considered to have suffered from severe social impairment in each centre, and the differences were statistically significant in Prague, between schizophrenia and psychotic depression. In Taipei, the differences between schizophrenia and other psychosis almost reached the 0.01 level of significance ($0.01 < p\ 0.025$).

8.3.6 Percentage of follow-up period out of hospital

Table 8.15 indicates, within individual centres, the percentage distribution of patients psychotic diagnostic group by percentage of the follow-up period spent out

TABLE 8.14. PRESENCE OR ABSENCE OF SEVERE SOCIAL IMPAIRMENT BY PSYCHOTIC DIAGNOSTIC GROUP. INTRA-CENTRE COMPARISON.

Centre	Diagnostic group	No. of patients	No severe impairment (%)	Severe impairment (%)	Total (%)
Aarhus	Schizophrenia	48	67	33	100
	Mania	17	82	18	100
	Other psychoses	18	78	22	100
Agra	Schizophrenia	89	82	18	100
	Mania	18	94	6	100
Moscow	Schizophrenia	68	79	21	100
	Psychotic depression	15	87	13	100
Taipei	Schizophrenia	80	80	20	100
	Other psychoses	26	100	-	100
Prague	Schizophrenia	54	67	33	100
	Psychotic depression	19	89	11	100

TABLE 8.15. PERCENTAGE DISTRIBUTION OF PATIENTS IN EACH PSYCHOTIC DIAGNOSTIC GROUP BY PERCENTAGE OF FOLLOW-UP PERIOD SPENT OUT OF HOSPITAL.

Intra-centre comparisons

Centre	Diagnostic group	No. of patients	Percentage of follow-up period spent out of hospital					Total	Mean (days)
			1 >90%	2 75-90%	3 50-75%	4 25-50%	5 <25%		
Aarhus	Schizophrenia	47	36	31	11	11	11	100	538
	Mania	17	47	35	12	6	-	100	650
	Other psychoses	17	82	6	6	-	6	100	649
Agra	Schizophrenia	92	63	32	3	2	-	100	668
	Mania	18	67	28	5	-	-	100	667
Moscow	Schizophrenia	66	44	39	12	2	3	100	616
	Psychotic depression	13	62	8	15	-	15	100	568
Taipei	Schizophrenia	79	58	28	10	4	-	100	639
	Other psychoses	26	85	11	-	4	-	100	673
Prague	Schizophrenia	38	26	34	21	16	3	100	546
	Psychotic depression	17	47	35	18	-	-	100	646

of the hospital. As the percentage time out of hospital is likely to be affected by differences in sociocultural factors and availability of services, no analyses were carried out for all centres combined. No consistent trends across the centres appear with regard to differences among the diagnostic groups, but the numbers of patients involved in each centre are small.

8.3.7 Overall outcome

As described in Chapters 6 and 7, three factors concerning the course and outcome of the IPSS patients were combined to form overall outcome groups. The 'best' outcome group is group 1 and the worst is group 5.

8.3.7.1 All centres combined

Table 8.16 presents the percentage distribution of patients in each psychotic diagnostic group by overall outcome group.

The differences among the four diagnostic groups with regard to the distribution of patients into the five overall outcome groups are statistically significant. It can be seen that the schizophrenic group had the lowest percentage of patients in the best outcome group, and the highest percentage in the worst outcome group. The manic group had the highest percentage of patients in the best group and the lowest percentage in the worst group.

Combining the two best groups (groups 1 and 2) and the two worst groups (groups 4 and 5), it is noted that the schizophrenic group has the lowest percentage of patients in the two best groups and the highest percentage in the two worst groups.

The manic patients have the highest percentage in the two best groups, and the lowest percentage in the two worst groups.

The differences among the manic, psychotic depressive and other psychoses groups were not statistically significant.

Thus, it can be seen that in terms of overall outcome grouping, the schizophrenic patients had the worst outcome. The manic patients had the best outcome, and the patients in the psychotic depressive and other psychoses groups were intermediate, although the differences among the manic, psychotic depressive and other psychoses groups were not significant.

8.3.7.2 Intracentre comparisons

Table 8.17 presents the same analysis for those intracentre comparisons that were possible.

Schizophrenia – mania. In Aarhus, the differences between schizophrenia and mania with regard to the distribution of patients into the five overall outcome groups were statistically significant. A higher percentage of manic patients fell into the two best groups and a higher percentage of schizophrenic patients fell into the two worst

TABLE 8.16. PERCENTAGE DISTRIBUTION OF PATIENTS IN EACH PSYCHOTIC DIAGNOSTIC GROUP BY OVERALL OUTCOME GROUP.

Overall outcome groups

Diagnostic group	No. of patients	1 Very favourable	2 Favourable	3 Intermediate	4 Unfavourable	5 Very unfavourable	Total
Schizophrenia	543	26	25	20	11	18	100
Psychotic depression	70	39	31	19	4	7	100
Mania	51	49	31	12	6	2	100
Other psychoses	57	39	28	19	11	3	100

TABLE 8.17. PERCENTAGE DISTRIBUTION OF PATIENTS IN EACH PSYCHOTIC DIAGNOSTIC GROUP BY OVERALL OUTCOME GROUP.

Overall outcome groups

Centre	Diagnostic group	No. of patients	1 Very favourable	2 Favourable	3 Intermediate	4 Unfavourable	5 Very unfavourable	Total
Aarhus	Schizophrenia	48	6	29	17	17	31	100
	Mania	17	41	29	24	-	6	100
	Other psychoses	18	28	33	17	11	11	100
Agra	Schizophrenia	88	48	18	13	6	15	100
	Mania	18	55	33	6	6	-	100
Moscow	Schizophrenia	66	9	39	32	9	11	100
	Psychotic depression	15	40	26	20	7	7	100
Taipei	Schizophrenia	78	15	23	27	20	15	100
	Other psychoses	24	46	21	21	12	-	100
Prague	Schizophrenia	44	14	20	27	9	30	100
	Psychotic depression	18	17	44	28	-	11	100

groups. The same trend was noted in Agra, but the differences did not reach the level of statistical significance.

Schizophrenia – psychotic depression. In Moscow, the differences between the schizophrenic and psychotic depressive groups were not statistically significant. A higher percentage of psychotic depressives than of schizophrenics fell into the best group, although the percentages of schizophrenics and psychotic depressives falling into the two worst groups were similar. In Prague, a higher percentage of psychotic depressives than of schizophrenics fell into the best two groups and a higher percentage of schizophrenics than of psychotic depressives fell into the two worst groups, although the differences were not statistically significant.

Schizophrenia—other psychoses. Table 8.17 indicates that in both Aarhus and Taipei, schizophrenics tended to have a poorer outcome than patients in the other psychoses group in terms of overall outcome grouping. In both centres a higher percentage of patients in the other psychoses group than in the schizophrenic group fell into the two best overall outcome groups, while a higher percentage of schizophrenic patients than of patients in the other psychoses group fell into the two worst groups. The differences did not reach the 0.01 level of significance, although the difference in Taipei almost reached that level ($p < 0.05$).

Thus, the intracentre comparisons support the finding from comparisons for all centres combined that schizophrenics had a poorer outcome than patients in the other psychotic diagnostic groups in terms of overall outcome grouping.

8.4 COURSE AND OUTCOME IN TERMS OF CENTRES IN DEVELOPED AND DEVELOPING COUNTRIES

Since the analyses presented in Chapter 6 suggested that schizophrenic patients from the centres in developing countries, particularly from Ibadan and Agra, tended to have a less severe two-year course and outcome than schizophrenic patients from the centres in developed countries, it was felt that it would be interesting to compare the course and outcome of schizophrenic and affective psychoses on each of the variables in terms of this dichotomy. It was quite striking that for every variable, the outcomes of schizophrenic patients and patients with affective psychoses were statistically significantly different in the centres in developed countries but not in the centres in developing countries. However, even in the developing centres, on every variable the schizophrenic had a more severe course and outcome than the patients with affective psychoses, even if these differences did not reach the level of statistical significance.

8.5 SUMMARY OF COMPARISONS OF COURSE AND OUTCOME AMONG DIFFERENT DIAGNOSTIC GROUPS

The previous four sections have compared the course and outcome of IPSS patients given initial evaluation diagnoses of schizophrenia, psychotic depression, mania, other psychoses, and non-psychotic conditions during a two-year follow-up period. The following major points stand out from these comparisons

1. Schizophrenic patients had a course and outcome which was different from, and worse than, the course and outcome of patients in the other three psychotic diagnostic groups. They tended to have the longest episodes of inclusion, the highest percentage of the follow-up period spent in a psychotic episode, the most severe pattern of course, the highest percentage of patients with severe social impairment during the follow-up period, the highest percentage of patients who were psychotic at the time of second-year follow-up, and the worst outcome in terms of overall outcome grouping.

2. Among the psychotic diagnostic groups, the manic patients tended to have the best outcome, although the differences among the manic, psychotic depressive, and other psychoses groups were statistically significant only for the length of the episode of inclusion and pattern of course. Manic patients had the shortest episodes of inclusion, and the psychotic depressive patients were very close to the manic patients, having shorter episodes of inclusion than the patients in the other psychoses group. In terms of pattern of course, the manic and psychotic depressive groups had relatively high percentages of patients with subsequent psychotic episodes followed by either full or partial remission, while the other psychoses group had a relatively high percentage of patients still in the episode of inclusion at the time of follow-up. The manic patients tended to spend a smaller percentage of the follow-up period in a psychotic episode than the patients in the other two groups and had the highest percentage of patients in the two best overall outcome groups and the lowest percentage in the two worst overall outcome groups.

3. When patients with an initial evaluation diagnosis of schizophrenia had episodes after the episode of inclusion, the vast majority had schizophrenic episodes. The vast majority of patients with an initial evaluation diagnosis of psychotic depression or mania who had subsequent episodes had affective psychotic episodes. However, 16 per cent of schizophrenic patients who had subsequent episodes had only affective psychotic episodes, and five of the 32 manic patients who had subsequent episodes had definitely or probably schizophrenic episodes.

Patients in the other psychoses group who had subsequent episodes had a variety of types of episodes, most of them being of the schizophrenic type.

4. Intracentre comparisons for the most part supported the findings from analyses for all centres combined. Although the intracentre differences between diagnostic groups were not always statistically significant, they were almost always in the direction of schizophrenics having a more severe course and outcome than patients in the other diagnostic categories.

5. When the course and outcome of schizophrenic patients and patients with either psychotic depression or mania were compared in the centres in developed countries and in those in developing countries, for every outcome variable there were statistically significant differences between the schizophrenia and affective psychoses groups in the centres in the developed countries, and no statistically significant differences between the diagnostic groups in the centres in the developing countries.

6. Considering the broad areas of psychopathology represented by the groups of units of analysis, the schizophrenic, psychotic depressive, manic, and other psychoses groups of patients were similar to one another at the time of second year follow-up, with generally low levels of psychopathology, more than minimal scores on only a few negative and non-specific symptoms, and little in the way of positive psychotic symptomatology. Comparison of the profiles of only those patients who were psychotic at second-year suggested that at the time of second-year follow-up patients with initial evaluation diagnoses of psychotic depression and mania had more affective and less negative symptomatology than patients with an initial evaluation diagnosis of schizophrenia. However, the numbers of patients in these categories were not large enough to make statistical comparisons. When the frequency of symptoms on a more specific level, the units of analysis level, is considered, the most frequently positive sympsoms at the time of second-year follow-up were negative and non-specific symptoms for the schizophrenic group, affective symptoms for the psychotic depressive and manic groups, and both non-specific and affective symptoms for the other psychoses group.

7. A significantly higher percentage of patients diagnosed as schizophrenic at initial evaluation than of patients diagnosed as psychotically depressed at initial evaluation were psychotic at second-year follow-up. For all diagnostic groups, a relatively high percentage of patients who were psychotic on initial evaluation were asymptomatic at the time of second-year follow-up, ranging from 28 per cent for the other psychoses group to 39 per cent for the psychotic depressive group.

8. When second-year follow-up CATEGO classes were compared across initial evaluation clinical diagnoses, it was found that only 10 per cent of initial evaluation psychotic depressive patients fell into a CATEGO class representing a definite psychosis on second-year follow-up, compared to 40 per cent of initial evaluation schizophrenics; 18 per cent of initial evaluation schizophrenics fell into CATEGO class S at second-year follow-up compared to 3 per cent of initial evaluation psychotic depressive patients who fell into this class at follow-up. The percentage of patients in the manic and other psychoses groups at initial evaluation who fell into CATEGO classes representing definite schizophrenia and definite psychosis were 12 per cent and 30 per cent respectively for mania and 9 per cent and 33 per cent for the other psychoses group. 22 per cent of psychotic depressive patients, 10 per cent of manic patients, 9 per cent of other psychoses patients and 7 per cent of schizophrenic patients fell into a CATEGO class representing a retarded or neurotic depression at second-year follow-up.

The implication of these findings for the hypotheses listed at the beginning of Chapter 6 will be discussed in Chapter 11.

CHAPTER 9

The Concordant Group and the Subgroups of Schizophrenia

Using results of analyses presented in Volume 1 of the report of the IPSS (WHO, 1973), a concordant group of schizophrenics was defined in terms of the results of three separate methods of classification – original clinical diagnosis, CATEGO classification, and cluster analysis. The concordant group was defined as consisting of all patients whose original diagnosis was schizophrenia, who fell into CATEGO class S, and who also belonged to one of those clusters which contained a statistically significantly higher number of schizophrenics than would have been expected by chance. There were 306 such concordant schizophrenics.

It was felt that such a concordant group has the advantage of being comprised of patients who had been diagnosed in a standardized fashion according to clinical assumptions and who belonged to clusters that statistically selected out schizophrenics. It was noted that if it could be shown that such a group of patients existed in all countries and that it had a specific clinical picture and course of illness which differentiated it from other groups of schizophrenic patients, then a description of the characteristics of that group might serve as a beginning for a transculturally applicable definition of schizophrenia.

Analyses reported in Volume 1 demonstrated that when the psychopathological characteristics of the concordant group were compared with those of the schizophrenic group of patients who had a centre clinical diagnosis of schizophrenia, but did not fall into CATEGO class S or into one of the clusters which selected out schizophrenic patients (discrepant schizophrenics), the concordant schizophrenics scored much higher on delusions, hallucinations and flatness of affect, while the discrepant schizophrenics scored higher on depressive symptomatology.

When the psychopathological characteristics of the concordant group were compared to those of the psychotically depressed group, it was noted that the concordant group showed even less similarity to the psychotically depressed group than the group of all schizophrenics did to the psychotically depressed group.

There were concordant schizophrenics in every one of the field research centres, and when the concordant groups in each of the centres were compared, they were found to be highly similar to one another. Thus, on the basis of initial evaluation data, it was concluded that it was possible to identify a concordant group of schizophrenic patients who had a distinctive pattern of symptomatology, that this pattern was consistent across centres, and that there were patients belonging to this group in every centre in the study.

226

The second-year follow-up data can now be considered to determine whether the two-year course of illness of the concordant group differs significantly in any respect from the two-year course of illness of the other schizophrenics in the study.

Volume 1 of the report also considered the usefulness of the diagnostic distinctions among subgroups of schizophrenia. It was noted that when broad areas of psychopathology were considered, the symptom profiles of different subgroups of schizophrenia within the same centre were similar to one another. In fact, intracentre similarity of different subgroup profiles was in general higher than intercentre similarity for most of the individual subgroups. It was also suggested that the symptomatic features which distinguish schizophrenic subgroups might be found in the finer subdivisions of symptomatology. The current chapter will consider the question of whether there are any significant differences among the schizophrenic subgroups with regard to two-year course and outcome.

9.1 THE CONCORDANT AND NON-CONCORDANT GROUPS

In order to consider how the two-year course and outcome of the concordant group compares with that of the non-concordant groups, the analyses carried out for the entire schizophrenic group described in Chapter 6 were repeated for these two groups.

9.1.1 Symptomatic picture at the time of second-year follow-up

9.1.1.1 Symptom profiles – Groups of Units of Analysis (GUAs)

Figure 9.1 presents the symptom profiles on 27 GUAs for the concordant and noncordant groups at second-year follow-up, for all centres combined. It can be seen from the figure that the profiles are quite similar to one another. The concordant schizophrenics had slightly higher scores on auditory hallucinations and characteristic auditory hallucinations and a slightly lower score on flatness of affect than the non-concordant schizophrenics. An analysis of variance indicated that the shapes of the profiles were not significantly different from one another. A rank order correlation coefficient was calculated (Kendall's τ) for the comparison of the two profiles, and this indicated that there was a high degree of similarity between the profiles. ANOVA analysis was also carried out for those intracentre comparisons in which there were 15 or more patients in both groups. This was possible in Aarhus, Agra, Ibadan, Cali and Taipei, and in none of these centres was there a significant difference between the profiles of the concordant and non-concordant groups. Although the overall profiles showed no differences within individual centres, there were some interesting differences within centres on particular groups or units. Thus, for example, in Aarhus, there were rather large differences between concordant and non-concordant schizophrenics on the scores on the following GUAs: experiences of control (31 for concordant schizophrenics and 8 for non-concordant schizophrenics), auditory hallucinations (30 for concordant, 0 for non-concordant), characteristic hallucinations (23 for concordant, 1 for non-

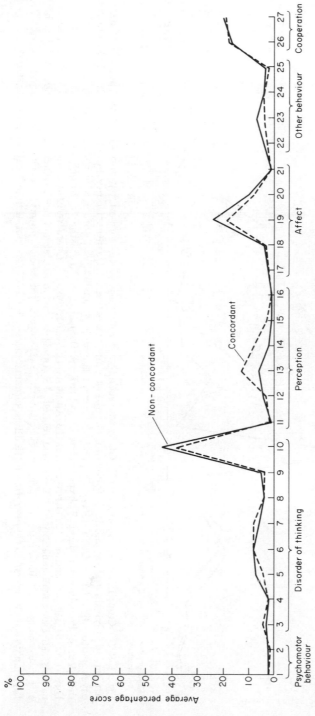

Figure 9.1   Comparison of scores on 27 GUAs at second-year follow-up of concordant group (348 patients) and non-concordant group (194 patients). Groups of units of analysis: 1 Quantitative psychomotor disorder. 2 Qualitative psychomotor disorder. 3 Quantitative disorder of form of thinking. 4 Qualitative disorder of form of thinking. 5 Affect-laden thoughts. 6 Predelusional signs. 7 Experiences of control. 8 Delusions. 9 Neurasthenic complaints. 10 Lack of insight. 11 Distortion of self-perception. 12 Derealization. 13 Auditory hallucinations. 14 'Characteristic' hallucinations. 15 Other hallucinations. 16 Pseudohallucinations. 17 Depressed–elated. 18 Anxiety, tension, irritability. 19 Flatness. 20 Incongruity. 21 Other affective change. 22 Indication of personality change. 23 Disregard for social norms. 24 Other behavioural change. 25 Psychophysical disorders. 26 Co-operation difficulties, circumstances-related. 27 Co-operation difficulties, patient-related

228

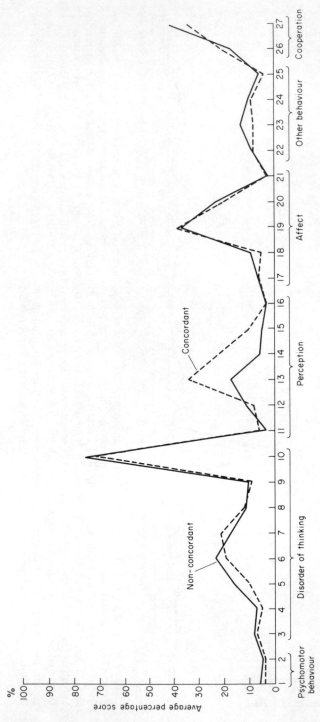

Figure 9.2 Comparison of scores on 27 GUAs at second-year follow-up of concordant patients (127) and non-concordant patients (75) considered psychotic at follow-up. Groups of units of analysis: 1 Quantitative psychomotor disorder. 2 Qualitative psychomotor disorder. 3 Quantitative disorder of form of thinking. 4 Qualitative disorder of form of thinking. 5 Affect-laden thoughts. 6 Predelusional signs. 7 Experiences of control. 8 Delusions. 9 Neurasthenic complaints. 10 Lack of insight. 11 Distortion of self-perception. 12 Derealization. 13 Auditory hallucinations. 14 'Characteristic' hallucinations. 15 Other hallucinations. 16 Pseudohallucinations. 17 Depressed—elated. 18 Anxiety, tension, irritability. 19 Flatness. 20 Incongruity. 21 Other affective change. 22 Indication of personality change. 23 Disregard for social norms. 24 Other behavioural change. 25 Psychophysical disorders. 26 Co-operation difficulties, circumstances-related. 27 Co-operation difficulties, patient-related

concordant), and flatness of affect (42 concordant, 24 for non-concordant). In Agra, there were differences on auditory hallucinations (19 *vs.* 1), and characteristic hallucinations (9 *vs.* 0); in Cali, on experiences of control (10 *vs.* 3) and auditory hallucinations (13 *vs.* 4); in Ibadan, on auditory hallucinations (4 *vs.* 13), and flatness of affect (3 *vs.* 13); in London, on affect-laden thoughts (2 *vs.* 22), and lack of insight (16 *vs.* 44); in Moscow, on delusions (10 *vs.* 3), auditory hallucinations (13 *vs.* 2), characteristic hallucinations (12 *vs.* 1), and incongruity of affect (46 *vs.* 26); in Taipei, on quantitative disorder of form of thinking (13 *vs.* 4), flatness of affect (13 *vs.* 27) and patient-related co-operation difficulties (5 *vs.* 19). In most of these comparisons the concordant schizophrenics scored higher on hallucination and delusion items and lower on affective symptomatology, which was also the case at initial evaluation.

The second-year follow-up profiles of only those patients who were considered to be psychotic at the time of second-year follow-up, according to the criteria described in Chapter 5, were also compared between initial evaluation concordant and non-concordant groups. The profiles are presented in Figure 9.2. It can be seen that the profiles are quite similar, except that the concordant group has higher scores on auditory and characteristic hallucinations than the non-concordant group. ANOVA analysis indicated that the shapes of the profiles are not significantly different, and τ analysis indicates that the profiles are highly similar. There were not enough patients followed up in both groups in individual centres to carry out intracentre comparisons.

9.1.1.2 Symptom profiles – 15 most frequent Units of Analysis (UAs)

Table 9.1 presents the 15 most frequent units of analysis at second-year follow-up for each group for all centres combined. It can be seen that there is a great similarity between the concordant and non-concordant groups as 11 units were among the 15 most frequent for both groups. It is interesting that the four units among the 15 most frequent for the concordant group which were not among the 15 most frequent for the non-concordant group were all units indicating auditory hallucinations. This supports the findings at the GUA level that the concordant group appears to demonstrate more hallucinations at the time of second-year follow-up than the non-concordant group, even if the profiles as a whole are quite similar to one another.

Intracentre comparisons were possible in five centres, Aarhus, Agra, Cali, Ibadan and Taipei. In Aarhus, Agra and Cali, the concordant group had several hallucination units among the 15 most frequent, while the non-concordant had no such units among the 15 most frequent. In Ibadan and Taipei, both groups had hallucination units among the 15 most frequent. In Aarhus, 11 of the 18 most frequent UAs (18 because of tie scores for 15th to the 18th) were among the 18 most frequent for the non-concordant group. In Agra, there were many differences between the two groups, as only seven of the 21 most frequent (tie scores for units 14 to 21) were among the 18 most frequent for the non-concordant group. Ten of the 15 most frequent UAs for the concordant group in Cali were among the 26

TABLE 9.1.   15 MOST FREQUENT UNITS OF ANALYSIS AT THE TIME OF 2ND
YEAR FOLLOW-UP.   COMPARISON BETWEEN CONCORDANT AND
NON-CONCORDANT GROUP.   FIGURES IN BRACKETS SHOW THE
PERCENTAGE POSITIVE RATINGS OF THE UNIT OF ANALYSIS
WITHIN THE RESPECTIVE GROUP OF PATIENTS.

All Centres	
Conc. N=194	Non-conc. N=348
Lack of insight (38.7)	Lack of insight (44.5)
Suspiciousness (28.9)	Flatness (29.9)
Poor rapport (25.3)	Poor rapport (26.7)
Inadequate description (22.7)	Inadequate description (26.7)
Unwilling to cooperate (22.2)	Unwilling to cooperate (25.6)
Flatness (21.6)	Suspiciousness (23.0)
Ideas of reference (19.1)	Apathy (19.3)
Presence of auditory halluc. (18.0)	Ideas of reference (17.5)
Presence of verbal halluc. (17.5)	Delusions of reference (13.8)
Apathy (17.5)	Restricted speech (13.2)
Voices speak to patient (16.0)	Hypochondriacal delusions (13.2)
Delusions of reference (14.9)	Autism (12.4)
Delusions of persecution (14.4)	Delusions of persecution (11.8)
Frequent auditory halluc. (14.4)	Delusional mood (10.9)
Autism (13.4)	Incongruity of affect (10.6)

A A R H U S

Conc. N = 19	Non-conc. N = 29
Poor rapport (78.9)	Poor rapport (62.1)
Suspiciousness (63.2)	Lack of insight (58.6)
Flatness (63.2)	Inadequate description (34.5)
Lack of insight (57.9)	Flatness (31.0)
Inadequate description (47.4)	Unwilling to cooperate (31.0)
Restricted speech (42.1)	Suspiciousness (31.0)
Thought alienation (42.1)	Restricted speech (31.0)
Thoughts spoken aloud (36.3)	Autism (27.6)
Pres. of verbal halluc. (36.8)	Obsessive thoughts (24.1)
Voices speak full sentences (36.8)	Incongruity of affect (20.7)
Pres. of auditory hall. (36.8)	Self-depreciation (20.7)
Voices speak to patient (36.8)	Derealization (20.7)
Autism (31.6)	Apathy (17.2)
Unwilling to cooperate (31.6)	Distractibility (17.2)
Disorder of pitch (26.3)	Ideas of reference (13.8)
Self-depreciation (26.3)	Delusional mood (13.8)
Voices comment on patient's thoughts (26.3)	Disorder of pitch (13.8)
Voices speak thoughts (26.3)	Thought alienation (13.8)

A G R A	
Conc. N = 26	Non-conc. N = 62
Lack of insight (26.9)	Lack of insight (30.6)
Pres. of auditory halluc. (26.9)	Inadequate description (27.4)
Pres. of verbal halluc. (26.9)	Apathy (27.4)
Voices speak to patient (23.1)	Flatness (25.8)
Flatness (23.1)	Poor rapport (19.4)
Apathy (23.1)	Restricted speech (17.7)
Frequent audit. halluc. (23.1)	Unwilling to cooperate (16.1)
Inadequate description (23.1)	Hypochondriacal delusions (16.1)
Delusions of persecution (19.2)	Autism (14.5)
Voices speak full sentences (19.2)	Self-neglect (14.5)
Ideas of reference (15.4)	Speech dissociation (12.9)
Suspiciousness (15.4)	Irrelevance (12.9)
Delusions of reference (15.4)	Ideas of reference (11.3)
Fantastic delusions (11.5)	Suspiciousness (9.7)
Worries (11.5)	Delusions of persecution (9.7)
Voices comment on patient's thoughts (11.5)	Disorder of pitch (9.7)
Voices speak thoughts (11.5)	Early waking (9.7)
Visual hallucinations (11.5)	
Diminished appetite (11.5)	
Decreased interest· (11.5)	
Decreased libido (11.5)	

```
                              C A L I
Conc.    N = 43               Non-conc.    N = 34
```

Conc. N = 43	Non-conc. N = 34
Lack of insight (41.4)	Lack of insight (35.3)
Suspiciousness (27.9)	Poor rapport (32.4)
Situation anxiety (25.6)	Hypochondriacal delusions (32.4)
Poor rapport (20.9)	Ideas of reference (29.4)
Unwilling to cooperate (20.8)	Autism (26.5)
Ideas of reference (18.6)	Inadequate description (26.5)
Hypochondriacal delusions (18.6)	Delusions of reference (20.6)
Pres. of verbal halluc. (16.3)	Situation anxiety (20.6)
Voices speak to patient (16.3)	Delusional mood (17.6)
Pres. of auditory halluc. (16.3)	Gloomy thoughts (14.7)
Thought alienation (14.0)	Flatness (11.8)
Delusions of reference (14.0)	Apathy (11.8)
Frequent audit. halluc. (14.0)	Unwilling to cooperate (8.8)
Autism (14.0)	Suspiciousness (8.8)
Inadequate description (14.0)	Elated thoughts (8.8)
	Hopelessness (8.8)
	Delusions of grandeur (8.8)
	Pres. of delusional system (8.8)
	Distractibility (8.8)
	Special mission delusions (8.8)
	Observed elated mood (8.8)
	Anxiety (8.8)
	Haughtiness
	Increased interest
	Disregard of norms
	Suggestibility (All 8.8)

I B A D A N

Conc. N = 29	Non-conc. N = 34
Sleep problems (13.8)	Lack of insight (23.5)
Delusions of persecution (10.3)	Flatness (14.7)
Hypochondriacal delusions (10.3)	Unwilling to cooperate (14.7)
Lack of insight (10.3)	Gloomy thoughts (14.7)
Early waking (10.3)	Pres. of verbal halluc. (14.7)
Unwilling to cooperate (10.3)	Pres. of auditory halluc. (14.7)
Suspiciousness (6.9)	Inadequate description (11.8)
Poor rapport (6.9)	Suspiciousness (11.8)
Inadequate description (6.9)	Apathy (11.8)
Pres. of auditory halluc. (6.9)	Delusions of reference (11.8)
Voices speak to patient (6.9)	Delusions of persecution (11.8)
Frequent audit. halluc. (6.9)	Perplexity (11.8)
Gloomy thoughts (6.9)	Thoughts spoken aloud (11.8)
Delusional mood (6.9)	Voices speak to patient (11.8)
Self-depreciation (6.9)	Nonverbal audit. halluc. (11.8)
Voices speak full sentences (6.9)	Frequent audit. halluc. (11.8)
Voices discuss patient (6.9)	Depressed mood (11.8)
Voices comment on patient's thoughts (6.9)	Anxiety (11.8)
Voices speak thoughts (6.9)	

	T A I P E I
Conc. N = 30	Non-conc. N = 31

Lack of insight (53.3)	Lack of insight (64.5)
Suspiciousness (46.7)	Suspiciousness (41.9)
Unwilling to cooperate (43.2)	Ideas of reference (38.7)
Poor rapport (40.0)	Unwilling to cooperate (35.5)
Inadequate description (36.7)	Flatness (32.3)
Apathy (30.0)	Inadequate description (29.0)
Flatness (26.7)	Poor rapport (25.8)
Autism (26.7)	Delusions of persecution (25.8)
Restricted speech (26.7)	Delusions of reference (25.8)
Distractibility (23.3)	Presence of verbal halluc. (22.6)
Delusions of persecution (20.0)	Voices speak to patient (22.6)
Hypochondriacal delusions (20.0)	Presence of auditory halluc. (22.6)
Ideas of reference (16.7)	Frequent auditory halluc. (19.4)
Speech dissociation (16.7)	Apathy (19.4)
Frequent auditory halluc. (13.3)	Delusional mood (19.4)
Presence of verbal halluc. (13.3)	
Blocking (13.3)	
Olfactory hallucinations (13.3)	
Perplexity (13.3)	

most frequent (11 units tied for 15th) for the non-concordant group in that centre. Nine of the 19 most frequent UAs in Ibadan were among the 18 most frequent for the non-concordant group, while 11 of the 19 most frequent for the concordant group in Taipei were among the 15 most frequent for the non-concordant group. Thus, there was considerable similarity between the concordant and non-concordant groups on the UA level in Aarhus, Taipei and Cali centres, although there were many differences between the two groups in Agra and Ibadan.

The 15 most frequent UAs were also compared between concordant and non-concordant schizophrenics for those patients who were considered to be psychotic at the time of second-year follow-up according to the criteria described in Chapter 6. There was considerable similarity between the two groups on this level as they shared ten units among the 15 most frequent. However, there is again the interesting finding that the five units among the 15 most frequent for the concordant group and not among the 15 most frequent in the non-concordant group are units reflecting auditory hallucinations.

Intracentre comparisons were not possible for the psychotic concordant and non-concordant patients because of the small numbers of patients involved.

9.1.1.3 Presence or absence of psychotic and other symptoms at second-year follow-up

The concordant and non-concordant groups were compared with regard to the percentage who were psychotic; symptomatic, but not psychotic; or asymptomatic at the time of second-year follow-up, using the criteria described in Chapter 6. The results are presented in Table 9.2.

There are no significant differences for all centres combined nor for any intracentre comparisons between concordant and non-concordant groups, in centres where there were enough patients in both groups to carry out statistical analysis.

9.1.2 Course of illness between initial evaluation and second-year follow-up

The course of illness of the concordant schizophrenic group during the interval between the initial evaluation and the second-year follow-up was compared with that of the non-concordant group in terms of the same criteria as described in Chapter 6. There were no significant differences between the two groups, either for all centres combined or within individual centres on any variable except for type of subsequent episode.

9.1.2.1 Type of subsequent episode

Of the 177 initial evaluation schizophrenics that were known to have had subsequent episodes, 76 were in the concordant group and 101 were in the non-concordant group. Table 9.3 indicates the percentage distribution of these groups by type of subsequent episode; 87 per cent of the concordant group of schizophrenics who had subsequent episodes had at least one subsequent definitely

TABLE 9.2. PRESENCE OR ABSENCE OF PSYCHOTIC OR OTHER SYMPTOMS AT 2ND YEAR FOLLOW-UP IN THE CONCORDANT AND NON-CONCORDANT GROUPS OF SCHIZOPHRENIC PATIENTS.

Centre	No. of patients		Percentage with psychotic symptoms		Percentage symptomatic, but not psychotic		Percentage asymptomatic		Total	
	conc.	non-conc.	conc.	non-conc.	conc.	non-conc.	conc.	non-conc.	conc.	non-conc.
Aarhus	19	29	79	52	16	38	5	10	100	100
Agra	26	62	35	31	11	13	54	56	100	100
Cali	43	34	35	32	30	41	35	27	100	100
Ibadan	29	34	24	26	17	18	59	56	100	100
London	12	9	-	-	-	-	-	-	-	-
Moscow	13	53	-	34	-	64	-	2	-	100
Taipei	30	31	37	45	37	29	26	26	100	100
Washington	11	54	-	41	-	26	-	33	-	100
Prague	11	42	-	36	-	47	-	17	-	100
All centres	194	348	39	37	25	34	36	29	100	100

TABLE 9.3. PERCENTAGE DISTRIBUTION OF FOLLOWED-UP SCHIZOPHRENICS WITH SUBSEQUENT EPISODES, BY TYPE OF EPISODE. CONCORDANT AND NON-CONCORDANT GROUPS.

	Centre	No. of patients	Type of subsequent episodes					Both 1+2	1 or 2 +3	Both 1+4	Both 3+4	Total
			1	2	3	4	5					
Concordant	All centres	76	46	40	7	5	-	1	-	-	1	100
	Cali	20	30	55	15	-	-	-	-	-	-	100
Non-concordant	All centres	101	29	37	23	2	4	1	2	2	-	100
	Moscow	24	29	21	42	4	-	-	4	-	-	100

Types of episodes: 1 = only definitely schizophrenic episodes.

2 = only probably schizophrenic episodes.

3 = only affective psychotic episodes.

4 = only non-psychotic episodes.

5 = only other psychotic episodes.

or probably schizophrenic episode, and 8 per cent had at least one subsequent affective psychosis episode. On the other hand, 71 per cent of non-concordant schizophrenics had at least one subsequent definitely or probably schizophrenic episode, and 25 per cent had at least one subsequent affective psychosis episode. These differences are statistically significant.

Thus, it appears that when concordant schizophrenics had subsequent episodes, they were more likely to have schizophrenic episodes and less likely to have affective psychotic episodes than non-concordant schizophrenics.

9.1.3 Summary

The above analyses indicate that on most course and outcome measures, there were no significant differences between the concordant and non-concordant groups. However, the two groups did differ significantly on type of subsequent episodes, and did demonstrate some differences in symptomatic picture at the time of second-year follow-up. When concordant schizophrenics had subsequent episodes, they were more likely to have schizophrenic episodes and less likely to have affective episodes than non-concordant schizophrenics. Although the overall profiles of the concordant and non-concordant schizophrenics were similar to one another at the time of second-year follow-up, the concordant schizophrenics demonstrated more hallucinatory symptoms than did the non-concordant schizophrenics.

9.2 THE SUBGROUPS OF SCHIZOPHRENIA

In Volume 1 of the report of the IPSS (WHO, 1973), it was noted that the symptomatic profiles of groups of patients divided according to subgroups of schizophrenia were not significantly different from one another at the level of groups of units of analysis. Some differences at the unit of analysis level were reported. It was felt that it would be instructive to compare the subgroups in terms of symptomatic picture at the time of second-year follow-up, and in terms of two-year course and outcome.

9.2.1 Symptomatic picture at the time of second-year follow-up

An analysis of variance was carried out to compare the shapes of the second-year symptom profiles of the various initial evaluation schizophrenic subgroups on the level of groups of units of analysis. The results indicated that there were no significant differences between subgroups either for all centres combined or for any comparisons that were possible within individual centres.

Since initial evaluation results suggested the possibility of differences among subgroups in terms of UAs, which are more specific than GUAs, the 15 most frequent units of analysis at the time of second-year follow-up were compared among diagnostic subgroups. Table 9.4 presents the 15 most frequent UAs for each diagnostic subgroup, and Table 9.5 indicates the number of UAs that were among the 15 most frequent for both members of each possible pair of subgroups.

TABLE 9.4. 15 MOST FREQUENTLY POSITIVE UNITS OF ANALYSIS AT 2ND YEAR FOLLOW-UP; COMPARISON AMONG SUBGROUPS OF SCHIZOPHRENIA. FIGURES IN BRACKETS SHOW THE PERCENTAGE POSITIVE RATINGS OF THE UNIT OF ANALYSIS WITHIN THE RESPECTIVE SUBGROUP OF SCHIZOPHRENIA.

Rank order	Simple	Hebephrenic	Catatonic	Paranoid
1	Inadequate description (50.0)	Lack of insight (55.7)	Lack of insight (28.2)	Lack of insight (48.9)
2	Lack of insight (40.0)	Poor rapport (44.3)	Unwilling to cooperate (20.5)	Suspiciousness (34.6)
3	Poor rapport (40.0)	Inadequate description (39.3)	Inadequate description (20.5)	Unwilling to cooperate (29.8)
4	Unwilling to cooperate (35.0)	Flatness (37.7)	Poor rapport (17.9)	Poor rapport (28.7)
5	Flatness (30.0)	Suspiciousness (36.1)	Flatness (15.4)	Flatness (28.2)
6	Autism (30.0)	Unwilling to cooperate (31.1)	Apathy (12.8)	Ideas of reference (25.5)
7	Restricted speech (25.0)	Autism (26.2)	Delusional mood (10.3)	Inadequate description (25.5)
8	Speech dissociation (25.0)	Ideas of reference (23.0)	Perplexity 10.3	Delusions of reference (19.1)
9	Apathy (25.0)	Apathy (23.0)	Restricted speech (7.7)	Pres. of auditory hall. (19.1)
10	Irrelevance (20.1)	Pres. of verbal hall. (21.3)	Speech dissociation (7.7)	Delusions of persecution (17.0)
11	Ideas of reference (20.0)	Pres. of auditory hall. (21.3)	Irrelevance (7.7)	Pres. of verbal hall. (17.0)
12	Derealization (20.0)	Voices speak to patient (19.7)	Suspiciousness (7.7)	Apathy (16.0)
13	Obsessive thoughts (15.0)	Restricted speech (18.0)	Delusions of persecution (7.7)	Autism (16.0)
14	Incongruity of affect (15.0)	Frequent auditory hall. (18.0)	Delusions of reference (7.7)	Voices speak to patient (16.0)
15	Self-neglect (15.0)	Incongruity of affect (18.0)	Hypochondriacal del. (7.7)	Restricted speech (13.3)
	Situation anxiety (15.0)	Distractibility (18.0)	Derealization (7.7)	Frequent auditory hall. (13.3)
	Giggling to self (15.0)	Delusions of reference (18.0)	Situation anxiety (7.7)	
	Distractibility (15.0)		Autism (7.7)	

TABLE 9.4. continued

241

Rank order	Acute	Latent	Schizo-affective	Other specified	Unspecified
1	Lack of insight (25.0)	Lack of insight (68.4)	Lack of insight (27.3)	Lack of insight (48.9)	Lack of insight (42.4)
2	Hypochondriacal (18.3)	Flatness (47.4)	Suspiciousness (18.2)	Apathy (37.8)	Flatness (42.4)
3	Flatness (13.3)	Poor rapport (42.1)	Flatness (15.6)	Poor rapport (35.6)	Inadequate description (42.4)
4	Ideas of reference (11.7)	Mannerisms (36.8)	Early waking (15.6)	Flatness (33.3)	Apathy (36.4)
5	Suspiciousness (11.7)	Apathy (36.8)	Worse in morning (15.6)	Unwilling to cooperate (28.9)	Restricted speech (30.3)
6	Situation anxiety (11.7)	Disorder of pitch (31.6)	Delusions of reference (13.0)	Suspiciousness (24.4)	Poor rapport (30.3)
7	Hopelessness (10.0)	Inadequate description (31.6)	Unwilling to cooperate (13.0)	Inadequate description (24.4)	Suspiciousness (27.3)
8	Delusions of reference (10.0)	Unwilling to cooperate (26.3)	Inadequate description (13.0)	Mannerisms (22.2)	Unwilling to cooperate (27.3)
9	Apathy (10.0)	Suspiciousness (21.1)	Ideas of reference (13.0)	Worse in morning (22.2)	Delusions of persecution (24.2)
10	Poor rapport (10.0)	Irritability (21.1)	Self-depreciation (11.7)	Gloomy thoughts (17.8)	Disorder of pitch (21.2)
11	Unwilling to cooperate (10.0)	Incongruity of affect (21.1)	Hypochondriacal del. (11.7)	Depressed mood (17.8)	Speech dissociation (18.2)
12	Inadequate description (10.0)	Abnormal tidiness (21.1)	Delusional mood (10.4)	Self-neglect (17.8)	Ideas of reference (18.2)
13	Gloomy thoughts (8.3)	Worse in morning (21.1)	Gloomy thoughts (10.4)	Ideas of reference (15.6)	Irrelevance (18.2)
14	Elated thoughts (8.3)	Restricted speech (15.8)	Elated thoughts (10.4)	Hypochondriacal del. (15.6)	Delusions of control (15.2)
15	Depressed mood (8.3)	Elated thoughts (15.8)	Delusions of persecution (9.1)	Incongruity of affect (15.6)	Incongruity of affect (15.2)
	Tension (8.3)	Obsessive thoughts (15.8)	Poor rapport (9.1)	Lability of affect (15.6)	Autism (15.2)
	Anxiety (8.3)	Hypochondriacal del. (15.8)			Self-neglect (15.2)
		Disregard of norms (15.8)			

TABLE 9.5. NUMBER OF UNITS OF ANALYSIS AMONG THE 15 MOST FREQUENT FOR BOTH MEMBERS OF EACH POSSIBLE PAIR OF SUBGROUPS OF SCHIZOPHRENIA, AT TIME OF 2ND YEAR FOLLOW-UP.

	Simple	Hebephrenic	Catatonic	Paranoid	Acute	Latent	Schizo-affective	Other specified	Unspecified
Simple	-	11	12	9	8	9	6	9	13
Hebephrenic	11	-	10	15	9	9	8	9	11
Catatonic	12	10	-	11	10	9	10	8	12
Paranoid	9	15	11	-	9	8	9	8	11
Acute	8	9	10	9	-	9	11	11	8
Latent	9	9	9	8	9	-	9	11	10
Schizo-affective	6	8	10	9	11	9	-	10	8
Other specified	9	9	8	8	11	11	10	-	10
Unspecified	13	11	12	11	8	10	8	10	-

Although there is considerable similarity among the subgroups, certain differences can be noted. Thus, the simple, latent, and 'other specified' subgroups do not have any units reflecting hallucinations or delusions among the 15 most frequent at the time of second-year follow-up. The schizo-affective, 'other specified', and acute subgroups have more affective symptomatology at the time of second-year follow-up than the other subgroups. The hebephrenic subgroup is characterized by a relatively high percentage of patients with auditory hallucinations but no unit reflecting delusions among the 15 most frequent, while the catatonic subgroup has no hallucination unit among the 15 most frequent. The paranoid subgroup has a relatively high percentage of patients with delusions of reference and persecution. The catatonic, acute and schizo-affective subgroups in general have lower percentage of patients with symptoms at any given rank level than the other diagnostic groups.

Negative and non-specific symptoms such as flatness of affect, poor rapport, lack of insight and co-operation difficulties ranked high among all subgroups at the time of follow-up.

It can be seen from Table 9.5 that the two subgroups that were most dissimilar with regard to the 15 most frequent UAs at the time of second-year follow-up were simple schizophrenia and schizo-affective schizophrenia, and the two subgroups that were most similar in this respect were hebephrenic schizophrenia and paranoid schizophrenia.

Thus, it appears that although at both initial evaluation and second-year follow-up, there are no significant differences among schizophrenic subgroups on the broad level of psychopathology represented by the groups of units of analysis, there are suggestions of differences at the more specific level of units of analysis. The differences at the time of second-year follow-up appear to be mainly in hallucinations, delusions, and affective symptoms, and in degree of psychopathology.

9.2.2. Course of illness between initial evaluation and second-year follow-up

9.2.2.1 All centres combined

To determine whether there were differences among the subgroups with regard to the course of illness between initial evaluation and second-year follow-up, the subgroups were compared with one another in terms of the same course and outcome criteria described in Chapters 6, 7 and 8.

Length of episode of inclusion. Table 9.6 indicates the percentage of followed-up patients in each of the subgroups of schizophrenia that fell into each of the five lengths of episode of inclusion categories.* The differences among the subgroups with regard to the distribution of patients into the five outcome categories are

---

* Throughout this section, figures are omitted for 295.6, residual schizophrenia, since there was only one patient in this subgroup followed up.

244

TABLE 9.6. PERCENTAGE DISTRIBUTION OF PATIENTS BY LENGTH OF EPISODE OF INCLUSION, SUBGROUPS OF SCHIZOPHRENIA. ALL CENTRES COMBINED.

Subgroup of schizophrenia	No. of patients	<1 month	1-3 months	3-9 months	9-18 months	>18 months	Total	Mean
Simple	21	10	14	5	-	71	100	18.1
Hebephrenic	73	18	25	14	5	38	100	11.7
Catatonic	40	40	28	17	-	15	100	5.9
Paranoid	206	23	28	14	4	31	100	9.7
Acute	55	34	38	11	2	15	100	5.2
Latent	20	40	40	-	5	15	100	5.6
Residual	1	-	-	-	-	100	100	25.0
Schizo-affective	73	32	33	19	4	12	100	5.5
Other specified	49	49	23	13	2	13	100	5.1
Unspecified	32	19	25	16	-	40	100	11.5

TABLE 9.7.   PERCENTAGE DISTRIBUTION OF PATIENTS BY PERCENTAGE OF THE FOLLOW-UP PERIOD SPENT
IN PSYCHOTIC EPISODES;   SUBGROUPS OF SCHIZOPHRENIA.   ALL CENTRES COMBINED.

Subgroup of schizophrenia	No. of patients	1 -5%	2 6-15%	3 16-45%	4 46-75%	5 76-100%	Total	Mean
Simple	17	12	17	6	-	65	100	55.3
Hebephrenic	70	9	13	24	11	43	100	52.7
Catatonic	40	27	25	30	3	15	100	26.8
Paranoid	202	14	21	25	7	33	100	42.8
Acute	52	23	33	23	8	13	100	25.9
Latent	17	23	53	6	6	12	100	18.4
Residual	1	-	-	-	-	100	100	(100.0)
Schizo-affective	69	22	25	29	10	14	100	25.1
Other specified	42	24	19	38	5	14	100	20.3
Unspecified	33	12	15	27	6	40	100	44.3

statistically significant. It can be seen that simple schizophrenics had the longest episodes of inclusion, with 71 per cent having an episode of inclusion which lasted more than 18 months, and only 10 per cent having an episode of inclusion lasting less than one month. Three other subgroups also had relatively high percentages of patients for whom the episode of inclusion lasted more than 18 months and relatively low percentages of patients for whom it lasted less than one month: hebephrenic, paranoid and unspecified schizophrenics. On the other hand, subgroups which were characterized by a relatively high percentage of patients with short episodes of inclusion and a relatively low percentage of patients with long episodes of inclusion were catatonic, acute, latent, schizo-affective, and 'other specified' schizophrenia.

Thus, it appears that with regard to the criterion of length of episode of inclusion, there were two categories of subgroups. The simple, hebephrenic, paranoid, and unspecified schizophrenics had a relatively poor outcome, and the catatonic, acute, latent, schizo-affective, and 'other specified' schizophrenics had a relatively good outcome.

Percentage of follow-up period spent in psychotic episodes. The percentage distribution of patients in each schizophrenic subgroup by percentage of the follow-up period spent in psychotic episodes is presented in Table 9.7. The differences among the subgroups are statistically significant. It can be seen from this table that patients in the simple, hebephrenic, paranoid, and unspecified subgroups spent relatively high percentages of the follow-up period in psychotic episodes while patients in the catatonic, acute, latent, schizo-affective and other specified subgroups spent relatively short percentages of the follow-up period in psychotic episodes.

It therefore appears that with regard to the criterion of percentages of follow-up period spent in psychotic episodes there were two categories of subgroups. The simple, hebephrenic, paranoid and unspecified schizophrenics were psychotic for a relatively higher percentage of the follow-up period, while the catatonic, latent, acute, schizo-affective and other specified schizophrenics were psychotic for a relatively low percentage of the follow-up period.

Pattern of course. Table 9.8 presents the percentage distribution of patients in each schizophrenic subgroup of type of pattern of course. The differences in the distributions among the subgroups are statistically significant.

It can be seen that the simple, hebephrenic, paranoid, and unspecified schizophrenic subgroups were characterized by a relatively high percentage of patients who remained in the episode of inclusion throughout the follow-up period, and a relatively low percentage of patients in whom the episode of inclusion was followed by a full remission lasting throughout the follow-up period. The catatonic, acute, and schizo-affective schizophrenic subgroups were characterized by a relatively high percentage of patients in whom the episode of inclusion was followed by a full remission lasting throughout the follow-up period and a relatively low percentage of patients in whom the episode of inclusion lasted throughout the

TABLE 9.8. PERCENTAGE DISTRIBUTION OF PATIENTS BY PATTERN OF COURSE GROUP. SUBGROUPS OF SCHIZOPHRENIA, ALL CENTRES COMBINED.

Subgroup of schizophrenia	No. of patients	1 Only episode of inclusion full remission	2 Only episode of inclusion incomplete remission	3 Subsequent non-psychotic episodes full remission	4 Subsequent non-psychotic episodes, incomplete remission	5 Subsequent psychotic episodes, full remission	6 Subsequent psychotic episodes, incomplete remission	7 Still in episode of inclusion	Total
Simple	22	14	14	-	-	4	4	64	100
Hebephrenic	72	21	10	-	-	4	26	39	100
Catatonic	43	47	2	-	-	21	16	14	100
Paranoid	205	25	17	-	1	9	17	31	100
Acute	52	37	13	-	-	21	13	16	100
Latent	20	10	50	-	10	-	15	15	100
Residual	2	-	-	-	-	-	50	50	100
Schizo-affective	75	36	20	-	1	16	16	11	100
Other specified	46	17	24	-	-	9	37	13	100
Unspecified	33	27	12	-	-	12	9	40	100

follow-up period. A high percentage of patients in the latent schizophrenia group had an episode of inclusion which was followed by a partial remission lasting throughout the follow-up period. The other specified schizophrenic group was characterized by a high percentage of patients with subsequent psychotic episodes followed by partial remissions.

Thus, it appears that the simple, hebephrenic, paranoid and unspecified schizophrenics tended to have a relatively severe pattern of course, while the catatonic, acute and schizo-affective schizophrenics tended to have a less severe pattern of course.

Degree of social impairment during the two-year follow-up period. The percentage of patients in the various schizophrenic subgroups who were considered to have suffered from severe social impairment during the two-year follow-up period are presented in Table 9.9. The differences among the subgroups are statistically significant.

It can be seen from this table that the simple schizophrenic subgroup had the highest percentage of patients (55 per cent) considered to have suffered from severe social impairment during the follow-up period. Unspecified schizophrenia and hebephrenic schizophrenia were the other two subgroups with relatively high percentages of patients with such impairment (34 per cent and 30 per cent respectively). Catatonic, acute, latent, and schizo-affective subgroups were characterized by low percentages of patients with severe social impairment, while paranoid and 'other specified' schizophrenia were intermediate in this respect.

TABLE 9.9.   PRESENCE OR ABSENCE OF SEVERE SOCIAL
IMPAIRMENT.   SUBGROUPS OF SCHIZOPHRENIA.
ALL CENTRES.

Subgroup of schizophrenia	No. of patients	No severe impairment %	Severe impairment %	Total %
Simple	22	45	55	100
Hebephrenic	73	70	30	100
Catatonic	43	86	14	100
Paranoid	208	74	26	100
Acute	58	88	12	100
Latent.	19	100	-	100
Residual	1	-	100	100
Schizo-affective	80	86	14	100
Other specified	46	76	24	100
Unspecified	35	66	34	100

Overall Outcome. Overall outcome groupings for the schizophrenic subgroups are compared in Table 9.10. The differences among the subgroups are statistically significant. It can be seen that the simple schizophrenic subgroup is the subgroup with the worst overall outcome, with the highest percentage of patients in the worst-outcome group and a low percentage in the best outcome group. The hebephrenic and unspecified subgroups were also characterized by a high percentage of patients in the worst overall outcome group. Catatonic, acute and schizo-affective schizophrenia were characterized by a low percentage of patients in the worst-outcome group and a high percentage in the best-outcome group. The paranoid subgroup was intermediate with regard to the percentages of patients in the various outcome groups. Latent and 'other specified' schizophrenia had low percentages of patients in both the best and worst overall outcome groups.

Summary of analyses for all centres combined. The simple schizophrenic subgroup thus had the worst outcome for all the criteria noted above. Three other subgroups were usually associated with poor outcome — hebephrenic, paranoid, and unspecified schizophrenia. Of these, paranoid schizophrenia usually had a somewhat better outcome than the others. Three subgroups had a relatively good outcome on most of the criteria — catatonic, acute and schizo-affective. Two subgroups, latent, and other specified, had variable outcomes on the different criteria. There were insufficient numbers of followed-up patients in the residual schizophrenia subgroup for any conclusion to be drawn about the type of two-year course and outcome. The analyses for all of the variables were repeated, comparing the simple-hebephrenic-paranoid-unspecified group, on the one hand, with the catatonic-acute-schizo-affective group on the other hand. For every variable the differences between the two groups were statistically significant.

9.2.2.2 Intracentre comparisons

Since it is possible that different centres may have used the subcategorization of schizophrenia differently, it is useful to consider differences in the course and outcome of different diagnostic subgroups within the same centre. Unfortunately, it was not possible to make many such comparisons because there were usually not many subgroups within individual centres with sufficient numbers of patients followed up to allow comparisons. It was possible to make the following comparisons: in Agra, catatonic *vs.* schizo-affective, catatonic *vs.* unspecified, and schizo-affective *vs.* unspecified; in Cali, hebephrenic *vs.* paranoid, hebephrenic *vs.* acute, and paranoid *vs.* acute; in Ibadan, paranoid *vs.* schizo-affective; in Taipei, simple *vs.* paranoid; and in Prague, paranoid *vs.* schizo-affective.

The Agra catatonics were characterized by a lower percentage of patients still in the episode of inclusion and a higher percentage of patients who had subsequent psychotic episodes with full remissions after episodes than Agra schizo-affective or unspecified schizophrenics. The unspecified schizophrenics in Agra also had a lower percentage of patients in whom the episode of inclusion was followed by a full remission which lasted throughout the follow-up period than did Agra catatonics.

TABLE 9.10. PERCENTAGE DISTRIBUTION OF PATIENTS BY OVERALL OUTCOME GROUPS. SUBGROUPS OF SCHIZOPHRENIA, ALL CENTRES COMBINED.

Subgroup of schizophrenia	No. of patients	Overall outcome groups					Total
		1 Very favourable	2 Favourable	3 Intermediate	4 Unfavourable	5 Very unfavourable	
Simple	20	15	30	5	5	45	100
Hebephrenic	69	11	19	22	22	26	100
Catatonic	40	50	20	15	3	12	100
Paranoid	198	23	20	23	14	20	100
Acute	51	39	33	12	10	6	100
Latent	19	15	63	11	11	-	100
Residual	1	-	-	-	-	(100)	(100)
Schizo-affective	70	33	30	22	4	11	100
Other specified	43	19	30	35	2	14	100
Unspecified	32	22	18	16	16	28	100

The paranoid subgroup in Prague was characterized by a higher percentage of patients who were still in the episode of inclusion at second-year follow-up or who had subsequent psychotic episodes without full remissions, and a lower percentage of patients in whom the episode of inclusion was followed by a full remission which lasted throughout the follow-up period than schizo-affective schizophrenics in the same centre.

In Agra, the unspecified group had a higher percentage of patients with severe social impairment than either the catatonic or the schizo-affective subgroups, while in Taipei, the hebephrenic subgroup had a higher percentage of patients with severe social impairment than the paranoid subgroup.

The Agra catatonic subgroup had a much higher percentage of patients in the best overall group and a lower percentage of patients in the worst overall outcome group than did the unspecified subgroup in that centre. A higher percentage of hebephrenic than of paranoid patients in Taipei fell into the worst overall outcome group, while a lower percentage of hebephrenics than of paranoid patients fell into the best overall outcome group in that centre.

9.3 SUMMARY

The follow-up phase of the IPSS thus presents some support for certain aspects of the subclassification of schizophrenia. Although considering broad areas of psychopathology there were no significant differences among the subgroups at the time of second-year follow-up, consideration of more specific symptom levels suggested that there are differences among the subgroups at follow-up. The two-year course and outcome data also suggest differences among the subgroups. In particular, it appears that simple, hebephrenic, paranoid, and unspecified schizophrenics had the worst two-year course and outcome, while catatonic, acute and schizo-affective schizophrenics had the best course and outcome.

CHAPTER 10

Predictors of Course and Outcome in Schizophrenia and Affective Psychoses

10.1 INTRODUCTION

Follow-up information on the 906 patients collected in the nine field research centres was used to explore the predictive power of a large number of variables in relation to different measures of course and outcome. In comparison with many earlier studies of prognostic indicators in the functional psychoses the IPSS data offered several advantages: (a) they were collected in a prospective study; (b) the initial evaluation and the follow-up reassessment of psychopathology were carried out by well-trained investigators using a standardized research instrument; (c) the reliability of the clinical evaluation procedures had been assessed, within and between the research centres; (d) the study population included patients from nine different cultures, a fact which provided the unique opportunity to relate prognostic factors to the setting in which the disorder occurred.

In assigning a significance to the results reported in this chapter, three general considerations should be kept in mind:

1. The study is based on a series of clinically diagnosed patients who have been identified through the psychiatric services and not on epidemiological samples. Therefore the findings about predictors of course and outcome should not be generalized to varieties of the schizophrenic and other functional psychotic disorders that may have remained outside the scope of the present study.

2. Predictions in psychiatry are usually of an actuarial nature. They are derived empirically from observations on groups of patients who initially have certain characteristics in common and who, in the course of time, may develop different kinds of outcome. The actuarial nature of prediction in psychiatry makes extrapolation from prognosis of the group to prognosis of the individual uncertain, except for the few instances in which predictor-outcome relationships represent strong cause-and-effect relationships (as in some organic lesions of the brain).

3. The reported results refer to the two-year prognosis, which, in terms of E. Bleuler's (1916) distinction between *ultimate* prognosis (*Richtungsprognose*) and *interim* prognosis (*Streckenprognose*), corresponds to the latter category.

The view prevailing since Kraepelin (1913) is that the two major diagnostic entities – schizophrenia and manic-depressive psychosis – differ qualitatively in their ultimate prognosis. The outlook in schizophrenia (except for the nosologically

253

disputed schizo-affective subtype) is regarded as generally poor, involving chronicity, social impairment and change of personality, while in manic-depressive psychosis the personality is expected to remain socially intact, in spite of the high risk of recurrent attacks. However, this widely held, and taught, view of qualitatively contrasting prognoses in schizophrenia and affective disorders has found so far only limited factual support.

With regard to the short-term or interim prognosis, it is assumed that most cases of depressive or manic attacks remit fully, with or without specific treatment, but the duration of the episode can vary considerably depending on age, previous personality, genetic constitution, and possibly the kind of treatment applied. The interim prognosis is less clear in schizophrenia where the prediction of the outcome of an individual attack (especially if it is a first or a second one) and of the subsequent course of the illness can be extremely difficult. The variety of courses that disorders diagnosed as schizophrenic take after the initial stage is documented in the literature reviewed in Chapter 2 and this great variability has been attributed to a no less varied assortment of prognostic factors. However, most of the previous studies on prognosis in the functional psychoses have operated with unstandardized diagnostic concepts, predictors, and characteristics of course and outcome whose assessment is not directly replicable and comparison of results from different studies is therefore difficult.

The present chapter reports on different approaches that were used to test on the available IPSS materials some of the assumptions and hypotheses mentioned above. First the hypotheses about predictors of course and outcome in schizophrenia and affective psychoses will be summarised (section 10.2); then the data and analyses used to test some of these hypotheses described (section 10.3); next the results of analyses will be presented first for schizophrenia (section 10.4), and then for affective psychosis (section 10.5); finally, these results will be discussed and the conclusions which were reached summarized (section 10.6).

10.2 HYPOTHESES ABOUT PREDICTORS OF COURSE AND OUTCOME

10.2.1 Predictors in schizophrenia

Although direct comparisons between different previous studies on prognosis in schizophrenia are difficult because of lack of uniform criteria for the assessment of course, outcome and predictor variables, it is possible to outline broad areas of agreement between different studies and to derive hypotheses, many of which could be tested on data from the two-year follow-up phase of the IPSS. Table 10.1 is a summary of such hypotheses and presents a list of variables suggested in the literature as potential predictors to 'good' and 'poor' prognosis in schizophrenia.

10.2.2 Predictors in affective psychoses

One of the reasons for the original nosological separation of affective psychoses from schizophrenia has been their tendency to more favourable course and

TABLE 10.1.   SUMMARY OF HYPOTHESES ON PREDICTORS OF COURSE AND OUTCOME
IN SCHIZOPHRENIA DERIVED FROM PREVIOUS STUDIES.

Variables	Good Prognosis	Poor Prognosis
Socio-demographic		
Age at onset	above 20-25	below 20
sex	inconclusive evidence	inconclusive evidence
socio-economic status	average, high	low
occupational record	stable	irregular
level of education	uncertain	uncertain
urban/rural residence	uncertain	uncertain
belonging to minority group	no	yes
other adverse social factors	absent	present
Past history and personality		
family history of mental illness	affective	schizophrenic
previous personality*	syntonic,affective	schizoid
somatotype*	pyknic	asthenic,leptosome
behaviour disorder in past	uncertain	uncertain
intelligence level	not subnormal	subnormal
psychosexual adjustment	at least one lasting hetero-sexual relation-ship	no lasting hetero-sexual relation-ship
past physical illnesses	uncertain	uncertain
past psychotic illness	affective	schizophrenic
past neurotic illnesses	obsessional	uncertain
precipitating factors	present	absent
type of onset	acute, sudden	insidious
rate of progression of symptoms	rapid,florid	slow, barren
length of episode prior to assessment	months or less	years
Presenting psychopathology		
psychological intelligibility of symptoms*	present	absent
state of consciousness, sensorium	clouding,confusion	clear
affective symptoms	depression, elation, fear	absent
affective blunting or incongruity	absent	present
neurotic symptoms	obsessional, hysterical,anxiety	absent
catatonic symptoms	excitement, agitation	stupor in absence of affective features
speech, thinking	flight of ideas, incoherence	poverty of speech
depersonalization and derealization (in Langfeldt's sense)	absent	present
thought insertion, broadcast, hearing, spoken aloud, etc.	uncertain	uncertain
hallucinations	visual	bodily, esp. sexual, haptic, olfactory
"characteristic" hallucinations (voices discussing patient, etc.)	uncertain	uncertain
predelusional experiences	delusional mood, misidentification	uncertain
ideas of reference	uncertain	uncertain
delusions	guilt,grandeur, fantastic, hypo-chondriacal	body change, sex change,influence, passivity,persecution
systematization of delusions	absent	present
early signs of autism	absent	present

* not tested in the analysis reported below.

outcome, and in clinical practice the detection of affective symptoms in an otherwise schizophrenic picture usually mitigates against a poor prognosis.

On the other hand, although the prognosis of affective psychoses is generally accepted to be more favourable than the prognosis of schizophrenia, depressive psychotic illnesses may run a disabling chronic course without displaying at any stage symptoms characteristic of schizophrenia. Little is known about the determinants and predictors of the unfavourable course in such cases. Therefore, an attempt was made to explore possible predictors in the patients with diagnosis of depressive affective psychoses (ICD 296.0, 296.2 and 298.0) who had been included in the IPSS for comparative purposes.

For several reasons, among which the small size of this group, and the limitation of age (15 to 44) are particularly important, those patients do not represent the whole range of affective disorders, and the predictors which were identified refer only to patients with affective illnesses who are in the same age groups as the schizophrenic patients in the IPSS series.

A hypothesis which could be tested was that predictors of poor outcome in schizophrenia would also be predictors of unfavourable course and outcome in affective psychoses in patients of comparable age. However, since affective illnesses are usually self-limiting in time, the type of onset and the duration of the episode prior to the initial assessment could be expected to have less, if any, prognostic significance in affective psychoses — for example, slow onset and long duration of the episode prior to the initial assessment would not necessarily predict unfavourable course and outcome.

10.2.3 Predictors of course and outcome of schizophrenia in different cultures

Culture, difficult as it may be to define, is assumed to have an impact on the course and outcome of functional psychotic disorders (Jablensky and Sartorius, 1975). Some studies (Raman and Murphy, 1972) suggest that the prognostic indicators in schizophrenia may vary in different cultural settings. Two hypotheses related to such issues could be tested in a preliminary way in the context of the IPSS: (a) the particular culture in which a schizophrenic disorder occurs can modify in some distinct way the prognosis of the disorder, and (b) there are differences among the centres of the study with regard to the variables which predict best the two-year course and outcome of schizophrenia.

10.3 IPSS DATA AND ANALYSES USED IN THE STUDY OF PREDICTORS

10.3.1 Description of variables studied

The study of prediction involves the search for relationships between a set of independent variables (predictors) and a set of dependent variables (course and outcome).

The predictor variables were selected from the items of information collected in a standardized way on each patient at the initial evaluation. The question of the

TABLE 10.2.   PREDICTOR VARIABLES AND NUMBER OF PATIENTS ON WHOM FOLLOW-
UP DATA ON SUCH VARIABLES WERE AVAILABLE.

Groups	Description	Subdivisions	Source of information	No. of patients Schizo-phrenia		Affective psychosis	
				N	%	N	%
A. socio demographic variables	Age	1=15-24	PSE,PH,SD*	248	40	27	20
		2=25-34		222	37	56	40
		3=35-44		137	23	56	40
				607	100	139	100
	Sex	0=male	PSE,PH,SD	303	50	53	38
		1=female		305	50	86	62
				608	100	139	100
	Marital status	1=single,never married	PSE,PH,SD	327	54	31	22
		2=married		247	41	98	71
		3=other; widowed, divorced, separated		34	5	10	7
				608	100	139	100
	Type of household	0=living alone	SD	57	9	8	6
		1=living not alone		549	91	130	94
				606	100	138	100
	Current residence	0=urban	SD	523	86	109	78
		1=rural		82	14	30	22
				605	100	139	100
	Socio-economic status of patient	1=high	SD	72	13	30	22
		2=middle		233	42	70	52
		3=low		253	45	34	26
				558	100	134	100
	Patient's education level	1=no schooling	SD	59	10	13	9
		2=up to three years at school		41	7	4	3
		3=4-12 years		403	67	88	64
		4=13+ years		98	16	32	24
				601	100	137	100
	Patient's type of occupation	1=never worked, unemployed,students, housewives,pensioners	SD	183	33	31	28
		2=manual or production process workers, craftsmen,labourers		145	26	23	20
		3=sales and service workers		74	14	14	13
		4=farmers and related occupations		23	4	9	8
		5=managerial and clerical occupations		69	13	14	13
		6=professionals		54	10	21	18
				548	100	112	100
	Occupational history	1=never had a job	SD	126	21	29	21
		2=has worked in the past but not in the last 12 months		129	21	30	22
		3=has worked in last 12 months		352	58	79	57
				607	100	138	100
	Current social isolation	1=none or mild	SD	292	52	102	78
		2=moderate		98	17	11	8
		3=severe		176	31	18	14
				566	100	131	100

TABLE 10.2. continued

Groups	Description	Subdivisions	Source of Information	No. of patients			
				Schizophrenia		Affective psychosis	
				N	%	N	%
B. past history variables	Mental illness of parents, spouse, children or other relatives	0=absent 1=present	PH	435 158 593	73 27 100	90 46 136	66 34 100
	History of behaviour symptoms (no. of positive entries)	0 1 2 3 4 5 6 7 8 9 10	PH	331 108 65 44 25 9 10 2 – – 1 595	56 18 11 7 4 2 2 – – – – 100	84 21 15 5 6 1 1 – – – – 133	63 16 11 4 4 1 1 – – – – 100
	Serious physical illness in the past;stigmata or permanent disability	0=absent 1=present	PH	568 33 601	95 5 100	130 8 138	94 6 100
	Effects of unfavourable environment	0=no 1=yes	PH	562 32 594	95 5 100	133 4 137	97 3 100
	Overall rating of psychosexual adjustment	1=no difficulties 2=some difficulties 3=marked difficulties	PH	325 82 73 480	68 17 15 100	101 17 7 125	81 14 5 100
	Past treatment or contact with medical services because of psychiatric disorder	0=no 1=yes	PH	366 241 607	60 40 100	57 82 139	41 59 100
	Past treatment or contact with other persons or organizations because of psychiatric disorder	0=no 1=yes	PH	420 139 559	75 25 100	83 31 114	73 27 100
	Events preceding onset of current episode	0=no 1=yes	PH	308 257 565	55 45 100	64 66 130	49 51 100

TABLE 10.2. continued

Groups	Description	Subdivisions	Source of infor- mation	No. of patients Schizo- phrenia		Affective psychosis	
				N	%	N	%
C.Variables related to episode of inclusion	Type of onset	0=sudden 1=slow, insidious	PH	80 527 607	13 87 100	31 104 135	23 77 100
	Duration of episode prior to initial evaluation	1=less than a week 2=1 week 3=8 weeks 4=6 months 5=1 year 6=2 years 7=5 years or more	PH	57 149 187 76 63 43 22 597	8 25 31 13 12 7 4 100	12 46 52 14 7 4 2 137	9 34 38 10 5 4 - 100
Symptomat- ology at initial evaluation	27 Groups of Units of Analysis (GUAs)		PSE	543		133	
	129 Units of Analysis (UAs)		PSE	543		133	
Field research centres (FRCs)	Aarhus Agra Cali Ibadan London Moscow Taipei Washington Prague			48 92 78 63 58 69 80 65 55 608	8 15 13 10 10 11 13 11 9 100	33 25 5 6 9 17 12 5 27 139	24 18 4 4 6 12 9 4 19 100

* PSE = Present State Examination; PH = Psychiatric History;
  SD = Social Description.

reliability of their assessment has been discussed in Volume 1 of the IPSS report (WHO, 1973). In the selection of potential predictors, the literature on prognosis in the functional psychoses, as well as the clinical experience of the investigators participating in the study, were taken into consideration. The choice of variables was also influenced by the nature and limitation of the data collected during the initial evaluation phase.

The 47 predictor variables* are listed in Table 10.2 which also indicates the source of information on each variable and the number of followed-up patients on whom data related to each predictor were available.

*Strictly, there were 54 variables, since the subdivisions of marital status and occupation were dichotomized and used as separate variables. The 129 units of analysis (UAs) are not included in this number because they are contained in the 27 groups of units of analysis (GUAs). Results of analyses using the 129 UAs are described in Section 10.4.3.

TABLE 10.3.   DEPENDENT VARIABLES (COURSE AND OUTCOME) USED IN THE
ANALYSIS OF PREDICTORS.

	No. of patients with initial diagnosis of schizophrenia and affective psychoses on whom follow-up data were available.			
	Schizo-phrenia (ICD 295.0-9)		Affective psychoses (ICD 296.0-9 and 298.0)	
	N	%	N	%
1. Length of episode of inclusion				
0-28 months	565		133	
2. Proportion of follow-up period during which patient was in psychotic episodes 0.0 - 100.0	559		133	
3. Pattern of course				
3.1=full remission after episode of inclusion, no further episodes	154	27	43	32
3.2=incomplete remission after episode of inclusion, no further episodes	94	17	22	16
3.3=one or more non-psychotic episodes after episode of inclusion, full remissions between all episodes	-	-	2	1
3.4=one or more non-psychotic episodes after episode of inclusion, at least one incomplete remission	5	1	-	-
3.5=one or more psychotic episodes after episode of inclusion, full remission between all episodes	63	11	37	27
3.6=one or more psychotic episodes after episode of inclusion, at least one incomplete	104	18	24	18
3.7=still in episode of inclusion	150	26	8	6
Total	570	100	136	100
4. Type of subsequent episode				
4.1=definitely schizophrenic	64	40	1	1
4.2=probably schizophrenic	68	42	6	10
4.3=affective	28	18	55	89
Total	160	100	62	100
5. Level of social functioning				
5.1=no or mild impairment	184	32	55	40
5.2=medium impairment	264	45	66	48
5.3=severe impairment	137	23	16	12
Total	585	100	137	100
6. Overall outcome groups				
6.1=very favourable	138	25	53	40
6.2=favourable	135	25	43	33
6.3=intermediate	110	20	20	15
6.4=unfavourable	62	11	7	6
6.5=very unfavourable	98	19	8	6
Total	543	100	131	100

All predictor variables were divided into three classes:

Class A: Sociodemographic variables;

Class B: Past history variables;

Class C: Variables related to the episode of inclusion

At a certain stage of the analysis, the nine centres were also used as a special group of predictors.

TABLE 10.4. INTER-CORRELATIONS BETWEEN THE COURSE AND
OUTCOME MEASURES USED IN THE ANALYSIS OF
PREDICTORS (SPEARMAN'S r).

Schizophrenia

Variables No.*	1	2	5	6
1	-	.910	.388	.723
2		-	.379	.752
3.1			-.370	-.559
3.2			-.001	-.095
3.3			.0	.0
3.4			.132	.050
3.5			-.082	-.160
3.6			.011	.050
3.7			.393	.695
5			-	.735
6				-

Affective psychosis

Variables No.*	1	2	5	6
1	-	.878	.364	.541
2		-	.440	.646
3.1			-.302	-.462
3.2			.040	.071
3.3			-.082	-.086
3.4			.0	.0
3.5			-.040	-.135
3.6			.198	.335
3.7			.276	.455
5			-	.517
6				-

* See Table 10.3.

Course and outcome variables were defined in the same way as in Chapters 6, 7, 8 and 9. They are listed in Table 10.3 together with the scale values used in the analysis of prediction. Data on the reliability of assessment of each course or outcome variable can be found in Chapter 4. The intercorrelations between the individual course and outcome variables are shown on Table 10.4.

10.3.2 Analyses used in the study of predictors

The statistical model of regression was chosen as the principal tool in the analysis of predictors of course and outcome. Discriminant function analysis and other correlational methods were used in some instances and their description is given in Section 10.4.3.

Regression analysis permits an evaluation of the nature and strength of the relationship between a set of predictor variables and each of the categories describing course and outcome. A simple example can illustrate the basic ideas underlying this technique.

The time patients spend out of hospital during a given period can vary from 0 to 365 days per year and this variation might be due, for example, to differences in the patients' age, because, the older patients tend to stay in hospital longer. This would mean that within each age group the variation with regard to the outcome variable 'time spent out of hospital' is much smaller than the variation for all patients taken together. The variance of the outcome category (time out of hospital) which remains after the removal of the effect of the predictor variable (age in this example) is called residual variance, and the percentage of the total variance explained by the predictor a coefficient of determination.* The coefficient of determination can serve as an indicator of the predictive power of a variable only if the relationship between this variable and the outcome characteristic is of a linear nature. If it is not, a suitable transformation has to be found.

The same basic ideas hold if the above simple regression model is replaced by a multiple regression model, by including several, rather than just one, predictor variables.

If the set of potential predictors consists of many variables, it is possible that only a small subset of four or five predictor variables may explain as much of the variance as the whole set of, say 20 or more. If such is the case, it would be of interest to identify those 'best' predictors, and the technique of stepwise multiple regression is an appropriate tool for this purpose.

In this procedure, the predictor which has the highest correlation with the outcome variable is entered first into the regression model, and the coefficient of determination (R^2) is calculated for this predictor variable. In the next step, the predictor which is entered into the equation is the one which has the highest correlation with the outcome variable, after the effects of the first predictor have been removed. The R^2 now indicates the percentage of the variation of the outcome variable which can be explained jointly by the two predictors in the equation. The same operation is repeated in successive steps.

Meaningful results can only be obtained if predictors and outcome variables are measured on ordinal scales. Nominal variables, such as marital status with its usual levels of 'single', 'married', 'divorced' etc. can be split for the purposes of those analyses into several dichotomous categories — for example 'single' with levels 'no' and 'yes', and so on.

The total number of patients available for analysis was relatively large: for example, the number of followed-up schizophrenic patients was over 500. For this reason the question of statistical significance was of little practical relevance, since

*R^2, or the squared coefficient of correlation between the predictor and the outcome variable.

even very small correlation and regression coefficients would turn out to be significantly different from zero. Tests of significance in this analysis would not contribute to the interpretation of the results and, therefore, are not reported.

Analyses were performed separately for patients who, on initial evaluation, had received a clinical diagnosis of schizophrenia (ICD 295.0-9) and for patients with initial diagnosis of affective psychosis (ICD 296.0-9 and 298.0).

The stepwise multiple regression analysis of the predictors was carried out in several stages. In the first three stages, each of the three classes of variables (A = sociodemographic characteristics, B = past history characteristics, and C = characteristics of the inclusion episode) was analysed separately to examine its relationship to course and outcome variables. Out of the resulting three sets of predictors, those were taken into the next stage of analysis, which reached highest levels of prediction (i.e. R^2) within their own class. In most instances, the predictors which emerged from the first five steps of the regression accounted for most of the variance that could be explained by the whole set of predictors. Five such 'best' predictors were taken from each class (A, B and C) and used as a 'battery' in the next stage of the analysis. Thus, at the fourth stage (stage D), all the 15 'best' predictors obtained up to this point were entered into the regression analysis and five of them which turned out to have the highest R^2 were considered a final set of best predictors.

For every course and outcome variable the analysis was repeated, taking the nine centres of the study as an additional set of potential predictors which was added to the variables in each of the classes A, B and C. With regard to each of the centres, a patient was rated simply as either being, or not being there. The purpose of this extension of the analysis was to examine the possible effects of unspecified but potentially relevant culture-related variables covered by the 'label' of the centre.

Each variable emerging from the analyses reported below predicts symmetrically, that is the presence/absence, or high/low score on a given characteristic, indicate contrasting trends of course and outcome. For convenience, only one direction of the prediction is indicated in the tables by (−) or (+) for 'poor' and 'good' prognosis, respectively. The order in which the predictors are listed in the tables does not necessarily imply a ranking according to their predictive power, but reflects the sequence in which they have been entered into the multiple regression equation.

10.4 PREDICTORS OF TWO-YEAR COURSE AND OUTCOME OF PATIENTS WITH CLINICAL DIAGNOSIS OF SCHIZOPHRENIA (ICD 295)

10.4.1 Analyses using data from all centres

The results of the stepwise multiple regression analysis of the predictor variables are described separately with regard to each course and outcome variable.

10.4.1.1 Prediction of the length of the episode of inclusion

The length of the episode of inclusion is a continuous variable (0-28 months).* Table 10.5 presents the obtained best predictors for this measure. The results of the analysis performed for this variable are described more extensively, to avoid repetition of technical details in subsequent sections.

Socio-demographic characteristics. If the centres are not included as variables in the analysis, 18 predictors explain 11 per cent of the outcome variance.† Five of them — social isolation, marital status, sex, occupation and educational level — explain 9 per cent and the contribution of the remaining 13 to the prediction of the length of the episode is marginal (2 per cent).

The estimated degree of social isolation of the patient was rated by the interviewer during the initial evaluation on a simple five-point scale. The analysis showed that ratings of severe social isolation made at the beginning of the study turned out to be associated with a greater length of the episode of inclusion, and ratings of mild or no social isolation with shorter episodes of inclusion.

The marital-status category 'widowed, divorced or separated' was associated with a longer duration of the inclusion episode. The 'single' marital status category, described in previous studies as a predictor of poor outcome, was also associated with a greater length of the episode of inclusion but its contribution to the prognosis was small (the addition of 'single' marital status to the five best predictors would increase the amount of explained variance by only 0.3 per cent).

Male sex, predicting longer inclusion episodes (and, respectively, female sex predicting shorter inclusion episodes) was found to have the same predictive power as the marital status 'widowed, divorced or separated'.

Type of occupation was predictive mainly with regard to two of the occupational categories, both of them related to a shorter duration of the inclusion episode — professional and managerial or clerical occupations (the latter category appeared at step 6 of the analysis).

Higher level of education predicted a greater length of the inclusion episode. This finding is contrary to what would be expected and a plausible explanation, suggested by another analysis, will be described below.

Changes in the composition of the set of predictors occurred as the centres were added as predictors to the other variables in the analysis. First, the proportion of variance explained now by all predictors increased to 17 per cent, and the variance explained by the first five of them to 12 per cent. This means that the centre variables contained additional predictive information. Second, when centres were entered as variables the predictive power of some class A predictors changed.

*The 'length of the episode of inclusion' was calculated in months between the date of the initial examination of the patient and the end of the episode of inclusion. The real beginning of the episode is reflected in the predictor variable 'length of the episode prior to initial evaluation' calculated in months between the reported beginning of the episode and the initial examination date.

†The term 'outcome variance' is used in this chapter for convenience only. Strictly speaking, most of the dependent variables reflect characteristics of the two-year course of the illness.

TABLE 10.5. PREDICTION OF THE LENGTH OF THE EPISODE OF INCLUSION.* PATIENTS WITH INITIAL CLINICAL DIAGNOSIS OF SCHIZOPHRENIA.

Predictor class	A. Socio-demographic characteristics		B. Past history characteristics		C. Characteristics of inclusion episode		D. 15 best predictors (A, B and C combined)	
	FRCs excluded	FRCs included	FRCs excluded	FRCs included	FRCs excluded	FRCs included	FRCs excluded	FRCs included
5 best predictors	social iso-lation (-)	social iso-lation (-)	mental illness in family (-)	Ibadan (+)	duration of episode prior to IE (-)	duration of episode prior to IE (-)	duration of episode prior to IE (-)	duration of episode prior to IE (-)
	marital sta-tus: widowed divorced or separated(-)	Ibadan (+)	poor psycho-sexual adjust-ment (-)	mental illness in family (-)	derealization (GUA 12) (+)	Ibadan (+)	Social iso-lation (-)	social iso-lation (-)
	male sex (-)	Aarhus (-)	history of behaviour disorder (-)	poor psycho-sexual adjust-ment (-)	insidious onset (-)	Moscow (+)	derealization (GUA 12) (+)	derealization (GUA 12) (+)
	occupation: professional (+)	Washington (-)	unfavourable environment (-)	Taipei (-)	cooperation difficulties, circumstances related (GUA 26) (+)	derealization (GUA 12) (+)	past psychia-tric treat-ment (-)	past psychia-tric treat-ment (-)
	higher educa-tional level (-)	male sex (-)	past psychia-tric treat-ment (-)	absence of precipitating stress (-)	depressed /elated (GUA 17) (+)	Agra (+)	history of behaviour disorder (-)	history of behaviour disorder (-)
% variance explained by 5 best	9	12	7	8	10	14	15	15
% variance explained by all	11	17	7	11	13	19	19	20

* (+) indicates good prognosis, i.e. predicts a shorter episode of inclusion.
  (-) indicates poor prognosis, i.e. predicts a longer episode of inclusion.

Generally, such changes in the multiple regression analysis were (a) inclusion of one or more centres among the best predictors, while other predictors changed positions but retained the order in which they appeared; (b) replacement of one or more predictors by one or more centres with a change of order of some of the original predictors.

In the resulting new set of five best predictors, three of the original variables were replaced by centres. The Ibadan centre was a predictor of shorter inclusion episodes, and the Aarhus and Washington centres were predictors of longer inclusion episodes. Two of the original predictors: social isolation and male sex, both associated with longer inclusion episode, retained their predictive value. This indicates that the two variables were strongly associated with the length of the inclusion episode and that this association was not the result of their correlation with other variables — particular centres, for example.

Marital status 'widowed, divorced or separated' lost some of its predictive power (appearing now at step 6), but more considerable change occurred with occupation and educational level, whose predictive power was greatly reduced (educational level even failed to enter the regression equation). This could mean that the predictive information contained, for instance in the variable level of education, was also contained in some, or all, of the three centre variables (Ibadan, Aarhus and Washington).

Past history characteristics When centre variables were not included in the analysis, the first five predictors explained practically the same proportion of the outcome variance (7 per cent) as the whole set of eight predictors.

History of mental illness in the family* had the highest correlation with the length of the inclusion episode, and predicted longer episodes.

Psychosexual adjustment (assessed on the basis of 19 separate history items) and history of behaviour symptoms at any age (for example, night terrors, sleepwalking, bedwetting, temper tantrums, panic attacks, truancy from school or work, aggressiveness toward people or things, running away from home, petty stealing, frequent lying, hyperactivity and others) are variables which describe facets of the premorbid personality. Difficulties in psychosexual adjustment predicted longer inclusion episodes, and absence of such difficulties predicted shorter inclusion episodes.

History of behaviour symptoms was rated on a continuun (number of symptoms) and the symptom count turned out to be positively correlated with the length of the inclusion episode.

Unfavourable environment prior to the onset of illness (that is, belonging to a minority group or a particular religious sect, being forced to leave home or emigrate, living in an alien culture) emerged as another predictor of longer inclusion episodes.

History of past psychiatric treatment, that is, contacts with medical agencies for

---

*In the psychiatric history schedule used at the initial evaluation this item was formulated as 'mental illness or handicap of parents, spouse, children or other relatives in household'. It does not, therefore, necessarily imply a hereditary predisposition.

treatment of psychiatric disorder was also associated with longer episodes of inclusion.

The introduction of the centres into the analysis resulted in a reduction of the predictive power of the variables 'history of behaviour symptoms', 'unfavourable environment' and 'past psychiatric treatment', and in the identification of three new predictors. The Ibadan centre appeared as the strongest predictor of shorter inclusion episodes, while the Taipei centre appeared as a predictor of longer episodes of inclusion.

Precipitating stress (physical, psychological or environmental) preceding the episode of inclusion also emerged as a strong predictor. Absence of stress predicted longer inclusion episodes and presence of stress predicted shorter episodes.

Characteristics of the episode of inclusion. This class of predictors includes mental state variables — scores on 27 groups of units of analysis* obtained from initial evaluation data, as well as type of onset, duration of the episode prior to the initial evaluation, and course of the episode before the initial evaluation.

The five best predictors of the length of the inclusion episode (explaining 10 per cent of the variance) were: duration of the episode prior to the initial evaluation, scores on derealization, type of onset, scores on co-operation difficulties, circumstances-related, and scores on presence of depression or elation.

The best predictor among them was the 'duration of the episode prior to the initial evaluation', positively correlated with the length of the episode after the initial evaluation. Long duration of the episode before the initial assessment predicted long duration of the same episode after the initial assessment, and conversely, short duration before the initial evaluation predicted short duration after the initial evaluation.

Insidious or slow onset of the episode was associated with longer episodes, while sudden onset predicted shorter episodes.

Among the mental state variables, derealization (GUA 12) contributed most to the prediction. High scores on this variable were associated with shorter inclusion episodes. Presence of depression or elation (GUA 17) predicted shorter inclusion episodes, if scored high on the initial evaluation, and longer inclusion episodes if scored low.

Co-operation difficulties, circumstances-related (GUA 26) predicted shorter inclusion episodes if scored high, and longer inclusion episodes if scored low. This variable comprises three rather different units of analysis (organic effects of biological treatment, untoward environmental circumstances and speech impediments), of which side effects of biological treatment (for example extrapyramidal rigidity due to medication) might be the unit actually contributing to the prediction.

The addition of all remaining variables in this class would increase the amount of variance explained by only 3 per cent.

---

*See Table 4.2 for list of GUAs and their composition in terms of units of analysis.

When the centres were entered into the analysis, the variables duration of the episode of inclusion prior to initial evaluation and derealization (GUA 12) retained their predictive value. Three centres appeared among the best predictors — Ibadan, Moscow, and Agra, and all of them were associated with shorter inclusion episodes.

The 15 best predictors. When the five best predictor variables from each of the preceding analyses were taken together as a battery and their predictive power analysed, a final set of five best predictors was obtained which explained 15 per cent of the outcome variance (compared to 19 per cent explained by all 15). The strongest among the predictors, explaining almost 6 per cent of the variance, was the duration of the episode prior to initial evaluation. The remaining four were: social isolation, derealization, history of past psychiatric treatment, and history of behaviour symptoms.

The addition of the centres as predictor variables in this analysis did not result in any changes in the set of five best predictors.

This suggests that the obtained final set of five predictors of the length of the episode of inclusion had comparable prognostic significance in all the centres of the collaborative study.

10.4.1.2 Prediction of the proportion of the follow-up period during which the patients were in psychotic episodes

This measure expresses in percentages the proportion of the two-year follow-up period during which the patient was in psychotic episodes, regardless of the length of individual episodes and their number. The results are presented in Table 10.6.

The technique and sequence of the statistical analysis have already been described and therefore only a brief summary of the results is given.

Sociodemographic characteristics. The variable with the highest correlation with the proportion of time during which the patients were in psychotic episodes is again social isolation.

Past history characteristics. History of past psychiatric treatment, psychosexual adjustment, unfavourable environment, history of past contact for psychiatric problems with other agencies (not medical services) and history of mental illness in the family, were the five best predictors before the inclusion of the centre variables into the analysis.

The variable 'history of past contact for psychiatric problems with other agencies', predicting a lower proportion of the follow-up period spent in psychotic episodes, includes contacts with private psychiatrists, own doctor, child guidance clinic, priest, medicine man, etc. The introduction of the centre variables results in the elimination of this variable from the regression equation and the inclusion, among the five best predictors, of three centres in developing countries: Ibadan, Agra and Cali, all associated with a lower proportion of the follow-up period spent in psychotic episodes.

TABLE 10.6. PREDICTION OF THE PROPORTION (OR %) OF THE FOLLOW-UP PERIOD, SPENT IN PSYCHOTIC EPISODE(S).*
PATIENTS WITH INITIAL CLINICAL DIAGNOSIS OF SCHIZOPHRENIA.

Predictor Class	S. Socio-demographic characteristics		B. Past history characteristics		C. Characteristics of inclusion episode		D. 15 best predictors (A, B and C Combined)	
	FRCs excluded	FRCs included	FRCs excluded	FRCs included	FRCs excluded	FRCs included	FRCs excluded	FRCs included
5 best predictors	social isolation (-) marital status:widowed,divorced or separated (-) educational level (-) occupation: professional (+) male sex (-)	social isolation (-) Ibadan (+) marital status:widowed, divorced or separated (-) Moscow (+) Washington (-)	past psychiatric treatment (-) poor psychosexual adjustment (-) unfavourable environment (-) past contacts for psychiat. problem, other agencies (+) mental illness in family (-)	Ibadan (+) Agra (+) past psychiatric treatment (-) absence of precipitating stress (-) mental illness Cali (+)	duration of episode prior to IE (-) insidious onset depressed/elated (GUA 17) (+) indications of personality change (GUA 22) (-) cooperation difficulties, (GUA 12) (+) circumstances related (GUA 26) (+)	duration of episode prior to IE (-) Ibadan (+) Agra (+) Moscow (+) derealization (GUA 12) (+) insidious onset (-)	social isolation (-) duration of episode prior to IE (-) past psychiatric treatment (-) Male sex (-) insidious onset (-)	social isolation (-) duration of episode prior to IE (-) past psychiatric treatment (-) Ibadan (+) male sex (-)
% variance explained by 5 best	9	12	6	10	9	14	12	13
% variance explained by all	10	15	7	13	11	17	15	17

*(+) indicates good prognosis, i.e. predicts low % of follow-up period spent in psychotic episode(s).
(-) indicates poor prognosis, i.e. predicts high % of follow-up period spent in psychotic episode(s).

The other two variables among the five best predictors are: 'history of past psychiatric treatment' and 'absence of precipitating stress', both predicting a higher proportion of the follow-up period spent in psychotic episodes.

Characteristics of the inclusion episode. Duration of the episode of inclusion prior to the initial evaluation, type of onset, and the GUA's depressed-elated symptoms (GUA 17), indications of personality change (GUA 22) and co-operation difficulties, circumstances-related (GUA 26) explain 9 per cent of the outcome variance.

Score on indications of personality change (including odd appearance and behaviour, change of interests, change of sex behaviour, autism, abnormal tidiness and social withdrawal) appeared initially as a strong predictor but, on introduction of the centres in the analysis, lost significance. A similar change occurred with type of onset.

Three centres (Ibadan, Agra and Moscow) and score on derealization (GUA 12), all predicting less time in psychotic episodes, entered the set of the five best predictors. 'Duration of the episode of inclusion prior to the initial evaluation' retained the highest correlation with the dependent variable.

The 15 best predictors. Social isolation, duration of the episode of inclusion prior to the initial evaluation, history of past psychiatric treatment, sex and type of onset explain 12 per cent of the outcome variance. If centres are introduced as predictor variables, 13 per cent of the variance can be explained by the five best predictors which now include the Ibadan field research centre (associated with good prognosis) but do not include type of onset.

10.4.1.3 Prediction of the pattern of course of the disorder

Among the different types of course, several paterns* of particular clinical interest were analysed individually.

Predictors of pattern of course 1: full remission after the inclusion episode, no further episodes. This most favourable subsequent course of the disorder was assessed to have occurred in 27 per cent of the followed-up patients with an initial diagnosis of schizophrenia. The results of the regression analysis of its predictors are presented in Table 10.7.

The amount of variance explained by five predictors is almost the same (15 to 16 per cent) within each of the three classes of predictor variables — sociodemographic characteristics, past history characteristics, characteristics of the inclusion episode, as well as in the group of the 15 best predictors if the centres are included in the analysis. Better prediction (22 per cent of the outcome variance) can be obtained if all the 15 best predictors are used.

If the centres are not in the analysis the five best predictors from classes A, B

*Each pattern of course was scored as a dichotomous variable (present/absent).

TABLE 10.7. PREDICTION OF COURSE: PATTERN 1 (FULL REMISSION AFTER THE INITIAL EPISODE, NO FURTHER EPISODE*). PATIENTS WITH INITIAL CLINICAL DIAGNOSIS OF SCHIZOPHRENIA.

Predictor Class	A. Socio-demographic characteristics		B. Past history characteristics		C. Characteristics of inclusion episode		D. 15 best predictors (A, B and C combined)	
	FRCs excluded	FRCs included	FRCs excluded	FRCs included	FRCs excluded	FRCs included	FRCs excluded	FRCs included
5 best predictors	marital status: married	Ibadan	no past psychiatric treatment	Agra	sudden onset	Agra	sudden onset	Ibadan
	lower educational level	marital status: married	past contact for psychiatric problem, other agencies	Ibadan	no indications of personality change (GUA 22)	Ibadan	No past psychiatric treatment	Sudden onset
	younger age	not Moscow	good psychosexual adjustment	precipitating stress	short duration of episode prior to IE	short duration of episode prior to IE	no indications of personality change (GUA 22)	no past psychiatric treatment
	no social isolation	not Aarhus	no mental illness in family	no past psychiatric treatment	rapid development of symptoms prior to IE	no indications of personality change (GUA 22)	marital status: married	short duration of episode prior to IE
	occupation: farmers	not unemployed housewife, pensioner or student	no history of behaviour disorder	not Moscow	no neurotic complaints (GUA 9)	not Moscow	short duration of episode prior to IE	marital status: married
% variance explained by best 5	10	15	8	16	10	17	14	15
% variance explained by all	11	20	9	18	12	19	18	22

* Presence of the listed characteristics predicts future course pattern 1.

and C combined are: sudden onset, no past history of psychiatric treatment, low score on indications of personality change (GUA 22), marital status – married, and short duration of the inclusion period prior to the initial evaluation.

When the centres are entered, the final set of five best predictors contains Ibadan (highest correlation with this pattern of course), sudden onset, no past psychiatric treatment, short duration of the inclusion episode prior to the initial evaluation, and marital status – married.

Predictors of pattern of course 5: one or more psychotic episodes after the inclusion episode, full remissions between all episodes. The level of prediction for this pattern of recurrent disorder (observed in 11 per cent of the followed-up schizophrenic patients) is relatively low: only 12 per cent of the variance can be explained by the 15 best predictors taken together, and the five best predictors explain 8 per cent of the variance (Table 10.8).

If the centres are included, the five best predictors are: female sex, high score on depressed-elated symptoms (GUA 17), Ibadan, occupation – managerial or clerical, and a high score on neurotic complaints (GUA 9).

Predictors of pattern of course 6: one or more psychotic episodes after the inclusion episode but not full remissions The 15 best predictors taken together explain 12 per cent of the variance of this pattern of course (observed in 18 per cent of the followed-up patients) and the final set of five best predictors explains 8 per cent of the variance (Table 10.9).

With the centres included in the analysis, the final set of five best predictors consists of: not Ibadan, not Agra, marital status – not widowed, divorced or separated, Moscow and Aarhus.

Four out of the five best predictors are centres. The likelihood for pattern of course 6 to be observed in Ibadan and Agra is very small, while it is high in Moscow and Aarhus. The difference between Ibadan and Agra, on the one hand, and Moscow and Aarhus on the other hand, might be due to the latter two centres' facilities for more frequent follow-up contacts with their patients after discharge from hospital (seeing a patient frequently increases the probability that some symptoms would be detected and recorded even in a state of remission).

Predictors of pattern of course 7: still in the episode of inclusion This pattern of course (observed in 26 per cent of the followed-up patients) consists of an uninterrupted continuous illness extending over a period of two or more years. It is predicted by a set of five variables explaining 14 per cent of the variance, or by a set of 15 variables accounting for 19 per cent of the variance (Table 10.10)

The inclusion of the centres in the analysis as predictor variables does not change the set of the final five best predictors. Therefore the five variables predicting pattern of course 7 do not appear to be correlated with any particular centre.

The final predictor set includes: long duration of the episodes prior to the initial evaluation, social isolation, marital status – widowed, divorced or separated, a low score on derealization (GUA 12) and a history of behaviour symptoms.

TABLE 10.8. PREDICTION OF COURSE: PATTERN 5 (ONE OR MORE PSYCHOTIC EPISODES AFTER INCLUSION EPISODE FULL REMISSIONS). PATIENTS WITH INITIAL CLINICAL DIAGNOSIS OF SCHIZOPHRENIA.

Predictor Class	A. Socio-demographic characteristics		B. Past history characteristics		C. Characteristics of inclusion episode		D. 15 best predictors (A, B and C combined)	
	FRCs excluded	FRCs included	FRCs excluded	FRCs included	FRCs excluded	FRCs included	FRCs excluded	FRCs included
5 best predictors	occupation: managerial or clerical	Ibadan	no history of behaviour disorder	no history of behaviour disorder	depressed/elated (GUA 17)	Ibadan	female sex	female sex
	lower educational level	occupation: managerial or clerical	past psychiatric treatment	past psychiatric treatment	sudden onset	depressed/elated (GUA 17)	depressed/elated (GUA 17)	depressed/elated (GUA 17)
	no social isolation	urban residence	good psychosexual adjustment	Ibadan	"characteristic" hallucinations (GUA 14)	sudden onset	occupation: managerial, clerical	Ibadan
	urban residence	not Washington	past physical illness or disability	Cali	short duration of episode prior to IE	rapid development of symptoms prior to IE	neurotic complaints (GUA 9)	occupation: managerial, clerical
	female sex	female sex	no precipitating stress	past physical illness or disability	neurotic complaints (GUA 9)	neurotic complaints (GUA 9)	no precipitating stress	neurotic complaints (GUA 9)
% variance explained by 5 best	3	6	3	3	4	5	7	8
% variance explained by all	4	7	3	5	6	9	10	12

274

TABLE 10.9. PREDICTION OF COURSE: PATTERN 6 (ONE OR MORE PSYCHOTIC EPISODES AFTER INCLUSION EPISODE, AT LEAST ONE INCOMPLETE REMISSION*). PATIENTS WITH INITIAL CLINICAL DIAGNOSIS OF SCHIZOPHRENIA.

Predictor Class	A. Socio-demographic characteristics		B. Past history characteristics		C. Characteristics of inclusion episode		D. 15 best predictors (A, B and C combined)	
	FRCs excluded	FRCs included	FRCs excluded	FRCs included	FRCs excluded	FRCs included	FRCs excluded	FRCs included
5 best predictors	good socio-economic status	Moscow	no past contacts for psychiatric problems, other agencies	Moscow	cooperation difficulties, circumstances related (GUA 26)	Moscow	good socio-economic	not Ibadan
	occupation: not farmer	not Ibadan	no mental illness in family	not Ibadan	qualitative psychomotor disorder (GUA 2)	not Ibadan	no past contacts for psychiatric problem, other agencies	not Agra
	marital status: not widowed, divorced, separated	marital status: not widowed, divorced, separated	poor psycho-sexual adjustment	not Agra	predelusional signs (GUA 6)	Aarhus	female sex	marital status: not widowed, divorced or separated
	female sex	not Agra	no unfavourable environment	no mental illness in family	no psycho-physical symptoms (GUA 25)	anxiety, tension, irritability (GUA 18)	marital status: not widowed, divorced, separated	Moscow
	occupation: no social isolation	occupation: professional	past physical illness or disability	Aarhus	anxiety, tension, irritability (GUA 18)	neurotic complaints (GUA 9)	no psycho-physical symptoms (GUA 25)	Aarhus
% variance explained by 5 best	4	8	5	1	4	7	6	8
% variance explained by all	5	10	5	1	6	9	8	12

* Presence of the listed characteristics predicts future course pattern VI.

TABLE 10.10. PREDICTION OF COURSE: PATTERN 7 (STILL IN EPISODE OF INCLUSION).* PATIENTS WITH INITIAL CLINICAL DIAGNOSIS OF SCHIZOPHRENIA.

Predictor Class	A. Socio-demographic characteristics		B. Past history characteristics		C. Characteristics of inclusion episode		D. 15 best predictors (A, B and C combined)	
	FRCs excluded	FRCs included	FRCs excluded	FRCs included	FRCs excluded	FRCs included	FRCs excluded	FRCs included
5 best predictors	social isolation	social isolation	mental illness in family	not Ibadan	long duration of episode prior to IE	long duration of episode prior to IE	long duration of episode prior to IE	long duration of episode prior to IE
	marital status: widowed, divorced, separated	not Ibadan	history of behaviour disorder	history of behaviour disorder	course prior to IE: initial deterioration then unchanged	not Ibadan	social isolation	social isolation
	male sex	Washington	unfavourable environment	mental illness in family	not depressed /elated (GUA 17)	insidious onset	marital status: widowed, divorced, separated	marital status: widowed, divorced, separated
	occupation: not managerial or clerical	Aarhus	poor psycho-sexual adjustment	unfavourable environment	insidious onset	insidious onset	no derealization (GUA 12)	no derealization (GUA 12)
	occupation: not professional	male sex	past psychiatric treatment	poor psycho-sexual adjustment	no derealization (GUA 12)	no derealization (GUA 12)	history of behaviour disorder	history of behaviour disorder
% variance explained by 5 best	9	12	7	8	10	12	14	14
% variance explained by all	11	16	7	10	13	17	18	19

* Presence of the listed characteristics predicts future course pattern VII.

10.4.1.4 Prediction of the clinical type of subsequent psychotic episodes

Stepwise multiple regression analysis was carried out in order to determine the predictors of the clinical type of subsequent psychotic illnesses in the subgroup of patients ($n = 177$) who had an initial clinical diagnosis of schizophrenia and had both remissions and further psychotic episodes after the inclusion episode (Table 10.11).

Predictors of definitely schizophrenic subsequent episodes (64 patients). The following variables emerged as best predictors: low socioeconomic status, absence of precipitating stress at the beginning of the inclusion episode, social isolation, long duration of the inclusion episode prior to the initial evaluation and occupation – professional.

The last variable (occupation) was replaced by the Prague centre when the centres were included – that is, it appeared to be correlated with one particular centre, which contained a high proportion of patients with definitely schizophrenic subsequent episodes.

Predictors of probably schizophrenic subsequent episodes (68 patients). Presence of precipitating stress at the beginning of the inclusion episode, high score on psychophysical symptoms (GUA 25), no past history of physical illness or disability, occupation – not professional, and not being a Taipei patient explained 13 per cent of the variance.

Predictors of affective subsequent episodes (28 patients). Of all schizophrenic patients who had psychotic relapses after the initial episode, 16 per cent had only affective episodes.

When the centres were included in the analysis, the following variables emerged as best predictors explaining 23 per cent of the variance with regard to this type of episode: a low score on auditory hallucinations (GUA 13), history of past physical illness or disability, marital status – not single, the Cali centre and absence of a history of behaviour symptoms.

It should be noted that absence of precipitating stress is among the best predictors of definitely schizophrenic subsequent episodes, and presence of precipitating stress is among the best predictors of probably schizophrenic subsequent episodes. Similarly, presence of a past history of physical illness or disability predicts affective subsequent episodes, while absence of such a history is predictive of probably schizophrenic episodes.

10.4.1.5 Prediction of the level of social functioning

The level of social functioning was assessed and rated on the basis of the narrative description of the patient's follow-up social history and was defined as degree (presence or absence) of social impairment.* The following results were obtained for the different classes of predictor variables (Table 10.12).

*Presence was defined as moderate or severe social impairment, absence as none or mild impairment. See also Chapter 4 for reasons for this dichotomy.

TABLE 10.11.   PREDICTION OF THE TYPE OF SUBSEQUENT PSYCHOTIC EPISODES: BEST PREDICTORS (CLASS A, B, C).   PATIENTS WITH INITIAL DIAGNOSIS OF SCHIZOPHRENIA.

Definitely Schizophrenic Episodes

	FRCs excluded	FRCs included
5 best predictors	low socio-economic status	low socio-economic status
	no precipitating stress	no precipitating stress
	social isolation	Prague FRC
	longer duration prior to IE	social isolation
	occupation: professional	longer duration of episode prior to IE
% variance explained by 5 best	25	26
% variance explained by all	33	38

Probably Schizophrenic Episodes

	FRCs excluded	FRCs included
5 best predictors	precipitating stress	precipitating stress
	psychophysical symptoms (GUA 25)	psychophysical symptoms (GUA 25)
	no past physical illness or disability	no past physical illness or disability
	occupation: not professional	occupation: not professional
	higher educational level	not Taipei FRC
% variance explained by 5 best	13	13
% variance explained by all	16	18

Definitely Affective Episodes

	FRCS excluded	FRCS included
5 best predictors	no auditory hallucinations (GUA 13)	no auditory hallucinations (GUA 13)
	past physical illness or disability	past physical illness or disability
	marital status: not single	marital status: not single
	good psychosexual adjustment	Cali FRC
	depressed/elated (GUA 17)	no history of behaviour disorder
% variance explained by 5 best	22	23
% variance explained by all	25	32

278

TABLE 10.12.   PREDICTION OF LEVEL OF SOCIAL FUNCTIONING.*   PATIENTS WITH INITIAL DIAGNOSIS OF SCHIZOPHRENIA.

Predictor Class	A. Socio-demographic characteristics		B. Past history characteristics		C. Characteristics of inclusion episode		D. 15 best predictors (A, B and C combined)	
	FRCs excluded	FRCs included	FRCs excluded	FRCs included	FRCs excluded	FRCs included	FRCs excluded	FRCs included
5 best predictors	social isolation (-)	social isolation (-)	past psychiatric treatment (-)	Ibadan (+)	duration of episode prior to IE (-)	duration of episode prior to IE (-)	social isolation (-)	social isolation (-)
	higher educational level (-)	Ibadan (+)	poor psychosexual adjustment (-)	past psychiatric treatment (-)	flatness of affect (GUA 19) (-)	Ibadan (+)	duration of episode prior to IE (-)	duration of episode prior to IE (-)
	occupation: managerial or clerical (+)	Taipei (+)	mental illness in family (-)	poor psychosexual adjustment (-)	insidious onset (-)	London (-)	past psychiatric treatment (-)	Ibadan (+)
	occupation: professional (+)	occupation: managerial or clerical (+)	unfavourable environment (-)	past physical illness or disability(+)	other behavioural symptoms (GUA 24) (-)	insidious onset (-)	marital status married (+)	past psychiatric treatment (-)
	marital status married (+)	higher educational level (-)	past physical illness or disability (+)	unfavourable environment (-)	psycho-physical symptoms (GUA 25) (+)	flatness of affect (GUA 19) (-)	past physical illness or disability(+)	past physical illness or disability (+)
% variance explained by 5 best	16	18	8	14	8	16	20	22
% variance explained by all	18	23	9	18	10	19	25	27

* (-) indicates poor prognosis, i.e. predicts social impairment.
  (+) indicates no or mild social impairment.

Sociodemographic characteristics. If the centres are not in the analysis the variables which explain 16 per cent of the outcome variance are: social isolation (predicts impairment), good educational level (predicts impairment), occupation – managerial, clerical or professional (predicts no or mild impairment) and marital status – married (predicts no or mild impairment).

If the centres are included in the analysis together with the sociodemographic variables, the five best predictors are: social isolation, Ibadan (predicts no or mild impairment), Taipei (predicts no or mild impairment), occupation – managerial or clerical, and good education level. One should note that a managerial or clerical occupation (usually requiring good education) predicted no or mild impairment while a good education level predicted social impairment. Considering that each predictor contributes to the prediction by means of its partial correlation with the outcome variable (excluding the effects of its intercorrelations with other predictors), this apparent contradiction can be resolved. In this particular instance, a skilled occupation would be associated with lower probability of severe social impairment, because achieving such a level would normally require a relatively long period of good social functioning in the patient's past. Achieving a certain level of education, on the other hand, does not necessarily presuppose a long history of good social functioning. Further, ratings of more severe social impairment, would be made in cases where a gross discrepancy between achieved educational level and actual level of functioning had been observed.

Past history characteristics. History of past psychiatric treatment, poor psychosexual adjustment, history of mental illness in the family and unfavourable environment predicted social impairment. The fifth among the best predictors – past history of physical illness or disability – was associated with a good prognosis regarding social functioning.

The inclusion of the centres in the analysis showed that Ibadan had the highest correlation with good social functioning. History of past physical illness or disability remained among the best predictors together with past psychiatric treatment, poor psychosexual adjustment and unfavourable environment. The final set of five variables explains 14 per cent of the variance.

Characteristics of the inclusion episode. Among class C variables the following emerged as predictors of social functioning: long duration of the inclusion episode prior to the initial evaluation (poor prognosis), a high score on flatness of affect (GUA 19 – poor prognosis), insidious onset (poor prognosis), a high score on other behaviour symptoms* (GUA 24 – poor prognosis) and a high score on psychophysical symptoms (GUA 25 – good prognosis).

The inclusion of the centres markedly improved the prediction – from 8 to 16 per cent for the five best predictors and from 10 to 19 per cent for the total set of predictor variables. Duration of the episode of inclusion prior to the initial evaluation retained its high correlation with social functioning. The other four predictors

*Included are: talking to self, disorder of pitch, giggling to self and demonstrative behaviour.

were: Ibadan (good prognosis), London (poor prognosis), insidious onset (poor prognosis), and flatness of affect (poor prognosis).

The 15 best predictors. The five variables achieving maximum prediction among the sets of best predictors from each class were: social isolation, duration of the inclusion episode prior to the initial evaluation, history of past psychiatric treatment, marital status – married, and past history of physical illness or disability. These variables accounted for 20 per cent of the outcome variance. The level of prediction was marginally improved, when centres were included in the regression analysis. The final set of five best predictors consisted of social isolation (poor prognosis), long duration of the inclusion episode prior to the initial evaluation (poor prognosis), Ibadan (good prognosis), history of past psychiatric treatment (poor prognosis), and past history of physical illness or disability (good prognosis).

10.4.1.6 Prediction of the overall two-year outcome

Overall outcome is a composite measure defined by: (a) the proportion of the follow-up period during which patients were in psychotic episodes; (b) presence or absence of social impairment on follow-up, and (c) occurrence or non-occurrence of full remissions during the two-year period. The five outcome groups described in Chapter 6 were rank-ordered on a scale ranging from a very favourable (category 1) to a very unfavourable (category 5) overall outcome. The results of the analysis are presented in Table 10.13.

Sociodemographic characteristics. Social isolation (poor outcome), high educational level (poor outcome), marital status – widowed, divorced or separated (poor outcome), and occupation – professional, managerial or clerical (good outcome) emerged as best predictors when centres were not included in the analysis. Together, they accounted for 12 per cent of the outcome variance.

When the centres were included, the set of five best predictors explaining 16 per cent of the variance consisted of: Ibadan (good outcome), social isolation (poor outcome), marital status – widowed, divorced or separated (poor outcome), Aarhus (poor outcome), and occupation – never worked, unemployed, housewives, pensioners and students (poor outcome).

Past history characteristics. The five best predictors (centres not included) which explained 9 per cent of the outcome variance were: history of past psychiatric treatment (poor outcome), poor psychosexual adjustment (poor outcome), history of behaviour symptoms (poor outcome), unfavourable environment (poor outcome), and past contact with other agencies because of psychiatric problems (good outcome).

When centres were included in the analysis, the variance explained by the five best past history predictors was 16 per cent. Ibadan and Agra had the highest correlations with overall outcome (both predicting favourably). The remaining three predictors were history of past psychiatric treatment, absence of precipitating stress and unfavourable environment (all three associated with poor outcome).

TABLE 10.13.   PREDICTION OF OVERALL OUTCOME.*   PATIENTS WITH INITIAL CLINICAL DIAGNOSIS OF SCHIZOPHRENIA.

Predictor Class	A. Socio-demographic characteristics		B. Past history characteristics		C. Characteristics of inclusion episode		D. 15 best predictors (A, B and C combined)	
	FRCs excluded	FRCs included	FRCs excluded	FRCs included	FRCs excluded	FRCs included	FRCs excluded	FRCs included
5 best predictors	social isolation (-)	Ibadan (+)	past psychiatric treatment (-)	Ibadan (+)	duration of episode prior to IE (-)	duration of episode prior to IE (-)	social isolation (-)	social isolation (-)
	higher educational level (-)	social isolation (-)	poor psychosexual adjustment (-)	Agra (+)	insidious onset (-)	Ibadan (+)	duration of episode prior to IE (-)	duration of episode prior to IE (-)
	marital status:widowed, divorced or separated (-)	marital status:widowed, divorced or separated (-)	history of behaviour disorder (-)	past psychiatric treatment (-)	flatness of affect (GUA 19) (-)	Agra (+)	past psychiatric treatment (-)	Ibadan (+)
	occupation: professional (+)	Aarhus (-)	unfavourable environment (-)	absence of precipitating stress (-)	psycho-physical symptoms (GUA 25) (+)	flatness of affect (GUA 19) (-)	marital status:widowed, divorced, separated (-)	past psychiatric treatment (-)
	occupation: managerial or clerical (+)	unemployed, housewives, pensioners, students (+)	past contact for psychiat. problem, other agencies (+)	unfavourable environment (-)	indications of personality change (GUA 22) (-)	derealization (GUA 12) (+)	history of behaviour disorder (-)	marital status: widowed, divorced, separated (-)
% variance explained by 5 best	12	16	9	16	12	19	19	22
% variance explained by all	14	21	10	19	15	22	23	26

* (+) and (-) indicate, respectively, "good" and "poor" prognosis with regard to the variable "overall outcome".

Characteristics of the inclusion episode. When centres were not included, the five best predictors explaining 12 per cent of the variance were: long duration of the inclusion episode prior to the initial evaluation (poor outcome), insidious onset (poor outcome), a high score on flatness of affect (GUA 19 – poor outcome), a high score on psychophysical symptoms (GUA 25 – good outcome) and a high score on indications of personality change (GUA 22 – poor outcome).

The inclusion of the centres in the analysis increased the proportion of explained variance to 19 per cent for five predictors (or 22 per cent if all predictors in the analysis are considered). The duration of the inclusion episode prior to the initial evaluation retained its highest correlation with overall outcome. Ibadan and Agra appeared among the five best predictors (both associated with favourable outcome). The other two among the five best predictors were a high score on flatness of affect (GUA 19 – poor outcome) and a high score on derealization (GUA 12 – good outcome).

The 15 best predictors. The regression analysis of the three sets of best predictors in classes A, B and C resulted in the following set of five best predictors explaining 19 per cent of the outcome variance (centres not included): social isolation, long duration of the episode of inclusion prior to the initial evaluation, history of past psychiatric treatment, marital status – widowed, divorced or separated, and history of behaviour symptoms. Presence of these factors was associated with poor prognosis while their absence predicted a favourable overall outcome.

When centres were included in the analysis, the final set of five best predictors of overall outcome consisted of *social isolation* (poor outcome if present, good outcome if absent), *duration of the inclusion episode prior to the initial evaluation* (long duration predicts poor outcome, short duration predicts good outcome), *Ibadan* (predictor of good outcome), *history of past psychiatric treatment* (poor outcome if present, good outcome if absent), and *marital status – widowed, divorced or separated* (yes – poor outcome, no – good outcome).

With these five predictors, 22 per cent of the outcome variance could be explained. All the 15 predictors could explain 26 per cent of the outcome variance. The multiple correlation coefficient with overall outcome is 0.466 for the five best predictors and 0.506 for the 15 best predictors.

10.4.2. Predictors of two-year course and outcome of schizophrenia in different cultural and social settings

The analyses described in the preceding sections were performed with pooled data on patients from all centres of the study. In addition to the identification of sets of predictors for each course and outcome dimension, it was demonstrated that the inclusive variable 'centre' had a predictive power on its own, that is, it accounted for a proportion of the variance of course and outcome. Since the centres as variables might reflect different cultural settings in which schizophrenic patients were selected, assessed and followed up, it was considered important to explore further the factors associated with the two-year prognosis of the patients in the different centres and in groups of centres.

TABLE 10.14. PREDICTION OF OVERALL OUTCOME WITHIN CENTRES IN WHICH SUFFICIENT NUMBERS OF PATIENTS WITH FOLLOW-UP DATA WERE AVAILABLE. (5 OUT OF 15 BEST PREDICTORS).

FRC	Agra	Cali	Ibadan	London	Moscow	Taipei
5 best predictors	flatness of affect (GUA 19) (-)	marital status: widowed, divorced, separated (-)	duration of episode prior to IE (-)	social isolation (-)	occupation: professional (+)	duration of episode prior to IE (-)
	psychophysical symptoms (GUA 25) (+)	social isolation (-)	psychophysical symptoms (GUA 25) (+)	psychophysical symptoms (GUA 25) (+)	flatness of affect (GUA 19) (-)	past psychiatric treatment (-)
	history of behaviour symptoms (-)	slow, insidious onset (-)	profession: managerial or clerical (+)	occupation: managerial or clerical (+)	occupation: managerial or clerical (+)	history of behaviour symptoms (-)
	duration of episode prior to IE (-)	occupation: professional (+)	past psychiatric treatment (-)	duration of episode prior to IE (-)	indications of personality change (GUA 22) (-)	occupation: managerial or clerical (+)
	past contact for psychiatric problems, other agencies (+)	occupation: managerial or other clerical (+)	flatness of affect (GUA 19) (-)	occupation: professional (+)	psychophysical symptoms (GUA 25) (+)	occupation: professional (+)
% variance explained by 5 best	51	22	26	57	39	28
% variance explained by all	59	23	28	61	41	32

* (+) and (-) indicate, respectively, "good" and "poor" prognosis with regard to the variable "overall outcome".

10.4.2.1 Predictors within individual centres of the study

An analysis of the prediction of course and outcome within centres was possible in those centres where sufficient numbers of schizophrenic patients had been evaluated and followed up, that is, in centres where the number of patients was greater than the number of variables used in the multiple regression analysis.

In view of this constraint, only the 15 best predictors identified among the sociodemographic, past history and inclusion episode variables were used in the within-centre analysis, and the composite measure 'overall outcome' was selected as a dependent variable.

Table 10.14 indicates the five variables which explained most of the overall outcome variance within each of the six centres in which stepwise multiple regression analysis was possible. Three conclusions can be drawn from this table:

1. The proportion of the variance explained by the predictors within individual centres is markedly higher than within the pooled series of all patients. This cannot be attributed simply to the higher ratio of predictor variables/number of patients in the within-centres analysis, since in two of the centres (Agra and Moscow) in which this ratio was lowest, the percentage variance explained was high, and in Ibadan, where the ratio was high, the percentage variance explained was low. The generally high proportion of predictor-explained variance within the centres was most probably related to the greater homogeneity of patient series in each centre, with regard to overall outcome.

2. The sets of five best predictors in the individual centres are different. Three variables (duration of episode prior to initial evaluation, occupation, and score on psychophysical symptoms) appear among the best predictors in four centres; one variable (flatness of affect) in three centres, and three variables identified in the analyses of pooled data (educational level, effects of unfavourable environment, and psychosexual adjustment) do not appear among the best predictors in any of the six centres. Since the cut-off of the number of predictors at 5 is an arbitrary one, no definitive conclusions should be made about 'importance' of individual predictors within each centre, but consideration should be given to trends for predictor variables to appear in more than one centre.

3. With the exception of Agra, the amount of variance explained by the predictors was higher in the two centres in developed countries (London and Moscow) than in the three centres in developing countries. This is consistent with other results which will be discussed below. It is interesting, however, that the centres in which the highest proportions of patients with good outcome were observed (Ibadan, Agra and Cali) differed so much with regard to the amount of variance explained by the 15 best predictors. Since Agra is the exception from the general trend of lower percentages of predictor-explained variance in centres in developing countries, one could conclude that the 15 predictors turned out to correlate highly with two-year prognosis in Agra patients, while in Ibadan and Cali important potential predictors remained untapped by the set of variables used in the analysis.

TABLE 10.15.   PREDICTION OF THE LENGTH OF THE EPISODE OF INCLUSION.*
                PATIENTS WITH INITIAL CLINICAL DIAGNOSIS OF
                SCHIZOPHRENIA.
                FIELD RESEARCH CENTRES IN DEVELOPING COUNTRIES (NO. OF
                PATIENTS = 125) AND IN DEVELOPED COUNTRIES (NO. OF
                PATIENTS = 161).

	FRCs in developing countries	FRCs in developed countries
5 best predictors	marital status: widowed, divorced or separated (-)	social isolation (-)
	duration of episode prior to IE (-)	history of behaviour disorder (-)
	cooperation difficulties, circumstances-related (GUA 26) (+)	duration of episode prior to IE (-)
	social isolation (-)	derealization (GUA 12) (+)
	derealization (GUA 12) (+)	occupation: professional (+)
% variance explained by 5 best	13	28
% variance explained by all	15	33

* (+) indicates good prognosis, i.e. predicts a shorter episode
    of inclusion.

  (-) indicates poor prognosis, i.e. predicts a longer episode
    of inclusion.

10.4.2.2 Predictors in centres in developing and developed countries

The findings which indicate consistent differences of two-year course and outcome of schizophrenic patients in centres in developing and developed countries* (see Chapter 6) suggest the possibility that these differences could be predicted by different sets of variables among those assessed on initial evaluation in the two groups of centres.

To test this hypothesis, stepwise multiple regression analysis of the predictors was performed separately for the two groups of centres — in developing countries (Agra, Cali and Ibadan) and in developed countries (Aarhus, London, Moscow, Washington and Prague). The course and outcome measures used in this analysis were length of the inclusion episode, proportion of the follow-up period during which the patients were in psychotic episodes, level of social functioning, and overall outcome. The results are shown in Tables 10.15, 10.16, 10.17, and 10.18.

Two conclusions can be made on the basis of these results. Firstly, the

*Taipei was not included in this analysis since it was difficult to place in either group.

TABLE 10.16.   PREDICTION OF THE PROPORTION (OR %) OF THE FOLLOW-UP
               PERIOD SPENT IN PSYCHOTIC EPISODE(S).*
               PATIENTS WITH INITIAL CLINICAL DIAGNOSIS OF
               SCHIZOPHRENIA.
               FIELD RESEARCH CENTRES IN DEVELOPING COUNTRIES (NO. OF
               PATIENTS = 123) AND IN DEVELOPED COUNTRIES (NO. OF
               PATIENTS = 131).

	FRCs in developing countries	FRCs in developed countries
5 best predictors	marital status: widowed, divorced or separated (-)	social isolation (-)
	duration of episode prior to IE (-)	duration of episode prior to IE (-)
	social isolation (-)	indications of personality change (GUA 22) (-)
	cooperation difficulties, circumstances-related (GUA 26) (+)	occupation: professional (+)
	indications of personality change (GUA 22) (-)	male sex (-)
% variance explained by 5 best	14	24
% variance explained by all	17	26

* (+) indicates good prognosis, i.e. predicts low % of FU-period.

proportion of variance explained by the predictors is consistently and considerably higher for patients in the centres in developed countries. It ranges from 24 to 30 per cent for the five best predictors and from 26 to 34 per cent for 15 best predictors. In the developing countries the corresponding ranges are 13 to 21 per cent and 15 to 23 per cent. This fact confirms the impression of a trend in this direction, conveyed by the results of the within-centre analysis of predictors. The difference in proportions of variance explained is quite big and unrelated to the numbers of patients in the two groups of centres (the total number of patients in the centres in developed countries was greater than in the centres in developing countries). Therefore, it seems possible that this difference is related to the nature of the predictor variables selected for the analysis. The selection of predictors was guided by hypotheses derived mainly from studies done on patient groups in developed countries. Other variables (including culture-related ones) which had not been included or considered to a sufficient extent in the present study, might be important predictors of course and outcome of schizophrenia in cultures other than European and North American.

Secondly, there are both differences and similarities in the composition of the

TABLE 10.17. PREDICTION OF SOCIAL FUNCTIONING.*
              PATIENTS WITH INITIAL CLINICAL DIAGNOSIS OF
              SCHIZOPHRENIA.
              FIELD RESEARCH CENTRES IN DEVELOPING COUNTRIES AND
              IN DEVELOPED COUNTRIES.

	FRCs in developing countries	FRCs in developed countries
5 best predictors	social isolation (-)	social isolation (-)
	duration of episode prior to IE (-)	duration of episode prior to IE (-)
	higher educational level (-)	flatness of affect (GUA 19) (-)
	psychophysical symptoms (GUA 25) (+)	past physical illness or disability (+)
	mental illness in family (-)	occupation: professional (+)
% variance explained by 5 best	21	24
% variance explained by all	23	29

* (-) indicates poor prognosis, i.e. predicts social impairment.

(+) indicates prediction of no or mild social impairment.

sets of five best predictors for each measure of course and outcome when the two groups of centres are compared.

The following variables are among the five best predictors in developing countries only and do not appear among the five best predictors in developed countries in any of the analyses: marital status — widowed, divorced or separated, a high score on co-operation difficulties (GUA 26), educational level, history of mental illness in the family, and past contacts with other agencies because of psychiatric problems.

Four variables appeared among the five best predictors in developed countries only: male sex, history of physical illness or disability, occupation — professional, and occupation — managerial or clerical.

Finally, five variables are among the best predictors in both developing and developed countries: social isolation, duration of the inclusion episode prior to the initial evaluation, a high score on indications of personality change (GUA 22), a high score on derealization (GUA 12), and a high score on psychophysical symptoms (GUA 25).

Two of the variables listed above — social isolation, and duration of the inclusion episode prior to the initial evaluation, appear consistently among the five best predictors for every measure of course and outcome in both groups of countries.

TABLE 10.18.   PREDICTION OF OVERALL OUTCOME.*
PATIENTS WITH INITIAL CLINICAL DIAGNOSIS OF
SCHIZOPHRENIA.
FIELD RESEARCH CENTRES IN DEVELOPING COUNTRIES (NO.
OF PATIENTS = 128) AND IN DEVELOPED COUNTRIES (NO.
OF PATIENTS = 129).

	FRCs in developing countries	FRCS in developed countries
5 best predictors	marital status: widowed, divorced or separated (-)	social isolation (-)
	social isolation (-)	duration of episode prior to IE (-)
	duration of episode prior to IE (-)	occupation: managerial or clerical (+)
	past contacts for psychiatric problem, other agencies (+)	psychophysical symptoms (GUA 25) (+)
	higher educational level (-)	occupation: professional (+)
% variance explained by 5 best	17	30
% variance explained by all	18	34

* (-) and (+) indicate, respectively, "good" and "poor" prognosis
   with regard to the variable "overall outcome".

10.4.3 Initial symptomatology as a predictor of two-year course and outcome in schizophrenia

The analysis of predictors described in the preceding sections indicated that up to one-fifth of the variance of course and outcome could be explained by five variables only and that the addition of further predictors resulted in relatively small gains. Since a considerable proportion of the course and outcome variance remained unexplained, it could be expected that other, hitherto unused information, might increase the level of prediction, if it could be identified.

Individual symptoms assessed on initial evaluation were felt to be a potential source of such additional predictive information, since the groups of units of analysis (GUA) which were used in the statistical procedures reported above reflected larger areas of psychopathology and were obtained by condensing symptomatological data (units of analysis)* in which some useful information might have been lost. An additional reason for exploring the predictive value of

*The units of analysis (UAs) were condensed from Present State Examination (PSE) items rated at the initial evaluation, on the basis of statistical measures of association and clinical considerations. The procedure is described in detail in Volume 1 of the IPSS report. The descriptive content of the UAs corresponds closely to clinical symptoms.

TABLE 10.19.   LIST OF SELECTED SYMPTOMS (UNITS OF
ANALYSIS) ASSESSED ON INITIAL
EVALUATION AND EXPECTED TO BE OF
PROGNOSTIC VALUE.

Unit of Analysis No.	Symptom	Prognostic score if present	Prognostic score if absent
1	Overactivity	+1	0
7	Stereotypies	-1	0
10	Posturing	-1	0
11	Mannerisms	-1	0
12	Hallucinatory behaviour	-1	0
13	Waxy flexibility	-1	0
15	Flight of ideas	+1	0
16	Pressure of speech	+1	0
19	Restricted speech	-1	0
28	Gloomy thoughts	+1	0
29	Elated thoughts	+1	0
30	Hopelessness	+1	0
33	Delusional mood	+1	0
38	Thought alienation	-1	0
39	Thoughts spoken aloud	-1	0
40	Delusions of control	-1	0
41	Delusions of persecution	-1	0
42	Delusions of guilt	+1	0
45	Delusions of grandeur	+1	0
47	Delusional system	-1	0
51	Fantastic delusions	+1	0
52	Sexual delusions	-1	0
54	Obsessive thoughts	+1	0
58	Hypochondriasis	+1	0
60	Lack of insight	-1	+1
61	Changed appearance	-1	0
62	Derealization	+1	0
73	Hallucinations from body	-1	0
74	Voices comment patient	-1	0
76	Visual hallucinations	+1	0
77	Tactile hallucinations	-1	0
79	Sexual hallucinations	-1	0
80	Somatic hallucinations	-1	0
32	Special depression	+1	0
84	Depressed mood	+1	0
85	Observed elated mood	+1	0
91	Anxiety	+1	0
92	Flatness of affect	-1	0
93	Apathy	-1	+1
94	Ecstatic mood	+1	0
101	Lability of affect	+1	0
105	Autism	-1	+1
110	Social withdrawal	-1	+1
6	Talking to self	-1	0
99	Giggling to self	-1	0
100	Demonstrative	+1	0
112	Worse in morning	+1	0
123	Poor rapport	0	+1
126	Unwilling to cooperate	-1	0
127	Inadequate description	-1	0

symptoms was the fact that many previous studies on prognosis in the functional psychoses have dealt extensively with symptoms as predictors, so that comparisons with results from those studies were possible.

Two approaches were used to explore the predictive value of symptoms.

Firstly, 50 symptoms (units of analysis) among those assessed on initial evaluation were selected on the basis of theoretical and clinical considerations, and

TABLE 10.20.   LIST OF OTHER VARIABLES ASSESSED ON INITIAL
                 EVALUATION AND EXPECTED TO BE OF PROGNOSTIC
                 VALUE.

Variable	Level	Prognostic Score
Age	15 - 24	-1
	25 - 34	0
	35 - 44	+1
Marital Status	single	-1
	married	+1
	other	0
Socio-economic Status	high	+1
	middle	0
	low	-1
Occupational History	never had job	-1
	worked but not in last 12 months	-1
	worked in last 12 months	+1
Social Isolation	none or mild	+1
	moderate	0
	severe	-1
History of Behaviour Symptoms	0 - 3 symptoms	0
	4 - 10 symptoms	-1
Psychosexual Adjustment	no difficulty	+1
	some	0
	marked	-1
Past Psychiatric Treatment	yes	-1
	no	+1
Precipitating Stress	yes	+1
	no	-1
Type of Onset	sudden	+1
	slow	-1
Duration of Episode Prior to Initial Evaluation	0 - 6 months	0
	6 months or more	-1

each patient was assigned a prognostic score depending on the presence or absence of such symptoms. Correlations between prognostic scores and the course and outcome variables were then calculated.

Secondly, multivariate statistical techniques were applied in order to derive empirically sets of units of analysis predicting course and outcome.

10.4.3.1 Predictions based on prognostic scores

Proceeding from the hypotheses summarized in Table 10.1, 50 units of analysis were selected as potential predictors. The presence or absence of each symptom was rated +1, −1 or 0, depending on its hypothetical good or bad prognostic significance. So for example, if the patient had a positive score on overactivity (UA

1), a rating +1 was made because earlier studies found that overactivity predicts good prognosis. Presence of apathy (UA 93) was rated −1 (poor prognosis), absence of apathy +1 (good prognosis), etc. A rating of 0 was assigned if either the presence or the absence of a symptom was considered to be of no specific prognostic importance. The resulting checklist of symptoms and their ratings is presented in Table 10.19. An analogous checklist of potential prognostic indicators and ratings was compiled also for variables other than mental state symptoms (Table 10.20).

Each patient was rated for presence or absence of the listed variables and two scores — one on mental state symptoms and one on other prognostic variables, were obtained by summing up the ratings. Each score could have a positive or a negative sign. The hypothesis to be tested statistically was that positive scores would correlate with favourable outcome, and negative scores would correlate with unfavourable outcome.

A total of 476 patients with initial clinical diagnosis of schizophrenia were rated in this way and the correlation coefficients calculated separately for negative, positive and total scores in this analysis (Kendall's τ) are presented in Table 10.21.*

Low positive and high negative scores obtained using the checklist shown in Tables 10.19 and 10.20 were associated with poor course and outcome; high positive and low negative scores were associated with good outcome.

The magnitude of the correlations was small, although many of them were significant at the 0.01 level. The correlations between non-mental state scores and course and outcome measures were considerably higher than the correlations between scores on mental state symptoms and course and outcome.

This result shows that prediction based on simple prognostic scores based on the assumption that all predictor variables are of equal weight is of a limited value and can only indicate the general qualitative direction of the prognosis.

10.4.3.2 Identification of predictive symptoms through multivariate statistical techniques

In order to explore the potential predictive value of the 129 symptoms, the measures of *pattern of course* and *overall outcome* were selected as dependent variables. Only data on patients assessed to fall within the extreme and contrasting categories of the two variables — pattern of course 1 and 2 versus 7, and overall outcome categories 1 versus 5, were used in the analysis. Multiple linear regression on these selected measures of course and outcome was performed with the 129 units of analysis. A multiple correlation coefficient R was obtained, the squared value (R^2) of which indicates the proportion of the variance of the dependent variables which could be explained by all the 129 symptoms taken together.

The proportion of the variance explained by the 129 units of analysis was high. For pattern of course 1 and 2 versus 7, the multiple correlation coefficient was

*A negative sign of the correlation between a positive score and the course and outcome variables means that the positive score was associated with better course or outcome. A positive correlation between a negative score and the course and outcome variables means that the negative score is associated with poor course or outcome.

TABLE 10.21. CORRELATION BETWEEN PROGNOSTIC SCORES AND OUTCOME (KENDALL'S TAU).

	Total score on symptoms	Total score on other variables	Positive score on symptoms	Positive score on other variables	Negative score on symptoms	Negative score on other variables
Length of inclusion episode	-.036	-.161*	-.047	-.139*	.004	.179*
Percentage time in psychotic episodes	-.040	-.133*	-.005	-.123*	.042	.147*
Pattern of course	+.001	-.181*	-.009	-.198*	.006	.168*
Social functioning	-.085*	-.207*	-.078*	-.201	.052	.212*
Overall outcome	-.051	-.185*	-.033	-.176*	.047	.204*

* Indicates significance at α = .01 level (1-sided test).

0.6651 which corresponds to 44.2 per cent explained variance. For overall outcome 1 versus 5, the multiple correlation coefficient was 0.8232 which corresponds to 67.8 per cent explained variance. This means that a large proportion of the variation between extreme and contrasting types of course and outcome can be explained by symptomatological differences among patients on initial evaluation.

The degree of discrimination between these extreme patient groups which could be obtained by using symptoms was assessed by discriminant function analysis. This multivariate method was used extensively to analyse the predictive validity of diagnostic groupings and it is described in some detail in Chapter 11. Its important property in the present context is the possibility to transform for each patient the scores on all the units of analysis into a single score on a composite variate and to plot these individual patient scores as frequency distributions for different patient groups.

The results of the discriminant function analysis showed clearly that: (a) the distribution of patients with favourable pattern of course 1 and 2 was distinct, and had a different mean from the distribution of patients with the unfavourable pattern of course 7; and (b) the distribution of patients belonging to the best overall outcome category 1 was distinct, and had a different mean from the distribution of patients belonging to the worst outcome category 5.

The distance between the means of the distributions can be expressed numerically by a distance coefficient D which was 1.69 for the two distributions of pattern of course and 3.54 for the two distributions of overall outcome*. These results confirmed further the possibility to separate the patients with contrasting patterns of two-year course and overall outcome on the basis of their initial symptomatology (see Figures 10.1 and 10.2).

One could expect that among the 129 symptoms, some would contribute more and some would contribute less to the prediction of the contrasting types of course and outcome. Symptoms with potentially greater predictive weight were identified among the 129 units of analysis according to two criteria: (a) size of their partial regression coefficient, and (b) variation (F-ratio). Twenty symptoms with high regression coefficients and relatively low degree of variation were selected from each of the two analyses described above. These symptoms, having high partial correlation coefficients with the course and outcome variables, contributed more than the remaining symptoms to the multiple correlation between all the 129 symptoms and the course and outcome variables. However, the predictive value that any individual symptom might have independently of its membership in the set of 129 symptoms for which multiple correlation coefficients were determined, cannot be inferred from its partial regression coefficient.

The estimation of the predictive power of different individual symptoms, or symptom patterns in this model of analysis, would require the computation of correlation coefficients between every possible subset of the 129 UAs and the measures of course and outcome, which is practically unfeasible.

---

*D-values greater than 1.0 are usually accepted as indicative of good discrimination between two groups.

```
PATTERN 1-2 VS. 7  , 129 UA - I.E., 50'S
FREQUENCY CISTRIBUTIONS FOR BOTH GRCUPS
NUMBER  OF CASES FOP GROUP1:      227          NUMBER OF CASES FCR GROUP2:    129
RANGE OF THE VARIABLE:  0.143178E 02           ONE STEP REPRESENTS:  0.238631E CO


 -8.09|XX
 -7.86|
 -7.62|
 -7.38|
 -7.14|
 -6.90|
 -6.66|
 -6.42|
 -6.19|
 -5.95|
 -5.71|
 -5.47|
 -5.23|
 -4.99|
 -4.75|
 -4.51|XX
 -4.28|
 -4.04|XXXXXXX
 -3.80|XXXXXXXXXXXX
 -3.56|XXXXX
 -3.32|XXXXXXXXX
 -3.08|XXXXXXXXXXXXXXXXXXX
 -2.84|XXXXXXXXX
 -2.61|BXXXXXXXXXXX
 -2.37|BXXXXXXXX
 -2.13|XXXXXXXXXXXXXXXXXXXXX
 -1.89|BXXXXXXXXXXXXXXXXXXXX
 -1.65|BXXXXXX
 -1.41|BBBBBXXXXXXXXXXX
 -1.17|BBBBXXXXXXXXXXXXXXXXXX
 -0.94|BBBBBXXXXXX
 -0.70|BBBXXXXXXXXXXX
 -0.46|BBBBBBBBXXXXXX
 -0.22|BBBBBXXXXXXX
  0.02|BBBBBBBBOOOLOOCO
  0.26|BBBBBBBOOOOOOOOOOOOO
  0.50|BBBBBBBBBOCO
  0.73|BBBBBBBOOOOOOOOCOOOO
  0.97|BBBBBBBBBBOCOOCO
  1.21|BBBBBOOCOJOOCCOOO
  1.45|BBBBBBBBBBOC OOOOOO
  1.69|BBBBBOOCOOOOOCOOOOOO
  1.93|BBBBBBBOOOO
  2.17|BBOCOOOOOOOOOOCO
  2.41|BBOOOOOOOOCOOOOOOOO
  2.64|BBOCOOOOOJOCC
  2.88|COOOOOOOOOOOOOOOO
  3.12|BBOOOOCOOOO
  3.36|BBOOOOOOOOC O
  3.60|COOOOOOO
  3.84|COOOOOO
  4.08|OOOO
  4.31|OOOO
  4.55|COOCO
  4.79|C
  5.03|CCOC
  5.27|
  5.51|
  5.75|
  5.98|COO
```

Figure 10.1   Discriminant function scores. Distribution of schizophrenic patients with pattern of course 1 and 2(X) and pattern of course 7(0) according to discriminant function scores on symptoms assessed on initial evaluation. Distance between the two distributions $D = 1.69$.

```
CVERALL CUTCCME 1 VS. 5, 5C'S, 129 LA-IE
FRECUENCY DISTRIBUTIONS FGR BOTH GROUPS
NUMBER  CF CASES FOR GROUP1:      127          NUMBER OF CASES FGR GROUP2:     78
RANGE OF THE VARIABLE:  0.291950E C2           ONE STEP REPRESENTS:  0.486583E CC

 -15.47|XXXX
 -14.98|
 -14.49|
 -14.01|
 -13.52|
 -13.03|XXXX
 -12.55|XXXXXXXXX
 -12.06|XXXXXXXX
 -11.57|
 -11.C9|XXXX
 -10.60|XXXX
 -10.12|XXXX
  -9.63|XXXXXXXX
  -9.14|XXXXXXXX
  -8.66|XXXXXXXXXXXXXXXXXXXXXXXXXXXX
  -8.17|XXXXXXXXXXXX
  -7.68|BBXXXXXX
  -7.20|XXXXXXXXXXXXXXXXXXXXXXX
  -6.71|XXXXXXXX
  -6.22|XXXXXXXXXXXXXXXXXXX
  -5.74|XXXXXXXXXXXXXXX
  -5.25|XXXXXXXXXXXXXXXXXXXXXXXXXX
  -4.76|XXXXXXXXXXXXXXXXXX
  -4.28|XXXXXXXXXXXXXXXXXXX
  -3.79|XXXXXXXXXXXX
  -3.30|XXXXXXXX
  -2.82|BBXX
  -2.33|XXXXXXXX
  -1.84|XXXX
  -1.36|
  -0.87|BBXXXXXX
  -0.38|BBBBBXXXXXXXX
   C.10|BBXX
   C.59|XXXX
   1.C8|BBBBO
   1.56|CCOCOOOOOO
   2.05|CC
   2.54|BBBBBXXX
   3.02|CC
   3.51|CCOCOOOOOOOO
   4.00|CCOCOOOOO
   4.48|CCOCOOOOOOCOOOOOOOOOOOOOOOOOOOO
   4.97|CCCCOOOOOOOOOCOOO
   5.46|COOCOOOOO
   5.94|CCCOOOOOOOOOOOO
   6.43|OOOCOOOOOOOCOOOCOOOO
   6.92|CCCCOOOOOOOCC
   7.40|COOCOOOOOOOCOOOOOOOOOO
   7.89|COOCOOOO
   8.38|OCOOOOOCOOLOOC
   8.86|OCOCOOOOOJLCOOOOOOO
   9.35|CCOGOOOOOOCOOC
   9.83|COOOOOOOOOOOCOOOOOOOOO
  10.32|CCCGOOOOO
  10.81|OCCOOCOCOOLO
  11.29|OC
  11.78|CCCGOOOOO
  12.27|
  12.75|CC
  13.24|CCCCOOCO
```

Figure 10.2 Discriminant function scores. Distribution of schizophrenic patients falling into overall outcome categories 1(X) and 5(0) according to discriminant function scores on symptoms assessed on initial evaluation. Distance between the two distributions $D = 3.54$

TABLE 10.22. 30 PREDICTIVE SYMPTOMS (UNITS OF ANALYSIS) RANKED ACCORDING TO MAGNITUDES OF PARTIAL REGRESSION COEFFICIENTS AND F-RATIO VALUES. (RESULTS OF MULTIPLE LINEAR REGRESSION ANALYSIS FOR PATTERN OF COURSE 1 & 2 OR 7 IN SCHIZOPHRENIC PATIENTS).

Rank	Units of Analysis	Pattern 1 & 2 (+)* Pattern 7 (-)
1	Early waking	+
2	Irritability	-
3	Speech dissociation	-
4	Restricted speech	+
5	Derealization	+
6	Repetitive movements	-
7	Flatness of affect	-
8	Biological treatment	+
9	Auditory pseudohallucinations	-
10	Gustatory hallucinations	-
11	Fantastic delusions	-
12	Loss of emotions	-
13	Voices comment on patient's thoughts	+
14	Neologisms	+
15	Non-verbal auditory hallucinations	-
16	Delusions of grandeur	-
17	Depressed mood	+
18	Apathy	+
19	Perseveration	+
20	Delusions of control	+
21	Pressure of speech	-
22	Constipation	+
23	Stereotypies	+
24	Tension	+
25	Sexual delusions	+
26	Delusions of persecution	+
27	Change of sex behaviour	-
28	Nihilistic delusions	+
29	Sleep problems	+
30	Groaning	+

*(+) predicts pattern of course 1 (full remission after episode of inclusion, no further episodes) or 2 (incomplete remission after episode of inclusion, no further episodes).

(-) predicts pattern of course 7 (still in episode of inclusion).

TABLE 10.23.　30 PREDICTIVE SYMPTOMS (UNITS OF ANALYSIS)
RANKED ACCORDING TO MAGNITUDE OF
REGRESSION COEFFICIENTS AND F-RATIO VALUES.
(RESULTS OF MULTIPLE LINEAR REGRESSION
ANALYSIS FOR OVERALL OUTCOME CATEGORIES
1 OR 5 IN SCHIZOPHRENIC PATIENTS).

Rank	Units of Analysis	Outcome 1 (+)* Outcome 5 (-)
1	Irritability	-
2	Fantastic delusions	-
3	Loss of emotions	-
4	Voices speaking own thoughts	-
5	Flatness of affect	-
6	Derealization	+
7	Delusional mood	-
8	Negativism	+
9	Obsessive thoughts	-
10	Delusions of persecution	+
11	Observed elated mood	-
12	Lack of concentration	-
13	Speech impediments	+
14	Auditory pseudohallucinations	-
15	Increased interest	-
16	Ambivalence	+
17	Change of interest	-
18	Early waking	+
19	Environmental circumstances	+
20	Lability of affect	+
21	Abnormal tidiness	+
22	Repetitive movements	-
23	Break of self-identity	+
24	Mutism	-
25	Worse in morning	-
26	Perplexity	+
27	Situation anxiety	-
28	Hallucinations from body	+
29	Speech dissociation	-
30	Own thoughts spoken aloud	+

* (+) predicts overall outcome category 1 (very
　　favourable outcome).

　(-) predicts overall outcome category 5 (very
　　unfavourable outcome).

298

TABLE 10.24.   20 SYMPTOMS (UNITS OF ANALYSIS) EMERGING
AS BEST PREDICTORS OF PATTERN OF COURSE
1 & 7 IN SCHIZOPHRENIC PATIENTS.   (RESULTS
OF STEPWISE MULTIPLE REGRESSION ANALYSIS).

Multiple Regression Step No.	Units of Analysis	R^2	Pattern 1&2 (+)* Pattern 7 (-)
1	Early waking	.045	+
2	Tension	.072	+
3	Autism	.085	-
4	Gustatory hallucinations	.099	-
5	Distractibility	.113	+
6	Groaning	.123	+
7	Demonstrative	.134	+
8	Social withdrawal	.144	-
9	Undecided	.153	+
10	Suicidal thoughts	.161	-
11	Compliance	.169	+
12	Speech impediments	.175	-
13	Change of sex behaviour	.181	-
14	Distortion of time perception	.187	+
15	Hallucinations from body	.192	+
16	Frequent auditory hallucinations	.198	
17	Waxy flexibility	.203	-
18	Speech dissociation	.208	-
19	Neologisms	.215	+
20	Klang associations	.221	+

R^2 for 80 units of analysis = .4220

* (+) predicts pattern of course 1 (full remission after
    episode of inclusion no further episodes) or
    2 (incomplete remission after episode of inclusion,
    no further episodes).
  (-) predicts pattern of course 7 (still in episode of
    inclusion).

A substitute for such an estimation could be the determination of the predictive power (that is, the multiple correlation with course and outcome) of increasingly larger subsets of symptoms by stepwise multiple regression which selects the 'optimum' combinations of symptoms among subsets of any size and stops at the level beyond which addition of further symptoms does not improve the prediction.

Stepwise multiple regression analysis of the 129 symptoms was carried out for pattern of course 1 and 2 versus 7, and overall outcome 1 versus 5. Tables 10.22, 10.23, 10.24 and 10.25 show: (a) the 30 symptoms with highest partial correlation coeffients and acceptable degree of variation (*F*-ratio); (b) the first 20

TABLE 10.25. 2O SYMPTOMS (UNITS OF ANALYSIS) EMERGING
AS BEST PREDICTORS OF OVERALL OUTCOME
CATEGORIES 1 OR 5 IN SCHIZOPHRENIC
PATIENTS. (RESULTS OF STEPWISE MULTIPLE
REGRESSION ANALYSIS).

Multiple Regression Step No.	Units of Analysis	R^2	Outcome 1 (+)* Outcome 5 (-)
1	Early waking	.073	+
2	Suicidal thoughts	.105	-
3	Overactivity	.133	+
4	Flatness of affect	.155	-
5	Worries	.183	-
6	Change in sex behaviour	.206	-
7	Ambivalence	.227	+
8	Mutism	.244	-
9	Negativism	.267	+
10	Derealization	.287	+
11	Repetitive movements	.307	-
12	Fantastic delusions	.324	-
13	Speech dissociation	.337	-
14	Situation anxiety	.349	-
15	Speech impediments	.363	+
16	Mannerisms	.374	+
17	Lability of affect	.383	+
18	Haughtiness	.398	-
19	Delusions of persecution	.408	+
20	Social withdrawal	.417	-

R^2 for 86 units of analysis = .6609

* (+) predicts overall outcome category 1 (very favourable outcome).
  (-) predicts overall outcome category 5 (very unfavourable outcome).

symptoms emerging as best predictors from the stepwise multiple regression analysis (together with the proportion of the variance explained by increasingly large subsets of symptoms at each step of the regression).

There is some degree of overlap between the two lists. Many of the symptoms appearing among the best predictors are clearly related to clinically meaningful areas of psychopathology, such as personality change, catatonic phenomena, delusions, hallucinations and affective symptoms.

In clinical terms these lists state that symptoms of a florid clinical picture (for example perplexity, experiences of derealization, overactivity,) and affective symptoms (for example, depression, early waking) predict good outcome; symptoms of a 'negative' clinical picture, such as flatness of affect or personality change (changes of interests, of sexual behaviour, haughtiness), and or social withdrawal, predict poor outcome. Some delusions and hallucinations are

300

associated with good (for example, delusions of persecution) others with poor outcome (for example, fantastic delusions). The same is true for hallucinations. First-rank symptoms in K. Schneider's sense appear both among predictors of poor outcome and among those predicting good outcome.

Another finding of the stepwise multiple regression analysis which deserves to be discussed briefly, is the shape of the curve indicating the relationship between the number of symptoms in the analysis and the proportion of variance explained by them.

In Figure 10.3 the maximum level of prediction that can be achieved with all the 129 UAs is indicated by a straight horizontal line. The ascending curve represents prediction based on an increasing number of symptoms (stepwise multiple regression). The graph shows that a relatively large number of units of analysis is required if a high level of prediction is to be achieved.

This curve is very different from the curve of the prediction based on sociodemographic or past history variables (described in preceding sections) which reaches levels close to the maximum prediction with relatively few predictor variables and does not rise further if more variables are added. This fact suggests that, even if the predictive potential of symptomatology may be high, a large number of symptoms would have to be considered simultaneously, in order to reach an acceptable level of prediction.

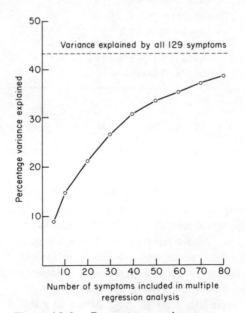

Figure 10.3   Percentage variance explained by sets of symptoms of different size, results of stepwise multiple regression analysis for patients with schizophrenia, pattern of course 1 and 2, and 7

10.5 PREDICTION OF COURSE AND OUTCOME IN AFFECTIVE PSYCHOSES

Stepwise multiple regression analysis was carried out in the sequence described in the preceding sections, in order to examine the predictive value of the variables in classes A, B and C in patients who had a clinical diagnosis of affective psychosis* on initial evaluation.

The objective of the analysis was to determine whether different sets of variables predicted course and outcome in schizophrenia and in affective psychoses.

10.5.1 Predictors of the length of the episode of inclusion

Five variables — poor psychosexual adjustment (predicts longer episode), social isolation (longer episode), history of past psychiatric treatment (predicts shorter episode), a high score on GUA 25 — psychophysiological symptoms† (longer episode) and a high score on GUA 19 — flatness of affect (shorter episode) explain 34 per cent of the outcome variance if the centres are not included in the analysis.

If the centres are included as predictors, the proportion of variance explained by the final set of five best predictors rises to 40 per cent (or 61 per cent if 15 best predictors are used). The final five best predictors include: poor psychosexual adjustment (predicts longer episode), London (longer episode), Cali (longer episode), a high score on GUA 25 — psychophysical symptoms‡ (longer episode) and a high score on GUA 24 — other behavioural symptoms (longer episode). The variable past psychiatric treatment did not enter the regression equation when the centres were introduced.

10.5.2 Predictors of the proportion of the follow-up period spent in psychotic episodes

The sets of five best predictors, with and without the centres, as well as the proportion of variance explained, were very similar to the results obtained for length of the inclusion episode. Poor psychosexual adjustment emerged again as the predictor best correlated with the proportion of time spent in psychotic episodes.

10.5.3 Predictors of the pattern of course

The three patterns of course — 1, 5 and 7 — can be regarded as clinically distinct, and the variables predicting each of them are described below.

---

*Groups of patients with diagnosis ICD 296.0-9 and 298.0 were combined in order to obtain a sufficient number of cases for analysis.
†Early waking, worse in morning, worse in evening, diminished appetite, sleep problems, increased appetite, increased libido, decreased energy, decreased libido, constipation.
‡Talking to self, disorder of pitch, giggling to self, demonstrative behaviour.

10.5.3.1 Predictors of pattern of course 1: full remission after the inclusion episode, no further episodes

This pattern is predicted by the following five variables which explain 25 per cent of the variance: rural residence, young age, occupation – other than sales and services, past physical illness or disability and absence of mental illness in the family. The best predictors do not appear to be correlated with any particular centre.

10.5.3.2 Predictors of pattern of course 5: one or more psychotic episodes after the inclusion episode, full remissions between all episodes

This pattern of recurrent psychosis is predicted best (23 per cent explained variance) by the following five variables: low score on neurotic complaints (GUA 9), history of mental illness in the family, low score on flatness of affect (GUA 19), good psychosexual adjustment and history of past psychiatric treatment. The set of predictors remains unchanged if the centres are included in the analysis.

10.5.3.3 Predictors of pattern of course 7: still in the episode of inclusion at follow-up

Poor psychosexual adjustment, presence of other hallucinations* (GUA 15), no past psychiatric treatment, social isolation and presence of qualitative thought disorder† (GUA 4) together explain 27 per cent of the variance. If the centres are included in the analysis, the set of five best predictors includes Cali, London and Washington, poor psychosexual adjustment and absence of a history of past psychiatric treatment. These five variables account for 40 per cent of the variance.

10.5.4 Predictors of the level of social functioning

If the centres are not included, the following five predictors explain 27 per cent of the variance: past physical illness or disability (predicts absence of impairment) young age (no impairment), poor psychosexual adjustment (predicts impairment), occupation – sales and services (predicts impairment) and occupation – manual workers, labourers, etc. (predicts impairment).

When the centres are included in the analysis, only one change occurs – London emerges as a predictor of social impairment, and the occupational category sales and services is eliminated from the predictor set. The final five best predictors explain 35 per cent of the outcome variance.

10.5.5 Predictors of the overall outcome

The five best predictors of the overall outcome (centres not included) which explain 27 per cent of the variance are: poor psychosexual adjustment (predicts

*Visual, tactile, olfactory, sexual, somatic and gustatory hallucinations.
†Neologisms, klang associations, speech dissociation, irrelevance, blocking, stereotypes of speech and echolalia.

unfavourable outcome), young age (favourable outcome), occupation — managerial or clerical (favourable outcome), rural residence (favourable outcome) and a high score on indications of personality change (GUA 22 — unfavourable outcome).

The inclusion of the centres in the analysis results in a final set of five best predictors explaining 32 per cent of the variance (45 per cent can be explained if 15 predictors are used): London (predicts unfavourable outcome), poor psychosexual adjustment (unfavourable outcome), young age (predicts favourable outcome), GUA 1 — quantitative psychomotor disorders* (unfavourable outcome) and occupation — managerial or clerical (favourable outcome).

The duration of the episode of inclusion prior to the initial evaluation — a predictor variable of considerable importance in schizophrenia, is not among the best predictors of any of the outcome measures in affective psychoses. Another important predictor — history of past psychiatric treatment, appears to be associated with a shorter inclusion episode and a tendency to recurrences in the group.

10.6 DISCUSSION AND CONCLUSIONS

10.6.1 Constraints in the interpretation of findings

Several constraints concerning the data and the methods used in the analysis will be examined before discussing the theoretical significance and the practical implications of the results described in this chapter.

Firstly, the patient cohorts examined and followed up in the IPSS are not necessarily representative of all patients suffering from schizophrenia or affective psychosis in the catchment areas of the centres in the nine countries. This issue was discussed in Volume 1 of the IPSS report (WHO, 1973). On the other hand there was no evidence that the patients followed up differed in any significant way from those that could not be re-examined or about whom there was no follow-up information.

Secondly, the reliability of the sociodemographic description and past history of data on initial examination has been assessed less stringently than that collected with the PSE (see Chapter 3). However, since considerable effort was applied to standardize the instruments of the assessment, and to train the investigators to use them reliably, it would be justified to estimate that the reliability of the assessment of sociodemographic and past history items could not be very much lower than the reliability of the PSE assessment which was measured and found to be relatively high. The fact that in the analysis, some of the sociodemographic and past history variables consistently emerge as good predictors, makes it unlikely that these data might have been heavily contaminated by random error of assessment.

Thirdly, not all assumptions of the method of multiple regression analysis were fully met by the available data. This applied particularly to the metric of the variables consistently emerge as good predictors, makes it unlikely that these data and in order to achieve an approximation to this, some variables had to be

*Overactivity, retardation, stupor and repetitive movements.

dichotomized, which may have resulted in either overestimates or underestimates of the predictive power of some of them.

Fourthly, since the regression model is based on correlation, the variance of outcome explained by a given set of predictors holds for groups of patients but not necessarily for the prediction of prognosis on the basis of such predictors present in individual patients.

10.6.2 Application of the predictors to the individual patients in the study

The two last constraints suggest that an internal validation of the predictors obtained through multiple regression analysis would be desirable, and that a procedure which is independent of the process of derivation of predictors should be applied. For the purpose of such cross-validation, the five best predictors of overall outcome where used as a rating scale and each individual patient with a diagnosis of schizophrenia received a score ranging from 0 to 5, depending on how many of the predictors of good, respectively poor outcome had been assessed as present on initial evaluation. Correlations (Kendall's τ) were then calculated between these scores and the measures of two-year overall outcome for the patients within each centre as well as for all schizophrenic patients in the follow-up study. Such correlations were calculated separately for all patients with clinical diagnosis of schizophrenia, for patients classified into the CATEGO class S, and for patients who were clinically diagnosed as schizophrenic but did not fall into CATEGO class S.

The results of this analysis are presented on Table 10.26. For all followed-up schizophrenic patients the correlation between predictor score and overall outcome was highly significant ($p < 0.001$). Within individual centres, the correlations were statistically significant in all but two of the centres (Aarhus and Prague). Comparisons between the predictor score/outcome correlations for schizophrenics classified as CATEGO class S, and those not falling into class S, show that in all but three centres (Agra, London and Moscow) they were higher for the group of CATEGO class S patients.

Three conclusions can be drawn from these data: (a) with regard to the group of followed-up schizophrenic patients as a whole, the predictors identified by multiple regression analysis correlate significantly with overall outcome; (b) in two of the centres the correlation did not reach a level of significance which suggests that the five best predictors used in this analysis were not the 'best' with regard to these two centres; (c) the predictors tend to correlate better with outcome in the group of CATEGO class S patients than in the schizophrenics who do not fall into that class, which is an indication that CATEGO class S patients may be a more homogeneous group in terms of outcome than the rest of the schizophrenic patients. The explanation of the higher correlations for schizophrenics other than class S in Agra might be that they in fact formed a special group (the majority of them fell into CATEGO class M) which though different from class S patients, was quite homogeneous. As to the London schizophrenics other than class S, the correlation between the predictor scores and outcome in this group was probably affected by

TABLE 10.26. CORRELATION BETWEEN OVERALL OUTCOME AND SCORES ON BEST PREDICTORS BY CENTRES (KENDALL'S TAU CORRELATION COEFFICIENTS).

Centres	Patients with clinical diagnosis of schizophrenia (ICD 295)	Patients in CATEGO class S	Schizophrenics in CATEGO classes other than class S
1. Aarhus	.17	.21	.15
2. Agra	.19*	.14	.32*
3. Cali	.25**	.29**	.05
4. Ibadan	.41**	.42***	.33
5. London	.41***	.40***	.65
6. Moscow	.18*	.24	.24
7. Taipei	.22**	.28**	.11
8. Washington	.39**	.60**	.13
9. Prague	.20	.24	.13
ALL	.33***	.35***	.28***

```
*    :  5%    )
**   :  1%    )  Rejection levels
***  :  0.1%  )
```

random factors, since the number of such patients was small and the coefficient of correlation did not reach statistical significance.

10.6.3 Summary of the findings and conclusions about predictors of course and outcome

The aim of the identification of predictors of course and outcome was to estimate the extent to which the variation of the two-year course and outcome could be attributed to the variation of specific variables assessed on initial evaluation.

Identification of predictors is of considerable theoretical and practical importance. Predictors could be used, for example as sampling criteria among other relevant variables, in studies designed to assess the effects of treatment and other factors on the course and outcome of schizophrenia; better knowledge about them could also contribute to the testing of hypotheses about the aetiology and pathogenesis of schizophrenia and other mental disorders.

All the limitations of the data and the methods considered, the evidence from the analysis of the prediction of two-year course and outcome in patients with initial clinical diagnosis of schizophrenia and affective psychosis suggests that the short-term prognosis of patients with functional psychoses in nine different countries was related to a number of specific characteristics of the patients and their environment which were present before or at the time the initial assessment was made. The main findings supporting this conclusion are as follows:

1. No single variable, and no combination of a few 'key' variables, can explain a large proportion of the variation of any of the course and outcome measures in schizophrenia; in other words, no characteristics of the patient, of the environment, or of the initial manifestations of the disorder considered in isolation would be effective predictors of the subsequent course and outcome of the illness.

The amount of variance of any of the course and outcome variables: length of episode of inclusion, percentage of time spent in psychotic episodes, pattern of course, level of social functioning and overall outcome, that could be explained by an optimal combination of five predictors, ranged from 8 to 22 per cent. If 15 predictors were used instead of five, this amount would increase to 27 per cent.*

In most instances increasing the number of predictors beyond five gave diminishing returns in terms of variance explained and therefore a prediction based on only five prognostic factors was almost as effective as a prediction based on several times as many variables. An exception to this was provided by the symptoms as predictors, which will be discussed separately.

2. In terms of predictive power, that is, the proportion of the variance explained, the three classes of predictor variables investigated — sociodemographic characteristics, past history characteristics and characteristics of the inclusion episode, were quite similar, and no particular class of variables appeared to be decisively more 'prognostic' than the others. The small differences in the level of prediction achieved by the three classes of predictors could be attributed to the different number of variables in each class. It could be expected that, everything else being equal, a large number of variables taken together would predict better than a small number of variables.

3. The addition of the field research centres as a special set of variables improved to some degree the level of prediction, by explaining in most instances another 1 to 3 per cent of the residual variance. This fact and the changes in the predictive power of some variables which occurred after the inclusion of the centres into the analysis suggest that other predictive factors may exist, which had not been specified, assessed or included in the analysis. Such factors could be, for example, characteristics related to particular cultures, and the finding that the centres are, in fact, predictors of course and outcome, should lead to further investigations in this respect.

On the whole, two of the centres in developing countries, Ibadan and Agra appeared in many of the analyses among the five best predictors of favourable course and outcome, while some centres in the developed countries, London and Aarhus, for example tended equally often to be predictors of unfavourable course and outcome. This finding is in agreement with the data reported in the preceding

---

*Clinical type of subsequent episodes could be predicted with a higher percentage of variance explained (up to 26 per cent for five predictors and 38 per cent for 15 predictors). However, the number of patients in each of the different categories by type of subsequent episodes was relatively small; therefore these percentages should not be compared with results obtained for course and outcome variables involving large numbers of patients.

chapters, which indicate that patients with initial evaluation diagnosis of schizophrenia in the developing countries had more favourable two-year course and outcome than patients in the developed countries.

4. The amount of course and outcome variance which could be explained by the best predictors was different for the groups of schizophrenic patients in the developing and in the developed countries. It was considerably higher in the developed countries, ranging from 24 to 30 per cent for a set of five best predictors and from 26 to 34 per cent for a set of 15 best predictors. The corresponding ranges for all patients in the developing countries were 13 to 21 per cent and 15 to 23 per cent.

This finding may seem to be in contradiction with the data in Table 10.26 which show that in two centres in developed countries – Aarhus and Prague – the correlations between predictor scores of individual patients and overall outcome fell short of statistical significance. The contradiction is however an apparent one, if it is considered that the variables on which the patients were scored to obtain these correlation coefficients were derived by multiple regression from the pooled data from all centres without including in the analysis the centres themselves as variables. Therefore, if some centres were strongly associated with particular trends of outcome – as some of the centres in developing countries actually were – the sets of predictors obtained from pooled data would include some variables associated with outcome in such centres. The greater 'weight' of the centres in developing countries in relation to the identification of predictors through multiple regression is further increased by the smaller number of followed-up schizophrenics in Aarhus and Prague, compared to the other centres.

On the other hand, the higher percentage of outcome variance explained by the predictors in the centres in developed countries was obtained when all the centres were split into the two groups of developing and developed countries. All this taken into consideration, the finding of a considerable difference between the two groups of centres with regard to the predictability of course and outcome by the variables utilized in the reported analyses, can be accepted as real.

Among the possible explanations of this difference, one hypothesis may deserve special attention. The data collection methods and instruments used in the study, as well as the selection of items for the prediction analysis, were based mainly on knowledge about prognosis of schizophrenia in Europe and North America. These variables may not be the most relevant ones for the prediction of course and outcome of patients in cultures other than European and North American, while variables untapped by the study or not included in the analysis, might be of greater prognostic value regarding these groups of patients. The fact that centres in the developing countries emerge more often as strong predictors of course and outcome, than centres in the developed countries, would support this hypothetical explanation.

5. The sets of best predictors for the different positively intercorrelated measures of outcome: length of episode of inclusion, proportion of time spent in psychotic episodes, impairment of social functioning and overall outcome, were on the whole, very similar. Several variables: social isolation, length of the inclusion

episode prior to the initial evaluation, history of past psychiatric treatment, marital status, history of behaviour symptoms and occupation, appeared among the best predictors in most of the analyses. The fact that these variables appear so consistently as best predictors is even more remarkable if it is considered that some of them (for example, social isolation) were 'soft data' and strict standardization of their assessment had not been made. Some of these variables — history of behaviour symptoms (at any time in the past) and social isolation — are related to aspects of personality adjustment and functioning; other variables — marital status and occupation — characterize in a general way the social context of the individual; and the remaining two — length of the episode before the inclusion into the study and history of past psychiatric treatment — reflect the temporal pattern of the illness itself. Clearly, these three pairs of variables would be considered as prognostically important by most clinical psychiatrists, but the fact that they were identified by a statistical method in a case material collected in nine different cultures suggests that these predictors may be related to basic patterns of the evolution of the disorder that are not dissimilar in the different cultures.

6. Among the characteristics of the inclusion episode, those that appear in sets of best predictors of course and outcome in schizophrenia are items related to major aspects of psychopathology and, primarily, to temporal and qualitative features of the evolution and symptomatology of the disorder. Thus, duration of the illness before the initial assessment and the type of its onset are measures of the acuteness, respectively chronicity, of the disorder, while the scores on depression — elation symptoms, derealization, psychophysical symptoms and indications of personality change provide a general but informative description of the essential symptomatology. Derealization, which appears often among the best predictors, and is associated with good prognosis, merits a special mention.* The introspective awareness of derealization phenomena and the ability to describe them during an interview may be a sensitive indicator of other characteristics of personality and psychopathology: intelligence level, education, acuteness and, possibly, presence of a strong affective component of the disorder, which all mitigate against unfavourable outcome. Psychophysical symptoms (for example, early waking, worse in morning, changes in appetite, sleep, libido, decreased energy, etc.) are also associated with a good prognosis, and clearly related to presence of an affective disturbance.

In contrast, indications of personality change and flatness of affect, which predict unfavourable course and outcome, are important diagnostic characteristics of an already chronic disorder which the majority of psychiatrists would classify as schizophrenic.

In summary, it can be said that in patients with a clinical diagnosis of schizophrenia, chronicity and social impairment in the future can be predicted by

*It must be emphasized that derealization, as defined in the PSE, is different from Langfeldt's (1976) concept of derealization. The latter refers essentially to the description of the delusional and hallucinatory distortion of the patient's awareness of reality which occurs predominantly in schizophrenic psychoses. Derealization in the context of the PSE, consists of diagnostically non-specific phenomena, such as feelings of unreality or changed appearance of things, people or familiar surroundings, changes in the subjective time perception, etc., without loss of insight.

levels of chronicity and social impairment already present, while absence of chronicity and impairment on the initial assessment, acute onset and mixture of affective symptoms, predict a more favourable course of the disorder.

7. Interesting differences can be found among the sets of variables predicting patterns of course 1, 5 and 7 in patients with a clinical diagnosis of schizophrenia.

Pattern of course 1 (single episode followed by a full remission for the rest of the follow-up), which was particularly common in Ibadan, is predicted, among other things, by young age, good premorbid personality (that is, no indications of personality change, good psychosexual adjustment, and no social isolation), marital status – married, no mental illness in the family, no past psychiatric treatment, sudden onset and short duration of the episode before the initial assessment, presence of precipitating stress and rapid development of the symptoms.

Pattern of course 5 (recurrent illnesses with full remissions), which is regarded as more characteristic of the affective psychoses than of schizophrenia, is predicted by several indicators of good premorbid personality, by female sex, acute nature of the episodes and presence of neurotic and affective symptoms. Both the pattern of course and the set of variables predicting it suggest that this group of schizophrenic illnesses bears considerable resemblance to the stereotype of an affective psychosis.

Pattern of course 7 (continuous illness for a period of two years of more), is by contrast, predicted mainly by the already discussed indicators of chronicity, by male sex, poor personality adjustment and by the absence of affective features or derealization.

Similarly, in the prediction of the clinical type of the subsequent episodes, definitely schizophrenic, probably schizophrenic, and affective subsequent episodes are associated with sets of predictors which include variables indicating presence or absence of chronicity and variables indicating presence or absence of affective features.

The finding that a majority (367 patients) of the followed-up schizophrenics fell into three quite distinct categories of pattern of course, and that these three categories were predicted by different variables assessed on initial evaluation raises once again the question which recurs in the literature on schizophrenia: in what sense is schizophrenia, as defined by agreed clinical criteria, a homogeneous disease category? There have been many attempts to split the entity defined by Kraepelin and Bleuler into hypothetical different diseases on the basis of clinical, genetic or other assumptions. The findings reported here do not justify far-reaching conclusions to be made on the basis of IPSS material, but they suggest that the pattern of course is an important dimension which should be considered in the taxonomy of schizophrenia, in addition to symptomatologically defined subgroups. Future research into the relationships between the cross-sectional and longitudinal aspects of the disorder may result in a new taxonomy of schizophrenia which would facilitate the search for specific aetiological factors.

8. Two conclusions stand out with regard to the specific contribution of the presenting symptomatology to the prediction of course and outcome in schizophrenia.

Firstly, the analyses carried out at the level of symptoms (units of analysis) tend, on the whole, to support the qualitative hypotheses (see Table 10.1) about the predictive value of individual symptoms: symptoms regarded in the literature as broadly descriptive of schizophrenic psychoses and symptoms characteristic of negative clinical picture (for example, flatness of affect) predict unfavourable course and outcome, and symptoms related to affective disorders and 'florid acute' clinical picture (for example, overactivity and perplexity) predict favourable course and outcome in schizophrenia patients.

Secondly, though aggregates of symptoms explain considerable part of outcome variance, no individual symptoms, and no combination of 'key' symptoms, could explain a high proportion of the course and outcome variance.

This fact, however, would not justify a general conclusion that the predictive value of symptomatology in psychiatric disorders is low. The IPSS patients were selected for the study because of the presence of certain psychotic symptoms, but the subsequent investigation did not aim at comparing their course and outcome with groups of individuals who did not have psychotic symptoms. Rather, one of the aims of the follow-up study was to identify among the various symptoms of schizophrenic patients those predicting course and outcome better than others. Therefore the conclusions about the prognostic value of symptoms refer only to patients already identified as suffering from schizophrenia.

In fact, when information on the presence or absence of a large number of symptoms was used, a substantial proportion of the variance could be explained if all symptoms were included simultaneously in a multivariate statistical analysis. This showed that, while individual symptoms were not sufficiently 'prognostic', the comprehensive symptomatological description of the patient could contribute significantly to the prediction of course and outcome.

9. The analysis of prediction of course and outcome of patients who, on initial evaluation, had a diagnosis of affective psychosis (depression or mania) showed that less favourable two-year course and outcome is associated with some of the indicators of poor premorbid personality adjustment: for example, poor psycho-sexual adjustment and history of behaviour symptoms.

Mental illness in the family, history of past psychiatric treatment and presence of neurotic symptoms were among the predictors of future recurrences, while social isolation and presence on initial evaluation of overt psychotic symptomatology (hallucinations and qualitative thought disorder, for example) were among the predictors of continuous, uninterrupted course of the illness.

The duration ot the episode of inclusion prior to the initial assessment was not among the best predictors of course and outcome in affective psychosis. History of past psychiatric treatment was predictive of shorter length of the episode of inclusion and of a recurrent pattern of course (while in schizophrenia it was among the predictors of chronicity).

In conclusion, the results of the analysis of the predictors of the two-year course and outcome of the IPSS patients with initial clinical diagnosis of schizophrenia or affective psychosis appear to support many of the hypotheses on prognostic factors in the functional psychoses, derived from previous studies. The IPSS data, however, throw additional light on several important aspects of prognosis. The data (a) demonstrate the multivariate determination of prognosis (b); permit to identify specific predictors which merit further study; (c) indicate areas where other potential predictors may be found — for example, the sociocultural environment; and (d) suggest possibilities of improving the instruments for standardized assessment of psychiatric patients, by making them more sensitive to prognostically important characteristics of the patients' personality, environment and psychopathology.

CHAPTER 11

Approaches toward Assessment of the Predictive Validity of Systems of Classification of Schizophrenia and Other Functional Psychoses

11.1 INTRODUCTION

One of the major purposes of classification in the field of mental disorders is to serve as a tool of communication. In order to be useful, a classification should involve explicit and simple decision rules that can be applied reliably by different users. Furthermore, its categories should be related to observable phenomena and convey information relevant to the needs in the particular area of its application. A classification which is useful for one purpose may not be relevant for another purpose, and different classification schemes may have to be developed to meet different needs.

The evolution of classifications in psychiatry conformed to such principles to a limited extent. The development of taxonomies of the mental disorders has been more influenced by a variety of theoretical assumptions and aspirations for a 'natural' classification, than by pragmatic considerations of the purpose for which a classification is needed. This has resulted in a proliferation of classification schemes which makes communication difficult and is reminiscent of an earlier situation about which D. H. Tuke (1892) wrote that 'the wit of man has rarely been more exercised than in the attempt to classify the morbid mental phenomena covered by the term insanity'.

Critics (such as Menninger, 1959) have pointed out many of the shortcomings of existing classifications in psychiatry. Classifications, however, are needed and there is evidence (for example the wide acceptance of ICD-8) that the interest in developing a common language in the field of mental disorders is growing. This need is being reinforced by the availability of new, effective therapeutic techniques whose administration requires a more accurate assessment of the indications for specific treatment or rehabilitation measures (examples are the pharmacotherapy of depressive disorders or the social treatment and rehabilitation in schizophrenia).

The efforts to improve the existing classification concepts call for an objective assessment of their applicability and usefulness. This is particularly important in the field of the functional psychoses where the possibilities for an independent validation of the clinical diagnosis – by, say, using biological indicators, are still very limited and where the current taxonomy has been continuously challenged since its inception. The importance of the task of assessing the classification of the functional psychoses can also be seen in a crosscultural perspective (Sartorius, 1976). For example, the Kraepelinian classification of such disorders and its derivatives, having arisen from observations in European settings, may not be fully applicable in non-European settings. Considering the magnitude of the mental health problems in the developing world, and in particular that the frequency of psychotic illnesses there is comparable to psychotic morbidity in technologically advanced societies, it is apparent that too little has been done so far to assess the validity of current classification concepts when applied to patients with functional psychoses in those countries which include the majority of the world's population.

The opportunity to explore certain aspects of the validity of classifications of schizophrenia and the other functional psychoses in the framework of the International Pilot Study of Schizophrenia was of particular interest. A more extensive assessment of such classifications will be undertaken on completion of the five-year follow-up of the study patients. However, the two-year follow-up material provided some ground for a preliminary testing of hypotheses and for a trial of different methodological approaches to the evaluation of validity of classifications.

11.2 CLASSIFICATION SYSTEMS USED IN THE STUDY AND CRITERIA FOR THE ASSESSMENT OF THEIR VALIDITY

Four different systems of classification were used in the initial evaluation phase of the study: clinical diagnosis (coded in the ICD system), computer-simulated diagnosis (the CATEGO programme), a statistical clustering method (McKeon's clusters), and the assignment of schizophrenic patients to a concordant or a discrepant group on the basis of the results of all of the three previous classifications. The classification procedures involved in each of these four systems have been described extensively in Volume 1 of the IPSS report (WHO, 1973), and only a brief overview of their actual or potential applications will be given here as a background for the discussion of findings about their validity.

11.2.1 Clinical diagnosis and the International Classification of Diseases (ICD)

The current ICD-8 taxonomy of the functional psychoses is derived essentially from the dichotomy of deteriorating and non-deteriorating psychotic illness recognized by many nineteenth century clinicians and reflected in Kraepelin's definitions of 'dementia praecox' and 'manic-depressive insanity'. In post-Kraepelinian psychiatry the underlying nosological principle which emphasizes course and outcome as the main criteria of the validity of the diagnostic and classificatory groupings of functional psychotic disorders, has been criticized or modified but never fully rejected, nor, for that matter, fully accepted. The ICD-8 system, based on clinical diagnosis, is being widely used for statistical reporting on mental disorders. Some of its shortcomings (for example it was not designed for use in outpatient settings, lacks adequate provisions for coding severity of illness, impairments or disabilities) come to the foreground with the expansion of the public health functions of psychiatry, or in some particular branches of research. However, the ICD system is open to modifications and improvements, and an objective assessment of the validity of its categories designed for classifying patients with functional psychoses (295 to 299) would be an important contribution to their further revision.

11.2.2 Computer-simulated diagnosis (CATEGO)

This system (Wing, Cooper and Sartorius, 1974) categorizes psychiatric patients into a number of classes among which several correspond closely to the clinical diagnostic groupings of the functional psychoses. The decision rules incorporated in the computer program are a reflection of the hierarchical diagnostic reasoning and weighting of symptoms in clinical practice. By standardizing entirely the inferential procedures involved in making a diagnosis and allocating automatically patients to classification categories, the reliability of the computerised classification process depends only on the quality of the PSE ratings which are used as input for the program. The uses of the CATEGO classification are mainly scientific (such as description of psychopathology, measurement of symptomatic change, standardization of the selection of patients for various investigations, studies of psychiatric taxonomy) but it may also have educational and clinical applications.

11.2.3 Statistical clusters (McKeon's method)

This classification technique rests on purely mathematical assumptions and treats all symptoms and other patient characteristics as having equal weights. It belongs to the family of numerical taxonomy methods (Sokal and Sneath, 1963) which have found applications in other branches of science (such as botany and zoology). Its potential uses in psychiatry are insufficiently explored. The computational process involved and the difficulty of interpreting statistical clusters in terms of familiar clinical concepts and observations are constraints for their use as an alternative to existing clinical classifications. However, as a research tool, statistical clustering methods may generate new hypotheses by grouping together patients on the basis of similarities which cannot be inferred from clinical considerations.

11.2.4 Concordant–non-concordant groups of schizophrenic patients

These groups were defined in the initial evaluation phase (see Volume 1 of the IPSS report) in order to select patients in whom the diagnosis of schizophrenia is least dependent on variations and inconsistencies on the part of the diagnostician. Thus, concordant schizophrenic patients were those who had a clinical diagnosis of schizophrenia, who had been assigned to the CATEGO class S, and who were included in the three McKeon clusters (4, 5 and 7) which turned out to select out schizophrenic patients in excess of statistical chance. This group could be expected to be symptomatically more homogeneous than the rest of the schizophrenic patients and to provide a point of departure toward a transculturally applicable definition of schizophrenia, since concordant patients were found to exist in each of the centres of the study.

The two main assumptions behind classifying patients into the diagnostic categories of schizophrenia and other functional psychoses are that: (a) patients allocated to the same group will have similar clinical manifestations at one point in time and these manifestations will be different from manifestations in other groups; (b) patients belonging to the same group will have similar course and outcome of their illnesses which will be different from the course and outcome in other groups.

These assumptions correspond to two criteria of validity: content validity and predictive validity, and the degree to which these criteria are met by the systems of classification used in the IPSS can be determined.

The initial phase of the IPSS provided evidence that the clinical characteristics of the patients with a diagnosis of schizophrenia in nine different countries are similar but distinguishable from the clinical characteristics of the other major non-organic psychoses. The data from the two-year follow-up can be used to consider whether the course and outcome of schizophrenic patients in the different countries is similar and distinguishable from the course and outcome of patients with other functional psychoses. It is clear that a two-year follow-up is not sufficiently long to make definitive conclusions about the validity of classification concepts, but considering the current state of knowledge this would be a significant step forward.

The assessment of validity of the different systems of classification proceeded in two ways. Firstly, the predictive validity of clinical diagnosis was considered in terms of the specific hypotheses listed at the beginning of Chapter 6, which outline some of the features generally accepted to be characteristic of the course and outcome of schizophrenia. In this context, the results of the analyses presented in Chapters 6 to 9 will be examined in order to determine if they provide support for these hypotheses.

Secondly, the four systems of classification were tested by means of a multivariate statistical technique — discriminant function analysis, which permits the simultaneous evaluation of a great number of variables relevant to the allocation of patients to diagnostic categories or clusters.

11.3 CLINICAL DIAGNOSIS AT INITIAL EVALUATION AS A PREDICTOR OF COURSE AND OUTCOME

The hypotheses about the course and outcome of schizophrenia will be examined in the light of the findings for groups of patients identified according to the clinical ICD diagnosis made at the field research centre (FRC) at the time of the initial evaluation.

The discussion in this section will concentrate on findings about individual variables and the extent to which each of them supports the hypotheses.

11.3.1 Impairment of social functioning

The first hypothesis was the following: that a high percentage of patients diagnosed as schizophrenic will be severely socially impaired in their subsequent lives, and that the percentage of schizophrenic patients with such disability will be higher than the percentage of socially impaired patients in whom diagnoses of other functional psychoses were made.

Results of analyses in Chapters 6 and 7 indicate that 23 per cent of the patients given an initial evaluation diagnosis of schizophrenia were considered to have suffered from severe social impairment during the follow-up period. This was more than twice the percentage of patients with social impairment in any other psychotic group. There was a considerable variation among individual centres with regard to the percentage of schizophrenic patients who were socially impaired on follow-up: the percentage was high in London (38 per cent), Aarhus (33 per cent), Prague (33 per cent) and Washington (32 per cent), while it was quite low in Ibadan (5 per cent). Those intracentre comparisons that were possible indicated that within individual centres a higher percentage of schizophrenics than of patients with other psychotic diagnoses suffered from severe social impairment during the follow-up period.

Thus, the findings offer some support for the hypothesis that a higher percentage of schizophrenic patients than of patients in other psychotic diagnostic groups are likely to have severe social impairment during the follow-up period, both across all centres and within individual centres. However, it was also clear that a high percentage of schizophrenic patients did not suffer from severe social impairment during the two year follow-up period, and that the percentage of schizophrenic patients who suffered such impairment varied greatly from centre to centre. The average percentage of patients with severe impairment from Ibadan, Agra and Cali, all centres in developing countries, was half as high as the average percentage for the patients in the other six centres.

11.3.2 Percentage of follow-up time with psychotic symptoms

The second hypothesis was: a high percentage of patients diagnosed as schizophrenic will have psychotic symptoms for a considerable part of their subsequent lives, and schizophrenic patients will usually be psychotic for a larger proportion of the follow-up period than patients with other functional psychoses.

On the average, the schizophrenic patients spent 37.1 per cent of the follow-up period in psychotic episodes, close to twice the average percentage of the follow-up period spent in psychotic episodes for the other diagnostic groups. The schizophrenic group had a higher percentage of patients in psychotic episodes for a high percentage of the follow-up period (28 per cent for more than 75 per cent of the follow-up period and 35 per cent for more than 45 per cent of the follow-up period), and a lower percentage of patients in psychotic episodes for a low percentage of the follow-up period (17 per cent for 5 per cent or less of the follow-up period and 39 per cent for 15 per cent or less).

There was considerable variation among centres with regard to the percentage of the follow-up period that schizophrenic patients spent in psychotic episodes. A relatively high percentage of schizophrenics were in psychotic episodes for a very short time (5 per cent or less of the follow-up period) in Ibadan (29 per cent), Agra (27 per cent), Cali (21 per cent) and Washington (20 per cent), while a relatively low percentage were in psychotic episodes for this proportion of the follow-up period in Taipei (7 per cent), Prague (7 per cent), London (9 per cent), Aarhus (13 per cent) and Moscow (14 per cent). On the other hand, in Aarhus 48 per cent of the patients and in Washington 47 per cent were in psychotic episodes for a long period of time (more than 75 per cent of the follow-up period). Only 7 per cent of the Ibadan patients were in a psychotic episode for more than 75 per cent of the time.

Thus, the IPSS results offer support for the hypothesis. However, it should be noted that 17 per cent of schizophrenic patients spent less than 5 per cent of the follow-up period in psychotic episodes and 30 per cent spent less than 15 per cent and that the centres varied markedly with regard to this measure. The average percentage of the follow-up period spent in psychotic episodes for schizophrenics in the three centres in developing countries was 26.5 per cent while for those from the other six centres, it was 44.8 per cent.

11.3.3 Remissions after acute psychotic episodes

The third hypothesis was: the majority of schizophrenic patients will not have full remissions after acute psychotic episodes, and a smaller percentage of schizophrenic patients will have such remissions than of patients with other functional psychoses.

In 27 per cent of the schizophrenic patients followed up, the episode of inclusion was followed by a full remission and no subsequent episodes, while in an additional 11 per cent there were subsequent psychotic episodes followed by full remissions, making for a total of 38 per cent of schizophrenic patients with full remissions after psychotic episodes. The corresponding percentage was 46 per cent for the psychotic depressive group, 80 per cent for the manic group, and 45 per cent for the other psychosis group. The same differences were noted for those intracentre comparisons that were possible.

Thus, the IPSS findings tend to support this hypothesis. However, it should be noted that in two centres, a large majority of schizophrenic patients had full remissions after psychotic episodes – Ibadan (80 per cent) and Agra (65 per cent). In Agra the manic group was the only group with enough followed-up patients to compare with the schizophrenic group; 94 per cent of the manics had full remissions after psychotic episodes, so it appears that even in Agra the hypothesis tends to hold up. In Ibadan there were no other diagnostic groups with a large enough number of patients followed up to make comparisons.

11.3.4 Symptomatic improvement

The fourth hypothesis was: the percentage of schizophrenic patients who show symptomatic improvement over time will be lower than the percentage of patients with other functional psychoses showing such improvement.

This hypothesis can be considered in terms of the percentages of patients found to be psychotic at the time of second-year follow-up, and the percentages of patients still in the episode of inclusion at the time of second-year follow-up.

11.3.4.1 Percentage of patients psychotic at second-year follow-up

Using the criteria for psychosis described in section 5.1.2 it was found that 37 per cent of all schizophrenics followed up were psychotic at the time of the second-year follow-up, compared to 14 per cent for the psychotic depression group, 25 per cent for the mania group, and 28 per cent for the other psychosis group. The differences between schizophrenia and the other diagnostic groups also held up for those intracentre comparisons that were possible. There was considerable variation among the individual centres with regard to the percentage of schizophrenic patients followed up that were psychotic at the time of the second-year follow-up, ranging from 61 per cent in Aarhus to 25 per cent in Ibadan.

11.3.4.2 Percentage of patients still in the episode of inclusion at the time of second-year follow-up

A second way of considering this hypothesis is to compare the diagnostic groups in terms of the percentage of patients still in the episode of inclusion at the time of second-year follow-up. Of the schizophrenic patients followed up 26 per cent were still in the episode of inclusion at the time of second-year follow-up, compared to 7 per cent for the psychotic depression group, 2 per cent for the mania group, and 15 per cent for the other psychosis group. The differences between schizophrenia and the other psychotic diagnostic groups were also noted in intracentre comparisons. There was a wide variation among the individual centres with regard to the percentage of schizophrenic patients still in the episode of inclusion at the time of second-year follow-up, ranging from 50 per cent in Aarhus to 7 per cent in Ibadan.

Thus, the follow-up data supports the hypothesis when the percentage of patients psychotic at the time of second-year follow-up, and the percentage of patients still in the episode of inclusion at the time of the second-year follow-up are considered.

11.3.5 Subsequent symptomatology

The fifth hypothesis was: when patients initially diagnosed as schizophrenic have symptoms subsequently during their lives, they will be similar to one another in the type of symptoms that they demonstrate, and the symptoms they have will be different from the symptoms that patients initially given a diagnosis of one of the other functional psychoses will have later in their lives.

The analyses described in Chapters 6 and 7 indicate that at the time of the second-year follow-up the level of psychopathology in the schizophrenic patient groups in the nine centres was, in general, low, and consisted mainly of 'negative' or non-specific symptoms such as flatness of affect, poor rapport, apathy, lack of insight, and cooperation difficulties. The level of psychopathology was particularly low in the schizophrenic groups in Agra, Cali and Ibadan. Considering the broad areas of psychopathology represented by the groups of units of analysis, the schizophrenic, psychotic, depressive, manic, and other psychosis groups are similar to one another at the time of second-year follow-up, with generally low levels of psychopathology, higher than minimal scores on only a few negative and non-specific symptoms, and little in the way of positive psychotic symptomatology. When the frequency of symptoms on a more specific level, the UA level, is considered, it is seen that the most frequently found symptoms at the time of second-year follow-up were negative or non-specific symptoms for the schizophrenic group, affective symptoms for the psychotic depressive and manic groups, and both non-specific and affective symptoms for the other psychosis group.

Of the schizophrenic patients who were considered to have had episodes of illness after the episode of inclusion, the vast majority had episodes considered to be either definitely or probably schizophrenic, although 18 per cent did have affective psychotic episodes. On the other hand, of the psychotic depressive and manic patients who had episodes after the episode of inclusion, the vast majority had affective psychotic episodes, although 5 of the 32 manics with subsequent episodes did have definitely or probably schizophrenic episodes.

Thus, the follow-up data provide some support for the hypothesis, indicating that schizophrenics at the time of second-year follow-up were in fact similar to one another, and also indicating that on specific levels of symptomatology there were some differences among the diagnostic groups in terms of the clinical picture that characterized them at the time of second-year follow-up. Furthermore, schizophrenic patients who had subsequent episodes tended to have schizophrenic episodes, and patients with affective psychoses who had subsequent episodes, tended to have affective psychotic episodes.

11.3.6 Types of subsequent episodes

The sixth hypothesis was: the symptoms that patients diagnosed as schizophrenic demonstrate later in their lives will be similar to the symptoms that they demonstrate at the time the diagnosis is made.

When initial evaluation profiles of schizophrenic patients were compared to the profiles of the same patients at the time of second-year follow-up, it was noted that there was considerable similarity between the symptomatological pictures of the groups of schizophrenic patients on the two occasions. At initial evaluation, the schizophrenic groups of patients had positive psychotic symptoms such as hallucinations and delusions; negative symptoms, such as flatness of affect; and non-specific symptoms such as anxiety, tension and irritability, lack of insight, and co-operation difficulties. At the time of second-year follow-up, the patients demonstrated much less pathology in all three types of symptoms, but the decrease was not marked in the positive psychotic symptoms. Thus, the similarity of the symptom profiles on the two occasions was primarily due to similarities in negative and non-specific symptoms.

When the same type of comparisons were carried out for only those initial evaluation schizophrenics who were psychotic at the time of second-year follow-up, it was found that the initial evaluation and second-year follow-up symptomatology of such patients was highly similar in all centres. This similarity was due to similarity in positive psychotic, negative, and non-specific symptoms.

The results of the CATEGO classification of patients on initial evaluation and second-year follow-up also indicated that those initial evaluation schizophrenic patients who were psychotic at the time of follow-up tended to present the same clinical type of psychosis on the two occasions. The percentage of such patients who were placed in the same CATEGO class on both occasions ranged between 72 per cent in Washington and 100 per cent in London.

These findings and the finding described under 11.3.5 above, that schizophrenic patients who had subsequent episodes during the follow-up period tended to have definitely or probably schizophrenic episodes provide considerable support for this hypothesis.

11.3.7 Relationship of the sociocultural setting to the course of schizophrenia

The seventh hypothesis was: the course of schizophrenia may vary according to the sociocultural setting in which it occurs.

This is a complex hypothesis to consider, and only a beginning can be made on the basis of the second-year follow-up findings. What stands out most clearly is that on virtually all of the course and outcome measures considered, on the average the schizophrenic patients in Agra, Cali and Ibadan had a better course and outcome than the schizophrenic patients in the other six centres. Another striking finding was that when the course and outcome of schizophrenia was compared to that of affective psychosis, the differences between these two diagnostic groups were statistically significant for every course and outcome variable in the groups of centres in developed countries, and were not significant for any course and outcome variable in the groups of centres in the developing countries.

There are many possible explanations for these findings and they will be discussed in Chapter 12.

On the whole, the IPSS data provided support for the hypothesis, but there are many additional hypotheses which will have to be tested in future studies if a clearer answer to the question of the relationship of culture to the course of schizophrenia is to be obtained.

11.3.8 Overall outcome

What is implicit in most of the hypotheses listed above is that schizophrenia has a poorer outcome than the outcome of other functional psychoses. The overall outcome groupings described in Chapters 6, 7 and 8 provide additional evidence that this is true. A higher percentage of schizophrenic patients than of patients in the other psychotic diagnostic groups fell into the two worst groups, and a lower percentage of schizophrenic patients than of patients in the other psychotic diagnostic groups fell into the two best groups.

In summary, most of the hypotheses about the course and outcome of schizophrenia listed at the beginning of Chapter 6 received at least some support from the IPSS two-year follow-up data, and it can be said in general that the course and outcome of schizophrenia during the two-year period was clearly different from and worse than that of other functional psychoses. Even so, some schizophrenics did have a very good outcome, and the overlap in terms of outcome between schizophrenia and the other functional psychoses was not of a negligible size. Schizophrenic patients from the centres in developing countries had a better course and outcome than schizophrenic patients from the other centres, which underlines the practical importance of crosscultural studies of course and outcome of mental disorders.

11.4 DISCRIMINANT FUNCTION ANALYSIS OF CLASSIFICATION SYSTEMS

11.4.1 The statistical technique of discriminant function analysis

It has been pointed out that a classification should be able to divide a set of objects into subsets that are mutually exclusive and jointly exhaustive (Hempel, 1959). This requirement cannot be fully met by classifications of mental disorders built on symptomatological distinctions because of the considerable overlap of symptoms and signs across the diagnostic categories. However, the different classifications systems can be compared to one another with regard to the extent to which meaningful distinctions between various characteristics of patients assigned to different diagnostic classes and categories within each system are possible.

If a diagnostic grouping of functional psychoses is to be accepted as valid, then the patients assigned to each particular group should be symptomatologically similar to each other and different from patients assigned to other groups at one point in time. If this is established, the next step in testing the validity of diagnostic distinctions would be to see if the groups of patients assigned to different diagnostic categories can be distinguished in terms of subsequent course and outcome. Moreover, it would be of considerable interest if the distinctions between diagnostic groups can be quantified, so that a direct comparison could be made among alternative classification systems in terms of discriminatory power.

It can hardly be expected that any single symptom (or unit of analysis) and any single course or outcome variable – for example, length of the episode of inclusion, would distinguish very clearly between patients assigned to the diagnostic categories of, say, schizophrenia and psychotic depression. Therefore, it would be more promising if the assessment of the distance between any two diagnostic groups is based on a simultaneous consideration of all relevant variables – for example the 129 units of analysis (UAs), or the 27 groups of units of analysis (GUAs), or all the measures of course and outcome.

A suitable statistical technique for this purpose is the discriminant function analysis. The main idea in this multivariate method is to replace a large group of measurements of patients' characteristics – for example the 129 UAs, or the set of course and outcome categories, by a single composite variable and measure the distance between two diagnostic entities in terms of this new variable. In this analysis, a weighted linear compound of patient's characteristics was chosen:

$$l_1 \cdot U_1 + l_2 \cdot U_2 + \ldots + l_{129} \cdot U_{129} = Z$$

323

```
50'S VS. (60,62,80), 129 UA - I.E.
FREQUENCY DISTRIBUTIONS FOR BOTH GROUPS
NUMBER  OF CASES FOR GROUP1:      507          NUMBER OF CASES FOR GROUP2:      71
RANGE OF THE VARIABLE:  0.218270E 02          ONE STEP REPRESENTS:  0.363783E 00

-11.48|XXXXXXXX
-11.12|XXXX
-10.75|
-10.39|
-10.03|XXXX
 -9.66|XXXX
 -9.30|
 -8.94|
 -8.57|XXXX
 -8.21|XXXXXXXX
 -7.84|XXXXXXXXXXXXXXXXXX
 -7.48|8XXX
 -7.12|XXXXXXXXXXXXXXXXXXXXXXXXXXXXXXXXXXX
 -6.75|XXXXXXXX
 -6.39|XXXXXXXXXXXXXXXXXXXXX
 -6.03|8XXXXXXXXXXXX
 -5.66|8XXXXXXXXXXXXXXXXXXXXXXXX
 -5.30|8XXXXXXXXXXX
 -4.93|
 -4.57|8XXXXXXXXXXXXXXXXXXXXXXXXX
 -4.21|8XXXXXXXXXXXXXXX
 -3.84|8XXXXXXX
 -3.48|00
 -3.12|8XXX
 -2.75|8888XXXXXXXXX
 -2.39|8888XXXX
 -2.02|888XXXXXXXXXXX
 -1.66|8888XXXX
 -1.30|8888XXXX
 -0.93|000000
 -0.57|88888XXXXXXXXXXXX
 -0.20|888800000
  0.16|00000000
  0.52|00000000
  0.89|000000000000
  1.25|0000000000000
  1.61|8888000000000
  1.98|000000000000
  2.34|0000000000000
  2.71|00000000000000000000
  3.07|0000000000000000
  3.43|0000000000000
  3.8C|0000000000000000000000
  4.16|0000000000000
  4.52|00000000000000000
  4.89|00000000000
  5.25|0000000000000
  5.62|0000000C
  5.98|0000000C0
  6.34|0000000
  6.71|00000
  7.07|0000000
  7.43|00000
  7.8C|0000C
  8.16|00
  8.53|00
  8.89|0
  9.25|0
  9.62|
  9.98|0
```

Figure 11.1   Discrimination between groups of patients with clinical diagnoses of schizophrenia ($n = 507$) and depressive psychoses ($n = 71$) in terms of 129 symptoms assessed on initial evaluation. Distance between the two distributions, $D = 2.830$; 0 = schizophrenia (ICD 295); X = depressive psychoses (ICD 296.0, 296.2, and 298.0)

where $U_1, U_2, \ldots, U_{129}$ are the 129 units of analysis, and $l_1, l_2, \ldots, l_{129}$, a set of suitably calculated weights. These weights are mathematically determined in a way aimed to maximize the distance between the patients in the two groups with respect to the linear compound Z.* The standardized distance between two diagnostic groups is a measure of the power of the discrimination between the patients belonging to each group, and is correspondingly designated as 'discriminatory power' (D) or 'Mahalanobis' distance'.

In most instances the frequency distributions of the linear compounds Z in the two groups obtained after discriminant analysis will still show some degree of overlap (as, for example, on Figure 11.1). The extent of this overlap represents another criterion of the discriminatory value of a diagnostic distinction, and a useful measure of this is the probability of misclassification.

If the two distributions of patients over the linear compound Z differ, then an arbitrary Z-value (Z_o) can be chosen so that any patient with a Z-value greater than Z_o will be assigned to group 2. In the case of overlapping distributions this rule will result in some patients who actually belong to group 1 being erroneously assigned to group 2, while other patients who belong to group 2 would be erroneously assigned to group 1. The percentage of cases in which this situation may occur can be expressed as probability of misclassification. For example, the error of classifying a depressed patient into the group of schizophrenics can be denoted as false-positive, and the error of assigning a schizophrenic patient to the group of psychotic depression can be denoted as false-negative. Then, the relationship between false positives and false-negatives for any selected Z_o will indicate the power of discrimination. On Figure 11.4 (page 329) any point on the curve indicates the expected ratio of false-positives and false-negatives for a given value of Z_o. The straight line shows this relationship in the case of a total overlap of the two distributions.

The false-positive/false-negative ratio can be interpreted as an indication of the kind of error one should be prepared to accept if a given classification is used, and the cost of the error is determined by the expected consequences of a false-positive versus a false-negative diagnosis. Thus, if it is considered very important not to miss schizophrenic patients, one can select a Z_o so that a maximum number of schizophrenic patients are classified correctly at the expense of a certain number of depressed patients being erroneously classified in the schizophrenic group.

The number of patients in the groups for which discriminant function analysis was performed was, in general, substantial. Thus, even a discrimination which would be considered poor for any practical or theoretical purpose might turn out to be statistically highly significant. For this reason, tests of significance would not be meaningful in this context, and will not be presented. On the other hand, the validity of such tests would be questionable anyway, since most of the original categories (for example, the 129 UAs) are dichotomous.

---

*In more precise terms, the distance is maximized with respect to a standardized linear compound Z, where standardization means that Z is divided by the pooled standard deviation of the two groups.

11.4.2 Content and predictive validity of the diagnostic distinction between schizophrenia and affective disorders

Being a cornerstone of the Kraepelinian classification of the functional psychoses, the distinction between schizophrenic and affective illnesses has been the focus of debate over decades. Although widely applied in clinical psychiatry, its validity has been questioned, because of observations indicating that the symptomatological overlap between the two groups may be more extensive than initially assumed, and because of the uncertain accuracy of the clinical prediction of course and outcome that can be achieved by using this classificatory distinction. However, there have been relatively few systematic studies designed to assess the validity of this classification and the results obtained are not conclusive.

The extent to which the two-year course and outcome in patients with a clinical diagnosis of schizophrenia or affective psychosis can be predicted by using different sets of patient characteristics, like symptoms, past history items, or demographic descriptors, was examined in Chapter 10. A large number of such characteristics of the patients were available on initial evaluation to the psychiatrists who were required to make a diagnostic assessment and assign each patient to an ICD classification category. It is difficult to know, however, which parts of the available data about the patients were actually used, or how they were used, in order to arrive at a diagnosis. Moreover, the scope and boundaries of the classification categories, as well as the rules for their use might have been interpreted differently by different diagnosticians in spite of the training they received to assess symptomatology in a standardized and reliable way.*

Therefore, the computer-simulated diagnostic procedure (CATEGO) was used to provide a parallel and standard classification of the same patients. As described in detail in Volume 1 of the IPSS report (WHO, 1973, Chapter 11) the CATEGO program rests on clinical diagnostic principles and classifies patients by using a hierarchy of decision rules. The input for the program consists only of information which was available to the psychiatrists when making a clinical diagnosis and classification; the psychiatrists, however, had at least the possibility of using in their diagnostic assessment considerably more information (recorded or not recorded) about the past history and the social situation of the patients than was included in the CATEGO input. The output of CATEGO — the diagnostic classes, are similar, but not identical to, relevant ICD categories as defined in the Glossary of Mental Disorders (WHO, 1974). Class S (see definition in Chapter 11, Volume 1 of the IPSS report) is an analogue of the ICD category of schizophrenia (295). In this analysis class S was combined with classes P and O (paranoid and other psychoses, respectively) which select out patients with disorders clinically close to schizophrenia but lacking 'nuclear' symptoms. Classes D, R, N (combined in this analysis and referred to as class D) are similar to the ICD categories for manic-depressive psychosis, depression (296.2), involutional depression (296.0) and reactive depressive

---

*One of the aims of the IPSS was to determine the magnitude and nature of such differences that may exist among psychiatrists in different countries (see Volume 1 of the IPSS report, page 391–2).

psychosis (298.0) combined.* CATEGO Class M is similar to ICD manic-depressive psychosis, manic type (296.1).

Because of their common ground in clinical nosology and diagnostic decision principles, the two systems of classification – ICD and CATEGO – will be examined statistically with regard to the extent of the distinctions they both make between schizophrenia and affective disorders.

11.4.2.1 Distinctions between ICD schizophrenia (295) and ICD depressive psychoses (296.0, 296.2 and 298.0)

All the 129 units of analysis considered, the two diagnostic groupings of patients – schizophrenia and depressive disorders – are clearly distinct in terms of symptomatology present on initial evaluation. Figure 11.1 shows that the patients assigned to each of two diagnostic entities form two separate distributions over the dimension of the discriminant function derived from the values of all the 129 units of analysis assessed on initial evaluation. The overlap between the two distributions is rather small and the coefficient of discrimination (D) in this comparison equals 2.830. Thus, the patients with a clinical diagnosis of schizophrenia and the patients with a clinical diagnosis of depressive psychosis, can be said to differ with regard to their overall symptomatology on initial evaluation.

When the same groups of patients were compared in terms of the symptoms (units of analysis) they had on the two-year follow-up evaluation, the coefficient of discrimination between the two diagnostic groups decreased its value to 1.702. Figure 11.2 shows that the overlap between the two diagnostic groupings on two-year follow-up is considerable, but the two ends of the distribution still consist entirely of schizophrenic and depressive patients respectively. This finding is in agreement with the analysis of symptomatology present on two-year follow-up described in Chapters 6 and 7 which demonstrated that: (a) the average level of symptomatology on follow-up was considerably lower than on initial evaluation, and (b) that a large proportion of those symptoms that were present on follow-up, were diagnostically non-specific.

Nevertheless, one may conclude from the discriminant function analysis, that even allowing for the overall reduction in frequency of symptoms, the two groups – schizophrenics and depressives – did not become symptomatologically homogenized on two-year follow-up, and in this sense, the initial classification of the patients into the two entities appears justified by follow-up reassessment.

However, the prediction of symptomatological differences to be found on follow-up assessment, that is at a certain point in time, is not sufficient to assess the validity of the initial classification of patients into a schizophrenic and a depressive group because it says little about the course and outcome of the disorders in the period between the initial and the follow-up assessments. Therefore, an important test of the validity of the schizophrenia-psychotic depression classification of

---

*The patients with an initial evaluation diagnosis of depressive neurosis (300.4) were not included in this ICD grouping of depressive disorders, since in all other analyses this group was defined as depressive psychosis group.

327

```
50'S VS. (60,62,80), 129 UA - 2FU.
FREQUENCY DISTRIBUTIONS FOR BOTH GROUPS
NUMBER OF CASES FOR GROUP1:      507            NUMBER OF CASES FOR GROUP2:      71
RANGE OF THE VARIABLE:  0.146402E 02            ONE STEP REPRESENTS:  0.244004E C0


-9.16|XXXX
-8.92|
-8.68|
-8.43|
-8.19|
-7.94|XXXX
-7.70|
-7.46|
-7.21|
-6.97|XXXX
-6.72|
-6.48|
-6.24|XXXXXXXX
-5.99|XXXXXXXX
-5.75|XXXXXXXX
-5.50|XXXXXXXX
-5.26|
-5.02|8XXX
-4.77|XXXXXXXX
-4.53|
-4.28|8XXX
-4.04|8XXXXXXXXXX XXXXXX
-3.80|
-3.55|88XXXXXXXXXXX
-3.31|
-3.06|88XX
-2.82|8XXX
-2.58|88XXXXXXXXXX XXXXXX
-2.33|88XXXXXX
-2.09|888XXXXXXXX XXXXXX
-1.84|8888XXXXXXXXXXXXX
-1.60|88888888XXX XXXXXXXXXX
-1.36|88888XXXXXXXX
-1.11|8888888X
-0.87|88880000000
-0.62|888888&888XXX
-0.38|88880000000
-0.14|88888880000000000
 0.11|8888888888 88888888888888888880000000000000000000
 0.35|88888888C00000C00000
 0.60|8888888883888000000000000000
 0.84|888888800000000000
 1.08|000000000000000C
 1.33|8888000C0000
 1.57|C000000JC000
 1.82|888800000000C
 2.06|C00000000
 2.30|C000000000JC0
 2.55|C000000
 2.79|C0C000
 3.04|00000C
 3.28|C00
 3.52|0C00
 3.77|C000
 4.01|000
 4.26|0
 4.50|0C0
 4.74|C
 4.99|
 5.23|0
```

Figure 11.2   Discrimination between groups of patients with clinical diagnoses of schizophrenia ($n = 507$) and depressive psychoses ($n = 71$) in terms of 129 symptoms assessed on follow-up evaluation. Distance between the two distribution, $D = 1.702$; 0 = schizophrenia (ICD 295); X = depressive psychoses (ICD 296.0, 296.2, and 298.0)

```
DISTRIBUTIONS ARE TRUNCATED ON THE LEFT
  50'S VS. (60,62,80), A2,A3,A4,A6,A7,A8, ALL FRC'S
FRECUENCY DISTRIBUTIONS FOR BOTH GROUPS
NUMBER  OF CASES FOR GROUP1:      507              NUMBER OF CASES FCR GROUP2:    67
RANGE OF THE VARIABLE:  0.290049E 01              ONE STEP REPRESENTS:  0.483414E-01


     2.44|BBXXXXXXX
     2.48|
     2.53|
     2.58|
     2.63|
     2.68|
     2.73|O
     2.77|C
     2.82|C
     2.87|
     2.92|
     2.97|
     3.02|O
     3.06|XXXX
     3.11|BBXX
     3.16|
     3.21|OO
     3.26|O
     3.31|BBBB
     3.35|BBBBBXXXX
     3.40|BBBBBBXXXXXXXXXXX
     3.45|BBBBOOO
     3.50|BBBBBBBBBBBBXXXXXX
     3.55|BBBBBBBBBBBBBBBBXXXXXXX
     3.60|BBBBBBBBBBBBBBBBBBBBBBBBBXXXXXXXXXXXXXXXXXX
     3.64|BBBBBBBBBBBBBBBBBBBBBBBOO
     3.69|BBBBBBBBBBBBBBBBBBXXXXXXXXXXXXXXXXXXXXXXXX
     3.74|BBBBBBBBBBBBBBXXXX
     3.79|BBBBBBBBBBBBBBBBBBBBXXXXXXXXXXXXX
     3.84|OOOCOOOOOOJOOOOC
     3.89|CCCCOOOO
     3.93|COOCOOOOOOCOO
     3.98|CCOOO
     4.03|BBBB
     4.08|CCOCOOO
     4.13|BBXX
     4.18|BBBXXXXXX
     4.22|BXXX
     4.27|CO
     4.32|BXXXXXXXX
     4.37|BXXX
     4.42|OOOO
     4.47|CO
     4.51|OOOO
     4.56|CCOOOO
     4.61|BBBBOOJOOOOCOOOOO
     4.66|OOOCO
     4.71|C
     4.76|O
     4.80|COOOO
     4.85|COO
     4.90|CO
     4.95|BBBBO
     5.00|CCOOOOO
     5.05|BBBBOOOOOOO
     5.09|COOCO
     5.14|
     5.19|
     5.24|C
     5.29|C
```

Figure 11.3   Discrimination between groups of patients with clinical diagnoses of schizophrenia ($n = 507$) and depressive psychoses ($n = 67$) in terms of six course and outcome measures. Distance between the two distributions, $D = 0.58$; 0 = schizophrenia (ICD 295); X = depressive psychoses (ICD 296.0, 296.2, and 298.0)

patients would be to see whether the two groups can be distinguished well with regard to the course and outcome variables: length of the episode of inclusion, proportion of the follow-up period spent in psychotic episodes, pattern of course, type of subsequent psychotic episodes, level of social functioning and overall outcome. Differences found between the two diagnostic groups with regard to each of the course and outcome variables taken separately were already described in section 11.3.

When all the course and outcome measures are used simultaneously and a single composite variable is derived from all of them, each patient is represented along the resulting dimension with his Z-score. Figure 11.3 shows the distribution of the schizophrenic and depressive patients over the course and outcome dimension. The two patient distributions overlap considerably and approximate to a single, unimodal distribution. The coefficient of discrimination is 0.58, and the probability of diagnostic misclassification of a patient, if his Z-score on course and outcome is used only, is over 35 per cent (Figure 11.4).

The analysis can be extended one step further by limiting the consideration to those patients only who were psychotic on two-year follow-up. Of the patients with initial clinical diagnosis of schizophrenia, 193 were psychotic *and* had sufficient data for discriminant function analysis. Only nine patients with initial diagnosis of depressive psychosis met the same criteria. Figure 11.5 shows that the discrimination between these two groups of patients in terms of symptoms present on

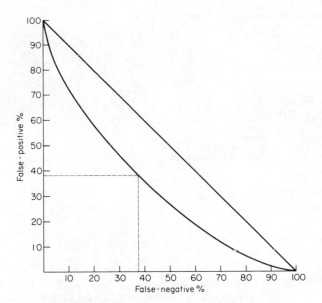

Figure 11.4   Probability of misclassification if patients' Z-score is based on all course and outcome measures (except 'type of subsequent episode'). Schizophrenia *vs.* psychotic depression

```
50'S VS. (60,62,80), 129 UA - 2FU., PSYCH. CNLY
FREQUENCY DISTRIBUTIONS FOR BOTH GROUPS
NUMBER  OF CASES FOR GROUP1:     193            NUMBER OF CASES FOR GROUP2:       9
RANGE OF THE VARIABLE:  0.600450E 02            ONE STEP REPRESENTS:  0.100075E 01


-45.21|XXXXXXXXXXXXXXXXXXXXXXXXXXXXXXX<XX
-44.21|
-43.21|
-42.21|
-41.21|XXXXXXXXXXXXXXXXXXXXXXXXXXXXXXXXX
-40.21|
-39.21|
-38.21|
-37.21|
-36.20|XXXXXXXXXXXXXXXXXXXXXXXXXXXXXXXX
-35.20|
-34.20|XXXXXXXXXXXXXXXXXXXXXXXXXXXXXXXXXX
-33.20|
-32.20|
-31.20|
-30.20|
-29.20|
-28.20|XXXXXXXXXXXXXXXXXXXXXXXXXXXXXXXX
-27.20|XXXXXXXXXXXXXXXXXXXXXXXXXXXXXXXX
-26.20|XXXXXXXXXXXXXXXXXXXXXXXXXXXXXXXXX
-25.20|
-24.20|
-23.19|
-22.19|
-21.19|
-20.19|
-19.19|
-18.19|
-17.19|
-16.19|
-15.19|00
-14.19|00XXXXXXXXXXXXXXXXXXXXXXXXXXXXXXXXXXXX
-13.19|
-12.19|
-11.19|00
-10.19|00
 -9.18|000000
 -8.18|XXXXXXXXXXXXXXXXXXXXXXXXXXXXXXXXXX
 -7.18|000
 -6.18|000000000
 -5.18|000000000000
 -4.18|0000000000000000
 -3.18|000000000000000
 -2.18|0000000000C000000
 -1.18|00000000000000000000000000000
 -0.18|000000000J000000000000000
  0.82|000000000J00000000000000000000000
  1.82|0000000000000000000000000000000000000
  2.82|000000000000C00000
  3.83|00000000000000
  4.83|000000000000000000
  5.83|0000000000000000
  6.83|00000
  7.83|000000000
  8.83|00000
  9.83|00000
 10.83|00000
 11.83|00
 12.83|00
 13.83|000
```

Figure 11.5   Discrimination between groups of patients with clinical diagnoses of schizophrenia ($n = 193$) and depressive psychoses ($n = 9$) who were psychotic on follow-up, in terms of 129 symptoms assessed at two-year follow-up evaluation. Distance between the two distributions, $D = 5.45$; 0 = schizophrenia (ICD 295); X = depressive psychoses (ICD 296.0, 296.2, and 298.0)

two-year evaluation is almost complete (D = 5.45), or that, in other words, schizophrenic patients who were psychotic on follow-up were symptomatologically distinct from depressive patients psychotic on follow-up. If the same patients are compared in terms of the symptomatology they had on initial evaluation (Figure 11.6) the two groups are also quite distinct (D = 6.69). The possibility that these patients may represent some special subgroups within the larger groups of schizophrenic and depressive patients was ruled out when the positions of these patients in the larger distributions shown on Figure 11.3 were identified. They seemed to be distributed more or less randomly and did not tend to cluster in any particular part of the distribution. However, the fact that these two subgroups of schizophrenic and depressive patients were symptomatologically distinct did not predict differences in their two-year course and outcome (Figure 11.3).

11.4.2.2 Distinctions between CATEGO schizophrenic psychoses (class S) and CATEGO depression (class D, R, N)

CATEGO class S (schizophrenic psychoses) has been defined by criteria such as to include patients who would be clinically diagnosed as schizophrenic by most psychiatrists.* In the analysis of the content and predictive validity of classification this group of IPSS patients was compared with the group of patients who, on the basis of the initial assessment, had been assigned by the computer program to either of the classes D, R and N, which include depressive disorders. Class D selects patients with depressive delusions or hallucinations; class R (retarded depression) includes patients with psychomotor retardation, ideas of guilt, self-depreciation, 'lost affect' or dulled perception; class N selects patients with depressed mood but without the symptoms which would qualify them for either of the classes D and R. Thus, the CATEGO depressive group comprises a wide range of depressive symptomatology. For the purpose of this analysis, the joint consideration of D, R and N, denoted for brevity as class D, was felt to be more justified, since the separation of the patients with overt psychotic symptoms (delusions or hallucinations) from the rest of the depressive patients would be regarded as artificial by many clinical psychiatrists. In addition, one might expect that such a grouping would represent a closer counterpart to the ICD grouping of 296.0, 296.2 and 298.0.†

The discrimination between class S patients, on one hand, and class D patients on the other hand, in terms of the composite variable derived from the ratings on the 129 units of analysis present on initial evaluation, is shown in Figure 11.7. The two groups are symptomatologically quite distinct, and the coefficient of discrimination is 3.41. This is not an unexpected finding, since the CATEGO class

---

*See Volume 1 of the IPSS report (WHO, 1973, page 253—5).
†Only a proportion of the patients classified into the psychotic depressive group (296.0, 296.2, 298.0) on initial evaluation had positive ratings on overt psychotic symptomatology. For example, delusions of self-depreciation ranked seventh, delusions of guilt 15th and hallucinations were not included at all among the 15 most frequent UAs at initial examination (see pages 200—203 of Volume 1 of the IPSS report).

```
50'S VS. (60,62,80), 129 UA - I.E., PSYCH. CNLY
FREQUENCY DISTRIBUTIONS FOR BOTH GROUPS
NUMBER  OF CASES FOR GROUP1:    193          NUMBER OF CASES FOR GROUP2:      9
RANGE OF THE VARIABLE:  0.677939E 02          ONE STEP REPRESENTS:  0.112990E 01


 -60.28IXXXXXXXXXXXXXXXXXXXXXXXXXXXXXXXXXXXX
 -59.15I
 -58.02I
 -56.89IXXXXXXXXXXXXXXXXXXXXXXXXXXXXXXXXXXXX
 -55.76I
 -54.63IXXXXXXXXXXXXXXXXXXXXXXXXXXXXXXXXXXXX
 -53.50IXXXXXXXXXXXXXXXXXXXXXXXXXXXXXXXXXXXXXXXXXXXXXXXXXXXXXXXXXXXXXXXXXXXXXXXXX
 -52.37I
 -51.24I
 -50.11I
 -48.98IXXXXXXXXXXXXXXXXXXXXXXXXXXXXXXXXXXXXXX
 -47.85IXXXXXXXXXXXXXXXXXXXXXXXXXXXXXXXXXXXXXXXXXXXXXXXXXXXXXXXXXXXXXXXXXXXXXXXXX
 -46.72IXXXXXXXXXXXXXXXXXXXXXXXXXXXXXXXXXXXX
 -45.59I
 -44.46I
 -43.33I
 -42.20I
 -41.07I
 -39.94I
 -38.81I
 -37.68I
 -36.55I
 -35.42I
 -34.29I
 -33.16I
 -32.03I
 -30.90I
 -29.77I
 -28.64I
 -27.51I
 -26.39I00
 -25.26I
 -24.13I
 -23.00I000000
 -21.87I000000
 -20.74I000
 -19.61I00
 -18.48I000000
 -17.35I00000000
 -16.22I00000
 -15.09I00000000
 -13.96I000000000000000
 -12.83I00000000000000
 -11.70I000000000000000000
 -10.57I00000000000000000
  -9.44I00000000000000000
  -8.31I0000000000000000000000000000
  -7.18I0000000000000000000000
  -6.05I0000000000000000000
  -4.92I0000000000000000000000000
  -3.79I00000000000000000
  -2.66I0000000000000000000000000
  -1.53I000000000000000000000000000
  -0.40I000000000
   0.73I000000000
   1.86I00000000
   2.99I00000000
   4.12I00
   5.25I000
   6.38I00000
```

Figure 11.6 Discrimination between groups of patients with clinical diagnoses of schizophrenia ($n = 193$) and depressive psychoses ($n = 9$) who were psychotic in follow-up, in terms of 129 symptoms assessed at two-year follow-up. Distance between the two distributions, $D = 6.69$; 0 = schizophrenia (ICD 295); X = depressive psychoses (ICD 296.0, 296.2, and 298.0)

```
CAT-S VS. CAT-D, 129 UA - I.E.
FREQUENCY DISTRIBUTIONS FOR BOTH GROUPS
NUMBER OF CASES FOR GROUP1:    423          NUMBER CF CASES FOR GROUP 2:    1
RANGE OF THE VARIABLE:  0.276167E 02         CNE STEP REPRESENTS:  0.460279E

 -8.20|XX
 -7.74|
 -7.28|XXXX
 -6.82|
 -6.36|XX
 -5.90|XXXXXX
 -5.44|
 -4.98|XXXXXXXXXXXX
 -4.52|XXXXXXXXXXXX
 -4.06|XXXXXXXXXX
 -3.60|XXXXXXXXXXXXXXXXXXXXX
 -3.14|XXXXXXXXX
 -2.68|XXXXXXXXXXXXXXXXXXXXXX
 -2.22|XXXXXXXXXXXXXXXX
 -1.76|XXXXXXXXXXXXXXXXXXX
 -1.30|XXXXXXXXXXXXXXX
 -C.84|XXXXXXXXXXXX
 -C.38|XXXXXXXXXX
  C.C8|0XXXXXXXXXXXXXXXXXXX
  C.54|0XXXXXXX
  1.01|00XXXXXXXXXXXXXXXXXXX
  1.47|0XXXXXXXXXXXXXXX
  1.93|XXXXXX
  2.39|0XXXXXXXXXXXX
  2.85|0000XXXX
  3.31|0XXXXXXXXXXXXXXX
  3.77|0XXXXXXX
  4.23|000
  4.69|000000XXX
  5.15|0
  5.61|0000
  6.07|000000
  6.53|00000
  6.99|0000
  7.45|000000000000
  7.91|000000000000
  8.37|C000000
  8.83|00000000000
  9.29|000000000000000
  9.75|000000000000000
 1C.21|000000000000000000000000
 1C.67|C0000000000
 11.13|000000000000
 11.59|000000000000000000000
 12.05|00000000000000
 12.51|000000000000000000000C
 12.97|0000000000000C000000
 13.43|00000000000000000
 13.89|000000000000
 14.35|CC000000000000
 14.81|00000000000000
 15.27|C0000000
 15.73|000000000000
 16.19|C0000000
 16.65|000
 17.11|00
 17.58|00
 18.04|0
 18.50|0
 18.96|0
```

Figure 11.7   Discrimination between groups of patients in CATEGO class S ($n = 156$) in terms of 129 symptoms assessed on initial evaluation. Distance between the two distributions, $D = 3.41$; 0 = CATEGO S; X = CATEGO D

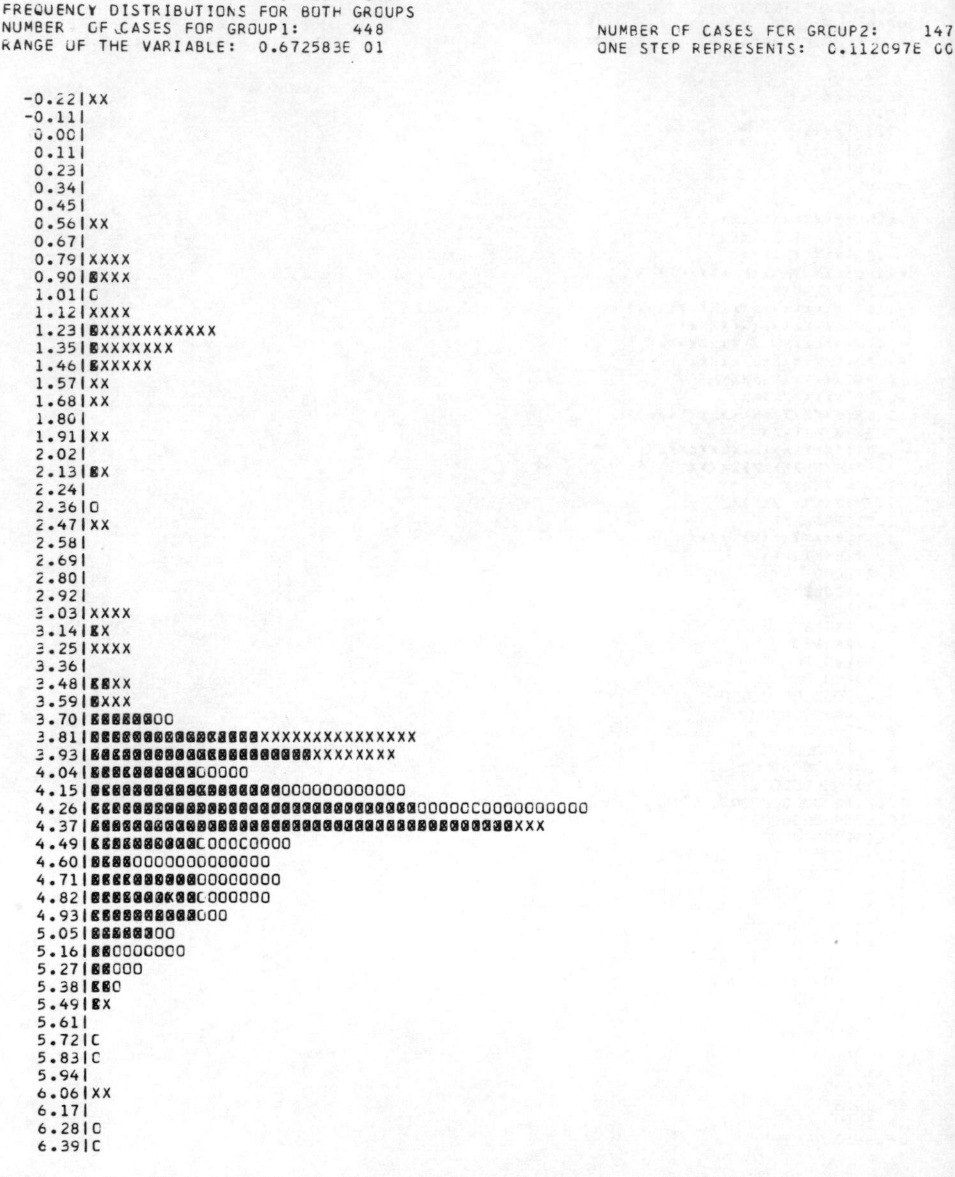

```
CATEGC-S VS. D; ALL BUT A5, ALL FRC'S
FREQUENCY DISTRIBUTIONS FOR BOTH GROUPS
NUMBER  CF CASES FOR GROUP1:     448          NUMBER CF CASES FCR GRCUP2:    147
RANGE UF THE VARIABLE:  0.672583E 01          ONE STEP REPRESENTS:  C.112C97E CC

  -0.22|XX
  -0.11|
   0.00|
   0.11|
   0.23|
   0.34|
   0.45|
   0.56|XX
   0.67|
   0.79|XXXX
   0.90|BXXX
   1.01|C
   1.12|XXXX
   1.23|BXXXXXXXXXXX
   1.35|BXXXXXXX
   1.46|BXXXXX
   1.57|XX
   1.68|XX
   1.80|
   1.91|XX
   2.02|
   2.13|BX
   2.24|
   2.36|0
   2.47|XX
   2.58|
   2.69|
   2.80|
   2.92|
   3.03|XXXX
   3.14|BX
   3.25|XXXX
   3.36|
   3.48|BBXX
   3.59|BXXX
   3.70|BBBBB000
   3.81|BBBBB00BBB0BBBBBXXXXXXXXXXXXXX
   3.93|BBBB00BBB0BBBBBB00BBBXXXXXXXX
   4.04|BBBBB00BB000000
   4.15|BBBB00BBB0BBBBB0B000000000000
   4.26|BBBBBB00BBB0BBBBBBBB0BBBBB0B00000C0000000000
   4.37|BBBBBB00BBB0BBBBBBBB0BBBBBBBB0BB000B0XXX
   4.49|BBBBBB00BBB0C000C0000
   4.60|BEBB0000000000000
   4.71|BBBBB0BBB000000000
   4.82|BBBBB0BBK00C000000
   4.93|BBBBB0BBB0000
   5.05|BBBBB000
   5.16|BB0000000
   5.27|BB000
   5.38|BB0
   5.49|BX
   5.61|
   5.72|C
   5.83|C
   5.94|
   6.06|XX
   6.17|
   6.28|0
   6.39|C
```

Figure 11.8   Discrimination between groups of patients in CATEGO class S ($n = 448$) and class D ($n = 147$) in terms of six course and outcome measures. Distance between the two distributions, $D = 0.80$; 0 = Class S patients; X = Class D patients

membership criteria were designed with the aim of achieving clear symptomato-logical discrimination between the diagnostic entities and were applied to the PSE ratings by a computer.

The CATEGO classification of the patients into class S or class D on initial evaluation also discriminates quite well the symptomatology which the two groups present on two-year follow-up evaluation, if only those patients are considered who were in a psychotic episode at the time of the follow-up assessment. The coefficient of discrimination is 4.51. The CATEGO class S and class D patients who were psychotic on follow-up had been also symptomatologically distinct on initial evaluation ($D = 5.90$).

The categorization of the patients into an S class and a D class on the basis of initial symptomatology, however, does not yield groups which are sufficiently distinct in terms of subsequent course and outcome. The discriminant function analysis of the two groups, performed with a composite of the course and outcome variables as the relevant dimension for discrimination, indicates a substantial overlap between the S and D groups (Figure 11.8). The coefficient of discrimi-nation ($D = 0.80$) is indeed higher than the coefficient of discrimination between ICD schizophrenic and ICD depressive patients in terms of course and outcome but nevertheless still below the level of acceptability for practical purposes and the probability of misclassification (Figure 11.9) is, in fact, higher (over 40 per cent). An interesting feature of the distribution on Figure 11.8 is the tendency toward bimodality. The area under the left-hand part of the curve is composed almost exclusively of class D patients with very favourable course and outcome. However,

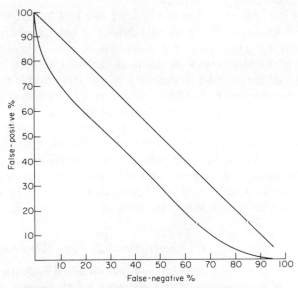

Figure 11.9   Probability of misclassification if patients' Z-score is based on all course and outcome measures (except 'type of subsequent episode'). CATEGO class S *vs.* CATEGO class D

in the right-hand part of the distribution, the majority of the depressive patients are intermingled with the majority of the schizophrenic patients and there are a few depressive patients even at the extreme right-hand end of the distribution, corresponding to poor course and outcome. The depressive patients located in this graph at the two extreme ends of the distribution were identified and their positions in the discriminant function distribution for symptomatology on initial evaluation were plotted on Figure 11.7 in order to see whether they would tend to cluster in separate areas of this distribution. No such tendency could be detected. Thus, depressive patients who differed most from one another in terms of course and outcome did not seem to differ among themselves with regard to their overall symptomatology on initial evaluation.

In order to test for possible differences between the two subgroups of class D patients in terms of individual symptoms, the 17 good-outcome patients were compared with the four poor-outcome patients with regard to the most frequent units of analysis. The symptoms which ranked 1 to 5 in the subgroups of the 17 good outcome patients were: depressed mood, gloomy thoughts, early waking, sleep problems, hypochondriasis, tension and worse in evening. The four poor-outcome patients were characterized by: depressed mood, hopelessness, self-depreciation, worse in morning, gloomy thoughts, special quality of depression, worries, lack of insight, anxiety, loss of emotions and social withdrawal. The small number of patients in the poor-outcome subgroup does not permit to draw definite conclusions, but the symptom scores suggest that these patients had more severe symptoms on initial evaluation than the group of depressive patients with favourable two-year course and outcome.

Summarizing the findings in Sections 11.4.2.1 and 11.4.2.2 one might conclude that the content validity of the diagnostic distinction between schizophrenic and depressive disorders is satisfactory, that is, the classification of patients into these two groups conveys information about measurable differences in the overall symptomatology of the patients so classified. It was also possible to demonstrate that such differences between the diagnostic groups are retained, if the symptomatology of the two groups at the two-year follow-up is compared.

The predictive validity of the classification of patients into a schizophrenic and a depressive group however, is less certain if non-symptomatic measures of two-year course and outcome are applied as a validity criterion. Prediction of course and outcome on the basis of a diagnostic classification of the patients into schizophrenia and depression would result in a misclassification for 35 to 40 per cent of the patients (see the misclassification probabilities).

11.4.2.3 Distinctions between ICD schizophrenia (295) and ICD mania (296.1)

Discriminant function analysis demonstrated that on initial evaluation, the overall symptomatology (129 units of analysis) presented by 49 patients with a clinical diagnosis of mania was different from the symptomatology of the patients with a clinical diagnosis of schizophrenia. Figure 11.10 shows that the two diagnostic groups form distributions with very little overlap (D = 3.92). The probability of

```
50.S VS. 61, 129 UA - I.E.
FREQUENCY DISTRIBUTIONS FOR BOTH GROUPS
NUMBER  OF CASES FOR GROUP1:      507          NUMBER OF CASES FOR GROUP2:
RANGE OF THE VARIABLE:  0.365138E 02          ONE STEP REPRESENTS:  0.608564E


 -21.07|XXXXXX
 -20.46|XXXXXX
 -19.85|
 -19.24|
 -18.63|XXXXXX(XXXXX
 -18.02|XXXXXXXXXXXX
 -17.42|
 -16.81|
 -16.20|XXXXXX
 -15.59|
 -14.98|XXXXXXXXXXXXXXXXXXX
 -14.37|XXXXXXXXXXXX
 -13.76|XXXXXXXXXXXXXXXXXX
 -13.16|XXXXXXXXXXXXXXXXXX
 -12.55|XXXXXX(XXXXX
 -11.94|XXXXXXXXXXXXXXXXXXXXXXXXX
 -11.33|XXXXXXXXXXXXXXXXXXXXXXXXX
 -10.72|BXXXXXXXXXXXXXXXXXX
 -10.11|XXXXXX
  -9.50|XXXXXX
  -8.90|XXXXXX(XXXXXXXXXXX
  -8.29|XXXXXX
  -7.68|BXXXXXXXXXXXXXXXXXX
  -7.07|XXXXXX
  -6.46|XXXXXXXXXXXX
  -5.85|BXXXXXXXXXXXX
  -5.24|0
  -4.64|C0000
  -4.03|BBBXXXXXXXXXX
  -3.42|00
  -2.81|000C0
  -2.20|0000
  -1.59|0000
  -C.98|00000000
  -0.38|C0000000
   0.23|BBBBBB000000
   0.84|C00000000
   1.45|BBBBBB0000C0000
   2.06|0000000000
   2.67|0000000000000000000
   3.28|C00C00C000C0000
   3.88|0000000000000000000000000
   4.49|C0000000000C00000000000000000C00
   5.10|0000000C000C0000000
   5.71|0000000000J0C000000
   6.32|00000000000000000
   6.93|0000000000000C0C00000
   7.54|00000000J00C00
   8.14|0000000000
   8.75|0000000000
   9.36|000C0000
   9.97|00000000
  10.58|C000
  11.19|0
  11.80|0
  12.40|C0
  13.01|00
  13.62|0
  14.23|
  14.84|0
```

Figure 11.10   Discrimination between groups of patients with clinical diagnosis of schizophrenia ($n = 50$) and mania ($n = 49$) in terms of 129 symptoms, assessed on initial evaluation. Distance between the two distributions, $D = 3.92$; 0 = schizophrenia (ICD 295); X = mania (ICD 296.1)

diagnostic misclassification of patients on the basis of symptomatology is only about 7 per cent.

The 12 patients with an initial evaluation diagnosis of mania, who were psychotic on two-year follow-up evaluation, could be distinguished quite clearly from the schizophrenic patients psychotic on follow-up, in terms of symptomatology present on follow-up evaluation ($D = 6.48$). Since the discrimination between these two groups of patients was even better when their symptoms on initial evaluation were compared ($D = 9.70$), the 12 manic patients' positions were identified in the distribution obtained for all patients on initial evaluation, in order to see whether the 12 patients tended to cluster in any particular part of the distribution. It was established that the patients who were psychotic on follow-up did not concentrate in any part of the distribution of *all* manic patients in terms of 129 units of analysis present on initial evaluation.

The initial diagnostic classification of patients into ICD schizophrenia (295) and ICD mania (296.1) discriminated relatively well ($D = 1.36$) subsequent course and outcome of these patients. The distribution of the two groups of patients over the discriminant function dimension combining course and outcome variables (Figure 11.11) shows a tendency toward bimodality.

The right-hand part of the distribution contains the majority of the schizophrenic patients, but also includes about one-half (23) of all the manic patients who had been followed up. The left-hand part of the distribution includes the remaining 27 manic patients and 48 schizophrenic patients.

The 48 poor course and outcome schizophrenic patients contained in the left-hand part of the distribution were compared with all the schizophrenic patients in terms of most frequent units of analysis present on initial evaluation. The poor course and outcome patients, compared with all schizophrenic patients on initial evaluation, had higher scores on all units of analysis (except lack of insight and inadequate description) that were among the most frequent ones in the two groups, but particularly so on hallucinations, delusions and the Schneiderian first-rank symptoms: thought alienation and thoughts spoken aloud.

11.4.2.4 Distinctions between CATEGO schizophrenic psychoses (class S) and CATEGO manic psychoses (class M)

Discriminant function analysis of symptomatology present on initial evaluation (129 units of analysis) indicates that the 98 CATEGO class M patients were clearly different from the 423 CATEGO class S patients ($D = 3.37$, Figure 11.12). Out of the patients who were psychotic on the second-year follow-up, the 24 class M patients were symptomatologically different ($D = 4.59$) from the 166 class S patients, when symptomatology present on the two-year assessment was the basis of discrimination. The coefficient of discrimination with regard to symptomatology was even higher ($D = 6.32$) when these two groups, that is class S and class M patients psychotic on follow-up, were compared in terms of units of analysis present on initial evaluation.

In spite of the good symptomatological differentiation between CATEGO class M

```
50'S VS. 61, A2,A3,A4,A6,A7,A8; ALL FRC'S
FREQUENCY DISTRIBUTIONS FOR BOTH GROUPS
NUMBER  CF CASES FOR GROUP1:    507          NUMBER OF CASES FCR GROUP2:     50
RANGE OF THE VARIABLE:  0.621655E 01          ONE STEP REPRESENTS:  0.103609E 00


  -4.65|BBBBBBXXXXXXXXXXXX
  -4.54|BXXXXXXXXXXX
  -4.44|
  -4.33|
  -4.23|BBBBXXXXXXXXXXXXXXXXXXXXXXXXXXXX
  -4.13|BBBBXXXXXXXX
  -4.02|BBBXXXXXXXXXXXXXXXXXXXXXXXX
  -3.92|BXXXXX
  -3.82|0
  -3.71|BBBBXXXXXXXX
  -3.61|BBBBXXXXXXXXXXXXXX
  -3.51|BXXXXXXXXXXX
  -3.40|BBXXXXXXXXXX
  -3.30|C
  -3.20|0
  -3.09|C
  -2.99|
  -2.88|
  -2.78|
  -2.68|
  -2.57|C
  -2.47|C
  -2.37|
  -2.26|
  -2.16|
  -2.06|
  -1.95|
  -1.85|
  -1.74|
  -1.64|
  -1.54|
  -1.43|
  -1.33|BBBBBBBBBBBBBBBBBBBBBBXXXXX
  -1.23|BXXXXXXXXXXX
  -1.12|
  -1.02|C
  -0.92|BBBBXXXXXXXX
  -0.81|BBBBBBBBBBBBBBBBBBBBBBBBBBBBBBBBBBBBBBBBBBBXX
  -0.71|BBBBBBCCC
  -0.60|BBBBBBBBBBBB00000000C
  -0.50|C00C000
  -0.40|C000000
  -0.29|BBBBBB00
  -0.19|BBBBBB0000000000000000
  -0.09|BBBBBBBBBXXXXXXXXX
   0.02|C0CC000CC
   0.12|C0CC000C0
   0.22|BBBBBB0000C00000000000000000
   0.33|CC0C0000G0J0C0GC00
   0.43|CC0C0000000000C00000000000C0000C0000
   0.53|CC0C0000000CC0
   0.64|C00CC0
   0.74|CC00
   0.85|CC
   0.95|C
   1.05|C
   1.16|
   1.26|
   1.36|C
   1.47|C
```

Figure 11.11   Discrimination between groups of patients with clinical diagnosis of schizophrenia ($n = 507$) and mania ($n = 50$) in terms of six course and outcome measures. Distance between the two distributions, $D = 1.36$; 0 = schizophrenia (ICD 295); X = mania (ICD 296.1)

```
CAT-S VS. CAT-M, 129 UA - I.E.
FRECUENCY DISTRIBUTIONS FOR BOTH GROUPS
NUMBER  OF CASES FOR GROUP1:      423              NUMBER OF CASES FOR GROUP2:      98
RANGE OF THE VARIABLE:  0.261471E 02               CNE STEP REPRESENTS:  0.435785E 00


-12.04|XXX
-11.60|XXX
-11.16|XXX
-1C.73|
-1C.29|XXXXXX
 -S.86|XXXXX
 -S.42|XXXXXXXXXXXXX
 -E.99|XXXXXX
 -E.55|XXXXXXXXX
 -E.11|XXXXXXXXXXXXXXXXXXXXXXXXX
 -7.68|XXXXXXXXXXXX
 -7.24|XXXXXXXXXXXXXXXXXXXXX
 -E.E1|XXXXXXXXXXXXXX
 -E.37|XXXXXXXXXXXXXXXXXXXXX
 -5.S3|XXXXXXXXXXXXXXXXXXXX
 -5.50|0XXXXXXXXXXXXXX
 -5.06|XXXXXXXXXXXXXX
 -4.63|0XXXXX
 -4.19|XXXXXXXXX
 -3.76|0XXXXX
 -3.32|XXXXXXXXXXXXXX
 -2.88|0XXXXXXXXXXXXXXXXXXXXXXXXXXXX
 -2.45|0XXXXX
 -2.01|000XXXXXXXXX
 -1.5E|000XXXXXX
 -1.14|0XX
 -C.71|000
 -C.27|0000
  C.17|0000XX
  C.60|0000
  1.04|00X
  1.47|000000
  1.S1|00000000
  2.35|0000000000
  2.78|000000000
  3.22|00000000000
  3.65|0000000000C00
  4.09|00000000000000
  4.52|000000000000000000
  4.96|C000000000000000000
  5.40|000000000000000000000
  5.83|0000000000
  6.27|00000000000000
  6.70|00000000000000
  7.14|00000000000000000
  7.57|000000000000000
  E.01|000000000000000
  E.45|000000000
  E.88|00000000000000000000000
  S.32|C00000000
  S.75|000000
 1C.19|000000
 1C.63|0000
 11.06|0000000
 11.50|C0000
 11.S3|000
 12.37|0
 12.80|00
 13.24|00
 13.68|0
```

Figure 11.12   Discrimination between patients in CATEGO class S ($n = 423$) and CATEGO class M ($n = 98$) in terms of 129 symptoms assessed on initial evaluation. Distance between the two distributions, $D = 3.37$; 0 = CATEGO S: X = CATEGO M

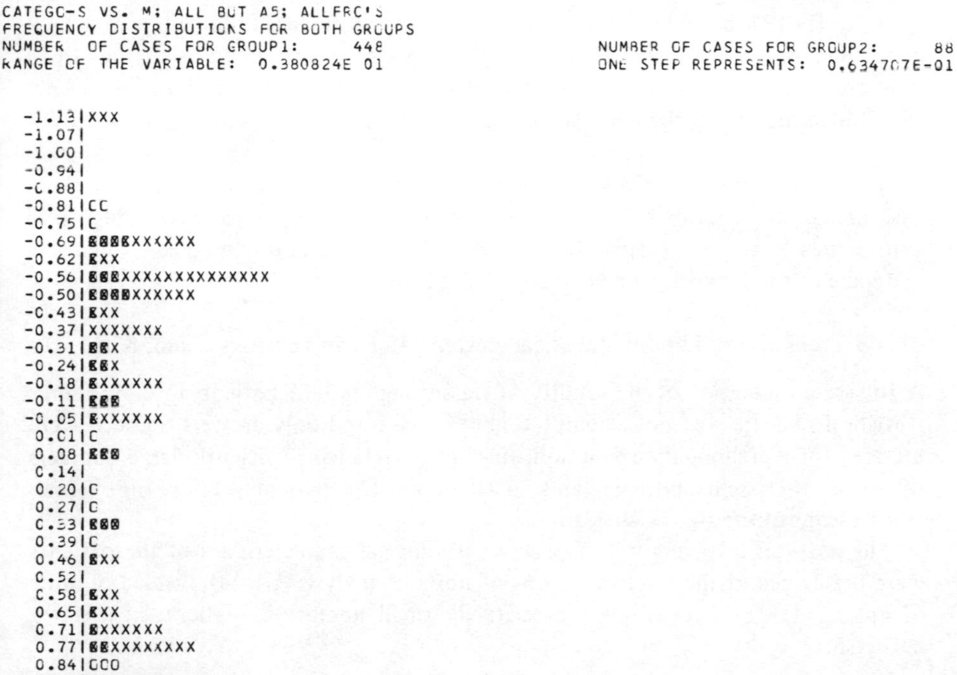

```
CATEGC-S VS. M: ALL BUT A5: ALLFRC'S
FREQUENCY DISTRIBUTIONS FOR BOTH GROUPS
NUMBER  OF CASES FOR GROUP1:     448          NUMBER OF CASES FOR GROUP2:     88
RANGE OF THE VARIABLE:  0.380824E 01          ONE STEP REPRESENTS:  0.634707E-01

  -1.13|xxx
  -1.07|
  -1.00|
  -0.94|
  -0.88|
  -0.81|CC
  -0.75|C
  -0.69|BBBBXX<XXX
  -0.62|BXX
  -0.56|BBBXXXXXXXXXXXXXX
  -0.50|BBBBXXXXXX
  -0.43|BXX
  -0.37|XXXXXXX
  -0.31|BBX
  -0.24|BBX
  -0.18|BXXXXXX
  -0.11|BBB
  -0.05|BXXXXXX
   0.01|C
   0.08|BBB
   0.14|
   0.20|C
   0.27|C
   0.33|BBB
   0.39|C
   0.46|BXX
   0.52|
   0.58|BXX
   0.65|BXX
   0.71|BXXXXXX
   0.77|BBXXXXXXXX
   0.84|CCO
   0.90|BBBBBBBXXXXXXX
   0.96|BBBOOOOCOOCC
   1.03|BBBBBBBBXXXXXXXXX
   1.09|BBBBBBBBBBBBXXXX
   1.15|BBBOOOOCOOC OCC
   1.22|BBBBBBBBBBBBBBBBBBBBBBBBBBBBBBBBXXXXXXXXX
   1.28|BBBBBX<XXXXXXXXX
   1.35|BBBBBBBBBBCCCCOOOO
   1.41|BBBBBBBBBBBBOOBOOOOOOOOO
   1.47|BBBBBBBBBBBOCOOOOO
   1.54|COOOOOOOOOOOOOCOOOOOO
   1.60|BBBBBBBBBBBBOOBCOO
   1.66|BBBCOOOOOOO
   1.73|BBBBBBBBBBO
   1.79|BBBBBBBBBBBOOOO
   1.85|OCCCOOOCOO
   1.92|BBBBBBBBCOO
   1.98|COOOOOOOC
   2.04|OC
   2.11|O
   2.17|C
   2.23|
   2.30|C
   2.36|
   2.42|
   2.49|
   2.55|C
   2.61|CO
```

Figure 11.13 Discrimination between patients in CATEGO class S (*n* = 448) and CATEGO class M (*n* = 88) in terms of six course and outcome measures. Distance between the two distribution, *D* = 0.67; 0 = CATEGO S: X = CATEGO M

and CATEGO class S patients, the assignment of the patients to either of the two classes on initial evaluation did not differentiate the patients belonging to the two groups with regard to their subsequent course and outcome ($D = 0.67$, Figure 11.13). The 24 class M patients who were psychotic on follow-up and whose symptomatology, both on initial and follow-up assessment, could be distinguished well from the symptomatology of the class S patients, were more or less evenly distributed among all the class M patients when the non-symptomatic measures of course and outcome were considered.

Thus, although the CATEGO classification achieved a very high level of discrimination in terms of overall symptomatology between patients categorized into classes M and S, its capacity to predict differences in the two-year course and outcome of these two diagnostic classes was limited.

11.4.3 Predictive validity of statistical clusters: McKeon's clusters 6 and, 8

A full-scale evaluation of the validity of classifying the IPSS patients into McKeon's statistical clusters was not attempted at this stage and only clusters 6 and 8 were selected for a preliminary evaluation, since they included sufficiently large numbers of both ICD schizophrenic and ICD depressive patients, to permit cross-comparisons of the two classifications.

The analyses involving use of psychopathological characteristics of the patients were performed at the level of groups of units of analysis (GUAs), instead of units of analysis (UAs), because of the relatively small number of patients in the two clusters.

11.4.3.1 Distinctions between McKeon's clusters 6 and 8

In terms of groups of units of analysis present on initial evaluation, the two clusters of patients could be distinguished from one another sufficiently well ($D = 1.63$, Figure 11.14). It is interesting to note that in contrast to the other classification comparisons reported above, the distance between the two clusters, in terms of GUAs increased slightly on the second-year follow-up ($D = 1.88$). If only those patients from clusters 6 and 8 are considered, who were found to be psychotic on follow-up (a total of 50), the coefficients of discrimination has a value of 2.87.

Because of the tendency of the two clusters to be distinct in terms of GUAs on both the initial evaluation and the two-year follow-up assessment it would be important to test whether cluster membership predicted differences in course and outcome. Figure 11.15 shows that the two clusters cannot be distinguished from one another, if a composite of six non-symptomatic course and outcome variables is used as the axis along which differentiation is sought ($D = 0.85$). Thus, membership in McKeon's clusters 6 or 8 does not predict differences in course and outcome.

11.4.3.2 Comparisons between schizophrenic and depressive patients within and across McKeon's clusters 6 and 8

Since clusters 6 and 8 appeared to select out patients who could be distinguished relatively well in terms of scores on groups of units of analysis (GUAs) on initial

```
MCK-6 VS. MCK-8, 27 GUA — I.E.
FRECUENCY DISTRIBUTIONS FOR BOTH GROUPS
NUMBER  OF CASES FOR GROUP1:      160              NUMBER OF CASES FOR GROUP2:      69
RANGE OF THE VARIABLE:  0.119434E 02              CNE STEP REPRESENTS:  0.199057E 00


 -7.16|XXXXXXXXX
 -6.96|XXXXXXXXX
 -6.76|
 -6.56|
 -6.36|XXXX
 -6.16|
 -5.96|
 -5.76|
 -5.56|00XXXXXXX
 -5.36|XXXXXXXXX
 -5.17|XXXX
 -4.97|00XXXXXXX
 -4.77|XXXX
 -4.57|XXXXXXXXXXXXXXXXX
 -4.37|00XXXXXXX
 -4.17|00XXXXXXXXXXXXXXXXXX
 -3.97|XXXXXXXXX
 -3.77|XXXXXXXXXXXXXXXXXXXXXX
 -3.57|XXXXXXXXXXXXX
 -3.37|0000000XXXXXXXXXXXXXXXXX
 -3.17|0000
 -2.98|000XX
 -2.78|0000000XXX
 -2.58|00XXXXXXX
 -2.38|00000000
 -2.18|0000000XXXXXXX
 -1.98|0000000000000000XXXXXXX
 -1.78|00000000
 -1.58|00000000000000
 -1.38|000000000000000XXXXXXX
 -1.18|0000000000000
 -C.99|00000000000000000000
 -C.79|00000000000000000000
 -0.59|00000000000000000000
 -0.39|0000000000000
 -C.19|0000000000
  C.01|000000000000000000000
  C.21|000000000000000000
  C.41|0000
  C.61|0000000000000
  C.81|C00000000
  1.01|0000000
  1.20|C00000
  1.40|C00000
  1.60|000000000
  1.80|C00000
  2.00|00
  2.20|
  2.40|00
  2.60|
  2.80|0000
  3.00|00
  3.19|
  3.39|
  3.59|
  3.79|
  3.99|
  4.19|
  4.39|
  4.59|00
```

Figure 11.14 Discrimination between patients in McKeon's cluster 6 ($n = 160$) and McKeon's cluster 8 ($n = 69$) in terms of 27 groups of units of analysis assessed on initial evaluation. Distance between the two distributions, $D = 1.63$; 0 = McKeon's cluster 6; X = McKeon's cluster 8

344

```
MCKEON-6 VS. MCKEON-8; A2,A3,A4,A6,A7,A8; ALL FRC'S
FREQUENCY DISTRIBUTIONS FOR BOTH GROUPS
NUMBER  OF CASES FOR GROUP1:     163              NUMBER OF CASES FOR GROUP2:     59
RANGE OF THE VARIABLE:  0.608819E 01             ONE STEP REPRESENTS:  0.101470E 00


  -2.24|88XXX
  -2.14|00
  -2.04|
  -1.93|XXXXX
  -1.83|XXXXX
  -1.73|
  -1.63|XXXXX
  -1.53|CO
  -1.43|XXXXX
  -1.32|88XXX
  -1.22|
  -1.12|
  -1.02|XXXXX
  -0.92|88XXX
  -0.82|XXXXX
  -0.72|XXXXX
  -0.61|CC
  -0.51|XXXXXXXXXX
  -0.41|8888XX4XXX
  -0.31|XXXXXXXXXX
  -0.21|8888883XXX
  -0.11|8888XXXXXX
  -0.01|88888880XXX
   0.10|000000
   0.20|88XXXXXXXX
   0.30|888888888883688XXXXXXX
   0.40|88888888688XXXXXX
   0.50|8888888888X000
   0.60|888888888888XXXXXXXXXXXXXXXXXXXXXXX<XXXXX
   0.70|888888868688X
   0.81|88868000C0
   0.91|8888888888C0000000000000
   1.01|888888888888X888800000000000000U0
   1.11|888888888888C0000J0000000000000000000
   1.21|888888888888X8888888888800
   1.31|88888000000000C000000
   1.41|8888800
   1.52|8888880000
   1.62|C000000
   1.72|00000
   1.82|CO
   1.92|8888800
   2.02|C00000000
   2.13|0000
   2.23|888880000
   2.33|0000
   2.43|CC
   2.53|
   2.63|
   2.73|
   2.84|
   2.94|
   3.04|
   3.14|
   3.24|
   3.34|
   3.44|
   3.55|
   3.65|
   3.75|00
```

Figure 11.15   Discrimination between patients in McKeon's cluster 6 ($n = 163$) and McKeon's cluster 8 ($n = 59$) in terms of six course and outcome measures. Distance between the two distributions, $D = 0.85$; 0 = McKeon's cluster 6; X = McKeon's cluster 8

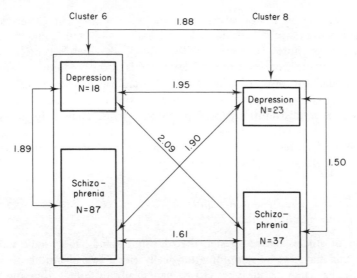

Figure 11.16   Distance relationships between groups of schizophrenic and depressive patients within McKeon's cluster 6 and 8. 27 GUAs on two-year follow-up

evaluation and on follow-up assessment, it was of considerable interest to see whether the groups of patients with clinical diagnosis of schizophrenia and depression belonging to the two clusters were symptomatologically more different from one another across the clusters rather than within each of the clusters. If schizophrenic and depressive patients within each of the clusters were less distant from each other than schizophrenic and depressive patients belonging to different clusters, and if such distance relationships could be found to exist on follow-up, the validity of clusters 6 and 8 would find support, as far as their capacity to predict clinically relevant symptomatological distinctions is concerned.

The distances at follow-up obtained by discriminant function analysis, between the schizophrenic and depressive subgroups within McKeon's clusters 6 and 8 are represented diagrammatically on Figure 11.16. While the distances between the schizophrenic and depressive subgroups within each of the clusters are identical or smaller than the distance between the two clusters, $(D = 1.88)$ the depressive subgroup of cluster 6 is slightly more distant from the schizophrenic subgroup of cluster 8 than the whole clusters are from each other. However, the distance between the depressive subgroup of cluster 8 and the schizophrenic subgroup of cluster 6 is practically equal to the distance between the two clusters.

Thus, the statistical clustering (referring specifically to clusters 6 and 8) did not seem to improve the symptomatological discrimination between those schizophrenic and depressive patients who had been selected out by the two clusters.

11.4.4 Predictive validity of the ICD subtypes of schizophrenia

Although a two-year period may not be long for potential differences of course and outcome to emerge in patients classified into different clinical subtypes of schizophrenia on initial evaluation, the findings described in Chapters 6 to 9 indicated the existence of substantial variation of the course and outcome of schizophrenic psychoses across and within the field research centres. This was considered a justification for a preliminary analysis of the predictive validity of the diagnostic subclassification of schizophrenia, in order to explore possible relationships between subtypes and two-year course and outcome. Because larger numbers of patients in the distributions to be compared by discriminant function analysis were required, several different ways of grouping the ICD subtypes of schizophrenia were attempted. General clinical, and not only statistical considerations were taken into account in defining each of the groupings.

11.4.4.1 Simple (295.0) and hebephrenic (295.1) schizophrenia compared with paranoid schizophrenia (295.3)

A number of studies have suggested that the simple and hebephrenic subtypes of schizophrenia may: (a) be symptomatologically closer to one another than each of them is to the paranoid subtype; (b) be genetically different from the paranoid forms; (c) have an earlier onset; and (d) tend to have different clinical prognosis in comparison with paranoid schizophrenia.

Data on 88 patients with an initial diagnosis of simple or hebephrenic schizophrenia, and on 179 with a diagnosis of paranoid schizophrenia were available for testing the predictive validity of this grouping.

Figure 11.17 shows the results of the discriminant function analysis, with a composite variable including six different measures of two-year course and outcome, as a dimension along which the two groups of patients were compared. The coefficient of discrimination achieved was 0.55 which means that the two groups overlap extensively with regard to their two-year course and outcome.

11.4.4.2 Simple (295.0) and hebephrenic (295.1) schizophrenia compared with the schizo-affective subtype of schizophrenia (295.7)

This comparison was based on the assumption that, within the schizophrenic psychoses, the simple and hebephrenic subtypes, on one hand, and the schizo-affective subtype, on the other hand, may be distinct with regard to prognosis. Figure 11.18 shows a relatively good discrimination ($D = 1.06$) between the two groups of patients in terms of course and outcome, which means that the two-year follow-up provides support for this assumption.

11.4.4.3 Paranoid schizophrenia (295.3) compared with the schizo-affective type of schizophrenia (295.7)

The results of the discriminant function analysis comparing in terms of course and outcome the 62 patients with an initial diagnosis of schizo-affective schizophrenia with the 179 patients diagnosed as paranoid schizophrenics indicated a significant overlap between the two groups (Figure 11.19, $D = 0.65$).

```
DISTRIBUTIONS ARE TRUNCATED ON THE RIGHT
50 & 51  VS.  53, A2,A3,A4,A6,A7,A8; ALL FRC'S
FREQUENCY DISTRIBUTIONS FOR BOTH GROUPS
NUMBER  OF CASES FOR GROUP1:       88          NUMBER OF CASES FOR GROUP2:    179
RANGE OF THE VARIABLE:  0.333555E 01          ONE STEP REPRESENTS:  0.555925E-01


  0.37|XX
  0.43|
  0.48|
  0.54|
  0.59|
  0.65|
  0.70|XX
  0.76|
  0.82|
  0.87|XX
  0.93|XX
  0.98|
  1.04|XXXXXXX
  1.09|XXXXX
  1.15|EEC
  1.20|XXX
  1.26|XX
  1.32|
  1.37|EEC
  1.43|EEEEEEEX
  1.48|EEEEEEEEEEKEEEX
  1.54|XXXXXXX
  1.59|EEEEEOO
  1.65|EEEEEEEEEXXXXXXXXXXXXX
  1.71|EEEEEEEEEEKEEEEEEEEEEEEEEEEEEXXXXXXXXXXX
  1.76|EEEEEEEEEEXX
  1.82|EEE
  1.87|XXXXXXXX
  1.93|XX
  1.98|EEEXXXXX
  2.04|XXXXX
  2.09|EEEEEOO
  2.15|EEC
  2.21|EEEXX
  2.26|EEEXXXXXXX
  2.32|EEEEEEE
  2.37|EEEEEEEEEOOCOOOCOO
  2.43|EEEEEEEEOOOCOCCCOO
  2.48|EEEEEEEEEEEEEEEEEEEOOOOOOO
  2.54|EEEEEEEXKEEEEEEEEEEEEEEEEEEEGOOOCOGOCOOOO
  2.59|EEEEEEEEEEEEEEEEEEOOOOOOOOO
  2.65|EEEEEEEEEEEEEEEEEOOOOOOOCOOOOO
  2.71|EEEEEOOCOOOOOOC
  2.76|XX
  2.82|EEECOOOCOOXCCC
  2.87|XXX
  2.93|XXX
  2.98|XX
  3.04|
  3.10|XX
  3.15|
  3.21|
  3.26|
  3.32|
  3.37|
  3.43|
  3.48|
  3.54|EEE
  3.60|
  3.65|COOCCOCCOO
```

Figure 11.17   Discrimination between a group ($n = 88$) including simple (ICD 295.0) and hebephrenic (ICD 295.1) subtypes and a group ($n = 179$) including the paranoid (ICD 295.3) subtype of schizophrenia in terms of six terms and outcome measures. Distance between the two distributions, $D = 0.55$; 0 = simple and hebephrenic schizophrenia; X = paranoid schizophrenia

```
50 & 51   VS.   57, A2,A3,A4,A6,A7,A8; ALL FRC'S
FREQUENCY DISTRIBUTIONS FOR BOTH GROUPS
NUMBER  OF CASES FOR GROUP1:        88          NUMBER OF CASES FOR GROUP2:    62
RANGE OF THE VARIABLE:  0.438613E 01            ONE STEP REPRESENTS:  0.731022E-01

    -2.75|XXXXX
    -2.67|XXXXXXXXXX
    -2.60|XXXXXX<XXX
    -2.53|XXXXX
    -2.45|CCO
    -2.38|XXXXXXXXXX
    -2.31|
    -2.23|XXXXXXXXXXXXXX
    -2.16|
    -2.09|CCO
    -2.01|
    -1.94|OOO
    -1.87|
    -1.80|EEOXX
    -1.72|EEEXXXXXXX
    -1.65|EEEEEEEEEEXXXXXXXXXXXXX
    -1.58|EEEEEEEEXXXXXXXX
    -1.50|XXXXX
    -1.43|EEEEEEEEEEXEEEXXXXXXXXXXXXXXXXXX<XXXXXX
    -1.36|EEEXX
    -1.28|EEEEEEEEEEEEEEEX
    -1.21|EEEXX
    -1.14|COO
    -1.06|EEEEEEEXXX
    -0.99|EEEEEEEXXX
    -0.92|EEEXX
    -0.85|XXXXXXXXXXXXXXX
    -0.77|EEEXX
    -0.70|COO
    -0.63|EEEXXXXXXX
    -0.55|EEEEEEOOOOO
    -0.48|EEEEEOO
    -0.41|COOOOOO
    -0.33|EEEXXXXXXX
    -0.26|EEEXX
    -0.19|COO
    -0.11|EEEEEEEXXX
    -0.04|EEEEEEOOOOO
     0.03|
     0.11|
     0.18|
     0.25|
     0.32|OOOOOOO
     0.40|
     0.47|XXXXX
     0.54|
     0.62|
     0.69|
     0.76|EEEEEOOOOOCOOCOOOOOO
     0.84|EEEEEEEEEECOOOCOOOOOOOOOOOOOOOCOOOOOOOCO
     0.91|EEEEOOOOOCOOO
     0.98|EEEEEOOOOOCOOC
     1.06|OCOCOOOOOO
     1.13|COOOOOO
     1.20|COOOOOOOOOOOO
     1.27|EEEEEOOOOO
     1.35|OCO
     1.42|
     1.49|COOCOOOOOO
     1.57|CCO
```

Figure 11.18   Discriminating between a group ($n = 88$) including simple (ICD 295.0) and hebephrenic (ICD 295.1) subtypes and a group ($n = 62$) including the schizo-affective (ICD 295.7) subtype of schizophrenia in terms of six course and outcome measures. Distance between the two distributions, $D = 1.06$; 0 = simple and hebephrenic schizophrenia; X = schizo-affective schizophrenia

```
53 VS. 57      , A2,A3,A4,A6,A7,A8; ALL FRC'S
FREQUENCY DISTRIBUTIONS FOR BOTH GROUPS
NUMBER  CF CASES FOR GROUP1:    179              NUMBER CF CASES FCR GROUP2:    62
RANGE OF THE VARIABLE:  0.334483E 01             ONE STEP REPRESENTS:  0.557472E-01

  -3.29|CC
  -3.23|
  -3.18|&&XXX
  -3.12|XXXXAXXAXXX
  -3.07|CC
  -3.01|&&XXXXXXXX
  -2.95|&&&&&XXXXXXAXXXXXXXXXXXXX
  -2.90|CCOCO
  -2.84|&&&&&OOOOO
  -2.79|&&&XXXXXXXXXXXX
  -2.73|&&&&&&&&&&&>XXXXXXXXXXXXXXXXXXXXXXXXXX
  -2.68|&&&&&&&&&&&XXXXXXXXXXXXX
  -2.62|&&&&&&&&&&XXXXX
  -2.56|&&&&&&&&&&&&&&XX
  -2.51|&&&&&OOC
  -2.45|&&&&&OOO
  -2.40|&&XXXXXXXXXXXXXX
  -2.34|&&&&&OOOOOCC
  -2.29|&&&&&&&&XXXXXXX
  -2.23|&&&&&&&&&&
  -2.17|&&&&&OOCOOCO
  -2.12|&&&&&OOOOOCOOOO
  -2.06|&&&&&&&&XXXXXXX
  -2.01|&&&&&OOOOOOCO
  -1.95|&&&&&XXXXX
  -1.90|&&&&&OOOOOCOCOOO
  -1.84|&&&XXXXXXX
  -1.78|CCCCO
  -1.73|&&&&&&OO
  -1.67|OO
  -1.62|XXXXX
  -1.56|CCO
  -1.51|COOCCOCOOOO
  -1.45|CCCOOOJOOO
  -1.39|COOOOJJ
  -1.34|&&&&&XXXXXXXXXXXXXXX
  -1.28|COCCOOCO
  -1.23|&&&&&OOC
  -1.17|OCO
  -1.11|CCC
  -1.06|COO
  -1.0|CCOOOOOO
  -0.95|CO
  -0.89|OO
  -0.84|
  -0.78|OOOOOOO
  -0.72|XXXXX
  -0.67|
  -0.61|
  -0.56|
  -0.50|COUCO
  -0.45|
  -0.39|CC
  -0.33|CO
  -0.28|OCO
  -0.22|CO
  -0.17|
  -0.11|
  -0.06|
  -0.00|
```

Figure 11.19   Discrimination between a group ($n = 179$) of patients with a diagnosis of paranoid schizophrenia (ICD 295.3) and a group ($n = 62$) of patients with a diagnosis of schizo-affective schizophrenia (ICD 295.7) in terms of six course and outcome measures. Distance between the two distributions, $D = 0.65$; 0 = paranoid schizophrenia; X = schizo-affective schizophrenia

350

```
(50,51,53,59) VS. (52,54,57), A2,A3,A4,A6,A7,A8; ALL FRC'S
FREQUENCY DISTRIBUTIONS FOR BOTH GROUPS
NUMBER  OF CASES FOR GROUP1:      298            NUMBER OF CASES FOR GROUP2:    149
RANGE OF THE VARIABLE:  0.341469E 01             ONE STEP REPRESENTS:  0.569115E-01


    -2.66|8888R0
    -2.60|8XXXXX
    -2.54|8XXX
    -2.49|8XXXXXXX
    -2.43|XXXXXXXX
    -2.37|XXXXXXXX
    -2.32|888X
    -2.26|88XX
    -2.20|R88RXXXXXX
    -2.15|8888888RXXXXXXXXXXXXXXXXXXXXXXXX
    -2.09|R8888888R8888R88R88X
    -2.03|88888R8RXXXXXX
    -1.98|8888888R88RXXXXXXXXXX
    -1.92|888R00000000R
    -1.86|88XXXXXXXXXXXXXX
    -1.81|00000
    -1.75|8888R000
    -1.69|888RXXX
    -1.63|88888RX
    -1.58|888RX
    -1.52|88888R0
    -1.46|8888RXXXXX
    -1.41|8R8888R000
    -1.35|88888R8RXXXXXXXXX
    -1.29|888R8R00000000
    -1.24|R88888R8R888XXXXXXX
    -1.18|88R00
    -1.12|888R
    -1.07|000000R
    -1.01|00000R
    -0.95|0000000
    -0.89|888RR8R
    -0.84|8888R8R00000R
    -0.78|8888R00000R( )000000
    -0.72|88R8R000
    -0.67|8888R00
    -0.61|00000
    -0.55|0
    -0.50|XX
    -0.44|R80000000
    -0.38|888888R88888R00
    -0.33|8888R88R8R0
    -0.27|88R0000
    -0.21|0000
    -0.15|00000
    -0.10|00000000
    -0.04|000000R0
     0.02|8X
     0.07|0
     0.13|0000000
     0.19|88R0
     0.24|
     0.30|
     0.36|
     0.41|
     0.47|
     0.53|
     0.59|
     0.64|
     0.70|0
```

Figure 11.20   Discrimination between a group ($n = 298$) including simple (ICD 295.0), hebephrenic (ICD 295.1), paranoid (ICD 295.3), and unspecified (ICD 295.9) subtypes and a group ($n = 149$) including catatonic (ICD 295.2), acute (ICD 295.4) and schizo-affective (ICD 295.7) subtypes of schizophrenia in terms of six course and outcome measures. Distance between the two distributions, $D = 0.71$; 0 = 295.0, 295.1, 295.3, 295.9 (ICD): X = 295.2, 295.4, 295.7 (ICD)

11.4.4.4 Catatonic (295.2), acute (295.4) and schizo-affective (295.7) schizo-phrenia compared with simple (295.0), hebephrenic (295.1), paranoid (295.3) and unspecified (295.9) schizophrenia

The reason for grouping together in this analysis the catatonic, acute and schizo-affective subtypes was that these three subtypes of schizophrenia were assumed to be more often associated with an acute onset and, hence, might be expected to have a better prognosis than the rest.

This assumption was not quite borne out by the results of the discriminant function analysis ($D = 0.71$) but the discrimination tends to be slightly better than the discrimination between the paranoid subtype and either of the two other groups (simple plus hebephrenic, and schizo-affective) with which comparisons were made (Figure 11.20).

In summary, the preliminary results of the discriminant function analysis of the validity of the subtypes of schizophrenia are compatible with a hypothesis of a course and outcome continuum within the clinical subclassification of schizo-phrenia. The simple and hebephrenic subtypes, on one hand, and the schizo-affective subtype, on the other hand, seem to occupy the two ends of a continuum, with the paranoid subtype occupying an intermediate position.

The fact that the discrimination, in terms of course and outcome, between simple and hebephrenic schizophrenia, on one hand, and schizo-affective psychoses, on the other hand, is relatively good, while neither of these two groupings can be sufficiently distinguished from the paranoid subtype, can be seen as supporting such an assumption.

Furthermore, the discrimination between simple and hebephrenic schizophrenia on one hand, and schizo-affective psychoses on the other hand, is higher than the discrimination between all schizophrenic psychoses and the depressive psychoses (see Table 11.1, page 358). This finding also suggests a course and outcome continuum of the subtypes of schizophrenia, in which patients with schizo-affective illnesses would be expected to concentrate in that area of the distribution of the schizophrenic patients which would overlap with the distribution of the depressive psychotic patients when course and outcome are the axis of the comparison. Further analyses designed to test this hypothesis will be carried out on the basis of the five-year follow-up data.

11.4.5 Distinctions between concordant and non-concordant schizophrenic patients

In terms of symptomatology (129 units of analysis) present on initial evaluation the concordant schizophrenic patients could be distinguished clearly from the non-concordant schizophrenic patients ($D = 2.37$, Figure 11.21). The discrimi-nation between the two classificatory groups, in terms of units of analysis present on the two-year follow-up assessment, was also very high ($D = 3.23$) if only those patients who were psychotic on follow-up were considered. The same patients (those found to be psychotic on follow-up) formed two quite distinct distributions ($D = 5.52$) where their symptomatology on initial evaluation was compared.

```
CCNC. VS. NON-CONC., 129 UA - I.E.
FREQUENCY DISTRIBUTIONS FOR BOTH GROUPS
NUMBER  OF CASES FOR GROUP1:     184                 NUMBER OF CASES FOR GROUP2:    323
RANGE OF THE VARIABLE:  0.192945E 02                 CNE STEP REPRESENTS:  0.321575E 00


   -4.45|XX
   -4.13|X
   -3.81|X
   -3.49|X
   -3.17|X
   -2.85|
   -2.52|XXXXXX
   -2.20|XX
   -1.88|XXX
   -1.56|XXXXXXX
   -1.24|XXXXXXX
   -0.92|XXXXXXXXXX
   -C.59|XXXXXXXXXXX
   -C.27|XXXXXXX
    C.05|XXXXXXXXX
    C.37|XXXXXXXXXXXXXXX
    C.69|XXXXXXXXXXXXXXXXXXX
    1.01|XXXXXXXXXXXXXXXXXXXXXXXXXX
    1.33|XXXXXXXXXXXXXXX
    1.66|0000XXXXXXXXXXX
    1.98|0000XXXX
    2.30|XXXXXXXXXXXXXXXXXXXX
    2.62|00XXXXXXXXX
    2.94|XXXXXXXXXX
    3.26|000XXXXXXXXXXXX
    3.59|0000000XXXX
    3.91|00XXXXXXXXXXXX
    4.23|0000000
    4.55|0000000000000
    4.87|00XX
    5.19|00000000
    5.51|000000000000
    5.84|00000000000
    6.16|00000CC00000000
    6.48|00000000000000
    6.80|000000000000000000000C00
    7.12|000000000000000000
    7.44|000000C0000000000C000000
    7.77|0000000
    8.09|000000000000000
    8.41|0000000000
    8.73|00000000000000000
    9.05|CC00000000000000000000000C0000000
    9.37|CC0000000000000000
    9.70|00000000000
   10.02|C00000000000000
   10.34|C0000
   10.66|C0000
   10.98|000
   11.30|00
   11.62|000
   11.95|
   12.27|
   12.59|
   12.91|00
   13.23|00
   13.55|
   13.88|00
   14.20|
   14.52|00
```

Figure 11.21   Discrimination between the group of concordant ($n = 184$) and the group of non-concordant ($n = 323$) schizophrenic patients in terms of 129 symptoms assessed on initial evaluation. Distance between the two distributions, $D = 2.37$; 0 = concordant patients; X = non-concordant patients

```
DISTRIBUTIONS ARE TRUNCATED ON THE LEFT
CONCORDANT VS. NON-CONCORD.; ALL BUT A5, ALL FRC'S
FREQUENCY DISTRIBUTIONS FOR BOTH GROUPS
NUMBER  OF CASES FOR GROUP1:      197              NUMBER OF CASES FOR GROUP2:     310
RANGE OF THE VARIABLE:  0.246137E 01               ONE STEP REPRESENTS:  0.410228E-01


   -0.24|XXXXXXXX
   -0.20|X
   -0.15|
   -0.11|
   -0.07|
   -0.03|XX
    0.01|
    0.05|X
    0.09|X
    0.13|BC
    0.17|X
    0.21|
    0.26|
    0.30|
    0.34|XXX
    0.38|BB
    0.42|BO
    0.46|BBOCO
    0.50|BBBBBXXXXX
    0.54|BBB
    0.58|BBBBBBXXXX
    0.62|BBBBBXXXXXXXXX
    0.67|BBBBBOOCO
    0.71|BBBXXXXX
    0.75|BBXXXXXXXXX
    0.79|BBBBBX
    0.83|BBBBBBBBOOOOOC
    0.87|BBBBBBBBBBBBBBBO
    0.91|BBBBBBXXXXX
    0.95|BBBBBBBBBXXXXXXXX
    0.99|BBBBBBBBBBBBBBBBOOOOOOO
    1.03|BBBBBBBBBBBBBBBBOOOOOO
    1.08|BBBBBBBBBBBBBBBBBBBBBBBBBBBBBBBBBBBBXXXXXX
    1.12|BBBBBBBBBBBBBBBBBBBBBBBBB
    1.16|BBBBBBBBBBBBBBBBOOOOOOOO
    1.20|BBBBBBBBBBBBBBB
    1.24|BBBBBOOCOOCOOC
    1.28|BBBBBBBBBOO
    1.32|BBBOOOOOO
    1.36|BBOOOOOO
    1.40|BBBCO
    1.45|BBBBOOOO
    1.49|BBBXXXX
    1.53|BBBX
    1.57|BB
    1.61|BCO
    1.65|BB
    1.69|CO
    1.73|XX
    1.77|BCO
    1.81|X
    1.86|
    1.90|BC
    1.94|
    1.98|CO
    2.02|
    2.06|
    2.10|CC
    2.14|CO
    2.18|BO
```

Figure 11.22   Discrimination between the group of concordant ($n = 197$) and the group of non-concordant ($n = 310$) schizophrenic patients in terms of six measures of course and outcome. Distance between the two distributions, $D = 0.38$; 0 = concordant; X = non-concordant

The concordant and non-concordant groups, however, overlapped almost completely when two-year course and outcome were taken as a criterion of predictive validity (D = 0.38, Figure 11.22). This means that the classification of schizophrenic patients into a concordant and a non-concordant group on initial evaluation was not predictive of differences in the two-year course and outcome of the schizophrenic patients.

It could be expected that the concordant group, being symptomatologically more homogeneous (and conceivably excluding such patients who would not be diagnosed as schizophrenic if more stringent criteria were consistently applied), would be separated in terms of course and outcome, from the patients with an initial evaluation diagnosis of psychotic depression better than the group of all patients with a clinical diagnosis of schizophrenia. This expectation was met by the data only marginally. The coefficient of discrimination (course and outcome considered) between the concordant group of schizophrenic patients and the psychotic depression group was 0.69, which is not much higher than the coefficient of discrimination between all schizophrenia patients and the psychotic depressive patients (0.58).

11.4.6 Predictive validity of distinctions within the group of affective disorders

The only diagnostic distinctions within the group of the affective disorders which were considered suitable for analysis in the context of the two-year follow-up data were those between ICD mania (296.1) and ICD depressive psychoses (296.0, 296.2 and 298.0), on one hand, and CATEGO classes M and D on the other hand.

Figure 11.23 shows that the discrimination in terms of two-year course and outcome between patients with initial clinical diagnosis of mania, and patients with initial clinical diagnosis of a depressive psychosis, is relatively good (D = 1.18).

The CATEGO classification of patients on initial evaluation into classes M and D is less predictive of differences between class M and class D patients in terms of subsequent course and outcome (D = 0.79, Figure 11.24).

11.5 COMPARISON OF THE PREDICTIVE POWER OF THE FOUR CLASSIFICATIONS

All the findings described so far concerned the degree to which it is possible to separate the symptomatology, course and outcome of patients who, on initial evaluation, had been allocated to a number of classification groups by four different methods. The discriminant function in each of the analyses was defined so as to obtain maximum separation of each pair of two groups of patients, and the results of this statistical procedure were expressed as a coefficient of discrimination (D) indicating the distance between the two groups, and as a probability of misclassification of patients. It was also pointed out that discrimination (or distance) coefficients greater than 1.0 could be accepted as high enough to indicate that the discrimination could be practically important.

```
61 VS. (60,62,80), A2,A3,A4,A6,A7,A8; ALL FRC'S
FREQUENCY DISTRIBUTIONS FOR BOTH GROUPS
NUMBER  CF CASES FOR GROUP1:       67              NUMBER CF CASES FCR GRGUP2:      50
RANGE OF THE VARIABLE:  0.510365E 01              ONE STEP REPRESENTS:  C.850608E-C1

   -4.50|XXXXXX
   -4.42|XXXXXX
   -4.33|8883XXXXXXXXXXXXXXXXXXXXXXXXXXXXXXXXXX
   -4.25|XXXXXX
   -4.16|COOOOOOOG
   -4.08|XXXXXXXXXXXX
   -3.99|8888XXXXXXXXXXXXXX
   -3.91|8888XXXXXXXXXXXXXXXXXXXXXXX
   -3.82|XXXXXXXXXXXX
   -3.74|XXXXXXXXXXXX
   -3.65|CCOC
   -3.57|XXXXXX
   -3.48|XXXXXXXXXXXX
   -3.40|CCOC
   -3.31|
   -3.23|
   -3.14|XXXXXX
   -3.06|
   -2.97|
   -2.89|
   -2.80|
   -2.72|
   -2.63|
   -2.55|
   -2.46|
   -2.38|
   -2.29|8888XXXXXXXXX
   -2.21|888888000
   -2.12|88888888XXXXXXXXX
   -2.04|COOC
   -1.95|0000
   -1.87|COOC
   -1.78|88888888888888888888888888000000CO
   -1.70|888888888888XXXXX
   -1.61|XXXXXXXXXXXXXXXXX
   -1.53|88888800000000000000000
   -1.44|CCOCOOOCO
   -1.36|CCCCOOOOOOOOOOOOO
   -1.27|
   -1.19|88888800000000
   -1.10|888888000
   -1.02|000000000G
   -0.93|CCOOOOOOO
   -0.85|888888888XXX
   -0.76|88888800C
   -0.68|888888GC00000
   -0.59|CGOGOOOOO
   -0.51|8888888000000000C000
   -0.42|OCOGOOOOOOOGCO
   -0.34|
   -0.25|CCOC
   -0.17|OOOO
   -0.08|COOC
    C.00|CCOO
    0.09|
    0.17|
    0.26|
    0.34|CCCC
    0.43|
    0.51|CCOO
```

Figure 11.23   Discrimination between groups of patients with clinical diagnosis of mania ($n = 67$) and depressive psychoses ($n = 50$) in terms of six measures of course and outcome. Distance between the two distributions, $D = 1.18$; 0 = depressive psychosis; X = mania

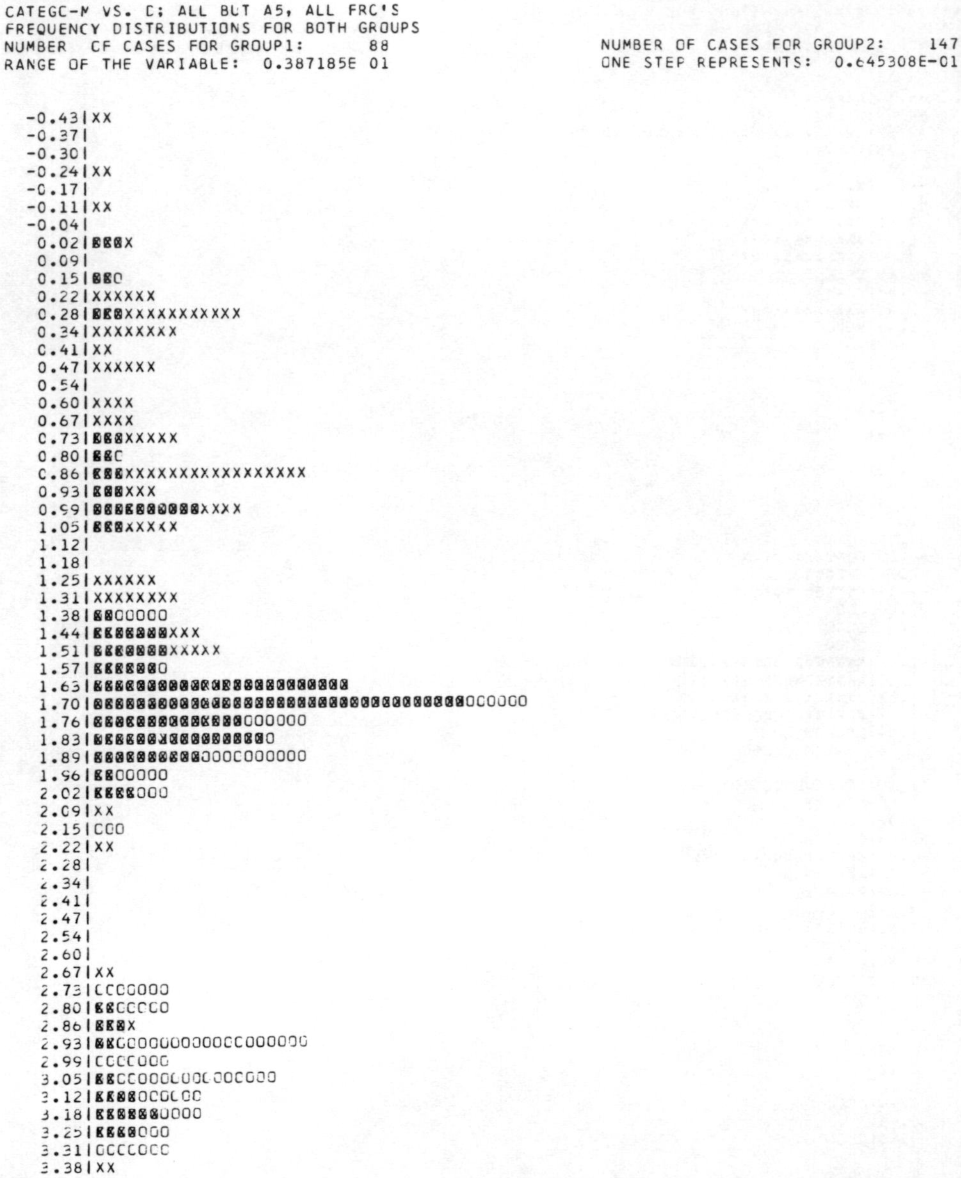

356

```
CATEGC-M VS. C; ALL BUT A5, ALL FRC'S
FREQUENCY DISTRIBUTIONS FOR BOTH GROUPS
NUMBER  CF CASES FOR GROUP1:        88        NUMBER OF CASES FOR GROUP2:     147
RANGE OF THE VARIABLE:  0.387185E 01          ONE STEP REPRESENTS:  0.645308E-01

 -0.43|XX
 -0.37|
 -0.30|
 -0.24|XX
 -0.17|
 -0.11|XX
 -0.04|
  0.02|BBBX
  0.09|
  0.15|BBC
  0.22|XXXXX
  0.28|BBBXXXXXXXXXXXX
  0.34|XXXXXXXX
  C.41|XX
  0.47|XXXXXX
  0.54|
  0.60|XXXX
  0.67|XXXX
  C.73|BBBXXXXX
  0.80|BBC
  C.86|BBBXXXXXXXXXXXXXXXXXX
  0.93|BBBXXX
  0.59|BBBBBBBBBBXXXX
  1.05|BBBXXXXX
  1.12|
  1.18|
  1.25|XXXXX
  1.31|XXXXXXXX
  1.38|BBOOOOO
  1.44|BBBBBBBXXX
  1.51|BBBBBBBXXXXX
  1.57|BBBBBBO
  1.63|BBBBBBBBBBBXBBBBBBBBBBBB
  1.70|BBBBBBBBBBBXBBBBBBBBBBBBBBBBBBBBBBBBBBBBBBOCOOOO
  1.76|BBBBBBBBBBBBXBBBOOOOOO
  1.83|BBBBBBXBBBBBBBBBO
  1.89|BBBBBBBBBBOOOCOOOOOO
  1.96|BBOOOOO
  2.02|BBBBOOO
  2.09|XX
  2.15|COO
  2.22|XX
  2.28|
  2.34|
  2.41|
  2.47|
  2.54|
  2.60|
  2.67|XX
  2.73|CCOOOOO
  2.80|BBCCCCO
  2.86|BBBX
  2.93|BBCOOOOOOOOOOCCOOOOOO
  2.99|CCCCOOO
  3.05|BBCCOOOCOOCOOCOOO
  3.12|BBBBOCOLOO
  3.18|BBBBBBOOOO
  3.25|BBBBOOO
  3.31|CCCCOCC
  3.38|XX
```

Figure 11.24 Discrimination between patients in CATEGO class M ($n = 88$) and CATEGO class D ($n = 147$) in terms of six course and outcome measures. Distance between two distributions, $D = 0.79$; 0 = CATEGO class M; X = CATEGO class D

However, the distance coefficients obtained in the different discriminations cannot be directly compared with each other, and hence, no comparisons of the predictive and discriminatory power of the different methods of classifying psychiatric patients would be possible my means of simply comparing the values of D.

The discriminatory power expressed by D, is the difference between the means of the two compared groups, in terms of Z-scores, divided by their pooled standard deviation. The 'weight' of a difference, however, depends also on the size of the sample on which the calculation is based. Thus, the same coefficient of discrimination in terms of Z-score values derived from 129 units of analysis would be of different importance, if it is based on a relatively small (say, 60) or relatively large (600) group of patients. A measure of the relative importance of the distance between two groups therefore should take the sample size into account.

In univariate problems Student's t statistic is usually used to measure distance in terms of its standard error. A corresponding statistic in the multivariate case could be denoted by T. It is the square root of the optimum ratio of between-groups to within-groups variance of the linear compound from both groups. If n_1 and n_2 are the respective sample sizes, T and D are related through the formula:

$$T = \sqrt{D \frac{n_1 n_2}{n_1 + n_2}}$$

By using the T statistic, it is possible to compare more reliably the discrimination between groups obtained with the four different systems of classification utilized in the study. To facilitate such comparisons, the results of discriminant function analysis for different pairs of classificatory categories and groupings are summarized in Tables 11.1 and 11.2. Table 11.1 is based on discriminant function analysis in terms of: (a) the 27 groups of units of analysis, and (b) the six course and outcome measures. Table 11.2 shows discriminant function results in terms of the 129 units of analysis (symptoms) for those categories in which the number of patients justified the use of a large number of variables (that is, the requirement that the number of patients should exceed considerably the number of variables was met). In both tables, the distance coefficients (Mahalanobis distance $- D$) and the T statistics are given. While D is a measure of the absolute overlap, respectively distinctions obtained between different pairs of groupings, T is an indication of the degree to which such distances were exposed to random variation (the greater T, the less the random variation). Practically all T's were statistically highly significant. However, even a statistically significant discrimination between two groups may not be satisfactory for a specific purpose, for example, for determining the prognosis of a group of patients — if an unacceptably large proportion of individuals would be misclassified.

TABLE 11.1. DISTANCE COEFFICIENTS(D) AND T-STATISTIC VALUES CHARACTERIZING THE DEGREE OF DISCRIMINATION BETWEEN PAIRS OF PATIENT GROUPS ACHIEVED BY DIFFERENT CLASSIFICATIONS.

Classification	Symptomatology (27 groups of units of analysis)								Course and Outcome	
	All Patients				Patients psychotic on F.U.					
	on I.E.		on F.U.		on I.E.		on F.U.			
	D	T	D	T	D	T	D	T	D	T
	(1)	(2)	(3)	(4)	(5)	(6)	(7)	(8)	(9)	(10)
ICD Categories										
Schizophrenia (295.0-9) - depressive psychoses (296.0, 296.2, 298.0)	2.20	11.72	1.00	7.87	3.44	5.44	2.17	4.32	0.58	5.86
Schizophrenia (295.0-9) - mania (296.1)	2.08	9.64	1.25	7.47	3.29	6.10	2.83	5.66	1.36	7.87
Depressive psychoses (296.0, 296.2, 298.0) - Mania (296.1)	2.45	8.97	1.15	6.14	-	-	-	-	1.18	5.81
CATEGO										
Class S - Class D	2.62	17.27	2.66	10.82	2.66	8.45	1.45	6.42	0.80	9.41
Class S - Class M	1.99	12.57	2.20	8.11	2.20	6.79	1.98	6.44	0.67	7.02
Class D - Class M	1.66	10.00	1.12	8.21	2.71	6.10	2.44	5.78	0.79	6.59
McKeon's clusters										
Cluster 6/cluster 8	1.63	8.86	1.19	9.52	3.62	7.03	2.87	6.26	0.85	6.07
Cluster 6 schizophrenics/cluster 8 depressives	2.65	6.01	1.90	5.88	-	-	-	-	0.94	4.05
Cluster 8 schizophrenics/cluster 6 depressives	5.03	7.65	2.09	5.03	-	-	-	-	1.39	3.83
Concordant group of schizophrenics										
concordant-non-concordant schizophrenics	1.62	13.79	0.75	7.11	1.74	8.89	1.24	7.49	0.38	6.77
concordant schizophrenics-depressive psychoses	3.84	14.02	1.27	8.07	6.63	7.29	3.11	4.99	0.69	5.87
ICD schizophrenia subtypes										
simple and hebephrenic-paranoid	1.77	7.92	1.30	7.14	1.45	5.98	1.88	6.79	0.55	5.70
simple and hebephrenic-schizoaffective	1.15	8.08	0.94	6.92	3.15	5.85	4.57	7.05	1.06	6.21
paranoid-schizoaffective	1.52	8.66	1.07	7.26	2.38	5.68	1.75	4.87	0.65	5.47
simple+hebephrenic+paranoid+unspecified - catatonic+acute+schizoaffective	1.20	11.08	0.89	9.54	1.64	6.77	1.32	6.08	0.71	8.40

359

TABLE 11.2. DISTANCE COEFFICIENTS (D) AND T-STATISTIC VALUES CHARACTERIZING THE DEGREE OF DISCRIMINATION BETWEEN DIAGNOSTIC GROUPS IN TERMS OF 27 GROUPS OF UNITS OF ANALYSIS.

Diagnostic groups	Symptomatology (27 groups of units of analysis)							
	All Patients				Patients psychotic on F.U.			
	on I.E.		on F.U.		on I.E.		on F.U.	
	D	T	D	T	D	T	D	T
	(1)	(2)	(3)	(4)	(5)	(6)	(7)	(8)
ICD categories								
Schizophrenia (295.0-9) – Depressive psychoses (296.0, 296.2, 298.0)	2.83	13.28	1.70	10.30	6.69	7.58	5.45	6.85
Schizophrenia (295.0-9) – Mania (296.1)	3.92	13.23	2.23	11.02	9.72	10.47	6.48	8.56
Depressive psychoses (296.0, 296.2, 298.0) – Mania (296.1)	-	-	-	-	-	-	-	-
CATEGO								
Class S – Class D	3.41	19.71	1.74	14.08	5.90	12.58	4.51	11.00
Class S – Class M	3.37	16.37	1.55	11.11	6.32	11.51	4.58	9.81

11.5.1 Discrimination between patient groups in terms of two-year course and outcome (predictive validity of classification categories)

Table 11.1 shows clearly that the discriminatory power of all the classification methods with regard to the two-year course and outcome of the patients in the study is more restricted than their capacity to separate patient groups in terms of symptomatology. Groups of patients allocated on initial evaluation to different classification categories differ among themselves more with regard to their symptomatology – both initial and subsequent, than with regard to course and outcome.

Considering both D and T, the best prediction of course and outcome on the basis of classification on initial evaluation is achieved by the CATEGO classes S and D ($D = 0.80$, $T = 9.41$) and the next highest by the two groups of ICD subtypes of schizophrenia – simple, hebephrenic, paranoid and unspecified, on one hand, and catatonic, acute and schizo-affective, on the other hand ($D = 0.71$, $T = 8.40$).

The lowest levels of discrimination in terms of course and outcome are obtained with the comparison of schizophrenic and depressive patients across the statistical clusters 6 and 8 ($T = 4.05$ and 3.83, respectively). The prediction of course and outcome on the basis of the whole clusters, however, is considerably better ($D = 0.85$, $T = 6.07$).

Regarding the subclassification of schizophrenia, the D- and T-values for the comparisons: simple and hebephrenic/paranoid; simple and hebephrenic/schizo-affective; and paranoid/schizo-affective, are consistent with the idea that, prognostically, the three groupings can be ordered along a continuum ranging from unfavourable to relatively favourable course and outcome (see Section 11.4.4). The fact that the distance between simple-cum-hebephrenic schizophrenia and schizo-affective schizophrenia is greater than the distance between all ICD schizophrenia and ICD psychotic depression, but less than the distance between CATEGO class S and CATEGO class D, can be interpreted as an indication that the ICD clinical diagnostic category of schizophrenia included a proportion of patients (mainly schizo-affective) who are practically indistinguishable from depressive psychotic patients with regard to course and outcome. CATEGO, using narrower criteria for defining schizophrenia, probably places such patients in the depressive group (class D), which is indeed larger than the ICD psychotic depression group.

Within the group of schizophrenic patients, the prediction is good with a dichotomy based on the following grouping of clinical subtypes: simple, hebephrenic, paranoid and unspecified, on one hand, and catatonic, acute and schizo-affective, on the other hand. Since the relatively big group of paranoid schizophrenic patients was practically equidistant in position between the simple-cum-hebephrenic and the schizo-affective groups, it could be assumed that the good discrimination between these latter two groups of clinical subtypes is due to a prognostic similarity among the schizo-affective, acute and catatonic patients, rather than to a homogeneity of course and outcome of the simple, hebephrenic, paranoid and unspecified subtypes. The fact that groups of clinical subtypes of schizophrenia provide a better predictive discrimination of course and outcome than the concordant/non-concordant classification of schizophrenic patients also suggests that in making a subtype diagnosis, psychiatrists may be using information, or clues, that are relevant to the prognosis but have not been utilized in the computer classification procedures.

11.5.2 Discrimination between patient groups in terms of symptomatology (content validity of classification categories)

Table 11.1 indicates a trend in the direction of better discrimination between patients in different classification groups in terms of the 27 groups of units of analysis than in terms of course and outcome measures. The trend is more marked if the material is analysed by 129 units of analysis (symptoms) rather than by groups of units, for those categories which contained a sufficient number of patients (Table 11.2). This finding suggests that some information contributing to better discrimination is lost when the symptoms are condensed into groups of units of analysis.

On the whole, the symptomatological discrimination between patient groups on initial evaluation was better than on follow-up reassessment with regard to both groups of units of analysis and units of analysis. This is consistent with the findings about the symptom profiles of the patient groups on the two occasions which were reported in the preceding chapters and which indicated that patients assigned to different diagnostic groups on initial evaluation were considerably less dissimilar on follow-up because of quantitative (fewer symptoms) and qualitative (less florid symptoms) changes in symptomatology occurring over the two-year period. The tendency for patients to be symptomatologically less dissimilar on follow-up could not be explained only as a result of many patients being in remissions at the time of the two-year re-examination, since the same trend could be observed in those patients who were found to be psychotic on follow-up. An exception from this general trend was the discrimination between the group of simple and hebephrenic schizophrenic patients, on one hand, and the group of schizo-affective patients, on the other hand. The symptomatological distance between the patients in these two groupings (patients psychotic on follow-up) was greater on two-year reassessment than on initial evaluation. This might be the effect of an evolution toward a more definite affective symptomatology in some of the patients diagnosed initially as schizo-affective.

Tables 11.1 and 11.2 permit a preliminary evaluation of the content validity of the major diagnostic group of schizophrenia as defined by the different classification schemes used on initial examination. The content validity of a classification category can be said to be satisfactory if the symptomatology of the patients assigned to it does not overlap to a great extent with the symptomatology of patients assigned to other categories.

Three classification categories − the ICD clinical diagnosis of schizophrenia the CATEGO class S, and the group of concordant patients were used in the initial phase of the study to delimit the nosological entity of schizophrenia from other psychoses included in the investigation. The distance coefficients and the values of the T-statistic shown in the two tables indicate that all three classification categories for schizophrenia achieved their purpose with regard to the symptomatological separation of patients assigned to them from patients in other groups. Taking an average of the distance coefficients obtained in four comparisons of patients with depressive psychoses (on initial evaluation and on follow-up, for all patients and for those who were psychotic on follow-up) it is possible to say that the differentiation was highest between the concordant group of schizophrenics and the patients with clinical diagnosis of depressive psychosis (mean D = 3.71), followed by the CATEGO class S/class D discrimination (mean D = 2.37), and the discrimination between patients with clinical diagnosis of schizophrenia and clinical diagnosis of depressive psychosis (mean D = 2.20).

On the other hand, the differentiation of schizophrenic psychoses from mania was somewhat better for groups defined by clinical diagnosis of schizophrenia and mania (mean D = 2.36) than by CATEGO class S and class M (mean D = 2.09).

Within the group of schizophrenic psychoses, it is possible to examine the symptomatological differentiation obtained by using the different diagnostic subtype categories, or combinations of them. The most pronounced symptomatological distinction within the group of patients with clinical diagnosis of schizophrenia was that between the combined subgroup of simple and hebephrenic schizophrenics and the subgroup of schizo-affective patients (mean D = 2.45) followed by the distinctions between (a) paranoid and schizo-affective patients; (b) the combined subgroup of simple and hebephrenic and the paranoid patients; and (c) the combined subgroup of simple, hebephrenic, paranoid and unspecified schizophrenics and the combined group of catatonic, acute, and schizo-affective patients. The latter two groups were least distinct from one another in terms of symptomatology (27 groups of units of analysis), but they showed considerable differences of course and outcome. The best discrimination within schizophrenia, in terms of both symptomatology and course and outcome, was that between simple and hebephrenic patients, on one hand, and the schizo-affective patients, on the other hand.

The distinction between concordant and non-concordant schizophrenics in terms of symptomatology, course and outcome was of a somewhat lower order (mean D = 1.33) than the discriminations obtained with the ICD clinical subtypes. Considering the good discrimination obtained between the subset of concordant schizophrenics and the depressive patients, this finding suggests that while the concordant patients seemed to be rather homogeneous with regard to symptomatology, course and outcome, the non-concordant patients varied considerably and therefore should not be regarded as a distinct, clinically meaningful subgroup of schizophrenia.

11.6 DISCUSSION AND CONCLUSIONS

The foregoing description of the results of the discriminant function analysis of different pairs of diagnostic of statistical categories within four different systems of classification of patients suffering from functional psychoses leads to one general conclusion. All the classification systems compared – clinical ICD diagnosis,

TABLE 11.3. DISTRIBUTION OF PATIENTS CLASSIFIED INTO
DIFFERENT DIAGNOSTIC GROUPS (ICD) BY QUINTILES
OF THE DISCRIMINANT FUNCTION, AND MISCLASSIFI-
CATION RATES, FOR THE 6 COURSE AND OUTCOME
MEASURES.

Class (quintile)	Schizophrenia N	%	Depressive psychoses N	%	Misclassifi-cation rate
1	70	14	16	24	
2	268	53	41	62	
3	48	9	7	10	37%
4	91	18	2	3	
5	30	6	1	1	
Total	507	100	67	100	

$$x^2 = 15.15 \qquad P \le .01$$

Class (quintile)	Schizophrenia N	%	Mania N	%	
1	31	6	17	34	
2	25	5	9	18	
3	36	7	6	12	26%
4	226	45	17	34	
5	189	37	1	2	
Total	507	100	50	100	

$$x^2 = 73.02 \qquad P \le .005$$

Class (quintile)	Mania N	%	Depressive psychoses N	%	
1	4	6	14	28	
2	3	4	12	24	
3	6	9	6	12	29%
4	30	45	13	26	
5	24	36	5	10	
Total	67	100	50	100	

$$x^2 = 28.25 \qquad P < .005$$

CATEGO, McKeon's statistical clusters and the concordant—non-concordant grouping, discriminate relatively well and reliably the symptomatological character-istics of the patients assigned to different classification groups at initial evaluation. At the same time all classifications could predict that patients who happened to be in a psychotic episode two years after the initial evaluation would be symptomato-logically different from each other, if they had been classified into different groups on initial evaluation. All the classifications, however (with the exception of certain distinctions within CATEGO and ICD, discussed above), predicted less well the two-year course and outcome of the patients, if non-mental state measures, such as length of the inclusion episode, proportion of the follow-up period spent in psychotic episodes, pattern of course, social functioning and overall outcome were considered. In other words, while the content (symptom-related) validity of the classifications of functional psychoses used in the study was supported, the predictive (course and outcome-related) validity of the same classifications with regard to a two-year follow-up period appeared to be limited.

This conclusion seems to contradict some of the findings described in previous chapters which showed that the course and outcome of patients in different diagnostic groups were significantly different. In particular, the comparisons between course and outcome measures in patients with clinical diagnosis of schizophrenia and patients with clinical diagnosis of depressive psychosis, indicated significant differences between them – the schizophrenic patients having worse two-year course and outcome on practically all measures. Since these significant differences were obtained in univariate comparisons which examined the two groups with regard to each individual dimension of course and outcome, one might suspect that the results indicating a relatively low degree of discrimination between the two diagnostic groups in terms of a multivariate composite dimension of course and outcome might be somehow linked to the nature of the statistical technique in the analysis. That no such contradiction however exists can be seen from Table 11.3.

In this table, the range of the discriminant function in each of the comparisons for course and outcome between schizophrenia/depressive psychoses, schizophrenia/mania, and mania/depressive psychoses, was split into five quintiles and the number of patients in each of the diagnostic categories under comparison was treated as a univariate frequency distribution. The two distributions were then compared using a chi-square test (Bonferroni's modification). The results in Table 11.3 show that there were statistically significant differences between the distribution in all three pairs of diagnostic categories, but that the difference between schizophrenic and depressive psychotic patients was at a somewhat lower level of significance.

However, the finding of significant differences between schizophrenic and depressive patients in terms of course and outcome says little about how important – theoretically and practically – such differences might be. To throw some light on this question, Table 11.3 includes also the proportions of patients who would be misclassified with regard to course and outcome if no other information but the diagnostic category to which they are allocated is used to classify them. The figures suggest that about one-third of the patients would be misclassified with regard to prognosis of course and outcome if only the diagnostic categories were taken as a basis for making the prognosis.

In interpreting these results, it should be remembered that the data on which conclusions about the validity of classification of the functional psychoses are based have been obtained in a standardized and reliable way from a crosscultural context, including patients from nine different countries. The international and crosscultural character of the study was a stringent test of the validity of diagnostic classifications, because data on patients from quite diverse geographical, socio-economic and cultural areas were pooled and analysed. Confirmation of validity of a classification for a population of patients so heterogeneous presents a strong support for the classification. At the same time, the limitations of IPSS data described earlier (for example, difficulty in estimating how representative the groups of patients were) and the nature of the course and outcome measures used in the follow-up study make it necessary to study further the important issue of validity of classifications using follow-up data obtained in the five-year IPSS follow-up and other prospective studies.

CHAPTER 12

Discussion and Conclusions

In the follow-up phase of the IPSS, the collaborating investigators set out to overcome some of the methodological problems of previous follow-up studies of schizophrenia outlined in Chapter 2, and to add to existing knowledge about the course and outcome of schizophrenia and other functional psychoses. The previous chapters have presented a large amount of data concerned with how the follow-up study was carried out and what happened to the IPSS patients during the two years after their initial evaluation. These data will now be considered in terms of the aims of the follow-up phase, as stated in Chapter 1. For the purposes of discussion, these aims can be restated as follows:

1. To assess and compare the nature of the course and outcome of schizo-phrenia and other functional psychoses within and between cultures.

2. To determine whether it is possible to identify predictors of particular types of course and outcome.

3. To approach the assessment of validity of the classification of the functional psychoses.

4. To determine the feasibility of carrying out a follow-up study of patients suffering from schizophrenia and other functional psychoses in the nine different centres.

5. To determine if it is possible to develop procedures for the standardized and reliable follow-up evaluation of patients with functional psychoses which will be applicable in different cultures.

6. To identify hypotheses about the nature of schizophrenia which can be tested in future studies.

12.1 THE COURSE AND OUTCOME OF SCHIZOPHRENIA AND OTHER FUNCTIONAL PSYCHOSES

12.1.1 Schizophrenia

A major aim of the IPSS was to evaluate the course and outcome of schizophrenic patients. The second-year follow-up data led to conclusions about the variability of course and outcome among schizophrenic patients in the study; the variability of course and outcome according to centre; temporal consistency of the symptom-atology of schizophrenic patients; and the cross-sectional symptomatic picture of schizophrenic patients in the nine centres two years after their initial evaluation.

12.1.1.1 Variability of course and outcome of schizophrenia

One of the major findings of the current study is that there is a great variability of course and outcome among schizophrenic patients. The review of the previous literature in Chapter 2 pointed out that one could make a case for either releatively poor or relatively good course and outcome for schizophrenic patients depending on which previous study is selected, and suggested some of the methodological problems that have accounted for this state of affairs. The current study indicates that schizophrenic patients who are homogeneous with regard to their initial clinical picture and who correspond rather closely to the strict concept of schizophrenia inherent in the CATEGO program have a rather wide variety of courses during a two-year follow-up period.

Some of the patients diagnosed as schizophrenic on initial evaluation had an extremely good two-year course and outcome; 32 per cent of those followed up were totally asymptomatic at second-year follow-up, and 12 per cent of those followed up had an episode of inclusion lasting for less than one month followed by a full remission which lasted throughout the follow-up period. More than one-quarter spent less than 15 per cent of the follow-up period in a psychotic eipsode, did not suffer from social impairment, and had full remissions after episodes. More than half fell into the two best overall outcome groups. Although two years is a relatively short period in the course of schizophrenic illness, the two-year follow-up results certainly give strong support to the concept that some schizophrenic patients do extremely well after their acute episodes of illness and do not progress into chronic states of symptomatic or functional impairment, at least not initially. This is particularly significant, since the initial evaluation profile analysis and the results of CATEGO analysis indicate that the vast majority of these schizophrenic patients meet rather strict criteria for the diagnosis of schizophrenia.

On the other hand, it is also clear that despite all of the recent advances of psychopharmacology and social and other therapies for schizophrenia, there is a large number of schizophrenics in the study who had a severe two-year course and outcome. Thus almost a fifth of the patients were either in a psychotic episode for more than three-quarters of the follow-up period and suffered severe social impairment or were psychotic for 46 to 75 per cent of the follow-up period without full remission and with severe social impairment. More than a quarter of the schizophrenic patients followed up were still in the episode of inclusion at the time of follow-up. More than half of the patients were either still in the episode of inclusion at the time of second-year follow-up or had had subsequent psychotic episodes during the follow-up period.

The results of the IPSS data thus indicate that the variability in the course and outcome of schizophrenic patients reported by various investigators is not entirely the result of lack of specificity of diagnostic criteria or methodological difficulties, but seems to reflect a true range of types of course and outcome. The predictive factors which may be related to the different types of course and outcome will be discussed in section 12.2 below.

12.1.1.2 Variability of course and outcome according to centre

The present study has provided an opportunity to compare the course and outcome of schizophrenic patient groups similar in their symptomatology at the beginning of the follow-up period.

There appear to be clear differences in the course and outcome of schizophrenia in the different centres of this study, with patients in centres in developing countries on the average having a better course and outcome than those in centres in developed countries.* This is a major result of the follow-up phase of the IPSS relevant to the study of the relationship between culture and mental disorder.

It is quite clear that Ibadan schizophrenic patients had the best course and outcome of schizophrenia patients in the various centres. Of the initial evaluation schizophrenic patients in Ibadan followed-up 58 per cent were asymptomatic at the time of second-year follow-up; 36 per cent had an episode of inclusion which lasted less than one month followed by full remission lasting throughout the follow-up period, and almost half had an episode of inclusion that lasted less than three months followed by a full remission and no further episodes. Ninety-seven per cent remained out of the hospital for more than three-quarters of the follow-up period and approximately two-thirds were in a psychotic episode for 15 per cent or less of the follow-up period. Only 5 per cent of Ibadan patients fell into the worst overall outcome group.

Agra patients had the next best course and outcome for most of the factors considered. For example, more than a quarter of Agra schizophrenics followed up had an episode of inclusion which lasted less than one month followed by full remission lasting throughout the follow-up period, and 40 per cent had an episode of inclusion which lasted less than three months followed by full remission without subsequent episodes. Nearly half of Agra schizophrenics were asymptomatic at the time of the two-year follow-up, and over half were in a psychotic episode for 15 per cent or less of the follow-up period.

At the other extreme it was quite clear that the patients in Aarhus had the worst course and outcome. Half of Aarhus schizophrenics followed up were still in the episode of inclusion at the time of second-year follow-up; 61 per cent were psychotic at the time of the follow-up and only 8 per cent were asymptomatic at that time.

For all variables considered, the schizophrenic patients in Ibadan, Agra and Cali, all centres in developing countries, tended to have a better outcome on average than the schizophrenic patients in the other six centres.†

*The terms 'developed' and 'developing' countries, now in common usage in international relations, have been used in this study without attempting to specify in detail the different dimensions of 'development'. Generally they refer to economic, sociopolitical and cultural differences between countries. The investigation of the association between groups of specific characteristics of 'development' and the course and outcome of mental disorders would be an important task for future studies.
†An exception to these findings was that the group of schizophrenics in Cali approximated centres in developed countries in the outcome variable 'pattern of course'.

These results could be due to the inclusion of different types of patients in the series of the various centres or to actual differences in the course and outcome of the same types of patients.

Factors which may have contributed to the inclusion of different types of schizophrenic patients in the developed and developing centres include the following:

1. The centres in developing countries in general had very large catchment areas serving extremely large populations. It is possible that as a result of a relative shortage of beds those patients who tended to be admitted to the hospitals at these centres may have been more acutely disturbed than the patients admitted to hospitals in the other centres. Since some previous studies have indicated that acutely disturbed patients are more likely to have good course and outcome than patients who are not so acutely disturbed at the time of admission, such a factor, if it did exist at the centres in this study, could have had an effect on the results of course and outcome studies.

2. Although the initial evaluation symptom profiles of the schizophrenic patient groups in all centres were significantly similar to one another when the PSE ratings were used to generate the profiles, it is possible that in fact the symptom pictures may have been somewhat different. It has been demonstrated that the PSE was used reliably in this study, during the initial evaluation and follow-up phases. However, it is possible that the actual symptom pictures of the schizophrenic patients may not have been as uniform as the PSE ratings suggested (for example, because of intraindividual variations of raters over time). Similarity in levels of reliability obtained in exercises conducted throughout the study speaks against a major influence of this type of factor.

3. It is also possible that different emphasis may have been placed on the relationship between certain symptoms in arriving at a diagnosis. Although the PSE may have reflected the presence of delusions, hallucinations, and affective symptoms in an individual patient, the degree to which different investigators may have felt that the affective symptoms were secondary to the delusions and hallucinations instead of the reverse, may have differed from centre to centre. Similarly the weight that investigators placed on evidence of prior chronicity or precipitating events in making a diagnosis may have varied.

4. It is also possible that at the time of follow-up, patients or informants in some centres were more accurate, more reliable, or more willing to describe symptoms and episodes than in other centres. Such factors might have the effect of obscuring similarities in the course and outcome of schizophrenic patient groups in various centres.

5. Finally, it must be remembered that little is known about the degree to which the patients from the centres included in this study are representative of all patients in the centre or in the culture. Therefore caution is necessary in generalizing the findings to make conclusions about the effect of culture on course and outcome.

Despite all of these cautions it is likely that the course and outcome of schizophrenia in the different centres actually do vary and that the course and outcome of schizophrenia are less severe in developing countries than in developed countries.

It is therefore necessary to consider possible explanations for such a phenomenon. There are at least three:

1. It may be that the structural elements of different cultures differ in important ways which have an effect on the outcome of schizophrenic patients. For example, differences in the intensity of family bonds, in the type of family structure, or in the socioeconomic features of the culture may make it more or less difficult for a schizophrenic patient to return to the community and remain in remission. It is possible that a schizophrenic patient returning into a rural community in which he receives considerable family and community support and in which he is not so directly exposed to the stresses of competing in a highly industrialized society may have a better chance of remaining in remission than the same patient would in another sociocultural setting.

2. It is possible that treatment modalities are difficult in different cultures. In both Ibadan and Agra there is a strong emphasis on maintaining the contact between the patient and his family during the acute phase of his illness, and family members often live together with and take care of the patient during the time of the patient's hospitalization. It is feasible that this has some effect on at least the relatively short-term course and outcome of schizophrenia. As the treatment variable was not extensively studied during the IPSS little can be said about what other differences may have existed among the centres with regard to the nature of the treatment offered to schizophrenic patients, but this variable cannot be excluded as a possible source of differences in course and outcome.

3. Finally, the possibility must be considered that patients who present with the same symptomatology may in fact be suffering from disorders with very different biological bases, and that the patients in different cultures may differ with regard to the distribution of different disorders that may present with 'schizophrenic symptomatology', and therefore with regard to patients that may be expected to have a good or bad outcome.

At this point it is possible to state that IPSS results clearly provide support for the contention that the course and outcome of schizophrenia is affected by sociocultural conditions and lead to hypotheses that can be tested in subsequent studies.

12.1.1.3 Temporal consistency of symptomatology

The demonstration of the fact that schizophrenic patients tend to have the same types of symptoms at different points of time, particularly when they are in acute episodes of illness, would support the value of distinguishing such patients from others who are less likely to demonstrate such symptoms later in their lives, solidifies the argument that schizophrenia exists as a distinct entity and serves as a contribution to developing satisfactory and generally acceptable classification systems in psychiatry.

When the initial evaluation and second-year follow-up profiles of schizophrenic patients were compared to one another, it was found that the profiles were for the most part similar to one another and that the similarity was due mainly to similarities in negative and non-specific symptoms. When the same comparisons were done for only those patients who were psychotic at the time of second-year follow-up, again the initial evaluation and second-year follow-up profiles were significantly similar, and this time the similarities appeared to be in positive, negative, and non-specific symptoms.

Another indication of the temporal consistency of schizophrenic symptomatology can be seen from the comparison of CATEGO classifications on first and second-year follow-up. As was pointed out in Chapter 6, the percentage of initial evaluation schizophrenic patients considered to be psychotic on follow-up who fell into into the same CATEGO class on both occasions was quite high, ranging from 72 per cent in Washington to 100 per cent in London. This suggests that when schizophrenic patients are psychotic they tend to have the same type of clinical picture which they had at the other times they were psychotic.

This finding is further confirmed by the analysis carried out on psychotic episodes that occurred during the interval between initial evaluation and second-year follow-up. It was found that of those schizophrenic patients who did have subsequent psychotic episodes after the episode of inclusion the vast majority had definitely or probably schizophrenic episodes, although 16 per cent did have subsequent affective psychotic episodes.

The initial evaluation results of the IPSS indicate that schizophrenic patients with similar symptoms could be found in all of the centres involved in the study. The follow-up study demonstrated the temporal consistency of symptoms in those patients.

12.1.1.4 Cross-sectional picture of symptomatology

The results described in Chapter 6 indicate that at the time of second-year follow-up the level of psychopathology among patients considered to be schizophrenic at initial evaluation was low. Scores were particularly low on such positive psychotic symptoms as delusions, characteristic auditory hallucinations, other hallucinations and distortions of self-perception. Those symptoms which tended to be present were primarily negative and non-specific symptoms such as flatness of affect, lack of insight, and difficulties in co-operating.

Centre-by-centre comparisons of the shapes of the symptom profiles of the schizophrenic patient groups were carried out, and ANOVA analysis indicated that the only centre in which the profiles showed significant differences from the profiles of other centres was Moscow. This result is rather consistent with the results of Volume 1 of the IPSS report (WHO, 1973) where it was pointed out that the diagnosis of schizophrenia in Moscow appeared to be based on somewhat different criteria from other centres, with a greater emphasis on the course of illness.

Using the operational criteria outlined in Appendix 3 the 543 schizophrenic patients followed up were divided into three groups: psychotic, non-psychotic and asymptomatic. It was found that 202 patients were psychotic at the time of follow-up, 169 were symptomatic but not psychotic, and 172 were asymptomatic. Most of the pathology in the profile of the entire schizophrenic group was accounted for by the 202 psychotic patients. Centre-by-centre comparisons of the symptom profiles of the schizophrenic patients who were psychotic at second-year follow-up indicate that there were no significant differences among the profiles, although τ analysis did indicate a relatively low degree of similarity between the profiles of the Washington patients and those of some of the other centres.

Washington, in addition to Moscow was the centre in which schizophrenic patients appeared to be somewhat different symptomatologically from patients in other centres at initial evaluation.

Thus, it can be concluded that schizophrenic patients in the nine centres tended for the most part, two years after initial evaluation, to remain similar to one another, with psychotic patients resembling other psychotic patients and non-psychotic patients resembling other non-psychotic patients.

12.1.2 The course and outcome of schizophrenia compared with that of other functional psychoses

As discussed in Chapters 6 and 11, one prevalent hypothesis about schizophrenia has been that schizophrenic patients have a more severe course and outcome than patients with other functional psychoses. This view is based mainly on clinical impressions, since there are surprisingly few studies which have compared the course and outcome of schizophrenia with those of other disorders using a standardized and reliable methodology. The results of the current study do provide some support for this view. Although a not inconsiderable number of schizophrenic patients had a very good two-year course and outcome, as a group the schizophrenic patients did more poorly over the two-year follow-up period than patients with other functional psychoses. As a group they had the longest episodes of inclusion, the highest percentage of the follow-up period spent in a psychotic episode, the most severe pattern of course, the highest percentage of patients with severe social impairment during the follow-up period, the highest percentage of patients who were psychotic at the time of second-year follow-up, and the worst outcome in terms of overall outcome. Intracentre comparisons for the most part supported the findings from analyses for all centres combined. Although the intracentre differences were not always statistically significant, they were almost always in the direction of schizophrenic patients having a more severe course and outcome than patients in other diagnostic groups.

Among the patients in the psychotic diagnostic groups the manic patients tended to have the best outcome, although the differences among the manic, psychotic-depressive and other psychosis groups were statistically significant only for the length of the episode of inclusion and the distributions by pattern of course.

The degree of variability of outcome among patients with diagnosis of affective psychoses on initial evaluation was less marked than among patients with schizophrenic psychoses on initial evaluation. Although some patients with affective psychoses had a bad outcome, it was a rather small percentage, while a very high percentage of such patients had a relatively good outcome on most course and outcome variables.

When the course and outcome of schizophrenia were compared to those of affective psychoses in centres in developing and developed countries, it was found that the differences between the two diagnostic groups were statistically significant for every course and outcome variable for the group of centres in developed countries, and were not significant for any course and outcome variable in the group of centres in the developing countries. In the developing country centres the schizophrenic patients did have a more severe course and outcome than patients with affective psychoses for every outcome variable, but the differences did not reach the level of statistical significance. This suggests that although there are differences between the course and outcome of schizophrenic and affective psychoses in the developing country centres, these differences are much less marked than they are in the developed country centres. This is a striking finding which may be the result of any one of, or a combination of, a number of factors. It may be that the cultural influences on the mode of presentation of psychosis in developing countries makes it more difficult to distinguish between schizophrenia and affective psychosis during the acute phase of illness. Another possible explanation is that the influence of cultural factors on the course and outcome of psychotic patients in developing countries is so marked that it tends to diminish the differences in outcome among different psychotic groups. It may also be, as was hypothesized in the previous section, that there are several different biological bases to schizo-phrenia and that the schizophrenic patients in developing and developed countries may differ with regard to the distribution of different disorders which may present with schizophrenic symptomatology, with the result that the relationship between the course and prognosis of schizophrenia and affective psychoses differs in developing and developed countries. As the differences appear to be mainly the result of a less severe course of the schizophrenic patients in the centres in the developing countries, rather than differences in the course of the patients with affective psychoses in the two groups of centres, all of the factors mentioned in section 12.1.1 as possible explanations for the differences in the course of schizophrenia in the two groups of centres may also play a part in the differences between the course and outcome of the two diagnostic groups in the two groups of centres. Thus, this finding gives rise to many interesting hypotheses which can be tested in future studies.

It must again be emphasized that the degree to which the patients in this study, particularly the patients with affective psychoses, are representative of all patients in the relevant diagnostic groups is not known. However, in view of the fact that there exist so few studies in which the course and outcome of schizophrenia has been compared in a standardized way and particularly in view of the fact that comparisons in a variety of cultures using the same methodology are virtually non-existent, it can probably be said that the current study provides the best evidence to date that schizophrenia has a more severe course and outcome than those of other psychoses, particularly the affective psychoses, within developed countries, and that the differences are less marked in developing countries.

Although as a group the schizophrenic patients had a more severe course and outcome than the patients with psychotic depression, there was considerable overlap between the two diagnostic groups. The discriminant function analyses described in Chapter 11 indicate that when a composite score on course and outcome measures is used as the only discriminator between schizophrenia and psychotic depression, the probability of misclassification is relatively high (a minimum of about 40 per cent). On the other hand, the composite course and outcome score was a relatively good discriminator between schizophrenia and mania.

Thus, the two-year course and outcome data indicate that the course and outcome of schizophrenia and mania differ, and that there is little overlap between the two diagnostic groups with regard to course and outcome. They. also indicate that the course and outcome of schizophrenia differ from those of psychotic depression, although there is considerable overlap between the course and outcome of patients in these two diagnostic groups.

It will be interesting to see what happens to the relationship between the course and outcome of IPSS patients with schizophrenia and affective psychoses over time. If it is true that schizophrenia has a worse long-term course and outcome, then it would be expected that at the five-year follow-up the differences between these diagnostic groups would be greater, and that there would be less overlap between the course and outcome of schizophrenia and psychotic depression.

12.2 PREDICTORS OF COURSE AND OUTCOME

Although the range of variability in the course and outcome of schizophrenia has not generally been assumed to be as broad as suggested by the results of the two-year follow-up of the IPSS, the concepts of good and bad outcome of schizophrenia have been present in the literature for a long time, and many attempts have been made to identify various symptomatic, past history and sociodemographic factors that are highly correlated with good or bad outcome. The results of these studies are summarized in Chapter 10. The initial evaluation and two-year follow-up phases of the IPSS provide data which make it possible to consider the degree of the variance in the course and outcome of schizophrenia patients and patients with affective psychosis in this study that is explained by such predictors. These data have the advantage over the data used in many previous studies of predictors in that (a) they were collected in a prospective study; (b) both the initial evaluation and follow-up reassessment of psychopathology were carried out by well-trained investigators with the use of standardized research instruments; (c) the reliability of the clinical evaluation procedures was assessed both within and across research centres; and (d) they relate to patients from nine different parts of the world, adding a crosscultural dimension to the investigation of predictors.

The methodology of the analyses of predictive power is described in detail in Chapter 10. The major results can be considered under two major headings, those that provide information about the degree of the variance explained by generally recognized predictors and those that provide information about what appear to be the best sociodemographic, past history, and episode of inclusion predictors.

12.2.1 Degree of variance explained by predictors

No single predictor variable and no combination of a few 'key' predictor variables was capable of explaining a large proportion of the variance of any of the course and outcome measures for the schizophrenic patients. Thus the amount of the variance of any of the course and outcome variables that could be explained by an optimal combination of five predictors with the highest predictive power ranged from 8 to 22 per cent. When the 15 best predictors were used instead of the best five, the highest percentage of the variation explained by these predictors on any course and outcome measure was 27 per cent.

This finding has two important implications. The first is that no individual factor and no combination of a small number of factors appear to be capable of having a strong determining influence on the course and outcome of schizophrenia. The second is that a large part of the variance in the course and outcome of the schizophrenic patients was accounted for by factors not included among the predictors examined in this study. In considering what such factors might be, at least three possibilities immediately suggest themselves. The first is the treatment variables. No attempt was made to standardize the treatment of the patients in this study or to assess in a standardized way the differences in treatments given to the patients. Some probable areas of difference are apparent. Thus, in some centres, such as Ibadan and Agra, the involvement of the family in the direct care of the patient during the acute phase of illness was probably greater than in some of the other centres. The degree to which comprehensive rehabilitation services were available to the IPSS patients probably also differed among centres. Other less apparent differences may have existed.

Another factor which may account for some of the unexplained variance is that of intervening variables. Little information is available in this study, or in most other follow-up studies of schizophrenia, about how the patients differ with regard to what has happened to them in terms of important life events in the interval between initial evaluation and follow-up. Thus, differences in such factors as death or other loss of supportive relatives, friends or employers, changes in family financial status, and other life crises may account for an important part of the variance in course and outcome, but little information about this parameter is available.

It is also possible that some of the unexplained variance is the result of sociocultural factors not yet clearly delineated. This possibility is suggested by the fact that the introduction of the centres into the analyses as predictor variables generally increased the amount of the variance explained by some 1 to 3 per cent.

Finally, it is possible that some of the unexplained variance is the result of differences in the biological bases of variance disorders that present with the final common pathway of schizophrenic symptomatology.

12.2.1.1 *The relative predictive power of the three classes of predictors*

An important finding that emerged from the predictor analyses was the fact that the three classes of predictors — characteristics of the episode of inclusion (including type of onset, duration of episode prior to initial evaluation, and initial evaluation symptomatology on the level of 27 groups of units of analysis), sociodemographic variables (for example, age, sex, marital status, degree of social isolation, socioeconomic status, educational level, occupation) and past history variables (for example, history of past treatment or contact because of psychiatric disorder, history of behavioural problems, psychosexual difficulties, history of mental illness in relatives) – are about equal with regard to their predictive power.

12.2.1.2 Power of predictors in developing and developed countries

It is noteworthy that the amount of course and outcome variance that could be explained by the best predictors was different for the groups of schizophrenic patients in the developing and developed countries. The predictive power was considerably higher in the developed countries, where the five best predictors accounted for 24 to 30 per cent of the variance on course and outcome measures and the 15 best predictors accounted for 26 to 34 per cent of the variance. In comparison, in the centres in developing countries the best five predictors accounted for 13 to 21 per cent of the variance while the best 15 predictors accounted for 15 to 23 per cent of the variance.

This finding suggests that it is important to consider further the question of whether variables relevant for the prediction of course and outcome in one culture are equally relevant in other cultures. The data collection methods used in this study and the selection of items for the prediction analysis were based primarily on knowledge about variables described as prognostic in European and North American psychiatry. The finding that they have greater predictive power for the course and outcome of schizophrenia in developed countries than in developing countries is therefore not entirely surprising. It is quite possible that other variables not considered in the current or previous follow-up studies may be more relevant predictors for schizophrenia within the developing countries. The fact that on many of the analyses some of the centres emerged as strong predictors, accounting for a significant part of the otherwise unexplained variance, suggests that in these centres there are some factors with predictive power that are not described by any of the predictive variables studied.

12.2.1.3 Predictive power in schizophrenia and affective psychoses

In general, the proportion of the variance accounted for by the best five and the best 15 predictors was higher in the case of the affective psychoses than in the case of schizophrenia. Thus, for example, the best five predictors of overall outcome explain 32 per cent of the variance for patients with affective psychoses and 22 per cent for schizophrenia. The comparable figures for the best 15 predictors are 45 per cent and 26 per cent.

There are several possible explanations for this finding. One factor may be the smaller number of depressive patients involved in the analyses, as the closer the number of patients is to the number of variables, the higher the percentage of the variance explained by the variables. Another possibility is that the patients with affective psychosis in this study were more homogeneous with regard to the underlying bases of the disorder than the schizophrenic patients.

12.2.2 Specific predictors

The multiple regression analyses described in Chapter 10 allow conclusions to be made about which predictors within each class of predictors are the best predictors, and about the relationship between individual centres and prognosis.

12.2.2.1 Sociodemographic predictors

Three sociodemographic predictors appear consistently among the best predictors for all course and outcome measures: social isolation, which is associated with a poor outcome, marital status—widowed, divorced or separated, which is associated with a poor outcome, and marital status—married, which is associated with a good outcome. These predictors usually remained among the best sociodemographic predictors when the centres were added as variables, indicating that their predictive power was not associated only with particular centres. They also appeared consistently among the five best predictors when all three classes of predictors were considered together.

Other sociodemographic predictors which appeared often, but less consistently than those mentioned above, were high educational level and male sex, both associated with a poor outcome, and professional occupation associated with a good outcome.

Social isolation was one of the most consistently good predictors of outcome of any of the three classes of predictors. This is particularly noteworthy because the estimate of the patient's degree of isolation at initial evaluation was made by a psychiatric social worker on a five-point scale and the social worker was instructed to use his judgement to assess the degree of social isolation in the light of his experience and knowledge of conditions in the catchment area. Since differences in interpreting what was social isolation might be expected under such circumstances it is interesting that the predictive power of social isolation did not seem to be related to any particular centre. The consistency with which this factor appears as a predictor of poor outcome underlines it as an important area for further investigation. Thus, it will be useful to determine in more detail exactly what has gone into the evaluation of social isolation.

The finding that being married tended to be associated with good outcome, and being divorced, widowed or separated with a bad outcome, is consistent with findings of previous studies. The fact that the relationship between marital status and outcome did not appear to be associated only with particular centres suggests that such factors were important in all centres in the study. It also underlines the effects of relationships within the family on the outcome of schizophrenia as an important area for future investigation.

The association of male sex with a poor outcome and of a professional occupational level with a good outcome are not so surprising in light of previous hypotheses and studies, but the finding that high educational level is associated with poor outcome is perhaps somewhat surprising. This association occurred primarily in Ibadan, as indicated by the fact that this variable usually dropped out of the list of best predictors and was replaced by the variable 'Ibadan' when the centres were included in the analyses. The investigators from Ibadan noted that students and those just completing higher education there are under considerable academic stress and pressure to obtain good jobs, and that this may explain this finding. This question will be further explored in Ibadan in a future substudy.

12.2.2.2 Past history predictors

Three past history predictors consistently emerged among the best predictors of this class for all outcome measures: history of past psychiatric treatment, poor psychosexual adjustment, and unfavourable environment, all associated with poor outcome. Another variable, history of behaviour disorder (for example, enuresis, temper tantrums, night terrors, truancy, stealing, aggressive or destructive actions, hyperactivity), was also associated with poor outcome on a number of outcome measures. Of all these variables, past history of psychiatric treatment was the one which also appeared consistently among the best five predictors for all three classes of predictors combined.

The finding that history of past psychiatric treatment was a predictor of poor outcome among the schizophrenic patients in the study suggests that patients who have had previous periods of illness are more likely to do poorly than those that have not. The exclusion criteria of the IPSS were designed in part to exclude chronic patients from the study. Nevertheless, this finding suggests that relative chronicity was a predictor of poor outcome.

The presence of a history of behaviour symptoms and poor psychosexual adjustment probably reflect disturbances of premorbid personality, and the finding that they predict outcome is consistent with previous studies which indicate that patients with premorbid personality problems do less well than patients with a good premorbid personality adjustment.

The variable 'unfavourable environment' consisted of four items — 'forced to leave home and/or emigrate', 'effects of alien culture', 'effects of belonging to a particular religious sect', and 'effects of belonging to a minority group'. The finding that this variable predicts poor outcome therefore suggests that cultural alienation may be related to poor outcome of schizophrenia. This area will be an important one to investigate further in future studies.

12.2.2.3 Characteristics of the episode of inclusion

The items within this class of predictors were symptoms (on the level of 27 groups of units and analysis) and other factors directly related to the episode of inclusion such as the duration of the episode of inclusion prior to initial evaluation and the type of onset of the episode of inclusion (for example, sudden, insidious etc). Two factors appeared among the best predictors consistently: duration of the length of episode of inclusion prior to initial evaluation (long duration associated with a poor outcome) and insidious onset (associated with a poor outcome). Other predictors included derealization and affective symptoms which were associated with a good outcome, and flatness of affect, which was associated with a poor outcome. Other symptoms which appeared as good predictors for some of the outcome variables were psychophysiological symptoms and cooperation difficulties, circumstances-related, associated with a good outcome, and indication of personality change, associated with a bad outcome.

The finding that a long duration of the episode of inclusion before initial evaluation and insidious onset of the episode of inclusion emerged consistently as predictors supports the concept that the less acute the onset of schizophrenia and the longer the period of time that elapses between onset of symptoms and initiation of treatment, the worse the outcome.

The fact that affective symptoms were associated with a good outcome and flatness of affect and indications of personality change with a bad outcome is of course consistent with the prevalent views that the stronger the affective component of a schizophrenic illness the better the prognosis, while the more affective responsiveness and personality structure are disturbed the worse the prognosis. The frequent emergence of the symptom derealization as a predictor of good outcome is more surprising. It should first of all be noted that derealization as defined in the PSE evaluation is different from Langfeldt's concept of derealization, which refers mainly to a psychotic disturbance of the patient's perception of reality usually associated with schizophrenia. Derealization in the PSE refers to feelings of unreality or changed appearance of things, people, or familiar surroundings, and changes in subjective time perception, but not necessarily reflecting a break with reality. It is possible that the ability to notice and communicate to others the derealization phenomena covered by the PSE item may reflect other aspects of personality and psychopathology such as level of intelligence, severity of the disorder, acuteness of the disorder and so on, which in themselves mitigate against unfavourable outcome.

Since the group of units of analysis 'psychophysiological symptoms' included symptoms that usually reflect an affective component of the illness (for example, early waking, symptoms worse in the morning, disturbances of sleep, appetite, and libido), it is understandable that this symptom was associated with good outcome.

One factor which may seem noteworthy on first glance is that symptoms did not often emerge as very good predictors. Thus, it is factors related to the type of onset of the episode of inclusion that are the best predictors in this class of predictors, while derealization is the only symptom that enters into the combined best five predictors for all classes considered together.

However, it should be noted that the predictor analysis was carried out on the level of 27 groups of units of analysis, while many of the symptomatic features which would be expected to distinguish among types of outcome can be assessed only at the level of the 129 units of analysis. For example, although delusions (a group of units of analysis) may not be a good predictor of outcome, either grandiose delusions or persecutory delusions (both units of analysis) might be good predictors. In fact when the 129 units of analysis were used in multiple regression analysis of the extremes of the pattern of course outcome measure for schizophrenic patients, it was found that the proportion of the variance explained by the 129 units of analysis was very high. For the comparison of pattern of course groups 1 and 2 versus group 7, the multiple correlation coefficient was 0.6651 which means that 129 UAs accounted for 44.2 per cent of the variance. The predictors with high partial regression coefficients and F-ratio values are presented in Chapter 10.

It must also be remembered that symptomatic factors have already gone into defining the schizophrenic group of patients. The fact that schizophrenic patients in the study had a worse course and outcome than patients with affective psychoses indicates that the symptoms distinguishing the two groups of patients have considerable predictive power.

12.2.2.4 Overall best predictors

For each course and outcome variable, the five best predictors identified for each of the three classes of predictors were analysed to arrive at a list of the five best predictors of any class for the outcome variable. Three variables appeared as good predictors for most of the outcome variables: social isolation, long duration of the length of the episode of inclusion prior to the initial evaluation, and past history of psychiatric treatment, all associated with a poor outcome. Three other variables also emerged often as good overall predictors: history of behaviour disorder, associated with a bad outcome, type of onset (sudden associated with a good outcome, insidious with a bad outcome), and marital status (married associated with a good outcome and widowed, divorced and separated associated with a poor outcome). The significance of each of these findings is discussed above.

12.2.2.5 Prediction of outcome in different centres

The design of the IPSS provided an opportunity to consider the important question of whether variables which are good predictors of outcome are the same in different cultures. Three sets of analysis of the follow-up phase data give information about this question.

After the best predictors in each of the three classes of predictors were determined, the individual field research centres were added as variables. That is, belonging to the Ibadan field research centre, for example, was considered as a variable along with the variables already identified as best predictors within the class. When this was done, in many cases one or more field research centres replaced one or more of the variables as a best predictor. This means either that the predictors replaced were highly correlated with the centres which replaced them or that the centres themselves were such stronger predictors of outcome than any of the predictors within the class assessed that they outweighed some of them. Thus, Ibadan consistently appears as a good predictor of good outcome on many of the course and outcome variables, while a number of the other centres also appear, although less frequently.

To test the hypothesis that the best predictors might be different in different cultures, the multiple regression analyses were repeated for the group of centres in developed countries and for the group of centres in the developing countries. The results indicated that some of the best predictors were consistently good predictors in both types of centres, while others were good predictors only in one or the other type of centre.

Two variables appeared consistently among the five best predictors for every course and outcome measure in both groups of countries: social isolation and duration of the inclusion episode prior to the initial evaluation. There were three other variables among the best predictors for at least one outcome variable in both groups of centres: a high score on indications of personality change, a high score on derealization, and a high score on psychophysiological symptoms.

On the other hand, the following variables were among the best five predictors only in developing countries and did not appear among the best five predictors for any of the outcome variables in the centres in the developed countries: marital status — widowed, divorced, or separated, a high score on cooperation difficulties, educational level, history of mental illness in the family, and past contacts with other agencies because of psychiatric problems.

Four variables were among the five best predictors for at least one outcome variable in the group of centres in developed countries only: male sex, history of physical illness or disability, professional occupation, and managerial or clerical occupation.

These results suggest that while some predictors, particularly social isolation and the duration of the episode of inclusion prior to initial evaluation, are good predictors in both groups of centres, there are also considerable differences between the two groups of centres with regard to the best predictors of outcome.

As mentioned above, the degree of the variance in outcome explained by the best predictors was consistently higher for schizophrenic patients in the developed countries than for those in the developing countries.

Stepwise multiple regression analysis of the 15 best predictors of overall outcome was also carried out within each of the centres having a sufficient number of followed-up patients to satisfy the requirements of this statistical technique. The results, presented in Chapter 10, also suggest that there are differences among centres with regard to the variables which are the best predictors of outcome in different cultures.

12.2.2.6 Best predictors of outcome for affective psychoses

Another question of considerable interest is whether the predictors of good and bad outcome are similar across diagnoses. The IPSS follow-up data make it possible to compare the best predictors of outcome for schizophrenic patients with the best predictors for patients with affective psychoses. When the five best predictors for all classes of predictors combined are compared between the two diagnostic groups, it appears that there is a considerable difference in the best predictors.

No predictor appeared consistently among the best five for every outcome variable in both diagnostic groups. The only variable among the five best predictors for every outcome measure among depressive patients was poor psychosexual adjustment. Though this variable was not among the best five overall predictors for any outcome measure for the schizophrenic patients it was consistently among the five best past history variables for the schizophrenic patients. Thus, this aspect of premorbid personality adjustment seems to be a predictor of poor outcome for both diagnostic groups.

Only four predictors were among the best predictors for at least one outcome measure for both diagnostic groups: social isolation, which was consistently a predictor of poor outcome for schizophrenics and less consistently for patients with affective psychoses, past history of physical illness or disability, which was a good predictor for both groups, and past history of psychiatric treatment and flatness of affect, which predicted in opposite directions for the two diagnostic groups. Thus, past psychiatric treatment was a predictor of poor outcome for schizophrenic patients and a predictor of good outcome for depressive patients. This is not so surprising, since previous episodes of illness generally are assumed to carry a poorer prognosis for schizophrenic patients than for patients with affective psychosis. On the other hand, the fact that flatness of affect is a predictor of good outcome for patients with affective psychoses is puzzling.

There were a large number of variables among the best predictors for only one of the two diagnostic groups. The most striking differences were the fact that long duration of the episode of inclusion prior to the initial evaluation and insidious onset, both predictors of poor outcome for many outcome measures in schizophrenia, were not among the best predictors for any outcome measure for patients with affective psychoses. Other variables which were good predictors only for schizophrenia were male sex and marital status – married, while variables which were good predictors only for affective patients included young age, rural residency, no mental illness in the family, non-auditory hallucinations, qualitative thought disorder, and occupational categories of sales and service and manual worker.

The number of patients with affective psychoses in the study is relatively small and little is known about how representative they are of all affective psychoses in the respective centres. Therefore, these results must be considered with caution. However, they do suggest the possibility that the best predictors of outcome are different for schizophrenia and affective psychoses.

12.2.2.7 General conclusions about predictors

The IPSS findings have offered considerable support for a number of hypotheses about the relationship between specific predictors and prognosis of schizophrenia. Factors often considered to be prognostic of good outcome, such as affective symtomatology, acute onset of illness, evidence of good premorbid personality adjustment, and being married, did in fact appear as good predictors of good outcome, while other factors often considered to be predictive of poor outcome, such as insidious onset, long duration of illness before initiation of treatment, evidence of difficulties of premorbid personality adjustment, and being widowed, divorced or separated were in fact good predictors of poor outcome. At the same time a number of new findings appeared. The two-year follow-up results suggest that the best predictors of outcome of schizophrenia differ among centres, and particularly between centres in developing and developed countries. Furthermore, the results suggest that the predictive factors identified for study in European and North American cultures may not be very suitable for the study of prognosis in other cultures.

The follow-up data also suggest that a large part of the variance of the course and outcome of schizophrenia is due to factors which have not yet been identified, and emphasize that no one variable and no combination of a few variables identified thus far has a very determining influence on the course and outcome of schizophrenia.

Furthermore, the results indicate that those factors which are good predictors of course and outcome for schizophrenia do not appear to be good predictors for other disorders such as the affective psychoses.

It must be remembered that two years is a short period of time in the course of schizophrenia, and the current results can only be considered to be tentative, based as they are on interim course and outcome. As a result of the uncertainty about the degree to which the IPSS patients are representative of other patients with schizophrenia and other functional psychoses in the populations served by the centres, generalizations from the IPSS material should be made with considerable caution. However, despite these cautions, a number of interesting hypotheses about the relationship between sociodemographic, past history, and symptomatic variables and the course and outcome of schizophrenia in several different cultures have been generated.

12.3 APPROACHES TOWARD THE ASSESSMENT OF DIAGNOSTIC VALIDITY

Although existing classification concepts and practices have been criticized for practical and theoretical shortcomings, classification continues to play an important role in psychiatry, in relation to the planning and monitoring of mental health services, teaching and research. Efforts to improve the existing classifications of mental disorders would require an empirical assessment of their usefulness, reliability and validity.

The classification categories for the major psychiatric disorders — schizophrenia and affective psychoses — have been in use for several decades, but studies attempting to evaluate their validity in a systematic way have been rare. Moreover, very little has been done to assess the applicability and validity of the classification concepts originated by Kraepelin and other psychiatrists in Europe, to psychiatric patients in cultures other than European and North American.

In view of this fact, the opportunity provided by the IPSS to carry out a study of the validity of diagnostic categories in a crosscultural context, was important and in a sense unique. Although a two-year period of follow-up is too short to permit a definitive assessment of diagnostic validity, the preliminary analysis which was carried out led to results which may provide a basis for further investigations.

The four different classification systems used in the initial evaluation of the IPSS patients were clinical diagnosis (recorded according to the International Classification of Diseases (ICD), eighth revision – WHO, 1967); computer–simulated reference diagnosis (the CATEGO program – Wing, Cooper and Sartorius, 1974), a statistical clustering method (McKeon, 1967), and the assignment of the schizophrenic patients to a concordant or a non-concordant group on the basis of the results of all the three classifications listed above (see Volume 1 of the IPSS report – WHO, 1973).

These classification systems were assessed and, to the degree that was possible, compared with one another in terms of predictive and content validity. Predictive validity in this investigation referred to the extent to which allocation of patients to different diagnostic categories on initial evaluation predicted differences in the two-year course and outcome of the patients. Content validity was related to the degree to which patients allocated to different diagnostic categories showed different patterns of symptomatology at initial evaluation and on follow-up. The investigation was carried out by means of discriminant function analysis which allowed to consider statistically a large number of variables related to the symptomatology, course and outcome of the patients.

12.3.1 Predictive validity of diagnostic distinctions

The predictive validity of diagnosis was assessed by comparing pairs of diagnostic groups as defined in the different classification systems employed in the study, according to the degree of discrimination that could be achieved between the patients in the two groups in terms of six measures of course and outcome condensed into a single composite variate (for a description of the technique of analysis, see Chapter 11). Several conclusions were reached.

1. The degree of discrimination was relatively low for all pairs of diagnostic categories compared. This means that a multivariate prediction of course and outcome – that is, a prediction of the position of the patients on each of the six dimensions of course and outcome, would result in a misclassification of a considerable proportion of the patients, if the prediction is based on diagnosis only. In other words, there was a sizeable overlap of the distributions of patients with different diagnoses over a discriminant function dimension defined by the six course and outcome measures.

2. Although the level of discrimination was low, some diagnostic and classification categories were more strongly associated with course and outcome than others. Thus, the distinction between schizophrenia and mania with regard to course and outcome was relatively good (distance coefficient of 1.36) while the distinction between schizophrenia and depressive psychoses was poor (distance coefficient of 0.58) and would lead to a misclassification (into prognostic groups) in 35 to 40 per cent of the patients. A better discrimination between depressive and

schizophrenic patients could be achieved if only the concordant group of schizophrenics was included in the comparison. The distinction between patients in CATEGO class S and class D in terms of course and outcome and outcome was better than between the clinical diagnostic groups of schizophrenia and depressive psychosis.

3. When alternative classifications of subgroups of patients within the diagnostic category of schizophrenia were examined, the ICD clinical subtypes turned out to be better discriminators of prognosis than the concordant/non-concordant classification. This finding could be the result of: (a) psychiatrists using for their clinical diagnosis of a particular subtype of schizophrenia items of information which were prognostically important but were not included in the decision rules and statistical considerations playing a role in the classification of the patients into concordant and non-concordant groups; (b) the lack of internal homogeneity and the greater variability of the non-concordant groups of schizophrenics which was obtained through exclusion of the concordant patients.

The finding that many of the diagnostic distinctions can result in the misclassification of a proportion of patients with regard to two-year course and outcome does not mean that the diagnostic groups overlap completely and that there are no differences between patients classified into different diagnostic categories in terms of prognosis. As already emphasized, the schizophrenic patients had consistently worse course and outcome characteristics than the patients suffering from psychotic depression or mania. The differences between the diagnostic groups retained their statistical significance when a multivariate approach was used to evaluate course and outcome. However, the finding of statistical significance does not necessarily imply a theoretical or practical importance of the differences found, and this fact was illustrated by the misclassification rate obtained for each pair of diagnostic groups. In conclusion, it can be said that with regard to two-year course and outcome the predictive validity of the different classification categories – clinical diagnosis, computer-simulated diagnosis, statistical clusters, and the concordant/non-concordant classification of schizophrenics, received support as far as statistical significance is concerned, but few of these categories could separate sufficiently high proportions of patients in terms of measures of course and outcome.

12.3.2 Content validity of diagnostic distinctions

Content validity of diagnostic distinctions was also assessed pairwise, but in this analysis the multivariate dimension on which the distributions of patients allocated to different diagnostic groups were plotted consisted of the composite scores on all the 27 groups of units of analysis. In some instances, when the number of patients was sufficiently large, the analysis was repeated with the 129 units (symptoms) instead of groups of units. The main conclusions from this investigation were as follows.

1. The content validity of most classification categories was high – that is, the

differences of symptomatology (described in a multivariate way including simultaneously a very large number of symptoms or groups of symptoms) were considerable between the diagnostic categories and there was little overlap. This represented a general trend observed on both initial evaluation and follow-up. However, if the symptomatological discrimination between diagnostic group on initial evaluation and on follow-up is compared, some decrease will be noted, indicating that patients allocated to different diagnostic groups were becoming less different from each other in the course of time. This could not be explained by the fact that many patients were in a state of remission during the follow-up examinations, because the decrease of the symptomatological distance between the diagnostic groups was also present in the subgroups of patients who were psychotic on follow-up.

2. With regard to the symptomatological distinctions between patients with schizophrenia and depressive psychoses, the highest discrimination achieved was between the group of concordant schizophrenics and the group of depressive patients. CATEGO classes S and D were second best in this respect, and the clinical diagnostic groups were third. The clinical categories however achieved a better discrimination between schizophrenic and manic patients than did the CATEGO classes S and M.

3. For those pairs of diagnostic groups in which it was possible to repeat the analysis of the level of 129 symptoms instead of 27 groups of units (clinical groups of schizophrenia and depressive psychoses, and CATEGO classes S and D), the discrimination achieved with symptoms was better. This increase was particularly marked in the distinction between CATEGO classes S and D. This finding suggests that some discriminatory items of information may have been lost when symptoms were condensed into 27 groups of units of analysis.

4. Within the group of schizophrenic patients the highest level of symptomatological discrimination was obtained with the subgroup of simple and hebephrenic schizophrenics compared with the subgroup of paranoid schizophrenics. The differences between concordant and non-concordant schizophrenic patients were also considerable but did not achieve the same level.

Generally, the results of the preliminary investigation of the validity of diagnostic and classification categories used in the IPSS suggest that classifications and diagnoses are better predictors of symptomatology that patients may develop at different points in time than of non-symptomatic dimensions of course and outcome. The results also indicate that classificatory categories which predict course and outcome better than others, are not necessarily those which predict symptomatology better than others, and vice versa. No single classification system among of the four used in the study appeared to be unqualifiably superior to alternative systems on all criteria. However, the fact that diagnostic categories could discriminate with statistical significance between groups of patients in a cross-cultural study is important, since such a study is a more stringent test of diagnostic validity than assessments of diagnosis within a specific cultural setting.

12.4 FEASIBILITY OF CARRYING OUT A LARGE-SCALE TRANSCULTURAL FOLLOW-UP STUDY OF PATIENTS WITH FUNCTIONAL PSYCHOSES

12.4.1 Finding and re-evaluating patients

In the planning of large-scale transcultural psychiatric studies, it is extremely useful to have some idea of how many patients it may be possible to find and re-evaluate during follow-up phases in various cultures. Little information concerning this point is available from the literature. The IPSS results suggest that despite the multitude of problems involved in the long-term follow-up of patients in any centre these can, for the most part, be overcome, even in centres in which local geographical and sociocultural factors make such follow-up particularly difficult. The fact that it was possible to trace 97.1% of the original 1202 patients in the study and to reinterview 75.5 per cent with a standardized instrument for the assessment of present mental state two years after their initial evaluation must indeed be encouraging to transcultural researchers. This is particularly so because there were no clear differences between centres in developed and developing countries with regard to the numbers of patients who could be traced and reinterviewed. It was possible to obtain social and past psychiatric history material about all the patients reinterviewed. In addition there were 93 patients not reinterviewed about whom it was possible to obtain detailed psychiatric and social history material from other sources, so that detailed follow-up information was obtained for about 77.1 per cent of the original material.

Although it was thus feasible to trace and obtain information about a high percentage of patients, it must be pointed out that a very great effort was required to obtain this information. More than 2100 hours were spent assessing IPSS patients with two-year follow-up schedules and almost 4000 manhours were spent carrying out home visits. In some centres it was particularly difficult to arrange for patients to come to the field research centre during the follow-up period, and home visits were essential to the success of the project in these countries; for example, it was necessary to carry out 104 home visits in Ibadan.

These findings have important implications for the planning and management of such large-scale studies as they identify factors that should be taken into consideration when funding and staffing decisions are made.

The major reason for which patients were not reinterviewed was lack of sufficient personnel. In countries without case registers and in which local factors such as a geographically large catchment area, poor transportation facilities, lack of street designations, and major seasonal variations which make travel to or from a centre difficult during long periods of time exist, considerable effort must be made to carry out follow-up evaluation. Although centres in developing countries were just as able to locate patients as centres in developed countries, it was often quite difficult to make arrangements to do so. It was felt by the investigators that under such circumstances it was particularly important to have staff who had been with the study throughout its entire duration, and who were very familiar with the geographical and sociocultural conditions of the catchment area of the centre.

Thus, it should not be assumed that since a two-year follow-up was quite feasible in the IPSS that follow-ups in various cultures will be feasible under other conditions. It is clear from the IPSS experience that in projects in which it is hoped that large numbers of patients from a variety of cultures can be followed up over relatively long periods of time, considerable funds and manhours must be devoted to accomplish such follow-ups.

It has sometimes been assumed that it would be more difficult to find non-psychotic patients than psychotic patients on follow-up because they would be less likely to keep in contact with psychiatric facilities. Although the IPSS has been primarily concerned with schizophrenic patients, the results of the two-year follow-up suggest that it is no more difficult to find and reinterview non-psychotic patients and that there is no difference between schizophrenic patients and patients with affective psychoses with regard to the ease with which they can be followed up.

12.4.2 Feasibility of maintaining coordination and organizational continuity

There has been virtually no previous experience with attempts to maintain the organizational continuity of a project involving the psychiatric assessment of large numbers of patients in a variety of centres over the world over long periods of time. It is a reassuring finding that the IPSS has demonstrated that it was feasible to maintain coordination and organizational continuity within and among the widely separated teams of researchers throughout the two-year follow-up period. Of the 20 collaborating investigators from the field research centres involved in the project in 1967, 16 were still with the project to the end of 1973, that is to the end of the period of second-year follow-up data analysis.

Undoubtedly such continuity was possible largely because of the decision to utilize local personnel for the study. Such a policy would seem to be of great importance for transcultural research studies intended to include follow-up studies, since local personnel are likely to remain in the centre throughout the length of the follow-up periods. Furthermore, such a policy makes it possible for new investigators joining the study to be trained at the centre, making it easier to maintain continuity.

One of the outgrowths of the maintenance of the same investigators throughout the study was the fact that their extended collaboration with one another provided opportunities for the discussion of research areas of common interest and as a result such investigators began to develop a number of substudies arising out of their IPSS work. Thus, the organizational coordination and continuity of the IPSS has led to the beginnings of a network of research centres interested and trained in transcultural psychiatric work. This, of course, was one of the initial aims of the study and this aim has been achieved to a very great extent.

The presence of such a network also provided an opportunity for the development of training programmes for researchers interested in transcultural psychiatric work and a formal joint training programme in epidemiological and social psychiatry in IPSS centres has now been made available to young mental health workers throughout the world.

Three aspects of the organization of the IPSS were of particular importance to maintaining co-ordination: (a) the existence of central co-ordination of the study from WHO headquarters in Geneva; (b) the possibility for regular, frequent contact among the collaborating investigators; and (c) the development of special studies within the main study which stimulated collaborators to work closely together on particular areas of special mutual interest.

12.5 DEVELOPMENT OF INSTRUMENTS AND PROCEDURES FOR FOLLOW-UP STUDIES

One of the major aims of the IPSS has been to determine whether it is possible to develop applicable, standardized instruments which can be used to assess reliably the current mental status, past psychiatric history and social history of patients in various cultures. The initial evaluation of the study indicated that the Present State Examination (PSE) was readily applicable in all the cultures of the study and that it could be used reliably by psychiatrists in the different centres for the assessment of a patient's current mental status.

During the follow-up phase of the study, the PSE was again found to be applicable in all of the centres of the study. However, two major points were made by the investigators concerning the applicability of the PSE as an assessment instrument during a follow-up period in which the majority of the patients were not acutely ill. The first point is that some patients who were felt to have residual minor symptoms and impairments of functioning did not score positively on any of the PSE items. The psychiatrists' clinical sense told them that the patient was not completely recovered although the PSE ratings did not indicate any psychopathology. These observations by the IPSS psychiatrists suggest the need for the further development of assessment instruments for evaluating patients during the non-acute stages of their disorder. Such schedules may need to place more emphasis on subtle and minor degrees of psychopathology, and particularly on such negative symptoms as lack of ability to enjoy life, lack of ability to form meaningful relationships with others, and lack of ability to function satisfactorily at a level that might be expected for their educational and sociocultural background.

The second problem noted was that in a number of instances the interviewer felt that a symptom covered by the PSE was present, but that the patient had learned to deny the symptom and answered in the negative all probes concerning the presence of this symptom. An example is the schizophrenic patient who still has delusions, but who had learned that it is best not to tell anyone about them. Often such a patient gives a few clues in his non-verbal manner or in the manner in which he denies the presence of such symptoms that he is in fact still deluded, and this contributes to the interviewer's sense that this patient is not in fact asymptomatic although the PSE ratings may indicate that he is.

The assessment of the reliability of the PSE at follow-up underlined some of the difficulties of assessing reliability of an instrument during a follow-up phase, when it can be expected that for most patients few symptoms will be present. In such a situation it is difficult to determine whether positive and negative agreement on ratings should be considered separately and to decide what level of agreement is indicative of significant reliability. On the one hand, since most items will be rated negatively, agreement on negative ratings may not indicate as much about reliability as agreement on positive ratings. On the other hand, the ability of psychiatrists to agree that a symptom is not present is certainly an important part of their reliability. In addition to these problems, there are a number of areas of confusion concerning the assessment of the reliability of the use of assessment instruments that stem from the fact that such instruments are used for different purposes and the fact that there are different types of reliability. In an attempt to resolve a number of these problems, a new method of assessing had to be developed for the IPSS. Using this method it could be shown that the reliability of the second-year follow-up assessment of psychopathology with the PSE was high (see Chapter 4 for details).

12.5.1 Follow-up psychiatric history and follow-up social description schedules

There had been considerable experience with the use of the PSE within individual cultures for some ten years prior to the IPSS. However, there were no standardized instruments for the evaluation of psychiatric history and social history for which a similar body of experience was available. Therefore new schedules were developed specifically for the IPSS. As was the case with the development of the initial evaluation schedules, emphasis at this stage of instrument development was placed on developing applicable, useful, and adequate items rather than on assessment of metric characteristics of the schedules. In general, these schedules were found to be applicable under field conditions at the field research centres though some difficulties were noted. On the basis of the experience gained modifications were introduced into the follow-up schedules used in the five-year follow-up concerning, for example, the assessment of the pattern of course, types of intervening episodes, occupational history and assessments of the individual's adjustment in areas such as relationship with others, overall outcome, and treatment compliance.

Thus, it can be concluded that the IPSS experience has demonstrated the applicability of a standardized assessment instrument for the follow-up evaluation of mental status (the PSE) in a variety of cultures, and the fact that it can be used reliably by psychiatrists in these cultures in a follow-up study. Furthermore, initial steps have been made toward developing transculturally applicable past history and social history schedules, but significant problems remain in this area, and it is hoped that improvements made during the development of the five-year follow-up schedule will help to resolve them.

12.6 CONCLUSIONS AND HYPOTHESES

The results described above provide considerable support for the usefulness of the conventional system of clinical classification and for the hypotheses and suppositions that underlie that system, and at the same time point out some of its shortcomings. One of the basis suppositions underlying the clinical classification of the functional psychoses is that the classification of patients into separate groups on the basis of differences in symptomatology is useful for predicting what will happen to these patients in the future. Several of the follow-up findings indicate that this is in fact the case. The demonstration that the schizophrenic group of patients had a more severe course and outcome than the other patients in the study indicates that symptomatological differentiations are of importance. The finding that when schizophrenic patients have subsequent episodes the episodes are schizophrenic in type and when patients with affective psychotic episodes have subsequent episodes the episodes are affective in type also indicates the predictive usefulness of the clinical system of classification. It is also encouraging to find that symptoms are not only good discriminators between schizophrenia and affective psychosis on initial evaluation, but also between the patients in each of those groups who were psychotic on second-year follow-up. The fact that course and outcome discriminated better between CATEGO class S and CATEGO class D patients than between patients with clinical diagnoses of schizophrenia and psychotic depression indicates that the more strictly diagnostic categories are defined the greater their usefulness in predicting course and outcome.

The initial evaluation phase of the IPSS indicated that it was possible to identify patients in each of the three major psychotic categories – schizophrenia, mania, and psychotic depression – symptomatologically similar within each category and different from patients in the other categories. The two-year follow-up phase indicates that there were important differences in the course and outcome of the schizophrenic patients and the patients with affective psychoses, although there were areas of considerable overlap, particularly between schizophrenia and psychotic depression.

With regard to the subclassification of schizophrenia, it was noted in Volume 1 of the IPSS report that on the level of broad areas of psychopathology such as the 27 groups of units of analysis (GUAs) the symptom profiles of the subgroups did not appear to be very different from one another, although there were indications that on a more specific level such as the 129 units of analysis (UAs) there were some important differences. The follow-up results provide some additional support for some aspects of the subclassification of schizophrenia. In particular, it appears that simple, hebephrenic, paranoid and unspecified schizophrenics had the worst two-year course and outcome while catatonic, acute and schizo-affective schizophrenics had the best course and outcome. When discriminant function analysis was carried out on the basis of initial evaluation symptomatology (129 UAs) of these two groups of subgroups, there was good discrimination between them. Discriminant function analysis on the basis of a combined course and outcome score suggested that the simple and hebephrenic subtypes on the one hand, and the schizo-affective subtype on the other hand, seem to occupy the two ends of a continuum, with the paranoid subtype occupying an intermediate position.

Although there has recently been increasing realization that schizophrenia is not always characterized by a chronic disabling course, the view that schizophrenia usually has a poor outcome, while affective psychoses usually have a good outcome

is still quite prevalent. The lack of standardized assessment and diag
procedures has often made it difficult to answer the question of whether
outcome schizophrenic patients differ from other schizophrenics, and there has
been a certain amount of circular reasoning by which patients with a good outcome
are by definition considered not to be schizophrenic. The results of the two-year
follow-up indicate that, at least as far as short-term course is concerned,
symptomatologically similar schizophrenic patients may differ greatly with regard to
course and outcome. This finding, of course, focuses additional interest on the
question of what factors are associated with the different types of outcome. The
results of the IPSS also provide some indications about particular factors which
should be explored further. The striking finding that the course and outcome of
schizophrenia differs in the different centres of the study, and particularly that it
appears to be less severe in the developing centres, suggests the importance of
further investigations concerning the interaction between culture and the course of
the disorder.

At this point we can only speculate that 'culture' in a global sense has an effect
on the course of schizophrenia. It is now possible and necessary to explore this
possibility in well-planned studies and if it is confirmed to attempt to identify
which culture-specific factors have such an effect.

The consistent finding that certain social variables are good predictors of
outcome and that such variables are just as good predictors as symptomatic
variables underlines this as an important area for future research. Variables such as
social isolation and marital status appeared as strong predictors of various outcome
measures in various cultures. More detailed studies are needed about the
relationship of outcome to such factors as the patient's integration within the
family, the structure of the family, the family's integration within the social
structure, and the effect of the patient's illness on the family, the level of economic
development within the culture, degree of social mobility within the culture, and
the type of health-care systems available.

It is apparent that some of the important areas of future study will need to be
included in the context of large-scale international studies, while others can be
examined in smaller local studies. The IPSS has demonstrated how a large-scale
international study generates many hypotheses which can be examined in more
detail on a local level. Crossculturally applicable instruments have been developed
during the course of the IPSS which can now be used in a variety of cultures. For
some of the areas important for future research, instruments which have been
demonstrated to be crossculturally applicable do not exist. For example,
instruments which can be used to assess the functioning of the family in a variety of
cultures will need to be developed before detailed cross-cultural studies of the
interaction between the family and schizophrenia can be undertaken.

Future work in the IPSS and studies which have arisen out of the IPSS will focus
on the following main areas:

1. On the consideration of the nature of the longer-term course of schizophrenia
and other functional psychoses in different cultures. Evaluation of the five-year
follow-up data will make it possible to determine if trends noted on the basis of the

two-year follow-up data continue. For example, it will be important to determine whether the marked variability in the two-year course and outcome of schizophrenia persists five years after the initial evaluation. Similarly, it will be important to see whether the degree of overlap in course and outcome of schizophrenia and affective psychoses becomes less over time. The relationship between the length of the follow-up and the differences among centres will also be examined, to determine whether the effect of culture-specific factors is more marked in terms of short-term outcome than in terms of long-term outcome.

2. On the evaluation of the question of whether and to what extent the conclusions drawn on the basis of the study of the IPSS patients can be extended to other groups of schizophrenic patients.

3. On the confirmation of the initial findings that the course and outcome of schizophrenia is different in different cultures.

4. On the identification of specific features of particular cultures which have an effect on the course of schizophrenia.

5. On the investigation of how particular social and biological variables produce an effect on the outcome of schizophrenia.

6. On the identification of predictors of outcome which are more relevant to cultures outside of Europe and North America than those currently identified.

7. On the development of instruments which will be applicable and reliable for the crosscultural evaluation of specific factors related to the course and outcome of schizophrenia and other functional psychoses.

There are a large number of hypotheses generated by the IPSS that can be tested in future phases of the IPSS and investigations that have arisen out of it.

1. Culture has an important effect on the course and outcome of schizophrenia (see Cooper and Sartorius, 1971).

2. The course and outcome of schizophrenia may be less favourable in sociocultural settings characterized by a high level of economic development, vertical social mobility, small average family size, social isolation of psychiatric patients and well-crystallized community stereotypes of the mentally ill, and may be more favourable in sociocultural settings characterized by mainly agricultural economy, little vertical social mobility, extended families, psychiatric services which include the active participation of the family, and the absence of specific community stereotypes of the mentally ill.

3. Many of the factors within cultures having an effect on the course of schizophrenia are as yet unknown, and can be discovered through intensive studies within particular cultures.

4. Variables relevant to the prognosis of schizophrenia in some cultures are not relevant in other cultures.

5. Variables other than those usually considered to be important for explaining the variability in the course and outcome of schizophrenia are likely to be of major importance, and may include such factors as differences in intervening life events affecting schizophrenic patients.

395

6. Social variables have as high a degree of prognostic importance for the outcome of schizophrenia as symptomatic variables.

7. The differences in the course and outcome of schizophrenia and other functional psychoses will increase over time, and factors which are good predictors of short-term course and outcome will be good predictors of longer-term course and outcome.

8. The relative contribution of biological and sociocultural and individual factors to the development course and outcome of schizophrenic can be assessed in comparative and crosscultural studies.

9. The effect of culture on course and outcome changes over time in one of the following ways:

> (a) the effect of culture on course and outcome diminishes over time so that after initial effects are produced the degree of differences in different cultures stabilizes over time;
> (b) the effect of culture increases over time, so that the degree of difference in the course of schizophrenia in different cultures increases over time;
> (c) initial effects disappear ultimately so that the nature of course and outcome in different cultures equalizes over time.

It is felt by the collaborating investigators that by raising these hypotheses and providing initial methodology and approaches to testing them, the IPSS has contributed to the understanding of the nature and comparability of schizophrenia in different cultures and has provided groundwork for developing a temporally and culturally relevant concept of schizophrenia.

APPENDIX 1

Summary of Course and Outcome of Patients Excluded from Further Analysis

Centre	Patient no.	Sex	Age at initial evaluation	Initial evaluation diagnosis	Reasons for exclusion	Two-year course and outcome
Aarhus	114	M	44	296.9 Endogenous depression; ideas of insufficiency; morbid jealousy	History of psychomotor epileptic attacks (EEG confirmed)	No further hospitalization; uninterrupted outpatient treatment for mild anxiety and headaches; continuous presence of neurotic symptoms. Receiving disablement pension, unemployed. Mild social impairment
Aarhus	121	F	30	294.4	Puerperal psychotic illness, diagnosed at initial evaluation (acute excitement and confusion following postpartum thrombophlebitis)	Recovered completely from postpartum psychosis but developed another similar episode eighteen months after in connection with surgery for ovarian cyst, recovered again and was symptom free throughout the rest of follow-up. No social impairment
Aarhus	149	F	17	294.4	Puerperal psychosis (acute excitement and confusion) Mental retardation	Psychotic relapse occurred one month after recovery from initial episode, probably in connection with febrile illness; discharged after three months inpatient treatment, then symptom free during the rest of the follow-up. No social impairment

Centre	Patient no.	Sex	Age at initial evaluation	Initial evaluation diagnosis	Reasons for exclusion	Two-year course and outcome
Aarhus	160	M	19	299	Generalized epileptic seizures during childhood	Three readmissions during follow-up; charged with indecent exposure on several occasions. Psychotic throughout follow-up (hallucinated, paranoid, subjective thought disorder); no remissions. Abnormal EEG on several occasions. Severe social impairment
Aarhus	212	F	35	298.9/7.9 Paranoid psychogenic	Dexedrine abuse. Borderline mental retardation	No further psychotic episodes; was, however, readmitted because of a variety of physical complaints of probable psychogenic origin. Final diagnosis of personality disorder (immature) made. Moderate social impairment
Agra	108	F	40	295.3	Puerperal psychotic illness with depression and *Dermatozoenwahn*	Initial psychotic episode continued over a year; on discharge from hospital was treated on outpatient basis by a faith healer; was apparently symptom free during second-year follow-up. No abnormality recorded on follow-up examination. Mild social impairment
Cali	124	M	21	295.2	Suspected epilepsy (EEG data but never convulsive fits)	Psychotic initial evaluation episode cleared up within a month after; no relapses; no epileptic fits; occasional complaints of forgetfulness. No social impairments

135	Cali	M	16	295.4	EEG data suggesting epilepsy	Continuous presence of severe neurotic symptoms throughout follow-up; two readmissions for a week each; under constant outpatient observation and treatment Has had anti-epileptic medication for most of the follow-up period but had no convulsive seizures Final diagnosis: psychotic organic brain syndrome associated with epilepsy Moderate social impairment
138	Cali	F	38	295.7	Epilepsy suspected on clinical grounds	Repeated attacks of impulsive behaviour, excitement, hallucinations, followed by amnesia Never hospitalized, did not take any medication No social impairment Possible temporal lobe epilepsy
230	Cali	M	18	295.4	Abuse of marihuana since the age of 12	Discharged after three weeks hospital treatment, seen as outpatient during next four months; no readmissions; no further psychotic episodes Continued smoking marihuana and taking Seconal and Mandrax Signs of some personality deterioration Mild social impairment
175	Ibadan	F	31	294.4	Acute excitement with hallucinations and paranoid ideas developed *post partum*	Discharged with some residual symptoms after one month inpatient treatment; seen as outpatient over following six months Second psychotic episode with same features developed one year later; treated by a native healer No further information available Patient died in January 1971 of unknown causes

Centre	Patient no.	Sex	Age at initial evaluation	Initial evaluation diagnosis	Reasons for exclusion	Two-year course and outcome
London	159	M	30	295.3	EEG and psychological test evidence for early brain damage Borderline mental retardation	Initial evaluation psychotic episode cleared up after three months hospital treatment. Was symptom-free but on Modecate for next seven months Developed a depressive episode, was readmitted to hospital where psychometric testing and EEG revealed brain damage Was discharged after four months and remained apparently well during the rest of follow-up Mild social impairment
London	221	M	30	295.3	Continued use of heroin and hashish	Discharged after three months of hospital treatment No further psychotic episodes but history of regular use of narcotic drugs No data on social functioning
Moscow	178	F	29	300.0	Suspected postencephalitic state	Discharged with residual neurotic symptoms after five months of hospital treatment Exacerbation of non-psychotic symptoms nine months after discharge. Rehospitalized for three months but neurotic symptoms and physical complaints throughout follow-up Neurological signs suspect of residual brain damage Moderate social impairment

Centre	No.	Sex	Age	Code	Diagnosis	Course and outcome
Moscow	180	F	44	306.3	Paralysis agitans	Discharged four-and-a-half months after initial evaluation with a deteriorating neurological disorder; Readmitted five months later; a diagnosis of paralysis agitans made on admission Transferred to a general hospital, remained hospitalized during the rest of the follow-up Depression and anxiety associated with severe physical deterioration Severe social impairment
Moscow	194	F	34	298.0	Thyrotoxicosis	Discharged from hospital after six months hospitalization but neurotic symptoms continued throughout follow-up Thyrotoxicosis has been discovered as an underlying cause and has been treated on an outpatient basis Moderate social impairment
Moscow	217	F	20	294.4	Psychotic episode developed post partum	Discharged after three months of hospitalization with a few residual symptoms that cleared up without maintenance treatment Has been symptom-free during the rest of follow-up No social impairment
Taipei	180	M	26	295.4	Alcohol dependence	Discharged from hospital one month after initial evaluation and treated on outpatient basis for another one month No psychotic relapses during follow-up but continuing regular alcohol abuse and compulsive gambling No social impairment

Centre	Patient no.	Sex	Age at initial evaluation	Initial evaluation diagnosis	Reasons for exclusion	Two-year course and outcome
Washington	114	M	21	295.3	Suspected amphetamine abuse	No readmissions Sketchy data but no evidence of further psychotic episodes No social impairment
Washington	169	F	27	295.3	Psychotic episode developed *post partum*	Insufficient information Probably had several exacerbations of symptoms
Washington	203	F	44	300.4	Alcohol dependence and thyrotoxicosis	Has had eight hospitalizations and three suicide attempts during follow-up period; treated for depression Moderate social impairment
Washington	209	F	20	295.4	Occasional abuse of hallucinogenic drugs (mescaline, hashish)	Had a further psychotic episode apparently caused by injection of mescaline; was hospitalized Mild social impairment
Washington	231	F	26	294.4	Psychotic episode developed *post partum*	Has had exacerbations of symptoms, no evidence that she was ever symptom-free Social impairment present but not possible to specify in degree
Prague	110	F	26	295.3	Psychotic episode developed *post partum*	Died on 8 October 1969 in hospital from acute heart failure

APPENDIX 2

Summary of Data on Patients who Died during the Follow-up Period

Centre	Patient no.	Sex	Age at initial evaluation	Initial evaluation diagnosis	Date of initial evaluation	Course	Date of death	Cause of death
Aarhus	107	F	21	296.2	18 April 1968	Committed suicide four months after initial evaluation during an exacerbation of her depression	15 August 1968	Medicamentous self-poisoning
Aarhus	188	M	39	295.3	3 December 1968	Was discharged free of psychotic symptoms 18 days after initial evaluation; had outpatient treatment New psychotic episode (paranoid) developed one year after initial evaluation On second discharge put on lithium because of suspected manic-depressive basis of his symptoms Non-psychotic until November 1970 when the patient developed acute coronary occlusion and died in a general hospital	5 November 1970	Coronary thrombosis
Aarhus	205	F	44	295.3	8 December 1968	Discharged from hospital two weeks after initial evaluation with residual psychotic symptoms (withdrawn negativistic); was semi-stuporous Died as a result of physical illness (pneumonia)	2 February 1969	Widespread pneumonia

Centre	Patient no.	Sex	Age at initial evaluation	Initial evaluation diagnosis	Date of initial evaluation	Course	Date of death	Cause of death
Agra	117	M	18	295.1	4 May 1968	Discharged unimproved against medical advice two weeks after initial evaluation; readmitted six weeks later and discharged again after 50 days of hospital treatment as 'improved' No data about his condition in 1969; in July 1970 admitted again with a physical illness of unspecified previous duration and deteriorated mental state Physical condition believed to be typhoid; had several Jacksonian fits *ante mortem*; died in his home in July 1970	July 1970	Acute physical illness (typhoid fever?)
Agra	186	F	25	295.2	10 September 1968	Continuous psychotic illness, discharged with minimal improvement after 19 months of treatment Died of unknown cause in her home in November 1970	November 1970	Unknown
Agra	190	F	18	295.9	6 September 1968	Continuously ill since initial evaluation, readmitted to hospital for two-and-a-half months in 1969, treated by faith-healers on discharge; several times attempted suicide In February 1970 set fire to herself and died	February 1970	Suicide (burns)
Agra	215	F	35	295.9	20 December 1968	Discharged from hospital two months after initial evaluation, apparently symptom-free until her death in June 1970 (death occurred in general hospital to which she was admitted for unspecified physical illness which developed about a month after childbirth)	June 1970	Unspecified physical illness accompanied by jaundice

Center	ID	Sex	Age	Code	Date	Description	Date of death	Cause
Cali	190	F	37	295.4	18 December 1968	Patient committed suicide through hanging one-and-a-half months after initial evaluation	6 February 1969	Suicide (hanging)
Ibadan	141	M	40	295.7	8 October 1968	No follow-up information except that the patient died after a short illness	February 1970	Unknown
Ibadan	154	M	22	295.3	16 November 1968	Discharged four months after initial evaluation with residual symptoms, psychotic relapse in September 1969, treated by native healers; probably no full recovery Died of unknown causes during second year after initial evaluation	Unknown	Unknown
Ibadan	175	reported in Appendix 1						
Ibadan	197	F	30	295.3	15 January 1969	Died three months after initial evaluation of unknown causes	April 1969	Unknown
London	180	M	44	298.3	25 September 1968	Discharged from hospital ten months after initial evaluation with residual symptoms; psychotic relapse two months later; was readmitted, then absconded and committed suicide by jumping in front of a train	12 November 1969	Suicide (jumped in front of a train)
London	182	M	38	295.3	16 September 1968	Uninterrupted chronic psychotic illness with personality deterioration and severe social impairment Committed suicide	February 1970	Suicide
London	189	M	24	295.3	18 October 1968	Uninterrupted psychotic illness; developed depressive symptoms and suicidal ideation Nine months after initial evaluation absconded and committed suicide	12 August 1969	Suicide (drowning)
Moscow	149	M	19	295.5	1 September 1968	No follow-up information available Died of drowning under unknown circumstances	June 1969	Drowning (suicide?)

Centre	Pati-ent no.	Sex	Age at initial evalua-tion	Initial evaluation diagnosis	Date of initial evaluation	Course	Date of death	Cause of death
Moscow	179	F	36	295.5	14 October 1968	No follow-up information available; died of unspecified heart disease	2 December 1970	Heart disease (unspecified)
Taipei	111	F	38	295.3	20 May 1968	Discharged from hospital after one-and-a-half months of treatment with residual paranoid symptoms; was never entirely symptom-free Run over by a train 20 months after initial evaluation	5 February 1970	Accident?
Taipei	117	M	27	295.3	25 May 1968	Continuously ill after initial evaluation until his death three months later (run over by train)	September 1968	Suicide? Accident?
Taipei	220	M	19	295.1	12 September 1968	Continuous illness; mild social impairment; exacerbation of symptoms In December 1970 talked of suicide, was found drowned in a river a few days later	December 1970	Suicide? (drowning)
Washing-ton	140	M	28	295.4	30 August 1968	Committed suicide a few days after completion of initial evaluation	September 1968	Suicide (unknown method)

Prague	108	F	28	298.9	26 April 1968	Committed suicide (date unknown) together with boyfriend	Unknown	Suicide (unknown method)
Prague	110	reported in Appendix 1						
Prague	135	F	33	295.7	24 July 1968	Patient died probably in a car accident	Unknown	Unknown (accident?)
Prague	218	F	30	295.7	26 March 1969	Discharged two months after initial evaluation in full remission but had a psychotic relapse six months later and several hospitalizations. Discharged herself against medical advice in September 1970 and committed suicide by gas	26 September 1970	Suicide (self-poisoning with gas)

APPENDIX 3

Classification of Patients on the Basis of PSE Ratings

List of criteria applied in the analysis of two-year follow up data to classify patients as 'psychotic', 'symptomatic but not psychotic' and 'asymptomatic', on the basis of Present State Examination (PSE) ratings.

A.3.1 PSYCHOTIC

A patient was considered psychotic if he had a positive score on *any one* of the following units of analysis (UAs):

UA no.	Description
3	Stupor
38	Thought alienation
39	Thoughts spoken aloud
40	Delusions of control
41	Delusions of persecution
42	Delusions of guilt
43	Delusions of self-depreciation
44	Nihilistic delusions
45	Delusions of grandeur
46	Delusions of reference
47	Presence of delusional system
48	Hypochondriacal delusions
49	Delusions of special mission
50	Religious delusions
51	Fantastic delusions
52	Sexual delusions
53	Delusions of impending doom
66	Presence of verbal hallucinations
67	Voices speak to patient
68	Voices speak full sentences
69	Non-verbal auditory hallucinations
70	Presence of auditory hallucinations
72	Voices discussing patient
73	Hallucinations from body

74	Voices comment on patient's thoughts
75	Voices speak thoughts
76	Visual hallucinations
77	Tactile hallucinations
78	Olfactory hallucinations
79	Sexual hallucinations
80	Somatic hallucinations
81	Gustatory hallucinations

A patient was also considered psychotic if he had a positive score on *at least one* unit of analysis within three or more of the following groups of units of analysis:

UA no.		*Description*
(a)	5	Compliance
	7	Stereotypies
	8	Odd appearance and behaviour
	9	Grimacing
	10	Posturing
	11	Mannerisms
	12	Hallucinatory behaviour
	13	Waxy flexibility
(b)	20	Neologisms
	21	Klang association
	22	Speech dissociation
	23	Irrelevance
	25	Blocking
	26	Stereotypy of speech
	27	Echolalia
(c)	61	Changed appearance
	62	Derealization
	63	Looking at self
	64	Break of self-identity
	65	Distortion of time perception
(d)	28	Gloomy thoughts
	29	Elated thoughts
	30	Hopelessness
	31	Suicidal thoughts
	32	Special depression
	84	Depressed mood
	85	Observed elated mood
	111	Early waking
(e)	92	Flatness
	95	Incongruity of affect
(f)	6	Talking to self
	105	Autism

(g)	34	Ideas of reference
	33	Delusional mood
(h)	1	Overactivity
	2	Retardation
	15	Flight of ideas
	18	Mutism

A.3.2 ASYMPTOMATIC

A patient was considered asymptomatic (symptom-free) if *no positive score* on any unit of analysis was present.

A.3.3 SYMPTOMATIC BUT NOT PSYCHOTIC

A patient was considered symptomatic but not psychotic if he could not be classified into either category 1 or category 2 on the basis of his scores on units of analysis.

.

APPENDIX 4

Composition of CATEGO Classes used in the Analysis of the Two-year Follow-up Data

Broad class	Component classes	Description	Diagnostic equivalents
S	(1) S+	Corresponds to the core group of schizophrenic conditions characterized by the following symptoms: (a) thought intrusion, broadcast or withdrawal; (b) delusions of control; (c) voices discussing patient in third person or commenting on thoughts or actions; (d) other, not affectively based auditory hallucinations; (e) other delusions. Presence of any of the first three symptoms, or presence of both (d) and (e) qualifies a patient for this class	ICD 295.0–9 sluggish shift-like } schizophrenia periodic
	(2) S?	A less certain counterpart of S+, in which voices experienced as speaking directly to the patient, but not characteristic of either depression or mania, are the only psychotic symptoms present	
	(3) O+ O?	Other psychotic conditions characterized mainly by: (a) catatonic symptoms; (b) behaviour indicative of hallucinations	ICD 295.0 295.2
	(4) P+ P?	Paranoid psychoses characterized by: (a) delusions (other than first-rank, as in S+); (b) hallucinations (other than auditory)	ICD 297.0 297.9 298.2, 3.9 } paranoid psychoses 299
M	(1) M+	Manic and mixed affective psychoses characterized by: (a) euphoria or elation; (b) ideomotor pressure; (c) grandiose ideas; (d) grandiose delusions; (e) flight of ideas; (f) overactivity Symptom (d) must be present, together with at least one other in the absence of symptoms from class S+	ICD 296.1 296.3 298.1

Broad class	Component classes	Description	Diagnostic equivalents
	(2) M?	Symptoms similar to those defining class M+ but there is minimal euphoria or elation	
D	(1) D+	Depressive psychoses characterized by: (a) depressive mood; (b) depressive delusions or hallucinations Both symptoms must be present, in the absence of symptoms from class S+ or M+	ICD 296.2 298.0
	(2) D?	Depressive mood must be present, as well as delusions or hallucinations, but the latter do not have a distinctive depressive quality. Symptoms from class S+ or M+ must be absent	
	(3) R+	Retarded depression characterized by: (a) depressed mood; (b) retardation; (c) guilt, self-depreciation etc.; (d) agitation Symptom (a) must be present, together with one of the others, in the absence of depressive delusions or other psychotic symptoms	ICD 296.2 298.0 300.4
	(4) N+	Neurotic depressive states, characterized by: (a) depressed mood; (b) anxiety Symptom (a) must be present, in the absence of psychotic symptoms, or symptoms characteristic of class R+	ICD 300.4
'Other'		Conditions which cannot be allocated to any of the above classes	

APPENDIX 5

Definition and Measurement of Reliability for Dichotomous Variables

A.5.1 INTRODUCTION

The instruments whose reliability and validity are to be assessed are rating scales designed to record the patients' symptomatological profiles and the course and outcome of their disorders. As in problems of validity, it is not meaningful to discuss the reliability of instruments without reference to the purpose for which they will be used. For example, it might be of interest to study the distribution of a variable in a population, for example, the degree of social impairment among schizophrenic patients. The problem then would be to obtain a reliable estimate of the proportion of the schizophrenics with defined degrees of social impairment.

The reliability required of an instrument measuring social impairment in a patient population should not be as high as in the case when this instrument would be used in order to assess an individual patient and initiate some kind of therapeutic or rehabilitative action on the basis of the outcome of the measurement. For most of the analyses presented in the present volume the problem was to compare several defined groups of patients in terms of specified variables. For example, the field research centres in developing and developed countries could be compared, with respect to course and outcome of the various disorders. The group of patients with diagnosis of schizophrenia at the time of the initial examination could be compared with the group of patients with a diagnosis of mania in terms of symptomatology. Generally, the instruments designed to assess course and outcome or symptomatic profiles are required to be reliable in the sense that they should be capable to measure differences between patient groups if there *are* real differences.

Rating scales in psychiatry are applied to three types of problems:

1. The problem of determining the distribution of a variable (such as degree of social impairment, diagnosis) in a population.

2. The problem of classifying patients into specified categories (such as mild or severe social impairment, diagnosis of schizophrenia or mania, etc.).

3. The problem of discriminating between different groups (such as patients in particular field research centres, diagnostic groups) by means of various characteristics (for example, symptomatology, course and outcome).

Different levels of reliability would be adequate for each of these problems. In the present context, reliability is discussed only in relation to discrimination problems.

415

A.5.2 A MODEL FOR RATING DICHOTOMOUS PSYCHIATRIC ITEMS

Rating scales whose individual items are dichotomies, that is, can be described as either present or absent, were of particular interest in the IPSS. The following model can be used resting on certain assumptions to describe the actual rating process:

1. A patient has, at least at a specific point in time, a *real* profile (such as of symptomatology), regardless of whether it can be measured or not.

2. Each item of the profile can be described by a dichotomy (a symptom is either present or absent).

3. There exists an instrument capable to measure a patient's profile.

4. For each profile item there exists one probability quantifying the instrument's capacity to assess correctly the item's presence or absence.

This model is almost identical with the classical rating model described by Guilford and Fruchter (1973), and the reliability of dichotomous measurement can be denoted by π.

The first assumption states that the rating scales mentioned above are meaningful from the point of view of psychopathology. The instrument for assessing the patients' symptomatology, the Present State Examination (PSE), is supplemented with a glossary giving definitions of the items contained in the schedule. All psychiatrists participating in the study have discussed and agreed on those definitions. Postulating a 'real' profile in this sense simply means that these definitions are accepted as meaningful and relevant, at least in the opinion of the psychiatrists involved.

The fourth assumption requires particular attention. Assuming that there exists only one probability of correct assessment means that it is equally likely to assess correctly the presence or absence of a symptom. The independence of the measurement's reliability from the real content of the item, which is postulated in Guilford's model, is problematic in the case of dichotomous items such as psychiatric symptoms and signs. For example, it may be fairly easy for two raters to agree on the absence of hallucinations from the body (unit of analysis number 73) but much more difficult to assess the presence of such a symptom, in particular if it is of a rare occurence (hallucinations from the body were rated as present in less than 1 per cent of the total series of patients). Therefore, it is necessary to examine more closely the case where the probability of a correct assessment depends upon the content of the symptom, that is, whether it is really absent or present.

If a sufficiently large number of patients are rated for presence/absence of a particular item, the following characteristics of this 'population' could be distinguished:

P_m : the proportion of patients in whom the item was measured to be present;

A_m : the proportion of patients in whom the item was measured to be absent;

P_r : the proportion of patients with the item really present;

A_r : the proportion of patients with the item really absent;

π : the probability that the measured value of the item agrees with the real one. Hence, $1 - \pi$ is the probability that the measured value does not agree with the real one.

It is evident (because of the assumption underlying the model) that

$$A_m = 1 - P_m \quad \text{and} \quad A_r = 1 - P_r \quad\quad (A.5.2.1)$$

To find the relationship between P_m, P_r, A_m, A_r and π the following notation is used:

$P(S_m = T/S_r = 1)$ = probability that the measurement gives the true result under the condition that the real content of the symptom is 1, or present;

$P(S_m = T/S_r = 0)$ = probability that the measurement gives the true result under the condition that the real content of the symptom is 0, or absent;

$P(S_m = W/S_r = 1)$ = probability that the measurement is wrong under the condition that the real content of the symptom is 1, or present;

$P(S_m = W/S_r = 0)$ = probability that the measurement is wrong under the condition that the real content of the symptom is 0, or absent;

$(A.5.2.2)$

$P(S_m = T, S_r = 1)$ = probability that the measurement gives the true result and the symptom is really present;

$P(S_m = T, S_r = 0)$ = probability that the measurement gives the true result and the symptom is really absent;

$P(S_m = W, S_r = 1)$ = probability that the measurement gives the wrong result and the symptom is really present;

$P(S_m = W, S_r = 0)$ = probability that the measurement gives the wrong result and the symptom is really absent.

With these abbreviations the following equations hold:

$$P_m = P(S_m = T, S_r = 1) + P(S_m = W, S_r = 0) = P(S_m = T/S_r = 1)P_r + P(S_m = W/S_r = 0)A_r.$$

Hence

$$P_m = \pi P_r + (1 - \pi)A_r, \quad\quad (A.5.2.3)$$

418

and analogously

$$A_m = \pi A_r + (1 - \pi)P_r \qquad\qquad (A.5.2.4)$$

For $\pi = 1$, that is, absolute reliability of the instrument, $P_m = P_r$ and $A_m = A_r$. On the other hand, however, $\pi = 0$ implies $P_m = A_r$ and $A_m = P_r$ which indicates that the instrument measures with certainty a symptom as absent when, in fact, it is present, and vice versa. An unreliable instrument is characterized by a π-value of ½. In such a situation, regardless of how the real item is distributed, the measured frequency of how the real item is distributed, the measured frequency of present and absent items is $P_m = A_m = $ ½. In general if $\pi > $ ½ the instrument reflects correctly the pattern of the distribution of the item in the population (if in reality there are more patients who do have than patients who do not have the symptom, the measured frequency of patients with the symptom present will also be greater than that of patients with the symptom absent). If $\pi = $ ½ the instrument cannot be used (it does not reflect the real situation). If $\pi < $ ½ the instrument reflects the opposite pattern of the item's distribution in the population. It should be noted, however, that for the type of problems discussed in the present volume the cases $\pi > $ ½ and $\pi < $ ½ are equivalent. With regard to the discrimination between defined groups of patients on the basis of the item profile it is irrelevant whether the rating scale measures the true content of an item or consistently gives its mirror image.

The question of an acceptable order of magnitude for the reliability π is already answered by the above discussion. It must be greater than ½. If that is the case, the patterns of the real and measured group profiles would be the same. In other words, if two groups of patients (such as schizophrenics and manics) differ with respect to their real profiles, they are also different in regard to their measured profiles. This can be shown formally (S and M stand for schizophrenia and mania respectively) as follows:

The conditions

$$\pi > \tfrac{1}{2} \text{ and } P_r^S > P_r^M$$

imply

$$\pi > 1 - \pi \text{ and } P_r^S - P_r^M > 0$$

and hence

$$\pi(P_r^S - P_r^M) > (1 - \pi)(P_r^S - P_r^M) = (1 - \pi)(1 - P_r^M - 1 + P_r^S)$$
$$= (1 - \pi)(A_r^M - A_r^S);$$

therefore:

$$\pi P_r^S + (1 - \pi)A_r^S > \pi P_r^M + (1 - \pi)A_r^M$$

and because of equation (A.5.2.3)

$$P_m^S > P_m^M.$$

But the opposite is also true:

$$P_m^S > P_m^M \quad \text{and} \quad P_r^S > P_r^M$$

imply

$$\pi > \tfrac{1}{2}.$$

This can be seen as follows:

$$P_m^S = \pi P_r^S + (1-\pi)A_r^S > \pi P_r^M + (1-\pi)A_r^M = P_m^M$$

implies

$$\pi(P_r^S - P_r^M) > (1-\pi)(A_r^M - A_r^S)$$

and because of (A.5.2.1)

$$\pi(P_r^S - P_r^M) > (1-\pi)(P_r^S - P_r^M).$$

But

$$P_r^S > P_r^M$$

and hence

$$\pi > 1 - \pi$$

or

$$\pi > \tfrac{1}{2}.$$

In other words the measured proportions of patients in whom a particular symptom is present reflect correctly the real situation if and only if the reliability π is greater than $\tfrac{1}{2}$.

If π is close to $\tfrac{1}{2}$, however, the measured profiles will be close to each other even if the real profiles are markedly different.

On the basis of Figure A.5.1 it would be easy to state that the diagnostic groups are characterized by different symptomatologies, but it would be much more difficult to make an assessment from Figure A.5.2. Average symptomatological profiles of samples of patients are subject to random fluctuations and it would not be clear whether the discrepancies of the profiles in Figure A.5.2 are due

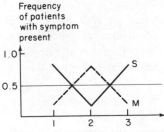

Figure A.5.1   *Real profiles* of two diagnostic groups S and M

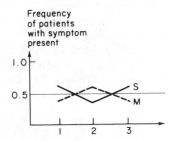

Figure A.5.2   *Measured profiles* of two diagnostic groups S and M if π is close to 0.5

to such fluctuations or reflect real differences in the group symptomatologies. The smaller the actual differences the more patients have to be rated in order to assess whether the differences are real or not. By increasing the reliability of a rating scale the number of patients to be rated in order to prove or to disprove differences in profile patterns can be decreased. This means that the determination of a 'sufficient' reliability of a valid instrument is a practical, rather than a theoretical problem.

A.5.3 THE PROBLEM OF ESTIMATING THE RELIABILITY

The sampling procedure for assessing the reliability of symptomatological and similar rating scales usually involves the independent rating of a patient by two or more psychiatrists in a simultaneous interview. The details of the design chosen in the IPSS to assess reliability are described in Chapter 4. Independent simultaneous ratings of the same patient by different observers allow to estimate the reliability coefficient π in the following way: K observers rate independently the same patient and this procedure can be termed a 'rating exercise'. The rating exercise is repeated several times and patients are examined independently by the group of K psychiatrists, and if M out of these L exercises are 'successful', the ratio $M/L = a$, that is, the proportion of 'successful' exercises can be calculated. It is evident that there is a direct relationship between the probability π of a correct assessment and the agreement ratio a (see Figure 4.2).

If the probability that one psychiatrist rates correctly is π, it is π^K that K psychiatrists rate correctly. But if K raters agree in their ratings this does not necessarily mean that their ratings were correct; all of them could have been wrong. The probability that one rater is wrong is $1 - \pi$, and that K raters are wrong simultaneously $(1 - \pi)^K$. Therefore, the probability is $\pi^K + (1 - \pi)^K$ that K raters agree in their judgments — that a rating exercise is 'successful'. The proportion of 'successful' rating exercises $a = M/L$ is an estimate of $\pi^K + (1 - \pi)^K$.

Since patients are assessed independently, that is, the rating of a particular patient is not influenced by the rating of any other patient, the number of successful exercises is binomially distributed with parameter $\pi^K + (1 - \pi)^K$. The solution π_0 of the equation

$$\pi^K + (1 - \pi)^K = a \qquad (A.5.3.1)$$

gives an estimate of π. Significance tests and confidence intervals for π can be obtained by standard statistical methods on the basis of the binomial distribution.

The relation (A.5.3.1) has been derived under the assumption that all raters have the same reliability π. If each of the K raters has an individual $\pi_i, i = 1, 2, \ldots, K$, the agreement ratio a estimates

$$\pi_1 \pi_2 \cdots \pi_K + (1 - \pi_1)(1 - \pi_2) \ldots (1 - \pi_K). \qquad (A.5.3.2)$$

These individual K parameters cannot be estimated on the basis of one agreement ratio. The solution of (A.5.3.1), however, gives an average for π_1, $\pi_2, \ldots, \pi_K$, which can be interpreted as a 'group-π'. In the case of a two-rater exercise, i.e. $K = 2$, it can be demonstrated easily that the group-π relates to π_1 and π_2 through the function group

$$\pi = \tfrac{1}{2} \pm \sqrt{(\tfrac{1}{2} - \pi_1)(\tfrac{1}{2} - \pi_2)}. \tag{A.5.3.3}$$

The group of K raters behaves as if each psychiatrist rated with the same reliability, equalling the group-π. For $K = 2$ this average is $\tfrac{1}{2}$ plus the geometric mean of the increments of the individual π-values over $\tfrac{1}{2}$ (see A.5.3.3).

If the π-values of the individual observers are similar, the group-π is a meaningful indicator of the average reliability of the group. On the other hand, if one rater consistently deviates in his rating behaviour, the group will reach complete agreement only rarely; in other words the agreement ratio would be very low and (A.5.3.1) would have no solution. For two-rater exercises (i.e. $K = 2$) with an agreement ratio of $a < \tfrac{1}{2}$ a group-π does not exist. In such a situation it would not be justified to continue the rating process before the reasons for the discrepant ratings have been analysed.

Another assumption of the above model was that the items are dichotomies. Although such a model would correspond to many existing psychiatric rating scales, particularly those designed to assess symptomatology, it is certainly not adequate in the case of instruments designed to assess course and outcome. One of the main categories describing the course of the disorder which is discussed in detail in Chapter 6 is 'pattern of course' with the following categories: (a) full remission after the episode of inclusion and no further episodes; (b) partial remission after the episode of inclusion and no subsequent episodes; (c) at least one non-psychotic episode after the episode of inclusion and full remissions between all episodes; (d) at least one non-psychotic episode after the episode of inclusion and no full remission between all episodes; (e) at least one subsequent psychotic episode and full remissions between all episodes; (f) at least one subsequent psychotic episode and no full remissions between all episodes; (g) still in the episode of inclusion at the time of the second year follow-up examination; (h) unknown. The methods described in the preceding paragraphs are not directly applicable to the evaluation of the reliability with which this category can be measured. Reliability measures for continuous variables, like the intraclass correlation coefficient or reliability indicators like Kendall's coefficient of concordance designed to deal with ordinal variables are also unsuitable. However, it can be shown that on the basis of rating exercises a rater's probability to make a correct assessment of the category's content can be estimated also for nominal, non-dichotomous variables. Assuming that the patient is to be classified into one out of S rather than two classes, and that the probability for a wrong classification is constant for all classes regardless of the real content of the category, it can be shown that the agreement ratio $a = M/L$ estimates

$$\pi^K + \frac{(1 - \pi)^K}{(S - 1)^{K-1}} = a = \frac{M}{L} \tag{A.5.3.4}$$

and π may be estimated by solving this equation. Similarly to (A.5.2.3) the relationship between π and the real and measured proportions of subjects in the different classes can be determined and one could demonstrate that the rating procedure is unreliable if $\pi = 1/S$. In this case, regardless of the real distribution of the item in the patients series, the same proportion of patients will be allocated to each class. The procedure therefore does not measure the real differences between diagnostic groups. On the other hand, if $\pi > 1/S$ the rating procedure can be used to discriminate between different patient groups on the basis of the nominal item with S classes described above.

(A.5.3.4) can be proved as follows: for a dichotomous item X the possible values are 0 or 1. For a polychotomous item X the real and measured values may be $X_r = i$ and $X_m = i$, $i = 1, 2, \ldots, S$ respectively, where S stands for the number of possible values of X. $P(X_m = i, X_r = j) = W_{ij}$ may be the probability that the value i is measured, while the real value of the item is j; similarly $P(X_m = i/X_r = j)$ denote the corresponding conditional probabilities for $i, j = 1, 2, \ldots, S$; $P(X_m = i)$ and $P(X_r = i)$ be the unconditional probabilities that the measured and real values of the item be $i (i = 1, \ldots, S)$. If a rater measures the item to have the value i, his assessment may be right or wrong so that

$$P(X_m = i) = P(X_m = i, X_r = i) + \sum_{j \neq i}^{S} P(X_m = i, X_r = j) \qquad (A.5.3.5)$$

which by the definition of conditional probabilities is

$$P(X_m = i) = W_{ii} P(X_r = i) + \sum_{j \neq i}^{S} W_{ij} P(X_r = j) \qquad (A.5.3.6)$$

W_{ii} is the probability for a rating to be correct and it is assumed that it does not depend upon $i (i = 1, \ldots, S)$. As in previous sections it will be denoted by π. Obviously $\sum_{j \neq i}^{S} W_{if} = 1 - \pi$ for all i and if it is assumed that all W_{ij} are equal to W, say, if follows that

$$W_{ij} = W = \frac{1 - \pi}{S - 1} \qquad (A.5.3.7)$$

Inserting (A.5.3.7) into (A.5.3.6) one obtains

$$P(X_m = i) = \pi P(X_r = i) + \frac{1 - \pi}{S - 1} [1 - P(X_r = i)], \qquad (A.5.3.8)$$

since

$$\sum_{j \neq i}^{S} P(X_r = j) = 1 - P(X_r = i). \text{ If } \pi = \frac{1}{S}, \ P(X_m = i) = \frac{1}{S},$$

regardless of the real value of the item, indicating that the rating procedure is unreliable. For $\pi > 1/S$ the measurements reflect the real situation. In a K-rater reliability exercise the probability is π^K that all the raters agree correctly, while it is $\sum_{j \neq i}^{S} [(1 - \pi)/(S - 1)]^K$ that all of them agree wrongly. Therefore, the probability for a reliability exercise to be successful is given by $\pi^K + (1 - \pi)^K/(S - 1)^{K-1}$

which can be estimated by the agreement ratio a as in the two-rater case:

$$a = \frac{M}{L} = \pi^K + \frac{(1 - \pi)^K}{(S - 1)^{K-1}} \tag{A.5.3.9}$$

In deriving the above relationships it has been assumed that regardless of the real content of the variables the probability for a wrong classification is constant for all classes. While such an assumption may adequately reflect the rating process in the case of purely nominal categories, it is problematic in the case of ordinal scale variables. If, for example, the variable to be rated is degree of social impairment (see Chapter 5) with levels 'no impairment', 'moderate', and 'severe impairment' it would be unrealistic to assume that a patient who is really severely impaired would be categorized with equal likelihood into the classes 'no impairment' and 'moderate impairment'. For those variables it is justified to calculate π through the formula for dichotomous variables (i.e. $\pi^K + (1 - \pi)^K = L/M$) which provides a conservative estimate for π.

References

Achté, K. A. (1967). On prognosis and rehabilitation in schizophrenia and paranoid psychoses, *Acta Psychiat. Neurol. Scand.*, Supplementum **125**, 33.

Arnold, O. H. (1955). *Schizophrener Prozess und Schizophrene Symptomgesetze* (Vienna: Maudrich).

Astrup, Ç. and Noreik, K. (1966). *Functional Psychoses – Diagnostic and Prognostic Models* (Springfield, IU.: Charles C. Thomas).

Barton, R. (1959). *Institutional Neurosis* (Bristol: Wright).

Bellak, L. (1948). *Dementia Praecox* (New York: Grune and Stratton).

Bennet, D. H. and Wing, J. K. (1963). Sheltered workshops for the psychiatrically handicapped. In: H. Freeman, and J. Farndale (eds.), *Trends in the Mental Health Services* (Oxford: Pergamon Press).

Bhaskaran, K., Dhawan, N., and Mohan, Y. (1972). A study of the effects of prolonged hospitalization on schizophrenia, *Ind. J. Psychiat.*, **14**, 106.

Birley, J. L. T. and Brown, G. W. (1970). Crises and life changes preceding the onset or relapse of acute schizophrenia, *Brit. J. Psychiat.*, **116**, 327.

Bleuler, M. (1972). *Die Schizophrenen Geistesstörungen im Lichte langjähriger Kranken – und Familiengeschichten* (Stuttgart: G. Thieme).

Bleuler, E. (1950). *Dementia Praecox or the Group of Schizophrenics* (New York: International Universities Press) (translation of the 1911 German edition).

Brown, G. W. (1959). Experiences of discharged chronic schizophrenic patients in various types of living groups. *The Millbank Memorial Fund Q.*, **37**, 105.

Brown, G. W. (1966). Comment on paper by Vaillant, G., The prediction of recovery in schizophrenia, *Int. J. Psychiat.*, **2**, 617.

Brown, G. W., Birley, J. L. T., and Wing, J. K. (1972). Influence of family life on the course of schizophrenic disorders: a replication, *Brit. J. Psychiat.*, **121**, 241.

Brown, G. W. and Birley, J. L. T. (1968). Crises and life changes and the onset of schizophrenia, *J. Health Soc. Beh.*, **9**, 203.

Brown, G. W., Bone, M., Dalison, B., and Wing, J. K. (1966). *Schizophrenia and Social Care* (London: Oxford University Press).

Brown, G. W., Monck, E. M., Carstairs, G. M., and Wing, J. K. (1962). The influence of family life on the course of schizophrenic illness, *Brit. J. Prev. Soc. Med.*, **16**, 55.

Carse, J., Panton, N. E., and Watt, A. (1958) The Worthing experiment, *Lancet*, **i**, 39.

Cooper, J. E. and Sartorius, N. (1977). Cultural and temporal variations in schizophrenia, *Brit. J. Psychiat.*, **130**, 50.

Cronbach, L. J. (1970). *Essentials of Psychological Testing* (New York: Harper and Row).

Douglas, J. W. B. (1960). Premature children at primary school, *Brit. Med. J.*, **1**, 1008.

Eitinger, L., Laane, C. L., and Langfeldt, G. (1958). The prognostic value of the clinical picture and the therapeutic value of physical treatment in schizophrenia and the schizophreniform states, *Acta Psychiat. Neurol. Scand.*, **33**, 33.

426

Ekblom, B. and Lassenius, B. (1964). A follow-up examination of patients with schizophrenia who were treated during a long period with psycho-pharmacological drugs, *Acta Psychiat. Scand.*, **40**, 249.

Ey, H. (1959). Unity and diversity of schizophrenia: clinical and logical analysis of the concept of schizophrenia, *Amer. J. Psychiat.*, **115**, 706.

Feinsilver, D. B. and Gunderson, J. G. (1972). Psychotherapy for schizo-phrenics — is it indicated? A review of the relevant literature, *Schizophrenia Bull.*, **7**, 11.

Goffman, E. (1961). Asylums (New York: Anchor, Doubleday).

Greenhouse S. W. and Geisser R. (1959). On methods in the analysis of profile data, *Psychometrika*, **24**, 95.

Grinspoon, L., Ewalt, J. R., and Shader, R. I. (1972). *Schizophrenia — Pharma-cotherapy and Psychotherapy* (Baltimore: Williams and Wilkins).

Groos, M. (1961). Discontinuation of treatment with ataractic drugs, *Recent Advances in Biological Psychiatry* (New York: Grune and Stratton).

Guilford, J. P., and Fruchter B. (1973). *Fundamental Statistics in Psychology and Education*, 5th edition, (New York: McGraw-Hill).

Gurland, B. J., Yorkston, N. J., Goldberg, K., Fleiss, J. L., Sloane, R. B., and Cristol A. H. (1972). The Structured and Scaled Interview to Assess Maladjustment (SSIAM): II. Factor analysis, reliability and validity, *Arch. Gen. Psychiat.*, **27**, 264.

Harris, A., Linker, I., Norris, V., and Shepherd, M., (1956). Schizophrenia — a prognostic and social study, *Brit. J. Soc. Prev. Med.*, **10**, 107.

Hempel, C. G. (1959). Introduction to problems of taxonomy. In: Zubin J. (ed.), *Field Studies in the Mental Disorders* (New York: Grune and Stratton).

Henisz, J. A. (1966). A follow-up study of schizophrenic patients, *Comprehensive Psychiat.*, **12**, 524.

Hirsch, S., Gaind, R., Rohde, P., Stevens, B., and Wing, J. K. (1973). Outpatient maintenance treatment of chronic schizophrenics with fluphenazine decanoate injections: a double-blind placebo trial, *Brit. Med. J.*, **1**, 633.

Hogarty, G. E., Goldberg, S. C. and the collaborative study group (1973). Drugs and sociotherapy in the aftercare of schizophrenic patients, *Arch. Gen. Psychiat.*, **28**, 54.

Holmboe, R. and Astrup, C. (1957). A follow-up study of 255 patients with acute schizophrenia and schizophreniform psychoses, *Acta Psychiat. Neurol. Scand.*, Supplementum 115, **32** (Copenhagen: Munksgaard).

Jablensky, A., and Sartorius, N. (1975) Culture and schizophrenia, *Psychological Medicine*, **5**, 113.

Johnson, Eva (1958). A study of schizophrenia in the male, *Acta Psychiat. Neurol. Scand.*, Supplementum 125, **33** (Copenhagen: Munksgaard).

Jones, F. H. (1974). Current methodologies for studying the development of schizophrenia — a critical review, *J. Nervous Mental Dis.*, **157**, 154.

Kant, O. (1940). Types and analyses of the clinical pictures of recovered schizo-phrenics, *Psychiat. Q.*, **14**, 676.

Kant, O. (1941a). Study of a group of recovered schizophrenic patients, *Psychiat. Q.*, **15**, 262.

Kant, O. (1941b). A comparative study of recovered and deteriorated schizophrenic patients, *J. Nervous Mental Dis.*, **93**, 616.

Katz, M. M., Sanborn, K. O., and Gudeman, H. (1967). Characterizing differences in psychopathology among ethnic groups in Hawaii, *Annual Meeting of the Association for Research on Mental and Nervous Diseases, Dec. 1–2* (New York, NY).

Kenniston, K., Boltex, S., and Almond, R. (1971). Multiple criteria of treatment outcome, *J. Psychiat. Res.*, 8, 107.

Kraepelin, E. (1913). *Psychiatrie, Ein Lehrbuch für Studierende und Ärzte*, 8. Aufl. III Band (Leipzig: Barth).

Lambo, T. A. (1968). Schizophrenia, its features and prognosis in the African, *Deuxième colloque africaine de psychiatrie* (Paris: Association Universitaire pour le Developpement de l'Enseignement et de la Culture en Afrique et à Madagascar).

Langfeldt, G. (1937). The prognosis of schizophrenia and the factors influencing the course of the disease, *Acta Psychiat. Neurol. Scand.*, Supplementum 13 (Copenhagen: Munksgaard).

Langfeldt, G. (1956). The prognosis of schizophrenia, *Acta Psychiat. Neurol. Scand.*, Supplementum 110 (Copenhagen: Munksgaard).

Langfeldt, G. (1960). Diagnosis and prognosis of schizophrenia, *Proc. Roy. Soc. Med.*, 53, 1047.

Leff, J. P. and Wing, J. K. (1971). Trial of maintenance therapy in schizophrenia, *Brit. Med. J.*, 3, 599.

Liebermann, Y. I. (1974). On the problem of incidence in schizophrenia (data from a clinical-epidemiological investigation), *Zh. nevropatol. i psihiat. im. Korsakova*, 74: 8, 1224.

Lord, F. M., and Novick, M. R. (1968). *Statistical Theories of Mental Test Scores* (Reading, Mass.: Addison-Wesley).

Lyerly, S. B. (1973). *Handbook of Psychiatric Rating Scales*, 2nd edition (NIMH).

McKeon, J. J. (1967). *Hierarchical Cluster Analysis. (Washington: George Washington University Biometric Laboratory).*

Malamud, W. and Render, N. (1939). Course and prognosis in schizophrenia, *Amer. J. Psychiat.*, 95, 1039.

May, P. R. A., Tuma, A. H., and Kraude, W. (1965). Community follow-up of treatment of schizophrenia – issues and problems, *Amer. J. Orthopsychiat.*, 35, 754.

Mayer-Gross, W., Slater, E., and Roth, M. (1954). *Clinical Psychiatry.* (London: Baillière, Tindall and Cassel).

Menninger, K. A. (1959). The psychiatric diagnosis, *Bulletin of the Menninger Clinic*, 23, 226.

Müller, V. (1951). Katamnestiche Erhebungen über den Spontanverlauf der Schizophrenie, *Monatschr. für Psychiat. Neurol.*, 22, 257.

Murphy, H. B. M. (1969). Ethnic variations in drug response: results of an international survey. *Transcultural Psychiat. Res. Rev.*, 6, 5.

Murphy, H. B. M., and Raman, A. C. (1971). The chronicity of schizophrenia in indigenous tropical peoples, *Brit. J. Psychiat.*, 118, 489.

Norris, V. (1959). *Mental Illness in London* (Maudsley Monographs No. 6) (London: Chapman and Hall).

Pfeiffer, W. M. (1967). Psychiatrische Besonderheiten in Indonesien, Beitrage zur vergleichenden Psychiatrie (ed. N. Petrilowitsch), *Akt. Fragen Psychiat. Neurol.*, 42, 877.

Raman, A. C., and Murphy H. B. M. (1972). Failure of traditional prognostic indicators in Afro-Asian psychotics: results of a long-term follow-up survey, *J. Nervous Mental Dis.*, 154, 238.

Rennie, T. A. C. (1939). Follow-up study of five hundred patients with schizophrenia admitted to the hospital from 1913–1923, *Arch. Neurol. and Psychiat.*, 42, 877.

Rin, H., and Lin, T.-Y. (1962). Mental illness among Formosan aborigines as compared to Chinese in Taiwan, *J. Mental Sci.*, **108**, 134.

Rupp, C. and Fletcher, E. K. (1939). A five to ten year follow-up study of 641 schizophrenic cases, *Amer. J. Psychiat.*, **96**, 877.

Sakurai, T., Shirafuji, M., Nishizono, M., Hasukawa, T., Kusuhara, T., Yoshinaga, G., and Hirohashi, S. (1964). *Saishin Ogaku (Osaka)*, **6**, 369.

Sartorius, N. (1976). Classification: an international perspective, *Psychiatric Annals*, **6**, 8.

Schofield, W., Hathaway, S. R., Hastings, D. W., and Bell, D. M. (1954). Prognostic factors in schizophrenia, *J. Consulting Psychol.*, **18**, 155.

Seibel, D. (1968). In: Whitla D. K. (ed.), *Handbook of Measurement and Assessment in Behavioral Sciences* (Reading, Mass.: Addison-Wesley).

Shepherd, M. (1957). *A Study of the Major Psychoses in an English County* (Maudsley Monographs No. 3) (London: Chapman and Hall).

Shepherd, M. (1958). The social outcome of early schizophrenia, *Psychiat. Neurol.*, **137**, 224.

Simon, W. and Wirt, R. (1961). Prognostic factors in schizophrenia, *Amer. J. Psychiat.*, **117**, 887.

Snezhnevskij, A. V. (ed.) (1972). *Schizofrenia: Multidisziplinarnoye Issledovanie* (Moscow: Medizina).

Sokal, R. R., and Sneath, P. H. A. (1963). *Principles of Numerical Taxonomy*. San Francisco: W. H. Freeman).

Spitzer, R. L., Endicott, J., Fleiss, J. L., and Cohen, J. (1970). The Psychiatric Status Schedule: a technique for evaluating psychopathology and impairment in role functioning, *Arch. Gen. Psychiat.*, **23**, 41.

Stalker, H. (1939). Prognosis in schizophrenia, *J. Mental Sci.*, **85**, 1224.

Stephens, J. H. and Astrup, C. (1963). Prognosis in 'process' and 'non-process' schizophrenia, *Amer. J. Psychiat.*, **119**, 945.

Stephens, J. H., Astrup, C., and Mangrum, J. C. (1966). Prognostic factors in recovered and deteriorated schizophrenics, *Amer. J. Psychiat.*, **122**, 1116.

Stevens, B. (1973). Role of fluphenazine decanoate in lessening the burden of chronic schizophrenics on the community, *Psychol. Med.*, **3**, 41.

Strömgren, E. (1961). Recent studies of prognosis and outcome in the mental disorders, In: P. Hoch, and J. Zubin (eds.), *Comparative Epidemiology of the Mental Disorders* (New York and London: Grune and Stratton).

Thorndike, R. and Hagen, E. (1969) *Measurement and Evaluation in Psychology and Education*, 3rd edition (New York, London Sydney, Toronto: J. Wiley and Son).

Trashinsky, C. H. *et al.* (1962). Maintenance phenothiazine in after-care of schizophrenic patients, *Psychiat. W.*, **2**, 11.

Tuke, D. H. (1892). *A Dictionary of Psychological Medicine*, Vol. I (Philadelphia: P. Blackiston).

Vaillant, G. (1962). The prediction of recovery in schizophrenia, *J. Nervous Mental Dis.*, **135**, 534.

Vaillant, G. (1964). Prospective prediction of schizophrenic remission, *Arch. Gen. Psychiat.*, **11**, 509.

Varga, E. (1966). *Changes in the Symptomatology of Psychotic Patterns*, (Budapest: Akadémiai Kiado).

Welner, J. and Strömgren, E. (1958). Clinical and genetic studies on benign schizophreniform psychoses based on follow-up, *Acta Psychiat. Neurol. Scand.*, **33**, 377.

Wing, J. K. (1962). Institutionalism in mental hospitals, *Brit. J. Soc. Clin. Psychol.*, **1**, 38.

Wing, J. K. and Brown, G. W. (1970). *Institutionalism and Schizophrenia* (London: Cambridge University Press).

Wing, J. K., Birley, J. L. T., Cooper, J. E., Graham, P., and Isaacs, A. D. (1967). Reliability of a procedure for measuring and classifying 'present psychiatric state', *Brit. J. Psychiat.*, 113, 499.

Wing, J. K., Cooper, J. E., and Sartorius, N. (1974). *The Measurement and Classification of Psychiatric Symptoms* (London: Cambridge University Press).

Author Index

Achte 22, 25, 37
Almond 13
Arnold 28
Astrup 20, 22, 25, 35, 37, 39

Barton 17
Bellak 11
Bennett 17
Bhaskaran 17
Birley 16
Bleuler, E. 11, 19, 20, 22, 29, 34, 309
Bleuler, M. 11, 12, 23, 24, 25, 26, 27, 31, 43
Boltex 13
Brown 13, 16, 17, 22, 24, 29, 43

Carse 17
Cooper, J. E. 63, 315, 385, 394
Cronbach 63

Dhawan 17
Douglas 15

Eitinger 34, 35
Ekblom 17
Evensen 19
Ewalt 17
Ey 28, 29

Feinsilver 17
Fletcher 20, 24
Fruchter 64, 66

Geisser 115
Gillespie 20
Goffman 17
Greenhouse 115
Grinspoon 17
Gross 17
Gudeman 41
Guilford 64, 66
Gunderson 17
Gurland 74

Hagen 62
Harris 13
Hempel 322
Henderson 20
Henisz 22
Hirsch 17
Hogarty 17
Holmboe 20

Jablensky 256
Johnson 20, 24
Jones 14

Kant 34, 36
Katz 41
Kenniston 13
Kraepelin 11, 19, 22, 28, 33, 34, 253, 309, 314, 325, 384
Kraude 15

Laane 34, 35
Lambo 41
Langfeldt 11, 19, 20, 22, 25, 32, 33, 34, 36, 37, 253, 308, 380
Lassenius 17
Leff 17
Leonhard 23, 35
Liebermann, Y. I. 29
Lin 41
Lord 65
Lyerly 63

Malamud 20, 24
Mangrum 37
Matussek 19
May 15
Mayer-Gross 22
Menninger 313
Meyer 20, 22
Mohan 17
Müller 28
Murphy 40, 41, 256

Noreik   22, 25, 39
Norris   39, 40
Novick   65

Panton   17
Pfeiffer   41

Raman   40, 256
Render   20, 24
Rennie   20, 24
Rin   41
Roth   22
Rupp   20, 24

Sakurai   41
Sanborn   41
Sartorius   63, 256, 314, 315, 385, 394
Schofield   38
Schneider   300
Seibel   62
Shader   17
Shepherd   12, 40
Simon   38
Slater   22

Sneath   315
Snezhnevskij   29
Sokal   315
Spitzer   74
Stalker   20
Stephens   35, 37
Stevens   17
Strömgren   11, 35

Thorndike   62
Troshinsky   17
Tuke   313
Tuma   15

Vaillant   36, 37
Varga   41, 42

Watt   17
Welner   35
Wing   16, 17, 63, 74, 315, 385
Wirt   38

Zablock   24

Subject Index

Abnormal tidiness, 70, 76, 270
Acuteness, 308, 380
Affect
    exaggerated expression of, 38
    flatness of, 7, 36, 73, 117, 119, 120,
        123, 126, 133, 141, 165, 167,
        193, 196, 198, 225, 226, 229,
        243
    incongruity of, 7, 70, 76, 86, 117,
        120, 133, 182, 196, 229
    lability of, 70, 76
    -laden thoughts, 7, 69, 83, 90, 117,
        120, 165, 167, 170, 180, 182,
        196, 229
Affective
    change, 7, 70, 83, 90, 165
    episodes, 62, 155
    psychosis, 4, 5, 6, 19, 39, 97, 98, 148,
        153, 155, 164, 176, 178, 191,
        192, 221, 222, 254, 301, 309,
        310, 325, 374, 377, 383, 384,
        389, 392
    symptoms/symptomatology, 119
        133, 223, 243, 299, 309
Age
    distribution, 100–101
    outcome in relation to, 161
    psychosis of old-, 40
Aggressive
    actions, 379
    behaviour, 18
Akinetic symptoms, 105
Alcohol dependence, 401, 402
Alcoholic hallucinosis, 26
Ambitendence, 70, 76
Ambivalence, 70, 76, 80
Amnesia, 399
Amphetamine abuse, 402
Analysis of variance (ANOVA), 115, 372
Anxiety, 70, 73, 76, 81, 83, 90, 119,
    120, 141, 167, 320, 336, 397
    situation-, 70, 76
Apathy, 70, 76, 123, 136, 141, 198,
    291, 319

Appetite
    changes in, 308
    diminished, 70, 77, 301
    disturbances of, 380
    increased, 70, 77, 301
Apprehension, 32
Asymptomatic (definition on the basis
    of PSE ratings), 411
Attention, 32, 57
    labile, 26
Autism, 32, 34, 36, 70, 76, 136, 255,
    270
    early infantile, 35

Bedwetting, 266
Behaviour disorders, 40, 105, 255, 379,
    381
Blocking (of thought), 69, 75, 302
Bonferroni's modification of Chi-square
    test, 116, 145, 364
Borderline psychosis, 3

Catastrophic schizophrenia, 30, 31
Catatonia, 26, 28, 41
Catatonic
    disturbances, 22
    phenomena, 299
    symptoms, 32, 33, 255
Catchment area, 50, 303, 370, 378, 388
CATEGO, 7, 8, 129, 314, 315, 321, 325,
    326, 331, 368, 372, 385–387,
    392
    classes, composition of, 413, 414
Changed appearance (as symptom), 69,
    75
Character disorders, 40
Chronic
    defect states, 41
    deterioration, 29, 31
    disorder, 308
    psychotic disorder, 26, 43
Chronicity, 254, 308–310, 370, 379
Classification, 313, 322, 367, 384, 386,
    392

Cluster analysis, 225
Clustering methods (technique), 71,
    315, 345
Compliance, 7, 69, 75
Concentration, lack of, 69, 75
Concordant/non-concordant groups of
    schizophrenics, 315, 316, 351,
    361, 362, 386, 387
Confabulation, 26
Confusion, 20, 25, 36, 37
    reactive-, 191
Confusional psychosis, 39
    states, acute, 41
Consciousness, state of, 32–34, 36, 255
Constipation, 70, 77, 301
Cooperation, 57, 73, 77, 86
    difficulties, 71, 72, 81, 83, 85, 86,
        89, 90, 117, 119, 120, 123,
        126, 133, 141, 144, 165, 167,
        180–182, 193, 198, 229, 243,
        270, 287, 319, 320, 372, 380,
        382
Coronary thrombosis, 493
Course, 14
    categories used to describe, 63, 92
    factors influencing, 32, 108
    insidious chronic, 28
    patterns of, 27, 31, 42, 61, 260, 270,
        291, 369, 373, 381
    phasic, 28
    shiftlike, 28
    type of, 28, 29, 43
Culture, 40, 41, 42, 63, 256, 306, 307,
    308, 321, 367, 370, 371, 379, 381,
    389, 391, 394, 395
Cycloid psychosis, 35

Decreased energy, 70, 77, 80, 301, 308
Defect, 19, 21, 23, 27, 29, 30, 31, 33,
    41
Delusional
    experiences, 32
    forms, 29
    mood, 7, 69, 73, 75, 136
    states, 42
Delusions, 4, 7, 17, 18, 22, 26, 33, 61,
    72, 79, 81, 83, 89, 90, 119, 123,
    126, 133, 141, 145, 148, 165, 170,
    193, 225, 229, 255, 299, 320, 331,
    370, 372, 390
    fantastic, 29, 300
    grandiose, 380
    hypochondriacal, 69, 75, 126
    nihilistic, 69, 75

of grandeur, 69, 75, 181
of guilt, 37, 69, 75, 80, 331
of impending doom, 69, 75
of persecution, 32, 69, 41, 123, 136,
    185, 198, 243, 300, 380
of reference, 69, 75, 136, 181, 198,
    243
of self-depreciation, 69, 75, 173, 181,
    198, 336
of special mission, 69, 75, 80
religious, 69, 75, 80
sexual, 69, 75, 80
systemization of, 255
Dementia, 28, 42
    persecutiva, 32, 33
    praecox, 11, 19, 33, 34
Demonstrative behaviour, 70, 76, 301
Depersonalization, 4, 26, 32, 33, 34, 35,
    255
Depressed mood, 7, 26, 70, 76, 83, 89,
    90, 165, 167, 170, 172, 180, 181,
    193
Depression, 26, 33, 37, 38, 70, 215, 299,
    308
    agitated, 5, 97, 98, 325
    endogenous, 397
    neurotic, 4, 130, 168, 191, 198, 199,
        223
    psychotic, 3, 4, 7, 8, 36, 115, 165,
        168, 176, 177, 178, 185, 193,
        198, 199, 201, 203, 208, 210,
        212, 215, 216, 218, 221, 222,
        223, 318, 329, 360, 375
    reactive, 5, 97, 98
    retarded, 130, 191, 198, 199, 223
    special, 70, 76
Depressive psychosis, 354, 362, 364,
    385, 386, 387, 392
Derealization, 7, 33, 34, 69, 76, 79, 80,
    81, 83, 90, 117, 133, 165, 167,
    182, 255, 265, 267, 268, 270, 272,
    287, 299, 308, 309, 380, 382
Dermatozoenwahn, 398
Diagnosis, criteria for, 12, 14, 15, 19,
    20, 22, 24, 40, 42, 368
    computer simulated, 7, 8, see also
        CATEGO
    distribution of patients by, 95–97
    standardization of, 43
Diagnostic Assessment Schedule (DA),
    10
Disability, 258, 276, 279, 280, 287, 302,
    314, 317, 382, 383
Discriminant function analysis, 261,

293, 316, 322–324, 326, 336, 375, 385, 392
Disorientation, 36, 37, 38
Distractibility, 69, 75
Double bookkeeping ('Doppelte Buchführung'), 26
Double blind trial, 17
Dreamlike thinking, 26
Drugs, 4, 17, 54, 105, 109

Early waking, 70, 72, 73, 76, 168, 173, 181, 299, 301, 308, 336, 380
Echolalia, 69, 75, 302
Ecstatic mood, 70, 76
Educational level, 38, 255, 257, 264, 265, 266, 279, 280, 284, 377, 378, 379, 382
Elated mood, 70, 76, 80, 89, 90, 165, 170, 180, 181, 193, 196
Elation, 70, 83, 308
Emotional blunting, 34
End state, 30
Endocrine disorders, 6
Enuresis, 379
Epilepsy, 4, 95
Epileptic
    attacks, 397
    psychosis, 40, 398, 399
    seizures, 398
Excitation, 25, 41
    reactive, 191
Exogenous psychosis, 26
Experiences of control, 7, 69, 83, 90, 120, 133, 148, 165, 229
Extrapyramidal rigidity, 267
Extroversion, 34

Factor analysis, 68
Faith healers, 104
Family, 13, 18, 26, 38, 42, 47, 104, 105, 110
First rank symptoms, 300, 338
Flatness of affect, 70, 72, 76, 83, 86, 89, 90, 279, 282, 284, 299, 301, 302, 308, 310, 319, 320, 372, 380, 383
Flight of ideas, 26, 69, 75
Fluphenazine, 17
Follow-Up Diagnostic Assessment Schedule (FUDA), 52
Follow-Up Psychiatric History Schedule (FUPH), 52, 391
Follow-Up Social Description Schedule (FUSD), 52

Functional psychoses, 1, 3, 6, 8, 9, 19, 22, 39, 40, 43, 45, 52, 58, 99, 108, 112, 114, 193, 196, 253, 256, 322, 325, 367, 373, 392

Giggling to self (as symptom), 70, 76, 80, 120
Grimacing (as symptom), 69, 75, 80
Groaning (as symptom), 71, 77, 80
Groups of Units of Analysis (GUA's), 69–71

Hallucinations, 4, 7, 18, 22, 26, 83, 90, 95, 126, 133, 141, 145, 148, 193, 225, 239, 255, 299, 300, 302, 310, 320, 331, 370
    auditory, 7, 32, 70, 71, 72, 76, 77, 80, 83, 90, 117, 119, 120, 133, 136, 165, 167, 180, 181, 196, 198, 226, 229, 236, 243
    body, 70, 76, 416
    characteristic, 70, 83, 90, 120, 133, 229, 255
    gustatory, 70, 76, 302
    internal (physical), 32
    olfactory, 70, 76, 302
    sexual, 70, 76, 302
    somatic, 70, 76, 302
    tactile, 70, 76, 80, 302
    visual, 32, 70, 76
Hallucinatory
    behaviour, 69, 75, 80
    states, 42
Hallucinogenic drugs, 402
Hashish, 400
Haughtiness (as symptom), 70, 76, 80, 299
Heroin, 400
History
    of mental illness in family, 38, 255, 266, 268, 279, 302, 377, 382
    premorbid, 14, 15, 37
Hopelessness, 69, 75, 168, 172, 336
Hyperactivity, 379
Hypochondriasis, 33, 136, 336
Hypomanic symptoms, 33
Hysterical
    episodes, 26, 33
    psychosis, 39

Ideas of persecution, 32–33
Ideas of reference, 7, 33, 36, 38, 69, 75, 255
Incoherence, 33

Incongruity, 70, 83, 90, 255
Insight, 7, 69, 72, 73, 75, 77, 83, 86,
    90, 117, 119, 120, 123, 126, 133,
    141, 165, 180, 181, 193, 196, 198,
    229, 243, 308, 319, 320, 336, 372
Institutionalization, harmful effects of,
    17
Intelligence, 255, 308
Interests
    changes of, 70, 76, 299
    decreased, 69, 75, 80
    increased, 71, 77, 80
International Classification of Diseases
    (ICD), 313–315, 326, 385–386
Involutional
    melancholia, 155, 165
    paraphrenia, 191
Irrelevance, 69, 75, 80, 302
Irritability, 70, 76, 83, 90, 141, 320

Kendall's coefficient of correlation, 84,
    89, 119, 170, 226, 291, 304, 421
Klang associations, 69, 75, 302

Lability of affect, 70
Libido
    changes in, 70, 77, 80, 301, 308
    disturbances of, 380
Life events, 16, 53, 376
Lithium treatment, 111
Loose associations, 36
Loss of emotions, 71, 77, 336

Mahalanobis' distance coefficient (D),
    324, 326, 329, 331, 335, 354, 357
Mania, 3, 97, 115, 180, 181, 182, 185,
    188, 190, 191, 193, 201, 203, 208,
    210, 213, 215, 216, 218, 221, 222,
    223, 319, 354, 362, 364, 375, 385,
    386, 392, 416
Manic-depressive psychosis, 40, 155,
    165, 253, 254, 325
Mannerisms, 7, 69, 75
Marijuana, 399
Marital status, 38, 99, 100, 101, 106,
    257, 264, 265, 266, 272, 279, 280,
    287, 308, 309, 377, 378, 381, 382
McKeon's clusters, 314, 315, 342, 345,
    385
Memory
    difficulties, 69, 75, 80
    hallucinations, 26
    illusions, 26
Mental retardation, 4, 397, 398, 400

Metabolic disorders, 6
Minority groups, 379
Morose mood, 70, 76
Mutism, 69, 75, 80

Negative symptoms, 56, 320
Negativism, 7, 69, 75
Neologisms, 69, 75, 80, 302
Neurasthenic complaints, 7, 69, 81, 90,
    112
Neuroleptic drugs, 17, 24
Neuroses, 5, 29, 32, 97, 98
    depressive, 5, 97, 98, 104
Neurotic
    complaints, 272, 302
    symptoms, 56, 119, 133, 168, 255,
        309, 310, 397, 399
Nosocomial factors, 13
Nuclear symptoms, 325
Nutritional disorders, 4

Obsessive thoughts, 69, 75
Odd appearance and behaviour (as
        symptoms), 70, 76
Onset
    acute, 16, 28, 30, 33, 34, 37
    chronic, 30
    insidious, 265, 279, 280, 283
    rapid, 38
    recent, 3
    sudden, 272, 309
    type of, 34, 38, 255, 256, 259, 270,
        308, 377, 379, 381
Organic
    brain disorders, 25
    brain syndrome, 399
    psychoses, 4
Organicity, 4
Orientation, 38
Outcome, 114
    overall, 280, 282, 284, 285, 291, 302,
        304, 307, 321, 373, 377
Overactivity, 69, 75, 77, 78, 80, 290,
        291, 299, 303, 310

Paralysis agitans, 401
Paranoia, 26, 191
Paranoid
    condition, 32
    dementia, 28
    psychosis, 4, 5, 130, 149, 181, 187
    reaction, acute, 191
    state, 4, 35, 97, 191
    symptomatology, 41

Passivity feelings, 32
Pathoplastic features, 33
Pearson's *r*, 65
Perplexity, 7, 69, 73, 75, 299, 310
Perseveration, 26, 71, 77
Personality
    change, 23, 41, 70, 83, 87, 89, 90,
        133, 254, 270, 272, 282, 287,
        299, 308, 309, 380, 382
    disorders, 5, 97, 98
    in manic depressive psychosis, 254
Phenothiazines, 41
Pitch, disorder of, 70, 76, 120, 301
Placebo, 17
Possession, 104
Postencephalitic state, 401
Postpartum psychosis, 397
Posturing, 69, 75, 80
Precipitating events, 36, 370
    factors, 34, 37, 255
    stress, 38, 265, 267, 270, 276, 280,
        309
Predelusional signs, 7, 69, 81, 83, 89,
    90, 117, 120, 133, 167
Premorbid
    history, 37
    personality, 34, 255, 266, 379, 383,
        384
Presenile psychoses, 3
Present State Examination (PSE), 6, 52,
    62, 68, 288, 308, 370, 380, 390
Pressure of speech, 69, 75
Process schizophrenia, 32
    symptoms, 33
Prognosis
    in functional psychoses, 254, 289
    interim, 254
    ultimate, 253
Prognostic
    factors, 31, 33, 36, 37, 38, 253, 254
    score, 290
Pseudohallucinations, 7, 70, 76, 83, 90
Psychiatric History Schedule (PH), 6, 10
Psychogenic
    psychoses, 26
    symptoms, 33
Psychometric theory, 62
Psychomotor disorders, 4, 7, 69, 83, 89,
    90, 170, 303
Psychoneuroses, 40
Psychophysical (psychophysiological)
    complaints, 7, 70, 81, 85, 87
    symptoms, 72, 83, 90, 165, 167, 196,
        276, 279, 280, 287, 308

Psychosexual adjustment, 255, 258, 265,
    266, 268, 269, 280, 284, 301, 302
    303, 309, 379, 383
Psychosomatic symptoms, 56, 168
Psychotherapy, 12, 25, 36
Psychotic (definition on the basis of
    PSE ratings), 409
Puerperal psychotic illness, 397, 398
Pyknic physique, 34

Rating scales, 304
Reactive depressive psychosis, 155, 165
    psychosis, 20, 35, 39, 191
Reality
    awareness of, 308
    loss of contact with, 32
Regression
    analysis, 262, 263, 266, 276, 285,
        291, 298, 300, 304, 307, 378,
        380, 382
    statistical model of, 261, 262, 303,
        304
Rehabilitation, 13, 17, 24, 376
Relapse, 16, 17, 19, 21, 23, 40, 64, 107,
    276
Reliability, concept of, 61–67
Religious
    healers, 109
    sects, 379
Remission, types of, 53, 54, 270
Repetitive movements, 69, 75, 303
Restricted speech, 49, 75, 126, 136
Retardation, 69, 75, 170, 173, 303

Schizoid personality, 35
Schizophrenia
    acute, 5, 17, 20, 98, 246, 248, 249
    atypical, 35
    catastrophic, 30, 31
    catatonic, 5, 97, 98, 243, 246, 248,
        249, 251
    chronic undifferentiated, 5
    concept of, 368, 395
    hebephrenic, 5, 28, 33, 97, 98, 243,
        246, 248, 249, 251, 346, 351,
        360, 362, 387, 392
    latent, 5, 35, 97, 98, 248
    malignant, 35
    paranoid, 5, 97, 98, 243, 246, 248,
        249, 251
    periodic, 5
    pseudoneurotic, 35
    pseudopsychopathic, 35

reactive, 32
schizoaffective, 5, 97, 98, 254, 346,
    351, 360—362, 392
shiftlike, 5
simple, 5, 20, 32, 97, 98, 243, 246,
    248, 249, 346, 351, 360—362,
    387, 392
subgroups (subtypes), 97, 239—241,
    345—351
systematic, 35
unspecified, 351, 360, 362, 392
Schizophrenic reaction, 26
Schizophreniform
    patients, 36, 37, 39
    psychoses, 32, 34, 35, 37
    symptomatology, 33
Self-neglect, 4, 70, 76
Self-perception (distortion of), 69, 83,
    90, 119, 133, 372
Senile psychosis, 3
Sensorium, 255
Sex, outcome in relation to, 161—163
Sex behaviour, changes of, 70, 76, 80
Sexual hallucinations, 70
Sleep
    disturbances, 380
    problems, 70, 72, 73, 77, 173, 181
Sleepwalking, 266
Social
    functioning, 53, 57, 92, 115, 175,
        189, 260, 276, 279, 285, 307,
        316
    impairment, 61, 62, 63, 116, 145,
        155, 156, 158, 159, 160, 163,
        164, 173, 176, 177, 190, 191,
        192, 201, 215, 216, 248, 254,
        276, 279, 280, 302, 308, 317,
        368, 373, 397, 398, 399, 400,
        401
    isolation, 257, 264, 265, 268, 269,
        276, 279, 280, 287, 301, 302,
        307, 308, 309, 310, 377, 378,
        381, 382, 383, 393, 394
    norms, disregard of, 70, 76, 80, 81,
        83, 90, 182, 193, 196
    withdrawal, 4, 41, 70, 76, 270, 299,
        336
Social Description Schedule (SD), 6, 10
Socioeconomic status, 38, 99, 100, 101,
    106, 255, 257, 276, 377
Somatotype, 255
Somnolence, 105
Spearman's coefficient of correlation,
    261

Speech
    disorders, 22, 69, 83, 90
    dissociation, 69, 75, 302
    impediments, 71, 77
Stereotypies, 38, 69, 75
    of speech, 69, 75, 302
Student's statistic (t), 357
Stupor, 25, 33, 69, 75, 170, 303
Suggestibility, 71, 77, 80
Suicide, 403—407
Suspiciousness, 71, 72, 73, 77, 123, 185,
    198
Symptom profile, 61, 64, 85, 91, 122,
    125, 132, 134—136, 165, 167,
    169—171, 178, 182, 193—196,
    226—229
Symptomatic but not psychotic
    (definition on the basis of PSE
    ratings), 411

Talking to self (as symptom), 70, 76,
    301
Tension, 38, 70, 76, 80, 83, 90, 119,
    141, 320, 336
Thinking, disorders of form of, 4, 69,
    83, 90, 105, 117, 196, 229
Thought
    alienation, 11, 69, 75, 136, 338
    broadcast, 225
    disorder, 18, 26, 32, 145, 302, 310,
        383, 398
    hearing, 26, 255
    projection, 32
    stealing, 32
Thoughts
    elated, 69, 75
    gloomy, 69, 73, 75, 136, 168, 172,
        198
    insertion, 255
    spoken aloud, 69, 75
    suicidal, 69, 75
Thyrotoxicosis, 401, 402
Time perception, distortion of, 69, 76,
    79, 80, 308, 380
Traditional healers, 106, 107
Treatment(s), therapy (ies), 1, 14, 15,
    16, 17, 18, 42, 53, 54, 106, 109,
    110
    biological, 71, 77, 86
    response, 38
    social, 17, 24, 25
Trifluoperazine, 17
Truancy, 379
Typhoid fever, 404

Undecided (as symptom), 69, 75
Units Of Analysis (UA's), 69–71

Validity,
  concept of, 62
  concurrent, 62
  construct, 62, 63
  content, 62, 316, 325, 361, 364,
    385, 386
  criterion-oriented, 62, 64
  predictive, 62, 64, 316, 325, 336,
    354, 360, 364, 385

Voices
  comment on patient's thoughts, 70,
    76, 80
  discussing patient, 70, 76
  speak full sentences, 70, 76
  speak thoughts, 70, 76
  speak to patient, 70, 76, 126, 136

Waxy flexibility, 69, 75
Worries, 69, 75, 336
Worse
  in evening (as symptom), 301, 336
  in morning (as symptom), 301, 308,
    336, 380